Neuropsychology of the Sense of Agency

Neuropsychology of the Sense of Agency

Editor: Rene Sinclair

AMERICAN
MEDICAL PUBLISHERS
www.americanmedicalpublishers.com

AMERICAN
MEDICAL PUBLISHERS
www.americanmedicalpublishers.com

Cataloging-in-Publication Data

Neuropsychology of the sense of agency / edited by Rene Sinclair.
p. cm.
Includes bibliographical references and index.
ISBN 979-8-88740-318-2
1. Neuropsychology. 2. Self-perception. 3. Locus of control.
4. Agent (Philosophy). 5. Psychiatry. I. Sinclair, Rene.
QP360 .N48 2023
612.8--dc23

American Medical Publishers,
41 Flatbush Avenue,
1st Floor, New York,
NY 11217, USA

ISBN 979-8-88740-318-2 (Hardback)

Contents

Preface

This book aims to highlight the current researches and provides a platform to further the scope of innovations in this area. This book is a product of the combined efforts of many researchers and scientists, after going through thorough studies and analysis from different parts of the world. The objective of this book is to provide the readers with the latest information of the field.

Sense of agency (SA), in neuropsychology refers to the subjective awareness of originating, executing, and controlling one's own volitional activities in the world. This also adds to the subjective phenomenon of self-consciousness by allowing oneself to feel separate from others. The sense of agency is crucial in cognitive development, particularly in the initial stage of self-awareness, which supports theory of mind capacities. SA is the manner in which self builds itself as an entity autonomous from the external world and from other agents. Differentiating oneself from others is one of the significant functions of human brain. Even slight impairments in this ability have profound effects on the functioning of the individual in the society. Furthermore, SA is also significant in law and ethical questions, which concerns guilt and responsibility. This book is compiled in such a manner, that it will provide in-depth knowledge about the neuropsychology of the sense of agency. It aims to serve as a resource guide for students and experts alike and contribute to the growth of the discipline. This book will serve as a reference to a broad spectrum of readers.

I would like to express my sincere thanks to the authors for their dedicated efforts in the completion of this book. I acknowledge the efforts of the publisher for providing constant support. Lastly, I would like to thank my family for their support in all academic endeavors.

Editor

1

From action intentions to action effects: how does the sense of agency come about?

Valérian Chambon[1,2,3]*†, Nura Sidarus[3]*† and Patrick Haggard[3]

[1] Laboratoire de Neurosciences Cognitives, INSERM U960, Paris, France
[2] Institut Jean Nicod, Ecole Normale Supérieure-EHESS, CNRS UMR-8129, Paris, France
[3] Institute of Cognitive Neuroscience, University College London, London, UK

Correspondence:
Valérian Chambon, Institut Jean Nicod, Ecole Normale Supérieure-EHESS, CNRS UMR-8129, 29, Rue d'Ulm, Paris 75005, France
e-mail: valerian.chambon@ens.fr
Nura Sidarus, Institute of Cognitive Neuroscience, University College London, Alexandra House, 17 Queen Square, London WC1N 3AR, UK
e-mail: n.sidarus.11@ucl.ac.uk
†These authors have contributed equally to this work.

Sense of agency refers to the feeling of controlling an external event through one's own action. On one influential view, agency depends on how predictable the consequences of one's action are, getting stronger as the match between predicted and actual effect of an action gets closer. Thus, sense of agency arises when external events that follow our action are consistent with predictions of action effects made by the motor system while we perform or simply intend to perform an action. According to this view, agency is inferred *retrospectively*, after an action has been performed and its consequences are known. In contrast, little is known about whether and how internal processes involved in the selection of actions may influence subjective sense of control, in advance of the action itself, and irrespective of effect predictability. In this article, we review several classes of behavioral and neuroimaging data suggesting that earlier processes, linked to fluency of action selection, *prospectively* contribute to sense of agency. These findings have important implications for better understanding human volition and abnormalities of action experience.

Keywords: fluency, action selection, agency, angular gyrus, human volition

ACTION-EFFECT LINK AND COMPARATOR MODELS: A RETROSPECTIVE ACCOUNT OF AGENCY

Agency is a key component of action experience. In a nutshell, agency refers to the sense of controlling one's own actions and, through these actions, events in the outside world. We rarely have an intense, clear phenomenology of agency, but we clearly recognize failures of agency when we experience actions that do not unfold as expected or fail to produce intended effects. One might even say that our sense of "authorship" becomes apparent only when it is falsified, resulting in a break of the flow from intentions to action effects that normally characterize experience. Thus, determining where the sense of agency comes from requires properly specifying where the break may occur along the intention-action-effect chain. Identifying the break may in turn depend on how we choose to specify the chain, and on the causal relation between its constituents (intention, action, effect).

On one influential view, agency implies a control mechanism that causally relates actions to their effects. More specifically, it implies a mechanism that has goals, and that controls actions to achieve them. This mechanism was first, and successfully, formalized as a *comparator model* (Wolpert et al., 1995; Miall and Wolpert, 1996). In its first incarnation, a comparator model translates intentions into outcomes, by continually monitoring whether action consequences occur, or do not occur, as predicted. Though originally formulated as models of motor control (Wolpert et al., 1995), comparator models have also been increasingly used to explain the subjective sense of agency (e.g., Blakemore et al., 2001). On the comparator account, agency is computed by matching predicted and actually experienced consequences of movement. In this framework, action effects are precisely those sensory events that can be predicted from one's intentions, using the specific intermediate mechanism of the comparator model (Wolpert et al., 1995; **Figure 1A**). Thus, the comparator model allows for two specific predictions. First, sense of agency should be strong when there is a close match between the predicted and the actual sensory consequences of an action, and should be reduced when predicted and experienced consequences do not match. Second, sense of agency necessarily occurs *late*, i.e., after an action has been performed, and sensory evidence about the consequences of action becomes available.

This view has received considerable empirical support from studies showing that spatial and temporal discrepancies between making an action and viewing visual feedback of the action reduce the sense that the observed action is one's own. Thus, introducing a spatial transformation between an action and its visual consequences reduces participants' sense of agency in proportion to

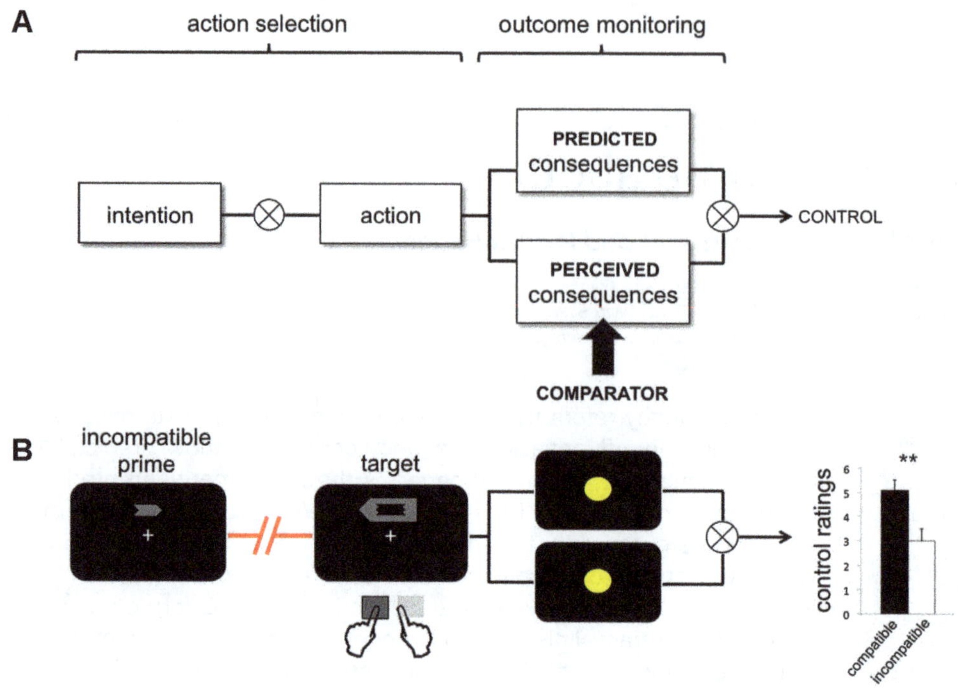

FIGURE 1 | (A) Intention-Action-Effect chain. The action-selection processes operate between the formation of the initial intention and action execution. Dysfluency of action selection signals a break in the intention-action link, that occurs prior to the action and its sensory consequences. After the action has been selected, predicted and perceived consequences of this action are compared. On the comparator account (in bold), sense of agency is strong when there is a match between predicted and actually experienced consequences of an action, and is reduced in the case of a mismatch. **(B)** Example trial from the prime-target incompatible condition, adapted from Chambon et al. (2013). Participants were instructed to respond to the target stimulus, and were not informed of the presence of the arrow primes. Action effects consisted of colored circles that appeared on the screen after a varying delay. In this condition, sense of agency decreases relative to the compatible condition, even though predicted and perceived action effects are the same (yellow circles).

the mismatch induced. In one typical task, participants received distorted visual feedback of their hand moving a joystick. When the movement of the virtual hand did not correspond to the subjects' movement (Farrer and Frith, 2002), or when an angular bias was introduced between the subject's and the virtual hand's movement, participants more readily attributed it to another agent (Fourneret and Jeannerod, 1998; Farrer et al., 2003; Synofzik et al., 2006; David et al., 2007). Note that manipulating temporal relations between actions and outcomes had similar effects (Franck et al., 2001; Leube et al., 2003; MacDonald and Paus, 2003; David et al., 2007, 2011; Farrer et al., 2008). The so-called "intentional binding" effect provides another line of evidence for the role of temporal contiguity between action and outcome in the building of agency. The intentional binding effect has been first reported by Haggard et al. (2002): it refers to the subjective compression of the temporal interval between a voluntary action and its external sensory consequences. Thus, actions are perceived as shifted in time towards the outcomes that they cause, while outcomes are perceived as shifted back in time towards the actions that cause them (see Moore and Obhi, 2012, for a review). This temporal attraction is absent in cases of involuntary or passive movement. Equally, when participants simply judge the interval between action and effect, their judgments show a perceptual compression absent for equivalent passive movements (Engbert et al., 2008). The intentional binding effect would constitute an implicit, but reliable, measure of agency, as it only occurs when events in the external environment are precisely recognized as the *consequences* of one's action.

On comparator accounts, a positive sense of agency is the default operation when no mismatch between predicted and current states occurs (see Synofzik et al., 2008). It is the experiential output of sub-personal processes that mostly run outside consciousness. Crucially, although sense of agency relies on real-time motor signals, it can only be computed after those signals are compared with reafferent feedback. Thus, a reliable, explicit sense of agency may only be formed when reafferent (visual, motor, or proprioceptive) signals become available for matching with intentions. Thus, one cannot feel agency over any event until that event has been registered and processed in the brain. As a consequence, agency can only be *retrospectively* attributed, although it is informed by *on-line* signals about motor guidance and control (Chambon and Haggard, 2013).

Note the retrospective account on agency has several advantages. First, it is grounded on several classes of converging behavioral and neuroimaging evidence. Second, it primarily relies on a computational model that provides a convincing explanation for the link between action and effect: action effects are sensory events that can be predicted from one's action plans.

However, an alternative possibility, that sense of agency is also generated *prospectively*, in advance of the action itself and before knowing the actual effect of actions, has received recent support (Wenke et al., 2010). On this view, selecting between alternative possible actions might itself generate a sense of agency. This view places a new emphasis on the intention-action, rather than the action-effect, link—i.e., on the process through which intentions are transformed into specific actions, to achieve desired effects. Importantly, this view suggests that agency may depend on real-time, prospective signals arising from internal circuits of action preparation, rather than on a *post-hoc*, retrospective comparison between predicted and current states of the environment.

INTENTION-ACTION LINK AND SELECTION FLUENCY: A PROSPECTIVE ACCOUNT OF AGENCY

Previous studies have shown that judgments of agency tend to be related to how participants think that they perform in a task (Metcalfe and Greene, 2007). Similarly, errors in task performance may lead to a *feeling* of dysfluency during the task, without any explicit awareness of an error, and without the ability to explicitly report the error. Thus, a feeling that something went "wrong" during the control of instrumental action may be sufficient to modulate later judgments of control, even without being able to identify or explicitly report the error. The term "epistemic feeling" has been coined to describe this subjective, on-line, experience of an error (Arango-Muñoz, 2010; Charles et al., 2013). Importantly, such on-line experience strongly influences the sense of agency, as shown by recent priming studies. Thus, Wenke and colleagues showed that the sense of agency could be modulated by using subliminal priming to affect the *fluency* of action selection processes (Wenke et al., 2010; Haggard and Chambon, 2012, for a review). Interestingly, this procedure enabled a manipulation of the subjective sense of agency, without manipulating the *predictability* of action outcomes. In this experiment, participants pressed left or right keys in response to left- or right-pointing arrow targets. Prior to the target, subliminal left or right arrow primes were presented, unbeknownst to the subject. Prime arrow directions were either identical (compatible condition) or opposite (incompatible condition) to the subsequent target (**Figure 1B**). Responding to the target caused the appearance of a color after a jittered delay. The color patch can thus be considered as the action outcome. The specific color shown depended on whether the participant's action was compatible or incompatible with the preceding subliminal prime, but did not depend on the prime identity or the chosen action alternative alone. Unlike previous studies, therefore, the primes did not predict action effects, nor could any specific color be predicted on the basis of the action chosen. Participants rated how much control they experienced over the different colors at the end of each block (Wenke et al., 2010).

Analyses of reaction times (RTs) showed that compatible primes facilitated responding whereas incompatible primes interfered with response selection. More importantly, priming also modulated the sense of agency over action effects: participants experienced more control over colors that followed actions compatible with the preceding primes than over colors that followed prime-incompatible actions. Thus subliminal priming made action selection processes more or less *fluent*, and this modulation of fluency affected the sense of agency over action outcomes.[1]

These results have several important cognitive implications. First, they suggest that the sense of agency depends strongly on processes of action selection that necessarily occur before action itself. Second, strong sense of agency may be associated with fluent, uncontested action selection. In contrast, conflict between alternative possible actions, such as that caused by incompatible subliminal priming, may reduce the feeling of control over action outcomes. Third, this prospective contribution of action selection processes to sense of agency is distinct from predicting the outcomes of action, since action outcomes were equally (un-) predictable for compatible and incompatible primes. That is, these primes did not prime effects of action as in previous studies (e.g., Wegner and Wheatley, 1999; Aarts et al., 2005; Linser and Goschke, 2007; Sato, 2009). Therefore, participants could not retrospectively base their control judgements on match between primes and effects alone. Rather, their stronger experience of control when primes were compatible could only be explained by the fluency of action selection—i.e., by a signal experienced *before* the action was made, and the effect was displayed.

Finally, participants did not consciously perceive the subliminal primes. Therefore, participants' sense of agency could not be based on (conscious) beliefs about the primes. Instead, action priming itself presumably directly influenced the subjective sense of agency. Pacherie (Pacherie, 2008; see also Synofzik et al., 2008) has suggested that action selection conflict need not necessarily be conscious (Morsella et al., 2009). Such conflict may elicit the feeling "that something is wrong", without necessarily leading to knowledge about *what* is wrong. Wenke et al.'s study shows that subjects can rely on this *implicit feeling* to make judgments about their own control over action effects.[2]

DISSOCIATING PROSPECTIVE SENSE OF AGENCY FROM MOTOR PERFORMANCE

Wenke et al.'s findings suggest that monitoring fluency signals generated *during* action selection could be an important marker for the experience of agency. However, it is also possible that

[1] Subliminal priming would facilitate action selection by reducing conflict between alternative action programmes (Fleming et al., 2009). This facilitation of premotor processing would precisely be experienced as a feeling of action *fluency*, while the opposite effect of conflict between alternative actions would be experienced as *dysfluency*. Note this suggestion is analogous to the well-accepted way that the feeling of "effort" is seen, as the experiential output of an increased demand in cognitive control (McGuire and Botvinick, 2010). Conversely, the literature usually defines fluency as an experiential consequence of smooth, *effortless* cognitive processing (e.g., Oppenheimer, 2008). In this sense, both terms are interchangeable—a fluent processing is an effortless processing–, and both may prospectively inform agency (e.g., Demanet et al., 2013).

[2] We take that selection fluency does not require to be *explicitly* represented to inform conscious experience of action. In fact, recent data suggest that fluency signals need to be kept implicit in order to influence agency on compatible trials—i.e., in order to be mistaken for actual control over action effects. Indeed, when primes are consciously perceived (i.e., presented at a supraliminal threshold), the compatibility effect is reversed: sense of agency is higher on *incompatible* trials (Damen et al., 2014).

participants might have estimated agency based on implicit monitoring of their own performance, such as their RTs. Since RTs are lower on compatibly primed trials (Dehaene et al., 1998; Schlaghecken and Eimer, 2000; Schlaghecken et al., 2008), participants would therefore feel more control on compatible trials, because they respond more rapidly. On this second view, agency would depend on *retrospective* monitoring of action execution performance (Marti et al., 2010), not on *prospective* monitoring of premotor fluency signals.

To distinguish between these two accounts of sense of agency, we used an experimental procedure that dissociated fluency of action selection from performance monitoring (Chambon and Haggard, 2012). Specifically, we increased the interval between mask and target to take advantage of a Negative Compatibility Effect (NCE) in priming. Longer mask-target latencies *increase* RTs following compatible primes, relative to incompatible primes (Schlaghecken et al., 2008). By combining this factor with Wenke et al.'s design for assessing sense of agency, it was possible to directly compare the contrasting retrospective (performance monitoring) and prospective (action selection) accounts. Specifically, if sense of agency depends on selection fluency, it should be greater when actions are compatibly (fluent condition) versus incompatibly (dysfluent condition) primed, irrespective of whether priming benefits (faster RTs) or impairs (slower RTs) performance. Alternatively, if sense of agency depends only on performance monitoring, it should be stronger for rapid versus slower responding, irrespective of whether priming is compatible or incompatible with the action executed.

Crucially, reversing the normal relationship between prime-target compatibility and RTs did not alter subjective sense of agency. Thus, in compatible NCE trials, participants experienced *stronger* control despite *slower* response times and higher error rates, compared to incompatible NCE trials (Chambon and Haggard, 2012; see also Stenner et al., 2014). These results suggest that the feeling of control normally experienced by subjects on compatible trials does not depend on retrospectively monitoring performance, thereby strengthening the evidence for a prospective contribution of action selection fluency to sense of agency.

In both Wenke et al.'s (2010) and Chambon and Haggard's (2012), experiments, priming did not influence the actual objective level of control that participants had over the colors presented after their actions. Indeed, the contingency between action and color effect was similar for compatibly-primed and incompatibly-primed trials. Importantly, the prospective sense of control identified in these experiments is therefore an illusion of control, since it is not based on differences in the actual statistical relation between action and effect. In other words, action selection is irrelevant to actual action-effect contingency, and thus to the agent's actual ability to drive external events. Although illusory, this prospective sense of control may nevertheless be a convenient proxy for actual control, because agents often just know what to do and what will happen next in most everyday life situations. In that sense, *fluent* action selection is generally a good *advance predictor* of actual statistical control over the external environment (Haggard and Chambon, 2012; Chambon et al., 2014). Prospective agency might thus reflect a learned experiential metacognition: if we can fluently select an appropriate action, then we are likely to get what we want, or fulfill our intentions.

As suggested above, internal signals of premotor fluency might not produce a strong conscious experience with distinctive content, but might influence the experience of surrounding events. Thus, fluency of action selection would not be experienced as such, but would presumably be experienced as something that goes "right" or "wrong" in the control of instrumental action, and thus seems relevant to sense of agency. In that sense, signals relating to the fluency of action selection would not be perceived for what they really are, but (mis-)attributed to the processes of actually controlling the action. Such a misattribution may foster the subject not to adjust her behavior accordingly. Indeed, it has been shown that behavioral adjustment does not only depend on the presence or absence of an error, but also on its cause (e.g., me vs. not-me) (Steinhauser and Kiesel, 2011). Thus, if participants misattribute dysfluency to lack of control on the selected action, and misattribute fluency to the process of actually controlling the action, then they should adjust their behavior less in the dysfluent, than in the fluent, condition—despite the fact that control is equally illusory in both conditions. Future work is required to test this assumption directly.

NEURAL SUBSTRATES OF PROSPECTIVE (FLUENCY-BASED) AGENCY

Taken together, these findings suggest that neural activity in action preparation circuits *prospectively* informs agency, independent of outcome predictability, and actual performance. Tracking dysfluency in action selection networks (Miele et al., 2011; Nahab et al., 2011) could be the basis for this prospective sense of agency. Recently, we adapted the prospective agency paradigm for functional neuroimaging (Chambon et al., 2013). Specifically, we studied whether the angular gyrus (AG), a parietal brain region which has been shown to compute *retrospective* agency by monitoring mismatches between actions and subsequent outcomes (Farrer et al., 2003, 2008), may also code for a *prospective* sense of agency, by monitoring action selection processes in advance of the action itself, and independently of action outcomes.

Behavioral results replicated those of Wenke and colleagues. Again, participants experienced greater control over action effects when the action was compatibly versus incompatibly primed (Chambon et al., 2013). More importantly, this prospective contribution of action-selection processes to sense of agency was accounted for by exchange of signals between specific frontal action selection areas and the parietal cortex. First, we found that activity in the AG was sensitive to mismatches, but not matches, between prime arrow and actual response to the target arrow. Moreover, this activity due to the prime-target mismatch predicted the magnitude of subsequent sense of agency: for incompatible trials only, activity in the AG decreased as sense of control over outcomes increased. Importantly, this neural coding of non-agency occurred at the time of action selection *only*, as in Wenke et al.'s original experiment.

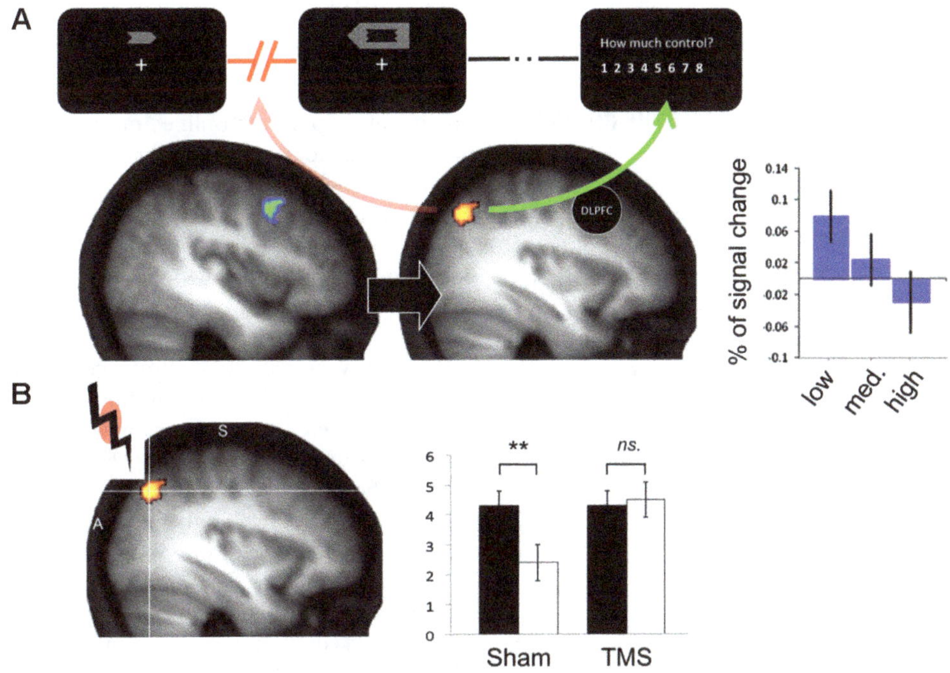

FIGURE 2 | (A) Sense of agency is accounted for by exchange of signals across a prefrontal-parietal network: decreased DLPFC activity (in blue) due to incompatible primes results in a concomitant increase in AG activity (in yellow), and a subjective loss of control. The right chart shows a negative modulation of AG activity as a function of the level of experienced control (from low to high; adapted from Chambon et al., 2013). **(B)** TMS-induced disruption of left AG at the time of action selection abolishes the compatibility effect on sense of agency (right chart).

Second, connectivity analyses (psycho-physiological interaction) revealed that activity in the AG (signaling non-agency) in incompatible trials was negatively correlated with activity in the dorso-lateral prefrontal area (DLPFC; **Figure 2A**). Previous studies of willed action also noticed the same frontoparietal correlation, namely, that increased activity in DLPFC was associated with decreased activity in the AG (Frith et al., 1991). Our results are directly analogous: compatible primes might partly engage circuits for willed action, while prime-target incompatibility might relatively decrease activity in this circuit (Wenke et al., 2010). Thus, DLPFC *deactivation* would signal dysfluency in the selection of willed action, as a consequence of prime-target incompatibility. Decreased DLPFC activity due to incompatible primes would in turn result in a concomitant increase in AG activity and a subjective loss of control. Overall, this suggests that AG may monitor signals relating to fluency or dysfluency of action selection emanating from DLFPC and use them to (pre)construct an experience of agency. Importantly, under this interpretation, this monitoring of fluency signals by AG would occur *prior* to actions and their sensory consequences. This prospective contribution of AG to sense of agency can thus be distinguished from other functions such as action outcome monitoring. Interestingly, Farrer et al. (2008) demonstrated a role of AG in action outcome monitoring, but found a bilateral AG activation, which was slightly more ventral than the AG found here. In Farrer et al.'s study, AG activation varied with mismatch between predicted and actual sensory consequences of an action, while AG activation in Chambon et al.'s study was elicited by a mismatch between a prime-induced intention and response to a target (Chambon et al., 2013). The different localization found in these two studies could thus reflect a subdivision within the inferior parietal cortex, with more dorsal AG being involved in detecting mismatch between intention and action, independent of action consequences (Chambon et al., 2013), while more ventral AG would be involved in retrospectively comparing predicted and actual consequences of an action (Farrer et al., 2008).

Monitoring of fluency signals by AG might provide the subject with an on-line, subjective marker of volition, prior to action itself. As such, this finding sketches an important qualification of recent *post-hoc* determinist views of action control (Ackerman et al., 2010). In its strongest form, determinist views suggest that human behavior is unconsciously determined by subtle changes in the stimulus environment. On this view, individuals are not even aware of how their behavior is shaped and transformed, although they can retrospectively integrate general information about past actions and environmental cues to make inferences and narrative explanations about their own behavior (Wegner, 2002). While participants, in both Wenke's and Chambon's experiments, did not have any conscious experience of the subliminal primes, they did have a real-time *subjective experience* of their own action generation, which reflected the prime's capacity to influence action selection. In this respect, the ability to monitor fluency signals generated *during* action selection in AG might be an important part of what makes our action intentional, and thus a key component of the experience of agency—defined as the feeling that we are intentionally making things happen by our own choices and actions.

A CAUSAL EVIDENCE FOR THE ROLE OF AG IN THE CODING OF PROSPECTIVE AGENCY

Although informative, this fMRI study was nevertheless limited in two key ways. First, the evidence was indirect, because of the correlational nature of fMRI. Secondly, it was not possible to pinpoint the precise *time* at which AG is involved in the prospective coding of agency owing to the relatively poor temporal resolution of fMRI. As we saw, the issue of timing is important for understanding *where* the sense of agency is computed within the intention-action-effect chain.

We recently addressed these two limitations by combining single-pulse transcranial magnetic stimulation (TMS) with subliminal priming of action selection and judgements of control over action effects. On two distinct experiments we assessed the effects of TMS over left AG on action selection processing, by linking TMS to either (i) the presentation of the arrow target; (ii) to action execution; or (iii) to the presentation of the action effect (color patch). We made specific predictions based on our previous fMRI findings. Because AG activation correlated with sense of agency only on incompatible trials, we assumed that this area monitored signals relating to selection fluency generated by DLPFC (Chambon et al., 2013). In this case, applying TMS over AG should prevent this region from monitoring any signals from DLPFC, and hence reduce the tendency for incompatibility primes to influence judgements of control.

Consistent with these predictions, we found that TMS over left AG abolished the compatibility effect (i.e., the difference between compatible and incompatible conditions) on sense of agency at the time of action selection *only* (**Figure 2B**), while TMS delivered shortly after presentation of the action effect did not alter experienced agency. Importantly, TMS had no effect on RTs. This suggests that TMS-induced disruption of AG did not interfere with action selection processing itself, but rather interfered with a circuit that monitors selection fluency to pre-construct the experience of control.

Previously it is has been suggested that the AG is involved in the retrospective construction of sense of agency by monitoring the consistency between predicted and actual sensory consequences of movements (David et al., 2008, for a review). When these predictions are violated sense of agency is reduced, and AG activity is increased. Results from our TMS study do not disagree with this view of AG function, but point to an additional role: by monitoring the consistency between action plans and required actions, the AG is also involved in *earlier* prospective aspects of sense of agency, relating to action selection and action programming.

Note the prospective *and* retrospective mechanisms have some general features in common. Both involve monitoring action-related signals or "cues" (such as re-afferent sensory feedback) as they become available, and comparing them with other relevant information for consistency (see Moore et al., 2009). We suggest that monitoring and checking is a very general function of the AG during instrumental action. Initial action intentions, such as those caused by subliminal primes in the series of studies described above, could be checked for compatibility with the action subsequently performed. These action selection cues may provide an important "online" marker of control as the action is unfolding. Not only would this provide an estimate of agency without the need to wait until sensory feedback becomes available but, as we have suggested (Chambon et al., 2013), it may protect against aberrant experiences of agency. For example, the sense of agency in patients with schizophrenia is characterised by excessive reliance on re-afferent sensory information generated by their actions, presumably due to poor, or unreliable, action selection processing (Voss et al., 2010). Prospective signals—such as fluency signals—may indeed provide an important counterweight to re-afferent information, and hence may protect against xenopathic experiences (e.g., loss of control over one's actions and thoughts) such as those experienced in passivity symptoms. At the same time, excessive reliance on these prospective signals may produce the opposite delusion of omnipotence, in which the mere decision to act is incorrectly assumed to produce successful action outcomes. This latter illusion appears to be common in historical despots but is interestingly absent in depressed people (Alloy and Abramson, 1979). A robust and reliable sense of agency may thus require a balanced—and probably context-dependent—mixture of both prospective and retrospective components. Future work is required to test whether other (contextual of individual) factors may influence the interplay between these two components. For example, it has been convincingly suggested that priming effects on the experience of agency depend on the *level* at which the agent represents her behavior (van der Weiden et al., 2010). Thus, while some people represent their own behavior at a low-level (i.e., the instrumental level: in terms of *how* an action is done), some others represent their behavior at a higher level (i.e., the outcome level: in terms of *why* an action is done). Interestingly, the former may depend more heavily on prospective cues to agency (e.g., selection fluency), whereas the latter may show excessive reliance on retrospective information—i.e., on general information about past actions and outcome-related cues.

LINKING FLUENCY TO OUTCOME PREDICTABILITY

Recent accounts of agency have highlighted that it results from the integration of various cues (Synofzik et al., 2008; Moore and Fletcher, 2012), which may emerge at different times (Farrer et al., 2013). Namely, it has been suggested that several agency cues may be weighted by their reliability in order to obtain a "Bayesian optimal" estimate of true agency (Moore and Fletcher, 2012). This view has received some support as studies have shown, for example, that changes in action-contingency affected the weighting of predictive and postdictive cues (Moore and Haggard, 2008; Wolpe et al., 2013). As outcome predictability was reduced, there was a greater reliance on *post-hoc*, inferential processes.

In the action priming studies described above, outcomes were fully contingent on a given action, in order to hold outcome predictability constant. However, it remained unclear whether action selection fluency would still be a relevant cue to agency in a context of greater uncertainty about action-outcome relations. Given our previous proposal that action selection fluency could serve as an advance predictor of successful action (Chambon and Haggard, 2012), one might predict that reducing action-outcome contingency would reduce the contribution of the prospective (fluency-based) relative to the retrospective (outcome-based) cue, to sense of agency. That is, if the outcome monitoring revealed that the action was in fact unsuccessful—i.e., outcomes did not match expectations, then the fluency of action selection would no longer be relevant.

To test this, we adapted our previous paradigm (e.g., Chambon et al., 2013) to involve a reduced contingency between actions and outcomes (Sidarus et al., 2013). Thus, a given action was associated with two possible colored outcomes on 66% of trials, but these colors would appear after the alternative action on the remaining 33% of trials. This allowed us to create situations in which outcomes could either match or mismatch expectations, given action-outcome contingencies. In addition, these outcomes would follow actions that were either compatibly or incompatibly primed. Therefore, we could assess the relative contribution of a prospective cue—action selection fluency, with a retrospective cue—outcome monitoring.

Results showed that participants' sense of agency was sensitive to manipulations of both the prospective and the retrospective cues. Compatibly primed actions were associated with higher control ratings than incompatibly primed actions. Additionally, participants reported a stronger sense of agency when the outcome was expected, compared to when the outcome was unexpected. More importantly, there was an interaction between the two variables. Incompatible action priming led to a significant reduction in control ratings when outcomes were unexpected, but not when outcomes were expected. At the same time, unexpected outcomes only reduced control ratings significantly when they followed incompatibly primed actions, and not compatibly primed actions (Sidarus et al., 2013). Thus, contrary to our predictions, selection fluency had a larger impact on sense of agency when outcomes were unexpected.

These findings reiterate the importance of action selection processes to the sense of agency. Even though outcomes were less predictable than in previous studies, we still found a similar effect of action priming on control ratings. What is more, the interaction between selection fluency and outcome expectation suggests that the sense of agency does not merely reflect information about action-outcome relations (e.g., Metcalfe and Greene, 2007). The sense of agency was drastically reduced only when both action selection was dysfluent *and* the outcome was unexpected. Prospective cues related to action selection fluency may thus make an independent contribution to the sense of agency from retrospective, outcome-based, cues.

Our findings are also not fully compatible with the cue integration models presently proposed for agency computation (Moore and Fletcher, 2012). Within this framework, it is the reliability of a given cue that determines its impact on the resulting sense of agency. Reliability is, however, a feature of the distribution of events. Thus, changes in cue reliability can only be assessed over a number of trials. Instead, our results suggest that the specific information carried by a given cue in a single trial can alter its weight relative to other cues. More complex Bayesian models of cue integration might be able to encompass these dynamic changes in cue weight. Yet, as mentioned above, perhaps a complete account of the sense of agency cannot be provided by simply maximising information about action-outcome relations.

These results overall support the idea that agency is the "default" assumption, which is only falsified, or reduced, when there is "sufficient" evidence against it.[3] In some circumstances, it might be adaptive to maintain a sense of agency in the face of unexpected outcomes. Our environment mostly does not afford us fully predictable and contingent relations between actions and outcomes, but rather these tend to be probabilistic in nature. As such, we can learn these predictive relations, but we must also admit that predictions may be violated either due to the known statistical relations (e.g., when it is 66%), or due to random or outlier events. This type of *expected uncertainty* (Yu and Dayan, 2005) suggests that a mismatch between prediction and outcome does not always imply that the environment has changed, and one is not in control. In these situations, agency may be retained depending on information from other available cues, namely internal signals related to action selection.

ACTION SELECTION, AGENCY, AND EXPERTISE

Interestingly, the experience associated to selection fluency (at least partly) overlaps with the phenomenal properties of what has been formalized as "flow" in positive psychology (Csikszentmihalyi, 1990). The flow is a particular mental state, described by expert people as a feeling of mindfulness and total commitment to the task at hand, often associated with an experience of a dilation of subjective time (Witt and Sugovic, 2010; see also Hagura et al., 2012). In some professional tennis players, for example, this feeling of "flow", resulting from a fluently selected (and perfectly executed) backhand stroke, may be associated with a "premonitory" anticipation of *where* the ball is going to hit the ground (Murphy and White, 1978). Consistently, our findings suggest that people may use the *fluency* (or ease) with which an action is selected as a good advance predictor of actual statistical control over the external environment.

Two hypotheses can be considered to account for the use of fluency signals in daily life. Using these signals adequately could first require learning *stable* relations between actions (e.g., the backhand stroke) and outcomes (e.g., where the tennis ball hit the court on average after that specific backhand). Indeed, simply having a feeling of fluently knowing which action to select does not guarantee the correct action outcome. Thus, fluency-based behaviors might only develop with expertise, once the brain has shifted from supervisory control to automatic or expert control. Under the expert regime, fluency would be used as an

[3]Whereas subjects experience less control when presented with incompatibly vs. neutrally-primed (using "neutral" primes constructed by superimposing left- and right-oriented primes), they do not feel more control when compatibly vs. neutrally-primed (Chambon and Haggard, 2012). These results are consistent with previous accounts suggesting that agency is a *default* experience. On this view, sense of agency would only really become apparent as a sense of *non-agency*, when the normal flow from our intentions to the effects of our actions is broken (Haggard, 2005; Chambon and Haggard, 2013).

implicit proxy for the current status (success or failure) of the action unfolding (Haggard and Chambon, 2012), and would substitute for explicit monitoring of the action-effect link through short-circuiting the process of "checking" the actual consequences of our actions.

In contrast, an alternative hypothesis would propose that we learn in our everyday lives to use fluency of action selection as a reliable cue to agency. Fluency signals may become a heuristics for assessing one's control over the external world, and we might even rely more on this heuristics in novel or uncertain situations. Before we know the statistical contingency between an action and its outcome in a given situation, we still have a sense of agency over what we do. Hence, we might rely on selection fluency to guide this sense of agency, until the more reliable action-outcome contingency cue is available. Although the Sidarus et al. (2013) study may provide some support for this alternative hypothesis, further research is needed to explore how the role of different agency cues may shift over time, during the learning of action-outcome relations. Similarly, high levels of expertise in complex tasks may involve the recruitment of different processes, and also affect the types of cues that inform the sense of agency.

ACKNOWLEDGMENTS

Valérian Chambon was supported by a Post-doctoral Fellowship of the Région Île-de-France (Paris), and by ANR-10-LABX-0087 IEC and ANR-10-IDEX-0001-02 PSL*. Nura Sidarus was supported by UCL Impact Scholarship and the Belgian Science Policy Office project "Mechanisms of conscious and unconscious learning" (IAP P7/33). Patrick Haggard was supported by an ESRC Professorial Fellowship, an ESRC/ESF ECRP Research Project, an ERC Advanced Grant (HUMVOL) and by EU FP7 Project VERE, Work Package 1.

REFERENCES

Aarts, H., Custers, R., and Wegner, D. M. (2005). On the inference of personal authorship: enhancing experienced agency by priming effect information. *Conscious. Cogn.* 14, 439–458. doi: 10.1016/j.concog.2004.11.001

Ackerman, J. M., Nocera, C. C., and Bargh, J. A. (2010). Incidental haptic sensations influence social judgments and decisions. *Science* 328, 1712–1715. doi: 10.1126/science.1189993

Alloy, L. B., and Abramson, L. Y. (1979). Judgment of contingency in depressed and nondepressed students: sadder but wiser? *J. Exp. Psychol. Gen.* 108, 441–485. doi: 10.1037/0096-3445.108.4.441

Arango-Muñoz, S. (2010). Two levels of metacognition. *Philosophia* 39, 71–82. doi: 10.1007/s11406-010-9279-0

Blakemore, S.-J., Frith, C. D., and Wolpert, D. M. (2001). The cerebellum is involved in predicting the sensory consequences of action. *Neuroreport* 12, 1879–1884. doi: 10.1097/00001756-200107030-00023

Chambon, V., Filevich, E., and Haggard, P. (2014). "What is the human sense of agency and is it metacognitive?," in *The Neuroscience of Metacognition*, eds S. M. Fleming and C. D. Frith (Berlin Heidelberg: Springer-Verlag), 321–342.

Chambon, V., and Haggard, P. (2012). Sense of control depends on fluency of action selection, not motor performance. *Cognition* 125, 441–451. doi: 10.1016/j.cognition.2012.07.011

Chambon, V., and Haggard, P. (2013). "Premotor or Ideomotor: how does the experience of action come about?," in *Action Science: Foundations of an Emerging Discipline*, eds W. Prinz, M. Beisert and A. Herwig (Cambridge, MA: MIT Press), 359–380.

Chambon, V., Wenke, D., Fleming, S. M., Prinz, W., and Haggard, P. (2013). An online neural substrate for sense of agency. *Cereb. Cortex* 23, 1031–1037. doi: 10.1093/cercor/bhs059

Charles, L., Opstal, F., van Marti, S., and Dehaene, S. (2013). Distinct brain mechanisms for conscious versus subliminal error detection. *Neuroimage* 73, 80–94. doi: 10.1016/j.neuroimage.2013.01.054

Csikszentmihalyi, M. (1990). *Flow: The Psychology of Optimal Experience.* New York: Harper and Row.

Damen, T. G. E., van Baaren, R. B., and Dijksterhuis, A. (2014). You should read this! Perceiving and acting upon action primes influences one's sense of agency. *J. Exp. Soc. Psychol.* 50, 21–26. doi: 10.1016/j.jesp.2013.09.003

David, N., Cohen, M. X., Newen, A., Bewernick, B. H., Shah, N. J., Fink, G. R., et al. (2007). The extrastriate cortex distinguishes between the consequences of one's own and others' behavior. *Neuroimage* 36, 1004–1014. doi: 10.1016/j.neuroimage.2007.03.030

David, N., Newen, A., and Vogeley, K. (2008). The "sense of agency" and its underlying cognitive and neural mechanisms. *Conscious. Cogn.* 17, 523–534. doi: 10.1016/j.concog.2008.03.004

David, N., Stenzel, A., Schneider, T. R., and Engel, A. K. (2011). The feeling of agency: empirical indicators for a pre-reflective level of action awareness. *Front. Psychol.* 2:149. doi: 10.3389/fpsyg.2011.00149

Dehaene, S., Naccache, L., Le Clec'H, G., Koechlin, E., Mueller, M., Dehaene-Lambertz, G., et al. (1998). Imaging unconscious semantic priming. *Nature* 395, 597–600. doi: 10.1038/26967

Demanet, J., Muhle-Karbe, P. S., Lynn, M. T., Blotenberg, I., and Brass, M. (2013). Power to the will: how exerting physical effort boosts the sense of agency. *Cognition* 129, 574–578. doi: 10.1016/j.cognition.2013.08.020

Engbert, K., Wohlschläger, A., and Haggard, P. (2008). Who is causing what? The sense of agency is relational and efferent-triggered. *Cognition* 107, 693–704. doi: 10.1016/j.cognition.2007.07.021

Farrer, C., and Frith, C. D. (2002). Experiencing oneself vs another person as being the cause of an action: the neural correlates of the experience of agency. *Neuroimage* 15, 596–603. doi: 10.1006/nimg.2001.1009

Farrer, C., Franck, N., Georgieff, N., Frith, C. D., Decety, J., and Jeannerod, M. (2003). Modulating the experience of agency: a positron emission tomography study. *Neuroimage* 18, 324–333. doi: 10.1016/s1053-8119(02)00041-1

Farrer, C., Frey, S. H., Van Horn, J. D., Tunik, E., Turk, D., Inati, S., et al. (2008). The angular gyrus computes action awareness representations. *Cereb. Cortex* 18, 254–261. doi: 10.1093/cercor/bhm050

Farrer, C., Valentin, G., and Hupé, J. M. (2013). The time windows of the sense of agency. *Conscious. Cogn.* 22, 1431–1441. doi: 10.1016/j.concog.2013.09.010

Fleming, S. M., Mars, R. B., Gladwin, T. E., and Haggard, P. (2009). When the brain changes its mind: flexibility of action selection in instructed and free choices. *Cereb. Cortex* 19, 2352–2360. doi: 10.1093/cercor/bhn252

Fourneret, P., and Jeannerod, M. (1998). Limited conscious monitoring of motor performance in normal subjects. *Neuropsychologia* 36, 1133–1140. doi: 10.1016/s0028-3932(98)00006-2

Franck, N., Farrer, C., Georgieff, N., Marie-Cardine, M., Daléry, J., d' Amato, T., et al. (2001). Defective recognition of one's own actions in patients with schizophrenia. *Am. J. Psychiatry* 158, 454–459. doi: 10.1176/appi.ajp.158.3.454

Frith, C. D., Friston, K., Liddle, P. F., and Frackowiak, R. S. J. (1991). Willed action and the prefrontal cortex in man: a study with PET. *Proc. R. Soc. Lond. B Biol. Sci.* 244, 241–246. doi: 10.1098/rspb.1991.0077

Haggard, P., and Chambon, V. (2012). Sense of agency. *Curr. Biol.* 22, R390–R392. doi: 10.1016/j.cub.2012.02.040

Haggard, P. (2005). Conscious intention and motor cognition. *Trends Cogn. Sci.* 9, 290–295. doi: 10.1016/j.tics.2005.04.012

Haggard, P., Clark, S., and Kalogeras, J. (2002). Voluntary action and conscious awareness. *Nat. Neurosci.* 5, 382–385. doi: 10.1038/nn827

Hagura, N., Kanai, R., Orgs, G., and Haggard, P. (2012). Ready steady slow: action preparation slows the subjective passage of time. *Proc. Biol. Sci.* 279, 4399–4406. doi: 10.1098/rspb.2012.1339

Leube, D. T., Knoblich, G., Erb, M., Grodd, W., Bartels, M., and Kircher, T. T. (2003). The neural correlates of perceiving one's own movements. *Neuroimage* 20, 2084–2090. doi: 10.1016/j.neuroimage.2003.07.033

Linser, K., and Goschke, T. (2007). Unconscious modulation of the conscious experience of voluntary control. *Cognition* 104, 459–475. doi: 10.1016/j.cognition.2006.07.009

MacDonald, P. A., and Paus, T. (2003). The role of parietal cortex in awareness of self-generated movements: a transcranial magnetic stimulation study. *Cereb. Cortex* 13, 962–967. doi: 10.1093/cercor/13.9.962

Marti, S., Sackur, J., Sigman, M., and Dehaene, S. (2010). Mapping introspection's blind spot: reconstruction of dual-task phenomenology using quantified introspection. *Cognition* 115, 303–313. doi: 10.1016/j.cognition.2010.01.003

McGuire, J. T., and Botvinick, M. M. (2010). Prefrontal cortex, cognitive control and the registration of decision costs. *Proc. Natl. Acad. Sci.* 107, 7922–7926. doi: 10.1073/pnas.0910662107

Metcalfe, J., and Greene, M. J. (2007). Metacognition of agency. *J. Exp. Psychol. Gen.* 136, 184–199. doi: 10.1037/0096-3445.136.2.184

Miall, R. C., and Wolpert, D. M. (1996). Forward models for physiological motor control. *Neural Netw.* 9, 1265–1279. doi: 10.1016/s0893-6080(96)00035-4

Miele, D. B., Wager, T. D., Mitchell, J. P., and Metcalfe, J. (2011). Dissociating neural correlates of action monitoring and metacognition of agency. *J. Cogn. Neurosci.* 23, 3620–3636. doi: 10.1162/jocn_a_00052

Moore, J. W., and Fletcher, P. C. (2012). Sense of agency in health and disease: a review of cue integration approaches. *Conscious. Cogn.* 21, 59–68. doi: 10.1016/j.concog.2011.08.010

Moore, J. W., and Haggard, P. (2008). Awareness of action: inference and prediction. *Conscious. Cogn.* 17, 136–144. doi: 10.1016/j.concog.2006.12.004

Moore, J. W., and Obhi, S. S. (2012). Intentional binding and the sense of agency: a review. *Conscious. Cogn.* 21, 546–561. doi: 10.1016/j.concog.2011.12.002

Moore, J. W., Wegner, D. M., and Haggard, P. (2009). Modulating the sense of agency with external cues. *Conscious. Cogn.* 18, 1056–1064. doi: 10.1016/j.concog.2009.05.004

Morsella, E., Wilson, L. E., Berger, C. C., Honhongva, M., Gazzaley, A., and Bargh, J. A. (2009). Subjective aspects of cognitive control at different stages of processing. *Atten. Percept. Psychophys.* 71, 1807–1824. doi: 10.3758/app.71.8.1807

Murphy, M., and White, R. (1978). *In the Zone, Transcendent Experience in Sports.* New York, NY: Penguin Arkana.

Nahab, F. B., Kundu, P., Gallea, C., Kakareka, J., Pursley, R., Pohida, T., et al. (2011). The neural processes underlying self-agency. *Cereb. Cortex* 21, 48–55. doi: 10.1093/cercor/bhq059

Oppenheimer, D. M. (2008). The secret life of fluency. *Trends Cogn. Sci.* 12, 237–241. doi: 10.1016/j.tics.2008.02.014

Pacherie, E. (2008). The phenomenology of action: a conceptual framework. *Cognition* 107, 179–217. doi: 10.1016/j.cognition.2007.09.003

Sato, A. (2009). Both motor prediction and conceptual congruency between preview and action-effect contribute to explicit judgment of agency. *Cognition* 110, 74–83. doi: 10.1016/j.cognition.2008.10.011

Schlaghecken, F., and Eimer, M. (2000). A central-peripheral asymmetry in masked priming. *Percept. Psychophys.* 62, 1367–1382. doi: 10.3758/bf03212139

Schlaghecken, F., Rowley, L., Sembi, S., Simmons, R., and Whitcomb, D. (2008). The negative compatibility effect: a case for self-inhibition. *Adv. Cogn. Psychol.* 3, 227–240. doi: 10.2478/v10053-008-0027-y

Sidarus, N., Chambon, V., and Haggard, P. (2013). Priming of action increases sense of control over unexpected outcomes. *Conscious. Cogn.* 22, 1403–1411. doi: 10.1016/j.concog.2013.09.008

Steinhauser, M., and Kiesel, A. (2011). Performance monitoring and the causal attribution of errors. *Cogn. Affect. Behav. Neurosci.* 11, 309–320. doi: 10.3758/s13415-011-0033-2

Stenner, M. P., Bauer, M., Sidarus, N., Heinze, H. J., Haggard, P., and Dolan, R. J. (2014). Subliminal action priming modulates the perceived intensity of sensory action consequences. *Cognition* 130, 227–235. doi: 10.1016/j.cognition.2013.11.008

Synofzik, M., Thier, P., and Lindner, A. (2006). Internalizing agency of self-action: perception of one's own hand movements depends on an adaptable prediction about the sensory action outcome. *J. Neurophysiol.* 96, 1592–1601. doi: 10.1152/jn.00104.2006

Synofzik, M., Vosgerau, G., and Newen, A. (2008). Beyond the comparator model: a multifactorial two-step account of agency. *Conscious. Cogn.* 17, 219–239. doi: 10.1016/j.concog.2007.03.010

van der Weiden, A., Aarts, H., and Ruys, K. I. (2010). Reflecting on the action or its outcome: behavior representation level modulates high level outcome priming effects on self-agency experiences. *Conscious. Cogn.* 19, 21–32. doi: 10.1016/j.concog.2009.12.004

Voss, M., Moore, J., Hauser, M., Gallinat, J., Heinz, A., and Haggard, P. (2010). Altered awareness of action in schizophrenia: a specific deficit in predicting action consequences. *Brain* 133, 3104–3112. doi: 10.1093/brain/awq152

Wegner, D. (2002). *The Illusion of Conscious Will.* Cambridge, MA: MIT Press.

Wegner, D., and Wheatley, T. (1999). Apparent mental causation: sources of the experience of will. *Am. Psychol.* 54, 480–492. doi: 10.1037//0003-066x.54.7.480

Wenke, D., Fleming, S. M., and Haggard, P. (2010). Subliminal priming of actions influences sense of control over effects of action. *Cognition* 115, 26–38. doi: 10.1016/j.cognition.2009.10.016

Witt, J. K., and Sugovic, M. (2010). Performance and ease influence perceived speed. *Perception* 39, 1341–1353. doi: 10.1068/p6699

Wolpe, N., Haggard, P., Siebner, H. R., and Rowe, J. B. (2013). Cue integration and the perception of action in intentional binding. *Exp. Brain Res.* 229, 467–474. doi: 10.1007/s00221-013-3419-2

Wolpert, D. M., Ghahramani, Z., and Jordan, M. I. (1995). An internal model for sensorimotor integration. *Science* 29, 1880–1882. doi: 10.1126/science.7569931

Yu, A. J., and Dayan, P. (2005). Uncertainty, neuromodulation and attention. *Neuron* 46, 681–692. doi: 10.1016/j.neuron.2005.04.026

2

A new comparator account of auditory verbal hallucinations: how motor prediction can plausibly contribute to the sense of agency for inner speech

Lauren Swiney[1]* and Paulo Sousa[2]

[1] School of Anthropology, Institute of Cognitive and Evolutionary Anthropology, University of Oxford, Oxford, UK
[2] Department of History and Anthropology, Institute of Cognition and Culture, Queen's University Belfast, Belfast, UK

***Correspondence:**
Lauren Swiney, School of Anthropology, Institute of Cognitive and Evolutionary Anthropology, University of Oxford, 51 Banbury Road, Oxford OX2, UK
e-mail: Lswiney01@qub.ac.uk

The comparator account holds that processes of motor prediction contribute to the sense of agency by attenuating incoming sensory information and that disruptions to this process contribute to misattributions of agency in schizophrenia. Over the last 25 years this simple and powerful model has gained widespread support not only as it relates to bodily actions but also as an account of misattributions of agency for inner speech, potentially explaining the etiology of auditory verbal hallucination (AVH). In this paper we provide a detailed analysis of the traditional comparator account for inner speech, pointing out serious problems with the specification of inner speech on which it is based and highlighting inconsistencies in the interpretation of the electrophysiological evidence commonly cited in its favor. In light of these analyses we propose a new comparator account of misattributed inner speech. The new account follows leading models of motor imagery in proposing that inner speech is not attenuated by motor prediction, but rather derived directly from it. We describe how failures of motor prediction would therefore directly affect the phenomenology of inner speech and trigger a mismatch in the comparison between motor prediction and motor intention, contributing to abnormal feelings of agency. We argue that the new account fits with the emerging phenomenological evidence that AVHs are both distinct from ordinary inner speech and heterogeneous. Finally, we explore the possibility that the new comparator account may extend to explain disruptions across a range of imagistic modalities, and outline avenues for future research.

Keywords: sense of agency, inner speech, comparator model, schizophrenia, efference copy, auditory verbal hallucination

INTRODUCTION

Patients seeking psychiatric help often describe unusual experiences and beliefs, such as reporting that their body is under the control of another agent, that they hear voices when there is no one there, or that thoughts are being inserted into their minds. Within psychiatry these reports are classified as delusions of alien control, auditory verbal hallucination (AVH) and delusions of thought insertion, respectively (*Diagnostic and Statistical Manual of Mental Disorders*; 5th ed.; *DSM-V, American Psychiatric Association, 2013*). Such symptoms provide significant weight towards a diagnosis of schizophrenia. While diagnostically distinct, it has been argued that these particular symptoms may share an etiological core, stemming from disruptions to the sense of agency, where the sense of agency refers to the experience of the self as causing and directing one's actions (e.g., Stephens and Graham, 2003; Jones and Fernyhough, 2007; Langland-Hassan, 2008; Synofzik et al., 2008a; Frith, 2012; Sousa and Swiney, 2013).

Over the last 25 years the comparator account has emerged as the dominant model of the sense of agency and its disruptions in schizophrenia. It draws on a well-established model of the motor control system that holds that the likely sensory consequences of a given motor act are predicted by a forward model, and that this prediction attenuates the actual incoming sensory information. The core idea of the comparator account is that a match between this prediction and the actual sensory information ordinarily gives rise to sense of self-agency. In schizophrenia, disruptions in the process of prediction are proposed to lead to a mismatch, giving rise to a sense of non-self agency (Frith et al., 2000a; Frith, 2005a,b, 2012).

The comparator account of the sense of agency most straightforwardly describes how bodily actions may come to be experienced as non-self produced, giving rise to reports of delusions of alien control (Frith, 2005a). From its inception, however, theorists have held out the possibility that the account could extend to mental acts such inner speech, potentially explaining symptoms of AVH and/or thought insertion (Feinberg, 1978; Frith, 1992, 2005b, 2012). This extension is based on the proposal that inner speech production may draw on the same mechanisms of motor control as bodily actions, and may therefore be subject to the same disruptions in motor prediction. Other theorists have recently taken up the task of providing a precise specification of how such disruptions might manifest relation to inner speech, giving rise to AVH (Seal et al., 2004; Jones and Fernyhough, 2007) or both AVH and thought insertion (Langland-Hassan, 2008).

The basic plausibility of extending the comparator account beyond bodily actions to explain misattributed inner speech is ubiquitously accepted both within the expanding literature on the sense of agency (e.g., Vosgerau and Newen, 2007; Synofzik et al., 2008a) and beyond (e.g., Carruthers, 2011; Whitford et al., 2012). Authors regularly appeal to the account as a plausible explanation for results from behavioral studies (e.g., Li et al., 2002; Johns et al., 2006). The account also forms the basis of a large-scale research program investigating the electrophysiological characteristics of the brain during speech and inner speech in schizophrenia (for a recent review see Ford and Mathalon, 2012). Even among those who critique the account on phenomenological grounds (Wu, 2012) or who argue that the account requires extensions (Synofzik et al., 2008a), the viability of the basic tenants of the comparator account—that inner speech is normally predicted and attenuated and that failures in this process contribute to misattribution—appears to be unproblematically accepted.

Counter to this consensus, we will argue that there are fundamental problems with the comparator account of misattributed inner speech as it has traditionally been formulated. These problems relate both to the plausibility of the account's specification of inner speech within the motor control system, and to the electrophysiological evidence widely taken to support the account. However, given the emerging evidence for the comparator account as it applies to misattributions of bodily actions in schizophrenia (for a recent overview see Frith, 2012), we acknowledge that the possibility of a unified account of symptoms such as delusions of alien control, AVH and thought insertion provides significant motivation to pursue a comparator account of misattributed inner speech. To this end, we outline a substantially new and revised account of how failures in motor production could give rise to misattributed inner speech. Our account is based on a plausible and cognitively justified model of the production of inner speech in the motor control system, and makes novel predictions about both the phenomenology and neural mechanisms associated with misattributed inner speech.

THE TRADITIONAL COMPARATOR ACCOUNT OF MISATTRIBUTED INNER SPEECH

THE COMPARATOR MODEL OF THE MOTOR CONTROL SYSTEM

Drawing from ideas on the importance of internal processes of comparison for regulation and control (Helmholtz, 1886; Holst and Mittelstadt, 1950; Sperry, 1950), experimental and computational work over the last years has contributed to our knowledge of the mechanisms constituting motor cognition—those that, at a subpersonal level, generate, control and monitor our physical movements (e.g., Kawato and Wolpert, 1998; Wolpert and Flanagan, 2001; Blakemore et al., 2002; Lindner et al., 2005; Wolpert et al., 2011). The result is the comparator model of motor control. The model posits a system that utilizes feedback and feedforward control loops in conjunction with three comparator mechanisms to direct, control and adjust motor actions. The fundamental job of the motor system is to generate movement by issuing motor commands (see **Figure 1**). If you want to lift your hand from your lap the motor control system generates the motor command that will guide your hand from your *actual state* (hand in the lap) to your *desired state* (hand above the lap). The representation of your actual state is derived from the current sensory experience of having your hand in your lap, and is therefore always an estimation. The representation of your desired state is based on your goal (to have the hand above the lap). These two representations (estimated actual state, desired state) are compared in the first comparator (C1) and sent to an inverse model that will specify the motor command necessary to get from the estimated actual state (hand in the lap) to the desired state (hand above the lap).

The system also uses the motor command to predict the sensory consequences of a given act; representing the *predicted state* (Miall et al., 1993; Wolpert and Ghahramani, 2000). This is achieved through the production of a duplicate of the motor command known as the efference copy. This efference copy is sent to a forward model that uses it to predict the sensory consequences of issuing the motor command (Holst and Mittelstadt, 1950). This predicted state is compared to the desired state in the second comparator (C2), allowing the motor command to be checked even before it is issued.

The predicted state is also compared to the incoming sensory information (the new actual state, relating to the hand now being above the lap) in the third comparator (C3), allowing for adjustments when the movement does not go according to plan. This comparison in the third comparator is often described in terms of a process of attenuation; the idea is that sensory information that is the result of self-generated movement is attenuated or "canceled out" by the matching predicted state. Evidence for this process includes our inability to tickle ourselves. The incoming sensory information (the tickle) is predicted by the motor control system and so is cancelled out or attenuated (Blakemore et al., 1998). This attenuation is also held to account for other aspects of our phenomenology, such as our experience of a stable visual field (Langland-Hassan, 2008). If you were to move one of your eyes indirectly, without issuing the relevant motor command, your visual experience is that the world (and not your eye) is moving. You can demonstrate this by covering one eye and then pressing gently on the side of the other; the visual scene appears to move. However, if you cover one eye and then move the other from side to side in the normal fashion (i.e., without the aid of your finger), you will have the normal sensation of vision with a stable visual field. The process of attenuation by the predicted state is not restricted to touch and vision; when we speak, the predicted auditory consequences are relayed to auditory sensory areas where incoming sound is attenuated (Greenlee et al., 2010).

The comparator model of motor control, and in particular the proposal of internal comparator mechanisms, has acquired considerable support (e.g., Kawato and Wolpert, 1998) and there is emerging evidence that such a model can be instantiated within the networks of the brain (Frith, 2005b; Ramnani, 2006; Knolle et al., 2012).

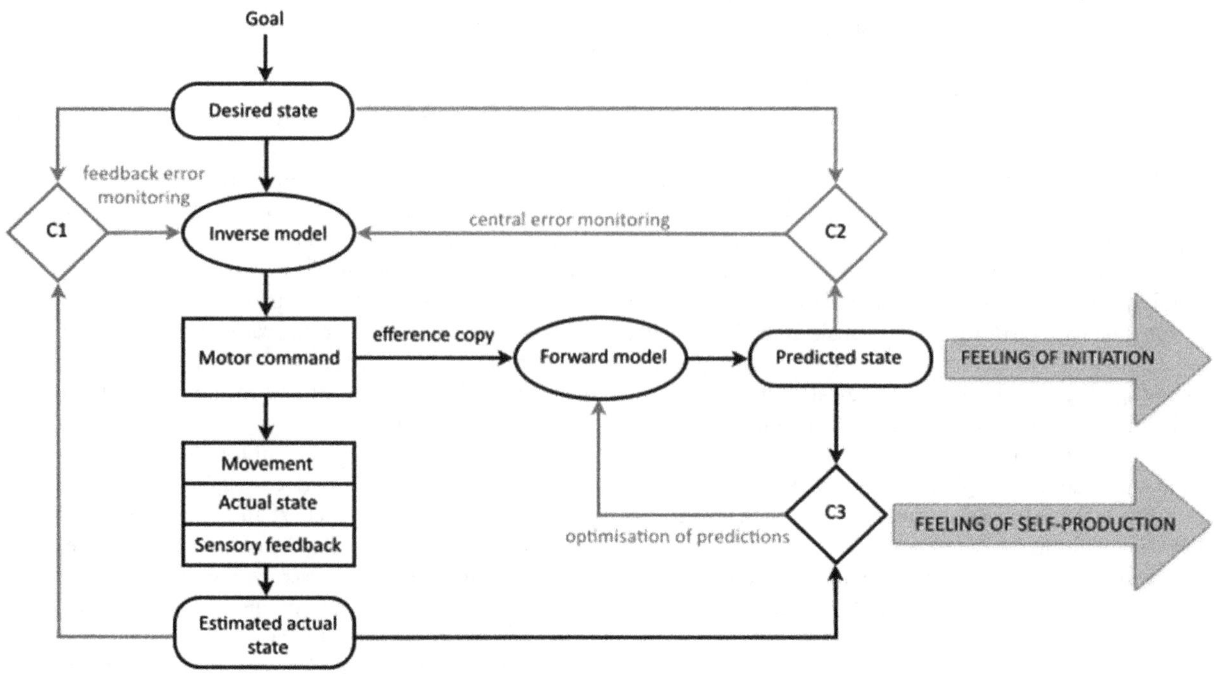

FIGURE 1 | The comparator model of the motor control system and the comparator account of the sense of agency for bodily action in normal cognition. Those processes central to the present discussion are in black, the remainder in gray. In this simple model of the motor control system three states are represented internally: the desired state, the predicted state, and the estimated current state. According to the comparator account of the sense of agency for bodily action, the production of the predicted state results in a *feeling of initiation*. Because the predicted state matches the sensory feedback from the new actual state, the comparison in comparator three, gives rise to a *feeling of self-production*. It is proposed that, in schizophrenia, disruptions to the predicted state lead to abnormalities in both the feeling of initiation and the feeling of self-production for bodily actions (for further details see main text; figure modified after Frith et al., 2000b; Blakemore et al., 2002; Synofzik et al., 2008a).

THE COMPARATOR ACCOUNT OF THE SENSE OF ABNORMAL AGENCY FOR BODILY ACTION

The comparator account of the sense of agency for bodily action proposes that as well as explaining the adjustment and control of motor action, the mechanisms of the motor control system can also provide an account of the sense of agency and its disruption in delusions of alien control (Frith et al., 2000a,b; Blakemore et al., 2002; Frith, 2005a, 2012). The account proposes that in normal cognition the generation of the predicted state underlies the sense of self-agency (see **Figure 1**). Firstly, during ordinary movement, the comparison of the predicted state to the incoming sensory information (in the third comparator, C3) should reveal a match, allowing self-generated movements to be distinguished from sensory feedback that is non self-generated, and giving rise to a *feeling of self-production*. In addition, the account holds that the mere generation of the predicted state may also contribute to the sense of agency, by giving rise to a *feeling of initiation* (Blakemore et al., 2002).

In schizophrenia, the predicted state is proposed to be faulty in some way, interfering with both of these aspects of the sense of agency and giving rise to delusions of alien control. Firstly, a faulty or absent predicted state leads to a lack of the feeling of initiation. Because the patient is not aware of having initiated the movement, "[i]t is as if the movement, although intended, has been initiated by some external force" (Blakemore et al., 2002, p. 240). Secondly, a faulty or absent predicted state would lead to a mismatch in the third comparator, meaning that the sensory consequences of the self-generated movement are not attenuated. It is proposed that this failure of attenuation leads to a feeling of non-self-production.

The account has received considerable empirical support from studies indicating that problems in predicting the sensory consequences of action are associated with schizophrenia (Blakemore et al., 2000; Shergill et al., 2005; Leube et al., 2010), as well as evidence of functional and structural abnormalities in schizophrenia in many of the brain regions suggested to play a role in motor prediction (for recent overviews of this evidence see Farrer and Franck, 2007; Voss et al., 2010; Pynn and DeSouza, 2013). There are also plausible neurobiological accounts consistent with the cognitive account (Fletcher and Frith, 2009; Whitford et al., 2012).

A popular way to classify accounts of the sense of agency has been to draw a distinction between "top-down" and "bottom-up" approaches. Top-down approaches are those that explain misattributions by appealing to disruptions in interpretive processes incorporating conceptual information about the self (e.g., Wegner, 2002; Stephens and Graham, 2003). By contrast, bottom-up approaches are those that explain misattributions of agency by appealing to disruptions in subpersonal, automatic, non-interpretive processes. This widespread distinction between top-down and bottom-up etiological accounts mirrors the recent explication of two distinct functional and representational levels at which the sense of agency can be usefully analyzed (Synofzik et al., 2008a). One is the level of *feeling* of agency, which is argued to represent the non-conceptual, low-level feeling of being the agent of an action, at which level the self can only be implicitly represented. The other is the level of *judgment* of agency, which refers to the interpretive, conceptual judgment of being the agent of an action at the level of the narrative self. One way that these levels have been elucidated has been to appeal to the experience of optical illusions (e.g., Bayne, 2011). The Müller-Lyer illusion consists of two lines of identical length; one of the lines has arrows on either end that point inwards, and the other has arrows that point outwards. Even when we are able to make the conceptual judgment that the two lines are of the same length (for instance, after we have measured them), we continue to have the visual experience of them as different lengths. Something like this distinction is understood to hold for subjective experiences such as the experience of agency for inner speech (Bayne, 2011). A person may reach the conceptual judgment that an episode of inner speech was self-produced (for instance, on the basis that there is no one else in the room), but they may nonetheless have the first-person *feeling* that the episode was non self-produced.

The comparator account of the sense of agency provides a bottom-up account that explains the cognitive generation of subpersonal *feelings* of agency. As such it has been criticized for suggesting that a non-conceptual feeling of non-self agency could fully account for a conceptual judgment of external agency (e.g., Synofzik et al., 2008a). However, it is worth noting that proponents of the comparator account have always maintained that additional disruptions to the patient's belief system are required to explain how the abnormal feelings of agency are interpreted in an irrational way (Blakemore et al., 2002; Frith, 2012). Most recently, Synofzik et al. have incorporated the comparator account of the sense of agency into their multifactorial weighting model (MWM). This model holds that a *variety* of top-down and bottom-up cues—including feelings of agency issuing from the motor control system—are ordinarily integrated to give rise to the sense of agency (Synofzik et al., 2008a,b, 2009a,b, 2013; Synofzik and Voss, 2010; Synofzik and Vosgerau, 2012).

THE COMPARATOR ACCOUNT OF THE SENSE OF ABNORMAL AGENCY FOR INNER SPEECH

Besides explaining misattributions of bodily actions such as delusions of control, proponents of the comparator model have often aimed to extend the account to explain the misattribution of mental acts (Feinberg, 1978, 2011; Frith, 1992, 2012). In recent years this has taken shape in the proposal that the same motor control-based disruption in predictive processes may impact the experience of inner speech, underlying symptoms of AVH and even thought insertion. Up to one fourth of our conscious mental life is comprised of "talking" to ourselves silently in our minds (Heavey and Hurlburt, 2008). Since AVH consists of reporting a voice when none is present, it is plausible that inner speech may form the basis of the hallucinatory experience. A variety of cognitive models have been proposed to explain how we might ordinarily come to have the subjective, internal experience of thought in natural language (e.g., Levelt, 1983; Kinsbourne, 2000; Fernyhough, 2004; Kosslyn, 2005; Carruthers, 2006; Baddeley, 2007). The comparator account of inner speech holds that similar motor control processes will underpin the production of sentences in natural language whether they are "spoken" internally or externally. On this basis, several theorists have provided detailed accounts of a comparator account for misattributed inner speech (Seal et al., 2004; Jones and Fernyhough, 2007; Langland-Hassan, 2008; Whitford et al., 2012). Jones and Fernyhough (2007) provide the clearest and most comprehensive explication of such an approach. Their account is outlined in **Figure 2**, showing both the specification of inner speech and the proposed disruptions in schizophrenia.

The basic proposal is that inner speech, like outer speech and other bodily acts, is a product of the motor control system in such a way that it is compared to, and attenuated by, a predicted state. The model holds that in the normal case of inner speech a goal generates a representation of the desired state, and a motor command is issued. The motor command results not only in the occurrence of the action (in this case, inner speech occurs) but also in the generation of the efference copy and predicted state.

Just as with the comparator account of the sense of agency for bodily actions, the approach holds that deficits in the predicted state result in an abnormal experience of agency. The account is a fairly direct transposition of the comparator account as it applies to bodily actions. Firstly, a failure to generate a predicted state results in a lack of feeling of initiation for the inner speech or, to use the term employed by Jones and Fernyhough (2007, p. 395), "no emotion of self-authorship". Secondly, the same failure to generate a representation of the predicted state results in a mismatch in the third comparator (C3), resulting in the episode of inner speech being classified as *non-self* in origin, or, to use Jones and Fernyhough's (2007, p. 395) phrase, resulting in an "emotion of other-authorship". These two factors are posited to combine to create a conscious experience of non-self agency, which is then interpreted by "top-down" factors, i.e., conscious judgments, to give rise to an explicit misattribution of agency.

PROBLEMS WITH THE TRADITIONAL COMPARATOR ACCOUNT OF MISATTRIBUTED INNER SPEECH

The basic explication of the comparator account applied to inner speech—that inner speech is normally predicted and attenuated and that failures in this process contribute to misattribution—is widely accepted both within the literature on the sense of agency and beyond (e.g., Li et al., 2002; Johns et al., 2006; Vosgerau and Newen, 2007; Synofzik et al., 2008a; Carruthers, 2011; Ford and Mathalon, 2012; Whitford et al., 2012). In contrast to this consensus, we argue that there are fundamental problems with the comparator account as it is currently specified. These problems mean that both the basic model of how inner speech is specified within the motor control system and the account of how deficits in prediction lead to misattributions of agency are untenable. The critique will focus on Jones and Fernyhough's version of the comparator account, but the main points apply to any version of

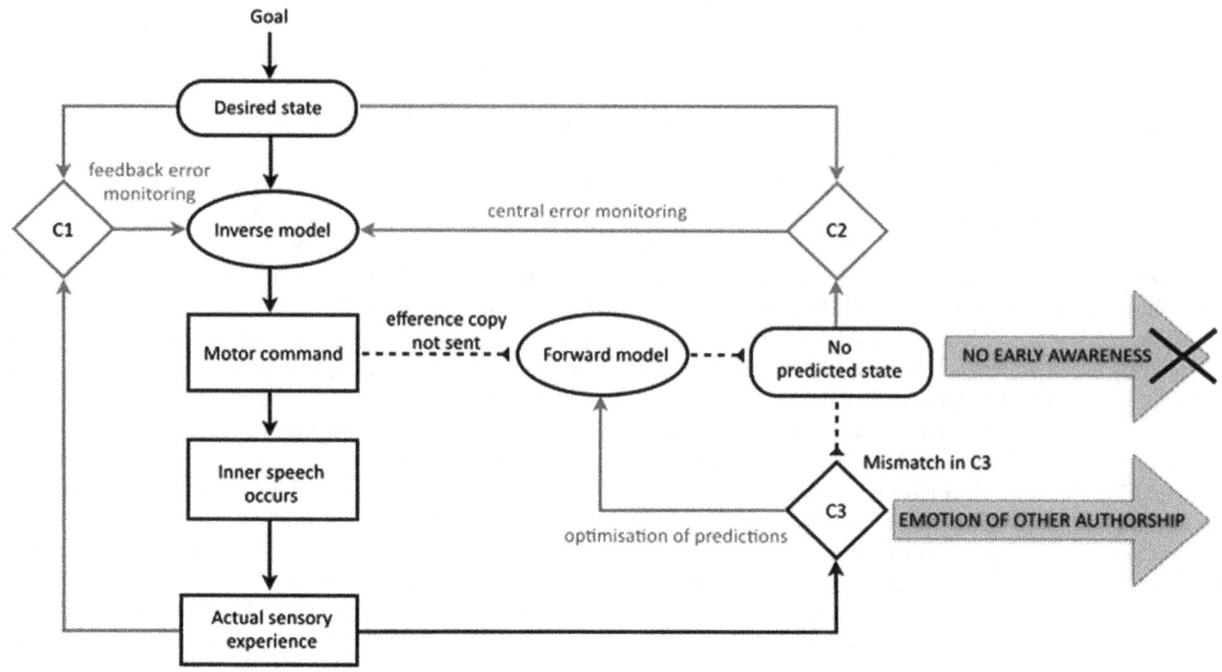

FIGURE 2 | The traditional comparator account of inner speech in the motor control system and the sense of agency for inner speech in schizophrenia, with relevant processes in black. The account holds that inner speech is, like overt speech, the direct product of the motor command, and that an efference copy is also produced. In pathology, a failure to send an efference copy of the motor command means that no predicted state is generated, leading to a *lack of early awareness* of the inner speech, and an *emotion of other authorship*. Based on Jones and Fernyhough (2007), with basic features of the motor control system as in **Figure 1** (based on Frith et al., 2000b; Blakemore et al., 2002; Synofzik et al., 2008a).

the account that maintains that inner speech is attenuated by a predicted state.

Before outlining our concerns with the current account, it is important to note that we will not challenge the basic proposal that the motor control system may be involved in the production of inner speech. Firstly, while the comparator model of the motor control system was originally posited to account for motor-to-somatosensory predictions in motor action, there is emerging electrophysiological and behavioral evidence that the extension of this model to motor-to-auditory predictions is plausible (Bäß et al., 2008; Greenlee et al., 2010; Weiss et al., 2011; Knolle et al., 2012). Secondly, there are several strands of evidence indicating that inner speech may be a product of the motor control system (for a review see Stephane et al., 2001). This includes developmental evidence that inner speech is related to early private speech (Berk, 1992), evidence of structural similarities between speech and inner speech (Dell and Repka, 1992), as well as brain imaging data which support the hypothesis that the same mechanisms are involved in both inner and outer speech (Jeannerod, 2006). Moreover, to accept a motor system route to inner speech does not rule out the possibility of alternative routes to verbal imagery, for example, involving the reconstruction of perceptual memories in modality specific cortices (Kosslyn et al., 2001; Kosslyn, 2005; Moulton and Kosslyn, 2009). The critique offered here therefore, relates not to *whether* inner speech is functionally specified in the motor system, but rather *how* it is specified.

PROBLEMS WITH THE SPECIFICATION OF INNER SPEECH IN THE TRADITIONAL COMPARATOR ACCOUNT

As described above, the existing comparator account of misattributed inner speech assumes that inner speech holds the same functional position in the motor control system as actual speech. This aspect of the account, and in particular the related proposition that inner speech is compared in the third comparator and attenuated by the predicted state, forms a crucial aspect of the approach's account of the etiology of AVH. Despite this, Jones and Fernyhough provide no clarification of the notion of inner speech they have in mind, nor of its cognitive specification. One clue comes from their diagrammatic representation of the model, which indicates that the occurrence of inner speech based on the motor command results in an "actual sensory experience" (see **Figure 2**). Despite this nomenclature, there is strong reason to believe that Jones and Fernyhough do *not* mean that the production of inner speech results in external sensory output (such as low level vocalization or muscle movements). Not only do they clearly refer to inner speech as "purely cognitive" throughout the article, they also expend considerable effort constructing an argument (drawing on a Vygotskian (Vygotsky, 1934/1987) developmental notion of private speech) for why we should expect a purely cognitive event such as inner speech to be the product of the motor control system in the first place. If they meant the inner speech output in their model to consist of low level vocalization with actual sensory consequences, then such arguments would not be required. If the notion of inner speech they have in mind is purely cognitive, then the output which they have labeled as "actual sensory consequence" would be better described as imagery (quasi-perceptual representation) of what the actual sensory consequences might have been had the speech been produced. Such a characterization would be in line with both their own description of inner speech as "purely cognitive" and with standard cognitive characterizations of inner speech (e.g., Carruthers, 2006; for an overview see Vicente and Martinez-Manrique, 2011).

Given the information provided by Jones and Fernyhough, this explication seems the most plausible way to characterize the notion of inner speech in their model. However, further questions remain. We leave open the question of the modality of inner speech in their account. It is likely that they would follow other theorists (e.g., Tian and Poeppel, 2012) in positing that this quasi-sensory representation could occur in either the auditory or the motoric and kinesthetic modalities, or in all three. More crucially, it is unclear under their account what mechanisms are supposed to generate the quasi-perceptual representation of inner speech. In the case of overt speech as specified in the original model of motor control, the motor command causes the bodily movement to occur, actual sensory consequences follow, and these are picked up by the sensory system and compiled into a representation (the "estimated actual sensory consequences", see **Figure 1**). In Jones and Fernyhough's model, the process by which the motor command leads to quasi-sensory representation of inner speech remains unspecified.

Moreover, it is unclear why there is a need to propose any new mechanisms for the generation of inner speech. If inner speech consists of a quasi-sensory representation of the likely consequences of a given act of speech, then the motor control system as originally specified already contains such a representation. Recall that, according to the original comparator model of the motor control system, an efference copy of the motor command is sent to the forward model, which generates representation of the predicted sensory consequences of performing the motor command. We know that this predicted state must be in the same representational format as the posited inner speech of Jones and Fernyhough, since, according to them, both are inputs to the third comparator. If the efference copy and forward model already issues a quasi-perceptual representation of the predicted sensory consequences of performing a given speech act, then would it not be more parsimonious to consider that *this* representation—the predicted state—would form the basis for inner speech? In the normal case of overt action, the predicted state is a subpersonal representation, but all that would be required to generate the conscious experience of inner speech would be to suppress the motor command and make the predicted state available to consciousness. Moreover, this specification of inner speech as derived from the predicted state is just as consistent with the motivations provided by the Vygostkian development view of language that Jones and Fernyhough offer. Firstly, inner speech is still a product of the motor control system. Secondly, the predicted state is compared to the desired state in the second comparator, providing a mechanism by which inner speech could be monitored and corrected.

In light of these issues, this traditional version of the comparator account of the sense of agency for inner speech faces several challenges. Either the notion of inner speech needs to be elaborated in order to explain how it is functionally different from the predicted state, or, if it is *not* different, there needs to be an explanation of why the motor control system would generate the same state twice, and what would be gained from comparing it to itself.

The alternative proposal we have offered—that the predicted state could form the basis for inner speech—is not only more parsimonious and well-defined than that provided by Jones and Fernyhough, but also more consistent with leading theorizing on motor imagery. As part of an extensive research program over a number of years, Marc Jeannerod (2006) has proposed an account of motor imagery based on the workings of the motor control system. According to this influential theory, motor imagery—conscious quasi-perceptual representation of motor acts—is derived from the predicted state. His account forms the basis for the specification of inner speech in at least one leading theory of the architecture of the mind (Carruthers, 2006). Recently, Tian and Poeppel (2012) have expanded on this approach to provide clear specification of how the forward model and predicted state of the motor control system could generate both the sensorimotor and auditory imagery associated with inner speech.

Our analysis of the traditional comparator account of misattributed inner speech suggests that the proposed specification of inner speech in the motor control system is problematic. This in turn calls into question the viability of the current comparator account as a model for misattributions of agency. If inner speech is, as we alternatively propose, derived from the predicted state, then it is not normally attenuated and a mismatch in the third comparator cannot account for its misattribution. It is possible that these problems with the traditional comparator account are at least implicitly recognized by some theorists. After initial enthusiasm in earlier versions of his account (Frith, 1992), Frith himself has become increasingly cautious about applying the comparator account to inner speech (Frith, 2012).

PROBLEMS WITH THE EVIDENCE FOR THE TRADITIONAL COMPARATOR ACCOUNT OF INNER SPEECH

Over the last 15 years a series of studies using electrophysiological techniques has probed the responsiveness of the brain to auditory probes during self-generated speech and inner speech. A primary aim of this research was to test the predictions of the comparator account as it applied to misattributed inner speech. Overall, the results have been interpreted as suggesting that inner speech is normally attenuated, and that there is a failure of attenuation of inner speech in patients with a diagnosis of schizophrenia (Ford et al., 2001a,b,c, 2007; Ford and Mathalon, 2004, 2005, 2012; Heinks-Maldonado et al., 2007). As such, the results appear to provide key evidence in favor of the current comparator account of misattributed inner speech.

In this section we closely examine the details of these studies and argue that there are problems with this common interpretation of the data. We suggest that even if we were to leave aside the analysis provided in the previous section and accept for the sake of argument that inner speech could plausibly be specified as functionally equivalent to overt speech in the motor control system, the data from these electrophysiological studies cannot be taken as supporting the traditional comparator account of inner speech.

The auditory N1 is a negative-going event related potential (ERP) generated in the auditory cortex by transient auditory stimuli, and has been the primary dependent measure on which the series of studies by Ford et al. have been based. It reaches its peak approximately 100 ms after stimulus onset and is measured by electroencephalography (EEG). Magnetoencephalographic (MEG) studies measuring the N1's magnetic counterpart, the N1m, have shown that, while a subject is talking, responsiveness of the auditory cortex to 1000 Hz tone probes is dampened and delayed compared to while a subject is reading silently (Numminen et al., 1999), or simply listening (Curio et al., 2000). In line with the comparator account of motor control, the reduction of N1m during talking in these studies was attributed to the dampening effect of the predicted state. These findings are consistent with a large body of research demonstrating the attenuation of sensory consequences during bodily action across modalities and across the animal kingdom (Crapse and Sommer, 2008).

Ford et al. expanded on this research to investigate N1 responsiveness to auditory stimuli not only in healthy controls, but also in patients with a diagnosis of schizophrenia. The majority of their studies focused on the differences in N1 responsiveness to auditory probes during overt talking as compared to a baseline condition during which subjects heard the auditory probes and were asked simply to focus on a fixation point. Ford et al. describe this as the Talk/Listen paradigm. In some studies the talking itself provided the auditory probe (and was played back during the listen condition). In other studies separate auditory probes were used (e.g., speech sounds [/ba/] and noises [broadband]).

Across these studies involving overt speech, healthy controls showed a significant difference in N1 responsiveness between the baseline and talking conditions, with N1 responsiveness to the auditory probe dampened while talking. In line with the comparator account of the motor control system and the previous research described above, these findings were interpreted as indicating that the predicted state attenuates incoming sensory information during speech.

By contrast, the patient group showed no such difference in N1 responsiveness between the talking and baseline conditions. This was taken to indicate a failure of attenuation of incoming sensory information, as predicted by the comparator account of misattributions of bodily agency in schizophrenia. While these results do provide good evidence of attenuation (and failure of attenuation) during overt speech, it is not straightforward to assume that they can be extrapolated to shed light on covert actions like inner speech. As noted in the previous section, it is problematic to presume that inner speech plays the same functional role in the motor control system as overt speech, and there is evidence that an alternative model of inner speech in the motor control may be appropriate. In the present context, to draw conclusions about the posited attenuation of inner speech from data relating to overt speech is to beg the question.

Given this, only evidence that inner speech is *itself* attenuated, and that failures of this attenuation are connected to schizophrenia, can be directly taken as evidence of the current comparator account of misattributed inner speech. Just one of the studies conducted by Ford et al. investigated levels of N1 responsiveness during inner speech (Ford et al., 2001a; Ford and Mathalon, 2004). Drawing on the type of comparator account of inner speech suggested by Jones and Fernyhough, the authors predict that engaging in inner speech will lead to a reduction in N1 responsiveness due to attenuation by the predicted state associated with the production of inner speech. As with the studies involving overt speech, during a baseline condition subjects simply focused on a fixation point and listened to the auditory stimuli. In the inner speech condition the participants engaged in what the authors refer to as "directed" inner speech by silently repeating statements (e.g., "That was really stupid"). In both the inner speech and baseline conditions, auditory probes were presented (e.g., speech sounds [/ba/], noises [broadband]) and N1 response to these stimuli was recorded.

The key results from the inner speech study were broadly similar to those from the studies involving overt speech. Firstly, in healthy controls the N1 responsiveness to the auditory probes was reduced in the inner speech condition as compared to the baseline condition. The authors take it that the production of inner speech in the motor control system in this condition has given rise to a predicted state, which has in turn attenuated not only the inner speech itself, but also N1 responsiveness. Thus, the result that N1 responsiveness was reduced during the inner speech condition in the control subjects has been taken to support to the basic proposition that inner speech is normally attenuated, as proposed in the traditional comparator account of misattributed inner speech.

In addition, the subjects with a diagnosis of schizophrenia demonstrated *no* difference in N1 responsiveness to the auditory probes between the inner speech and baseline condition. Ford et al. (2001a) suggest this may be because in the case of the inner speech produced by patients the predicted state "was not functioning properly" and so "auditory cortical responsiveness... might not have been dampened" (p. 1915). In line with the traditional comparator account of misattributed inner speech, this failure of attenuation of the N1 response is posited to reflect a failure of attenuation of inner speech itself, which contributes to symptoms such as AVH and thought insertion by causing a failure of the "self/other signal" (p. 1915) or as they put in a later description (Ford and Mathalon, 2004), leading to "the misperception that [. . .] thoughts have an external source" (p. 43).

These interpretations of the key data as being supportive of the current comparator account of misattributed inner speech have been repeated by Ford et al. in several reviews of the original study (e.g., Ford and Mathalon, 2012) and in turn referenced across the literature on the sense of agency for thought (e.g., Langland-Hassan, 2008). However, it is clear from a closer reading of Ford et al.' broader research program that this is not the only, or even the best, interpretation of the key data from the inner speech study. Firstly, it is important to note that the study does not directly measure attenuation of inner speech, but rather draws inferences about attenuation of inner speech from levels of N1 responsiveness. For this reason, interpretation of the N1 responsiveness data requires an *a priori* assumption about the posited nature and direction of the relationship between N1 responsiveness and any supposed inner speech attenuation.

Specifically, the interpretation described above rests on the assumption that a reduction in N1 responsiveness is the result of attenuation by the predicted state and can be taken as a direct indication that inner speech is itself also being attenuated. To put it another way, the interpretation rests on the assumption that a reduction in N1 responsiveness reflects a properly functioning predicted state and properly attenuated inner speech. Elsewhere in discussing the same series of studies, however, the authors make the opposite *a priori* assumption, positing that reduced N1 responsiveness could reflect a *failure* of predicted state, and as indicating that inner speech itself has *not* been attenuated (see details below). This is extremely problematic; if reduced N1 responsiveness can be plausibly interpreted as reflecting either a properly functioning predicted state or a failure of the predicted state, then it is impossible to draw firm conclusions about either the specification of inner speech (whether it is normally attenuated) or the role of prediction failure in schizophrenia from the N1 data gathered in these studies.

Given the seriousness of this problem, it is worth spelling out in detail this alternative contradictory framework as posited by the authors. Firstly, Ford et al. make clear that attenuation by the predicted state is not the only mechanism by which the dependent measure of N1 responsiveness may be reduced. Acoustic interference (for instance, listening to speech) is another possible mechanism for reduction of N1 responsiveness to auditory probes, because the auditory cortex is already engaged (Ford et al., 2001b; Ford and Mathalon, 2004). For instance, Ford et al. appeal to this mechanism to explain why, in a third listening condition, N1 responsiveness is at its lowest as compared to both baseline and speech conditions for both patients and controls, even though attenuation is clearly not at work (since the participants are not engaging in speech); the reduction is argued to be the result of acoustic interference from the short bursts of heard speech (Ford et al., 2001b, p. 547).

Importantly, they appeal to this process of acoustic interference again when explaining a set of findings from the baseline conditions within studies. In this case their appeal to acoustic interference has important implications for their interpretation of the relationship between inner speech, the predicted state and N1 responsiveness. Recall that in the baseline condition, individuals simply sit and listen to auditory probes. Across the various studies involving both overt and covert speech the level of baseline N1 responsiveness to auditory probes was lower in the patient groups than in the control group; that is, in the baseline condition the patient's N1 responsiveness seemed to have been dampened as compared to baseline responsiveness of control subjects. Ford et al. explain this finding by appealing to differential levels of acoustic interference from inner speech in the control and patient groups. This differential level comes not from different *amounts* of inner speech—as they say, it is "likely that both control subjects and patients engage in internal dialogue", during the baseline condition (Ford et al., 2001b, p. 547)—but rather from differences in the level of *attenuation* of the inner speech between the control and patient groups. Specifically, they posit that inner speech in the patient group is not attenuated (due to a failure of the predicted state, as proposed by the comparator account), meaning that it causes greater acoustic interference, thereby reducing N1 responsiveness. In the control group they posit that inner speech is correctly attenuated (in line with the comparator account) and therefore interferes with the N1 less, meaning N1 responsiveness is not reduced.

This explanation of the likely relationship between the attenuation of inner speech and N1 responsiveness offered in interpreting the data between the baseline conditions is in direct contradiction of the interpretation offered in relation to the key findings discussed above. In the key findings above Ford et al. interpret reduced N1 responsiveness (in the control group as compared to the patients in the inner speech condition) as reflecting *functioning* attenuation of inner speech; when inner speech is correctly attenuated by the predicted state, the N1 responsiveness is attenuated in the same way. But in discussing the baseline findings, Ford et al. posit the inverse relationship, whereby reduced N1 responsiveness (in the patient group as compared to the control group) reflects a *failure* of attenuation of inner speech; unattenuated inner speech interferes with the auditory cortex, reducing N1 responsiveness.

That these two proposals about the relationship between inner speech, attenuation by the predicted state and N1 responsiveness are both available is not in itself problematic; both are theoretically driven and internally consistent. What is problematic is the coexistence of them in interpretation of the same set of data without making their contradictions explicit. More simply, it is impossible to draw any conclusions about the compatibility of the key N1 responsiveness results with the comparator account of misattributed inner speech if reduced N1 responsiveness could plausibly indicate both *functioning* attenuation or a *failure* of attenuation of inner speech. Had the findings revealed the opposite pattern of findings for the key comparison between control and patients in the inner speech condition—i.e., had they found that N1 response was reduced in the patients rather than the controls—this too could have been deemed in keeping with the traditional comparator account of misattributed inner speech, simply by appealing to the alternative *a priori* assumption regarding the relationship between N1 responsiveness and inner speech attenuation.

The above analysis reveals one additional note of caution about interpreting the results from the inner speech study. It is clear that Ford et al. did not control for the possibility that subjects would engage in spontaneous inner speech during the baseline condition. In fact, as noted above, in discussing the differences between the baseline conditions in a similar study, Ford et al. *assume* that participants were engaging in inner speech during the baseline. This means that there are at least two alternative explanations for the key findings from the inner speech study. Firstly, the difference in patterns of N1 responsiveness could simply be due to differential levels of spontaneous inner speech in the baseline condition. Suppose, for instance, that patients tended to engage in spontaneous inner speech in the baseline condition while those in the control condition did not; the additional acoustic interference provided by inner speech in the control subjects would explain the reduction in N1 responsiveness in the inner speech as compared to the baseline condition, while the lack of difference between the two conditions in the patient groups would be attributable to the fact that N1 response was already affected by acoustic interference from inner speech in the baseline condition. Alternatively, it could be that levels of spontaneous inner speech were the same in both patients and controls, but that the level of attention differed between groups; if patients tended to pay more attention to their spontaneous inner speech the same pattern of key results would be expected. Notably, neither of these plausible explanations for the pattern of data from the inner speech study makes any appeal to mechanisms by which inner speech is predicted or attenuated, as posited by the traditional comparator account of misattributed inner speech.

The above analysis calls into question the leading evidence for the current comparator account of misattributed inner speech. As pointed out by Langland-Hassan (2008), there are other research programs employing brain imaging which demonstrate results *consistent* with the comparator account, but those other studies—showing, for example, that the nervous system in patients with AVH behaves as it would during normal speech perception (Dierks et al., 1999)—are also consistent with alternative models of AVH which do not appeal to a model of attenuated inner speech (e.g., Allen et al., 2008). To date, the results from across the Ford et al. studies have been held up as the leading evidence in favor of the current model. This analysis reveals that the common interpretation of these key data from the inner speech study as supporting the comparator account of misattributed inner speech is problematic. Not only is it impossible to conclude from these data that the attenuation of inner speech is faulty in schizophrenia, but it is also impossible to conclude that inner speech is normally attenuated.

A NEW COMPARATOR ACCOUNT OF MISATTRIBUTED INNER SPEECH

Given the emerging evidence that motor prediction failures are associated with symptoms of hallucination and delusion in schizophrenia (Frith, 2012), and the plausibility of the comparator account as it applies to bodily action, there is a strong motivation to seek a motor control based account of symptoms such as AVH. However, in the previous two sections we have pointed out fundamental flaws in the traditional comparator account of misattributed inner speech, and highlighted inconsistencies in the interpretation of the electrophysiological data commonly taken to support the account.

There is one existing alternative comparator account of the sense of agency for inner speech that (seemingly inadvertently) sidesteps these problems by re-conceptualizing the process of prediction in the motor control system as a process of filtering. Langland-Hassan (2008) suggests that the idea of prediction proposed by Miall et al. (1993) and Wolpert and Ghahramani (2000) is not the only way in which Sperry (1950) and Holst and Mittelstadt (1950) original model of the motor control system could be cashed out, arguing that in the case of visual and auditory modalities the motor control system could calculate the needed cancellation of the incoming sensory information without ever generating a full prediction of the actual input. Crucially, then, his filter model "does not require that the 'predictive' signal itself be a quasi-visual state" (Langland-Hassan, 2008, p. 383). This account may avoid some of the problems of the traditional comparator account by avoiding a proposal of "double prediction", but it does not provide a plausible alternative. Contemporary theory and research indicates that the idea of predictive forward models based on efference copies is ubiquitous across sensory domains (Pynn and DeSouza, 2013). Not only does Langland-Hassan's account stand counter to this evidence, but it also entails a rather puzzling and unjustified split in the functioning of the motor control system's forward modeling. While he proposes that prediction does not occur in the visual and auditory modalities, in the case of the somatosensory and kinesthetic domains Langland-Hassan holds that the conceptualization of forward modeling as a process of prediction is valid (Langland-Hassan, 2008, p. 381).

In this section we outline a new comparator account that we take to provide the most viable model of how prediction failures in the motor control system could give rise to misattributions of inner speech. Unlike the traditional comparator account it involves a clear and cognitively justified specification of inner speech, is in line with leading theories of motor imagery, and does not entail duplication of states in the motor control system. Unlike Langland-Hassan's account it does require a radical re-conceptualization of the forward-modeling processes of the motor control system.

The new account is based on a model of inner speech production derived from the motor imagery literature (Carruthers, 2006; Jeannerod, 2006; Tian and Poeppel, 2012) and is consistent with recent arguments that mental imagery is likely to be based on full-blown simulation (Moulton and Kosslyn, 2009). This model of ordinary inner speech assumes that inner speech is directly derived from the predicted state. Inner speech begins, like overt speech, in the formation of an intention (which can be a motor intention, see Pacherie, 2008), leading to the generation of the desired state and the required motor command. As in the case of actual speech, an efference copy of the motor command is sent to the forward model and a prediction of the sensory consequences of the given speech act is produced.

It is clear from recent research that the predicted state can comprise representations across sensory modalities, including somatosensory, visual and auditory (Cullen, 2004; Pynn and DeSouza, 2013). In line with the recent model of inner speech proposed by Tian and Poeppel (2012), the model outlined here holds that the prediction that forms the basis of inner speech can incorporate both somatosensory (articulation imagery) and auditory (hearing imagery) modalities (see also Tian and Poeppel, 2010). The predicted state, which during overt speech normally remains in subpersonal processing, is made available to higher levels of processing (for example, via global broadcasting, see Carruthers, 2006). This process results in the first-person conscious experience of the episode of inner speech. The proposal that the predicted state may form the basis of the sensory content of inner speech is supported by recent behavioral studies (Scott, 2013; Scott et al., 2013).

In contrast to overt speech, in the case of inner speech the motor command is suppressed. Because the motor command is suppressed, there are no actual sensory consequences and there is no comparison in the third comparator. However, in line with similar models of motor imagery (Grush, 2004; Jeannerod, 2006), and specifically inner speech (Tian and Poeppel, 2012), the present model holds that the comparison in the second comparator between the desired and predicted states still occurs. We propose that during ordinary inner speech the match between the desired state and the predicted state in the second comparator contributes to the sense of agency for inner speech. The idea that the comparison in the second comparator might contribute to the sense of agency is not new. In at least one discussion of the comparator account of the sense of agency for bodily action, Frith has indicated that as well as the sense of initiation (derived from the mere production of the predicted state) and the sense of self-production (derived from the match in the third comparator) the match between the intended and predicted state may evoke a sense of "being in control" (Frith, 2005b, see also Synofzik et al., 2008a, p. 221).

With this framework in place it is possible to provide a unified and plausible account of how failures in motor prediction could contribute to the misattribution of inner speech (**Figure 3**). Following the traditional comparator account, we propose that in schizophrenia there are disruptions somewhere in the process of efference copy production and forward modeling, leading to a faulty or inaccurate predicted state. We leave unspecified the precise nature of this fault. The faulty prediction is proposed to potentially occur across the various modalities that contribute to ordinary inner speech (e.g., auditory and somatosensory). Thus, the errors in prediction could encompass incorrect specification in one modality (i.e., predicting the speech as louder or quieter, faster or slower), or incorrect specification across modalities (i.e., predicting the speech as composed of more or less auditory imagery relative to motor imagery). In line with traditional versions of the comparator account the deficit in the predicted state is also proposed to be sporadic, meaning that the predicted state will be accurate most or some of the time. Finally, these sporadic errors in the predicted state will lead to instances of a mismatch in the second comparator, whereby the predicted state will no longer match the desired (intended) state.

The proposed deficit in the predicted state is likely to have at least two distinct consequences for the phenomenology of the associated inner speech. The first is that the prediction error would directly translate into the patient's conscious experience of the resultant inner speech. In comparison to their ordinary inner speech, the individual could find that they experience inner speech which is unusual across any of the dimensions associated with the prediction of the sensory consequences of speech; the inner speech could be unusually slow/fast, unusually loud/quiet, unusually auditory in nature, unusually clear/unintelligible etc. It is these characteristics, which would differ from the characteristics of ordinary, correctly predicted inner speech, that are proposed lead the inner speech to be experienced as another person's

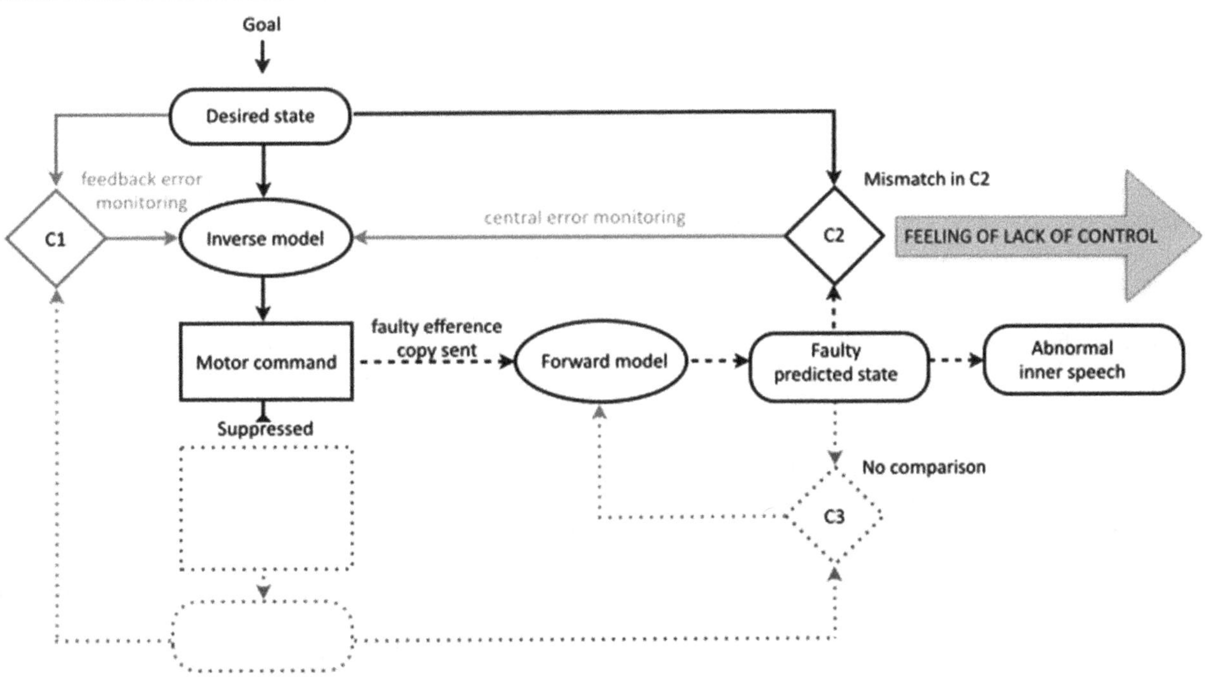

FIGURE 3 | The new comparator account of inner speech in the motor control system, also showing proposed disruptions to the experience of inner speech in schizophrenia. The efference copy allows the production of the predicted state to form the basis for conscious mental imagery (inner speech), while the motor command is suppressed (those aspects of the motor control system therefore not implicated in inner speech are shown dotted). In ordinary inner speech the match in comparator two between the predicted and desired states gives rise to a feeling of control. In schizophrenia, failures in the predicted state directly affect the conscious experience of the resultant inner speech (abnormal inner speech) *and* lead to a mismatch in the second comparator, leading to abnormalities in the feeling of intentional control.

voice. It is possible that the precise nature of the prediction errors would vary between, and even within, individuals, meaning that the proposed deficit could give rise to a wide variety of phenomenologically unusual cases of inner speech. Secondly, the mismatch in the second comparator between the desired state and the predicted state would mean that an unusual feeling of agency would accompany the associated inner speech, potentially a feeling that the inner speech is outside of intentional control. The sporadic nature of the deficit means that these experiences would be interspersed with episodes of phenomenologically ordinary inner speech accompanied by an ordinary feeling of agency.

THE NEW COMPARATOR ACCOUNT AND EVIDENCE FROM THE PHENOMENOLOGY OF AVH

A primary motivation for developing a comparator account of misattributed inner speech is to provide an etiological account of AVH in schizophrenia. The new account that we have proposed fits well with emerging evidence on the phenomenology of voice-hearing in schizophrenia. The account predicts that AVH would be experienced as outside of intentional control and unusual across a range of phenomenological dimensions related to sensory prediction. These predictions are in line with standard characterizations of AVH which hold that, along with a phenomenology of "externality", AVH are commonly experienced as both uncontrolled and compellingly perceptually real (Moritz and Larøi, 2008; Waters et al., 2012; Wu, 2012).

The account's predictions are also in line with a recent study which confirmed that AVH differ from patients' ordinary inner speech along a number of dimensions related to their perceptual phenomenology, including their speed (compared to a normal rate of speaker), intelligibility (understandable or garbled) and volume (Langdon et al., 2009). Moreover, while patients were able to describe the nature of various vocal characteristics of their AVH (the perceived gender, age, accent and class of the voices), the majority reported that their ordinary inner speech was free of such characteristics and "more like words in the head than a voice in the head" (Langdon et al., 2009, p. 661). As several theorists have concluded, the traditional comparator account of misattributed inner speech struggles to explain these phenomenological differences, since it predicts only differences in the experience of agency (Langdon et al., 2009; Wu, 2012).

In addition, our new account proposes that the precise effect of prediction failure could differ between individuals, and would therefore predict that AVH could vary across individuals in terms of any phenomenological dimension associated with prediction, including spatial location (predicting how close the voice will sound), identity of the voice (predicting the tone and timbre of speech), and reality (prediction of auditory characteristics in general). This is in line with the emerging evidence that voice-hearing in schizophrenia is a diverse and heterogeneous experience which varies along a number of phenomenological dimensions, including those commonly held to characterize the experience (Junginger and Frame, 1985; Chadwick and Birchwood, 1994; Oulis et al., 1995; Nayani and David, 1996; Leudar et al., 1997; Watkins, 1998; Stephane et al., 2003; Jones, 2008; Moritz and Larøi, 2008; Daalman et al., 2011; McCarthy-Jones and Fernyhough, 2011). For example, Stephane et al. (2003) found variation in terms of the clarity of AVH (ranging from clear, like external speech, to deep, like thinking in words), personification (e.g., whether it was a male or female voice), loudness (from not having loudness at all, to being softer than or as loud as normal speech), whether voices outside were within or outside of normal hearing range, and whether the voice was attributed to themselves or to another agent. The traditional comparator account of misattributed inner speech struggles to explain this variation between individuals.

OPEN QUESTIONS AND FUTURE RESEARCH

The new comparator account of misattributed inner speech draws on a significant reconceptualization of inner speech in the motor control system and makes novel predictions about the likely consequences of motor control failure, thus prompting new research questions and reshaping existing ones. The new model should be of particular interest to researchers investigating the neurocognitive basis of misattributions of both speech and inner speech within the comparator account framework. We have highlighted ambiguities in the way in which Ford et al. have interpreted their findings on the electrophysiological basis of inner speech, appealing both to the traditional view that inner speech is attenuated and an alternative view in which it is inner speech does the attenuating (see Section Problems with the Evidence for the Traditional Comparator Account of Inner Speech). It is hoped that the explication of a new comparator account may provide a clearer framework in which to interpret data from these and future studies.

Another question relates to the viability of the theoretical account of inner speech on which the account is based (e.g., Tian and Poeppel, 2012). Questions remain about how such a theoretical model of inner speech would be instantiated within the networks of the brain (for an overview of possible neural instantiation of the basic comparator account of motor control, see Ramnani, 2006), and how it relates to other models of verbal thought, inner speech and auditory imagery (e.g., Levelt, 1983; Kinsbourne, 2000; Fernyhough, 2004; Kosslyn, 2005; Kraemer et al., 2005; Carruthers, 2006; Baddeley, 2007; Leaver et al., 2009). The model of inner speech also faces phenomenological questions. If ordinary inner speech is derived from the predicted sensory consequences of a motor command to speak, why, for many individuals, is inner speech ordinarily experienced as silent (e.g., Langdon et al., 2009)? And while the new comparator account fits well with the phenomenology of voice-hearing in schizophrenia, there are some elements of the phenomenological data that it struggles to explain, such as apparent differences in the form, pragmatics and content of patients' inner speech and AVHs (Langdon et al., 2009). There are two possible approaches to making our new account compatible with this type of evidence. The first would be to appeal to a higher order conceptual process that interacts with the outputs of the motor control system such that it is only the combination of the two processes that leads to the experience of AVH. Under this picture, only inner speech that is both the product of faulty prediction *and* has a certain type of content (for example) would be experienced as a voice. This approach would be similar to Synofzik et al.'s multifactorial weighting model, which holds that a variety of top-down and bottom-up cues are integrated to give rise to the experience of agency (Synofzik et al., 2008a,b, 2009a,b, 2013; Synofzik and Voss, 2010; Synofzik and Vosgerau, 2012). Another approach would be to hold that top-down conceptual processes taking into account things like inner speech content and pragmatics could directly impact subpersonal processes, such that prediction errors would be more likely to occur in relation to certain episodes of inner speech.

There are also questions relating to the potential explanatory scope of the new account. In the present article we have focused on the account's ability to provide an etiological account of AVH, but it is possible that it might be extended to explain delusions of thought insertion or even other thought interference delusions such as thought influence or thought broadcasting. It is difficult to assess the extent to which the new comparator model can provide an explanation for delusions of thought interference because of the paucity of research into the phenomenology of these experiences. Based on the limited evidence currently available, we have previously argued that the phenomenology of thought insertion is best characterized in terms of an anomalous sense of agency for thought, meaning that the new comparator account may provide an account of these delusions (Sousa and Swiney, 2013). However, we argued more specifically that thought insertion is characterized by the sense that a thought as been *generated* or *produced* by another agent, rather than a sense of external intentional control (what we called intentional guidance, Sousa and Swiney, 2013). This more precise characterization is somewhat out of step with the predictions of the new comparator account proposed here. It also remains an open question as to whether inserted thoughts are experienced as perceptually unusual, as the new comparator account would predict.

A related question concerns the modal range of conscious mental imagery that might be affected by the disruptions proposed in the new account. The discussion so far has concentrated on how failures in the prediction of speech acts could give rise to anomalous inner speech, but there is reason to suspect that the account might extend to other types of imagery. Jeannerod (2006) detailed account of motor imagery entails that the full range of imagery (visual, kinesthetic, tactile) is derived from the predicted state of the motor control system, and there is evidence that conscious motor imagery is impaired or altered in schizophrenia across a variety of modalities. Recent research indicates that in schizophrenia imagined movements to grasp a target object show no reliable relationship to target size, suggesting an impairment in imagined movement (Danckert et al., 2002). Another study found that in contrast to patients without symptoms such as delusions of alien control and thought insertion, patients with such symptoms had slowed imagined pointing movements (Maruff et al., 2003). Finally, recent research has revealed that patients with schizophrenia were slower in imagining walking movements as compared to normal controls (Lallart et al., 2012). The researchers undertaking these studies have operated under a theoretical framework in which motor imagery is assumed to derive from the predicted state (as depicted in relation to inner speech in **Figure 3**). As such, the findings have been taken as providing support for the comparator account of misattributed bodily action, since they indicate problems with motor prediction. But considered in light of the model proposed here, they suggest that prediction failures may have direct consequences for phenomenology across a range of imagistic modalities. If this were the case, the explanatory scope of the account could be widened. For example, some cases of thought insertion appear to refer to "inserted" episodes of visual imagery (Mellor, 1970, p. 17). Also, if failures in the prediction of speech imagery contribute to the hallucination of voices, it is possible that other types of hallucinatory experiences could be explained by appeal to faults in the predictive processes underpinning other modalities of conscious motor imagery.

Finally, it is clear that even if a comparator account of misattributed inner speech is viable, disruptions to the predicted state will not be the only factor that contributes to pathological symptoms. As alluded to in previous versions of the comparator account and spelled out in a recent elaboration of the account (Synofzik et al., 2008a), subpersonal cues from the motor control system are likely to be only one cue contributing to the sense of agency for thought. The comparator account outlined here is intended only to provide a viable picture of how motor control prediction failures could conceivably contribute to misattributions; it is not intended as a full account of the sense of agency for mental acts.

CONCLUSIONS

Since its inception over 25 years ago the comparator account has come to dominate and define the expanding literature on the sense of agency, capturing the imagination of theorists from across the cognitive sciences. Its popularity stems in large part from its potential to provide a unified account of how failures in motor prediction could contribute to the etiology of both delusions of alien control and AVH in schizophrenia. In the case of AVH the comparator account has traditionally assumed that inner speech is cognitively specified in the motor control system in the same way as overt bodily actions, subject to the same processes of prediction and attenuation.

In the present paper we have challenged this traditional account, outlining problems with the specification of inner speech on which it is based and with the interpretation of the electrophysiological evidence commonly cited in its favor. We have provided a new comparator account of misattributed inner speech, appealing to the same failures in motor prediction, but relying on a different specification of inner speech within the motor control system. The new account makes novel predictions about the experience of misattributed inner speech that fit well with the phenomenological evidence on voice-hearing in schizophrenia. It also provides a framework for future neurocognitive research on the effect of motor prediction failures on inner speech.

REFERENCES

Allen, P., Larøi, F., McGuire, P., and Aleman, A. (2008). The hallucinating brain: a review of structural and functional neuroimaging studies of hallucinations. *Neurosci. Biobehav. Rev.* 32, 175–191. doi: 10.1016/j.neubiorev.2007.07.012

American Psychiatric Association. (2013). *Diagnostic and Statistical Manual of Mental Disorders* 5th Edn. Arlington, VA: American Psychiatric Publishing.

Baddeley, A. D. (2007). *Working Memory, Thought and Action.* USA: Oxford University Press.

Bäß, P., Jacobsen, T., and Schröger, E. (2008). Suppression of the auditory N1 event-related potential component with unpredictable self-initiated tones: evidence for internal forward models with dynamic stimulation. *Int. J. Psychophysiol.* 70, 137–143. doi: 10.1016/j.ijpsycho.2008.06.005

Bayne, T. (2011). "The sense of agency," in *The Senses*, ed F. Macpherson (Oxford: Oxford University Press), 355–374.

Berk, L. E. (1992). "Children's private speech: an overview of theory and the status of research," in *Private Speech from Social Interaction to Self-Regulation*, eds R. M. Diaz and L. E. Berk (Hillsdale, NJ: Lawrence Erlbaum Associates, Inc.), 17–53.

Blakemore, S., Smith, J., Steel, R., Johnstone, E., and Frith, C. (2000). The perception of self-produced sensory stimuli in patients with auditory hallucinations and passivity experiences: evidence for a breakdown in self-monitoring. *Psychol. Med.* 30, 1131–1139. doi: 10.1017/s0033291799002676

Blakemore, S.-J., Wolpert, D., and Frith, C. (1998). Central cancellation of self-produced tickle sensation. *Nat. Neurosci.* 1, 635–640. doi: 10.1038/2870

Blakemore, S.-J., Wolpert, D. M., and Frith, C. D. (2002). Abnormalities in the awareness of action. *Trends Cogn. Sci.* 6, 237–242. doi: 10.1016/S1364-6613(02)01907-1

Carruthers, P. (2006). *The Architecture of the Mind.* Oxford: Oxford University Press.

Carruthers, P. (2011). *The Opacity of Mind.* Oxford: Oxford University Press.

Chadwick, P., and Birchwood, M. (1994). The omnipotence of voices: a cognitive approach to auditory hallucinations. *Br. J. Psychiatry* 164, 190–201. doi: 10.1192/bjp.164.2.190

Crapse, T. B., and Sommer, M. A. (2008). Corollary discharge across the animal kingdom. *Nat. Rev. Neurosci.* 9, 587–600. doi: 10.1038/nrn2457

Cullen, K. E. (2004). Sensory signals during active versus passive movement. *Curr. Opin. Neurobiol.* 14, 698–706. doi: 10.1016/j.conb.2004.10.002

Curio, G., Neuloh, G., Numminen, J., Jousmaki, V., and Hari, R. (2000). Speaking modifies voice-evoked activity in the human auditory cortex. *Hum. Brain Mapp.* 9, 183–191. doi: 10.1002/(sici)1097-0193(200004)9:4<183::aid-hbm1>3.0.co;2-z

Daalman, K., Boks, M. P. M., Diederen, K. M. J., de Weijer, A. D., Blom, J. D., Kahn, R. S., et al. (2011). The same or different? A phenomenological comparison of auditory verbal hallucinations in healthy and psychotic individuals. *J. Clin. Psychiatry* 72, 320–325. doi: 10.4088/JCP.09m05797yel

Danckert, J., Rossetti, Y., d'Amato, T., Dalery, J., and Saoud, M. (2002). Exploring imagined movements in patients with schizophrenia. *Neuroreport* 13, 605–609. doi: 10.1097/00001756-200204160-00014

Dell, G. S., and Repka, R. J. (1992). "Errors in inner speech," in *Experimental Slips and Human Error: Exploring the Architecture of Volition*, ed B. Baars (New York: Plenum Press), 237–262.

Dierks, T., Linden, D., Jandl, M., Formisano, E., Goebel, R., Lanfermann, H., et al. (1999). Activation of Heschl's gyrus during auditory hallucinations. *Neuron* 22, 615–621. doi: 10.1016/s0896-6273(00)80715-1

Farrer, C., and Franck, N. (2007). Self-monitoring in schizophrenia. *Curr. Psychiatry Rev.* 3, 243–251.

Feinberg, I. (1978). Efference copy and corollary discharge: implications for thinking and its disorders. *Schizophr. Bull.* 4, 636–640. doi: 10.1093/schbul/4.4.636

Feinberg, I. (2011). Corollary discharge, hallucinations and dreaming. *Schizophr. Bull.* 37, 1–3. doi: 10.1093/schbul/sbQ135

Fernyhough, C. (2004). Alien voices and inner dialogue: towards a developmental account of auditory verbal hallucinations. *New Ideas Psychol.* 22, 49–68. doi: 10.1016/j.newideapsych.2004.09.001

Fletcher, P. C., and Frith, C. D. (2009). Perceiving is believing: a Bayesian approach to explaining the positive symptoms of schizophrenia. *Nat. Rev. Neurosci.* 10, 48–58. doi: 10.1038/nrn2536

Ford, J. M., and Mathalon, D. H. (2004). Electrophysiological evidence of corollary discharge dysfunction in schizophrenia during talking and thinking. *J. Psychiatr. Res.* 38, 37–46. doi: 10.1016/s0022-3956(03)00095-5

Ford, J. M., and Mathalon, D. H. (2005). Corollary discharge dysfunction in schizophrenia: can it explain auditory hallucinations? *Int. J. Psychophysiol.* 58, 179–189. doi: 10.1016/j.ijpsycho.2005.01.014

Ford, J. M., and Mathalon, D. H. (2012). Anticipating the future: automatic prediction failures in schizophrenia. *Int. J. Psychophysiol.* 83, 232–239. doi: 10.1016/j.ijpsycho.2011.09.004

Ford, J. M., Mathalon, D. H., Heinks, T., Kalba, S., Faustman, W., and Roth, W. T. (2001c). Neurophysiological evidence of corollary discharge dysfunction in schizophrenia. *Am. J. Psychiatry* 158, 2069–2071. doi: 10.1176/appi.ajp.158.12.2069

Ford, J. M., Mathalon, D. H., Kalba, S., Faustman, W. O., and Roth, W. T. (2001a). Cortical responsiveness during inner speech in schizophrenia: an event-related potential study. *Am. J. Psychiatry* 158, 1914–1916. doi: 10.1176/appi.ajp.158.11.1914

Ford, J. M., Mathalon, D. H., Kalba, S., Whitfield, S., Faustman, W. O., and Roth, W. T. (2001b). Cortical responsiveness during talking and listening in schizophrenia: an event-related brain potential study. *Biol. Psychiatry* 50, 540–549. doi: 10.1016/s0006-3223(01)01166-0

Ford, J. M., Roach, B., Faustman, W., and Mathalon, D. (2007). Synch before you speak: auditory hallucinations in schizophrenia. *Am. J. Psychiatry* 164, 458–466. doi: 10.1176/appi.ajp.164.3.458

Frith, C. D. (1992). *The Cognitive Neuropsychology of Schizophrenia.* Hove, UK: Lawrence Erlbaum Associates.

Frith, C. D. (2005a). The neural basis of hallucinations and delusions. *C. R. Biol.* 328, 169–175. doi: 10.1016/j.crvi.2004.10.012

Frith, C. D. (2005b). The self in action: lessons from delusions of control. *Conscious. Cogn.* 14, 752–770. doi: 10.1016/j.concog.2005.04.002

Frith, C. D. (2012). Explaining delusions of control: the comparator model 20 years on. *Conscious. Cogn.* 21, 52–54. doi: 10.1016/j.concog.2011.06.010

Frith, C. D., Blakemore, S.-J., and Wolpert, D. M. (2000a). Explaining the symptoms of schizophrenia: abnormalities in the awareness of action. *Brain Res. Brain Res. Rev.* 31, 357–363. doi: 10.1016/s0165-0173(99)00052-1

Frith, C. D., Blakemore, S.-J., and Wolpert, D. M. (2000b). Abnormalities in the awareness and control of action. *Philos. Trans. R. Soc. Lond. B Biol. Sci.* 355, 1771–1788. doi: 10.1098/rstb.2000.0734

Greenlee, J. D. W., Jackson, A. W., Chen, F., Larson, C. R., Oya, H., Kawasaki, H., et al. (2010). Human auditory cortical activation during self-vocalization. *PLoS One* 6:e14744. doi: 10.1371/journal.pone.0014744.

Grush, R. (2004). The emulation theory of representation: motor control, imagery and perception. *Behav. Brain Sci.* 27, 377–396; discussion 396–442. doi: 10.1017/s0140525x04000093

Heavey, C. L., and Hurlburt, R. T. (2008). The phenomena of inner experience. *Conscious. Cogn.* 17, 798–810. doi: 10.1016/j.concog.2007.12.006

Heinks-Maldonado, T. H., Mathalon, D. H., Houde, J. F., Gray, M., Faustman, W. O., and Ford, J. M. (2007). Relationship of imprecise corollary discharge in schizophrenia to auditory hallucinations. *Arch. Gen. Psychiatry* 64, 286–296. doi: 10.1001/archpsyc.64.3.286

Helmholtz, H. (1886). *Handbuch der Physiologischen Optik.* Leipzig: Voss.

Holst, E., and Mittelstadt, H. (1950). Das Reafferenzprinzip. *Naturwissenscaften* 37, 464–476. doi: 10.1007/bf00622503

Jeannerod, M. (2006). *Motor Cognition: What Actions Tell the Self.* Oxford: Oxford University Press.

Johns, L. C., Gregg, L., Allen, P., and McGuire, P. (2006). Impaired verbal self-monitoring in psychosis: effects of state, trait and diagnosis. *Psychol. Med.* 36, 465–474. doi: 10.1017/s0033291705006628

Jones, S. R. (2008). Do we need multiple models of auditory verbal hallucinations? Examining the phenomenological fit of cognitive and neurological models. *Schizophr. Bull.* 36, 566–575. doi: 10.1093/schbul/sbn129

Jones, S. R., and Fernyhough, C. (2007). Thought as action: inner speech, self-monitoring and auditory verbal hallucinations. *Conscious. Cogn.* 16, 391–399. doi: 10.1016/j.concog.2005.12.003

Junginger, J., and Frame, C. L. (1985). Self-report of the frequency and phenomenology of verbal hallucinations. *J. Nerv. Ment. Dis.* 173, 149–155. doi: 10.1097/00005053-198503000-00003

Kawato, M., and Wolpert, D. M. (1998). Internal models for motor control. *Novartis. Found. Symp.* 218, 291–304; discussion 304–307.

Kinsbourne, M. (2000). Inner speech and the inner life. *Brain Lang.* 71, 120–123. doi: 10.1006/brln.1999.2229

Knolle, F., Schröger, E., Baess, P., and Kotz, S. A. (2012). The cerebellum generates motor-to-auditory predictions: ERP lesion evidence. *J. Cogn. Neurosci.* 24, 698–706. doi: 10.1162/jocn_a_00167

Kosslyn, S. M. (2005). Mental images and the brain. *Cogn. Neuropsychol.* 22, 333–347. doi: 10.1080/02643290442000130

Kosslyn, S. M., Ganis, G., and Thompson, W. (2001). Neural foundations of imagery. *Nat. Rev. Neurosci.* 2, 635–642. doi: 10.1038/35090055

Kraemer, D. J. M., Macrae, C. N., Green, A. E., and Kelley, W. M. (2005). Musical imagery: sound of silence activates auditory cortex. *Nature* 434:158. doi: 10.1038/434158a

Lallart, E., Jouvent, R., Herrmann, F. R., Beauchet, O., and Allali, G. (2012). Gait and motor imagery of gait in early schizophrenia. *Psychiatry Res.* 198, 366–370. doi: 10.1016/j.psychres.2011.12.013

Langdon, R., Jones, S. R., Connaughton, E., and Fernyhough, C. (2009). The phenomenology of inner speech: comparison of schizophrenia patients with auditory verbal hallucinations and healthy controls. *Psychol. Med.* 39, 655–663. doi: 10.1017/s0033291708003978

Langland-Hassan, P. (2008). Fractured phenomenologies: thought insertion, inner speech and the puzzle of extraneity. *Mind Lang.* 23, 369–401. doi: 10.1111/j.1468-0017.2008.00348.x

Leaver, A. M., Van Lare, J., Zielinski, B., Halpern, A. R., and Rauschecker, J. P. (2009). Brain activation during anticipation of sound sequences. *J. Neurosci.* 29, 2477–2485. doi: 10.1523/JNEUROSCI.4921-08.2009

Leube, D. T., Knoblich, G., Erb, M., Schlotterbeck, P., and Kircher, T. T. J. (2010). The neural basis of disturbed efference copy mechanism in patients with schizophrenia. *Cogn. Neurosci.* 1, 111–117. doi: 10.1080/17588921003646156

Leudar, I., Thomas, P., McNally, D., and Glinski, A. (1997). What voices can do with words: pragmatics of verbal hallucinations. *Psychol. Med.* 27, 885–898. doi: 10.1017/s0033291797005138

Levelt, W. (1983). Monitoring and self-repair in speech. *Cognition* 14, 41–104. doi: 10.1016/0010-0277(83)90026-4

Li, C., Chen, M., Yang, Y., Chen, M., and Tsay, P. (2002). Altered performance of schizophrenia patients in an auditory detection and discrimination task: exploring the self-monitoring model of hallucination. *Schizophr. Res.* 55, 115–128. doi: 10.1016/s0920-9964(01)00203-1

Lindner, A., Thier, P., Kircher, T. T. J., Haarmeier, T., and Leube, D. T. (2005). Disorders of agency in schizophrenia correlate with an inability to compensate for the sensory consequences of actions. *Curr. Biol.* 15, 1119–1124. doi: 10.1016/j.cub.2005.05.049

Maruff, P., Wilson, P., and Currie, J. (2003). Abnormalities of motor imagery associated with somatic passivity phenomena in schizophrenia. *Schizophrenia Research* 60, 229–238. doi: 10.1016/s0920-9964(02)00214-1

McCarthy-Jones, S., and Fernyhough, C. (2011). The varieties of inner speech: links between quality of inner speech and psychopathological variables in a sample of young adults. *Conscious. Cogn.* 20, 1586–1593. doi: 10.1016/j.concog.2011.08.005

Mellor, C. (1970). First rank symptoms of schizophrenia. I. The frequency in schizophrenics on admission to hospital. II. Differences between individual first rank symptoms. *Br. J. Psychiatry* 117, 15–23.

Miall, R. C., Weir, D. J., Wolpert, D. M., and Stein, J. F. (1993). Is the cerebellum a smith predictor? *J. Mot. Behav.* 25, 203–216. doi: 10.1080/00222895.1993.9942050

Moritz, S., and Larøi, F. (2008). Differences and similarities in the sensory and cognitive signatures of voice-hearing, intrusions and thoughts. *Schizophr. Res.* 102, 96–107. doi: 10.1016/j.schres.2008.04.007

Moulton, S. T., and Kosslyn, S. M. (2009). Imagining predictions: mental imagery as mental emulation. *Philos. Trans. R. Soc. Lond. B Biol. Sci.* 364, 1273–1280. doi: 10.1098/rstb.2008.0314

Nayani, T., and David, A. (1996). The auditory hallucination: a phenomenological survey. *Psychol. Med.* 26, 177–189. doi: 10.1017/s003329170003381x

Numminen, J., Salmelin, R., and Hari, R. (1999). Subject's own speech reduces reactivity of the human auditory cortex. *Neurosci. Lett.* 265, 119–122. doi: 10.1016/s0304-3940(99)00218-9

Oulis, P. G., Mavreas, V. G., Mamounas, J. M., and Stefanis, C. N. (1995). Clinical characteristics of auditory hallucinations. *Acta Psychiatr. Scand.* 92, 97–102. doi: 10.1111/j.1600-0447.1995.tb09550.x

Pacherie, E. (2008). The phenomenology of action: a conceptual framework. *Cognition* 107, 179–217. doi: 10.1016/j.cognition.2007.09.003

Pynn, L. K., and DeSouza, J. F. X. (2013). The function of efference copy signals: implications for symptoms of schizophrenia. *Vision Res.* 76, 124–133. doi: 10.1016/j.visres.2012.10.019

Ramnani, N. (2006). The primate cortico-cerebellar system: anatomy and function. *Nat. Rev. Neurosci.* 7, 511–522. doi: 10.1038/nrn1953

Scott, M. (2013). Corollary discharge provides the sensory content of inner speech. *Psychol. Sci.* 24, 1824–1830. doi: 10.1177/0956797613478614

Scott, M., Yeung, H. H., Gick, B., and Werker, J. F. (2013). Inner speech captures the perception of external speech. *J. Acoust. Soc. Am.* 133, EL286–EL292. doi: 10.1121/1.4794932

Seal, M., Aleman, A., and McGuire, P. (2004). Compelling imagery, unanticipated speech and deceptive memory: neurocognitive models of auditory verbal hallucinations in schizophrenia. *Cogn. Neuropsychiatry* 9, 43–72. doi: 10.1080/13546800344000156

Shergill, S. S., Samson, G., Bays, P. M., Frith, C. D., and Wolpert, D. M. (2005). Evidence for sensory prediction deficits in schizophrenia. *Am. J. Psychiatry* 162, 2384–2386. doi: 10.1176/appi.ajp.162.12.2384

Sousa, P., and Swiney, L. (2013). Thought insertion: abnormal sense of thought agency or thought endorsement? *Phenomenol. Cogn. Sci.* 12, 637–654. doi: 10.1007/s11097-011-9225-z

Sperry, R. W. (1950). Neural basis of the spontaneous optokinetic response produced by visual inversion. *J. Comp. Physiol. Psychol.* 43, 482–489. doi: 10.1037/h0055479

Stephane, M., Barton, S., and Boutros, N. (2001). Auditory verbal hallucinations and dysfunction of the neural substrates of speech. *Schizophr. Res.* 50, 61–78. doi: 10.1016/s0920-9964(00)00150-x

Stephane, M., Thuras, P., Nasrallah, H., and Georgopoulos, A. (2003). The internal structure of the phenomenology of auditory verbal hallucinations. *Schizophr. Res.* 61, 185–193. doi: 10.1016/s0920-9964(03)00013-6

Stephens, G. L., and Graham, G. (2003). *When Self-Consciousness Breaks.* Cambridge, MA: MIT Press.

Synofzik, M., and Vosgerau, G. (2012). Weighting models and weighting factors. *Conscious. Cogn.* 21, 55–58. doi: 10.1016/j.concog.2011.09.016

Synofzik, M., Vosgerau, G., and Lindner, A. (2009a). Me or not me—an optimal integration of agency cues? *Conscious. Cogn.* 18, 1065–1068. doi: 10.1016/j.concog.2009.07.007

Synofzik, M., Vosgerau, G., and Newen, A. (2008a). Beyond the comparator model: a multifactorial two-step account of agency. *Conscious. Cogn.* 17, 219–239. doi: 10.1016/j.concog.2007.03.010

Synofzik, M., Vosgerau, G., and Newen, A. (2008b). I move, therefore I am: a new theoretical framework to investigate agency and ownership. *Conscious. Cogn.* 17, 411–424. doi: 10.1016/j.concog.2008.03.008

Synofzik, M., Vosgerau, G., and Newen, A. (2009b). Reply to Carruthers. *Conscious. Cogn.* 18, 521–523. doi: 10.1016/j.concog.2008.06.008

Synofzik, M., Vosgerau, G., and Voss, M. (2013). The experience of agency: an interplay between prediction and postdiction. *Front. Psychol.* 4:127. doi: 10.3389/fpsyg.2013.00127

Synofzik, M., and Voss, M. (2010). "Disturbances of the sense of agency in schizophrenia," in *Neuropsychology of the Sense of Agency*, ed M. Balconi (Milan: Springer), 145–154.

Tian, X., and Poeppel, D. (2010). Mental imagery of speech and movement implicates the dynamics of internal forward models. *Front. Psychol.* 1:166. doi: 10.3389/fpsyg.2010.00166

Tian, X., and Poeppel, D. (2012). Mental imagery of speech: linking motor and perceptual systems through internal simulation and estimation. *Front. Hum. Neurosci.* 6:314. doi: 10.3389/fnhum.2012.00314

Vicente, A., and Martinez-Manrique, F. (2011). Inner speech: nature and functions. *Philos. Compass* 6, 209–219. doi: 10.1111/j.1747-9991.2010.00369.x

Vosgerau, G., and Newen, A. (2007). Thoughts, motor actions and the self. *Mind Lang.* 22, 22–43. doi: 10.1111/j.1468-0017.2006.00298.x

Voss, M., Moore, J., Hauser, M., Gallinat, J., Heinz, A., and Haggard, P. (2010). Altered awareness of action in schizophrenia: a specific deficit in predicting action consequences. *Brain* 133, 3104–3112. doi: 10.1093/brain/awQ172

Vygotsky, L. S. (1934/1987). *Thought and Language.* Cambridge, MA: MIT Press (Original work published 1934).

Waters, F., Allen, P., Aleman, A., Fernyhough, C., Woodward, T. S., Badcock, J. C., et al. (2012). Auditory hallucinations in schizophrenia and nonschizophrenia populations: a review and integrated model of cognitive mechanisms. *Schizophr. Bull.* 38, 683–693. doi: 10.1093/schbul/sbs045

Watkins, J. (1998). *Hearing Voices.* Melbourne: Hill of Content.

Wegner, D. M. (2002). *The Illusion of Conscious Will.* Cambridge, MA: MIT Press.

Weiss, C., Herwig, A., and Schütz-Bosbach, S. (2011). The self in social interactions: sensory attenuation of auditory action effects is stronger in interactions with others. *PLoS One* 6:e22723. doi: 10.1371/journal.pone.0022723

Whitford, T. J., Ford, J. M., Mathalon, D. H., Kubicki, M., and Shenton, M. E. (2012). Schizophrenia, myelination and delayed corollary discharges: a hypothesis. *Schizophr. Bull.* 38, 486–494. doi: 10.1093/schbul/sbQ125

Wolpert, D. M., Diedrichsen, J. R., and Flanagan, J. R. (2011). Principles of sensorimotor learning. *Nat. Rev. Neurosci.* 12, 739–751. doi: 10.1038/nrn3112

Wolpert, D. M., and Flanagan, J. R. (2001). Motor prediction. *Curr. Biol.* 11, R729–R732. doi: 10.1016/S0960-9822(01)00432-8

Wolpert, D. M., and Ghahramani, Z. (2000). Computational principles of movement neuroscience. *Nat. Neurosci.* 3(Suppl.), 1212–1217. doi: 10.1038/81497

Wu, W. (2012). Explaining schizophrenia: auditory verbal hallucination and self-monitoring. *Mind Lang.* 27, 86–107. doi: 10.1111/j.1468-0017.2011.01436.x

3

Intentional binding effect in children: insights from a new paradigm

***Annachiara Cavazzana*[1]*, *Chiara Begliomini*[1,2] and *Patrizia S. Bisiacchi*[1,2]**

[1] *Department of General Psychology, University of Padua, Padova, Italy*
[2] *Center for Cognitive Neuroscience, University of Padua, Padova, Italy*

Correspondence:
Annachiara Cavazzana, Department of General Psychology, University of Padua, Via Venezia 8, 35131 Padova, Italy
e-mail: annachiara.cavazzana@gmail.com

Intentional binding (IB) refers to the temporal attraction between a voluntary action and its sensory consequence. Since its discovery in 2002, it has been considered to be a valid implicit measure of sense of agency (SoA), since it only occurs in the context of voluntary actions. The vast majority of studies considering IB have recruited young adults as participants, while neglecting possible age-related differences. The aim of the present work is to study the development of IB in 10-year-old children. In place of Libet's classical clock method, we decided to implement a new and more suitable paradigm in order to study IB, since children could have some difficulties in dealing with reading clocks. A stream of unpredictable letters was therefore used: participants had to remember which letter was on the screen when they made a voluntary action, heard a sound, or felt their right index finger moved down passively. In Experiment I, a group of young adults was tested in order to replicate the IB effect with this new paradigm. In Experiment II, the same paradigm was then administered to children in order to investigate whether such an effect has already emerged at this age. The data from Experiment I showed the presence of the IB effect in adults. However, Experiment II demonstrated a clear reduction of IB. The comparison of the two groups revealed that the young adult group differed from the children, showing a significantly stronger linkage between actions and their consequences. The results indicate a developmental trend in the IB effect. This finding is discussed in light of the maturation process of the frontal cortical network.

Keywords: sense of agency, intentional binding, voluntary action, development, frontal lobe

INTRODUCTION

The feeling of generating and controlling actions and their external effects is known as sense of agency (SoA; Haggard and Tsakiris, 2009). When we act, we are generally in control of what we are doing; therefore, we are aware and responsible for both our own actions and their consequences.

For many years, researchers have tried to identify appropriate measures to study this complex phenomenon. Two main research lines can be distinguished (Synofzik et al., 2008). The first refers to agency at its explicit level: usually, explicit agency is investigated by tasks in which participants have to verbally report whether they feel they are the authors of a certain effect or whether a presented sensory feedback of an action corresponds to the action made (Wegner and Wheatley, 1999; Aarts et al., 2005; Sato and Yasuda, 2005; Daprati et al., 2007; Metcalfe and Greene, 2007; Tsakiris et al., 2007; Farrer et al., 2008). However, we experience a continuous flow of actions and their effects in our everyday life, and we do know that we are the authors of an action without constantly giving explicit judgments. The second research line on SoA involves implicit measures, such as intentional binding (IB; Haggard et al., 2002). Such an effect occurs when a temporal compression phenomenon between voluntary action and its consequent effect is observed (e.g., actions are perceived as occurring later than they really do, while the sensory effect is perceived as occurring earlier). This effect seems to be limited to voluntary actions; in fact, IB is absent or reduced for situations in which the action is not driven by volition (e.g., passively-induced movement) or when no intentional agent is present (Haggard et al., 2002; Haggard and Clark, 2003; Engbert et al., 2008). Since its discovery, IB has been considered a valid quantitative index of SoA and has been applied to study agency, both in healthy individuals and clinical populations (for a review, see Moore and Obhi, 2012).

Up to the present moment, studies on SoA in general—and IB in particular—have concentrated most of their attention on searching for the underlying cognitive and neural mechanisms (David et al., 2008; Moore et al., 2010; David, 2012; Moore and Obhi, 2012; Kühn et al., 2013; Jo et al., 2014), without considering the aspect of ontogenetic development. A recent study conducted by Metcalfe et al. (2010) tried to study the possible differences in SoA across lifespans. The authors compared children, young adults, and older participants' performance using a computer game in which the task was to click on Xs and avoid Os. At times, the game included random distortions that decreased control. The participants had to judge how in control they felt and to rate their accuracy. The results showed that young adults were the most sensitive to discrepancies in control over their actions, as well as demonstrating their awareness of whether they were in control, compared to both children (8–10 years old) and older adults (mean age 75). Overall, these results showed that the metacognition of agency changes across the lifespan, suggesting a possible developmental trend. Although being the first to investigate age-related differences in SoA, this study used an explicit agency task, which may be influenced by different biases, such as prior expectations and beliefs about the task (Gawronski et al., 2007); thus, it says very little about the experience of agency, since it does not reflect or capture the feeling of agency that accompanies normal voluntary action (Synofzik et al., 2013).

In addition to Metcalfe et al.'s study, other studies have tried to investigate the emergence of agency. On one hand, studies focusing on the sense of the body (body awareness—for a review, see Rochat, 2010) and on the phenomenon of action–effect learning (Elsner and Aschersleben, 2003; Eenshuistra et al., 2004; Hauf et al., 2004; Elsner, 2007) show that: (i) the sense of body is already present in the first few months of life. Infants can therefore be considered agents in the world because they begin to gain control of their bodies and move voluntarily in the environment. In addition; (ii) action-effect learning seems to emerge even before the first year of age (Verschoor et al., 2010). On the other hand, other studies have shown that only 5-year-old children can report a mature experience of agency (Shultz et al., 1980; Astington, 2001; Lang and Perner, 2002). For example, Shultz et al. demonstrated that 5-year-old children are able to distinguish between a voluntary movement of the leg and a knee-jerk reflex However, all of the aforementioned studies—although aimed at studying the emergence of agency—are characterized by two important limits: (i) they contradict the fact that volition, which is strictly linked to the concept of agency, matures late during an individual's development (Haggard, 2008), when the brain, in particular the frontal areas, reaches its full maturation (Giedd et al., 1999; Sowell et al., 1999); and (ii) they focus on low-level processes implicated in agency that are considered to be necessary conditions for the appearance of goal-directed behavior and action control, but are not sufficient to explain SoA's complexity, which is rather a more sophisticated process. It includes in fact the ability to plan and control actions (planning, for example, to do something), but also the ability to identify actions' consequences in the external world inhibiting erroneous behavior. SoA is therefore linked to the concept of responsibility (Moll et al., 2007; Frith, 2013, 2014): we are aware and responsible of what our actions produce. If, for example, I fight with someone and decide to voluntarily hit him/her, I am aware of the consequences that my action could produce (e.g., this person could fall down and injure himself, and I am aware of this). However, if the agent is a child, this feeling of being responsible for action consequences may not emerge in the same way. Below a certain age, children are not considered responsible for their actions: the minimum age of responsibility is the topic of important legal debates and varies from 7–18 years old (Frith, 2013, 2014). The general idea is that children may not be considered to be fully responsible for their own actions—and consequently not complete "agents"—since their frontal lobes are not fully matured yet (Moll et al., 2007; Mackintosh, 2011; Frith, 2013, 2014). In this sense it could be interesting to know how and when SoA develop.

The general purpose of the present work is therefore to understand how IB, as an implicit measure of SoA, can develop in children, by corroborating the existing literature, going beyond the basic aspects of agency, and overcoming the limits of the verbal reports that characterize the explicit level of SoA. If this background feeling of agency is innate, we could expect the same pattern to be found in young adults, or rather the temporal compression between voluntary action and sensory effects; otherwise, if IB is something that we acquire during our development, we could expect some differences between young adults and children.

The present study consists of two main experiments. In the first experiment (Experiment I), we sought to develop a new paradigm in order to assess IB at the implicit level. This purpose stems from the fact that the majority of studies uses either (i) the rotating spot method used by Libet et al. in 1983 (Libet et al., 1983; Haggard et al., 2002; Haggard and Clark, 2003; Haggard and Cole, 2007) or (ii) direct numerical judgments of the time interval between an action and its effect (Engbert et al., 2007, 2008; Cravo et al., 2009; Humphreys and Buehner, 2009). However, these approaches do not fit our case, since the rotating clock method could raise some problems with children, given the fact that the acquisition of both clock and time knowledge changes and improves with age (Vakali, 1991). In addition, time interval paradigms do not allow for the separate measurement of action binding (i.e., the shift of the action towards the effect) and effect binding (i.e., the shift of the effect towards the action), which seem to rely on different neural mechanisms (Moore et al., 2010; Wolpe et al., 2013). Therefore, the aim of Experiment I was to replicate the IB effect in a group of young adults using a new and more suitable paradigm, in order to test it later in children (Experiment II). We considered the method developed by Soon et al. (2008) to study the brain processes associated with the preparation of intentional actions as a reference point using a stream of letters. In this way, both the problem of the predictability of numbers using a clock and the problem of inaccuracy in time judgments, which can occur with rotating stimuli (van de Grind, 2002), can be avoided. In the second experiment (Experiment II), we tested IB in a group of 10-year-old children in order to investigate whether such an effect has already emerged at this age.

EXPERIMENT I

The aim of Experiment I was twofold: (i) to create a paradigm suitable to test IB in children; and (ii) to test this paradigm in a group of young adults in order to verify the possibility of replicating the IB effect. In the case of replicating the IB effect in adults, the same paradigm would be adopted to test the IB effect in children in Experiment II.

METHOD

Participants

Twenty participants (16 females; mean age in years: 23, SD: 1.41; education in years: 16.6, SD: 0.94) took part in the study. All participants were right-handed, as measured by the Edinburgh Handedness Inventory (Oldfield, 1971), had normal or corrected-to-normal vision, and lacked neurological and psychiatric pathologies. The study was conceived according to the Declaration of Helsinki and was approved by the Ethics Committee of the University of Padua. All participants gave their informed, written consent to participate in the study.

Apparatus and procedure

The experiment took place in a dimly illuminated room. The stimuli were presented on a 17-inch monitor controlled by a Pentium four PC programmed with E-Prime two (Psychology Software Tools, Pittsburgh, PA). The participants were seated comfortably in a chair at a viewing distance of 60 cm from the monitor. They were asked to passively observe a stream of unpredictable white, capital consonants at the center of a black screen. In order to prevent the participants from responding immediately after the occurrence of the letters, a series of randomized white numbers was displayed before the letters' presentation (**Figure 1**). Each number and letter was presented separately and lasted for 150 ms, without time gaps in between. At the end of each trial, a set of response options (called "response mapping") appeared on the screen. Five letters were presented on the screen, including the target letter (i.e., the letter that was on the screen at the actual appearance of the event of interest). After each trial, the participants had to choose the correct consonant using the keyboard with their left hand. We decided to introduce "response mapping" in order to avoid the significant involvement of a memory retrieval component in the task.

The experiment consisted of 4 baseline conditions (BCs) and 6 experimental conditions (ECs), for a total of 10 conditions (**Table 1**).

Among the BCs (**Figure 2A**), only one event among voluntary action, involuntary action, Tone 1, or Tone 2 occurred per condition. The participants had to remember which consonant was on the screen when (1) they made a free voluntary key-press with their right index finger (acting as a baseline for voluntary action condition); (2) they felt their right index finger being passively moved down by a mechanical device (acting as a baseline for involuntary action condition); (3) they heard an auditory stimulus presented through headphones (1,000 Hz, 100-ms duration; baseline for tone condition: Tone 1); or (4) they heard another auditory control stimulus presented by headphones (same duration as Tone 1 but with a different pitch; baseline for tone control condition, Tone 2). In Condition (1), the participants had to wait until the letters' appearance before responding, in order to avoid response anticipation (i.e., a key-press performed immediately after the trial onset). In Condition (2), a mechanical device was applied to the right index finger of the participants. The device was connected and activated by computer at a random interval after the trial's onset. When the computer gave the input, the key and, consequently, the right index finger moved down, giving the participant the same physical perception as the voluntary key-press.

For the ECs, two events occurred per condition (**Figure 2B**). The participants had to judge (5) the onset of the voluntary action that produced Tone 1; (6) the onset of Tone 1 caused by the voluntary action; (7) the onset of the involuntary action that was followed by Tone 1; (8) the onset of Tone 1 activated

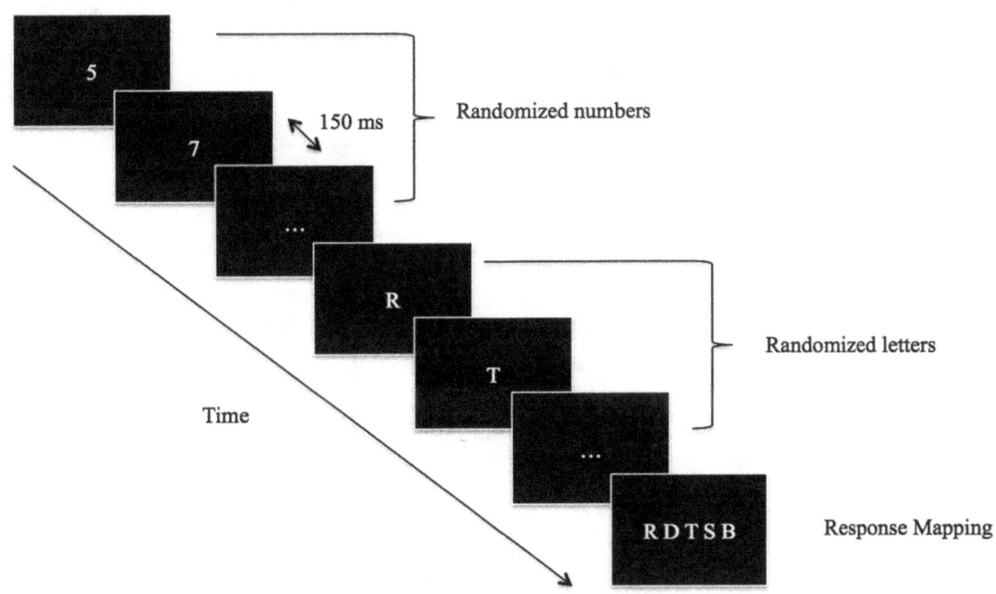

FIGURE 1 | Schematic illustration of the task structure. Participants passively observed a stream of numbers and letters that was updated every 150 ms. The frame with "..." represented here the continuous flow either of numbers or letters. After the appearance of the event of interest (Voluntary Action, Involuntary Action, Tone 1, Tone 2) a response mapping appeared and participants chose the letter that was on the screen at the occurrence of the event of interest (e.g., Voluntary Action, Involuntary Action, Tone 1, Tone 2).

Table 1 | Conditions (Baseline and Experimental) and event judged by the participants in each condition.

Condition	Event judged
Baseline Conditions	
1) Voluntary Action	Voluntary Action
2) Involuntary Action	Involuntary Action
3) Baseline Tone (Tone 1)	Baseline Tone (Tone 1)
4) Control Tone (Tone 2)	Control Tone (Tone 2)
Experimental Conditions	
5) Voluntary Action—250 ms—Tone 1	Voluntary Action
6) Voluntary Action—250 ms—Tone 1	Tone 1
7) Involuntary Action—250 ms—Tone 1	Involuntary Action
8) Involuntary Action—250 ms—Tone 1	Tone 1
9) Control Tone (Tone 2)—250 ms—Tone 1	Control Tone (Tone 2)
10) Control Tone (Tone 2)—250 ms—Tone 1	Tone 1

Among the baseline conditions, only one event occurred per condition (e.g., voluntary action, involuntary action, Tone 1, Tone 2). For the experimental conditions, two events occurred per condition. The time interval between the first event (the voluntary action, the involuntary action, or Tone 2) and the second event (Tone 1) was set at 250 ms.

by the involuntary action; (9) the onset of Tone 2 followed by Tone 1; (10) the onset of Tone 1 when activated by Tone 2. The time interval between the first event (the voluntary action, the involuntary action, or Tone 2) and the second event (Tone 1) was set at 250 ms.

Conditions involving the "involuntary action" and "Tone 2" were introduced as control conditions, in order to exclude the possible presence of IB in such conditions and investigate whether the results obtained for the voluntary action with the new paradigm were specific to SoA.

In all of the conditions, the stimuli were presented randomly, between 3 and 8 s after the trial onset. The stream of letters stopped randomly between 1.5 and 5 s after the event of interest. Thirty-three trials per condition were administered, for a total of 330 trials. The first three trials of each condition were discarded to allow for familiarization and were not included in the analysis. Each participant performed all of the conditions (BCs and ECs) in a different, random order over a single session.

DATA ANALYSIS

For each trial, we first calculated a judgment error (JE), which is the difference between the actual time of occurrence of the judged event and the perceived time of its occurrence. A negative JE was interpreted as anticipatory awareness of events (the participants perceived the event happening *before* it really did),

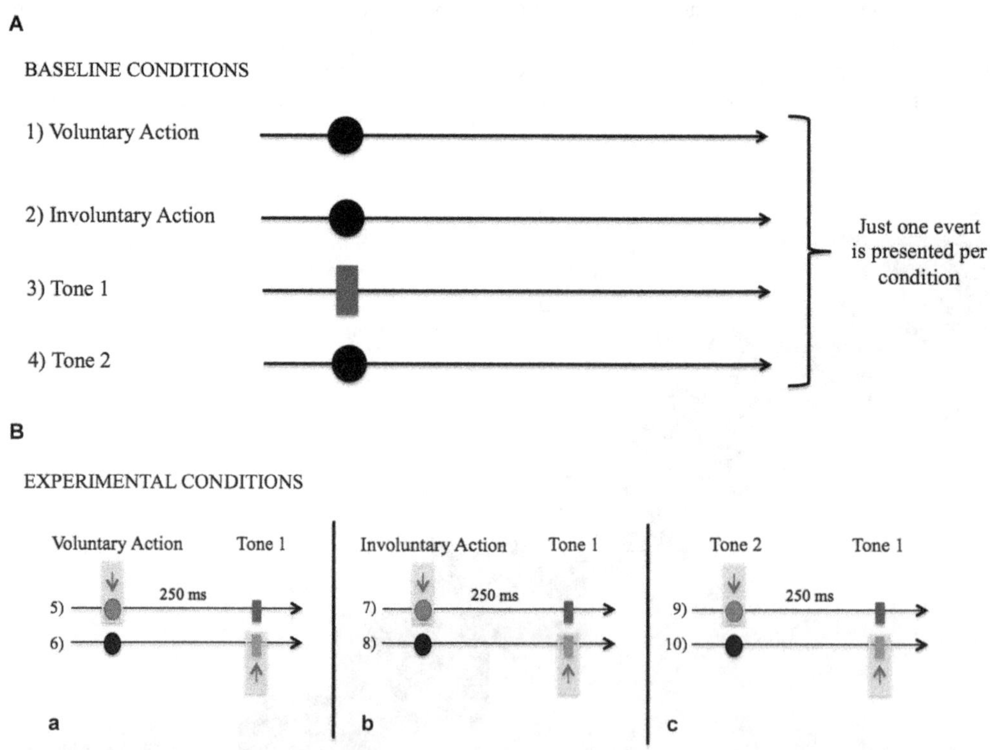

FIGURE 2 | (A) Schematic representation of the Baseline Conditions (BCs) in which only one event (Voluntary Action, Involuntary Action, Tone 1, Tone 2) occurred per condition. While viewing the stream of numbers and letters participants had to remember which consonant was on the screen when: (1) they made a voluntary key-press; (2) they felt their right index finger moved down passively; (3) they heard Tone 1; and (4) they heard Tone 2. **(B)** Schematic representation of Experimental Conditions (ECs). **(a)** Participants judged the letter that was on the screen either when they made the Voluntary Action (5) or heard the Tone 1 (6). **(b)** Participants judged the letter that was on the screen either when they felt their right index finger moved down passively (Involuntary Action, 7) or heard the Tone 1 (8). **(c)** Participants judged the letter that was on the screen either when they heard the Tone 2 (9) or the Tone 1 (10).

while a positive JE was interpreted as delayed awareness (the participants perceived the event happening *after* it really did). For each condition, a mean JE (mJE), including both negative and positive values, was obtained. We obtained a total of 10 mJEs, one for each condition. Since the numerical value of the mJE in a single condition is generally not informative and difficult to interpret, the differences between the mJE of an identical physical event in two different contexts (the BCs and ECs) were calculated (i.e., the perceptual shift) by subtracting the mJE of each event in the BC (voluntary action, involuntary action, Tone 1, or Tone 2) from the mJE of the same event in the EC. For example, the shift of the action towards the tone (i.e., action binding) was calculated by subtracting the mJE of the voluntary action in the BC from the mJE of the voluntary action in the EC, whereas the shift of the tone towards the action (i.e., tone binding) was found by subtracting the mJE of Tone 1 in the BC from the mJE of the same Tone 1 in the EC. Therefore, calculating the perceptual shifts was important to control for the cross-modal synchronization judgments, which differ widely across individuals. Finally, we also computed an overall binding measure (Haggard et al., 2002; Haggard and Clark, 2003; Engbert et al., 2008) by combining the first (i.e., the action binding) and the second event (i.e., the tone binding). By calculating 250 ms—(action binding–tone binding), the obtained value represents the perceived linkage between an action and an effect, and provides an implicit measure of SoA.

RESULTS

Table 2 summarizes the mJEs, perceptual shifts, and overall binding.

Using paired-sample t-tests, we first compared the mJE of a certain event in the BC with the mJE of the same event in the EC. For example, the mJE of a voluntary action in the BC was compared with the mJE of the voluntary action in the EC. Significant differences were only found in the context of voluntary action (voluntary action in the BC vs. voluntary action in the EC, $t_{19} = -5.633$, $p < 0.001$, and Tone 1 in the BC vs. Tone 1 in the EC, $t_{19} = 4.138$, $p = 0.001$) (**Figure 3**). Actions were therefore perceived later when followed by a tone, as compared to the BC, in which only the action was presented (**Figure 3A**). Differently, a tone was perceived earlier when it was activated by the action, in comparison to a BC where only the tone was presented (**Figure 3B**).

In order to control for cross-modal synchronization judgments, we then calculated perceptual shifts using a 3 ("type of context": voluntary, involuntary, and Tone 2) × 2 ("event judged": either the first or the second) repeated-measures ANOVA. First, no main effect of action type was found, $F_{(2,38)} = 0.782$, $p = 0.465$, $\eta_p^2 = 0.040$, while the effect of the "event judged" was significant, $F_{(1,19)} = 10.978$, $p = 0.004$, $\eta_p^2 = 0.366$, with a shift of the first event towards the second (28.09 ms) and vice versa (−32 ms). In addition, a significant interaction between these two factors emerged, $F_{(2,38)} = 21.697$, $p < 0.001$; $\eta_p^2 = 0.533$ (**Figure 4**). We thus conducted a *post-hoc* analysis applying Bonferroni correction for multiple comparisons, in order to examine the interaction in more detail. The *post-hoc* analysis revealed that the difference between the first and the second event judged was only significant in the case of voluntary action ($p < 0.001$). In addition, concerning the first event judged, a significant difference was found for voluntary action, in comparison with involuntary action ($p = 0.004$) and Tone 2 ($p < 0.001$). Involuntary action and Tone 2 were also significantly different ($p = 0.041$). Significant differences also emerged when comparing the second event judged (e.g., Tone 1) ("voluntary action context" vs. "involuntary action context", $p = 0.035$; "voluntary action context" vs. "two auditory stimuli context", $p = 0.002$). Such interactions occurred because voluntary actions lead to a perceptual shift of action towards tone and vice versa, whereas this effect was reduced for the involuntary action context and for the two auditory stimuli context.

The repeated-measures ANOVA found a significant effect of the overall binding (i.e., the perceived linkage between action and effect), $F_{(2,38)} = 21.697$, $p < 0.001$, $\eta_p^2 = 0.533$. *Post-hoc* comparisons showed a significant difference in both the voluntary and involuntary contexts ($p < 0.001$). In addition, the "voluntary context" and the "two auditory stimuli context" ($p < 0.001$) were also significantly different. No significant differences were found between the "involuntary context" and the "two auditory stimuli context" ($p = 0.205$).

In summary, temporal compression (IB effect) was only evident in the context of voluntary action. The overall binding data indicate that the participants perceived the interval between

Table 2 | mJEs, perceptual shifts and overall binding in young adults (Experiment I).

	Event judged	mJE (ms) ± sd	Mean shift (ms) ± sd	Overall binding (ms) ± sd
Baseline Conditions				
1) Voluntary Action (VA)	VA	14.25 ± 61.54		
2) Involuntary Action (IA)	IA	61.25 ± 59.98		
3) Baseline Tone (Tone 1)	Tone 1	40.75 ± 46.15		
4) Control Tone (Tone 2)	Tone 2	40.5 ± 44.36		
Experimental Conditions				
5) Voluntary Action—Tone 1	VA	90 ± 71.49	75.75 ± 60.14	98.75 ± 108.97
6) Voluntary Action—Tone 1	Tone 1	−34.75 ± 71.83	−75.5 ± 81.59	
7) Involuntary Action—Tone 1	IA	86.75 ± 62.5	25.5 ± 63.18	208.5 ± 93.16
8) Involuntary Action—Tone 1	Tone 1	24.75 ± 84.78	−16 ± 92	
9) Control Tone (Tone 2)—Tone 1	Tone 2	23.5 ± 39.8	−17 ± 46.52	262.5 ± 109.6
10) Control Tone (Tone 2)—Tone 1	Tone 1	36.25 ± 70.2	−4.5 ± 86.75	

In the Experimental Conditions the first event (voluntary action, involuntary action, Tone 2) is separated by the second event (Tone 1) by a fixed 250-ms interval.

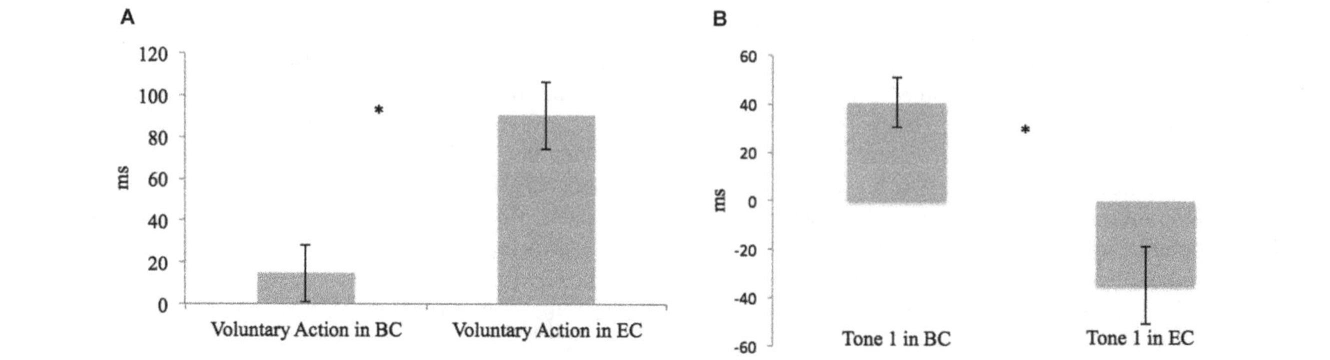

FIGURE 3 | (A) Differences in the mJE of Voluntary Action in BC *vs.* EC in the young adult group. Error bars represent SEM and * indicates the significantly difference between BC and EC ($p < 0.05$). Here participants perceived the onset time of voluntary action later when it was followed by the tone (Voluntary Action in EC), as compared to the BC in which only the action was presented (Voluntary Action in BC). **(B)** Differences in mJE of Tone 1 in BC vs. EC in the young adult group. Error bars represent SEM and * indicates the significantly difference between BC and EC ($p < 0.05$). Here, participants perceived the onset time of the Tone 1 earlier when it was activated by the voluntary action (Tone 1 in EC), in comparison to the BC where only the tone was presented (Tone 1 in BC).

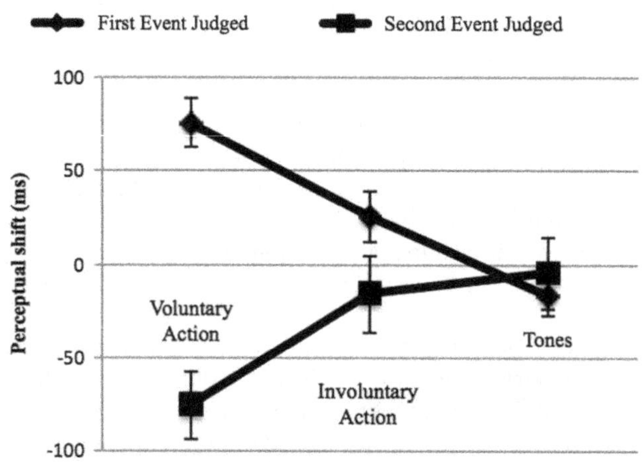

FIGURE 4 | Adults' perceptual shifts in the three main contexts: Voluntary Action, Involuntary Action and Tones (i.e., the two auditory stimuli context: Tone 2–Tone 1). Error bars represent SEM. The first event judged (♦) could be either the voluntary action, the involuntary action or the Tone 2. The second event judged (■) was always represented by Tone 1. Negative perceptual shifts indicate than an event is perceived earlier in an experimental condition than in the baseline condition; positive perceptual shifts indicate that an event is perceived later in an experimental condition than in the baseline condition. Only voluntary actions produce IB (left). On the middle and on the right the involuntary action and two tones contexts are represented respectively, showing no IB.

their action and its effect as significantly shorter than it really was, although no direct judgment of the time interval's duration was requested. Overall, our results revealed that, when participants were actively causing the beep (Tone 1), which was always presented 250 ms after their voluntary action, the onset of the voluntary action was perceived as occurring later, as if the action was "attracted" towards the tone. Analogously, the tone onset was perceived as "bound" to a voluntary action. This temporal compression phenomenon was only present in the case of voluntary action; when the beep followed the involuntary action or another control beep (Tone 2), such compression did not occur.

Using a new methodology, we replicated the IB effect and therefore proceeded to test IB in children (see Experiment II).

EXPERIMENT II

Given the positive results of Experiment I, we decided to use the new paradigm validated in Experiment I in order to test IB in children.

METHOD

Participants

Eighteen participants (14 females; mean age in years: 10, SD: 0.97; education in years: 5.05, SD: 0.87) took part in the study. All participants were right-handed, as measured by the Edinburgh Handedness Questionnaire (Oldfield, 1971), had normal or corrected to-normal vision, and lacked neurological and psychiatric pathologies. The study was approved by the Ethics Committee of the University of Padua and was conducted according to the Declaration of Helsinki. Informed consent was obtained from parents.

Apparatus and procedure

The apparatus and the procedure were the same as those used in Experiment I. In addition, the participants received basic neuropsychological screenings in order to exclude children with cognitive problems, which could interfere with the task. The tests included the Colored Progressive Matrices (Pruneti et al., 1996), the Trial Making Test (TMT; forms A, AB, and B—Scarpa et al., 2006), and the Bells Test (Biancardi and Stoppa, 1997).

RESULTS I: IB IN CHILDREN

All participants had an IQ above 100 and obtained normal scores on the TMT and Bells Test. **Table 3** presents their mJEs, perceptual shifts, and overall binding.

Table 3 | mJEs, perceptual shifts and overall binding in children (Experiment II).

	Event judged	mJE (ms) ± sd	Mean shift (ms) ± sd	Overall binding (ms) ± sd
Baseline Conditions				
1) Voluntary Action (VA)	VA	−19.72 ± 69.82		
2) Involuntary Action (IA)	IA	81.39 ± 47.95		
3) Baseline Tone (Tone 1)	Tone 1	79.17 ± 23.28		
4) Control Tone (Tone 2)	Tone 2	82.22 ± 49.44		
Experimental Conditions				
5) Voluntary Action—Tone 1	VA	1.67 ± 74.2	21.39 ± 72.86	169.17 ± 101.65
6) Voluntary Action—Tone 1	Tone 1	19.72 ± 67.11	−59.44 ± 64.39	
7) Involuntary Action—Tone 1	IA	72.5 ± 61.05	−8.89 ± 44.73	209.72 ± 93.23
8) Involuntary Action—Tone 1	Tone 1	30 ± 62.47	−49.17 ± 61.29	
9) Control Tone (Tone 2)—Tone 1	Tone 2	81.66 ± 33.91	−0.56 ± 52.07	208.33 ± 72.58
10) Control Tone (Tone 2)—Tone 1	Tone 1	36.94 ± 55.18	−42.22 ± 51.63	

In the Experimental Conditions the first event (voluntary action, involuntary action, Tone 2) is separated by the second event (Tone 1) by a fixed 250-ms interval.

We compared the mJE of each event in the BC with the mJE of the same event in the EC using paired-samples t-tests. Significant differences were only found in the perception of Tone 1 in the EC compared to the BC, in which the tone was presented alone. However, these differences were not limited to the case of the voluntary action ($t_{17} = 3.916$, $p = 0.001$) like in adults; they also extended to the case of the two control conditions: involuntary action ($t_{17} = 3.403$, $p = 0.003$) and Tone 2 ($t_{17} = 3.470$, $p = 0.003$). Tone 1 (i.e., the effect/beep) was therefore perceived earlier when it followed the voluntary action, the involuntary action, or Tone 2, as compared to the BC.

We also analyzed the perceptual shifts in order to investigate IB, as in Experiment 1. The repeated-measures ANOVA revealed no effect of action type, $F_{(2,34)} = 0.341$, $p = 0.713$, $\eta_p^2 = 0.020$, except for a main effect of the event judged ($F_{(1,17)} = 18.03$, $p = 0.001$, $\eta_p^2 = 0.515$) having a larger shift for the second event towards the first one (−50.28 ms vs. 3.98 ms). The interaction between the two factors was not significant, $F_{(2,34)} = 1.233$, $p = 0.304$, $\eta_p^2 = 0.068$ (**Figure 5**), indicating that no temporal compression occurred for the voluntary action.

When considering the overall binding, no differences were found between the three contexts ("voluntary action", "involuntary action", and the "two auditory stimuli context"), $F_{(2,34)} = 1.233$, $p = 0.304$, $\eta_p^2 = 0.068$.

The results showed that no IB was present in the 10-year-old children. Although a sort of minimal temporal compression seems to exist in the case of voluntary action, it does not reach significance, when compared to the two control conditions.

RESULTS II: BETWEEN-GROUP COMPARISONS

In order to better understand the lack of IB in children, we then proceeded to compare the degree of binding between the two groups. Concerning BCs, no differences were found in the "voluntary action condition", $t_{36} = 1.594$, $p = 0.120$, or in the "involuntary action condition", $t_{36} = -1.135$, $p = 0.264$. However, significant differences were found in the case of Tone 1, $t_{36} = -3.287$, $p = 0.003$, and Tone 2, $t_{36} = -2.742$, $p = 0.009$. In our study, adults perceived tones better than children.

Concerning ECs, on the other hand, significant differences were found in the perception of the voluntary action during the EC, $t_{36} = 3{,}736$, $p = 0.001$, as well as of Tone 1 following the voluntary action, $t_{36} = -2.408$, $p = 0.021$, and of Tone 2 in the EC, $t_{36} = -4.821$, $p < 0.001$.

The baseline differences in the perception of tones can explain the differences shown in the perception of Tone 1 following the voluntary action and Tone 2 in the EC, but they cannot account for the differences found in the case of the voluntary action. While the adults perceived voluntary actions significantly later (towards the tone) compared to the BC, in children, although the direction of the shift was opposite between BC (−19.72 ms) and EC (+1.67 ms), such changes did not reach a significant level. We therefore analyzed the perceptual shifts using 3 × 2 repeated measures ANOVA, using the group (children vs. young adults) as

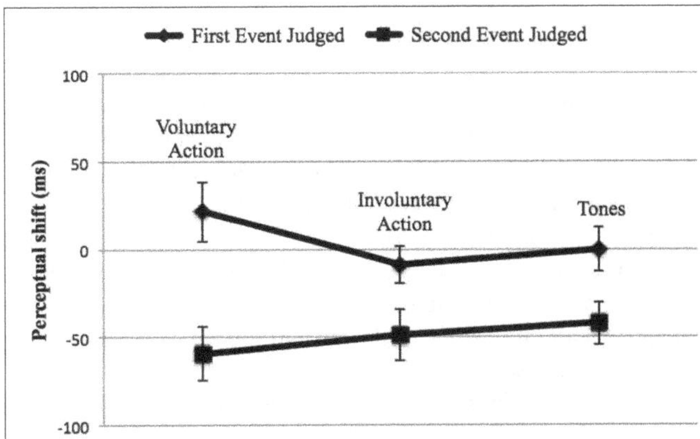

FIGURE 5 | Children' perceptual shifts in the three main context: Voluntary Action, Involuntary Action and Tones (i.e., the two auditory stimuli context: Tone 2–Tone 1). Error bars represent SEM. The first event judged (♦) could be either the voluntary action, the involuntary action or the Tone 2. The second event judged (■) was always represented by Tone 1. Negative perceptual shifts indicate than an event is perceived earlier in an experimental condition than in the baseline condition; positive perceptual shifts indicate that an event is perceived later in an experimental condition than in the baseline condition. No temporal compression occurred for the voluntary action.

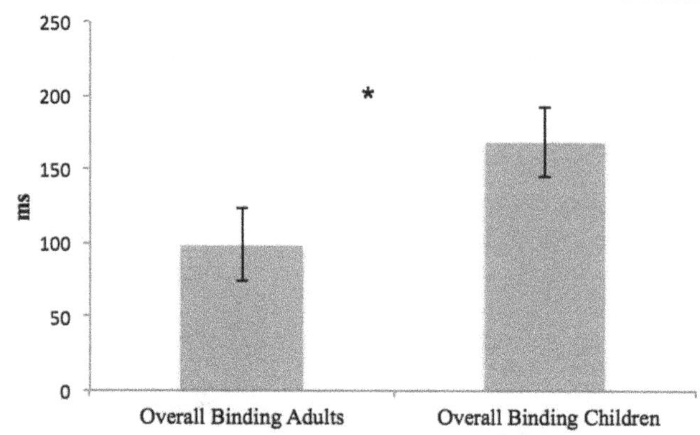

FIGURE 6 | Differences in the voluntary action overall binding between young adults and children. Error bars represent SEM and * indicates the significantly difference in overall binding between the two groups. Only adults present IB effect, showing temporal compression between voluntary action and its effect.

the between-factor. First, we did not find a significant main effect of group, $F_{(1,36)} = 4.012$, $p = 0.053$, $\eta_p^2 = 0.100$. A predicted and highly significant main effect of the judged event was observed, $F_{(1,36)} = 25.490$, $p < 0.001$, $\eta_p^2 = 0.415$, with the first event showing a delayed shift towards the second (16.03 ms) and vice versa (−41.14 ms). Most importantly, the interaction between group, type of action (voluntary, involuntary, and Tone 2), and judged event (first vs. second) was significant, $F_{(2.72)} = 5.242$, $p = 0.007$, $\eta_p^2 = 0.127$. The only significant difference between the two groups emerged in the case of the action-binding effect (i.e., the shift of the voluntary action towards the tone) ($p = 0.016$). No significant differences were found between the shifts in the other control contexts.

Also, the overall bindings were compared between the two groups. No main effect of group, $F_{(1,36)} = 0.066$, $p = 0.799$, $\eta_p^2 = 0.002$, was found, but a main effect of overall binding emerged, $F_{(2,72)} = 14.92$, $p < 0.001$, $\eta_p^2 = 0.293$: temporal compression was only present in the voluntary action context ($p < 0.001$). A significant interaction between overall binding and group emerged, $F_{(2,72)} = 5.242$, $p = 0.007$, $\eta_p^2 = 0.127$. Children and young adults only differed in the case of the "voluntary action context" ($p = 0.047$) (**Figure 6**).

To summarize, the only significant difference between adults and children regarded the "voluntary action context", in particular, the shift of the action towards the tone. No differences emerged in the case of the two control contexts. These data are important for explaining the lack of IB effect in children.

GENERAL DISCUSSION

The aim of the present study was to investigate the ontogenetic development of IB as an implicit measure of SoA, by taking advantage of its superiority over explicit tasks (verbal self-reports) (Wolpe and Rowe, 2014).

In Experiment I, a new, reliable paradigm for assessing IB was introduced and tested in a group of young adults. The results showed that only voluntary actions were perceived as occurring later in time than they really were (e.g., as more adjacent to the following tone in temporal terms); on the other hand, tones were perceived as occurring earlier than they really were (e.g., closer to actions in time). Such temporal compression was limited to the context of voluntary conditions. We considered these results as a proof of the IB effect.

In Experiment II, we tested the same paradigm considered in Experiment I in children. The results showed a reduction of IB, both in the context of "voluntary action" and in the two control conditions ("involuntary action" and "tones"). This lack of findings could be explained within the frame of the "warning-signal hypothesis" (Droit-Volet, 2003, 2011), which demonstrates that, when target stimuli are preceded by warning signals, the amount of time required for stimulus processing decreases and accuracy improves. In fact, when the children had to evaluate the second event in the ECs (e.g., Tone 1), judgment accuracy significantly increased in comparison to the BC, in which only Tone 1 was presented. In fact, in the BC conditions, children perceived Tone 1 after its real onset; when Tone 1 was activated by the voluntary action, it was perceived more accurately. The same pattern also emerged when Tone 1 followed the involuntary action and Tone 2. We therefore speculated that children could consider the first event (voluntary action, involuntary action, or Tone 2) to be a warning signal for the arrival of the subsequent tone. The warning-signal hypothesis found confirmation in developmental studies showing that a warning event can actually act as an attentional preparation cue and then lead to performance improvements (Droit-Volet, 2003, 2011). In fact, children are more accurate in judging the second event in the ECs compared to the BC, in which only one event is presented at random latencies. On the other hand, when an evaluation of the first event in the ECs is requested, no significant differences emerged, in comparison to the BCs. In this case, the children did not seem to consider the effect (e.g., Tone 1) following the voluntary action, the involuntary action, or Tone 2, and only focused their attention on the first event.

Another possible explanation that is worth taking into account refers to the "lack of inhibitory control", which is common in children. Several classic developmental studies have demonstrated that the ability to suppress irrelevant information becomes more efficient with age (Diamond and Doar, 1989; Durston et al., 2002). As a matter of fact, performance on Stroop, flanker, and go/no-go tasks continues to develop over childhood and does not reach its maximum until 12 years of age or later (Carver et al., 2001; Bunge et al., 2002; Durston et al., 2002). In our study, the children could have more accurately judged the onset of the second event in the ECs compared to the BCs because they were influenced by the presence of the first event, not because they treated the first event as a warning stimulus (warning signal theory: Droit-Volet, 2003, 2011). In fact, when Tone 1 was presented alone in the BC, it was perceived 79.17 ms after its real appearance. When it was activated by the first event in the ECs (voluntary action, involuntary action, or Tone 2), Tone 1 was perceived earlier and, consequently, more accurately, compared to the BC. When the children had to evaluate the second event in the ECs, they were not able to disengage their attention from the irrelevant stimulus (i.e., the first event), which was therefore not well-inhibited. For this reason, the second event was perceived earlier and consequently more accurately, compared to the BC.

Summarizing both hypotheses (the warning signal and the lack of inhibitory control) could represent a plausible explanation for our results. However, the lack of an inhibitory control hypothesis could better fit our data: in fact, in order to control the cross-modal estimations in timing judgments, we have to consider the perceptual shifts, not just the difference between the BC and the EC. **Figure 5** shows that the second event seems to be influenced by the first one: the effect (e.g., Tone 1) is perceived earlier towards the first event independently, by the context, and the shift is significantly different between the first and the second event, with a greater shift for the second one. It is therefore more likely that the children were unable to manage the interference caused by the first event and, consequently, to correctly evaluate the beep (e.g., Tone 1). Judging the second event correctly implies that attention has to be disengaged from the previously presented stimulus (i.e., the first event). This hypothesis finds confirmation in the literature from several studies reporting difficulties in suppressing activated, but irrelevant, information in children. In these cases, irrelevant information exploited resources that otherwise would be available to process relevant information, which led to global performance decreases (Tipper et al., 1989; Bjorklund and Harnishfeger, 1990; Rubia et al., 2000; Lorsbach and Reimer, 2011). A point worth mentioning is the fact that, in the case of the first event—in particular, the perception of the voluntary action—something different occurred compared to the two control conditions. Although this difference did not reach a significant level, it is worth underlining that the change in the case of voluntary action was greater in the BC (−19.72 ms) than in the EC (1.67 ms), When the children had to evaluate the consonant on the screen when they made the key-press in the BC, they perceived the onset of the voluntary action earlier than it really was. On the other hand, when the voluntary action caused the tone in the EC, the action was perceived later towards the tone, compared to the BC (1.67 ms). Also, the shift direction was different: in the BC, the voluntary action was perceived before it really occurred, while in the EC, it shifted towards the consequent tone. Such changes did not occur in the two control conditions. Therefore, it seems that a sort of temporal compression was developing in the children.

Considering the overall binding (i.e., the perceived linkage between action and effect), no differences emerged between the three different contexts (i.e., "the voluntary action context", "the involuntary action context", and "the two tones context"), although a sort of temporal compression seems to be present in the case of voluntary action. This lack of effect could be explained by looking at Droit-Volet's (2013) and Droit-Volet et al.'s (2004, 2007). First, the children could have encountered difficulties with this task (as a result of their limited attentional control capacities; for a review, see Brainerd and Dempster, 1995), particularly with the stream of visual letters, since the dominance of audition over vision has been reported in the processing of time (for a review, see Pouthas et al., 1993). In fact, auditory stimuli could be captured more easily compared to visual stimuli because audition is more specialized for processing temporal information. The second aspect refers to timing sensitivity, which increases with age and is not completely present in 8-year-olds (for a review, see Droit-Volet et al., 2006).

In addition, when comparing the data obtained from the adults and the children, the overall binding pattern of results within the two groups appears to be different. The two groups did not differ in terms of control conditions; rather, they only showed significant differences in the "voluntary action condition", suggesting that temporal compression only characterizes the adults' performance (**Figure 6**). On the other hand, when considering action and effect binding separately, the two groups only exhibited differences concerning action binding (i.e., the shift of the action towards the tone). This result can be explained by considering the two different processes implicated in action-and-effect binding (Moore et al., 2010; Wolpe et al., 2013). Effect binding seems to rely on a pre-activation mechanism (Waszak et al., 2012); the neural representation of a sensory outcome following a voluntary action is activated before its occurrence. When the predicted sensory event occurs, the perceptual threshold is reached faster than when the event is not predicted. Consequently, estimation errors are smaller in the ECs than they are in the BCs, leading to effect binding. On the other hand, action binding depends on both predictive motor control and inferential processes (Moore and Haggard, 2008). It could be possible that the pre-activation mechanism is already fully efficient in children, while mechanisms implicated in action binding are still being developed.

In conclusion, our research represents a substantial contribution to the comprehension of SoA mechanisms. First, we replicated the IB effect with a new paradigm that could represent an alternative to both the Libet clock and the time interval methods, thus avoiding the problems related to rotating stimuli and disentangling action binding from effect-binding processes respectively. In this sense, it is crucial to better investigate the contribution of predictive (e.g., motor command signals: Wolpert and Ghahramani, 2000; Blakemore et al., 2001) and reconstructive processes (the integration of external sensory feedback: Wegner, 2002) in children by varying the conditional probabilities of the tones and actions (Moore and Haggard, 2008). Second, our data improve and corroborate results from the literature on the ontogenetic development of agency, while going beyond its basic aspects (body awareness and action–effect learning). The use of IB as an implicit measure of SoA implies that more complex cognitive abilities are considered (i.e., executive functions), thus better depicting the complexity of SoA. In this sense, the present study is the first attempt to investigate IB as an implicit measure of SoA, in a group of children using an implicit measure of it. We found reduced IB effects in children. In fact, although the patterns of the adults and the children regarding the "voluntary action context" seemed to be similar, the results obtained from the children seem to suggest a tendency to be more focused on voluntary action, without taking the effects produced by it into account. If we consider IB to be an "adaptive illusion" that gives us a strong sense of causality and helps us to consider ourselves as responsible for certain effects, such an illusion does not seem to deceive children, maybe because the necessary cognitive skills have not been acquired yet (i.e., inhibitory control or the ability to attend selectively to critical stimuli while ignoring irrelevant information). These cognitive abilities, which belong to the executive functions' family, are generally connected with the functionality of frontal areas. Hence, it is possible that children may not possess IB because such areas, which are fundamental for the acquisition of the cognitive skills necessary to process IB, are not developed yet, like in adults. For all of these reasons, we suggest that IB may follow a developmental trend. It may be acquired gradually during ontogenesis, parallel with the maturation of the frontal cortical network. Since SoA and IB seem to share the same common cognitive mechanisms and neural networks (David et al., 2008; Moore et al., 2010; Moore and Obhi, 2012; Kühn et al., 2013; Wolpe et al., 2014), we could therefore speculate that, in conjunction with the reduction of IB, children also show diminished SoA, which does not allow them to understand the consequences of their actions. However, our results refer to IB, and speculations on SoA remain limited. The possible hypothesis of a link between reduced IB and the maturation of frontal areas in children remains an open issue that needs to be tested by means of neuroimaging techniques. Future studies are required to confirm our hypothesis, in order to provide a further step in the contextualization of SoA dynamics throughout age.

ACKNOWLEDGMENTS

We wish to thank Luca Semenzato and Jacopo Torre for their technical support. This study was partially supported by a grant from the Bial Foundation (84/12 to Patrizia S. Bisiacchi).

REFERENCES

Aarts, H., Custers, R., and Wegner, D. M. (2005). On the inference of personal authorship: enhancing experienced agency by priming effect information. *Conscious. Cogn.* 14, 439–458. doi: 10.1016/j.concog.2004.11.001

Astington, J. W. (2001). The future of theory-of-mind research: understanding motivational states, the role of language and real-world consequences. *Child Dev.* 72, 685–687. doi: 10.1111/1467-8624.00305

Biancardi, A., and Stoppa, E. (1997). Il test delle campanelle modificato: una proposta per lo studio dell'attenzione in età evolutiva. *Psichiatr. Infanz. E Adolesc.* 64, 73–84.

Bjorklund, D. F., and Harnishfeger, K. K. (1990). The resources construct in cognitive development: diverse sources of evidence and a theory of inefficient inhibition. *Dev. Rev.* 10, 48–71. doi: 10.1016/0273-2297(90)90004-n

Blakemore, S. J., Frith, C. D., and Wolpert, D. M. (2001). The cerebellum is involved in predicting the sensory consequences of action. *Neuroreport* 12, 1879–1884. doi: 10.1097/00001756-200107030-00023

Brainerd, C. J., and Dempster, F. N. (Eds.). (1995). *Interference and Inhibition in Cognition.* New York: Academic Press.

Bunge, S. A., Dudukovic, N. M., Thomason, M. E., Vaidya, C. J., and Gabrieli, J. D. (2002). Immature frontal lobe contributions to cognitive control in children: evidence from fMRI. *Neuron* 33, 301–311. doi: 10.1016/s0896-6273(01)00583-9

Carver, A. C., Livesey, D. J., and Charles, M. (2001). Age related changes in inhibitory control as measured by stop signal task performance. *Int. J. Neurosci.* 107, 43–61. doi: 10.3109/00207450109149756

Cravo, A. M., Claessens, P. M., and Baldo, M. V. (2009). Voluntary action and causality in temporal binding. *Exp. Brain Res.* 199, 95–99. doi: 10.1007/s00221-009-1969-0

Daprati, E., Wriessnegger, S., and Lacquaniti, F. (2007). Kinematic cues and recognition of self-generated actions. *Exp. Brain Res.* 177, 31–44. doi: 10.1007/s00221-006-0646-9

David, N. (2012). New frontiers in the neuroscience of the sense of agency. *Front. Hum. Neurosci.* 6:161. doi: 10.3389/fnhum.2012.00161

David, N., Newen, A., and Vogeley, K. (2008). The "sense of agency" and its underlying cognitive and neural mechanisms. *Conscious. Cogn.* 17, 523–534. doi: 10.1016/j.concog.2008.03.004

Diamond, A., and Doar, B. (1989). The performance of human infants on a measure of frontal cortex function, the delayed response task. *Dev. Psychobiol.* 22, 271–294. doi: 10.1002/dev.420220307

Droit-Volet, S. (2003). Alerting attention and time perception in children. *J. Exp. Child Psychol.* 85, 372–384. doi: 10.1016/s0022-0965(03)300103-6

Droit-Volet, S. (2011). "Child and time," in *Multidisciplinary Aspects of Time and Time Perception*, eds A. Vatakis, A. Esposito, M. Giagkou, F. Cummins and G. Papdelis (Berlin Heidelberg: Springer-Verlag), 151–173.

Droit-Volet, S. (2013). Time perception in children: a neurodevelopmental approach. *Neuropsychologia* 51, 220–234. doi: 10.1016/j.neuropsychologia.2012.09.023

Droit-Volet, S., Delgado, M., and Rattat, A. C. (2006). "The development of the ability to judge time in children," in *Focus on Child Psychology Research*, ed F. Columbus (NY: Nova Science Publishers, Inc.), 81–104.

Droit-Volet, S., Meck, W. H., and Penney, T. B. (2007). Sensory modality and time perception in children and adults. *Behav. Processes* 74, 244–250. doi: 10.1016/j.beproc.2006.09.012

Droit-Volet, S., Tourret, S., and Wearden, J. (2004). Perception of the duration of auditory and visual stimuli in children and adults. *Q. J. Exp. Psychol. A* 57, 797–818. doi: 10.1080/02724980343000495

Durston, S., Thomas, K. M., Yang, Y., Uluğ, A. M., Zimmerman, R. D., and Casey, B. J. (2002). A neural basis for the development of inhibitory control. *Dev. Sci.* 5, F9–F16. doi: 10.1111/1467-7687.00235

Eenshuistra, R. M., Weidema, M. A., and Hommel, B. (2004). Development of the acquisition and control of action-effect associations. *Acta. Psychol. (Amst)* 115, 185–209. doi: 10.1016/j.actpsy.2003.12.006

Elsner, B. (2007). Infants' imitation of goal-directed actions: the role of movements and action effects. *Acta. Psychol. (Amst)* 124, 44–59. doi: 10.1016/j.actpsy.2006.09.006

Elsner, B., and Aschersleben, G. (2003). Do I get what you get? Learning about the effects of self-performed and observed actions in infancy. *Conscious. Cogn.* 12, 732–751. doi: 10.1016/s1053-8100(03)00073-4

Engbert, K., Wohlschläger, A., and Haggard, P. (2008). Who is causing what? The sense of agency is relational and efferent-triggered. *Cognition* 107, 693–704. doi: 10.1016/j.cognition.2007.07.021

Engbert, K., Wohlschläger, A., Thomas, R., and Haggard, P. (2007). Agency, subjective time and other minds. *J. Exp. Psychol. Hum. Percept. Perform.* 33, 1261–1268. doi: 10.1037/0096-1523.33.6.1261

Farrer, C., Frey, S. H., Van Horn, J. D., Tunik, E., Turk, D., Inati, S., et al. (2008). The angular gyrus computes action awareness representations. *Cereb. Cortex* 18, 254–261. doi: 10.1093/cercor/bhm050

Frith, C. (2013). The psychology of volition. *Exp. Brain Res.* 229, 289–299. doi: 10.1007/s00221-013-3407-6

Frith, C. D. (2014). Action, agency and responsibility. *Neuropsychologia* 55, 137–142. doi: 10.4135/9781446219140.n6

Gawronski, B., LeBel, E. P., and Peters, K. R. (2007). What do implicit measures tell us?: scrutinizing the validity of three common assumptions. *Perspect. Psychol. Sci.* 2, 181–193. doi: 10.1111/j.1745-6916.2007.00036.x

Giedd, J. N., Blumenthal, J., Jeffries, N. O., Castellanos, F. X., Liu, H., Zijdenbos, A., et al. (1999). Brain development during childhood and adolescence: a longitudinal MRI study. *Nat. Neurosci.* 2, 861–863. doi: 10.1038/13158

Haggard, P. (2008). Human volition: towards a neuroscience of will. *Nat. Rev. Neurosci.* 9, 934–946. doi: 10.1038/nrn2497

Haggard, P., and Clark, S. (2003). Intentional action: conscious experience and neural prediction. *Conscious. Cogn.* 12, 695–707. doi: 10.1016/s1053-8100(03)00052-7

Haggard, P., Clark, S., and Kalogeras, J. (2002). Voluntary action and conscious awareness. *Nat. Neurosci.* 5, 382–385. doi: 10.1038/nn827

Haggard, P., and Cole, J. (2007). Intention, attention and the temporal experience of action. *Conscious. Cogn.* 16, 211–220. doi: 10.1016/j.concog.2006.07.002

Haggard, P., and Tsakiris, M. (2009). The experience of agency feelings, judgments and responsibility. *Curr. Dir. Psychol. Sci.* 18, 242–246. doi: 10.1111/j.1467-8721.2009.01644.x

Hauf, P., Elsner, B., and Aschersleben, G. (2004). The role of action effects in infants' action control. *Psychol. Res.* 68, 115–125. doi: 10.1007/s00426-003-0149-2

Humphreys, G. R., and Buehner, M. J. (2009). Magnitude estimation reveals temporal binding at super-second intervals. *J. Exp. Psychol. Hum. Percept. Perform.* 35, 1542–1549. doi: 10.1037/a0014492

Jo, H. G., Wittman, M., Hinterbrger, T., and Schmidt, S. (2014). The readiness potential reflects intentional binding. *Front. Hum. Neurosci.* 8:421. doi: 10. 3389/fnhum.2014.00421

Kühn, S., Brass, M., and Haggard, P. (2013). Feeling in control: neural correlates of experience of agency. *Cortex* 49, 1935–1942. doi: 10.1016/j.cortex.2012.09.002

Lang, B., and Perner, J. (2002). Understanding of intention and false belief and the development of self-control. *Br. J. Dev. Psychol.* 20, 67–76. doi: 10. 1348/026151002166325

Libet, B., Gleason, C. A., Wright, E. W., and Pearl, D. K. (1983). Time of conscious intention to act in relation to onset of cerebral activity (readiness-potential). The unconscious initiation of a freely voluntary act. *Brain* 106, 623–642. doi: 10. 1093/brain/106.3.623

Lorsbach, T. C., and Reimer, J. F. (2011). Developmental differences in the use of task goals in a cued version of the stroop task. *Br. J. Dev. Psychol.* 29, 138–147. doi: 10.1111/j.2044-835x.2010.02011.x

Mackintosh, N. (2011). *Brain Waves Module 4: Neuroscience and the Law.* London: Royal Society, 35.

Metcalfe, J., Eich, T. S., and Castel, A. D. (2010). Metacognition of agency across the lifespan. *Cognition* 116, 267–282. doi: 10.1016/j.cognition.2010.05.009

Metcalfe, J., and Greene, M. J. (2007). Metacognition of agency. *J. Exp. Psychol. Gen.* 136, 184–199. doi: 10.1037/0096-3445.136.2.184

Moll, J., Oliveira-Souza, R. D., Garrido, G. J., Bramati, I. E., Caparelli-Daquer, E. M., Paiva, M. L., et al. (2007). The self as a moral agent: linking the neural bases of social agency and moral sensitivity. *Soc. Neurosci.* 2, 336–352. doi: 10. 1080/17470910701392024

Moore, J., and Haggard, P. (2008). Awareness of action: inference and prediction. *Conscious. Cogn.* 17, 136–144. doi: 10.1016/j.concog.2006.12.004

Moore, J. W., and Obhi, S. S. (2012). Intentional binding and the sense of agency: a review. *Conscious. Cogn.* 21, 546–561. doi: 10.1016/j.concog.2011.12.002

Moore, J. W., Ruge, D., Wenke, D., Rothwell, J., and Haggard, P. (2010). Disrupting the experience of control in the human brain: pre-supplementary motor area contributes to the sense of agency. *Proc. Biol. Sci.* 277, 2503–2509. doi: 10. 1098/rspb.2010.0404

Oldfield, R. C. (1971). The assessment and analysis of handedness: the Edinburgh inventory. *Neuropsychologia* 9, 97–113. doi: 10.1016/0028-3932(71)90067-4

Pouthas, V., Droit, S., and Jacquet, A. Y. (1993). Temporal experiences and time knowledge in infancy and early childhood. *Time Soc.* 2, 199–218. doi: 10. 1177/0961463x93002002004

Pruneti, C. A., Fenu, A., Freschi, G., Rota, S., Cocci, D., Marchionni, M., et al. (1996). Update of the Italian standardization of the test of Raven Colored Progressive Matrices (CPM). *Boll. Psicol. Appl.* 217, 51–57.

Rochat, P. (2010). The innate sense of the body develops to become a public affair by 2-3 years. *Neuropsychologia* 48, 738–745. doi: 10.1016/j.neuropsychologia.2009. 11.021

Rubia, K., Overmeyer, S., Taylor, E., Brammer, M., Williams, S. C. R., Simmons, A., et al. (2000). Functional frontalisation with age: mapping neurodevelopmental trajectories with fMRI. *Neurosci. Biobehav. Rev.* 24, 13–19. doi: 10.1016/s0149-7634(99)00055-x

Sato, A., and Yasuda, A. (2005). Illusion of sense of self-agency: discrepancy between the predicted and actual sensory consequences of actions modulates the sense of self-agency, but not the sense of self-ownership. *Cognition* 94, 241–255. doi: 10.1016/j.cognition.2004.04.003

Scarpa, P., Piazzini, A., Pesenti, G., Brovedani, P., Toraldo, A., Turner, K., et al. (2006). Italian neuropsychological instruments to assess memory, attention and frontal functions for developmental age. *Neurol. Sci.* 27, 381–396. doi: 10. 1007/s10072-006-0717-5

Shultz, T. R., Wells, D., and Sarda, M. (1980). Development of the ability to distinguish intended actions from mistakes, reflexes and passive movements. *Br. J. Soc. Clin. Psychol.* 19, 301–310. doi: 10.1111/j.2044-8260.1980.tb00357.x

Soon, C. S., Brass, M., Heinze, H. J., and Haynes, J. D. (2008). Unconscious determinants of free decisions in the human brain. *Nat. Neurosci.* 11, 543–545. doi: 10.1038/nn.2112

Sowell, E. R., Thompson, P. M., Holmes, C. J., Jernigan, T. L., and Toga, A. W. (1999). In vivo evidence for post-adolescent brain maturation in frontal and striatal regions. *Nat. Neurosci.* 2, 859–861. doi: 10.1038/13154

Synofzik, M., Vosgerau, G., and Newen, A. (2008). Beyond the comparator model: a multifactorial two-step account of agency. *Conscious. Cogn.* 17, 219–239. doi: 10. 1016/j.concog.2007.03.010

Synofzik, M., Vosgerau, G., and Voss, M. (2013). The experience of agency: an interplay between prediction and postdiction. *Front. Psychol.* 4:127. doi: 10. 3389/fpsyg.2013.00127

Tipper, S. P., Bourque, T. A., Anderson, S. H., and Brehaut, J. C. (1989). Mechanisms of attention: a developmental study. *J. Exp. Child Psychol.* 48, 353–378. doi: 10.1016/0022-0965(89)90047-7

Tsakiris, M., Hesse, M. D., Boy, C., Haggard, P., and Fink, G. R. (2007). Neural signatures of body ownership: a sensory network for bodily self-consciousness. *Cereb. Cortex* 17, 2235–2244. doi: 10.1093/cercor/bhl131

Vakali, M. (1991). Clock time in seven to ten year-old children. *Eur. J. Psychol. Educ.* 6, 325–336. doi: 10.1007/bf03173154

van de Grind, W. (2002). Physical, neural and mental timing. *Conscious. Cogn.* 11, 241–264. doi: 10.1006/ccog.2002.0560

Verschoor, S., Weidema, M., Biro, S., and Hommel, B. (2010). Where do action goals come from? Evidence for spontaneous action-effect binding in infants. *Front. Psychol.* 1:201. doi: 10.3389/fpsyg.2010.00201

Waszak, F., Cardoso-Leite, P., and Hughes, G. (2012). Action effect anticipation: neurophysiological basis and functional consequences. *Neurosci. Biobehav. Rev.* 36, 943–959. doi: 10.1016/j.neubiorev.2011.11.004

Wegner, D. M. (2002). *The Illusion of Conscious Will.* Cambridge, MA: MIT Press.

Wegner, D. M., and Wheatley, T. (1999). Apparent mental causation: sources of the experience of will. *Am. Psychol.* 54, 480–492. doi: 10.1037/0003-066x.54. 7.480

Wolpe, N., Haggard, P., Siebner, H. R., and Rowe, J. B. (2013). Cue integration and the perception of action in intentional binding. *Exp. Brain Res.* 229, 467–474. doi: 10.1007/s00221-013-3419-2

Wolpe, N., Moore, J. W., Rae, C. L., Rittman, T., Altena, E., Haggard, P., et al. (2014). The medial frontal-prefrontal network for altered awareness and control of action in corticobasal syndrome. *Brain* 137, 208–220. doi: 10.1093/brain/awt302

Wolpe, N., and Rowe, J. B. (2014). Beyond the "urge to move": objective measures for the study of agency in the post-Libet era. *Front. Hum. Neurosci.* 8:450. doi: 10. 3389/fnhum.2014.00450

Wolpert, D. M., and Ghahramani, Z. (2000). Computational principles of movement neuroscience. *Nat. Neurosci.* 3, 1212–1217. doi: 10.1038/81497

4

The readiness potential reflects intentional binding

Han-Gue Jo[1,2], Marc Wittmann[3], Thilo Hinterberger[4] and Stefan Schmidt[1,2]*

[1] Department of Psychosomatic Medicine, University Medical Center Freiburg, Freiburg, Germany
[2] Institute for Transcultural Health Studies, European University Viadrina, Frankfurt (Oder), Germany
[3] Institute for Frontier Areas of Psychology and Mental Health, Freiburg, Germany
[4] Department of Psychosomatic Medicine, Research Section of Applied Consciousness Sciences, University Medical Center Regensburg, Regensburg, Germany

Correspondence:
Stefan Schmidt, Department of Psychosomatic Medicine, University Medical Center Freiburg, Hauptstraße 8, 79104 Freiburg, Germany
e-mail: stefan.schmidt@uniklinik-freiburg.de

When a voluntary action is causally linked with a sensory outcome, the action and its consequent effect are perceived as being closer together in time. This effect is called intentional binding. Although many experiments were conducted on this phenomenon, the underlying neural mechanisms are not well understood. While intentional binding is specific to voluntary action, we presumed that preconscious brain activity (the readiness potential, RP), which occurs before an action is made, might play an important role in this binding effect. In this study, the brain dynamics were recorded with electroencephalography (EEG) and analyzed in single-trials in order to estimate whether intentional binding is correlated with the early neural processes. Moreover, we were interested in different behavioral performance between meditators and non-meditators since meditators are expected to be able to keep attention more consistently on a task. Thus, we performed the intentional binding paradigm with 20 mindfulness meditators and compared them to matched controls. Although, we did not observe a group effect on either behavioral data or EEG recordings, we found that self-initiated movements following ongoing negative deflections of slow cortical potentials (SCPs) result in a stronger binding effect compared to positive potentials, especially regarding the perceived time of the consequent effect. Our results provide the first direct evidence that the early neural activity within the range of SCPs affects perceived time of a sensory outcome that is caused by intentional action.

Keywords: sense of agency, intentional binding, readiness potential, slow cortical potential, meditation

INTRODUCTION

The link between a voluntary action and its consequent effect leads to the experience of controlling one's own actions, i.e., the sense of agency. For over a decade there has been a growing interest in understanding a specific effect related to human agency, which was reported by Haggard et al. (2002) and termed "intentional binding". They showed that when a voluntary action causes a sensory outcome, the action and the consequent effect are perceived as being closer together in time than they really are. Action-binding (the temporal attraction of action towards its consequent effect) and effect-binding (the temporal attraction of the effect towards action) were measured separately in order to investigate the intentional binding effects (see **Figure 1**).

The intentional binding paradigm was applied in a number of experiments to study human agency, such as self-causation (Dogge et al., 2012), action selection (Barlas and Obhi, 2013), shared actions (Strother et al., 2010), uncertainty of the effect (Wolpe et al., 2013), emotional states (Yoshie and Haggard, 2013), affective valence (Takahata et al., 2012) and beliefs in free will (Aarts and van den Bos, 2011). Although many studies have assessed how intentional binding is modulated, the underlying neural mechanisms remain relatively unexplored (Moore and Obhi, 2012). Recently, a study investigated the contribution of specific brain areas on intentional binding (Moore et al., 2010). A transient disturbance of the activity in the pre-supplementary motor area (pre-SMA) by transcranial magnetic stimulation (TMS) reduced the temporal linkage between action and the effect. This was mainly due to the fact that the sensory consequence was perceived as less shifted in time towards action. In contrast, the disruption of the contralateral sensorimotor area had no or much less influence on the temporal binding effect. These results suggested that the pre-SMA plays a crucial part in intentional binding, especially on effect-binding. Because the pre-SMA is seen as a key structure involved in conscious intention to act (Fried et al., 1991; Lau et al., 2004) and intentional binding is specifically related to intentional action (Haggard et al., 2002), this brain area is likely to be associated with the binding effects.

The intentional binding experiment starts with a self-generated action. This is similar to the Libet-type experiment which assesses preconscious brain activation (readiness potential, RP), preceding a voluntary action (Libet et al., 1983). In the literature, the RP can be divided into two components based on the scalp distribution and the slope of negative potential (Shibasaki and Hallet, 2006). The early RP starts about 2 s before

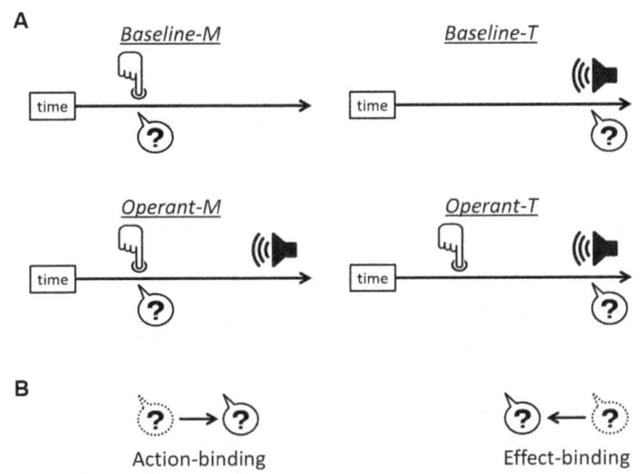

FIGURE 1 | Intentional binding paradigm. (A) In each task, participants reported either finger movement time or the onset time of the tone, indicated by the question marks. In operant tasks, i.e., *Operant-M* and *Operant-T*, a voluntary finger movement causes the tone effect 250 ms after. **(B)** Action-binding represents the temporal attraction of finger movement time towards the tone onset in *operant-M* relative to *baseline-M*, while effect-binding represents the temporal attraction of the tone onset time towards the onset of finger movement in *operant-T* relative to *baseline-T*.

a voluntary movement and consists of a prolonged and increasing negativity. This activity is localized in the bilateral pre-SMA. In contrast, the late RP has a steeper slope seen in the contralateral premotor cortex starting around −0.5 s before movement onset. Since the pre-SMA activity plays a crucial role in intentional binding (David et al., 2008; Moore et al., 2010), one can presume that the early RP might also be of importance for the temporal binding effect.

Many studies have implicated that the onset of the RP is a neural signature indicating initiation or preparation of a movement (for review, see Shibasaki and Hallet, 2006; Haggard, 2008), but recent studies suggested that the early RP is not necessarily causally related to movement preparation (Schurger et al., 2012; Jo et al., 2013, 2014). These studies rather suggest that a transient negativity of the continuously fluctuating slow cortical potentials (SCPs) facilitates the initiation of a movement in the near future. Only by averaging many single trials of this kind the early readiness potential emerges. These findings suggest that the emergence of conscious intention to act may differ in each trial as a result of differences in spontaneous brain states. Therefore, it may be more fruitful to investigate the temporal binding effect and the related brain dynamic on the level of single trials.

A number of studies have shown the positive effects of meditation on attention control and self-regulation (e.g., Jha et al., 2007; Tang et al., 2007; MacLean et al., 2010; an overview is provided in Wittmann and Schmidt, 2014). Thus, we were further interested in the effects of experience in contemplative practices on temporal attraction in an intentional binding paradigm. We hypothesized that experienced meditators would display a different temporal attraction as they are better in continuously keeping the focus of attention on the specific task conditions (Chan and Woollacott, 2007; Lutz et al., 2009; MacLean et al., 2010). Less temporal attraction in intentional binding would be indicative of less deviation from the timing of the actual event. Moreover, growing evidence of positive effects on neural systems involved in attention processes have been shown after meditation practice (Slagter et al., 2007; Lutz et al., 2009; Moore et al., 2012). Thus, different behavioral performance on intentional binding between meditators and non-meditators would be of interest regarding the question of the underlying neural mechanism of the temporal binding effect.

The aim of the present study is to investigate (i) whether the early neural activity preceding the voluntary action has an effect on intentional binding; and (ii) to explore its effect in experienced meditators by examining whether these brain correlates would be displayed differently as related to behavioral performance. In order to do so, we recorded electroencephalography (EEG) activity, while participants engaged in the intentional binding task, comparing a group of experienced meditators with matched non-meditating controls. Behavioral and electrophysiological data were analyzed on the basis of single trials.

METHODS

PARTICIPANTS

Twenty experienced mindfulness meditators (seven males; mean age 40.7 years, $SD = 7.5$, range 28–50 years) volunteered for the present study. They had at least 3 years of continuous experience in regular mindfulness meditation practice and had continuous meditation practice for at least 2 h per week during the last 8 weeks. Twenty matched controls in gender, age (mean age 40.3 years, $SD = 7.4$; $p = 0.278$) and education level, were recruited. Control subjects had never attended any course of meditation practice including Yoga, Tai-Chi and similar techniques. All participants had normal or corrected-to-normal vision and had no known psychological or neurological deficits. Participants were paid 10 € per hour for taking part in the experiment. The ethics committee of the University Medical Center Freiburg approved this study and written informed consent was obtained from all participants. Participants were invited to come twice within a period of 2 weeks to two different laboratories; first for the assessment of meditation experience cognitive performance, time perception, and personality, which will be reported elsewhere, and secondly for the Libet-type tasks with EEG recording (see below the apparatus and procedure).

SELF-REPORT MEASURES

The Freiburg Mindfulness Inventory (FMI; Walach et al., 2006) was administered to assess the level of self-reported mindfulness. It has a two-dimensional structure with the factor "presence" referring to the ability to attend to the present moment and the factor "acceptance" referring to a non-judgmental attitude (Kohls et al., 2009). A 14-item short version has been developed which was used here.

APPARATUS AND PROCEDURE

The experiment followed the procedure introduced by Haggard et al. (2002) as shown in **Figure 1**. Participants sat in front of a monitor and performed two baseline condition tasks (*baseline-M* and *baseline-T*) and two operant condition tasks (*operant-M* and *operant-T*) in a pseudo-random sequence. They were asked to report either the first moment of their finger movement (m-time) or the onset time of the tone (t-time). Each task contained forty trials.

In *baseline-M*, an analog clock (visual angle, 3° in diameter) was presented in the center of the screen. A clock-hand appeared after a short period (of 1–2 s delay) and started rotating clockwise with a revolution period of 2550 ms. Participants were asked to perform a voluntary movement (pressing the left mouse button) whenever they wanted to, but not earlier than after one full rotation of the clock-hand. After the button press, the clock-hand continued rotating for a short interval (between 1–2 s) and disappeared. Participants were then asked to indicate with the mouse pointer the clock-hand position on the clock circle at the moment when they started to move their finger to press the button. The *operant-M* condition was identical to the *baseline-M* condition apart from the fact that a 500 Hz tone (presented for 100 ms) followed the button press after a delay of 250 ms. The *operant-T* condition was identical to the *operant-M* condition, but participants were asked to indicate the onset time of the tone instead of the movement onset. In the *baseline-T* condition, participants performed no voluntary button press. Instead, a tone occurred at random times between 2.6 and 7.7 s after the clock-hand started rotating. After the tone, the clock-hand continued rotating for a short interval (between 1 and 2 s) and then disappeared. Participants were then asked to indicate the clock-hand position of the tone onset.

Because of EEG recordings (see below) participants were asked to focus on the center of the clock and to refrain from eye blinking during clock-hand rotation. Presentation of the clock and collection of the response data were performed by the E-Prime 2.0 software (Psychology Software Tools, USA). Before the experiment started, participants performed two blocks of a Libet-type task, which will be reported elsewhere, and then performed a few trials of practice for each task condition.

ELECTROPHYSIOLOGICAL RECORDINGS

EEG was recorded from a Quickamp amplifier using 64-channel active electrodes (Brain Products, Germany) in an acoustically and electromagnetically attenuated chamber. Ground electrode was placed on the forehead and an initial reference was placed at P9 according to the 10–20 system. Electrode impedance of all electrodes was kept under 5 kΩ. One channel electrooculography (EOG) was recorded to detect ocular artifacts. To estimate the onset of finger movement, a single axis accelerometer (1.7 g) was placed on the left mouse button to measure the exact onset time of the movement. All electrophysiological data were recorded at a sampling rate of 1000 Hz.

Pre-processing of data was performed with the help of EEGLAB version 12.02 (Delorme and Makeig, 2004). EEG records were down sampled to 250 Hz and re-referenced to linked mastoids. A band-pass filter from 0.01 to 45 Hz (zero-phase filter with −6 dB cutoff) was applied. Continuous EEG data was segmented into event-locked epochs ranging from 2.5 s before the event, either the onset of the button press or the tone, to 1 s after the event with baseline correction of the first 200 ms. Epochs affected by artifact (±100 μV) of any electrodes except ocular movement were excluded for further analysis. Remaining ocular artifacts were then corrected using independent component analysis (ICA). The trials with a button press during the first rotation of the clock-hand were also excluded. On average, 92.7% (*SD* = 8.6) epochs were analyzed.

Event-related EEG was measured as average over the nine electrodes around Cz (FC1, FCz, FC2, C1, Cz, C2, CP1, CPz, CP2). The amplitude of the RP was then quantified calculating the mean signal during the period from −0.2 to 0 s before this button press (or before the tone onset for *baseline-T* task). Next, the RP was divided into an early and a late component (see **Figure 2**). We calculated separate slopes for the each part of the RP. The late RP slope was computed by dividing the amplitude difference between the mean from −0.7 to −0.5 s and the mean from −0.2 to 0 s by 0.5 s. Thereby we have divided the estimated increase of the amplitude during the last 0.5 s by its duration. For the early RP we did the analogous calculation. Since the amplitude is by definition 0 for the first 200 ms due to baseline correction the overall increase was estimated by the mean amplitude from −1.0 to −0.8 s and then divided by 1.5 s, which is the duration of the early RP. In order to account for the slope of the early RP already contained in the late RP we finally subtracted the slope of the early RP from the late RP. By this procedure we can see whether there is an additional increase in the late RP compared to already ongoing trend.

To test whether ongoing potential shifts have different effects on temporal attraction, the slope of each epoch was estimated by fitting a first-order polynomial function to the average of nine electrodes before the events. According to either a negative or positive slope, each epoch was classified into either a negative or positive epoch, respectively, and then averaged for each subject.

DATA ANALYSIS

Analysis of medians rather than of simple means was applied in the present study as recommended for the Libet-type experiment (Pockett and Miller, 2007). The m-time and t-time were subtracted from the actual movement and the tone onset times, respectively. Action-binding was calculated by subtracting m-time during *baseline-M* from *operant-M*, and effect-binding was calculated by subtracting t-time during *baseline-T* from *operant-T*. Overall-binding is computed by subtracting effect-binding from action-binding. The reported times (i.e., m-time or t-time) and RP amplitudes were subject to a repeated measure ANOVA with type of reported time (m-time vs. t-time) and agency condition (baseline vs. operant) as within-subject variables, and the group (meditators vs. controls) as between-subject variables. Comparisons for matched pairs between groups were performed with paired t-test.

RESULTS

One control subject dropped out because of personal reasons. Therefore, comparison between groups was performed with 19 matched-pairs. Meditators on average had meditation experience

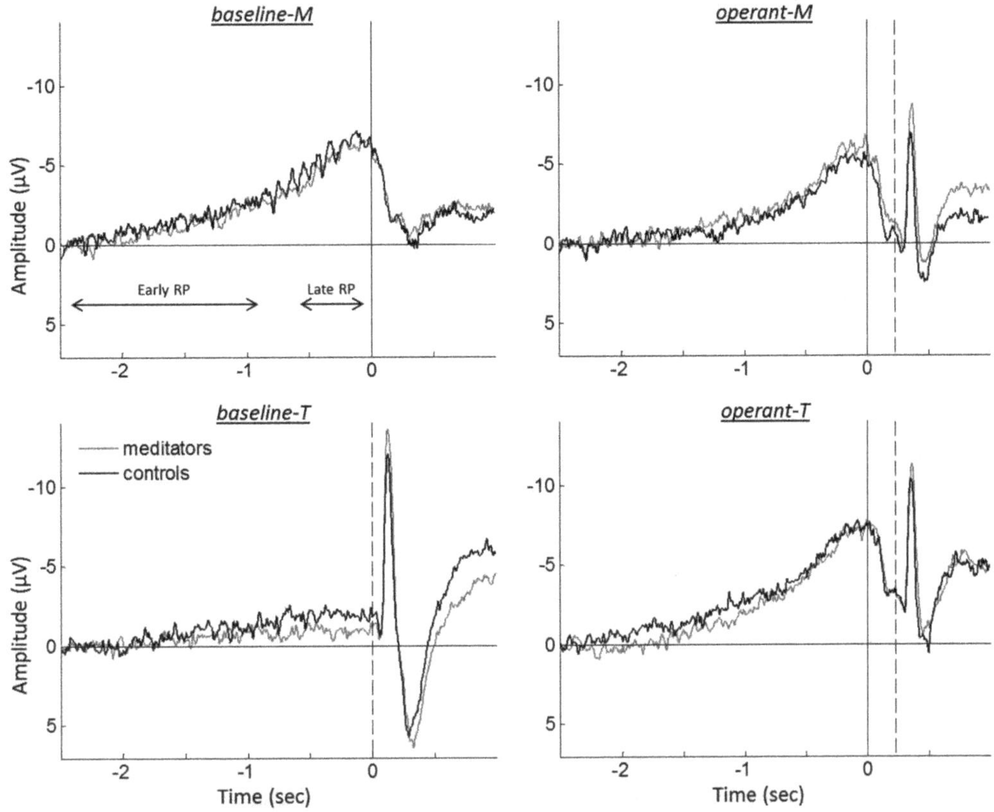

FIGURE 2 | Grand averaged event-related EEGs for meditators (gray traces) and controls (black traces), during intentional binding tasks. Solid vertical lines represent the onset of the finger movement, while dashed vertical lines indicate the tone onset. The division for the early RP and the late RP are represented by both-sided arrows.

of 10.1 years ($SD = 6.4$) and in the last 8 weeks had on average meditated for 7.6 h ($SD = 5.2$) a week.

SELF-REPORTED DATA

Scores of the self-report mindfulness scale revealed significant differences between the two groups (meditators, 44.4 ± 1.1; controls, 36.5 ± 1.2; $t_{(19)} = 4.991$, $p < 0.001$), indicative of higher "acceptance" (meditators, 24.8 ± 0.8; controls, 20.1 ± 0.7; $t_{(19)} = 4.670$, $p < 0.001$) and "presence" (meditators, 19.6 ± 0.4; controls, 16.4 ± 0.6; $t_{(19)} = 4.382$, $p < 0.001$) in meditators. This result shows that meditators report themselves to be more mindful than controls.

BEHAVIORAL DATA: REPORTED TIMES

A repeated measure ANOVA analysis revealed a significant interaction between reported time (m-time vs. t-time) and agency condition, $F_{(1,37)} = 14.961$, $p < 0.001$. To clarify this interaction, we examined the temporal binding effects for reported times, see **Table 1**. The reported time of the tone was shifted towards action in comparison to the baseline condition ($t_{(39)} = -5.293$, $p < 0.001$), showing effect-binding in 81.1% of the participants. In contrast, we found no significant difference in m-time between *baseline-M* and *operant-M* ($t_{(39)} = 0.336$, $p = 0.739$; action-binding being seen in 48.7% of the participants). That is, overall-binding was driven mainly by enhanced shift of t-time towards action in the *operant-T* task.

Notably, we found neither significant group effect nor group by task interactions (ANOVA analysis, all $p > 0.193$). Although on average we observed an earlier m-time in meditators than controls in both *baseline-M* and *operant-M* (see **Table 1**), further analysis

Table 1 | Means of reported times and temporal binding effects during intentional binding tasks.

		Meditators	Controls	*p*-value	All participants
m-time	baseline	−68.35(41.9)	−7.16(24.0)	0.198	−38.54(24.6)
	operant	−66.30(25.4)	−18.34(28.5)	0.248	−42.94(19.2)
Action-binding		2.05(26.8)	−11.18(8.6)	0.639	−4.40(14.2)
t-time	baseline	−32.88(11.3)	−32.40(18.8)	0.796	−32.64(11.7)
	operant	−131.58(27.6)	−122.82(28.1)	0.856	−127.31(19.4)
Effect-binding		−98.70(27.4)	−90.42(23.5)	0.774	−94.67(17.9)
Overall-binding		100.75(39.1)	79.24(24.1)	0.614	90.27(23.0)

The m-time and t-time are obtained by subtracting the actual event time from reported time in ms (SE). Action-binding and effect-binding indicate the mean shifts in time from baseline to operant tasks for m-time and t-time, respectively. Overall-binding is the difference between effect-binding and action-binding. p-values were calculated based on 19 matched-paired between groups.

of reported-times for all the tasks showed no difference between groups (two-tailed paired t-test, all $p > 0.198$).

We also conducted a one-way repeated measure ANOVA on mean waiting-time (the time from the start of a trial to the button press) with the self-generated movement tasks (*baseline-M*, *operant-M*, and *operant-T*) as a within-subject factors and group (meditators vs. controls) as between-subject variables. It revealed no task effect ($F_{(2,74)} = 0.465$, $p = 0.630$) and no group by task interaction ($F_{(2,74)} = 2.260$, $p = 0.111$). The mean waiting-times across participants were 7.21 s for *baseline-M*, 6.98 s for *operant-M*, 7.06 s for *operant-T*, and 5.06 s for *baseline-T*.

NEUROPHYSIOLOGIOCAL DATA: EVENT-RELATED EEG

Figure 2 shows the grand averaged event-related EEG for the different tasks. A repeated measure ANOVA analysis on the RP amplitudes revealed a significant interaction between the reported time and the agency condition, $F_{(1,37)} = 37.149$, $p < 0.001$. To further test this interaction, RP amplitudes were examined for reported times (i.e., *m*-time and *t*-time). While comparison between *baseline-M* and *operant-M* revealed no differences (*baseline-M*, -6.40 μV ± 0.81; *operant-M*, -5.66 μV ± 0.73; $t_{(39)} = -1.448$, $p = 0.156$), *operant-T* showed higher amplitude as compared to *baseline-T* (*baseline-T*, -1.37 μV ± 0.49; *operant-T*, -7.19 μV ± 0.75; $t_{(39)} = -7.330$, $p < 0.001$), indicating absence of the RP in *baseline-T*. However, we found neither significant group effect nor group by task interactions (ANOVA analysis, all $p > 0.260$), displaying no difference for each task (two-tailed paired t-test, all $p > 0.371$). Since we found no difference between groups in both behavioral data and EEG recordings, we pooled all participants for further comparisons of the tasks.

We next examined the relation of reported times to RP components, i.e., whether the early neural activity before the action influences the temporal attraction. A significant correlation was found in the *operant-T* condition, namely that the more negative the early RP, the larger the shift of *t*-time towards action ($r_{(32)} = 0.403$, $p = 0.022$; seven participants, including three meditators, who showed no effect-binding were excluded), However, we did not find this correlation in the late RP ($r_{(32)} = -0.173$, $p = 0.345$; see **Figure 3**). Notably, no significant correlations in the other three tasks were found regarding both the early and the late RPs (all $p > 0.215$), indicating the specificity of results for the *operant-T* condition. This result suggests that the perceived time of the consequent effect is related to the neural processes of the early RP, but not with the late RP.

To further test this implication, each single trial of the individual participants was classified regarding having a negative or positive slope of the epochs, and then averaged (**Figure 4**). In agreement with the previous study (Jo et al., 2013), we found a significant correlation of the ratio of positive epochs with the early RP slope (*baseline-M*, $r_{(39)} = 0.590$, $p < 0.001$; *operant-M*, $r_{(39)} = 0.644$, $p < 0.001$; *operant-T*, $r_{(39)} = 0.802$, $p < 0.001$; see **Figure 5**), demonstrating that smaller portions of positive epochs are related to larger negative early RP. However, we observed no correlation with the late RP (*baseline-M*, $r_{(39)} = 0.272$, $p = 0.094$; *operant-M*, $r_{(39)} = 0.224$, $p = 0.171$; *operant-T*, $r_{(39)} = 0.051$,

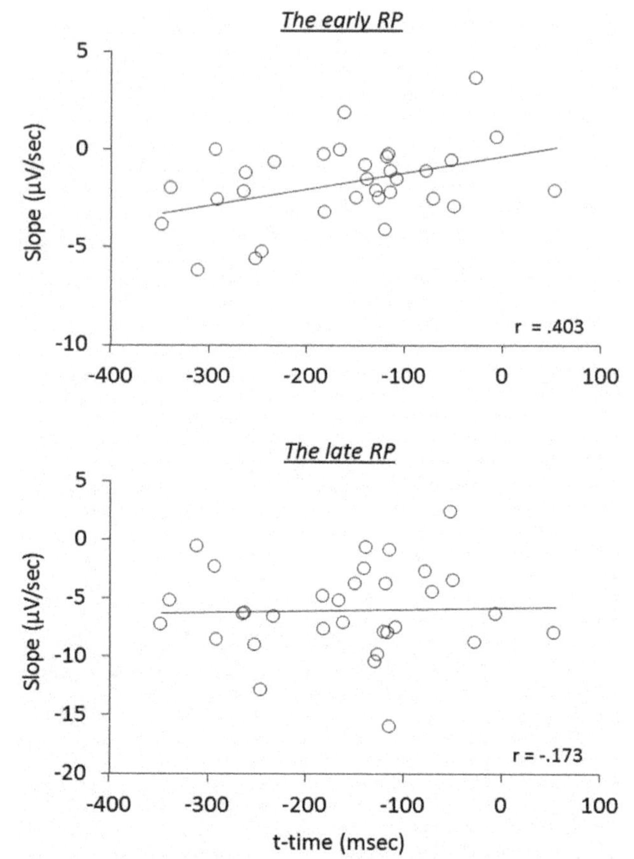

FIGURE 3 | The relation of the RP slopes to reported time of the tone during the *operant-T* task.

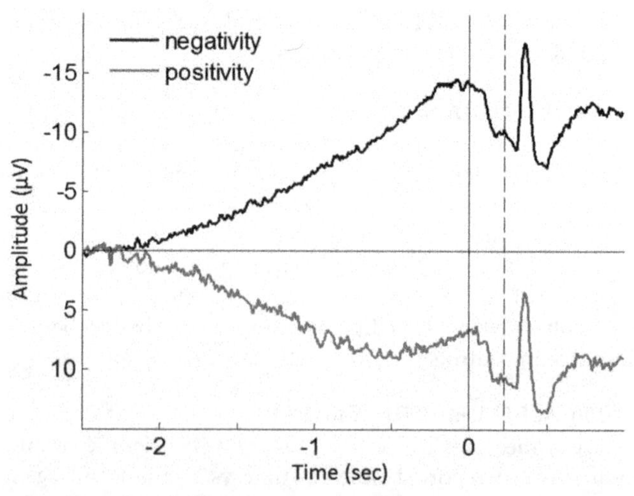

FIGURE 4 | Grand averaged ongoing negative potential (black trace) and positive potential (gray trace) during the *operant-T* task. Solid vertical line represents the onset of the finger movement, while dashed vertical line indicates the tone onset. The shift of perceived time of the tone towards action was increased in ongoing negativity ($p = 0.023$; see the text). The grand mean of the proportion of positive epochs is 30.91% ± 2.0, which results in prolonged ongoing negativity in the early RP (see **Figure 5**).

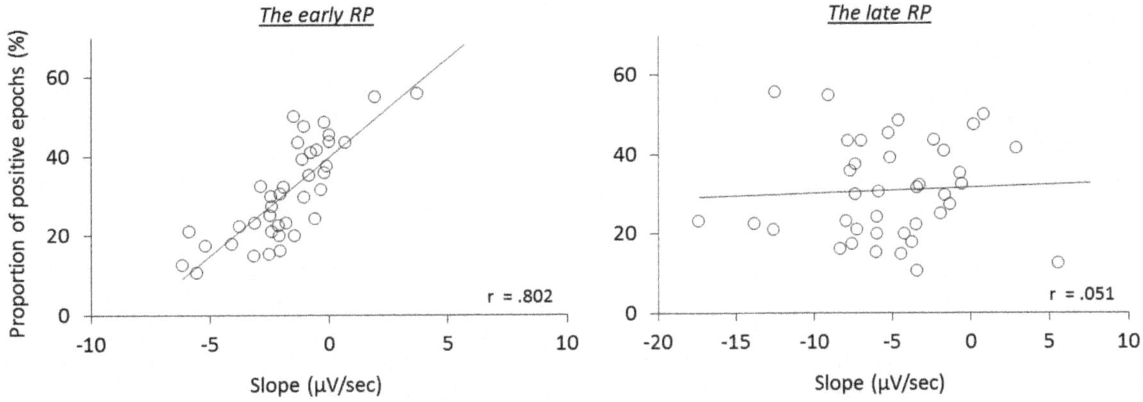

FIGURE 5 | The relation of the proportion of ongoing positive epochs to the RP slopes during the *operant-T* task.

$p = 0.758$). That is, the ongoing potential shifts are specifically related to the early part of the RP. We then performed paired t-tests to compare reported times between ongoing negative and positive slope epochs, and found a significant difference in the *operant-T* condition (negative, -131.8 ms $\pm$ 19.2; positive, -117.8 ms $\pm$ 19.2; $t_{(39)} = 2.370$, $p = 0.023$). The shift of t-time towards action was larger in negative slope epochs as compared to positive ones. This supports the relation that more negative amplitudes result in stronger effect-binding. Importantly, however, we did not find the difference in the other three tasks (*baseline-M*, $t_{(39)} = 0.079$, $p = 0.937$; *operant-M*, $t_{(39)} = -0.510$, $p = 0.613$; *baseline-T*, $t_{(39)} = -0.681$, $p = 0.500$), indicating that neither the reported time of action nor the effect that is isolated with intentional action was different between negative slope epochs and positive ones. Taken together, these results provide evidence that the early neural activity affects the perceived time of a sensory outcome that is caused by intentional action.

DISCUSSION

In the present study, we aimed to investigate (i) the RP correlates of the intentional binding effect; and (ii) to explore these correlates in experienced meditators compared to non-meditating controls. The latter comparison did not yield any significant effect, neither in the behavioral data nor in the neurophysiological ones. On the other hand, we found that the early neural activity correlates with reported time across all participants. This finding adds to the current discussion on the underlying neural mechanisms of the sense of agency.

It is of interest that we could replicate only effect-binding but not action-binding, the latter having been shown in several other studies (Dogge et al., 2012; Barlas and Obhi, 2013; Wolpe et al., 2013). This lack of replication might be explained by the following facts: Firstly, in the present study participants were asked to report "the first moment of their finger movement" rather than the time they pressed the button. Secondly, participants were asked to gaze at the center of the clock and refrain from eye-movement, i.e., they did not trace the clock-hand movement. These two aspects have been demonstrated to significantly affect the perceived time of the events in Libet-type experiments (Pockett and Miller, 2007). Nevertheless, it is important to note that a much stronger effect-binding compared to action-binding, as found here, has been consistently shown in many other studies (e.g., Haggard et al., 2002; Moore et al., 2010, 2012; Strother et al., 2010; Aarts and van den Bos, 2011; Barlas and Obhi, 2013; Yoshie and Haggard, 2013). One explanation of this typical finding in intentional binding studies could be that participants feel a stronger sense of agency when they are asked to focus on the consequent effect rather than focusing on the action.

Regarding the RP amplitude, we found that individuals who showed a larger negative amplitude of the early RP had a higher shift of reported time towards the action (effect-binding) in the condition when participants needed to focus on the consequent effect. Consistent with this result, the ongoing shifts of the SCP within participants had a significant influence on this type of reported time, with negative slopes of the early RP being related to a larger shift towards action. Importantly, these results were only found in the *operant-T* condition, demonstrating that the early neural activity prior to movement plays a significant role in the consequent effect especially with respect to the sense of agency. Since the early RP has been related to activity in the pre-SMA (Shibasaki and Hallet, 2006), our results showing that effect-binding is specific to the early RP, but not the late RP, support the previous study by Moore et al. (2010). They reported that the transient disruption of pre-SMA using TMS showed a reduced effect-binding but not a reduced action-binding. Notably, the disruption of contralateral sensorimotor areas, which have been discussed as providing the source of the late RP, had no significant influence on temporal binding. In other words, if the pre-SMA activity had a facilitating effect, enhanced temporal attractions would be expected as a result of increased effect-binding. Overall, the present data represent the first direct evidence that the early RP plays a crucial role in the temporal attraction contributing to the effect-binding.

Notably, we found that trial-to-trial variability of the ongoing shift of SCP determined the t-time even when the physical condition was held constant, i.e., within the *operant-T* task. While ongoing brain fluctuation was shown to affect intrinsic motor behavior (Fox et al., 2007; Jo et al., 2014) and the early RP could reflect ongoing fluctuating SCPs (Schurger et al., 2012; Jo et al., 2013), this observation raises the possibility that temporal attraction occurs differently in dependence of the status of spontaneous brain states. Additionally, one can assume that preceding brain activity has a stronger influence on effect-binding when the action is intrinsically generated rather than triggered by external imperative stimuli. For instance, stronger effect-binding was reported in the voluntary action condition as compared to an involuntary action, though inducing the belief of self-causation could modulate the effect-binding (Dogge et al., 2012). There is strong evidence indicating that negative deflections of the spontaneous fluctuating SCPs are associated with an increasing probability of neural firing (Birbaumer et al., 1990). Therefore an action is more likely to be executed during negative shifts of the SCP. In line with this, it has repeatedly been found that a conscious intention to act could arise more likely during an ongoing negativity of the SCP, which on average results in an increased negative RP (Schurger et al., 2012; Jo et al., 2013, 2014). Within this context, the present result of the relation between the early RP and the *t*-time further suggests that if a voluntary action follows an ongoing negative potential of SCP it will more likely lead to temporal attraction of the consequent effect than with positive deflections. That is, the neural representation of conscious intention to act, ongoing negative potentials of SCP, might be associated with an enhanced sense of agency by predicting possible consequent effects of action.

There is increasing evidence that the experience of agency is generated by both predictive and postdictive processes (Synofzik et al., 2013). Regarding predictive processes, the intentional motor representation before an action is related to the experience of agency for the given action. Regarding postdictive processes, anticipation of an action's outcome and the intention-outcome matching play the crucial role for inferring self-agency (Wegner and Wheatley, 1999). Although, many studies have repeatedly found these both effects in intentional binding (Moore and Obhi, 2012), there is still ongoing debate on whether temporal attraction is specific to intentional movement or a property of general causality perception between action and outcome (Buehner and Humphreys, 2009; Buehner, 2012). For instance, causality perception between action- and outcome-synchronized auditory signals modulated the intentional binding effect (Kawabe et al., 2013). The current finding of the relation between temporal attraction of the consequent effect and the early RP, but not with the late RP, suggests that the emergence of intention to act affects intentional binding.

In the *baseline-T* condition, we observed a slightly negative amplitude. But since there is no action preceding the tone no amplitude should be expected. A possible explanation could be that participants might have anticipated the external event. For instance, if participants learned the temporal expectancy of events, expectancy-related CNV (contingent negative variation) keeps rising until the time point of the expected event is reached even when no motor preparation is involved (Mento et al., 2013). Although the occurrence of the tones varies within an interval of 5 s, similar explanations can be applied to the result presented in the *baseline-T* condition. It should be noted, though, that the results of this task showed neither relation between event-related EEG and *t*-time nor differences in *t*-time between negative and positive epochs. Thereby one can conclude that the relation of ongoing potential shifts to *t*-time during *operant-T* are not likely due to temporal expectancy of the tone that is isolated from the sense of agency.

Although EEG recordings allow the examination of neural correlates with high temporal resolution, the temporal brain dynamics underlying human agency is not well understood (David, 2012). Several studies have observed that the brain predicts the sensory consequence of an action. The N1 amplitude was smaller in predictive sensory outcome when it was self-generated as compared to computer-generated feedback (Schafer and Marcus, 1973; Gentsch and Schütz-Bosbach, 2011; Hughes et al., 2013). Thus, N1 attenuation has been discussed as an indicator of the forward sensory model that combines self-generated motor commands and sensory information processes to predict sensory outcome. The same mechanism seems to hold in the intentional binding paradigm, as we observed sensory attenuation for the tone-evoked N1 that was self-generated (*operant-M* and *operant-T*) as compared to computer-generated (*baseline-T*; see **Figure 2**). However, the possibility cannot be ruled out that event-related EEG of the button press might affect the N1 amplitude.

One curious result of the present study is that the *operant-M* condition showed a lower RP amplitude as compared to the *operant-T* condition ($p = 0.015$), although both conditions contain the same action and the same consequent effect but differ in the reporting task. It can be speculated that in the different conditions participants might have changed their subjective criteria for performing a voluntary button press. Indeed, several participants reported that they tried to disregard the tone effect following their action in the *operant-M* condition. It could be that the consequent tone after the button press was seen as distractor since participants did not need to focus on it.

Regarding the group comparison, we found no differences between mindfulness meditators and controls. Meditators and controls showed the same temporal attraction in effect-binding and no action-binding. With respect to event-related EEG, no significant difference was found in the RP amplitudes for the entire tasks. We also examined whether there was any ongoing potential shift and early RP-related group differences, and found no group effect. It is possible that the selection criteria were not strong enough to recruit individuals who had sufficient experiences of mindfulness meditation. Although the FMI scores showed strong differences between groups, conceptual difficulties in the meaning of "mindfulness" and also comprehension disagreements of questionnaire items (Belzer et al., 2013) have led to doubts of whether it is possible to assess the experience of mindfulness through self-report items (Grossman, 2008). Thus, the self-report measure might not differentiate between "levels" of mindfulness but differences found here might describe different levels of conceptual knowledge. Another possible explanation is that meditators may have performed the task by focusing on their perceived time rather than the actual event time. For instance, we observed earlier *m*-time in meditators than controls in both *baseline-M* and *operant-M* conditions (see **Table 1**), though it revealed no significant difference. It might be that meditators reported the moment of "intention" to act, which is shortly before the actual movement onset. Therefore, further work may concern the possible divergences of subjective criteria, whether focusing on perceived-events or actual events.

In conclusion, our results do not support the hypothesis that mindfulness meditators would display different performance on the intentional binding paradigm as compared to controls. However, the present findings of the early RP correlates with the temporal attraction shed light on the underlying neural mechanism of human agency. Our results suggest that the early neural activity within the range of ongoing potential shifts affects the perceived time of the sensory outcome that is caused by intentional action.

ACKNOWLEDGMENTS

This work was supported by two grants from the FUNDAÇÃO Bial (#52/12 to Marc Wittmann and Stefan Schmidt, and #53/12 to Stefan Schmidt, Han-Gue Jo, and Marc Wittmann).

REFERENCES

Aarts, H., and van den Bos, K. (2011). On the foundations of beliefs in free will: intentional binding and unconscious priming in self-agency. *Psychol. Sci.* 22, 532–537. doi: 10.1177/0956797611399294

Barlas, Z., and Obhi, S. S. (2013). Freedom, choice and the sense of agency. *Front. Hum. Neurosci.* 7:514. doi: 10.3389/fnhum.2013.00514

Belzer, F., Schmidt, S., Lucius-Hoene, G., Schneider, J. F., Orellana-Rios, C. L., and Sauer, S. (2013). Challenging the construct validity of mindfulness assessment—a cognitive interview study of the Freiburg mindfulness inventory. *Mindfulness* 4, 33–44. doi: 10.1007/s12671-012-0165-7

Birbaumer, N., Elbert, T., Canavan, A. G. M., and Rockstroh, B. (1990). Slow potential of the cerebral cortex and behavior. *Physiol. Rev.* 70, 1–41.

Buehner, M. J. (2012). Understanding the past, predicting the future: causation, not intentional action, is the root of temporal binding. *Psychol. Sci.* 23, 1490–1497. doi: 10.1177/0956797612444612

Buehner, M. J., and Humphreys, G. R. (2009). Causal binding of actions to their effects. *Psychol. Sci.* 20, 1221–1228. doi: 10.1111/j.1467-9280.2009.02435.x

Chan, D., and Woollacott, M. (2007). Effects of level of meditation experience on attentional focus: is the efficiency of executive or orientation networks improved? *J. Altern. Complement. Med.* 13, 651–657. doi: 10.1089/acm.2007.7022

David, N. (2012). New frontiers in the neuroscience of the sense of agency. *Front. Hum. Neurosci.* 6:161. doi: 10.3389/fnhum.2012.00161

David, N., Newen, A., and Vogeley, K. (2008). The "sense of agency" and its underlying cognitive and neural mechanisms. *Conscious. Cogn.* 17, 523–534. doi: 10.1016/j.concog.2008.03.004

Delorme, A., and Makeig, S. (2004). EEGLAB: an open source toolbox for analysis of single-trial EEG dynamics including independent component analysis. *J. Neurosci. Methods* 134, 9–21. doi: 10.1016/j.jneumeth.2003.10.009

Dogge, M., Schaap, M., Custers, R., Wegner, D. M., and Aarts, H. (2012). When moving without volition: implied self-causation enhances binding strength between involuntary actions and effects. *Conscious. Cogn.* 21, 501–506. doi: 10.1016/j.concog.2011.10.014

Fox, M. D., Snyder, A. Z., Vincent, J. L., and Raichle, M. E. (2007). Intrinsic fluctuations within cortical systems account for intertiral variability in human behavior. *Neuron* 56, 171–184. doi: 10.1016/j.neuron.2007.08.023

Fried, I., Katz, A., McCarthy, G., Sass, K. J., Williamson, P., Spencer, S. S., et al. (1991). Functional organization of human supplementary motor cortex studied by electrical stimulation. *J. Neurosci.* 11, 3656–3666.

Gentsch, A., and Schütz-Bosbach, S. (2011). I did it: unconscious expectation of sensory consequences modulates the experience of self-agency and its functional signature. *J. Cogn. Neurosci.* 23, 3817–3828. doi: 10.1162/jocn_a_00012

Grossman, P. (2008). On measuring mindfulness in psychosomatic and psychological research. *J. Psychosom. Res.* 64, 405–408. doi: 10.1016/j.jpsychores.2008.02.001

Haggard, P. (2008). Human volition: towards a neuroscience of will. *Nat. Rev. Neurosci.* 9, 934–946. doi: 10.1038/nrn2497

Haggard, P., Clark, S., and Kalogeras, J. (2002). Voluntary action and conscious awareness. *Nat. Neurosci.* 5, 382–385. doi: 10.1038/nn827

Hughes, G., Desantis, A., and Waszak, F. (2013). Attenuation of auditory N1 results from identity-specific action-effect prediction. *Eur. J. Neurosci.* 37, 1152–1158. doi: 10.1111/ejn.12120

Jha, A. P., Krompinger, J., and Baime, M. J. (2007). Mindfulness training modifies subsystems of attention. *Cogn. Affect. Behav. Neurosci.* 7, 109–119. doi: 10.3758/cabn.7.2.109

Jo, H.-G., Hinterberger, T., Wittmann, M., Borghardt, T. L., and Schmidt, S. (2013). Spontaneous EEG fluctuations determine the readiness potential: is preconscious brain activation a preparation process to move? *Exp. Brain Res.* 231, 495–500. doi: 10.1007/s00221-013-3713-z

Jo, H. -G., Wittmann, M., Borghardt, T. L., Hinterberger, T., and Schmidt, S. (2014). First-person approaches in neuroscience of consciousness: brain dynamics correlate with the intention to act. *Conscious. Cogn.* 26, 105–116. doi: 10.1016/j.concog.2014.03.004

Kawabe, T., Roseboom, W., and Nishida, S. (2013). The sense of agency is action-effect causality perception based on cross-modal grouping. *Proc. Biol. Sci.* 280:20130991. doi: 10.1098/rspb.2013.0991

Kohls, N., Sauer, S., and Walach, H. (2009). Facets of mindfulness—results of an online study investigating the Freiburg mindfulness inventory. *Pers. Individ. Diff.* 46, 224–230. doi: 10.1016/j.paid.2008.10.009

Lau, H. C., Rogers, R. D., Haggard, P., and Passingham, R. E. (2004). Attention to intention. *Science* 303, 1208–1210. doi: 10.1126/science.1090973

Libet, B., Gleason, C. A., Wright, E. W., and Pearl, D. K. (1983). Time of conscious intention to act in relation to onset of cerebral activity (readiness-potential). The unconscious initiation of a freely voluntary act. *Brain* 106, 623–642. doi: 10.1093/brain/106.3.623

Lutz, A., Slagter, H. A., Rawlings, N. B., Francis, A. D., Greischar, L. L., and Davidson, R. J. (2009). Mental training enhances attentional stability: neural and behavioral evidence. *J. Neurosci.* 29, 13418–13427. doi: 10.1523/JNEUROSCI.1614-09.2009

MacLean, K. A., Ferrer, E., Aichele, S. R., Birdwell, D. A., Zanesco, A. P., Jacobs, T. L., et al. (2010). Intensive meditation training improves perceptual discrimination and sustained attention. *Psychol. Sci.* 21, 829–839. doi: 10.1177/0956797610371339

Mento, G., Tarantino, V., Sarlo, M., and Bisiacchi, P. S. (2013). Automatic temporal expectancy: a high-density event-related potential study. *PLoS One* 8:e62896. doi: 10.1371/journal.pone.0062896

Moore, A., Gruber, T., Derose, J., and Malinowski, P. (2012). Regular, brief mindfulness meditation practice improves electrophysiological markers of attentional control. *Front. Hum. Neurosci.* 6:18. doi: 10.3389/fnhum.2012.00018

Moore, J. W., and Obhi, S. S. (2012). Intentional binding and the sense of agency: a review. *Conscious. Cogn.* 21, 546–561. doi: 10.1016/j.concog.2011.12.002

Moore, J. W., Ruge, D., Wenke, D., Rothwell, J., and Haggard, P. (2010). Disrupting the experience of control in the human brain: pre-supplementary motor area contributes to the sense of agency. *Proc. Biol. Sci.* 277, 2503–2509. doi: 10.1098/rspb.2010.0404

Pockett, S., and Miller, A. (2007). The rotating spot method for timing subjective events. *Conscious. Cogn.* 16, 241–254. doi: 10.1016/j.concog.2006.09.002

Schafer, E. W. P., and Marcus, M. M. (1973). Self-stimulation alters human sensory brain responses. *Science* 181, 175–177. doi: 10.1126/science.181.4095.175

Schurger, A., Sitt, J. D., and Dehaene, S. (2012). An accumulator model for spontaneous neural activity prior to self-initiated movement. *Proc. Natl. Acad. Sci. U S A* 109, E2904–E2913. doi: 10.1073/pnas.1210467109

Shibasaki, H., and Hallet, M. (2006). What is the Bereitschaftspotential? *Clin. Neurophysiol.* 117, 2341–2356. doi: 10.1016/j.clinph.2006.04.025

Slagter, H. A., Lutz, A., Greischar, L. L., Francis, A. D., Nieuwenhuis, S., Davis, J. M., et al. (2007). Mental training affects distribution of limited brain resources. *PLoS Biol.* 5:e138. doi: 10.1371/journal.pbio.0050138

Strother, L., House, K. A., and Obhi, S. S. (2010). Subjective agency and awareness of shared actions. *Conscious. Cogn.* 19, 12–20. doi: 10.1016/j.concog.2009.12.007

Synofzik, M., Vosgerau, G., and Voss, M. (2013). The experience of agency: an interplay between prediction and postdiction. *Front. Psychol.* 4:127. doi: 10.3389/fpsyg.2013.00127

Takahata, K., Takahashi, H., Maeda, T., Umeda, S., Suhara, T., Mimura, M., et al. (2012). It's not my fault: posdictive modulation of intentional binding by monetary brains and losses. *PLoS One* 7:e53421. doi: 10.1371/journal.pone.0053421

Tang, Y., Ma, Y., Wang, J., Fan, Y., Feng, S., Lu, Q., et al. (2007). Short-term meditation training improves attention and self-regulation. *Proc. Natl. Acad. Sci. U S A* 104, 17152–17156. doi: 10.1073/pnas.0707678104

Walach, H., Buchheld, N., Buttenmüller, V., Kleinknecht, N., and Schmidt, S. (2006). Measuring mindfulness—the Freiburg mindfulness inventory (FMI). *Pers. Individ. Dif.* 40, 1543–1555. doi: 10.1016/j.paid.2005.11.025

Wegner, D. M., and Wheatley, T. (1999). Apparent mental causation. Source of the experience of will. *Am. Psychol.* 54, 480–492. doi: 10.1037/0003-066x.54.7.480

Wittmann, M., and Schmidt, S. (2014). "Mindfulness meditation and the experience of time," in *Meditation—Neuroscientific Approaches and Philosophical Implications. Studies in Neuroscience, Consciousness and Spirituality* (Vol. 2), eds S. Schmidt and H. Walach (Switzerland: Springer-Verlag), 199–210.

Wolpe, N., Haggard, P., Siebner, H. R., and Rowe, J. B. (2013). Cue integration and the perception of action in intentional binding. *Exp. Brain Res.* 229, 467–474. doi: 10.1007/s00221-013-3419-2

Yoshie, M., and Haggard, P. (2013). Negative emotional outcomes attenuate sense of agency over voluntary actions. *Curr. Biol.* 23, 2028–2032. doi: 10.1016/j.cub.2013.08.034

5

Action and perception in social contexts: intentional binding for social action effects

Roland Pfister[1]*, Sukhvinder S. Obhi[2], Martina Rieger[3,4] and Dorit Wenke[4,5]

[1] *Department of Psychology III, Julius Maximilians University of Würzburg, Würzburg, Germany*
[2] *Department of Psychology, Wilfrid Laurier University, Waterloo, ON, Canada*
[3] *Institute for Psychology, UMIT, University for Health Sciences, Medical Informatics and Technology, Hall in Tirol, Austria*
[4] *Department of Psychology, Max-Planck-Institute for Human Cognitive and Brain Sciences, Leipzig, Germany*
[5] *Department of Psychology, Humboldt University at Berlin, Berlin, Germany*

Correspondence:
Roland Pfister, Department of Psychology III, Julius Maximilians University of Würzburg, Röntgenring 11, 97070 Würzburg, Germany
e-mail: roland.pfister@psychologie.uni-wuerzburg.de

The subjective experience of controlling events in the environment alters the perception of these events. For instance, the interval between one's own actions and their consequences is subjectively compressed—a phenomenon known as intentional binding. In two experiments, we studied intentional binding in a social setting in which actions of one agent prompted a second agent to perform another action. Participants worked in pairs and were assigned to a "leader" and a "follower" role, respectively. The leader's key presses triggered (after a variable interval) a tone and this tone served as go signal for the follower to perform a keypress as well. Leaders and followers estimated the interval between the leader's keypress and the following tone, or the interval between the tone and the follower's keypress. The leader showed reliable intentional binding for both intervals relative to the follower's estimates. These results indicate that human agents experience a pre-reflective sense of agency for genuinely social consequences of their actions.

Keywords: intentional binding, action effects, social actions, action and perception, sense of agency

INTRODUCTION

The physical world is quite simple, at least when considering how it can be affected by one's own actions: Pressing a light switch in a dark hallway will turn on the light just as reliably as jumping into a puddle will make some water splash around. In other words: Every action an agent chooses to perform will produce certain effects in the environment, and these effects can be predicted with ease in many cases. Actively bringing about an action effect in the environment gives rise to *sense of agency*, the subjective experience of controlling one's actions and, through them, events in the outside world (Haggard and Tsakiris, 2009). A major precondition for sense of agency to arise is a high contingency between actions and following effects (Metcalfe and Greene, 2007; Moore et al., 2009a). As the above examples show, the physical world offers almost ideal preconditions for feeling control over various ensuing events, while at the same time being able to tell which events escape one's own influence.

By contrast, matters become more complicated when considering social consequences of own actions: Human actions often aim at changing the behavior of another agent, and in this situation, the action's exact effects do not only depend on the action itself but also on how the other agent actually responds to it. Interestingly, sense of agency has not yet been studied for actions that explicitly aim at influencing another agent's behavior. The present study therefore addressed this issue by measuring a specific, pre-reflective component of sense of agency that is known as *intentional binding* (Haggard et al., 2002). Before describing these experiments, we give a brief overview of different measures of sense of agency and of previous studies on sense of agency in social contexts that involved two individuals jointly producing a given effect.

MEASURING SENSE OF AGENCY

Sense of agency can be measured directly and indirectly (Haggard and Tsakiris, 2009). Direct measures of sense of agency are usually obtained via self-reports in terms of judgments of agency on a predefined rating scale (e.g., Wegner et al., 2004; Sato and Yasuda, 2005; Wenke et al., 2010). Obviously, these measures draw on reflective aspects of sense of agency that are available to introspection. Thus, they have often been viewed as capturing mainly processes of retrospective inference which compare the match between current intention and an experienced effect (e.g., Wegner, 2003).

Indirect measures, by contrast, aim to assess pre-reflective correlates of agency, and the phenomenon of intentional binding is one of these correlates (for an overview of indirect measures, see Haggard and Tsakiris, 2009). Intentional binding refers to the finding that the perceived time interval between voluntary actions and ensuing perceptual events is subjectively compressed (Haggard et al., 2002; Moore and Haggard, 2008; but see Buehner and Humphreys, 2009; Buehner, 2012). It has been argued that intentional binding strongly depends on pre-reflective processes that do not require self-referential processing. In particular, intentional binding was suggested to reflect the low-level sensorimotor basis of sense of agency (Moore and Obhi, 2012) and might primarily reflect what Synofzik et al. (2008) refer to as "feelings of agency." Compared to explicit self-report judgments, indirect measures of sense of agency such as intentional binding are assumed to be less affected by prior beliefs about who is in control (but see Desantis et al., 2011). Therefore, intentional binding and explicit agency judgments seem to capture at least partly different processes and might yield diverging results in some situations (Ebert and Wegner, 2010; for a review, see Moore and Obhi, 2012). This is not to say however that intentional binding depends on predictive processes alone. Previous studies have shown that intentional binding depends on both, efferent motor prediction and retrospective inference that occurs right after an agent experiences a certain effect to result from his or her action (Moore and Haggard, 2008; Moore et al., 2009a). Thus, our use of the term "pre-reflective" aims at distinguishing processes that are captured by indirect measures rather than by direct self-reports, without implying a particular interpretation in terms of predictive or retrospective mechanisms.

SENSE OF AGENCY IN SOCIAL INTERACTION

Previous studies on sense of agency in social interaction focused on settings that were explicitly designed to be highly ambiguous about which of two agents had caused a certain event. Such ambiguous settings allow investigating whether agents may attribute authorship for an event to themselves even if this event was actually caused by someone else. And indeed, such "vicarious" agency has been demonstrated in different experimental contexts (Nielsen, 1963; Wegner and Wheatley, 1999; Wegner et al., 2004). For instance, Wegner and Wheatley (1999) asked two actors to perform a joint (mouse) movement and each actor could stop the mouse cursor at a time of his or her choosing. After stopping, participants provided direct judgments of agency about the stopping action. Interestingly, they reported a high degree of agency even when the other actor had actually stopped the movement, provided that the effect of the stopping action (the mouse cursor resting on a particular object on the screen) corresponded to an auditory prime naming that object prior to the action.

In addition to introspective self-reports of sense of agency, Obhi and colleagues recently suggested that sense of agency in social situations may also include pre-reflective processes as measured via intentional binding (Strother et al., 2010; Obhi and Hall, 2011a,b). Similar to an experiment by Wegner and Wheatley (1999), the participants of Obhi and Hall (2011a) jointly engaged in a task (pressing the space bar on a computer keyboard), which in turn produced a joint effect (a tone). Both participants placed their index finger on one end of the space bar and were encouraged to press the key at a time of their choosing. If the other participant initiated the keypress first, they were to join in and press the space bar down as well. In addition to explicit judgments of agency, these authors also assessed intentional binding and found reliable binding effects for both, self-initiated and other-initiated actions. Interestingly though, explicit self-reports of agency differed, such that only those individuals who actually initiated the key press reported being responsible for the outcome. Overall, these results suggest that intentional binding might not be restricted to own actions. Instead, it might also occur for another person's actions, at least when agents jointly produce an effect that matches the individual's intention.

CONTROLLING OTHER PEOPLE: THE PRESENT EXPERIMENTS

In the present experiments, we investigated sense of agency in a different social situation: Rather than creating ambiguity about who had caused a certain effect in the environment, we set up a situation in which one of two agents clearly was the "leader" and prompted a second participant, the "follower," to carry out an action. That is, both agents performed their own distinctive actions *with the action of the follower being triggered by the leader action*. In fact, such situations are very common in everyday interactions. For example, someone might ask another person to open a window or, in organizational settings, a person higher up in the hierarchy might prompt his or her subordinates to carry out a certain task. In such situations, the leader clearly affects the follower's action although, of course, the follower is immediately responsible for initiating and performing it. As outlined above, the follower's action is not as predictable as action effects in the physical world tend to be, neither in terms of timing (contiguity) nor in terms of actual occurrence (contingency). It is thus unclear, whether pre-reflective components of sense of agency—as measured via intentional binding—arise for such social action effects. Finding intentional binding for the leader regarding the follower's action would indicate that the representation of the follower's action potentially affected low-level predictive motor processes, similar to situations in which one's own action causes predictable effects in the physical environment (Haggard et al., 2002).

Supporting evidence for this speculation comes from a recent study on the role of anticipated social action effects for effect-based action control (Pfister et al., 2013). In this study, two participants also worked on a task in which one of them was the designated leader and the other was the designated follower. The leader performed a long or short keypress in response to an imperative stimulus on a computer screen that only he or she was able to see. In different blocks, the follower either imitated the leader's action (e.g., performing a short keypress in response to a short keypress of the leader), or counter-imitated the leader's action (performing a long keypress in response to a short keypress of the leader). The leader showed better performance, i.e., faster responses, in the imitation condition as compared to the counter-imitation condition. Because the follower's imitation or counter-imitation response only occurred after the leader action, these findings indicate that anticipated changes of the follower's behavior affected the leader's action planning. The results of Pfister et al. (2013) thus suggest that social action effects may indeed become integrated in action control. This, in turn, might give rise to intentional binding for these effects (for additional comments on effect-based action control in social settings, see Ray and Welsh, 2011; Pfister et al., 2014). We tested this prediction in two experiments in which two participants acted interdependently in a simple action sequence (see **Figure 1**).

One participant, the leader, started the action sequence by pressing a key. After a variable interval, an effect tone was presented which served as a go signal for the follower to also press a key. The interval between the leader's keypress and the onset of the effect tone, termed the leader's action-tone-interval (L-ATI), as well as the interval between the tone and the follower's keypress, termed follower's tone-action-interval (F-TAI; i.e., his or

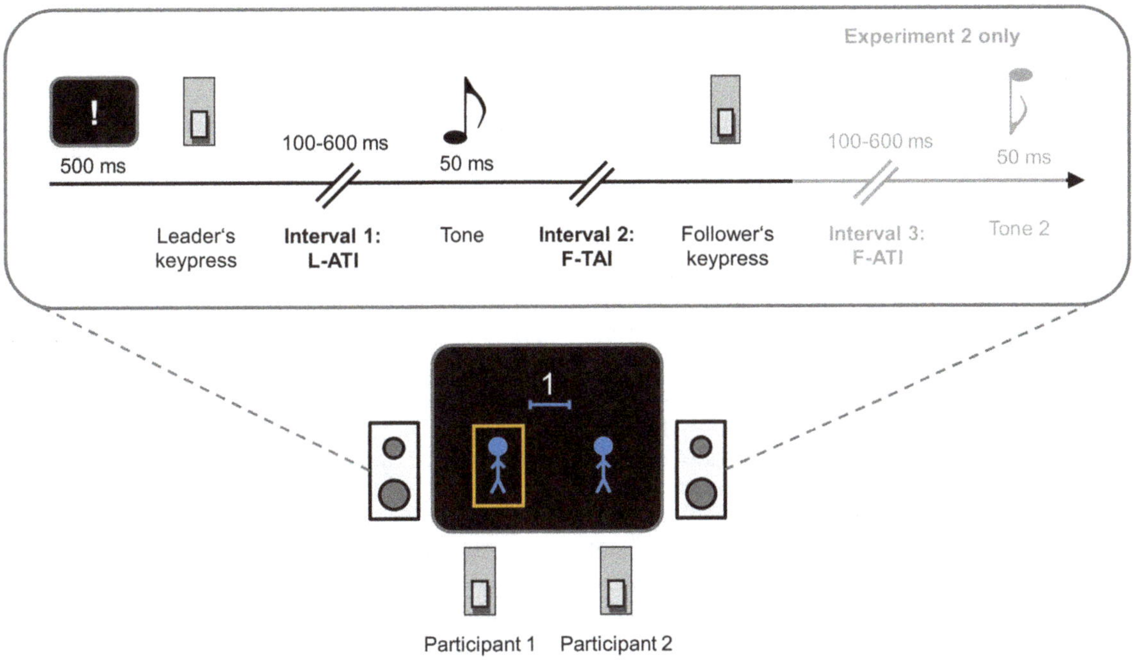

FIGURE 1 | Setup and trial procedure of Experiment 1 and 2. Participants sat next to each other and operated one response key each. One participant acted as the leader of an action sequence whereas the other participant acted as the follower: The leader initiated the action sequence at leisure after an exclamation mark had disappeared from the computer screen. The leader action triggered an effect tone after a variable action-effect interval of 100–600 ms. This tone also served as a go signal for the follower. The follower's action triggered an effect tone in Experiment 2, but not in Experiment 1. At the end of the trial, either the leader or the follower had to estimate the duration of either the leader's action-tone interval (L-ATI), the interval between the tone and the follower's action (F-TAI), or (Experiment 2 only) the follower's action-tone interval (F-ATI).

her response time) were estimated by both, leader and follower (for previous uses of interval estimation tasks in research on temporal binding, see Engbert and Wohlschläger, 2007; Engbert et al., 2007, 2008; Moore et al., 2009b; Wenke and Haggard, 2009; Humphreys and Buehner, 2010). Intentional binding for the leader would become evident in terms of giving shorter interval estimates than the follower. Based on the above argument, we expected to observe intentional binding for the leader not only for his or her action effect in the physical environment (the action-contingent tone), but also for the ensuing action of the follower.

EXPERIMENT 1: INTENTIONAL BINDING FOR SOCIAL ACTION EFFECTS

In Experiment 1, we investigated whether different roles in a social setting, i.e., being a leader or a follower, results in different representations of the actions conducted in this setting. Specifically, we were interested in whether the leader, whose action prompted the follower to react, would represent the follower's action in the same way the leader represents other effects of the own action. To investigate whether the representation of such action effects is mirrored in indirect measures of sense of agency, we assessed intentional binding in terms of direct interval estimates (see also **Figure 1**). The to-be-estimated interval on a given trial was prespecified, whereas a cue at the end of the trial indicated who was to judge. We expected intentional binding for the leader's effect tone to be mirrored in shorter interval estimates for the leader estimating the L-ATI than for the follower estimating the L-ATI. Further, if the follower's response is also coded as an additional action effect for the leader, the leader should perceive this event to occur earlier in time than the follower, giving rise to shorter estimates for the F-TAI, too. We thus predicted shorter interval estimates by leaders than by followers, not only with regard to the first interval (L-ATI) but, more importantly, also for the second one (F-TAI).

METHODS

Participants

Twenty-eight volunteers from the city of Leipzig were paid for participation (8 males; all right-handed; mean age = 22.9 years). All participants reported normal or corrected-to-normal vision and hearing and were naive as to the purpose of the experiment. The two participants of each session were of the same gender. The study was conducted in accordance with the Declaration of Helsinki and the procedures were approved by the local ethics committee.

Material, apparatus, and procedure

The two participants of each pair worked together in front of a 17″ monitor and operated one response key each with their right hand. The keys were mounted safely on the table and were connected to the computer via the parallel port. A second monitor was turned sideways to the experimenter and could not be observed by the participants.

Participants received written instructions and were told that their task was to estimate the length of either of the two intervals (in ms) and that the to-be-judged interval (i.e., either L-ATI or F-TAI) was constant for each block of trials. They were assigned to the roles of leader and follower and were informed that their roles would change after the first half of the experiment. Across participant pairs, we counterbalanced whether the left- or right-sitting participant started as leader.

Figure 1 shows a schematic of an experimental trial. Each trial started with the presentation of a white exclamation mark in the center of the screen (20 pt Arial font). After a delay of 500 ms, the exclamation mark disappeared and the program waited for the leader's key press. Leaders pressed their key at a time of their choosing. The leader's key press triggered an effect tone that appeared after a random action-tone interval between 100 and 600 ms drawn from a uniform distribution. This was done in order to match typical RTs of previous experiments with comparable settings (Engbert et al., 2007, 2008). However, participants were told that the interval varied between 1 and 1000 ms, and they were similarly informed that typical reaction times are in the range of up to 1000 ms. Sinusoidal tones with a duration of 50 ms and a frequency of 400 and 800 Hz served as auditory action effects. Tones were presented via two loudspeakers that stood to the right and to the left of the monitor, and the pitch of the tone depended on the key that was pressed. Because each pair of participants had a fixed sitting order and only operated one key each, this implied that the tones were participant-specific for the duration of the entire experiment. The assignment of tones to keys was counterbalanced across participant pairs.

The tone served as go-signal for the follower and the program waited for a maximum of 1000 ms for the follower's key press. Then, after an additional SOA of 500 ms, the judgment screen was presented (see **Figure 1**). The judgment screen consisted of two matchstick men and either the left or the right matchstick man was marked by an orange box to indicate the judge in the current trial. That is, participants only learned at the end of each trial whose turn it was to judge the interval, to ensure that both participants always paid attention to the events at all times. Additionally, the judgment screen contained a number above the matchstick men that reminded participants which interval to judge ("1" for the L-ATI, "2," for the F-TAI). The to-be-judged intervals were blocked such that participants knew in advance which interval to focus on. The order of to-be-judged intervals was counterbalanced across participant pairs, but remained constant for the two experimental halves for each pair.

Participants gave their interval judgments orally, and the experimenter noted the time estimates and initiated the next trial. Anticipations (leader actions before the exclamation mark disappeared, follower reactions before tone onset), omissions (follower's reaction time > 1000 ms), or wrong order of keystrokes (follower before leader), triggered a warning message on the screen and the next trial started afterward. These trials were removed from the analyses.

Each experimental half started with three different practice blocks that allowed participants to familiarize themselves with the task in each role (leader, follower). The first practice block comprised 10 trials in which participants only had to press the keys in the correct order without estimating the interval length. This block was followed by two additional training blocks of 20 trials (each pertaining to one of the intervals) during which the participants were instructed to make interval estimates. In these two training blocks, the experimenter gave vague feedback about the judgments by classifying the to-be judged intervals as short, medium, and long (and shorter/longer than the previous interval). To this end, the actual interval length was displayed on the experimenter's monitor throughout the experiment. Data of the training blocks were not analyzed.

After the training blocks, two test blocks of 20 trials each were performed for each interval (totaling to 20 interval estimates for each combination of interval and judge). Both blocks relating to a specific interval immediately followed each other and the sequence of intervals matched the sequence of the training blocks. Thus, if the participants judged the L-ATI in the first training block and F-TAI in the second training block, they started with two blocks of L-ATI judgments and continued with two blocks of F-TAI judgments. The interval sequence was counterbalanced across participant pairs. The fourth test block marked the end of the first half of the experiment and was followed by a longer break before participants continued with changed roles.

RESULTS

The first trial of each block and trials with errors (4.3%) were excluded from data analysis. For the remaining test trials, we computed binding scores by subtracting the actual interval length from the respective interval estimate; negative binding scores thus indicate a subjective compression of the interval. These binding scores were then subjected to an outlier correction for each participant and condition ($|z| > 2.5$; 1.0%).

Preliminary analyses examined the correlation of binding scores and actual interval lengths across all trials for each participant. These correlations were submitted to a Fisher-Z transformation, averaged across participants, and re-transformed afterward. This analysis yielded a strong mean correlation indicating more pronounced binding for longer intervals, $r = 0.60$, with the mean Z-value differing significantly from zero, $t_{(27)} = 11.28$, $p < 0.001$. Such a correlation might introduce potential confounds to any analysis of the raw binding scores because, unlike in most previous studies, our design did not allow for matching interval lengths across all conditions. This potential confound becomes evident when considering a session in which the particular follower responds very slowly as compared to most other participants: Such a slow response time (that cannot be manipulated experimentally) might be sufficient to introduce various biases in the obtained interval estimates from both participants and thus distort the pattern of results. We therefore decided to perform an analysis of regression residuals instead of analyzing the raw binding scores, even though the raw binding scores yielded a similar pattern (with profound underestimation for all conditions except for the follower estimating the F-TAI, see Table A1 in the Supplementary Material).

Such analyses of regression residuals are performed in two steps (cf. Maxwell et al., 1985; Pfister, 2011). In the first step, we calculated a linear regression for each individual participant to estimate the impact of the interval length on binding scores (irrespective of the experimental condition). The scores predicted by the regression analysis were then compared to the actual binding scores to calculate the regression residuals, i.e., the portion of the interval estimate that could not be accounted for by the interval length itself. We then submitted the mean regression residuals to a 2 × 2 repeated-measures ANOVA with the factors judge (leader vs. follower) and to-be-judged interval (L-ATI vs. F-TAI).

As hypothesized, participants gave shorter interval estimates for both intervals when acting as leader than when acting as follower (**Figure 2**, left panel), $F_{(1,27)} = 7.65$, $p = 0.010$, $\eta_p^2 = 0.22$. Additionally, the first interval was consistently judged to be shorter than the second interval by both judges, $F_{(1,27)} = 16.30$, $p < 0.001$, $\eta_p^2 = 0.38$. Both main effects were additive as indicated by a non-significant interaction ($F < 1$). Considered separately, one-tailed t-tests showed significant differences between leaders and followers both, for the L-ATI, $t_{(27)} = 1.89$, $p = 0.035$, $d = 0.36$, and the F-TAI, $t_{(27)} = 1.72$, $p = 0.048$, $d = 0.33$.

DISCUSSION

Experiment 1 investigated intentional binding for social action effects, i.e., responses of another agent. The results indicate that the leader of the action sequence did experience intentional binding for the follower's action. This finding is especially striking in light of previous research on the perceived timing of observed actions that are not performed in response to own actions (as in the present setup) but rather, independently of any other agent (Wohlschläger et al., 2003a,b). These previous studies found either no difference between the estimated onsets of own and observed actions, or even the reverse pattern, with observed actions being judged to occur later in time than own actions. The present setting thus clearly did not only compensate for this bias but shifted the pattern of estimates toward an underestimation of the follower's tone-action interval by the (observing) leader, as compared to the follower him- or herself. It thus seems as if pre-reflective components of sense of agency do indeed occur for social action effects even despite the challenges that come with the social setting.

On closer inspection, however, the design of Experiment 1 seems to lack a critical feature that is often present in real-world interactions outside the laboratory. For instance, when asking someone to open a window, the "follower" clearly achieves an action effect (i.e., the opened window), rather than simply performing a particular movement as was the case in Experiment 1. Experiment 2 thus introduced an additional component to the task: The follower's action now triggered a tone as well, and we obtained interval estimates for this interval in addition to the two intervals of Experiment 1. This setting thus provided the opportunity to replicate the central results of Experiment 1 (stronger F-TAI binding for leaders than for followers) while at the same time probing for differential binding for the third interval for the leader and the follower.

EXPERIMENT 2: INVESTIGATING THE FOLLOWER'S ACTION EFFECT

Experiment 2 extended the action sequence of Experiment 1 so that the follower now also produced an effect tone by her or his keypress and this tone differed in pitch from the leader's tone. As for the leader's effect tone, the follower's effect occurred after a variable interval and we label this interval the F-ATI. Participants either estimated the length of the L-ATI, the F-TAI, or F-ATI. Our main question was whether the results of Experiment 1 would replicate in this setting and whether the stronger intentional

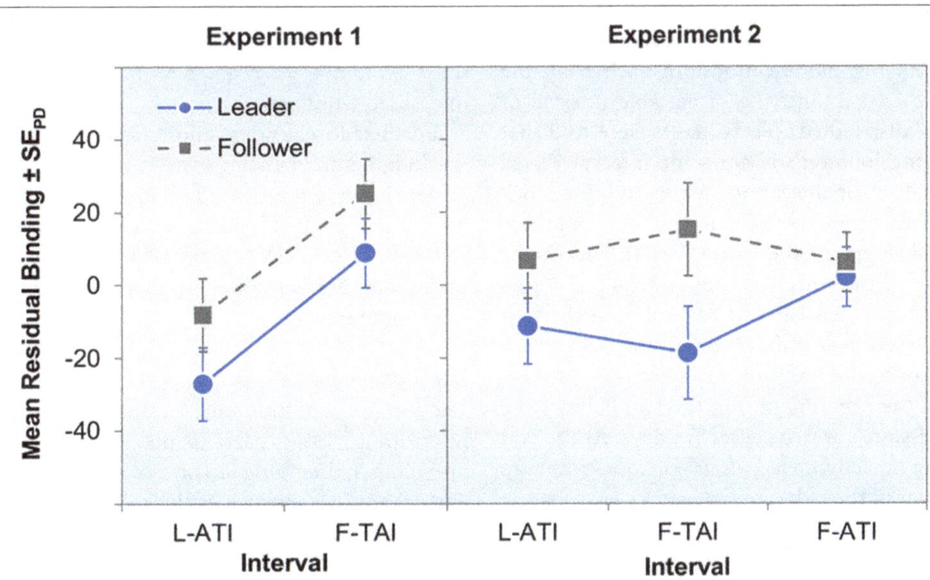

FIGURE 2 | Results of Experiment 1 (left panel) and Experiment 2 (right panel). The plots show the mean regression residuals for the leader's action-effect-interval (L-ATI), the interval between the leader's tone and the follower's action (F-TAI), and the follower's action-tone interval (F-ATI, Experiment 2 only). Negative values indicate shorter estimates and error bars represent standard errors of paired differences (SE_{PD}; Pfister and Janczyk, 2013), computed separately for each interval.

binding for leaders compared to followers would also transfer to the additional F-ATI.

This question is related to previous studies that found vicarious agency for the action effects of others in ambiguous situations (Wegner and Wheatley, 1999; Strother et al., 2010; Obhi and Hall, 2011a,b). In the present setup, however, it was clear that the follower ultimately triggered his or her effect tone. For such observed actions, it is not clear whether or not binding occurs, with some studies suggesting a negative answer (Engbert et al., 2007, 2008) and others suggesting a positive one (Obhi and Hall, 2011a, Experiment 2; Poonian and Cunnington, 2013; cf. also Buehner and Humphreys, 2009).

As a manipulation check, we further wanted to assess how leaders and followers conceptualized their own and the other agent's actions. To this end we developed and administered an *ad-hoc* questionnaire that was loosely based on action identification theory (Vallacher and Wegner, 1987, 1989) According to this theory, agents may construe own actions on different levels of goal-directedness, by either focusing on immediate movements or, alternatively, on more distal goals. Similarly, we aimed at assessing whether the participants of Experiment 2 construed the situation in terms of the responses or any of the corresponding action effects.

METHODS

Participants

Twenty-four volunteers were paid for participation (8 males; all right-handed; mean age = 23.7 years). They fulfilled the same criteria as in Experiment 1. All but one participant reported normal or corrected-to normal vision and hearing; the remaining participant reported an otitis of the middle ear in the second session and we therefore did not analyze his data.

Material, apparatus, and procedure

Experiment 2 employed the same design as Experiment 1 (see **Figure 1**) with the following modifications. In each trial, the follower's reaction produced a tone after a variable interval of 100–600 ms (uniformly distributed). Participants were told that both, the leader's and the follower's action-tone interval varied between 1 and 1000 ms. Participants started with a training block of 12 trials without interval estimates. Next, they underwent three blocks per to-be-judged interval—the L-ATI, F-TAI, and the F-ATI—whereas the order of intervals was counterbalanced across participant pairs. Each block consisted of 24 trials and the first block of each triplet served as a training block for the respective interval. The roles of leader and follower were still constant throughout one half of the experiment, but the two halves were now held as separate sessions on two successive days. At the end of each session, participants completed an *ad-hoc* questionnaire targeting their perception of the task (see the below).

Post-experimental questionnaire

Each participant of Experiment 2 judged leader and follower actions after both sessions. If the participant had been the leader in a session, he or she completed the questionnaire in the leader role ("How would you describe your own action?" and "How would you describe the follower's action?"), and if the participant had been the follower, he or she completed the questionnaire in the follower role. For each rating, they had to choose one out of six descriptions which best matched their perception of the leader and, separately, the follower role. The six items of the questionnaire described the actions as (1) *finger movement*, (2) *key press*, (3) *producing a signal for the follower* (leader) or *reacting to the leaders signal* (follower), (4) *starting an action sequence* (leader) or *finishing an action sequence* (follower), (5) *producing a tone*, and (6) *none of the above*. For follower actions, these items were ordered as described above, whereas for leader actions, the order was 1, 2, 5, 3, 4, and 6.

RESULTS

Residual binding scores

The analysis followed the same strategy as for Experiment 1 and all test trials with errors (3.1%) were excluded from data analysis. The remaining trials were outlier-corrected ($|z| > 2.5$; 1.1%) and entered a linear regression to estimate regression residuals. The analysis of regression residuals was again motivated by a substantial correlation of interval length and binding scores, $r = 0.49$, $t_{(22)} = 11.74$, $p < 0.001$ (see Table A1 in the Supplementary Material for the raw data). Residuals were submitted to a 2 × 3 repeated-measures ANOVA with the factors judge (leader vs. follower) and to-be-judged interval (L-ATI vs. F-TAI vs. F-ATI) and we used the multivariate approach to repeated-measures ANOVA to counter possible violations of sphericity.

The right panel of **Figure 2** shows the mean residual binding scores for all design cells. Leaders again perceived the intervals to be shorter than followers, $F_{(1,22)} = 8.02$, $p = 0.010$, $\eta_p^2 = 0.27$, and this effect was qualified by a marginally significant interaction, $F_{(1,21)} = 2.65$, $p = 0.094$, $\eta_p^2 = 0.20$. The main effect of interval did not approach significance ($F < 1$). The interaction was driven by manifest differences between leader and follower for the L-ATI, $t_{(22)} = 1.73$, $p = 0.049$, $d = 0.36$, and the F-TAI, $t_{(22)} = 2.65$, $p = 0.007$, $d = 0.55$, but not for the F-ATI, $t_{(22)} = 0.49$, $p = 0.313$, $d = 0.10$, as indicated by one-tailed t-tests.

Furthermore, leaders and followers differed slightly regarding the judgments of their "own" tone: Residual binding scores for leaders judging the L-ATI (−11 ms) were marginally significantly lower than residual binding scores of followers judging the F-ATI (−6 ms), $t_{(22)} = 1.92$, $p = 0.068$, $d = 0.040$, thus indicating an asymmetry in intentional binding when intervals of the same type were compared.

Questionnaire data

The main questionnaire results are shown in **Figure 3**. Interestingly, the participants' judgments mainly depended on whether they judged their own role or the role of the other participant, irrespective of the role itself. For observed actions—leader actions from the follower perspective and follower actions from the leader perspective–, participants mainly used the labels of keypresses (2) and, crucially, the task-related description of signaling a response or responding to the signal (3). The tendency toward this latter description was especially pronounced for leaders, suggesting that they indeed construed the follower response as an effect of their preceding action. For performed

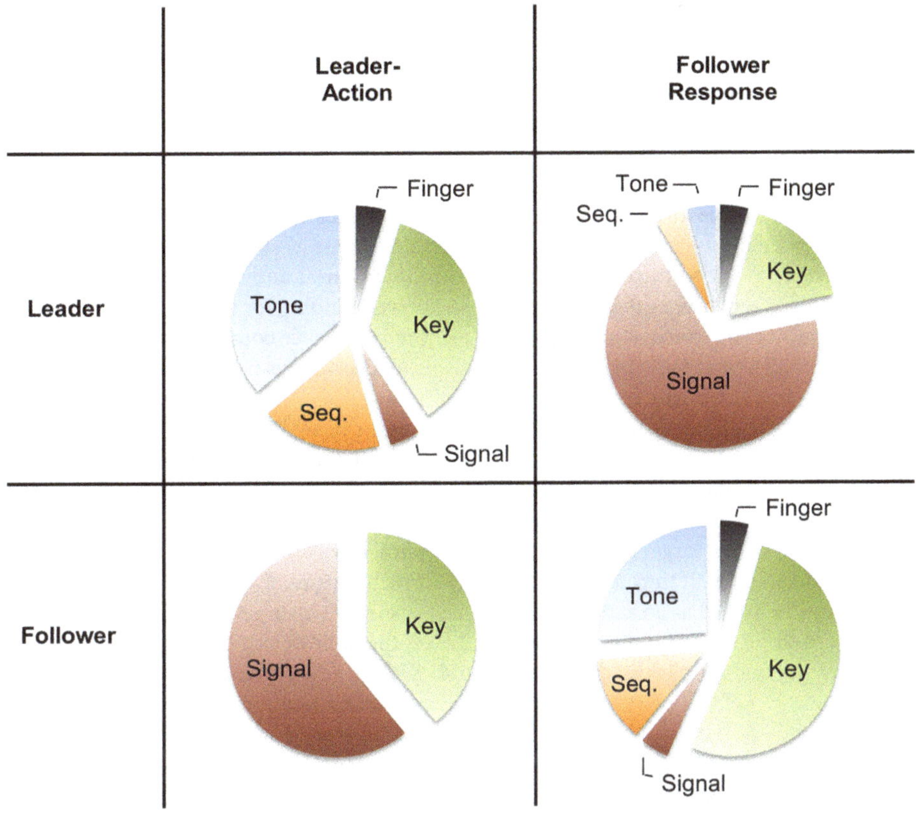

FIGURE 3 | Responses in the post-experimental questionnaire as judged from the leader's perspective (top row) and the follower's perspective (bottom row). The available answers to describe the respective actions were (1) *finger movement*, (2) *keypress*, (3) *signaling response/reacting to the signal*, (4) *initiating/completing an action sequence*, (5) *producing a tone*, and (6) *none of the above (chosen only once; not displayed)*.

actions—leader actions from the leader perspective and follower actions from the follower perspective—participants mainly used the labels of keypresses (2) and of producing a tone (5). Again, this latter option was chosen more often by leaders than by followers.

These impressions were confirmed by Cochran's Q-tests across the four conditions (leader judging the leader action, leader judging the follower action, follower judging the leader action, and follower judging the follower action). A separate test was conducted for each possible answer (1–6), when coding the presence of this answer as 1 and any other option as 0 for each condition. These tests showed significant between-conditions differences for answer 3 ("signal"), $Q_{(3)} = 34.94$, $p < 0.001$, and answer 5 ("tone"), $Q_{(3)} = 15.34$, $p = 0.002$, indicating that these options differed in frequency across the four conditions. Further, a marginally significant effect emerged for answer 2 ("keypress"), $Q_{(3)} = 6.44$. $p = 0.092$), whereas the remaining answers were distributed equally across the conditions ($ps > 0.141$).

DISCUSSION

Experiment 2 replicated the findings of Experiment 1 regarding the leader's intentional binding for the own action effect and the follower's action in terms of reduced interval estimates for both intervals. Additionally, the results of Experiment 2 did not yield any differences in intentional binding regarding the follower's action effect. More precisely, neither the leader nor the follower showed any indication of a subjective compression of the F-ATI. This finding might be taken to indicate that the followers did not experience much control over the effects that their actions produced. Such an interpretation would be in line with studies that showed the perceived timing of action effects to depend on causal beliefs about having control (Desantis et al., 2011; Haering and Kiesel, 2012), and the impact of causal beliefs for the processing of temporal delays in general (Greville et al., 2013). By contrast, it is less clear why leaders did not show intentional binding for the follower's action effects even though they clearly showed binding for the follower's action itself (as indicated by the lower F-TAI estimates for the leader as compared to the follower). It seems tempting to explain this null effect by assuming that the explicit knowledge of follower's causing the tone counter-acted intentional binding for the leader. A possible alternative explanation, however, is that the follower's action effects were merely too far removed temporally (Haggard et al., 2002; but see Humphreys and Buehner, 2009). Alternatively, or in addition, intentional binding might have been reduced by the fact that several events—the leader's effect tone and the follower's response—intervened between the leader's action and the followers' action effects.

The notion that action effects produced by another agent at one's command that are far removed from one's own prior actions are associated with reduced agency is interesting in the light of real-world scenarios involving the chain of command, such as in organizational hierarchies or in military decision making. It would be interesting to assess whether individuals higher up in the chain of command do indeed feel less agency for the actions committed by those lower down the chain, and whether those lower down the chain also feel less agency for the *consequences* of their actions when they are made in response to a leader's signal. The results from Experiment 1 of the present experiment seem to suggest that the greatest feeling of agency will be felt by the individual whose direct signal leads to the critical action. However, these ideas remain highly speculative and given that the present results do not allow for any firm conclusions regarding these points, or indeed the general idea of agency for actions taking place after many intervening steps, we will concentrate on the effects that were obtained for the L-ATI and the F-TAI in the following discussion.

A further interesting aspect of the data concerns the participants' responses to the *ad-hoc* questionnaire. Here, leaders described their follower's action by and large in task-related terms, i.e., as responses to the leader's signal. It thus seems as if the leaders construed the follower action indeed as an action effect of their actions which might have been promoted intentional binding for such social action effects. We will get back to this point in the following General Discussion.

GENERAL DISCUSSION

Two experiments investigated sense of agency for social action effects in a task in which participants either had the role of a leader or the role of a follower in an action sequence. The leader pressed a key to start off the sequence and produced an effect tone after a variable action-tone interval. This effect tone served as a go signal for the second participant (follower) who pressed his or her key as quickly as possible in response. In Experiment 2, but not in Experiment 1, the second keypress also triggered an effect tone. In different blocks of trials, the participants estimated the duration of three intervals: the L-ATI, the F-TAI, and (in Experiment 2) the F-ATI. Leaders judged the L-ATI and the F-TAI consistently shorter than their followers across both experiments, representing intentional binding for both intervals for the leader. Intentional binding, in turn can be seen as a pre-reflective component of sense of agency for the corresponding action effects (Moore and Obhi, 2012), i.e., the effect tone for the L-ATI and the follower action for the F-TAI.

The observation that the leader showed intentional binding (relative to the follower) not only for his or her own effect tone but also for the response of the follower, suggests that intentional binding does indeed occur when another person's action follows one's own action. The finding of intentional binding for such social action effects extends previous reports on the role of social action effects for effect-based action control (Pfister et al., 2013), by showing that such effects are not only included in action control but may also shape perception similarly to action effects in the physical environment. This notion is also mirrored in the questionnaire data where leaders described the follower response mainly in terms of reacting to the leader's signal.

It should be noted, however, that several factors in the employed design clearly worked in favor of finding binding effects for the leader role. One of these factors becomes evident when considering the exact operationalization of the two roles: Whereas the leader obviously could choose freely when to start the action sequence, the follower did not have this free "when" choice (for a general framework of "when" choices as compared to "what" and "whether" choices, see Brass and Haggard, 2008). Even though some results indicated comparable binding for free-choice and forced-choice responses (Wenke et al., 2009), other findings suggested that at least free "what" choices may promote intentional binding (Barlas and Obhi, 2013). It could thus be argued that the observed binding for social action effects mainly emerged because of the free choice component of the leader's task. Support for this speculation comes from recent findings that indicated the impact of free action choices on effect anticipations to mainly apply to situations in which action-effect relations are somewhat variable (Pfister et al., 2010; Pfister and Kunde, 2013)—and such a variability is clearly present for any type of social action effect due to reduced contingency and contiguity as compared to effects in the physical environment.

Furthermore, the leader's intentional binding of social action effects might also have been boosted by feelings of having power over the follower's behavior. Indeed, power priming has been shown to affect intentional binding, with low power priming decreasing intentional binding as compared to high power priming (Obhi et al., 2012). Whether or not the leaders actually experienced notable feelings of power over the follower's actions cannot be judged from the present experiments, but investigating the impact of power on the perception of social action effects seems to be a promising field for further inquiry.

The present observation of intentional binding for social action effects is also in line with studies that targeted brain activations for participants who performed interdependently on leader-follower tasks. For instance, Chaminade and Decety (2002) employed positron-emission tomography (PET) during a task in which participants moved a circle on a screen in two different conditions. In the leader condition, their own circle was followed by a second circle that was allegedly moved by somebody else, whereas in the follower condition, they were to follow computer-generated movements of the second circle that was said to be moved by another person. Leading and following gave rise to differential activity within the right intraparietal sulcus, a region that has often been associated with sense of agency (e.g., Farrer and Frith, 2002; Spengler et al., 2009). Although Chaminade and Decety did not asses any direct or indirect measures of sense of agency, their results could partly be seen as mirroring sense of agency for social action effects in the leader role, similar to the binding effects observed in our experiments.

The present results are only a first step toward understanding sense of agency for social action effects—a topic that clearly awaits further investigation. This investigation would ideally target sense of agency for social actions with various implicit and explicit measures and at the same time relate these measures to how social action effects are integrated in human motor control in general. A further interesting topic seems to be the impact of unexpected action effects on sense of agency in social settings relative to non-contingent action-effect relations in the physical world (Moore et al., 2009a; Wenke et al., 2009; Sidarus et al., 2013). Indeed, the possibility and problem-spaces relating to agency for actions in social contexts is largely unexplored and there are many exciting opportunities for further research.

In conclusion, social roles like being a leader or a follower while performing a task together have an impact on one's sense of agency, as intentional binding as a pre-reflective component of sense of agency occurs more strongly in the leader than in the follower. Most importantly, our results show that sense of agency does not only occur for physical effects in the environment, but also for social action effects, i.e., predictable actions of other agents.

ACKNOWLEDGMENTS

This publication was funded by a grant of the German Research Foundation (DFG) to Dorit Wenke (WE 2852/3-1), and by the DFG and the University of Wuerzburg in the funding programme Open Access Publishing.

REFERENCES

Barlas, Z., and Obhi, S. S. (2013). Freedom, choice, and the sense of agency. *Front. Hum. Neurosci.* 29:514. doi: 10.3389/fnhum.2013.00514

Brass, M., and Haggard, P. (2008). The what, when, whether model of intentional action. *Neuroscientist* 14, 319–325. doi: 10.1177/1073858408317417

Buehner, M. J. (2012). Understanding the past, predicting the future: causation, not intentional action, is the root of temporal binding. *Psychol. Sci.* 23, 1490–1497. doi: 10.1177/0956797612444612

Buehner, M. J., and Humphreys, G. R. (2009). Causal binding of actions to their effects. *Psychol. Sci.* 20, 1221–1228. doi: 10.1111/j.1467-9280.2009.02435.x

Chaminade, T., and Decety, J. (2002). Leader or follower? Involvement of the inferior parietal lobule in agency. *Neuroreport* 13, 1975–1978. doi: 10.1097/00001756-200210280-00029

Desantis, A., Roussel, C., and Waszak, F. (2011). On the influence of causal beliefs on the feeling of agency. *Conscious. Cogn.* 20, 1211–1220. doi: 10.1016/j.concog.2011.02.012

Ebert, J. P., and Wegner, D. M. (2010). Time warp: authorship shapes the perceived timing of actions and events. *Conscious. Cogn.* 19, 481–489. doi: 10.1016/j.concog.2009.10.002

Engbert, K., and Wohlschläger, A. (2007). Intentions and expectations in temporal binding. *Conscious. Cogn.* 16, 255–264. doi: 10.1016/j.concog.2006.09.010

Engbert, K., and Wohlschläger, A., and Haggard, P. (2008). Who is causing what? the sense of agency is relational and efferent-triggered. *Cognition* 107, 693–704. doi: 10.1016/j.cognition.2007.07.021

Engbert, K., Wohlschläger, A., Thomas, R., and Haggard, P. (2007). Agency, subjective time, and other minds. *J. Exp. Psychol. Hum. Percept. Perform.* 33, 1261–1268. doi: 10.1037/0096-1523.33.6.1261

Farrer, C., and Frith, C. D. (2002). Experiencing oneself vs. another person as being the cause of an action: the neural correlates of the experience of agency. *Neuroimage* 15, 596–603. doi: 10.1006/nimg.2001.1009

Greville, W. J., Cassar, A. A., Johansen, M. K., and Buehner, M. J. (2013). Structural awareness mitigates the effect of delay in human causal learning. *Mem. Cognit.* 41, 904–916. doi: 10.3758/s13421-013-0308-7

Haering, C., and Kiesel, A. (2012). Mine is earlier than yours: Causal beliefs influence the perceived time of action effects. *Front. Psychol.* 3:393. doi: 10.3389/fpsyg.201200393

Haggard, P., Clark, S., and Kalogeras, J. (2002). Voluntary action and conscious awareness. *Nat. Neurosci.* 5, 382–385. doi: 10.1038/nn827

Haggard, P., and Tsakiris, M. (2009). The experience of agency. *Curr. Dir. Psychol. Sci.* 18, 242–246. doi: 10.1111/j.1467-8721.2009.01644.x

Humphreys, G. R., and Buehner, M. J. (2009). Magnitude estimation reveals temporal binding at super-second intervals. *J. Exp. Psychol. Hum. Percept. Perform.* 35, 1542–1549. doi: 10.1037/a0014492

Humphreys, G. R., and Buehner, M. J. (2010). Temporal binding of action and effect in interval reproduction. *Exp. Brain Res.* 203, 465–470. doi: 10.1007/s00221-010-2199-1

Maxwell, S. E., Delaney, H. D., and Manheimer, J. M. (1985). ANOVA of residuals and ANCOVA: correcting an illusion by using model comparisons and graphs. *J. Educ. Behav. Stat.* 10, 197–209. doi: 10.3102/10769986010003197

Metcalfe, J., and Greene, M. J. (2007). Metacognition of agency. *J. Exp. Psychol. Gen.* 136, 184–199. doi: 10.1037/0096-3445.136.2.184

Moore, J. W., and Haggard, P. (2008). Awareness of action: Inference and prediction. *Conscious. Cogn.* 17, 136–144. doi: 10.1016/j.concog.2006.12.004

Moore, J. W., Lagnado, D., Deal, D. C., and Haggard, P. (2009a). Feelings of control: contingency determines experience of action. *Cognition* 110, 279–283. doi: 10.1016/j.cognition.2008.11.006

Moore, J. W., and Obhi, S. S. (2012). Intentional binding and the sense of agency: a review. *Conscious. Cogn.* 21, 546–561. doi: 10.1016/j.concog.2011.12.002

Moore, J. W., Wegner, D. M., and Haggard, P. (2009b). Modulating the sense of agency with external cues. *Conscious. Cogn.* 18, 1056–1064. doi: 10.1016/j.concog.2009.05.004

Nielsen, T. I. (1963). Volition: a new experimental approach. *Scand. J. Psychol.* 4, 225–230. doi: 10.1111/j.1467-9450.1963.tb01326.x

Obhi, S. S., and Hall, P. (2011a). Sense of agency and intentional binding in joint action. *Exp. Brain Res.* 211, 655–662. doi: 10.1007/s00221-011-2675-2

Obhi, S. S., and Hall, P. (2011b). Sense of agency in joint action: Influence of human and computer co-actors. *Exp. Brain Res.* 211, 663–670. doi: 10.1007/s00221-011-2662-7

Obhi, S. S., Swiderski, K. M., and Brubacher, S. P. (2012). Induced power changes the sense of agency. *Conscious. Cogn.* 21, 1547–1559. doi: 10.1016/j.concog.2012.06.008

Pfister, R. (2011). Gender effects in gaming research: a case for regression residuals? *Cyberpsychol. Behav. Soc. Netw.* 14, 603–606. doi: 10.1089/cyber.2010.0547

Pfister, R., Dignath, D., Hommel, B., and Kunde, W. (2013). It takes two to imitate: anticipation and imitation in social interaction. *Psychol. Sci.* 24, 2117–2121. doi: 10.1177/0956797613489139

Pfister, R., Dolk, T., Prinz, W., and Kunde, W. (2014). Joint response-effect compatibility. *Psychon. Bull. Rev.* 21, 817–822. doi: 10.3758/s13423-013-0528-7

Pfister, R., and Janczyk, M. (2013). Confidence intervals for two sample means: Calculation, interpretation, and a few simple rules. *Adv. Cogn. Psychol.* 9, 74–80. doi: 10.5709/acp-0133-x

Pfister, R., Kiesel, A., and Melcher, T. (2010). Adaptive control of ideomotor effect anticipations. *Acta Psychol.* 135, 316–322. doi: 10.1016/j.actpsy.2010.08.006

Pfister, R., and Kunde, W. (2013). Dissecting the response in response-effect compatibility. *Exp. Brain Res.* 224, 647–655. doi: 10.1007/s00221-012-3343-x

Poonian, S. K., and Cunnington, R. (2013). Intentional binding in self-made and observed actions. *Exp. Brain Res.* 229, 419–427. doi: 10.1007/s00221-013-3505-5

Ray, M., and Welsh, T. N. (2011). Response selection during a joint action task. *J. Mot. Behav.* 43, 329–332. doi: 10.1080/00222895.2011.592871

Sato, A., and Yasuda, A. (2005). Illusion of sense of self-agency: discrepancy between the predicted and actual sensory consequences of actions modulates the sense of self-agency, but not the sense of self-ownership. *Cognition* 94, 241–255. doi: 10.1016/j.cognition.2004.04.003

Sidarus, N., Chambon, V., and Haggard, P. (2013). Priming of actions increases sense of control over unexpected outcomes. *Conscious. Cogn.* 22, 1403–1411. doi: 10.1016/j.concog.2013.09.008

Spengler, S., von Cramon, Y. D., and Brass, M. (2009). Was it me or was it you? how the sense of agency originates from ideomotor learning revealed by fMRI. *Neuroimage* 46, 290–298. doi: 10.1016/j.neuroimage.2009.01.047

Strother, L., House, K. A., and Obhi, S. S. (2010). Subjective agency and awareness of shared actions. *Conscious. Cogn.* 19, 12–20. doi: 10.1016/j.concog.2009.12.007

Synofzik, M., Vosgerau, G., and Newen, A. (2008). Beyond the comparator model: a multifactorial two-step account of agency. *Conscious. Cogn.* 17, 291–239. doi: 10.1016/j.concog.2007.03.010

Vallacher, R. R., and Wegner, D. M. (1987). What do people think they're doing? action identification and human behavior. *Psychol. Rev.* 94, 3–15. doi: 10.1037/0033-295X.94.1.3

Vallacher, R. R., and Wegner, D. M. (1989). Levels of personal agency: Individual variation in action identification. *J. Pers. Soc. Psychol.* 57, 660–671. doi: 10.1037/0022-3514.57.4.660

Wegner, D. M. (2003). The mind's best trick: How we experience conscious will. *Trends Cogn. Sci.* 7, 65–69. doi: 10.1016/S1364-6613(03)00002-0

Wegner, D. M., Sparrow, B., and Winerman, L. (2004). Vicarious agency: experiencing control over the movements of others. *J. Pers. Soc. Psychol.* 86, 838–848. doi: 10.1037/0022-3514.86.6.838

Wegner, D. M., and Wheatley, T. (1999). Apparent mental causation. sources of the experience of will. *Am. Psychol.* 54, 480–492. doi: 10.1037/0003-066X.54.7.480

Wenke, D., Fleming, S. M., and Haggard, P. (2010). Subliminal priming of actions influences sense of control over effects of action. *Cognition* 115, 26–38. doi: 10.1016/j.cognition.2009.10.016

Wenke, D., and Haggard, P. (2009). How voluntary actions modulate time perception. *Exp. Brain Res.* 196, 311–318. doi: 10.1007/s00221-009-1848-8

Wenke, D., Waszak, F., and Haggard, P. (2009). Action selection and action awareness. *Psychol. Res.* 73, 602–612. doi: 10.1007/s00426-009-0240-4

Wohlschläger, A., Engbert, K., and Haggard, P. (2003a). Intentionality as a constituting condition for the own self–and other selves. *Conscious. Cogn.* 12, 708–716. doi: 10.1016/S1053-8100(03)00083-7

Wohlschläger, A., Haggard, P., Gesierich, B., and Prinz, W. (2003b). The perceived onset time of self- and other-generated actions. *Psychol. Sci.* 14, 586–591. doi: 10.1046/j.0956-7976.2003.psci_1469.x

6

Side effect of acting on the world: acquisition of action-outcome statistic relation alters visual interpretation of action outcome

Takahiro Kawabe*

NTT Communication Science Laboratories, Atsugi, Japan

***Correspondence:**
*Takahiro Kawabe, NTT Communication Science Laboratories, 3-1 Morinosato Wakamiya, Atsugi 243-0198, Japan
e-mail: kawabe.takahiro@lab.ntt.co.jp*

Humans can acquire the statistical features of the external world and employ them to control behaviors. Some external events occur in harmony with an agent's action, and thus, humans should also be able to acquire the statistical features between an action and its external outcome. We report that the acquired action-outcome statistical features alter the visual appearance of the action outcome. Pressing either of two assigned keys triggered visual motion whose direction was statistically biased either upward or downward, and observers judged the stimulus motion direction. Points of subjective equality (PSE) for judging motion direction were shifted repulsively from the mean of the distribution associated with each key. Our Bayesian model accounted for the PSE shifts, indicating the optimal acquisition of the action-effect statistical relation. The PSE shifts were moderately attenuated when the action-outcome contingency was reduced. The Bayesian model again accounted for the attenuated PSE shifts. On the other hand, when the action-outcome contiguity was reduced, the PSE shifts were greatly attenuated, and however, the Bayesian model could not accounted for the shifts. The results indicate that visual appearance can be modified by prediction based on the optimal acquisition of action-effect causal relation.

Keywords: action, causality, prediction, visual motion, sense of agency

INTRODUCTION

Humans can acquire statistical features of external events and use them to accommodate their behaviors. For example, statistical features in temporal (Miyazaki et al., 2006a; Acerbi et al., 2012) and spatial (Tassinari et al., 2006; Vilares et al., 2012) sensory stimuli can be acquired, and the acquired statistical features significantly alter manual responses in sensorimotor tasks. Moreover, acquiring statistical features for the temporal aspect of sensory signals can also affect temporal order judgments for the signals (Miyazaki et al., 2006b; Nagai et al., 2012; Yamamoto et al., 2012). These results suggest that the brain can use the acquired statistical features as prior knowledge about the external world to choose and execute appropriate responses to the world.

Such prior knowledge about the world can also alter visual perception (Freeman, 1994). For example, implicit prior knowledge about the position of a light source can affect the perception of three-dimensional surface shapes (Mamassian and Goutcher, 2001; Adams et al., 2004; Gerardin et al., 2010) [see Kersten et al. (2006) for a review]. Prior knowledge that affects the perception of the world can also be optimally learned (Orban et al., 2006).

Some visual events are caused by an agent's action. For example, we see a line being drawn on paper with the stroke of a pen. We obviously have prior knowledge about the relation between the action (i.e., drawing) and its outcome (a drawn line). So far, researchers (Körding and Wolpert, 2004) have focused on how the prior knowledge between an action and outcome could accommodate manual responses in a sensory motor task. On the other hand, another important question, which has not been addressed, is whether the acquisition of statistical relationships between an action and its outcome influence the interpretation of action outcome. In addition, it was also an open question whether such acquisition of action-effect statistical relationships was statistically optimal. In this work, three experiments were conducted to resolve these issues.

EXPERIMENT 1

BACKGROUND

The purpose of this experiment was to explore whether the acquisition of the statistical relation between an action and its outcome would distort the interpretation of the action outcome. Observers were asked to press assigned keys to trigger a drifting grating as an action outcome on a CRT display. The task of the observers was to report whether motion direction was upward or downward. As depicted in **Figure 1**, we spatially superimposed upward and downward drifting gratings and manipulated their luminance contrast (e.g., when the contrast of an upward grating was ω, the contrast for a downward grating was $1\text{-}\omega$). It was expected that judged motion direction in the superimposed grating would be consistent with the motion direction of the component drifting grating having stronger luminance contrast (**Figure 1A**, see also Movies 1 and 2). We also expected that a superimposed grating, where each component grating has the contrast of 0.5 would likely result in an ambiguous judgment of motion direction (**Figure 1B**, see also Movie 3). In the experiment, the luminance contrast in the superimposed drifting grating was dependent on which keys the observers pressed. For example, when the observers pressed left and right keys (though a reverse key mapping was also tested), the relative contrast of each component grating was chosen from a Gaussian distribution (i.e., prior distribution) where its mean was biased so that the downward grating on average had lower and higher relative contrast than the upward grating (**Figure 2A**). If the observers could really learn the statistical relation between key press and visual motion direction, the point of subjective equality (PSE) for motion direction would be biased repulsively from the mean of the prior distribution that was associated with either key. Moreover, employing a computational model based on Bayesian statistics, we tested whether the acquisition of action-effect statistical relation was statistically optimal.

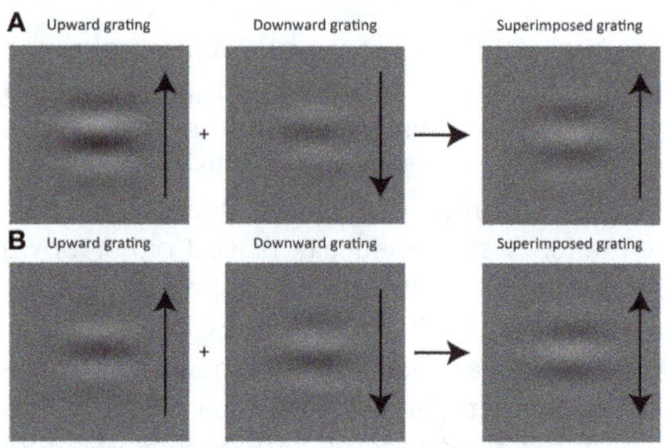

FIGURE 1 | Schematic illustrations of grating stimuli used in experiments. (A) When a high contrast upward (downward) grating is superimposed on a low-contrast downward (upward) grating, a percept of an upward (downward) grating results in. **(B)** If the contrast of an upward grating is equivalent to the one of a downward grating, a grating with ambiguous motion direction is perceived.

METHODS

Observers

Ten naive people (6 females and 4 males) served as observers. They reported they had normal or corrected-to-normal visual acuity. They were paid 1000 JPY for their participation. Ethical approval for this study was obtained from the ethical committee at Nippon Telegraph and Telephone Corporation (NTT Communication Science Laboratories Ethical Committee). The experiments were conducted according to the principles laid down in the Helsinki Declaration. Written informed consent was obtained from all participants in this study.

Apparatus

Stimuli were presented on a 21-inch CRT monitor (GDM-F500R, Sony) with the resolution of 1024 × 768 pixels (38 × 30 cm) and refresh rate of 100 Hz. A photometer (OP200-E, Cambridge Research Systems) linearized the luminance emitted from the monitor in a range from 0 to 106 cd/m^2. A computer (Mac Pro, Apple) controlled stimulus generation, stimulus presentation, and data collection. Stimuli were generated by using MATLAB and PsychToolBox 3 (Brainard, 1997; Pelli, 1997).

Stimuli

We used horizontally oriented sinusoidal drifting gratings as stimuli (**Figure 1**). Each grating was windowed by a two-dimensional Gaussian function with the standard deviation

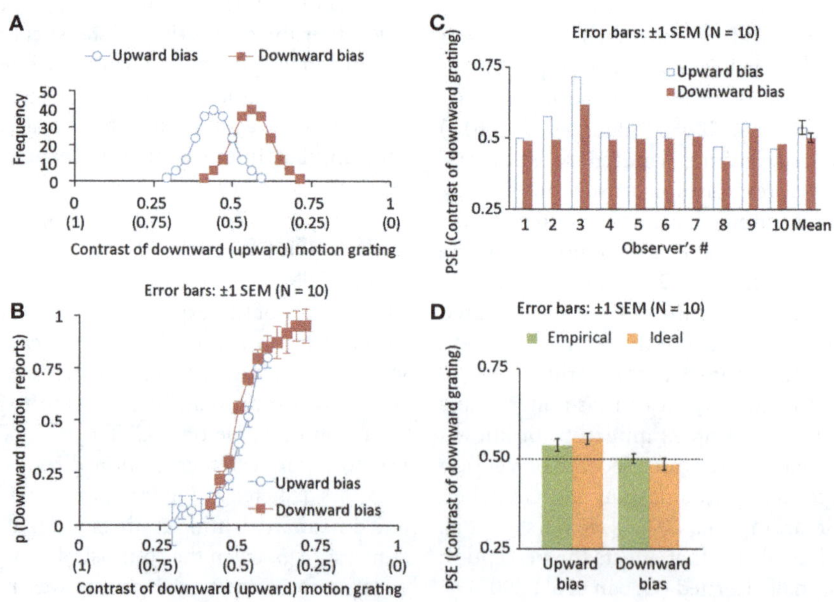

FIGURE 2 | (A) Distributions of luminance contrast for downward (and upward) drifting gratings in upward (blue, open disk maskers) and downward (red, open square markers) bias conditions. The mean of the distribution is deviated from 0.5 by 0.06 negatively and positively for upward- and downward-bias conditions. The standard deviation of the distribution was 0.06. **(B)** The proportion of trials wherein drifting direction was reported to be downward as a function of the luminance contrast of a downward grating in Experiment 1. **(C)** Individual and group data of empirical PSEs in Experiment 1. **(D)** Mean ideal and empirical PSEs in Experiment 1.

of 3.58 degrees of visual angle. The spatial frequency of the gratings was 0.22 cycles per degree. Each of eight frames of drifting gratings lasted for 100 msec. Because no temporal interval was inserted between successive frames, the whole drifting-grating presentation lasted for 800 msec. The phase of the grating was shifted upward/downward by 0.5π per frame, and thus, drifting frequency was 2.5 Hz. The drifting speed was 11.2°/s. In the upward-bias condition, the contrast of a downward grating was chosen from the following alternatives: 0.29, 0.32, 0.35, 0.38, 0.41, 0.44, 0.47, 0.50, 0.53, 0.56, and 0.59, which were presented 2, 6, 12, 24, 36, 40, 36, 24, 12, 6, and 2 out of 200 trials, respectively, (see **Figure 2A** for the contrast relationship between the upward- and downward-bias conditions). The frequency of trials as a function of the contrast of a downward grating followed a Gaussian distribution with a mean of -0.06 and a standard deviation of 0.06. In the downward-bias condition, the contrast of a downward grating was chosen from the following alternatives: 0.41, 0.44, 0.47, 0.50, 0.53, 0.56, 0.59, 0.62, 0.65, 0.68, 0.71, which were presented 2, 6, 12, 24, 36, 40, 36, 24, 12, 6, and 2 out of 200 trials, respectively (**Figure 2A**). The frequency of trials as a function of the contrast of a downward grating followed a Gaussian distribution with a mean of 0.06 and a standard deviation of 0.06. In each condition, values after subtracting the contrast of the downward grating from 1 were given as the luminance contrast of an upward grating. The downward grating was superimposed on the upward grating. Consequently, the superimposed grating was presented to the observer as a stimulus.

Procedure

Participants sat 70 cm from the CRT display. In each trial, they were asked to press one of two keys ("Z" and "M") with the index finger of the left and right hands, respectively. They were allowed to freely choose the key to press on their own. Pressing the key triggered the drifting grating in the display. For half of the observers, left and right keys produced the drifting grating with the relative contrast chosen from alternatives in the upward- and downward-bias conditions, respectively, and the reverse was true for the other half. The observers were asked to pay attention to the drifting grating, and after the disappearance of a drifting grating, to judge direction in which (upward or downward) the drifting grating moved. They pressed "T" and "V" keys when they saw upward and downward motion, respectively. No feedback was given to the observers. Digits were provided at the left and right bottom of the display to help the observers notice the number of trials in which they pressed "Z" and "M" keys. It took 30–40 min for each observer to complete an experimental session, which consisted of 400 trials. The order of trials was randomized.

RESULTS AND DISCUSSION

We calculated the proportion of trials in which downward motion was perceived as a function of the relative contrast of the downward-drifting grating, and averaged the proportion across observers (**Figure 2B**). We individually fitted a cumulative Gaussian function to the proportion data and computed the relative contrast causing 50% responses of downward motion as an empirical PSE for motion direction (Empirical PSE in **Figure 2C**). Consequently, the PSE was significantly different between upward- and downward-bias conditions [$t_{(9)} = 3.22$, $p < 0.011$, Cohen's $d = 0.57$]. Next, we tried to assess the difference between empirical and ideal PSEs. In a way similar to previous studies (Miyazaki et al., 2006a,b; Nagai et al., 2012; Yamamoto et al., 2012), we used a Bayesian model (see Appendix for the detail of the model) to estimate the ideal PSEs on the basis of the Bayesian statistics. Using the empirical and ideal PSEs as plotted in **Figure 2D**, we conducted a mixed two-way repeated measures ANOVA with the data source (model and empirical observers) as a between-subject factor and bias direction (upward and downward) as a within-subject factor. The main effect of the data source was not significant [$F_{(1, 18)} = 0.000$, $p = 0.98$]. On the other hand, the main effect of bias direction was highly significant [$F_{(1, 9)} = 55.131$, $p < 0.0001$]. Interaction between the two factors was also significant [$F_{(1, 18)} = 5.877, p < 0.03$]. Simple main effect of the data source was still not significant in the upward [$F_{(1, 18)} = 0.420, p > 0.05$] and downward [$F_{(1, 18)} = 0.378, p > 0.05$] bias conditions. Simple main effect of the bias direction was significant in the empirical [$F_{(1, 18)} = 12.504$, $p < 0.03$] and ideal [$F_{(1, 18)} = 48.505$, $p < 0.03$] observers. The results suggest that the human brain can acquire the statistical relation between an action and its outcome in a statistically optimal manner, and consequently alter the judgment for the appearance of the action outcome.

EXPERIMENT 2

BACKGROUND

The acquisition of an action-outcome relation will be strongly attenuated when the prior distribution (i.e., the Gaussian distribution of a relative contrast in a superimposed grating) is wide, consistent with a previous study (Miyazaki et al., 2006a). To confirm this prediction, using a new group of 10 observers (5 females and 5 males), we tested whether the PSE shift as observed in experiment 1 is reduced when the standard deviation of the prior distribution is increased from 0.06 to 0.15. (compare **Figure 2A** with **Figure 3A**). Except for the standard deviation manipulation, the stimuli and procedure were identical to those in experiment 1.

RESULTS AND DISCUSSION

We calculated the proportion of trials in which downward motion was perceived as a function of the contrast of the grating with a downward motion (**Figure 3B**), and calculated the empirical PSE as we did in experiment 1 (**Figure 3C**). The PSE was not significantly different between the two bias conditions [$t_{(9)} = 0.92$, $p = 0.38$]. To check the difference in the PSE between Experiments 1 and 2, we conducted a two-way mixed repeated measures analysis of variance (ANOVA) with distribution width as a between-subject factor and bias direction as a within-subject factor. The main effect of the distribution width was not significant [$F_{(1, 18)} = 0.018$, $p = 0.89$]. The main effect of the bias direction was significant [$F_{(1, 18)} = 9.338$, $p < 0.007$]. Interaction between the two factors was marginally significant [$F_{(1, 18)} = 3.083, p < 0.097$]. Based on the outcome of t-test and ANOVA, we suggest that the PSE shifts based on the acquisition of action-effect relations are moderated with a larger width of the prior distribution. To check whether the Bayesian model could account for the attenuation of the PSE shifts, we assessed

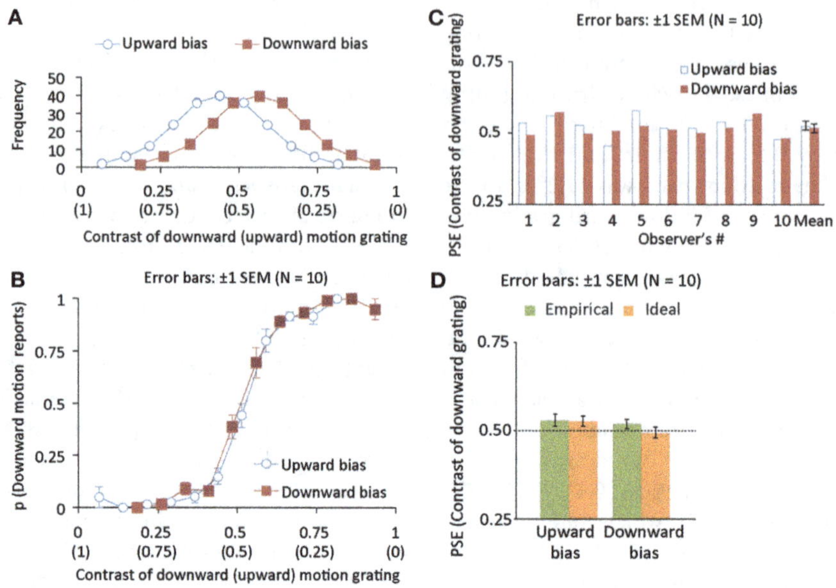

FIGURE 3 | (A) Distributions of luminance contrast for downward (and upward) drifting gratings in upward (blue, open disk maskers) and downward (red, open square markers) bias conditions. The mean of the distribution is deviated from 0.5 by 0.06 negatively and positively for upward- and downward-bias conditions. The standard deviation of the distribution was 0.15. **(B)** The proportion of trials wherein drifting direction was reported to be downward as a function of the luminance contrast of a downward grating in Experiment 2. **(C)** Individual and group data of empirical PSEs in Experiment 2. **(D)** Mean ideal and empirical PSEs in Experiment 2.

the statistical difference between ideal and empirical PSEs. Using the empirical and ideal PSEs as plotted in **Figure 3D**, we conducted a mixed two-way repeated measures ANOVA with the data source (model and empirical observers) as a between-subject factor and bias direction (upward and downward) as a within-subject factor. The main effect of the data source was not significant [$F_{(1,\ 18)} = 0.886, p = 0.3590$]. On the other hand, the main effect of bias direction was highly significant [$F_{(1,\ 9)} = 12.193$, $p < 0.0026$]. Interaction between the two factors was significant only marginally [$F_{(1,\ 18)} = 3.403, p < 0.082$]. The acquisition of the action-effect relation was not removed but attenuated with the large standard deviation of the prior distribution while our Bayesian model could account for the magnitude of the attenuation. Taken together, the results again indicate the optimal acquisition of the action-effect statistical relation.

EXPERIMENT 3

BACKGROUND

An external event is recognized as the outcome of one's own action when a temporal discrepancy between the action and the event is small (Berberian et al., 2012; Kawabe et al., 2013). An association between an action and its outcome is also established depending strongly on the temporal contiguity between them (Elsner and Hommel, 2004). Moreover, it is known that one critical determinant of associative learning is the temporal contiguity between the response and outcome (Wasserman and Miller, 1997). On the basis of these lines of evidence, we predicted that inserting a delay between an action and outcome might hamper the acquisition of an action-outcome statistical relation even when the prior distribution is sufficiently narrow because the delayed event following an agent's action is possibly no longer an action outcome for the brain (Berberian et al., 2012; Kawabe et al., 2013). Using a completely new group of 10 observers (6 females and 4 males), we examined whether human observers can acquire an action-effect statistical relation (**Figure 4A**) even when a 2-s delay is inserted between action and outcome.

RESULTS AND DISCUSSION

We calculated the proportion of trials in which downward motion was perceived as a function of the contrast of the grating with a downward motion (**Figure 4B**) and calculated the empirical PSE as we did in experiment 1 (**Figure 4C**). As a result, we found that the PSE was not significantly different between the two bias conditions [$t_{(9)} = 0.22, p = 0.83$]. To check the difference in the PSE between Experiments 1 and 3, we conducted a two-way mixed repeated measures analysis of variance (ANOVA) with action-effect delay (i.e., the delay was absent in Experiment 1 while was present in Experiment 3) as a between-subject factor and bias direction as a within-subject factor. The main effect of the presence/absence of the action-effect delay was not significant [$F_{(1,\ 18)} = 0.002,\ p = 0.96$]. The main effect of the bias direction was significant [$F_{(1,\ 18)} = 6.647,\ p < 0.019$]. Interaction between the two factors was significant [$F_{(1,\ 18)} = 5.117,\ p < 0.04$]. Simple main effect of the bias condition was significant only when there was no delay between action and outcome (i.e., in Experiment 1) [$F_{(1,\ 18)} = 11.421, p < 0.004$], but not when there was an action-outcome delay (i.e., in Experiment 3) [$F_{(1,\ 18)} = 0.050,\ p = 0.82$]. These results indicate that inserting a delay between action and outcome causes the significant attenuation in the acquisition of action-effect statistical relation. To see the

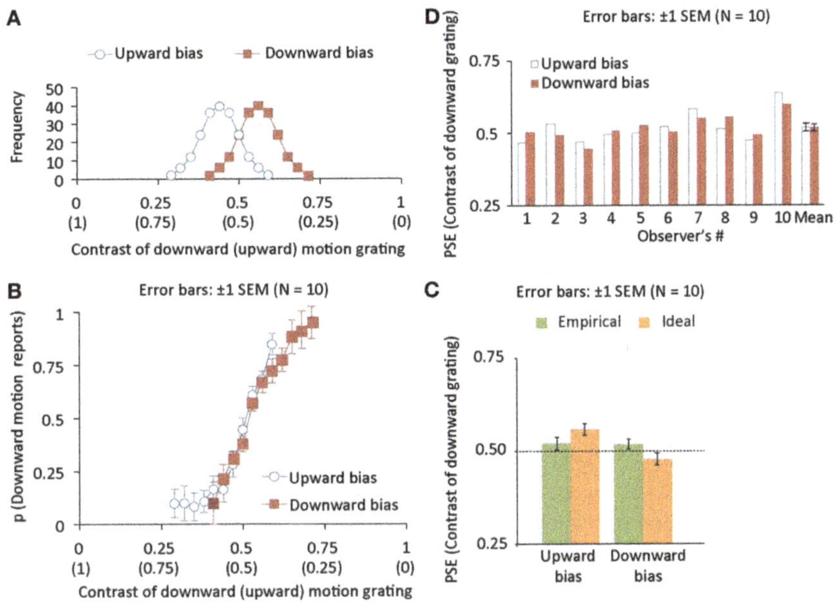

FIGURE 4 | (A) Distributions of luminance contrast for downward (and upward) drifting gratings in upward (blue, open disk maskers) and downward (red, open square markers) bias conditions. The mean of the distribution is deviated from 0.5 by 0.06 negatively and positively for upward- and downward-bias conditions. The standard deviation of the distribution was 0.06. **(B)** The proportion of trials wherein drifting direction was reported to be downward as a function of the luminance contrast of a downward grating in Experiment 3. **(C)** Individual and group data of empirical PSEs in Experiment 3. **(D)** Mean ideal and empirical PSEs in Experiment 3.

relation between ideal and empirical PSEs, we assessed the statistical difference between them. Using the empirical and ideal PSEs as plotted in **Figure 4D**, we conducted a mixed two-way repeated measures ANOVA with the data source (model and empirical observers) as a between-subject factor and bias direction (upward and downward) as a within-subject factor. The main effect of the data source was not significant [$F_{(1, 18)} = 0.001$, $p = 0.9711$]. On the other hand, the main effect of bias direction was highly significant [$F_{(1, 9)} = 52.314, p < 0.0000$]. Interaction between the two factors was highly significant [$F_{(1, 18)} = 46.369$, $p < 0.0001$]. Simple main effect of the bias direction was significant for the ideal PSEs [$F_{(1, 18)} = 98.593, p < 0.0001$], but not for the empirical PSEs [$F_{(1, 18)} = 0.090, p < 0.07681$]. The Bayesian model predicted the significant difference in the PSEs between two bias conditions while empirical data demonstrated that the PSEs were not different between the two conditions. To sum up, these results indicate the following two points; first, acquiring an action-outcome relation is strongly reduced when a large delay is inserted between an action and its outcome, and second, the large delay between action and outcome hinders the optimal acquisition of action- outcome statistical relationship. It has been suggested that a 2-s delay is sufficient to greatly reduce the sense of agency (or sense of causality) for external events (Berberian et al., 2012; Kawabe et al., 2013). Because an agent does not likely consider the event (i.e., drifting grating) as a causal outcome of her/his action when delay is inserted between an action and its outcome, only a weak acquisition of an action-outcome relation possibly results in.

GENERAL DISCUSSION

Consistent with previous studies (Körding and Wolpert, 2004), we observed that the human observers can optimally acquire the action-effect relationship. On the other hand, we recently found that the acquisition of an action-effect relation has a side effect: visual interpretation of action outcome is strongly modulated by the acquired relation between an action and its outcome. However, the acquisition effect on the interpretation of action outcome was moderately attenuated when the width of the distribution to be acquired was large, and moreover, was greatly attenuated when there was a temporal delay between the action and its effect. These results indicate that the acquisition of a statistical relation between an action and its outcome clearly depends on the consistency (experiment 2) and contiguity (experiment 3) between action and its effect.

It is already known that acquiring the statistical relation between visual events strongly alters the perception of motion direction (Gekas et al., 2013). Moreover, it has been shown that motion direction perception is strongly affected by an action-effect relation that is naturally acquired through one's development (Wohlschläger, 2000; Maruya et al., 2007). Beyond these studies, the present study suggests that such modulation of visual motion perception by action occurs as a result of motion prediction from the acquired statistical relation between an action and its outcome. A previous study (Jordan and Hunsinger, 2008) has reported that the learned pattern of action outcome can enhance the forward mislocalization of a moving target, but it did not address the statistical aspects of the action-outcome relation. We suggest that the successful acquisition of an action-outcome's statistical relationship can trigger the prediction for visual motion direction that is associated with action, and consequently alter the appearance of visual motion, while it is still unclear whether perceptual bias or response bias is triggered by the action-related prediction of visual motion. Anyway, we speculate that spontaneous cortical activities, which are promising neural correlates of prior representation (Berkes et al., 2011; De Lange et al., 2013), possibly mediate the expectation for motion direction on the basis of an action-outcome relationship.

An intriguing future issue is whether an endogenous action is a necessary factor for acquiring the action-outcome statistical relation. In learning the relation between action and its outcome, endogenous and exogenous actions respectively, contribute to ideomotor and sensorimotor learnings (Herwig et al., 2007; Herwig and Waszak, 2012). In particular, endogenous action seems to trigger a long-term association between an action and its outcome. In this respect, an endogenous action may be an important factor for efficiently learning the action-effect statistical relation. On the other hand, another line of research has demonstrated that human observers can learn the statistical relationship between spatial cues and a tactile temporal order judgment without executing any action (Nagai et al., 2012), suggesting that the statistical relation between external events can be acquired if subjective causality is established between two events. In the present study, we found that the acquisition of action-outcome statistical relation deteriorates when the congruency and temporal contiguity between action and outcome, which presumably play a fundamental role in causality perception, are reduced (Hume, 1888; Wegner, 2005; Woods et al., 2012; Kawabe, 2013; Kawabe et al., 2013). Thus, it is also possible that the perception of causality between an action and its outcome is one of the decisive factors for the acquisition of their statistical relation. Other lines of evidence have suggested that causality inference between events plays critical roles in the optimal integration of cross-sensory signals (Körding et al., 2007; Sato et al., 2007; Berniker and Körding, 2011). As such, we suggest that the perception of causality between an action and its outcome at least partly underlies the acquisition of the statistical relation between them, though we need to empirically dissociate the contribution of action from non-action factors to the acquisition of an action-effect relation.

REFERENCES

Acerbi, L., Wolpert, D. M., and Vijayakumar, S. (2012). Internal representations of temporal statistics and feedback calibrate motor-sensory interval timing. *PLoS Comput. Biol.* 8:e1002771. doi: 10.1371/journal.pcbi.1002771.

Adams, W., Graf, E. W., and Ernst, M. O. (2004). Experience can change the 'light-from-above' prior. *Nat. Neurosci.* 7, 1057–1058. doi: 10. 1038/nn1312

Berberian, B., Sarrazin, J.-C., Le Blaye, P., and Haggard, P. (2012). Automation technology and sense of control: a window on human agency. *PLoS ONE 7:e34075.* doi: 10.1371/journal.pone.0034075

Berkes, P., Orban, G., Lengyel, M., and Fiser, J. (2011). Spontaneous cortical activity reveals hallmarks of an optimal internal model of the environment. Science 331, 83–87. doi: 10.1126/science.1195870

Berniker, M., and Körding, K. (2011). Bayesian approaches to sensory integration for motor control. Wiley Interdiscip. Rev. Cogn. Sci. 2, 419–428. doi: 10.1002/wcs.125

Brainard, D. H. (1997). The psychophysics toolbox. Spat. Vis. 10, 433–436. doi: 10.1163/15685689 7X00357

De Lange, F. P., Rahnev, D. A., Donner, T. H., and Lau, H. (2013). Prestimulus oscillatory activity over motor cortex reflects perceptual expectations. *J. Neurosci.* 23, 1400–1410. doi: 10.1523/JNEURO SCI.1094-12.2013

Elsner, B., and Hommel, B. (2004). Contiguity and contingency in action-effect learning. *Psychol. Res.* 68, 138–154. doi: 10.1007/s00426-003-0151-8

Freeman, W. T. (1994). The generic viewpoint assumption in a framework for visual perception. *Nature* 368, 542–545. doi: 10.1038/368542a0

Gekas, N., Chalk, M., Seitz, A. R., and Series, P. (2013). Complexity and specificity of experimentally-induced expectations in motion perception. *J. Vis.* 13, 1–18. doi: 10. 1167/13.4.8

Gerardin, P., Kourtzi, Z., and Mamassian, P. (2010). Prior knowledge of illumination for 3D perception in human brain. *Proc. Natl. Acad. Sci. U.S.A.* 107, 16309–16314. doi: 10.1073/pnas. 1006285107

Gros, B. L., Blake, R., and Hiris, E. (1998). Anisotropies in visual motion perception: a fresh look. *J. Opt. Soc. Am. A Opt. Image Sci. Vis.* 15, 2003–2011. doi: 10.1364/ JOSAA.15.002003

Herwig, A., Prinz, W., and Waszak, F. (2007). Two modes of sensorimotor integration in intention-based and stimulus-based actions. Q. J. Exp. Psychol. 60, 1540–1554. doi: 10.1080/17470210601119134

Herwig, A., and Waszak, F. (2012). Action-effect bindings and ideomotr learning in intention and stimulus-based action. Front. Psychol. 3:444. doi: 10.3389/fpsyg. 2012.00444

Bayesian inference. *Annu. Rev. Psychol.* 55, 271–304. doi: 10.1146/ annurev. psych.55.090902.142005

Körding, K. P., Beierholm, U., Ma, W. J., Quartz, S., Tenenbaum, J. B., and Shams, L. (2007). Causal inference in multisensory perception. PLoS ONE 2:e943. doi: 10.1371/journal.pone.0000943

Körding, K. P., and Wolpert, D. M. (2004). Bayesian integration in sensorimotor learning. *Nature* 427, 244–247. doi: 10.1038/nature 02169

Mamassian, P., and Goutcher, R. (2001). Prior knowledge on the illumination position. Cognition 81, B1–B9. doi: 10.1016/S0010-0277 (01)00116-0

Maruya, K., Yang, E., and Blake, R. (2007). Voluntary action influences visual competition. Psychol. Sci. 18, 1090–1098. doi: 10.1111/j.1467-9280.2007.02030.x

Miyazaki, M., Nozaki, D., and Nakajima, Y. (2006a). Testing Bayesian models of human coincidence timing. J. Neurophysiol. 94, 395–399. doi: 10.1152/ jn.01168. 2004

Miyazaki, M., Yamamoto, S., Uchida, S., and Kitazawa, S. (2006b). Bayesian calibration of simultaneity in tactile temporal order judgment. Nat. Neurosci. 9, 875–877. doi: 10.1038/ nn1712

Nagai, Y., Suzuki, M., Miyazaki, M., and Kitazawa, S. (2012). Acquisition of multiple prior distributions in tactile temporal order judgment. Front. Psychol. 3:276. doi: 10.3389/fpsyg. 2012.00276

Naito, T., Saito, H., and Osaka, N. (2010). Direction anisotropy of human motion perception depends on stimulus speed. Vision Res 23, 1862–1866. doi: 10.1016/j.visres. 2010.06.007

Orban, G., Fiser, J., Aslin, R. N., and Lengyel, M. (2006). "Bayesian model learning in human visual perception," in Advances in Neural Information Processing Systems, eds Y. Weiss, B. Schölkopf, and J. Pratt (Cambridge, MA: Massachusetts Institute of Technology Press), 1043–1050.

Pelli, D. G. (1997). The videotool-box software for visual psychophysics: transforming numbers into movies. Spat. Vis. 10, 437–442. doi: 10.1163/15685689 7X00366

Sato, Y., Toyoizumi, T., and Aihara, K. (2007). Bayesian inference explains perception of unity and ventril-oquism aftereffect: identification of common sources of audiovisual stimuli. Neural Comput. 19, 3335–3355. doi: 10.1162/neco.2007. 19.12.3335

Tassinari, H., Hudson, T. E., and Landy, M. S. (2006). Combining priors and noise visual cues in a rapid pointing task. *J. Neurosci.* 26, 10154–10163. doi: 10.1523/JNE UROSCI.2779-06.2006

Vilares, I., Howard, J. D., Fernandes, H. L., Gottfried, J. A., and Körding, K. P. (2012). Differential representations of prior and likelihood uncertainty in the human brain. Curr. Biol. 22, 1–8. doi: 10.1016/j.cub. 2012.07.010

Hume, D. (1888). Hume's Treatise of Human *Nature.* ed L. A. Selby-Bigge Oxford, England: Clarendon Press. (Original work published 1739).

Jordan, J. S., and Hunsinger, M. (2008). Learned patterns of action-effect anticipation contribute to the spatial displacement of continuously moving stimuli. J. Exp. Psychol. Hum. Percept. Perform. 34, 113–124. doi: 10.1037/0096-1523.34.1.113

Kawabe, T. (2013). Inferring sense of agency from the quantitative aspect of action outcome. Conscious. Cogn. 22, 407–412. doi: 10.1016/j.concog. 2013.01.006

Kawabe, T., Roseboom, W., and Nishida, S. (2013). The sense of agency is action-effect causality perception based on crossmodal grouping. Proc. Biol. Sci. 280:20130991. doi: 10.1098/rspb. 2013.0991

Kersten, D., Mamassian, P., and Yuille, A. (2006). Object perception as

Wasserman, E. A., and Miller, R. R. (1997). What's elementary about associative learning. *Annu. Rev. Psychol.* 48, 573–607. doi: 10.1146/annurev. psych.48.1.573 Wegner, D. M. (2005). Preìcis of the illusion of conscious will. Behav. Brain Sci. 27, 649–692.

Wohlschläger, A. (2000). Visual motion priming by invisible actions. Vision Res. 40, 925–930. doi: 10.1016/ S0042-6989(99)00239-4

Woods, A. J., Lehet, M., and Chatterjee, A. (2012). Context modulates the contribution of time and space in causal inference. Front. Psychol. 3:371. doi: 10.3389/fpsyg.2012. 00371

Yamamoto, S., Miyazaki, M., Iwano, T., and Kitazawa, S. (2012). Bayesian calibration of simultaneity in audiovisual temporal order judgments. *PLoS ONE* 7:e40379. doi: 10.1371/journal.pone.0040379

APPENDIX

We checked whether the acquisition of the action-outcome relation was statistically optimal. In a way similar to previous studies (Miyazaki et al., 2006a,b; Nagai et al., 2012; Yamamoto et al., 2012), we used a Bayesian model, where the probability of possible true motion direction d_{true} given the sensed motion direction d_{sensed} is expressed as

$$p(d_{\text{true}}|d_{\text{sensed}}) = p_{\text{prior}}(d_{\text{true}})p(d_{\text{sensed}}|d_{\text{true}})/p(d_{\text{sensed}}) \quad (1)$$

where d_{sensed} denotes the sensory measurement of the true motion direction that distributes in a Gaussian manner with a mean of zero and a standard deviation of σ_{sensed}, and the p_{prior} (d_{true}) denotes the prior distribution for motion direction, which follows a Gaussian distribution expressed as

$$p_{\text{prior}}(d_{\text{true}}) = G\left(d_{\text{true}};\, \mu_{\text{prior}}, \sigma_{\text{prior}}\right) \quad (2)$$

where $\mu_{\text{prior}} = \pm 0.06$ in terms of the contrast of a downward drifting grating, and $\sigma_{\text{prior}} = 0.06$ in experiments 1 and 3 and 0.15 in experiment 2. Finally, the motion direction is optimally estimated so as to maximize the left side term $p(d_{\text{true}}|d_{\text{sensed}})$ in (1). Here, optimal judgment on motion direction is based on the weighted sum of μ_{prior} and d_{sensed}, which is expressed as

$$d_{\text{judged}} = (1 - \omega)\mu_{\text{prior}} + \omega d_{\text{sensed}} \quad (3)$$

where

$$\omega = \sigma^2_{\text{prior}} / \left(\sigma^2_{\text{prior}} + \sigma^2_{\text{sensed}}\right) \quad (4)$$

Moreover, a perceptual bias in vertical motion direction has been reported, which likely occurs independently from the weighted sum described above (Gros et al., 1998; Naito et al., 2010). We believed we should consider this factor of perceptual bias in our model. The perceptual bias β was calculated by averaging the deviations of PSEs from 0.5 in both upward and downward direction conditions. Thus, the final estimate of perceived motion direction is expressed as

$$d_{\text{judged}} = (1 - \omega)\mu_{\text{prior}} + \omega d_{\text{sensed}} + \beta \quad (5)$$

βs in Experiments 1, 2, and 3 were 0.020 (SEM: 0.019), 0.02 (SEM: 0.009), and 0.018 (SEM: 0.015), respectively. The positive βs indicate a consistent bias toward upward motion reports.

7

A formal model of interpersonal inference

Michael Moutoussis[1]*, Nelson J. Trujillo-Barreto[2], Wael El-Deredy[3], Raymond J. Dolan[1] and Karl J. Friston[1]

[1] *Wellcome Trust Centre for Neuroimaging, University College London, London, UK*
[2] *Brain Dynamics Department, Cuban Neuroscience Centre, Havana, Cuba*
[3] *School of Psychological Sciences, University of Manchester, Manchester, UK*

***Correspondence:**
Michael Moutoussis, Wellcome Trust Centre for Neuroimaging, University College London, 12 Queen Square, London WC1N 3BG, UK
e-mail: fzsemmo@gn.apc.org

Introduction: We propose that active Bayesian inference—a general framework for decision-making—can equally be applied to interpersonal exchanges. Social cognition, however, entails special challenges. We address these challenges through a novel formulation of a formal model and demonstrate its psychological significance.

Method: We review relevant literature, especially with regards to interpersonal representations, formulate a mathematical model and present a simulation study. The model accommodates normative models from utility theory and places them within the broader setting of Bayesian inference. Crucially, we endow people's prior beliefs, into which utilities are absorbed, with preferences of self and others. The simulation illustrates the model's dynamics and furnishes elementary predictions of the theory.

Results: (1) Because beliefs about self and others inform both the desirability and plausibility of outcomes, in this framework interpersonal representations become beliefs that have to be actively inferred. This inference, akin to "mentalizing" in the psychological literature, is based upon the outcomes of interpersonal exchanges. (2) We show how some well-known social-psychological phenomena (e.g., self-serving biases) can be explained in terms of active interpersonal inference. (3) Mentalizing naturally entails Bayesian updating of how people value social outcomes. Crucially this includes inference about one's own qualities and preferences.

Conclusion: We inaugurate a Bayes optimal framework for modeling intersubject variability in mentalizing during interpersonal exchanges. Here, interpersonal representations are endowed with explicit functional and affective properties. We suggest the active inference framework lends itself to the study of psychiatric conditions where mentalizing is distorted.

Keywords: free energy, active inference, value, evidence, surprise, self-organization, interpersonal, Bayesian

INTRODUCTION

There is growing interest in modeling behavioral and physiological responses with biologically grounded normative models, particularly in emerging disciplines such as neuroeconomics and computational psychiatry. The motivation for these developments rests upon characterizing behavioral phenotypes in terms of underlying variables that have a principled functional and—in some instances—neurobiological interpretation. Recently, optimal decision making has been formulated as a pure inference problem to provide a relatively simple (active inference) framework for modeling choice behavior and inference about hidden states of the world generating outcomes (Friston et al., 2013). This is a potentially important development because it provides a coherent and parsimonious (Bayes) optimal model of behavior. This normative model is consistent with classical treatments, such as expected utility theory and softmax response rules, without calling on *ad hoc* parameters like inverse temperature or temporal discounting. This means that, in principle, one can characterize people's behavior in terms of prior beliefs about the world (as well as the confidence or precision of those beliefs).

In this paper, we demonstrate that this approach can also be applied fruitfully when choices—and the underlying preferences—are based upon interpersonal beliefs about oneself and other people. Social cognition merits special analysis as it presents substantial challenges. An active inference framework can usefully address some of these, but not without new theoretical considerations. In what follows, we describe the sorts of beliefs that may underlie interpersonal exchange and use simulations of active inference to demonstrate the behaviors that ensue. In subsequent work, we hope to use these simulated choices to explain observed behavior so as to characterize subjects in terms of model parameters that encode interpersonal beliefs. The routines used for the simulations of this paper are available as part of the academic SPM freeware and can be adapted to a variety of games.

THEORIES OF AFFECTIVELY CHARGED BELIEFS ABOUT SELF AND OTHERS

Self- and other- representations often are heavily affect-laden and a vast literature is devoted to them. We cannot do justice to this entire field here and instead focus on four groups of theories about interpersonal representations. Firstly, "homeostatic" theories hold that an adequately positive self-representation is so important in itself that healthy humans will even sacrifice accurate explanations of social and psychological events to maintain positive self-representations. Classic psychological-defense theories (Ogden, 1983; Rycroft, 1995) and attribution theories (Bentall, 2003) fall into this group. These theories easily explain the biases that healthy people and psychiatric patients exhibit in seeing the self in rosy colors (e.g., grandiosity) or others in negative colors (e.g., racism) as self-representation-boosting manoeuvres. Hence, these theories also explain how the motives for one's behavior can be ulterior to the motives that the agent believes they are acting under. However, experimental support for these theories is incomplete (Moutoussis et al., 2013). Secondly, economic theories usually consider one's true preferences as known to the agent; while at the same time their behavior may be directed at instrumentally managing their reputation vis-a-vis others, including deceiving them (Camerer, 2003). Some social-psychological theories combine these utilitarian perspectives into one construct, social desirability, said to have both self-deceit and image-management components (Crowne and Marlowe, 1960). Thirdly, there are a group of theories that see many adult beliefs about the self and others as products of learnt information-processing, relatively divorced from current interests. Examples are the rigid "core beliefs" that people often hold about themselves according to some cognitive-behavioral theories (Waller et al., 2001) or the inaccurate beliefs formed when strong affects are said to overwhelm peoples' ability to think about their own mind and that of others (Allen et al., 2008). Finally, there are theories that take into account both the fluidity and uncertainty of person-representations (like many clinical and psychological theories) and an *explicit, current* functional role for them (like the neuroeconomic tradition). This is a smaller tradition, exemplified by the "sociometer theory of self-esteem" (Leary et al., 1995). Here a particular aspect of self-representation—self-esteem—predicts whether other people are likely to include or exclude one from social interactions. As access to human (e.g., friends, partners), material (e.g., work opportunities), safety and other resources can be dramatically reduced by social exclusion, self-esteem helps predict the success of social interactions. When it comes to other-representation, the "sinister attribution error" theory of apparently unwarranted suspiciousness (Kramer, 1994) formalizes a somewhat similar logic: that taking others to be less well-meaning than they are serves to minimize false-negative errors in the detection of social difficulties. However, the theories of Leary et al. and of Kramer are qualitative, insufficiently general, and have not been applied to interactive exchanges.

We seek to generalize the "sociometer theory" to encompass *all* self- and other- representations that can be reasonably inferred within interpersonal exchanges. In this paper, we provide a specific computational example of this. Psychologically it is easy to appreciate how making inferences about others helps to make predictions: For example, "a fair person will not exploit me." Similarly about the self, "honest people like me are trusted." However, interpersonal representations may come to serve as preferred outcomes themselves; for example, "I'd prefer to be a fair person and to deal with fair people." They may summarize (and even hide) social, cultural and ultimately evolutionary goals that are not otherwise explicitly represented.

COMPUTATIONAL CHALLENGES OF DECISION-MAKING IN SOCIAL EXCHANGES

One might expect people to maximize the overt benefits that they extract from social interactions, such as food or mates, by logically thinking through different policies and choosing the best. However, such a project faces serious challenges, of which we consider three. These motivate using interpersonal representations to make predictions about exchanges and active inference to infer both representations and policies.

The first challenge concerns the potentially *explosive complexity* of social cognition. As a key example, interpersonal cognition is recursive. In order to achieve maximum material benefit I need to predict how another person will react. To do this I need to imagine what they will decide. However, they should do the same—estimate what I intend to do. Therefore I have to estimate what they think that I intend to do. But they will do the same and so on, without a well-defined end. In contrast, real people in real situations only perform a very limited number of such recursive steps. We argue that using interpersonal beliefs can increase the effective depth of (otherwise costly) cognition.

The second concerns the *arbitrariness of the parameterization* of many decision-making schemes. As a central example, just one parameter is often used to describe the precision (inverse noisiness) of choices given the values attached to these choices. This precision parameter is then fitted to observed choice behavior in an agnostic manner. The parameter in question has been interpreted in a number of ways that are almost impossible to distinguish: sometimes it is cast as intrinsic noise or error rate, implying that agents are incapable of more precise or deterministic choices. Sometimes, it is used to motivate a form of exploration, implying that there is something unknown about the situation and it is best not to put all one's eggs in one basket. At other times, it is seen as a sensitivity that reflects the change in behavior for a change in returns. This last interpretation is closely related to choice matching, whereby the preferred frequency of different outcomes is an increasing function of their utility and not a winner-takes-all preference. In learning paradigms it is also difficult to separate estimates of precision from the learning rate (Daw, 2011). Parameterization of an agents' choices in terms of a single noisiness parameter thus conflates error, exploration, choice matching and, in practice, learning rates.

The active inference framework addresses this problem first by taking account of the fact that there is always uncertainty about outcomes. In a probabilistic sense, optimal outcomes are better quantified in terms of probability distributions, as opposed to scalar reward or utility functions. We can then separate the optimal precision over action choice (en route to the outcome), which describes *how to best get to the desired distribution* over outcomes, from the *preferred outcome distribution itself.* The former precision can itself be optimized given beliefs about hidden states of the world and controlled transitions among them—through formulating choice behavior in terms of beliefs over policies. The precision in question is the precision of (or confidence in) beliefs about alternative policies. It still weighs the choice between different policies, but it is no longer a free parameter! In contrast the precision over outcome preferences is a *reward sensitivity*, in principle *testable independently of the task* at hand. In the active inference framework there is no need for a learning rate parameter as such—the optimal change of beliefs is inferred at each step.

The third computational challenge rests on *the difficult calculations entailed in using a model of the world* to draw inferences. Social inferences, for example, present a difficult inverse problem when disambiguating the meaning of a particular social datum: for example, "my partner gave me nothing" may be important both for self-representation ("maybe because I am worthless") and for other-representation ("maybe because she is horrible"). The framework that we describe is well suited to deal with such ambiguities. Their resolution rests upon prior beliefs about social outcomes that can be updated on the basis of experience in a Bayes optimal fashion. This, like all statistical inversion of probabilistic models, is computationally challenging; the active inference framework suggests a practical solution based on so-called Variational Bayes (a ubiquitous instance of approximate Bayesian inference that finesses computational complexity). In this paper, we will use approximate Bayesian inference to show how interpersonal representations are accommodated in terms of prior beliefs; thereby providing a normative framework within which to parameterize different people and their interpersonal beliefs.

This paper comprises three sections. The first provides a brief introduction to active inference, with a special emphasis on how preferences and goals can be cast in terms of prior beliefs about eventual outcomes. This enables goal-directed behavior to be described purely in terms of inference about states of the world and subsequent behavior. The second section introduces a Trust game to illustrate the formal aspects of modeling interpersonal exchanges within this framework. The third (Results) section uses simulations of this game under active inference to highlight how interpersonal beliefs produce characteristic choice behaviors. We conclude with a discussion of putative applications of this approach to normative behavioral modeling.

METHODS

This section summarizes the building blocks of Active inference, which include the following: Adaptive agents are held to (i) set themselves desirable goals that they consider likely to achieve (ii) choose policies that maximize the likelihood of achieving these goals (iii) form beliefs about the world consistent both with their sensory observations and their goals. In this section, we also briefly describe a practical way of solving this inference problem, i.e., (iv) using an inference process that involves the passing of simple messages between cognitive modules. This Variational Bayes (VB) message passing or updating is a simpler and more biologically plausible method for performing approximate Bayesian inference than the schemes usually considered. We then formulate a model of a simple interpersonal exchange and describe its implementation so that others researchers can use it. The definition and meaning of the mathematical symbols we use is summarized in **Table 1**.

SUMMARY OF ACTIVE INFERENCE

Setting plausible goals

In active inference, action elicits outcomes that are the most plausible under beliefs about how they are caused. This approach contrasts with normative formulations in optimal decision theory, where actions are chosen to maximize the value of outcomes rather than plausibility. However, beliefs about outcomes are not motivationally neutral—an agent believes that her actions will lead to *good* outcomes. Therefore, if the prior beliefs about outcomes—the agent's goals or hopes—reflect the utility of those outcomes, then active inference can implement optimal policies, effectively seeking out the outcomes with the greatest utility.

In general, agents may have subtle reasons to distribute their prior beliefs over particular outcomes. They may, for example, use a matching law such as Herrnstein or softmax mapping to preserve ecological resources or to distribute goods among conspecifics. We model an agent's preference with a softmax function $\sigma(r(s_T), \beta)$ of objective returns r at the outcome time T, so that prior (utilitarian) beliefs for any agent or model m, are written as follows:

$$P(s_T|m) = \sigma(r(s_T), \beta) \tag{1}$$

This describes a probability distribution over states s_T at time T. Probability depends upon the return associated with each state. This classical utility function is expressed as a map from objective ultimate outcomes to prior beliefs, with the relative utility of different outcomes depending upon a sensitivity parameter β.

Choosing policies to achieve the plausible goals

Suppose that an agent believes that at time t they occupy a state s_t. They then need to choose a policy comprising a sequence of control states $\tilde{u} = \{u_t \cdots u_T\}$ that leads to the desired outcome distribution $P(s_T|m)$. If $\tilde{u}$ leads to a distribution over final or outcome states $P(s_T|s_t, \tilde{u})$, then success can be measured by the Kullback-Leibler divergence between the anticipated and desired distribution. The agent can then choose policies according to this measure of their likely success. Following Friston et al. (2013), we can express this formally as follows:

$$P(\tilde{u}|s_t, \gamma, m) = \tfrac{1}{Z}\exp(-\gamma D_{KL}[P(s_T|s_t, \tilde{u})||P(s_T|m)]) \tag{2}$$

Here, we have introduced a normalizing constant Z and a confidence or precision parameter γ. While the softmax parameter β in Equation 1. calibrates the relative utility of different outcomes, the precision parameter γ encodes the confidence that desired goals can be reached, based on current beliefs about the world and the policies available. Unless otherwise stated we will use the unqualified term "precision" for γ. Crucially, precision has to be inferred so that the confidence is optimal, in relation to the current state (context) and beliefs about the current state and future states.

Forming beliefs consistent with observations and goals

In our model, agents need to perform inference about certain quantities. An agent's knowledge of how they interact with the

Table 1 | Additional definitions and significance of symbols that appear in equations.

Symbol	Definition and significance	Formula where symbol first appears
P	Probability mass of a discrete random variable, or probability density of a continuous random variable	$P(s_T \mid m) = \sigma(r(s_T), \beta)$
s_T	Outcome state—a state that the agent may arrive at time T, the end of the exchange	
m	Model of the world according to the agent. It includes all the rules of how the dynamics of the world evolve, as well as the parameters of the world that don't change as the world evolves	
β	Inverse temperature over outcomes. It signifies how strongly prior (utilitarian) beliefs change as a function of the outcome measure in question (e.g., money) at the point of indifference.	
$\sigma(\vec{x}, \beta)$	The Gibbs softmax function. It ascribes to each component of $x_i \in \vec{x}$ a probability proportional to $\exp(\beta x_i)$	
$r(x)$	Return associated with state x.	
$u_t, \tilde{u}$	u_t is a control state—that is, a state that the agent believes s/he will deploy at time t. In general this does not necessarily determine what action will be realized at time t—the agent may not have full control over this. However in our agents do have such control, so u_t equates with the decision about the action to take. $\tilde{u}$ is the sequence of control states believed to be taken from now to the outcome (e.g.,: "I will type in all the letters of my password").	$\tilde{u} = \{u_t \ldots u_T\}$
γ	Precision of belief about control sequences. It signifies the confidence that the goal will be attained, if the best attainable combinations of control states are employed.	$P(\tilde{u} \mid s_t, \gamma, m) =$ $= \frac{1}{Z}\exp(-\gamma D_{KL}[P(s_T \mid s_t, \tilde{u}) \| P(s_T \mid m)])$
Z	Normalizing constant. In many cases we consider how strong beliefs are relative to each other; Dividing each by their sum Z ensures they add up to one, as probabilities should.	
$D_{KL}[P_0(x) \| P_1(x)]$	Kullback-Leibler divergence between a distribution $P_0(x)$ and another distribution $P_1(x)$. It is the expectation *with respect to* $P_0(x)$ of the difference in surprise inherent in encountering each possible value of x according to the two distributions.	
Pr	Probability value; $\Pr(x = a)$ is the probability that x takes the value a.	$P(\tilde{o}, \tilde{s}, \tilde{u}, \gamma \mid m) = \Pr(\{o_0, \ldots, o_t\} = \tilde{o},$ $\{s_0, \ldots, s_t\} = \tilde{s}, \{u_t, \ldots, u_T\} = \tilde{u}, \gamma)$
$P(\tilde{o}, \tilde{s}, \tilde{u}, \gamma \mid m)$	Probability density according to the generative model m; i.e., the world including the agent	$P(\tilde{o}, \tilde{s}, \tilde{u}, \gamma \mid m) =$ $= P(\tilde{o} \mid \tilde{s}, m)P(\tilde{u} \mid s_t, \gamma, m)P(\tilde{s} \mid m)P(\gamma \mid m)$
$Q(\tilde{s}, \tilde{u}, \gamma \mid \mu)$	Q is the belief that agent infers using the approximate inference scheme. Rather than being expressed in terms of probability distributions, it is expressed in terms of their "sufficient statistics" μ, such as its expectation. Not to be confused with $\boldsymbol{Q}$, the matrix representation of policy values.	$Q(\tilde{s}, \tilde{u}, \gamma \mid \mu) \approx \Pr(\{s_0, \ldots, s_t\} = \tilde{s}, \{u_t, \ldots, u_T\} = \tilde{u}, \gamma)$
$\mu = (\widehat{s}_0, \ldots, \widehat{s}_t, \widehat{u}, \widehat{\gamma})$	The specific instantiation of the sufficient statistics in our example.	$\mu = (\widehat{s}_0, \ldots, \widehat{s}_t, \widehat{u}, \widehat{\gamma})$
$H[P(x)]$	H is the Entropy of the distribution $P(x)$. It is a measure of the average surprise of this distribution	$-D_{KL}[P(s_T \mid s_t, \tilde{u}) \| P(s_T \mid m)] =$ $= H[P(s_T \mid s_t, \tilde{u})] + E_{P(s_T \mid s_t, \tilde{u})}[\ln P(s_T \mid m)]$
$E_{P(x)}[\ln P(x)]$	$E_{P(x)}[f(x)]$ signifies the Expectation of $f(x)$ under the probability distribution $P(x)$. In active inference $\ln P(x)$ is a measure of utility.	

world can be expressed as a joint distribution over these requisite quantities:

$$P(\tilde{o}, \tilde{s}, \tilde{u}, \gamma|m) = \Pr(\{o_0, \ldots, o_t\} = \tilde{o}, \{s_0, \ldots, s_t\} = \tilde{s}, \{u_t, \ldots, u_T\} = \tilde{u}, \gamma) \quad (3)$$

This probabilistic knowledge constitutes a generative model over observations, states, control and precision. This model is constituted by prior beliefs about policies $P(\tilde{u}|s_t, \gamma, m)$—as specified by Equation 2—state transitions, the likelihood of a sequence of observations stemming from those states and prior beliefs about precision:

$$P(\tilde{o}, \tilde{s}, \tilde{u}, \gamma|m) = P(\tilde{o}|\tilde{s}, m)P(\tilde{s}|\tilde{u}, m)P(\tilde{u}|s_t, \gamma, m)P(\gamma|m) \quad (4)$$

Agents can use this model to infer the hidden states of the world $\tilde{s} = \{s_0 \cdots s_t\}$; to determine where each policy, or sequence of choices, $\tilde{u} = \{u_t \cdots u_T\}$, is likely to lead; and to select the precision γ that encodes the confidence in policy selection. Agents can infer hidden states, their policy and precision from observed outcomes by inverting the model above. To do this they have two assets at their disposal: their observations $\tilde{o} = \{o_1 \cdots o_t\}$ and their model m of choice-dependent probabilistic state transitions.

To keep things simple, we assume a one-to-one mapping between observations and states of the world. This is encoded by an identity matrix **A** with columns corresponding to states, rows corresponding to observations and elements encoding the likelihood of observations—$P(\tilde{o}|\tilde{s}, m)$, under their model.

State transitions in an interpersonal world

We can describe the possible states of the world as a cross product between a subspace which is hidden and one which can be observed. An example of the former is "my partner is cooperative" whereas an example from the latter is "they will give me nothing." We model transitions between hidden states as constrained by the meaning of these subspaces. The part of the world-state that describes my partner's traits cannot change (otherwise they would not be traits). The part which describes their actions will be a probabilistic function of what I will do. As an example, the action "they will give me nothing" is probable if I follow a policy of giving them nothing myself.

Agents therefore describe changes in the world contingent upon what they do in terms of a 3-D transition matrix. This matrix $\boldsymbol{B}(u_t)$ has one "page" for each control state u_t that the agent can employ. Each page has columns of possible states at time t; and rows of the possible states at time $t+1$. The entries of $\boldsymbol{B}$ are the probabilities $P(s_{t+1}|s_t, \tilde{u})$. As the reader may have noticed, the policy-dependent probabilities in Equation 2 can be derived by the repeated application of $\boldsymbol{B}$.

A practical method for performing inference

If agents have at their disposal a function F that approximates how *in*consistent their beliefs and observations were, they can minimize F to maximize the chance of achieving their goals. A suitable function F is the free energy of observations and beliefs under a model of the world. The reader is referred to Friston et al. (2013) for a full explication of free energy in active inference. For our purposes, we just need to know that F provides a measure of the probability of the observations under the model $F \approx -\ln P(\tilde{o}|m)$. This means that minimizing free energy renders observations the least surprising, under my model: "Given that I am likely to be at work in an hour (belief under model of the world) it is not surprising that I'm in a train station (observation); it *would be surprising* if I headed for the cinema (belief about behavior)." The free energy defined by a generative model is thus an objective function with respect to optimal behavior—where optimality is defined by the agent's beliefs.

Posterior beliefs correspond to an *approximate posterior probability* over states, policies and precision. These beliefs are parameterized by sufficient statistics$\mu \in \mathbb{R}^d$ such that $Q(\tilde{s}, \tilde{u}, \gamma|\mu) \approx \Pr(\{s_0, \ldots, s_t\} = \tilde{s}, \{u_t, \ldots, u_T\} = \tilde{u}, \gamma)$. The free energy then becomes a function of the sufficient statistics of the approximate posterior distribution. This allows us to express approximate Bayesian inference in terms of free energy minimization:

$$\mu_t = \arg\min_{\mu} F(\tilde{o}, \mu) \quad (5)$$

where actions or choices are sampled from $\Pr(a_t = u_t) = Q(u_t|\mu_t)$. This means policies are selected that lead to the least surprising actions and outcomes. In summary, the optimization of sufficient statistics (usually expectations) rests upon a generative model and therefore depends on prior beliefs. It is these beliefs that specify what is surprising and consequently optimal behavior in both a Bayesian and utilitarian (optimal decision theory) sense.

A common scheme used to perform free-energy minimization is VB. Many statistical procedures used in everyday data analysis can be derived as special cases of VB. We will not go into technical details and interested readers can find a treatment of VB relevant to the present discussion in Friston et al. (2013). Here, we note that VB allows us to partition the sufficient statistics into three common-sense subsets: statistics describing beliefs about states of the world causing observations; statistics describing beliefs about the (future) policy $\tilde{u} = \{u_t \ldots u_T\}$ to be selected; and statistics describing beliefs about precision γ: $\mu = (\widehat{s}_0, \ldots, \widehat{s}_t, \widehat{u}, \widehat{\gamma})$. These statistics are updated with each new observation, using variational message passing (VMP). Each belief (about precision, about the state of the world etc.) is a probability distribution held in a "node" of a network of such beliefs, as in **Figure 1**. Each belief not only has a most-likely-value but also an uncertainty, and possibly other features, that describe the exact shape of the distribution. In our case, these features are encoded by the statistics above. In VMP, the belief distributions and their associated parameters (sufficient statistics) are chosen from amongst a rich and flexible—but not unlimited—vocabulary, the so-called conjugate-exponential belief networks. When one of the beliefs—say, the sensory state—is updated via an observation, it is no longer consistent with the others: the free energy increases. The "node" of the network representing this belief then sends information about its new content (e.g., the expectation or mean of the distribution) to all the other belief "nodes" with which it is connected. It also sends information about the beliefs on which it depends to nodes sending messages, which mandates a reciprocal or recurrent message passing. The recipient "nodes" then adjust

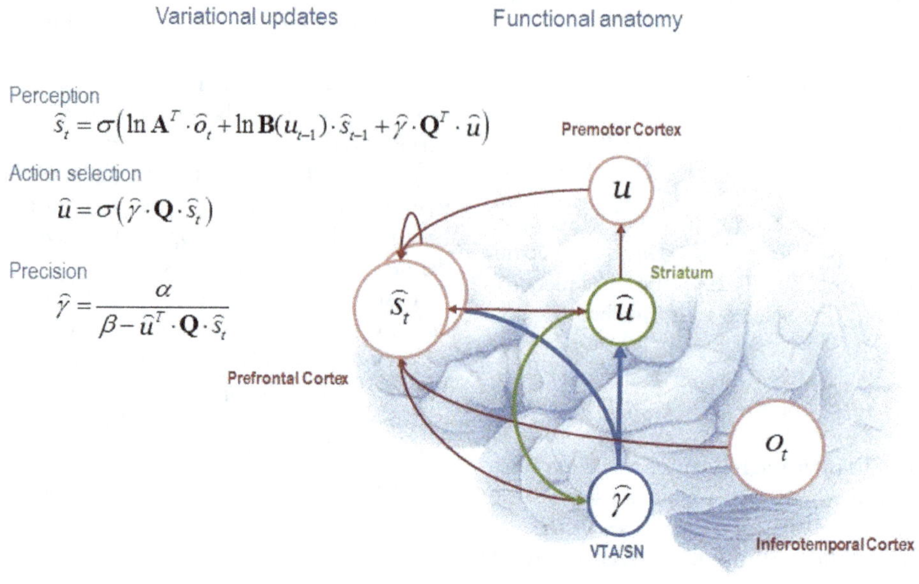

FIGURE 1 | This figure illustrates the cognitive and functional anatomy implied by the mean field assumption used in Variational Bayes. Here, we have associated the variational updates of expected states with perception, of future control states (policies) within action selection and, finally, expected precision with evaluation. The updates suggest the sufficient statistics from each subset are passed among each other until convergence to an internally consistent (Bayes optimal) solution. In terms of neuronal implementation, this might be likened to the exchange of neuronal signals via extrinsic connections among functionally specialized brain systems. In this (purely iconic) schematic, we have associated perception (inference about the current state of the world) with the prefrontal cortex, while assigning action selection to the basal ganglia. Crucially, precision has been associated with dopaminergic projections from ventral tegmental area and substantia nigra. See Friston et al. (2013), whence this figure has been adapted, for a full description of the equations.

their parameters, and thus change the beliefs they encode, so as to increase consistency with the source of the message. Of course, this may put them a little out of line with yet other beliefs. Hence messages propagate back and forth via all the connections in the network, changing the statistical parameters that the nodes hold, until free energy cannot be reduced any further and consistency is once again optimized (Winn and Bishop, 2005).

The simplicity and generality of this VMP scheme speaks to the biological plausibility of its neuronal implementation (Friston et al., 2013). A common objection to Bayesian schemes is that it is implausible that the brain performs long algebraic derivations, or alternatively high-dimensional numerical integration, every time a new task was at hand. However, evolution may have converged on the simplicity and efficiency of VMP—or at least something like it.

Figure 1 shows the architecture of variational updates for any generative model of choice outcomes and hidden states that can be formulated as a Markov decision process. The functional anatomy implied by the update equations is shown (schematically) on the right. Here the distributions over observations given hidden states are categorical and parameterized by the matrix **A** as above. Similarly, the transition matrices $\boldsymbol{B}(ut)$ encode transition probabilities from one state to the next, under the current control state of a policy ($\tilde{u} = \{u_t \cdots u_T\}$).

In the simulations that follow we used a prior over precision that has a gamma distribution with shape and scale parameters $\alpha = 8$ and $\theta = 1$. The matrix $\boldsymbol{Q}$ contains the values of the i-th policy from the j-th current state and corresponds to the divergence term in Equation 2. We see that expectations about hidden states of the world are updated on the basis of sensory evidence, beliefs about state transitions and value expected under allowable policies. Conversely, policies are selected on the basis of the expected value over hidden states, while precision is monotonically related to value expected over hidden states and policies. See Friston et al. (2013) for details.

INFERENCES ABOUT PEOPLE IN A MODEL TASK

The simplified trust game

To illustrate the basic features of this formulation we construct a model[1] of a simplified Trust Task based on the multi-round Investor-Trustee game (King-Casas et al., 2008). I (*self*) am to play consecutive rounds with the Trustee (*other*). At each round t I earn a wage w^{self}, usually set at 20 units of play money. I can then invest one of a discrete set of fractions $f^{self,\,low}, \ldots, f^{self,\,high}$ of my wage in a joint venture with the *other*. The investment is multiplied by a gain g, representing the surplus value created by the joint venture (usually $g = 3$). The *other* then returns a fraction of the *invested* amount. The round ends with the following returns:

$$\begin{aligned} r_t^{self} &= w^{self} - w^{self} f^{self} + w^{self} f^{self} f^{other} \\ r_t^{other} &= w^{self} f^{self} g - w^{self} f^{self} f^{other} \end{aligned} \qquad (6)$$

[1]Here we present the model step-by-step; see also the Discussion section regarding the rationale behind specific modeling choices.

Our Trust-Task is simpler than the standard Investor-Trustee game, with respect to the levels of investment and repayment available to the players. We make available only two levels, thus rendering a matrix representation of the exchange more straightforward and allowing experimenters to enforce (psychologically) interesting choices. The available response fractions f correspond only to *Cooperation* (action 1) or *Defection* (action 2). A matrix of monetary returns for *self* and *other* that can be used for this simplified task is shown in **Table 2**.

The task is a multi-round game—partners have to make decisions, taking into account long-term consequences of their choices. This is a difficult problem—and we will see that appropriate use of interpersonal representations may be used as a shortcut.

Interpersonal representations and prosocial utilities

We now consider the issue of how preferences are constituted in the generative model. To construct our minimal model, we assume the following:

1. *self* and *other* are each represented by a single scalar quantity—"how good one is." We will call this "esteem" so that e^s is how good the *self* is, while the esteem of the *other* is e^o.
2. A "good" person, with positive esteem, is more likely to cooperate with an average person, all other things being equal.
3. An average person is more likely to cooperate with a "good" person, other things being equal.

The observable component of world states is disclosed by action (u^o, u^s) and the hidden component (e^s, e^o) concerns the traits to be inferred. The fact that a "good" person is more likely to cooperate—and to *attract cooperation*—highlights the fact that esteem can augment the utility of cooperation. An analogous reasoning applies to defection.

Preferential biases induced by esteem can be specified in terms of an augmented return that includes the payoff and esteem. Following the format of **Table 2** we write:

$$\begin{aligned} r^s(u^o = 1, u^s = 1, e^s, e^o) &= \beta_r^s r_{22}^s + e^s + e^o \\ r^o(u^o = 1, u^s = 1, e^s, e^o) &= \beta_r^o r_{22}^s + e^s + e^o \end{aligned} \tag{7}$$

Table 3 gives the augmented returns for each combination of outcomes.

With this setup observable outcomes can take just 5 values: A "starting state" and four outcomes: $o_2 = \{u^s = 1, u^o = 1\}$, $o_3 = \{u^s = 2, u^o = 1\}$ and so on, for all combinations of cooperation and defection. For each round, each player has to model the transition probabilities $P(s_T|s_t, \tilde{u})$. If $r^o(u_t^o, u_t^s, e^s, e^o)$ denotes the augmented return for the *other*, *self* can use a softmax function to calculate the probabilities of actions taken by the *other* (following Equation 1):

$$P(u_t^o|u_t^s, e^s, e^o) = \frac{\exp(r^o)}{\sum_c \exp(r^o)} \tag{8}$$

However, this requires that *self* knows the beliefs of *other* about hidden esteems (e^s, e^o). We will assume that *self* uses beliefs about their esteem to model the beliefs of the *other*. We will see later that this is not an unreasonable assumption. Furthermore, we assumed that players can resolve just two levels of esteem $e^o = p$ (for prosocial) or $e^o = n$ (for non-social or antisocial). To further simplify things, we assume that the self esteem is neutral, $e^o = 0$. Prior beliefs about choices will then be influenced by "who I would like you to be" and "what I would like (us) to get." These simplifications create a discrete hidden state space with 10 states. These correspond to the five observable states, for each of the two levels of the other's esteem $e^o \in \{p, n\}$. The action chosen by *self* were sampled from posterior beliefs over choices based on the prior beliefs over policies of Equation 2. These prior beliefs depended on the utilities in **Table 3**.

IMPLEMENTATION OF THE TRUST GAME IN ITERATED PLAY

We implemented the multi-round version of the Trust game by using the posterior beliefs about the partner, at the end of each round, as the priors for the next round.

The software routines were written using the SPM academic freeware platform in matlab (MATLAB, 2012). The SPM platform, including the DEM toolbox used here, is available

Table 2 | Trust Task monetary returns matrix with only two choices for each partner.

	Other	
self	$u^o = 1$ (Cooperate: $f^{other,\,high}$)	$u^o = 2$ (Defect: $f^{other,\,low}$)
$u^s = 1$	r_{11}^s (e.g., =26)	r_{21}^s (e.g., =10)
(Cooperate: $f^{self,\,high}$)	r_{11}^o (e.g., =26)	r_{21}^o (e.g., =42)
$u^s = 2$	r_{12}^s (e.g., =21)	r_{22}^s (e.g., =18)
(Defect: $f^{self,\,low}$)	r_{12}^o (e.g., =7)	r_{22}^o (e.g., =10)

These returns are defined by payoffs $r_{11}^s > r_{12}^s \geq r_{22}^s > r_{21}^s$ for the self (in the Investor role) and $r_{21}^o > r_{11}^o \geq r_{22}^o > r_{12}^o$ for the other (in the Trustee role). The task is constructed as a sequential game, with my self playing first, and is typically asymmetric. In the example in brackets I have a "wage" of 20 units. I can choose to invest $f^{self,\,low} = 20\%$ or $f^{self,\,high} = 80\%$; the other can choose to return 40 or 140% of my investment. All amounts have been rounded.

Table 3 | Utility matrix for the simplified Trust task.

	Other	
self	$u^o = 1$ (Cooperate)	$u^o = 2$ (Defect)
$u^s = 1$	$\beta_r r_{11}^s + e^s + e^o$	$\beta_r r_{21}^s + e^s + e^o$
(Cooperate)	$\beta_r r_{11}^o + e^s + e^o$	$\beta_r r_{21}^o - e^s - e^o$
$u^s = 2$	$\beta_r r_{12}^s - e^s - e^o$	$\beta_r r_{22}^s - e^s - e^o$
(Defect)	$\beta_r r_{12}^o + e^s + e^o$	$\beta_r r_{22}^o - e^s - e^o$

*The entries of **Table 1** are weighted by a sensitivity parameter and then augmented by an interpersonal component to form socialized returns. The interpersonal component consists of the esteem for each partner plus the esteem for the other partner (weighted equally in this example). Positive esteems enhance cooperative utility whereas negative esteem increases the utility of defecting. We have assumed here that $\beta_r^s = \beta_r^o = \beta_r$.*

under GPL (GNU General Public License, version 3, 2007). It can be accessed via www.fil.ion.ucl.ac.uk/spm/software/spm12. Additional scripts are available from the corresponding author on demand, also under GPL.

RESULTS

In order to perform simulations we used the monetary values in **Table 1**. To calculate the numerical values corresponding to **Table 2**, we chose a value for β_r such that the resulting probabilities according to Equation 8 would be very distributed. Furthermore, for the purposes of this demonstration, we chose the *other* to be antisocial; i.e., have a negative esteem, and naïve; i.e., only influenced by immediate outcomes (as per Equation 8). The preferences (priors) that these choices translate into for the *other* are shown in **Figure 2A**. The *other* would prefer the self to cooperate and the *other* herself to defect (cd in **Figure 2A**). Their second best preference would be mutual cooperation (cc), which still has a substantial monetary outcome. The *other* is indifferent about the remaining two options, in which the *self* defects (dc, dd). In **Figure 2**, we have included the starting state (start) as a potential outcome—as is required by the model specification in the code we used. We set the starting state probability to zero, as it never actually materializes as an outcome and agents do not need to consider a preference for it.

The situation is a little more complicated, and more interesting, with respect to the goals of the *self* that this scheme gives rise to. These are shown in **Figure 2B**. Whereas our antisocial, naïve *other* did not consider separate states for prosocial vs. antisocial self, we endowed the *self* with preferences depending on the type of the *other* and hence we consider the full 10-state outcome space for each round of the exchange.

Figure 2B shows that the preference of the *self* for mutual cooperation is more pronounced if the *other* is prosocial. As one might expect, given an antisocial *other* the second-best preference for *self* is for the *other* to cooperate while *self* defects. More interestingly, given a prosocial *other* the second-best preference for the *self* is to cooperate, while the prosocial *other* defects. Heuristically, *self* is forgiving toward prosocial but not antisocial *others*.

A SINGLE-ROUND

The basic behavior of *self* when choosing a policy through free energy minimization is shown in **Figure 3**. Initially, *self* believes that the *other* is equally likely to be *p* or *n*. In other words, at the beginning of a series of exchanges, we assume people are agnostic as to the character or esteem of their opponent. Notice that although there are 10 hidden states, there are only five observable states—because the esteem (of the other) is hidden and has to be inferred.

At the first time step *self* just observes the starting state and believes the *other* is equally likely to be *prosocial* or *antisocial*, corresponding to hidden states 1 or 6. Still, under the influence of their utilitarian priors *self* assigns a higher probability to the cooperative policy (control state 1). With the parameters used in this example, this is a modest preference: as it happens, the

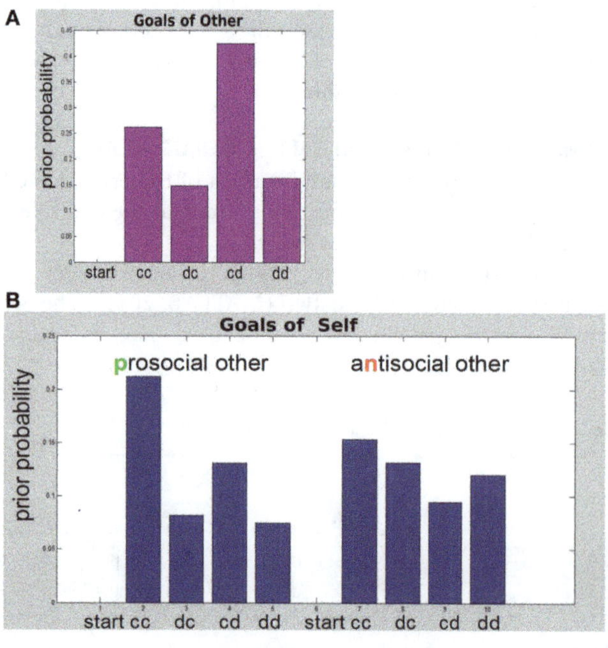

FIGURE 2 | Pattern of social utilities In $P(s_{T|m}) = \sigma(r^s(s_T), \beta)$. (A) Preferences of the *other*. This simple *other* only considers observable states of each round—the starting state (start), and each of the four *self*-action—*other*-action combinations shown in **Table 3**. The "start" state is only indicated for completeness: agents correctly never consider it as an outcome. **(B)** Preferences (goals) of the *self*. Preferences over all 10 hidden states are shown; See text for detailed description.

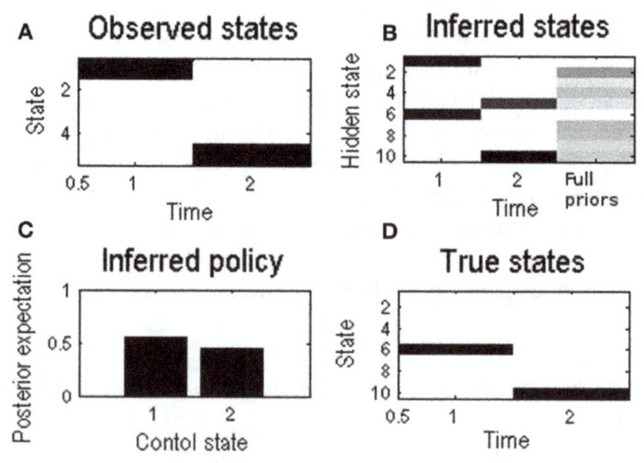

FIGURE 3 | Inferences made by *self* during a single round, where *self* initially believes that the *other* is just as likely to be prosocial as antisocial. The numbering of states from 1 to 10 corresponds to the 10 states in **Figure 2B. (A)** This shows that the observable state changed from state 1, the starting state, to 5, corresponding to mutual defection during this example round. **(B)** Initially the belief of *self* was equally shared between playing a prosocial partner or an antisocial partner (state 1 or 6). At the end of the round, belief was shared between mutual defection with a prosocial (s5) or antisocial (s10) partner, but no longer equally so. Defection made the *self* infer that the *other* was more likely to be antisocial: $P(s10) > P(s5)$. The column "Full priors" corresponds to **Figure 2B. (C)** Control state 1 (cooperation) is slightly favored despite agnosticism, at this stage, as to the type of the *other*. As it happened however the *self* still chose to defect, as choice is probabilistic **(D)**. The underlying true states: in this example the *other* is antisocial.

choice selected was to defect—to which the *other* responded by also defecting. *Self* therefore observes outcome state 5. Finally, on the basis of this outcome, *self* infers that they are more likely to be playing an *antisocial other*, which is the case. Clearly, in a single round, *self* cannot make use of this inference. However, if we now replace the prior beliefs about the *other* with the posterior beliefs and play a further round, we can emulate Bayesian updating of beliefs about the *other*. We now turn to the simulation of iterated play using this method of updating beliefs.

ITERATED PLAY

During iterated play, beliefs about the *other* evolve. This has a knock-on effect on the goals or priors for each round—that produce a progressive change in preferred policies as one learns about the *other* and adjusts one's behavior accordingly. The result of a multi-round game is shown in **Figure 4** and reveals several interesting features:

The agent infers fairly quickly that the *other* is antisocial and reduces cooperative play. In this example, they still engage a considerable amount of cooperative play – outcome state 4 in **Figure 4C** is self-cooperate, other-defect $o_4 = \{u^s = 1, u^o = 2\}$. These outcomes reflect the preference of *self*, not a lack of confidence or expected precision. The evolution of expected precision is interesting. Precision reflects whether the available policies can fulfill the goals or utilitarian priors. Initially, there was prior belief that fully cooperative play might be achieved, given the *other* might be prosocial. When it looked as if this was the case (outcome state 2 in **Figure 4C**), precision jumped optimistically (**4D**). However, overall, there is a slower increase in expected precision, as the agent realizes the true nature of the opponent (i.e., that the *other* is antisocial). This illustrative example highlights the important interplay between prior beliefs about outcomes, inference on hidden states or characteristics of opponents and, crucially, confidence in the ensuing beliefs.

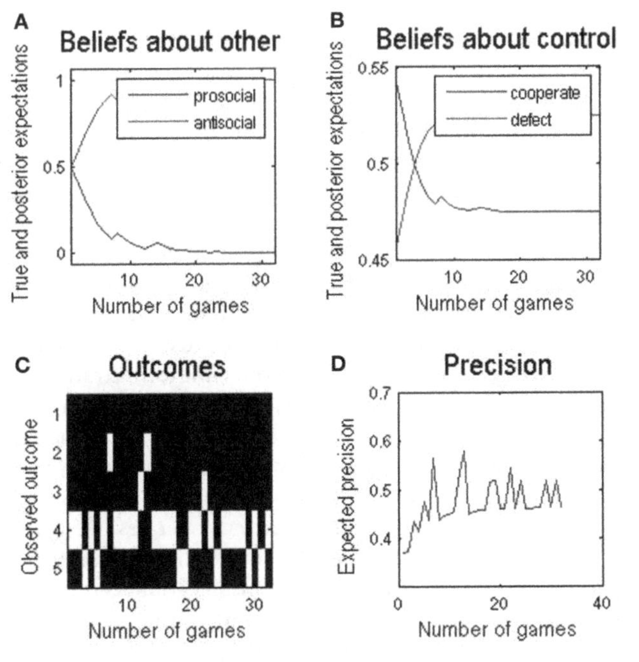

FIGURE 4 | (A) A sequence of 32 rounds of the simplified Trust task. Over the course of approximately 10 rounds, *self* becomes confident that *other* is antisocial. **(B)** This increasing belief results in a declining belief in (preference for) cooperating. **(C)** In this example the actions chosen are quite variable and: **(D)** expected precision changes relatively slowly. The variability of responses is due to the relatively weak preferences over different outcomes used here; this is to illustrate how one quantity (e.g., expected precision) changes with respect to another (e.g., players' choices) over a single round or over a sequence of rounds.

DISCUSSION

In this paper, we applied active inference to interpersonal decision making. Using a simple example, we captured key aspects of single and repeated exchanges. This example belongs to the large family of partially observable Markov decision problems (POMDP) but its solution is distinguished by explicit consideration of the agent's goals as *prior* distributions over outcomes. Because behavior depends upon beliefs, this necessarily entails beliefs that have precision. In other words, it is not sufficient simply to consider the goals of interpersonal exchange, one also has two consider the confidence that those goals can be attained. We have focused on optimizing this precision of beliefs about different policies—as opposed to sensitivity to different outcomes. In what follows, we consider the difference between sensitivity and precision. We then consider the nature of interpersonal inference and how it shapes decision-making. Finally, we discuss further developments along these lines.

SENSITIVITY OVER OUTCOMES vs. PRECISION OVER POLICY CHOICE

One of the key consequences of our formulation is the separation of choice behavior into two components. The first is inherent in the prior distribution itself, which reflects goals that are not directly represented in the exchange—as might be codified by various matching rules or exploratory drives. The second is optimized by the agent during the exchange itself in order to maximize utility or returns, in light of what is realistic. As described in Friston et al. (2013), this decomposition can be seen clearly by expressing the negative divergence—that constitutes prior beliefs—in terms of entropy (promoting exploration of allowable states) and expected utility:

$$-D_{KL}[P(s_T|s_t,\tilde{u})||P(s_T|m)] = H[P(s_T|s_t,\tilde{u})] + E_{P(s_T|s_t,\tilde{u})}[\ln P(s_T|m)] \quad (9)$$

Therefore minimizing the difference between attainable and desired outcomes can always be expressed in terms of maximizing expected utility, under the constraint that the entropy or dispersion of the final outcomes is as high as possible.

This separation of choice behavior—into (context-sensitive) beliefs about policies vs. (context invariant) beliefs about which outcomes are desirable—is reflected by an introduction of precision γ to complement the softmax sensitivity β. Both parameters play the role of precision or sensitivity (inverse temperature). β determines how sensitive prior beliefs are to rewards or the relative utility of different outcomes. However, this does not specify the confidence or precision that these outcomes can be attained.

This is where the precision parameter γ comes in—it encodes the confidence that desired outcomes can be reached, based on current beliefs about the world and allowable policies. For example, one can be very uncertain about the contingencies that intervene between the current state and final outcome, even if one is confident that a particular outcome has much greater utility than another.

Crucially, the precision of the probability distribution over alternative policies can itself be inferred in a Bayes-optimal sense. This represents a departure from classical formulations. It arises because we are formulating policy selection in terms of inference. Choices are based upon beliefs (or inference) and beliefs in turn are held with greater or lesser confidence. The Bayes-optimal selection of precision over policies is a key thing that the current formulation brings to the table, above and beyond classical formulations.

INTERPERSONAL REPRESENTATIONS AS MOTIVATING BELIEFS

Our modeling demonstrates that the formulation of interpersonal representations in terms of plausible and desirable outcomes accommodates a number of psychological findings and points to interesting theoretical and empirical questions.

First, our model replicates basic features of other successful models of interactive games. The 'esteem' traits in our model parallel the role of fairness-related coefficients in other models (Xiang et al., 2012). Second, our model infers the type of the partner (e.g., **Figure 4A**) and adjusts its policy so that it is not exploited (**Figure 4B**). Thirdly, posterior beliefs are based upon a generative model that entails beliefs about beliefs (utility functions) of others. This endows the generative model with an elemental theory of mind. Furthermore, Bayesian inference about esteem, and therefore intentions, constitute an elementary form of *mentalizing* (Allen et al., 2008).

In our case the fact that interpersonal representations contribute to the agent's beliefs about the desirability of outcomes *biases inference about states perceived* and actions selected. The perceptual update in **Figure 1** contains a contribution from precision. This is a remarkable effect of approximate Bayesian inference. In our example (**Figure 4B**) the result is that the agent is biased toward co-operativity, despite believing that the *other* is as likely to be uncooperative as not (**Figure 4A**). This is an interpersonal analog of optimism bias, or 'giving the benefit of the doubt'. There is experimental evidence in the Trust task that beliefs about prosocial traits in the *other* result in preference structures akin to the prosocial side of **Figure 2A**. When Investors are made to believe that the Trustee is of 'moral character' they entrust larger amounts (in our terms, cooperate in a sustained manner) even if the experimenter manipulates Trustee behavior so that the Investor does not make more money as a result (Delgado et al., 2005).

Our treatment suggests that interpersonal representations can help predict (and seek out) the outcomes of interactions. The idea that a self-esteem aspect of self-representation helps predict social outcomes is a central empirical finding of research by Leary and co-workers (Leary et al., 1995). Aspects of other-representation that help predict active social outcomes can be found in negative ideas about others, that healthy people harbor in certain contexts. As mentioned, exaggerated suspicion about others can serve to manage false-negative errors in the detection of social difficulties (Kramer, 1994). Computationally, more sophisticated agents can predict interactions better. Under certain constraints, however, interpersonal beliefs in the form of prosocial biases help achieve behavior that emulates such sophisticated thinking, a key theoretical finding of Yoshida and co-workers (Yoshida et al., 2008).

Interpersonal inference suggests that the use of self-representations to predict outcomes requires an *assessment of context*. In our Trust task, my partner and I can just consider one round in the future, provided we have inferred our types appropriately and, implicitly, the effective nature of the exchange (cooperative or competitive, etc.). Our simulation contains an interesting example of what happens if the wrong representations are assumed. The game is cooperative but, in our example, the other is antisocial (and unsophisticated). The *other*'s preference, stemming from their negative "niceness" (esteem), is to defect while the *self* cooperates, followed by mutual cooperation. Note that this preference structure is the only element in our naïve *other*'s cognitive machinery. When the *self* infers this preference structure they switch to a more uncooperative policy, thus undermining the *other*'s goals. Had the *other* been "nice" enough, or had they believed the *self* to be "nice" enough, the *self* would have inferred this and the *other*'s predictions, or goals, would be fulfilled.

We see that goals are not prescribed by immediate reward but by more generic beliefs. Clearly, there are an enormous number of forms for these beliefs that we could consider that help predict and realize different outcomes in different contexts. In the present context, one might consider the long-term payoffs that accrue from a collaborative policy for the agent or for everybody. Crucially, collaboration entails a consilience in terms of prosocial preferences or utility. The key thing about prosocial utility is that it can be symmetrical with respect to me and my opponent. For example, I may altruistically value the total reward accrued by myself and my opponent *if* I think they are prosocial, but only my own rewards if they are antisocial. In our simple illustration, and with the right choice of parameters, this would result in a very similar pattern of exchange to that seen in **Figure 3**. Alternatively, through some aversion to inequality, *self* might prefer equitable outcomes (irrespective of who gets most).

In our simulations the effect of esteem operates like a *social Pavlovian bias*, biasing beliefs irrespective of their consequences. A Pavlovian bias enhances certain actions in certain contexts. For example, it enhances passivity in a context of threat or vigorous approach in a context of opportunity, irrespective of instrumental outcomes. Our social Pavlovian bias promotes certain actions in the context of certain personal esteems irrespective of instrumental outcomes. Here, we chose a scheme of social Pavlovian biases that makes direct links between contemporary research into these fundamental biases (Guitart-Masip et al., 2012) and the large body of clinical- and social- psychological work on affectively charged representations of people. This work spans Aristotelian ethics, forensic psychotherapy (Gilligan, 2000) through to attribution theory (Thewissen et al., 2011).

We placed emphasis on prior beliefs as they may absorb various beliefs about long-term outcomes. These utilitarian beliefs entail the agents' cognitive-affective horizon, beyond which the agent has no knowledge and no control. This contrasts with the dynamics of the exchange, wherein the agent has both beliefs about states and beliefs about control. We envisage that the present approach will help disentangle these two components in the setting of interpersonal dynamics.

Although our ultimate aim is to study how self-representation is inferred under active inference, in this introductory study we have kept self-representation constant. Although we hope to examine this in future work here we note that a Bayesian framework naturally predicts that ordinary self-representation should be less responsive to evidence than the representation of others. Setting aside beliefs about changeability of the self, as well as the real possibility that aspects of self-representation may be learnt "once and for all" during childhood, inference about self-representations must take place on the basis of a much greater evidence base than inference about strangers. Therefore each new piece of evidence is expected to have less impact on self-representation than other-representation.

MODELING CHOICES, LIMITATIONS AND OUTLOOK

What does my partner think of me?

It may appear that we made a gross simplification in modeling the *self* using their own representation to estimate how the *other* sees the self. A more general formulation might be more conventional, where the beliefs of the *self* (self-representation and reputation with respect to others) are separate. Yet this is not a modeling choice made to make the model simpler. For example, clinical psychology indicates that beliefs about the *self* are highly correlated with beliefs about how others see the *self*. Moreover, patients with unwarranted beliefs about themselves and others that look "psychologically defensive" show no greater social desirability than healthy controls (Moutoussis et al., 2013). We suggest that the *self* uses beliefs about their esteem to model the beliefs of the *other*, a generalization of the "sociometer" theory with a view to testing the limits of this assumption's predictive power.

Depth-of-thought

Our model uses a very simple *other*, who makes no inferences about itself. Clearly, this is not a realistic simulation of *other*. Furthermore, our model *self* does did not explicitly calculate distant outcomes before applying the prior "horizon." The latter is partly justified as most people look to the future to quite a limited extent. In the Trust Task, only about a quarter of Investors show up to two levels of recursive interpersonal thought (Xiang et al., 2012). Having said this, further work needs to consider agents that explicitly simulate outcomes for a small number of steps into the future and apply inference and preferences to patterns of such outcomes.

Normative self-representations

We envisage that self representations would enter into the assessment of proximal gains in the light of long-term outcomes; for example, "What sort of person am I, if I treat the other player like this?"; "If that's the sort of person I am, how am I likely to be treated in the future?" This extension of the simple model above will be crucial if the *other* makes inferences about the *self*. Our long-term aim, test the hypothesis that the normative role of self-representation is to predict the likely outcomes of social interactions, is likely to require such complex thinking. We envisage that beliefs about the opponent can, through conditional dependencies among Bayesian estimates about me and my opponent, affect beliefs about me. This may be crucial for understanding psychopathology in interpersonal exchange.

Model parameterization

We discussed above that interpersonal, affectively charged representations may be parameterized in a number of related ways. We chose a very simple parameterization for the purposes of demonstration. In the light of a wider literature, the validity of different models for interpersonal representation and the relationships between them remain to be clarified. One important contribution of formal models, of the sort we have introduced here, is that they can provide quantitative predictions of choice behavior. In principle, this means that one can use observed choices to estimate the parameters of a given model and—more importantly—use Bayesian model comparison to adjudicate between different forms or hypothetical schemes.

SUMMARY

In conclusion, we have sketched an elementary model of *self* and *other* representation during interpersonal exchange; within which these representations have important functional roles. We have seen that it is fairly straightforward to place optimal decision schemes in an active inference framework. This involves replacing optimal policies, defined by utility functions, with prior beliefs about outcomes. The advantage of doing this is that one can formulate action and perception as jointly minimizing the same objective function, which provides an upper bound on surprise or (negative log Bayesian) model evidence. This enables optimal control to be cast as a pure inference problem, with a clear distinction between action and inference about (partially) observed outcomes. Using a simple example, we have demonstrated how desirable goals can embody and express prosocial preferences as well as beliefs about the type of an opponent. Specifically, we have shown how these beliefs can be updated during iterated play and how they can guide interpersonal choices. Although rudimentary, these simulations illustrate a formal basis for interpersonal inference.

AUTHOR CONTRIBUTIONS

Michael Moutoussis formulated the core hypotheses regarding interpersonal representation from both a clinical-psychological and a Bayesian perspective; formulated the test task and its parameterization; programmed the structure of the task; ran the simulations; and drafted much of the manuscript. Raymond J. Dolan provided supervision to Michael Moutoussis; provided management for the whole project; provided psychiatric expertise; and edited the manuscript. Nelson J. Trujillo-Barreto and Wael El-Deredy provided help with variational Bayesian modeling; and reviewed the manuscript. Karl J. Friston placed the hypotheses regarding interpersonal Bayesian inference within the framework of Active Inference; contributed heavily to the mathematical formulation; wrote and provided key code within the SPM environment for solving discrete partially observable Markov problems through the message-passing free-energy-minimization algorithm; edited the manuscript; and provided supervision to Michael Moutoussis.

ACKNOWLEDGMENTS

This work was funded by the Wellcome Trust ['Neuroscience in Psychiatry' strategic award, 095844/Z/11/Z]. This work was supported by the Wellcome Trust Ray Dolan holds a Senior Investigator Award [098362/Z/12/Z]. The Wellcome Trust Centre for Neuroimaging is supported by core funding from the Wellcome Trust [091593/Z/10/Z]. Michael Moutoussis also receives support by the Biomedical Research Council.

REFERENCES

Allen, J. G., Fonagy, P., and Bateman, A. (2008). *Mentalizing in Clinical Practice.* Arlington, VA: American Psychiatric Pub.

Bentall, R. P. (2003). *Madness Explained: Psychosis and Human Nature.* London: Penguin.

Camerer, C. F. (2003). *Behavioral Game Theory: Experiments in Strategic Interaction.* Princeton, NJ: Princeton University Press.

Crowne, D. P., and Marlowe, D. (1960). A new scale of social desirability independent of psychopathology. *J. Consult. Psychol.* 24, 349–354. doi: 10.1037/h0047358

Daw, N. D. (2011). "Trial-by-trial data analysis using computational models (Tutorial Review), Chapter 1," in *Decision Making, Affect, and Learning: Attention and Performance*, eds M. R. Delgrado, E. Q. Phelps, and T. W. Robbins (Oxford: OUP), 3–38.

Delgado, M. R., Frank, R. H., and Phelps, E. A. (2005). Perceptions of moral character modulate the neural systems of reward during the trust game. *Nat. Neurosci.* 8, 1097–6256. doi: 10.1038/nn1575

Friston, K. J., Schwartenbeck, P., FitzGerald, T., Moutoussis, M., Behrens, T., and Dolan, R. J. (2013). The anatomy of choice: active inference and agency. *Front Human Neurosci* 7:598. doi: 10.3389/fnhum.2013.00598

Gilligan, J. (2000). *The Emotions and Morality of Violence, Chapter 5,* ed G. Adshead (London: Jessica Kingsley), 103–138.

GNU General Public License, version 3. (2007). Available online at: http://www.gnu.org/licenses/gpl.html

Guitart-Masip, M., Huys, Q. J. M., Fuentemilla, L., Dayan, P., Duzel, E., and Dolan, R. J. (2012). Go and no-go learning in reward and punishment: interactions between affect and effect. *Neuroimage* 62, 154–166. doi: 10.1016/j.neuroimage.2012.04.024

King-Casas, B., Sharp, C., Lomax-Bream, L., Lohrenz, T., Fonagy, P., and Montague, P. R. (2008). The rupture and repair of cooperation in borderline personality disorder. *Science* 321, 806–810. doi: 10.1126/science.1156902

Kramer, R. M. (1994). The sinister attribution error: paranoid cognition and collective distrust in organizations. *Motiv. Emotion* 18, 199–230. doi: 10.1007/BF02249399

Leary, M. R., Tambor, E. S., Terdal, S. K., and Downs, D. L. (1995). Self-esteem as an interpersonal monitor: the sociometer hypothesis. *J. Pers. Soc. Psychol.* 68, 518–530. doi: 10.1037/0022-3514.68.3.518

MATLAB. (2012). *Version 7.14.0 (R2012a).* Natick, MA: The MathWorks Inc.

Moutoussis, M., El-Deredy, W., and Bentall, R. P. (2013). An empirical study of defensive avoidance in Paranoia. *Behav. Cogn. Psychoth.* 1–8. doi: 10.1017/S1352465813000805. [Epub ahead of print].

Ogden, T. H. (1983). The concept of internal object relations. *Int. J. Psychoanal.* 64, 227–241.

Rycroft, R. (1995). *A Critical Dictionary of Psychoanalysis.* 2nd Edn. London: Penguin.

Thewissen, V., Bentall, R. P., Oorschot, M., A., Campo, J., Lierop, T., van Os, J., et al. (2011). Emotions, self-esteem, and paranoid episodes: an experience sampling study. *Br. J. Clin. Psychol.* 50, 178–195. doi: 10.1348/014466510X508677

Waller, G., Shah, R., Ohanian, V., and Elliott, P. (2001). Core beliefs in bulimia nervosa and depression: the discriminant validity of young's schema questionnaire. *Behav. Ther.* 32, 139–153. doi: 10.1016/S0005-7894(01)80049-6

Winn, J., and Bishop, C. M. (2005). Variational message passing. *J. Mach. Learn. Res.* 6, 661–694. Available online at: http://search.ebscohost.com/login.aspx?direct=true&db=bth&AN=18003399&site=ehost-live

Xiang, T., Ray, D., Lohrenz, T., Dayan, P., and Montague, P. R. (2012). Computational phenotyping of two-person interactions reveals differential neural response to depth-of-thought. *PLoS Comput. Biol.* 8:e1002841. doi: 10.1371/journal.pcbi.1002841

Yoshida, W., Dolan, R. J., and Friston, K. J. (2008). Game theory of mind. *PLoS Comput. Biol.* 4:e1000254. doi: 10.1371/journal.pcbi.1000254

8

The joint Simon effect depends on perceived agency, but not intentionality, of the alternative action

Anna Stenzel[1]*, Thomas Dolk[2,3], Lorenza S. Colzato[4], Roberta Sellaro[4], Bernhard Hommel[4] and Roman Liepelt[1]*

[1] Institute for Psychology, University of Muenster, Muenster, Germany
[2] Department of Psychology, Max-Planck-Institute for Human Cognitive and Brain Sciences, Leipzig, Germany
[3] Research Group: Heterogeneity and Inclusion, Faculty of Human Science, University of Potsdam, Potsdam, Germany
[4] Institute for Psychological Research and Leiden Institute for Brain and Cognition, Leiden University, Leiden, Netherlands

***Correspondence:**
Anna Stenzel and Roman Liepelt, Institute for Psychology, University of Muenster, Fliednerstrasse 21, 48149 Muenster, Germany
e-mail: anna.stenzel@uni-muenster.de; roman.liepelt@uni-muenster.de

A co-actor's intentionality has been suggested to be a key modulating factor for joint action effects like the joint Simon effect (JSE). However, in previous studies intentionality has often been confounded with agency defined as perceiving the initiator of an action as being the causal source of the action. The aim of the present study was to disentangle the role of agency and intentionality as modulating factors of the JSE. In Experiment 1, participants performed a joint go/nogo Simon task next to a co-actor who either intentionally controlled a response button with own finger movements (agency+/intentionality+) or who passively placed the hand on a response button that moved up and down on its own as triggered by computer signals (agency−/intentionality−). In Experiment 2, we included a condition in which participants believed that the co-actor intentionally controlled the response button with a Brain-Computer Interface (BCI) while placing the response finger clearly besides the response button, so that the causal relationship between agent and action effect was perceptually disrupted (agency−/intentionality+). As a control condition, the response button was computer controlled while the co-actor placed the response finger besides the response button (agency−/intentionality−). Experiment 1 showed that the JSE is present with an intentional co-actor and causality between co-actor and action effect, but absent with an unintentional co-actor and a lack of causality between co-actor and action effect. Experiment 2 showed that the JSE is absent with an intentional co-actor, but no causality between co-actor and action effect. Our findings indicate an important role of the co-actor's agency for the JSE. They also suggest that the attribution of agency has a strong perceptual basis.

Keywords: joint Simon effect, joint action, social interaction, stimulus-response compatibility, agency

INTRODUCTION

As social beings, we are born into a social environment. Acting in and interacting with our surroundings shapes our behavior and cognition from the early beginning (Prinz, 2012). Previous research on single subjects has enormously improved our understanding of how perception and action are linked (i.e., by sharing common representations), how individuals select task-relevant information, predict upcoming actions, and integrate predicted effects of one's own and others' actions (Wilson and Knoblich, 2005). However, when and to what extent individuals mentally represent their own and others' actions is currently a matter of debate in cognitive science (Liepelt and Prinz, 2011; Guagnano et al., 2013; Welsh et al., 2013a,b).

One of the most popular paradigms to investigate the cognitive processes representing joint action in humans is the joint go/nogo Simon task (Sebanz et al., 2003), in which two individuals share the standard Simon task (Simon and Rudell, 1967; Simon, 1969; see Simon, 1990 for a review). In the standard Simon task, a single participant carries out spatially defined responses, such as left and right key presses, to non-spatial stimulus attributes (e.g., geometric forms) that appear randomly to the left or right side of a central fixation point. Even though stimulus location is completely task-irrelevant, responses are faster when they spatially correspond to the stimulus position, a phenomenon known as the Simon effect (see Hommel, 2011 for an overview). When the same participant responds to only one of the two stimuli by pressing for example the left key, thus rendering the task a go/nogo task, there is typically no Simon effect observable (Hommel, 1996). However, when the same go/nogo task is divided between two co-acting participants, so that each of them performs complementary go/nogo responses next to each other, the Simon effect is re-established across the dyad (Sebanz et al., 2003). This so-called joint Simon effect (JSE) is typically explained by the assumption that interacting individuals automatically co-represent the other person's action (action co-representation), so that performing the Simon task with another person is functionally equivalent to performing the entire standard two-choice Simon task alone (Sebanz et al., 2003, 2005; Knoblich and Sebanz, 2006).

Recent studies, however, showed that a Simon effect can also be observed when replacing the human co-actor in a joint go/nogo Simon task with an event-producing object, like a rotating wheel (Dolk et al., 2011, Experiment 3), a Japanese waving cat or a metronome (Dolk et al., 2013). Based on these findings, a "referential-coding" account has been suggested as an alternative explanation for the JSE. Given that self-generated and other-generated actions are cognitively represented by their sensory consequences, i.e., by using the same kinds of codes (Prinz, 1997; Hommel et al., 2001; Hommel, 2013), the co-actor's action can be considered as just any other event that needs to be differentiated for response coding (Guagnano et al., 2010; Dolk et al., 2011, 2013; Dittrich et al., 2012). As a consequence, the perception of concurrently activated (and thus cognitively represented) social or non-social events that share features with the events that a person produces (i.e., action) introduces a discrimination problem: to enable proper task performance the participant needs to discriminate between the event representations referring to one's own action and all other (concurrently) activated event representations. According to the referential coding account, the action discrimination problem can be resolved by emphasizing processing on event features that discriminate best in a given task context. As the relative spatial location of both alternative actions (distributed to the left and right side) is the most obvious discriminable event feature in the spatial Simon task, it provides a reasonable reference for coding the individual's own action (the single button press) as left or right relative to the alternative event (Dolk et al., 2013). This referential coding of actions in turn can lead to matches or mismatches between the spatial stimulus features and the spatial response features—a necessary condition for Simon effects to emerge (Kornblum et al., 1990; Hommel et al., 2001; Liepelt et al., 2011, 2013; Dittrich et al., 2013; Sellaro et al., 2013). Hence, referential coding assumes that the presence of an alternative action event that shares features with one's own action event is necessary for the JSE to occur, whereas the co-representation of the other's task or task rules is not.

According to the referential coding account, the need to discriminate one's own action event from alternative action events via spatial coding should be stronger the more similar both action events are (Colzato et al., 2012, 2013; Liepelt et al., 2012). In turn, more pronounced spatial coding should lead to a larger JSE (Guagnano et al., 2010; Dolk et al., 2011, 2013). Indeed, there are several recent studies demonstrating that the size of the JSE is modulated by a range of factors that are related to the similarity between the participant and the co-actor. For example, Tsai and Brass (2007) showed that the JSE only emerges when participants share a go/nogo Simon task with a virtual human co-actor (a video of a human hand), but not when the task was shared with a non-human co-actor (a video of a wooden hand). Stenzel et al. (2012) extended these findings by showing that a reliable JSE is observed when a human person shared a task with a real humanoid robot, but only when this person believed that the robot was functioning in a human-like, biologically inspired way, and not when the robot was believed to function like a machine. Both studies suggest that a higher similarity regarding the humanness of the participant and the co-actor leads to a larger JSE. Furthermore, Müller et al. (2011a) showed that actions of in-group members, i.e., a white participant sharing a task with a white virtual co-actor, produced a larger JSE than actions of out-group members, i.e., a white participant sharing a task with a black virtual co-actor. Other components referring to the quality of the interpersonal relationship between both interacting individuals have also been shown to modulate the size of the JSE. In a study by Hommel et al. (2009), for example, the JSE was only present when two actors were in a positive relationship, which might lead participants to perceive the other person as being more similar to themselves. All of these studies provide evidence that a greater similarity between two actors (e.g., regarding their humanness or group membership) leads to a larger JSE.

Atmaca et al. (2011) investigated the role of conceptual similarity between two co-actors defined in terms of similarity regarding intentionality. They used a go/nogo version of the Erikson Flanker task (Eriksen and Eriksen, 1974) that participants performed either alone or together with another person responding to the nogo-stimuli of the participant. In the Flanker task, participants respond to a central target letter that is flanked by task irrelevant letters to its left and right side. The flanking letters are either the same as the target letter (e.g., SSSSS, compatible trial) or different (e.g., HHSHH, incompatible trial). Participants showed a larger Flanker effect (i.e., faster responses in compatible than incompatible trials) when performing the go/nogo Flanker task together with another person than when performing the same task alone—a phenomenon known as the joint Flanker effect. When performing the task with a co-actor whose response button was controlled by a computer (unintentional co-actor condition) the Flanker effect was smaller than when performing the task with a co-actor who actively controlled her response button (intentional co-actor condition) (Atmaca et al., 2011, Experiment 4). Atmaca and colleagues suggested that humans only form shared task representations when perceiving another person as acting intentionally. However, recently Dolk et al. (2014) could show that—just like for the JSE—a joint Flanker effect can be induced even if the human co-actor is replaced by an event-producing object (a Japanese waving cat). The logic applied to explain the joint Flanker effect with referential coding goes as follows. As actions are coded on more dimensions in the presence of an event-producing human or object than in its absence, response competition is increased, and hence behavioral effects that rely on response competition (like the Flanker effect) are enhanced.

In line with the findings by Atmaca et al. (2011) other studies have suggested that the intentionality of a co-actor is a key conceptual feature modulating joint action effects with larger effect sizes for intentional than unintentional co-actors (Tsai et al., 2008; Müller et al., 2011b; Stenzel et al., 2012). The concept of intentionality comprises components like belief, desire, intention and awareness (Malle and Knobe, 1997). All of these mental states can be ascribed to other biological agents or technical systems that function according to biologically inspired algorithms, but clearly not to objects. The assumption that joint action effects can only be found for intentional co-actors is at odds with the outlined findings showing emerging Simon or Flanker effects for non-human event-producing objects (Dolk et al., 2011, Experiment 3; Dolk et al., 2013, 2014), and raises doubts in the crucial role of intentionality for joint action. Whereas intentionality, by definition, cannot be ascribed to objects, objects can be identified as the physical cause of an (action) effect (e.g., a ticking metronome is the causal source of peep tones or a Japanese cat the initiator of an arm movement). The process of identifying an agent as the initiator or causal source of an action has been defined as agency (Gallagher, 2000). In the present manuscript, we define the process of perceiving the physical causality between an initiator of an (action) effect and the effect, independently of whether the initiator is a human agent, non-human agent or object as the minimum-criterion of agency. The work of Albert Michotte (1963) suggests that ascribing causality to two events depends on perceptual features. In his famous launching effect, an object (the so called launcher) moves in the direction of another object, stops when making contact with it, whereupon the other object starts to move. Whether the first object is regarded as causing the movement of the second object has been found to depend on different perceptual parameters like the speed with which both objects move, the direction they move, and the time interval between the movement offset of the first object and the movement onset of the second. In light of these findings, and the finding that identifying an agent as the cause of an action effect is particularly likely when action and action effect appear in close temporal proximity (Haggard et al., 2002; Moore and Haggard, 2008), the ascription of agency could critically rely on perceiving the causality between initiator and action effect. For example, identifying a person as the initiator of a button press could rely on seeing how the finger of the person moves down in order to press the button.

In many previous studies that investigated the effects of intentionality on joint action, intentionality and agency were confounded. That is, intentional co-actor's could be clearly perceived as being the initiator of the action effect, while unintentional co-actor's were clearly not the initiator of the action effect. Related to this problem, intentional and unintentional experimental conditions did not only differ in conceptual features (i.e., intentionality), but often also regarding perceptual features. For example, in the study by Atmaca et al. (2011) the response button of the intentional co-actor differed in size, shape, and probably also in sound from the response button of the unintentional co-actor. In both conditions, response buttons were permanently visible to participants while performing the task. An open question is whether intentionality alone, in the absence of agency, can modulate joint action effects like the JSE.

In the present study, we aimed to disentangle the role of intentionality and agency in modulating the JSE. Further, we controlled for differences in perceptual features between manipulations of intentionality. In Experiment 1, we aimed to replicate the findings of Atmaca et al. (2011) for the joint go/nogo Simon effect while controlling for perceptual differences between conditions during task performance. We compared JSEs between a condition in which the co-actor intentionally controlled a response button and could be perceived to be the agent of the action (agency+/intentionality+ condition) and a condition in which the co-actor acted unintentionally and was clearly not the agent of the action, because the co-actor's hand rested on a response button that passively moved up and down on its own as triggered by the computer, so that the physical causality between the co-actor and the button movement was clearly disrupted (agency−/intentionality− condition). During the experiment, we controlled for perceptual differences (visual and auditory action effects) between both conditions by using boxes covering the hands of both persons and letting persons wear earplugs. In Experiment 2, we again included a control condition in which the co-actor acted unintentionally and was not the agent of the computer controlled button press (agency−/intentionality− condition). Performance in this condition was compared to a condition in which the co-actor was believed to control the response button with a Brain-Computer Interface (BCI) instead of manual responses, so that the co-actor could be regarded as intentionally controlling the response button, but the causal relationship between co-actor and action effect could not be perceived (agency−/intentionality+).

For Experiment 1, agency and intentionality make similar predictions. This would be a conceptual replication of the findings of Atmaca et al. (2011) for the JSE ($JSE_{agency+/intentionality+} > JSE_{agency-/intentionality-}$). For Experiment 2, the predictions do crucially differ for intentionality and agency. If the co-actor's intentionality is the underlying source for modulating joint action effects, we predicted a larger JSE when the co-actor acts intentionally than when the co-actor does not act intentionally ($JSE_{agency-/intentionality+} > JSE_{agency-/intentionality-}$). If, however, agency is the modulating factor of the JSE, we expect no differences in JSEs between conditions ($JSE_{agency-/intentionality+} = JSE_{agency-/intentionality-}$).

EXPERIMENT 1

The aim of Experiment 1 was to investigate whether a co-actor's agency and intentionality modulate the size of the JSE. Different from Atmaca et al. (2011), we controlled for perceptual differences between experimental conditions while participants were performing the task. Participants performed a joint go/nogo Simon task with a co-actor who either actively controlled a response button and could clearly be perceived as the agent of the button press (agency+/intentionality+ condition) or whose response button was controlled by the computer so that the co-actor was not the agent of the button press (agency−/intentionality− condition). We expected a larger JSE in the agency+/intentionality+ condition than in the agency−/intentionality− condition.

METHODS

Participants

A total of 32 healthy volunteers participated in Experiment 1. Sixteen participants were randomly assigned to the agency+/intentionality+ condition (15 female, mean age = 23.3 years, $SD = 4.8$ years) and 16 participants to the agency−/intentionality− condition (12 female, mean age = 21.7 years, $SD = 2.8$ years). All participants were right-handed, had normal or corrected-to-normal vision, were naive with regard to the hypothesis of the experiment, and received compensation for their participation.

Stimuli and apparatus

As stimuli we used a white square and a white diamond (2.2 × 2.2°, horizontal × vertical visual angle) on a black background, which were presented 5.4° to the left or right of a centrally presented white fixation cross (0.9 × 0.9°). All stimuli were displayed on an 18-inch CRT monitor at a viewing distance of approximately 60 cm.

For the agency+/intentionality+ condition we used two conventional response keys (one for the participant and the other for the co-actor). For the agency−/intentionality− condition we used one conventional response key for the participant and one response key that could be moved up and down by a trigger signal from the computer for the co-actor. Both response keys were placed 5 cm in front of the monitor and 27 cm from the midline of the monitor.

Task and procedure

The participant was always seated on the left side of the monitor and the co-actor (a confederate) on the right side (**Figure 1**). Both persons were asked to place their right index finger on the response button in front of them. The participant responded to the square, whereas the co-actor responded to the diamond. Participants either performed the task with a co-actor who actively controlled the response button (agency+/intentionality+ condition) or with a co-actor whose response button was controlled by the computer via trigger signals (agency−/intentionality− condition) (**Figure 1**). In the latter condition, the co-actor passively placed her index finger on the response button, which was automatically pulled down every time it was the co-actor's turn to respond. The response latency of the computer controlled response button varied randomly between 280, 320, and 360 ms. The participant actively controlled his/her response button in both conditions. Participants were randomly assigned to conditions.

As the conventional and the computer controlled response button differed in size and shape, response keys were covered with black boxes before the experimental task started to control for visual differences between both conditions during task performance (**Figure 1**). In addition, the participant and the co-actor wore earplugs in both conditions in order to control for the different sounds of the conventional and the computer controlled response key.

The instruction given to the co-actor was audible to participants in both conditions. In the agency+/intentionality+ condition, the instruction for the co-actor was to press the response button whenever a diamond appeared on the screen. In the agency−/intentionality− condition, the co-actor was instructed to position her response finger on the response button located in front of her. The co-actor was informed that the stimulus computer sent a trigger signal to start the movement of the button whenever a diamond appeared thereby controlling the response button. To familiarize participants with the task, the experiment started with a short instruction phase including the presentation of the two stimuli, their assignment to both actors, as well as the presentation of the conventional and the computer controlled response key. For the practice phase, the box that covered the hands during the experiment was removed so that the participant

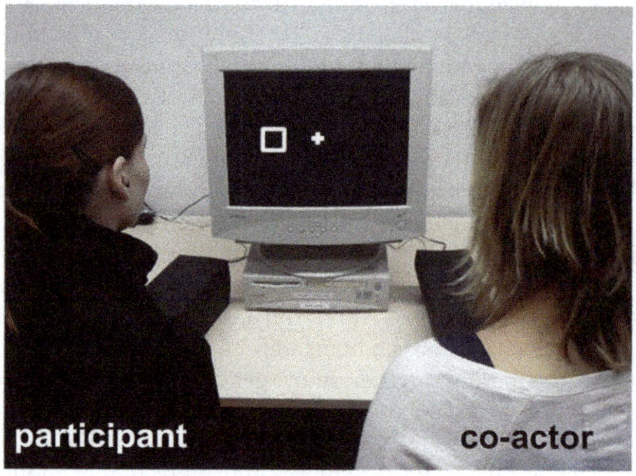

FIGURE 1 | Experimental setup used in Experiment 1. The participant (sitting on the left side of the monitor) shared a joint go/nogo Simon task with a co-actor (confederate) who either intentionally controlled a response button, and could be perceived as the initiator of the button press (agency+/intentionality+ condition) or whose response button was controlled by the computer so that the co-actor was not the initiator of the button press and did not respond intentionally (agency−/intentionality− condition). Perceptual differences between the response button of the actively responding co-actor and the computer controlled response button were controlled for during task performance by covering response hands and letting both persons wear earplugs, so that the setup shown on the picture applies to both, the agency+/intentionality+ and the agency−/intentionality− condition.

could clearly see that the co-actor actively responded in the agency+/intentionality+ condition, whereas the response button moved on its own when receiving a signal from the computer in the agency−/intentionality− condition.

There were two blocks of 64 trials separated by short breaks of 2 min. The two target stimuli appeared equally often in the left and right location which resulted in a total of 32 Stimulus-Response (S-R) compatible trials and 32 S-R incompatible trials for each person. The order of trials was randomized. Each trial began with the presentation of the fixation cross for 1000 ms. Afterwards the target stimulus was displayed together with the fixation cross for 150 ms. The response had to be given within a time interval of 1800 ms following stimulus offset during which the fixation cross was displayed. Following a response, feedback about the accuracy was provided for 300 ms: correct responses were followed by the fixation cross, incorrect responses by the word "Fehler" (error), and too slow responses by "zu langsam" (too slow). In the inter-trial-interval the fixation cross was displayed for 1000 ms.

As a manipulation check verifying that there is a difference between both conditions regarding the intentionality attributed to the co-actor, participants rated the items "The other person acted intentionally" (Item 1) and "The other person decided actively when to respond to a stimulus" (Item 2) after the experiment. Both items were rated on a five-point Likert scale ranging from 0 (= I strongly disagree) to 4 (= I strongly agree) with 2 indicating neither agreement nor disagreement. Participants in the agency+/intentionality+ condition showed significantly higher mean rating scores for both items than participants in the agency−/intentionality− condition [Item 1: 2.4 vs. 0.8, $t_{(30)} = 3.64$, $p = 0.001$; Item 2: 3.1 vs. 0.7, $t_{(30)} = 7.24$, $p < 0.0001$].

RESULTS

In accordance with previous studies (Röder et al., 2007; Liepelt et al., 2011), we excluded all trials in which responses were incorrect (1.5%), faster than 150 ms or slower than 1000 ms (0%) prior to the statistical analysis of reaction times (RTs). Responses were coded as compatible (stimulus ipsilateral to the correct response side) or incompatible (stimulus contralateral to the correct response side). We calculated a repeated measures analysis of variance (ANOVA) for RTs and errors with the within-subjects factor compatibility (compatible, incompatible) and the between-subjects factor condition (agency+/intentionality+, agency−/intentionality−). The JSE was calculated by subtracting mean RTs in compatible trials from mean RTs in incompatible trials. Additionally, we calculated Bayesian probabilities associated with the occurrence of the null (H_0) and alternative (H_1) hypotheses, given the observed data (see Wagenmakers, 2007; Masson, 2011). This method allows making inferences about both significant and non-significant effects by providing the exact probability of their occurrence, with values ranging from 0 (i.e., no evidence) to 1 (i.e., very strong evidence; see Raftery, 1995 for a coarse classification).

Reaction times

The 2 × 2 ANOVA revealed a significant main effect of compatibility, $F_{(1, 30)} = 14.22$, $p = 0.001$, partial $\eta^2 = 0.32$, $p(H_1|D) > 0.99$, indicating faster responses for S-R compatible trials (352 ms) than incompatible trials (361 ms). More importantly, the compatibility effect differed for the two conditions as indicated by a significant interaction of compatibility and condition, $F_{(1, 30)} = 6.55$, $p = 0.02$, partial $\eta^2 = 0.18$, $p(H_1|D) = 0.99$. Newman-Keuls *post-hoc* analyses revealed that the difference between compatible and incompatible trials was significant in the agency+/intentionality+ condition (16 ms, $p < 0.001$, $d = 0.93$) but not in the agency-/intentionality- condition (3 ms, $p = 0.40$, $d = 0.29$) (**Figure 2**). There was no significant main effect of condition, $F_{(1,30)} < 1$, $p = 0.96$, partial $\eta^2 < 0.001$, $p(H_0|D) = 0.85$.

Error rates

The main effects of compatibility, $F_{(1, 30)} < 1$, $p = 0.90$, partial $\eta^2 = 0.001$, $p(H_0|D) = 0.85$, and condition, $F_{(1, 30)} < 1$, $p = 0.68$, partial $\eta^2 = 0.006$, $p(H_0|D) = 0.84$, as well as the interaction of compatibility and condition, $F_{(1, 30)} = 1.40$, $p = 0.25$, partial $\eta^2 = 0.04$, $p(H_0|D) = 0.73$, were not significant.

DISCUSSION

In Experiment 1, we observed a significant JSE when interacting with a co-actor who actively controlled the response button (agency+/intentionality+ condition), but found no significant JSE when the co-actor's response button was controlled by the computer (agency−/intentionality− condition). The JSE in the agency+/intentionality+ condition was significantly enlarged as compared to the agency−/intentionality− condition, conceptually replicating the findings of Atmaca et al. (2011) for the joint go/nogo Simon effect. So, even in the absence of perceptual differences between co-acting agents, past perception of physical causality between co-actor and action effect and/or the ascription of intentionality to the co-actor appear to be sufficient in modulating the size of the JSE. Given that intentionality and agency were clearly confounded in this experiment, in a second experiment we aimed at separating both aspects by varying the co-actor's intentionally between conditions while keeping the physical causality between co-actor and action effect constant.

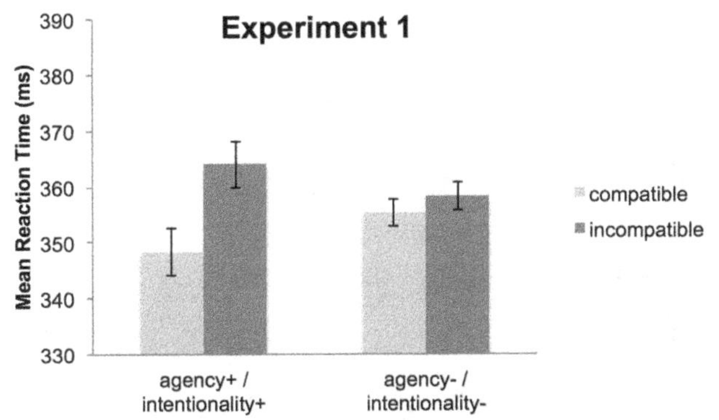

FIGURE 2 | Mean reaction times for Experiment 1. Depicted are compatible (light gray) and incompatible (dark gray) trials for the agency+/intentionality+ condition (left panel) and the agency−/intentionality− condition (right panel). Error bars represent standard errors of the mean differences (Pfister and Janczyk, 2013).

EXPERIMENT 2

The aim of Experiment 2 was to disentangle the effects of intentionality and agency on the JSE. We included a condition, in which the co-actor was believed to intentionally control the response button, but the causal relationship between agent and action effect could not be perceived, so that physical causality was disrupted (agency−/intentionality+ condition). In this condition, the co-actor was equipped with a cap used to measure electroencephalography (EEG) activity including two electrodes over the motor cortex. Participants were made to believe that the co-actor controlled the response button via a BCI by generating motor potentials whenever it was the co-actor's turn to respond. We again compared the size of the JSE in this condition to a condition in which the co-actor passively placed her finger on a computer controlled response button (agency−/intentionality− condition). In this condition, participants were told that the co-actor was wearing an EEG cap in order to measure electrical potentials in a motor observation task. To fully eliminate any perceptual differences between the agency−/intentionality+ and the agency−/intentionality− condition, the co-actor's response button was identical for both conditions (see **Figure 3**, co-actor side), so that only the belief about the co-actor's intentionality differed between conditions.

If the co-actor's intentionality modulated the size of the JSE in the previous experiment, we would expect a similar response time pattern as in Experiment 1 with a larger JSE when the co-actor acts intentionally than when acting unintentionally

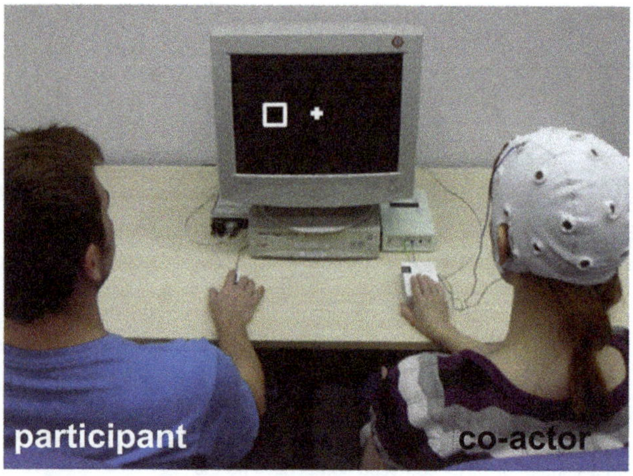

FIGURE 3 | Experimental setup used in Experiment 2. The participant (left side) shared a joint go/nogo Simon task with a co-actor (confederate, right side) wearing an EEG cap with electrodes attached to the motor cortex, and placing the finger underneath the moving part of a response device. The participant was either told that the confederate intentionally controlled the response button via a BCI so that the causal relationship between co-actor and action effect was not perceivable (agency−/intentionality+ condition) or that the response button was controlled by the computer (agency−/intentionality− condition). As the same response button was used for the co-actor in the agency−/intentionality+ and the agency−/intentionality− condition, the setup shown on the picture applies to both conditions.

($JSE_{agency-/intentionality+} > JSE_{agency-/intentionality-}$). If, however, the modulation of the JSE in Experiment 1 was driven by agency, we expect JSEs of comparable size in both conditions ($JSE_{agency-/intentionality+} = JSE_{agency-/intentionality-}$).

METHOD

Participants

Thirty-two new healthy volunteers participated in Experiment 2. Sixteen participants were assigned to the agency−/intentionality+ condition (13 female, mean age = 23.5 years, $SD = 3.7$ years) and 16 to the agency−/intentionality− condition (12 female, mean age = 23.9 years, $SD = 2.3$ years). All participants fulfilled the same criteria as participants in Experiment 1 and were treated in the same way.

Stimuli and apparatus

Stimuli and apparatus were the same as in Experiment 1. The co-actor (a confederate) wore an EEG cap equipped with one electrode over the left and one over the right motor cortex (**Figure 3**). The cable of the electrodes was connected to a box placed on the right side of the monitor (**Figure 3**). Participants were told that this box was connected to the stimulus computer, analyzing the electrical signals measured over the motor cortex.

Task and procedure

Task and procedure were the same as in Experiment 1 with the following exceptions concerning the co-actor. In both, the agency−/intentionality+ and agency−/intentionality− condition, the computer controlled response button was placed in front of the co-actor, and the co-actor passively placed her right hand on the response device (**Figure 3**). Note that in both conditions the finger of the co-actor was positioned about 2 cm below the moving part of the response device (**Figure 3**) in order to avoid any movements of the co-actor's finger which could have led to the false assumption that the co-actor was controlling the response button by finger movements. As the agency−/intentionality+ and the agency−/intentionality− condition were therefore perceptually identical, the left and the right response button were visible during the entire experiment. To manipulate the agency of the co-actor, we used a belief manipulation: in the agency−/intentionality+ condition, participants were told that the co-actor controlled the response button via a BCI. They were told that the co-actor had undergone multiple training sessions to be able to generate motor potentials by imagining a button press with the right index finger. Whenever these motor potentials measured over the motor cortex exceeded a certain threshold, a signal was sent to the response device as a starting signal to move. Hence, participants were led to believe that the co-actor intentionally controlled the response device via brain signals, but the physical causality between co-actor and action effect could not be perceived as the co-actor's finger was clearly placed below the response button on the response device. In the agency−/intentionality− condition, participants were told that the computer controlled the response button. As a cover story to explain why the co-actor wore an EEG cap during in the agency−/intentionality− condition, we explained that the study was about action observation of human and non-human actions, and that the goal of the study was to compare motor potentials elicited by the observation of a human response (the button press of the participant) to those elicited by the observation of a non-human response (the computer controlled response device). In both conditions, the experimenter presented pictures while instructing in order to support the belief manipulation. In the agency−/intentionality+ condition, participants were shown a schematic illustration of the BCI principle and a picture of a child using a BCI to operate a cursor on a monitor. In the agency−/intentionality− condition, the participant and the co-actor were shown a schematic illustration of an electrode over the cortex to explain the principle of measuring evoked potentials. In addition, a picture was shown in which a man equipped with an EEG cap observed a picture of a hand posture. Actually, in both conditions the response button was controlled by the computer.

We used the same manipulation check as in Experiment 1. Participants in the agency−/intentionality+ condition showed significantly higher rating scores for both items than participants in the agency−/intentionality− condition [Item 1: 2.3 vs. 0.8, $t_{(30)} = 3.22$, $p = 0.003$; Item 2: 2.6 vs. 0.8, $t_{(30)} = 3.75$, $p = 0.001$] indicating that the belief manipulation was successful.

RESULTS

For the statistical analyses of RTs, we again excluded all trials in which responses were incorrect (0.9%), faster than 150 ms or slower than 1000 ms (0%). We calculated a repeated measure ANOVA for RTs and errors with the within-subjects factor compatibility (compatible, incompatible) and

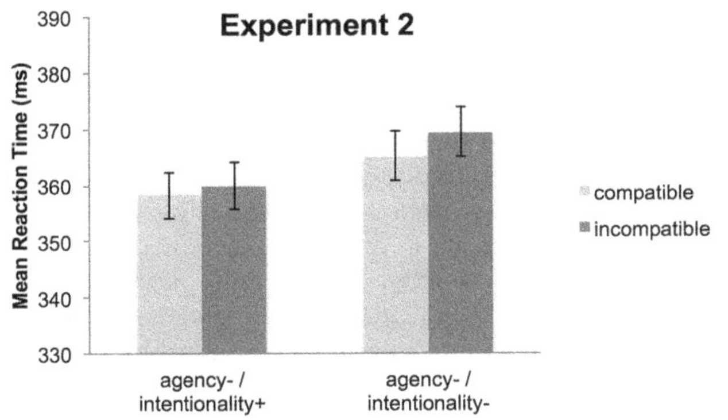

FIGURE 4 | Mean reaction times for Experiment 2. Depicted are compatible (light gray) and incompatible (dark gray) trials for the agency−/intentionality+ condition (left panel) and the agency−/intentionality− condition (right panel). Error bars represent standard errors of the mean differences (Pfister and Janczyk, 2013).

the between-subjects factor condition (agency−/intentionality+, agency−/intentionality−). As in Experiment 1, Bayesian probabilities associated with the occurrence of H_0 and H_1 were calculated.

Reaction times

The main effect of compatibility was not significant, $F_{(1, 30)} < 1$, $p = 0.33$, partial $\eta^2 = 0.03$, $p(H_0|D) = 0.77$, indicating comparable response times for S-R compatible trials (362 ms) and incompatible trials (365 ms) (**Figure 4**). The main effect of condition, $F_{(1, 30)} < 1$, $p = 0.54$, partial $\eta^2 = 0.01$, $p(H_0|D) = 0.82$, as well as the interaction between compatibility and condition, $F_{(1, 30)} < 1$, $p = 0.69$, partial $\eta^2 = 0.006$, $p(H_0|D) = 0.84$, were not significant.

Error rates

The main effect of compatibility, $F_{(1, 30)} = 4.2$, $p = 0.049$, partial $\eta^2 = 0.12$, but $p(H_1|D) = 0.60$, was significant indicating fewer errors for compatible (0.6%) than incompatible trials (1.3%). The main effect of condition, $F_{(1, 30)} < 1$, $p = 0.78$, partial $\eta^2 = 0.003$, $p(H_0|D) = 0.84$, as well as the interaction of compatibility and condition, $F_{(1, 30)} < 1$, $p = 0.77$, partial $\eta^2 = 0.003$, $p(H_0|D) = 0.84$, were not significant.

DISCUSSION

In line with the results from Experiment 1, no JSE was observed when participants assumed that the co-actor's response button was controlled by the computer (agency−/intentionality− condition). Importantly and different from Experiment 1, no JSE was induced by the co-actor who intentionally controlled her response button via a BCI, but the causal relationship between agent and action effects could not be perceived. As the results of the post-experimental ratings suggest that our belief manipulation was successful (i.e., participants stated that the co-actor acted intentionally in the agency−/intentionality+ condition), we conclude that agency—perceiving the co-actor as being the causal source of an action effect—seems to be a critical factor for the JSE.

GENERAL DISCUSSION

In the present study, we aimed to disentangle the role of agency and intentionality for the JSE. Whereas differences in intentionality were confounded with differences in agency in previous studies (e.g., Tsai and Brass, 2007; Atmaca et al., 2011), we aimed to solely test the effects of intentionality on joint action.

In Experiment 1, actively responding participants performed a joint go/nogo Simon task with a co-actor who responded actively or a co-actor whose response button was controlled by the computer. While controlling for perceptual differences between both conditions during task performance, participants had the opportunity to clearly perceive how the response button was controlled in each condition prior to task performance. When the participant and the co-actor both acted intentionally and physical causality could be perceived the JSE was highly significant, whereas no JSE was observed when the co-actor did not respond intentionally and physical causality was disrupted. In Experiment 2, we again included a condition in which the co-actor's response button was controlled by the computer, and the co-actor clearly was not the agent of the action effect. Performance in this condition was compared to a condition in which the co-actor controlled the response button intentionally via a BCI placing the response finger clearly below the button, so that the physical causality between co-actor and action effect was disrupted. In line with Experiment 1, we observed no JSE when the co-actor was believed to respond unintentionally and was not the agent of the button press (agency−/intentionality− condition). However, different from Experiment 1 no JSE was found for the intentional co-actor when participants did not perceive that the co-actor caused the button press, even though post-experimental questionnaires indicated that the co-actor was believed to intentionally control the response button via the BCI. These results suggest that perceiving the co-actor at least once as being the causal source of responses seems to be a necessary prerequisite for the emergence of a JSE in a real (vis-à-vis) interaction, and point to the co-actor's agency as a modulating factor for joint action effects. Intentionality alone does not seem to be sufficient to induce a JSE. Only when physical causality between co-actor and action effect can be perceived, a JSE seems to be observed.

In the present study, we did not include a condition in which the co-actor was the causal source of action effects, but acted unintentionally (i.e., a agency+/intentionality− condition). However, this condition has already been tested in previous studies using different event-producing objects that replaced the co-actor in joint action tasks (e.g., Dolk et al., 2011, 2013, 2014). By definition, intentionality cannot be ascribed to objects, but the objects used in these studies were the causal source of the respective (action) effects (e.g., the tone originated from the metronome), so physical causality between object and action effect was clearly present. Under these conditions a JSE has consistently been found, suggesting that agency can induce a JSE in the absence of intentionality.

Our findings are in line with the referential coding account (Dolk et al., 2011, 2013) predicting that a higher similarity (conceptual and perceptual) between alternative action events should lead to a larger JSE. When the participant's and the co-actor's action events were highly similar with regards to their conceptual features (i.e., both actors responded intentionally) and perceptual features (i.e., physical causality could be perceived for both actors) the JSE was highly significant, whereas no JSE was observed when both persons were dissimilar (i.e., the participant still acted intentionally and physically caused the action effect, but the co-actor acted unintentionally and physical causality was disrupted). A higher similarity between the action events of both actors induced a (stronger) discrimination problem, which could be resolved by emphasizing spatial action features leading to a JSE. In contrast, the need to emphasize discriminable action features seemed to be weaker and cognitively less demanding when the action features of the co-actor were clearly distinct. Interestingly, conceptual features alone (i.e., intentionality) did not induce a JSE, whereas similarity regarding perceptual features (i.e., visible physical causality) seems to be sufficient to induce a JSE (Dolk et al., 2011, 2013).

A study by Stenzel et al. (2012) compared the size of the JSE in a joint Simon task shared with a robot that was believed to function in a human-like way to a task shared with a robot believed to be controlled by the stimulus computer, and thus to function like a machine. In line with the present results, a JSE was present for the human-like robot which was believed to respond intentionally (i.e., the decision to respond was calculated by a neural network integrated in the robot's body on the basis of visual information recorded by the robot's cameras), and for which agency was clearly present (i.e., participants could see how the robot moved its finger down to press the response button). In contrast, for the machine-like robot, to which intentionality could not be ascribed (i.e., participants believed that responses were controlled by a fixed sequence of trigger signals originating from the stimulus computer, which was located outside of the robotic agent), no JSE was observed. As the machine-like robot condition was perceptually identical to the human-like robot condition, participants could see how the finger of the machine-like robot moved down to press the button, so that—based solely on these visual information—agency could also be attributed to the machine-like robot, and hence a JSE should have been observed. However, due to the belief manipulation used in the robot study the causal source of the action was spatially shifted away from the machine-like robot to the stimulus computer, which was located outside of the robot, so that based on this knowledge the robot could not be regarded as the causal source of the action. That is, the verbal instruction given to the participant disrupted the physical causality between robot and action effect, which could explain why no JSE was observed for this robot. From the perspective of the present findings, the finding of a JSE for the human-like robot may be better interpreted as the result of an interplay between intentionality and agency, and not solely on intentionality.

An interesting question for future research is whether gaining experience with a BCI would lead to a JSE in an agency−/intentionality+ condition like the one used in Experiment 2. As most people are currently not experienced in using BCIs, it might be rather difficult to get a notion of how a person using a BCI accomplishes it to control a response device solely based on the information provided by the experimenter. This might be especially hard because of two reasons. First, the ascription of physical causality seems to be strongly perceptually grounded (Michotte, 1963), so that the ascription of agency might be hard when the causality between agent and action effect cannot be perceived. Second, for human actors with whom we usually interact on a daily basis from very early age on, and on the basis of being humans ourselves, we had the opportunity to develop a fixed notion about how humans usually control actions, so that it might be difficult to get rid of this notion and develop a new understanding of action control using newly developed methods such as BCI. If participants would gain more experience in using BCIs themselves, i.e., gaining perceptual experience in controlling a given device with brain signals, knowing about the physical causality of such action-effect relations may foster recognizing a person using a BCI as being the initiator of action effects even in the absence of any directly perceived causality. This in turn might induce a JSE in a BCI condition like the one used in Experiment 2.

Based on the present findings we would argue that the concept of agency might be better suited than the concept of intentionality to explain the modulatory findings of the JSE in the previous study and potentially in previous studies using human co-actors (e.g., Sebanz et al., 2003, 2005; Vlainic et al., 2010; Liepelt et al., 2011), non-human co-actors (Müller et al., 2011b; Stenzel et al., 2012), and objects (Dolk et al., 2011, Experiment 3; Dolk et al., 2013, 2014). In contrast to intentionality, the attribution of agency—identifying the causal source of an (action) effect—can be applied to biological agents as well as to non-biological agents and objects (Pickering, 1995). As long as a human, a robot or an object is the causal source of an (action) effect and this causal relationship is clearly perceivable, and not otherwise disrupted by instruction, a joint action effect can be observed. Of course this is not to say that agency is the only modulating factor of joint action effects. Other factors that surely determine the size of the JSE refer to the degree of similarity on a perceptual level between the participant's and the co-actor's action effects (Sellaro et al., under revision) or the degree of similarity on more abstract levels like the personal relationship between both actors (Hommel et al., 2009).

Taken together, the results of the present study suggest that a co-actor's agency has a reliable influence on the joint go/nogo Simon effect. Further, our results suggest that in order to ascribe agency to an initiator of action effects, the causal relationship between the initiator and the action effect must be perceived (Michotte, 1963) suggesting a perceptual grounding of physical causality ascription.

AUTHOR CONTRIBUTIONS

Roman Liepelt, Anna Stenzel, and Bernhard Hommel contributed to the conception and design of the work. Anna Stenzel and Roberta Sellaro analyzed the data. Roman Liepelt, Anna Stenzel, Thomas Dolk, Lorenza S. Colzato, Roberta Sellaro, and Bernhard Hommel contributed to the interpretation of the work. Anna Stenzel and Roman Liepelt wrote the initial draft of the manuscript, which was critically revised by Roberta Sellaro, Thomas Dolk, Lorenza S. Colzato, and Bernhard Hommel. All authors approved the final version of the manuscript and are fully accountable for all aspects of the work.

ACKNOWLEDGMENTS

This study was supported by the German Research Foundation grants DFG LI 2115/1-1; 1-3 awarded to Roman Liepelt, and the Open Access Publication Fund of the University of Muenster. The authors would like to thank Benedikt Liesbrock for help with data acquisition.

REFERENCES

Atmaca, S., Sebanz, N., and Knoblich, G. (2011). The joint Flanker effect: sharing tasks with real and imagined co-actors. *Exp. Brain Res.* 211, 371–385. doi: 10.1007/s00221-011-2709-9

Colzato, L. S., de Bruijn, E., and Hommel, B. (2012). Up to "me" or up to "us"? The impact of self-construal priming on cognitive self-other integration. *Front. Psychol.* 3:341. doi: 10.3389/fpsyg.2012.00341

Colzato, L. S., van den Wildenberg, W., and Hommel, B. (2013). Increasing self-other integration through divergent thinking. *Psychon. Bull. Rev.* 20, 1011–1016. doi: 10.3758/s13423-013-0413-4

Dittrich, K., Dolk, T., Rothe-Wulf, A., Klauer, K. C., and Prinz, W. (2013). Keys and seats: spatial response coding underlying the joint spatial compatibility effect. *Atten. Percept. Psychol.* 75, 1725–1736. doi: 10.3758/s13414-013-0524-z

Dittrich, K., Rothe, A., and Klauer, K. C. (2012). Increased spatial salience in the social Simon task: a response-coding account of spatial compatibility effects. *Atten. Percept. Psycho.* 74, 911–929. doi: 10.3758/s13414-012-0304-1

Dolk, T., Hommel, B., Colzato, L. S., Schütz-Bosbach, S., Prinz, W., and Liepelt, R. (2011). How social is the social Simon effect? *Front. Psychol.* 2:84. doi: 10.3389/fpsyg.2011.00084

Dolk, T., Hommel, B., Prinz, W., and Liepelt, R. (2013). The (not so) Social Simon effect: a referential coding account. *J. Exp. Psychol. Hum.* 39, 1248–1260. doi: 10.1037/a0031031

Dolk, T., Hommel, B., Prinz, W., and Liepelt, R. (2014). The joint flanker effect: less social than previously thought. *Psychon. Bull. Rev.* doi: 10.3758/s13423-014-0583-8. [Epub ahead of print].

Eriksen, B. A., and Eriksen, C. W. (1974). Effects of noise letters upon the identification of a target letter in a nonsearch task. *Percept. Psychophys.* 16, 143–149. doi: 10.3758/BF03203267

Gallagher, S. (2000). Philosophical conceptions of the self: implications for cognitive science. *Trends Cogn. Sci.* 4, 14–21. doi: 10.1016/S1364-6613(99)01417-5

Guagnano, D., Rusconi, E., and Umiltà, C. A. (2010). Sharing a task or sharing space? On the effect of the confederate in action coding in a detection task. *Cognition* 114, 348–355. doi: 10.1016/j.cognition.2009.10.008

Guagnano, G., Rusconi, E., and Umiltà, C. (2013). Joint (mis-)representations: a reply to Welsh et al. *J. Motor Behav.* 45, 7–8. doi: 10.1080/00222895.2012.752688

Haggard, P., Aschersleben, G., Gehrke, J., and Prinz, W. (2002). "Awareness, binding and causation," in *Attention and Performance: Common Mechanisms in Perception and Action*, ed W. Prinz and B. Hommel (Oxford: Oxford University Press), 266–285.

Hommel, B. (1996). S-R compatibility effects without response uncertainty. *Q. J. Exp. Psychol.* 49, 546–571. doi: 10.1080/713755643

Hommel, B. (2011). The Simon effect as tool and heuristic. *Acta Psychol.* 136, 189–202. doi: 10.1016/j.actpsy.2010.04.011

Hommel, B. (2013). "Ideomotor action control: on the perceptual grounding of voluntary actions and agents," in *Action science: Foundations of an emerging discipline*, ed W. Prinz, M. Beisert, and A. Herwig (Cambridge, MA: MIT Press), 113–136.

Hommel, B., Colzato, L. S., and van den Wildenberg, W. P. M. (2009). How social are task representations. *Psychol. Sci.* 20, 794–798. doi: 10.1111/j.1467-9280.2009.02367.x

Hommel, B., Müsseler, J., Aschersleben, G., and Prinz, W. (2001). The theory of event coding (TEC): a framework for perception and action planning. *Behav. Brain Sci.* 24, 849–878. doi: 10.1017/S0140525X01000103

Knoblich, G., and Sebanz, N. (2006). The social nature of perception and action. *Curr. Dir. Psychol. Sci.* 15, 99–104. doi: 10.1111/j.0963-7214.2006.00415.x

Kornblum, S., Hasbroucq, T., and Osman, A. (1990). Dimensional overlap: cognitive basis for stimulus-response compatibility-A model and taxonomy. *Psychol. Rev.* 97, 253–270. doi: 10.1037/0033-295X.97.2.253

Liepelt, R., and Prinz, W. (2011). How two share two tasks: evidence of a Social Psychological Refractory Period effect. *Exp. Brain Res.* 211, 387–396. doi: 10.1007/s00221-011-2703-2

Liepelt, R., Schneider, J. C., Aichert, D., Wöstmann, N., Dehning, S., Möller, H. J., et al. (2012). Action blind: disturbed self-other integration in schizophrenia. *Neuropsychologia* 50, 3775–3780. doi: 10.1016/j.neuropsychologia.2012.10.027

Liepelt, R., Wenke, D., and Fischer, R. (2013). Effects of feature integration in a hands-crossed version of the social simon paradigm. *Psychol. Res.* 77, 240–248. doi: 10.1007/s00426-012-0425-0

Liepelt, R., Wenke, D., Fischer, R., and Prinz, W. (2011). Trial-to-trial sequential dependencies in a social and non-social Simon task. *Psychol. Res.* 75, 366–375. doi: 10.1007/s00426-010-0314-3

Malle, B. F., and Knobe, J. (1997). The folk concept of intentionality. *J. Exp. Soc. Psychol.* 33, 101–121. doi: 10.1006/jesp.1996.1314

Masson, M. E. J. (2011). A tutorial on a practical Bayesian alternative to null hypothesis significance testing. *Behav. Res. Methods* 43, 679–690. doi: 10.3758/s13428-010-0049-5

Michotte, A. (1963). *The Perception of Causality.* London: Methuen.

Moore, J., and Haggard, P. (2008). Awareness of action: inference and prediction. *Conscious. Cogn.* 17, 136–144. doi: 10.1016/j.concog.2006.12.004

Müller, B. C. N., Brass, M., Kühn, S., Tsai, C. C., Nieuwboer, W., Dijksterhuis, A., et al. (2011b). When Pinocchio acts like a human, a wooden hand becomes embodied. Action co-representation for non-biological agents. *Neuropsychologia* 49, 1373–1377. doi: 10.1016/j.neuropsychologia.2011.01.022

Müller, B. C. N., Kühn, S., van Baaren, R. B., Dotsch, R., Brass, M., and Dijksterhuis, A. (2011a). Perspective taking eliminates differences in co-representation of out-group members' actions. *Exp. Brain Res.* 211, 423–428. doi: 10.1007/s00221-011-2654-7

Pfister, R., and Janczyk, M. (2013). Confidence intervals for two sample means: calculation, interpretation, and a few simple rules. *Adv. Cogn. Psychol.* 9, 74–80. doi: 10.5709/acp-0133-x

Pickering, A. (1995). *The Mangle of Practice.* Chicago, University of Chicago Press.

Prinz, W. (1997). Perception and action planning. *Eur. J. Cogn. Psychol.* 9, 129–154. doi: 10.1080/713752551

Prinz, W. (2012). *Open Minds: The Social Making of Agency and Intentionality.* Cambridge, MA: MIT Press.

Raftery, A. E. (1995). "Bayesian model selection in social research," in *Sociological Methodology*, ed P. V. Marsden (Cambridge: Blackwell), 111–196.

Röder, B., Kusmierek, A., Spence, C., and Schicke, T. (2007). Developmental vision determines the reference frame for the multisensory control of action. *Proc. Natl. Acad. Sci. U.S.A.* 104, 4753–4758. doi: 10.1073/pnas.0607158104

Sebanz, N., Knoblich, G., and Prinz, W. (2003). Representing others' actions: just like one's own? *Cognition* 88, B11–B21. doi: 10.1016/S0010-0277(03)00043-X

Sebanz, N., Knoblich, G., and Prinz, W. (2005). How two share a task: co-representing stimulus-response mappings. *J. Exp. Psychol. Hum.* 33, 1234–1246. doi: 10.1037/0096-1523.31.6.1234

Sellaro, R., Treccani, B., Rubichi, S., and Cubelli, R. (2013). When co-action eliminates the Simon effect: disentangling the impact of co-actor's presence and task sharing on joint-task performance. *Front. Psychol.* 4:844. doi: 10.3389/fpsyg.2013.00844

Simon, J. R. (1969). Reactions towards the source of stimulation. *J. Exp. Psychol.* 81, 174–176. doi: 10.1037/h0027448

Simon, J. R. (1990). "The effects of an irrelevant directional cue on human information processing," in *Stimulus-response Compatibility*, ed R. W. Proctor and T. G. Reeve (New York, NY: North-Holland), 31–86.

Simon, J. R., and Rudell, A. P. (1967). Auditory S-R compatibility: the effect of an irrelevant cue on information processing. *J. Appl. Psychol.* 51, 300–304. doi: 10.1037/h0020586

Stenzel, A., Chinellato, E., Tirado Bou, M. A., del Pobil, Á. P., Lappe, M., and Liepelt, R. (2012). When humanoid robots become human-like interaction partners: co-representation of robotic actions. *J. Exp. Psychol. Hum.* 38, 1073–1077. doi: 10.1037/a0029493

Tsai, C. C., and Brass, M. (2007). Does the human motor system simulate Pinocchio's actions? Coacting with a human hand versus a wooden hand in a dyadic interaction. *Psychol. Sci.* 18, 1058–1062. doi: 10.1111/j.1467-9280.2007.02025.x

Tsai, C. C., Kuo, W. J., Hung, D. L., and Tzeng, O. J. (2008). Action co-representation is tuned to other humans. *J. Cogn. Neurosci.* 20, 2015–2024. doi: 10.1162/jocn.2008.20144

Vlainic, E., Liepelt, R., Colzato, L. S., Prinz, W., and Hommel, B. (2010). The virtual co-actor: the Social Simon effect does not rely on online feedback from the other. *Front. Psychol.* 1:208. doi: 10.3389/fpsyg.2010.00208

Wagenmakers, E.-J. (2007). A practical solution to the pervasive problems of p values. *Psychon. Bull. Rev.* 14, 779–804. doi: 10.3758/BF03194105

Welsh, T., Kiernan, D., Neyedli, H., Ray, M., Pratt, J., Potruff, A., et al. (2013a). Joint Simon effects in extrapersonal space. *J. Motor Behav.* 45, 1–13. doi: 10.1080/00222895.2012.746635

Welsh, T., Kiernan, D., Neyedli, H., Ray, M., Pratt, J., and Weeks, D. (2013b). On mechanisms, methods, and measures: a response to Guagnano, Rusconi, and Umiltà. *J. Motor Behav.* 45, 9–14. doi: 10.1080/00222895.2012.746560

Wilson, M., and Knoblich, G. (2005). The case for motor involvement in perceiving conspecifics. *Psychol. Bull.* 131, 460–473. doi: 10.1037/0033-2909.131.3.460

9

Cortical information flow during inferences of agency

Myrthel Dogge[1]*, Dennis Hofman[2], Maria Boersma[2], H. Chris Dijkerman[2] and Henk Aarts[2]

[1] Department of Psychiatry, University Medical Center Utrecht, Utrecht, Netherlands
[2] Department of Psychology, Utrecht University, Utrecht, Netherlands

***Correspondence:**
Myrthel Dogge, Brain Center Rudolf Magnus, University Medical Center Utrecht, Room A.01.206, PO Box 85500, Utrecht, 3508 GA, Netherlands
e-mail: m.dogge@umcutrecht.nl

Building on the recent finding that agency experiences do not merely rely on sensorimotor information but also on cognitive cues, this exploratory study uses electroencephalographic recordings to examine functional connectivity during agency inference processing in a setting where action and outcome are independent. Participants completed a computerized task in which they pressed a button followed by one of two color words (red or blue) and rated their experienced agency over producing the color. Before executing the action, a matching or mismatching color word was pre-activated by explicitly instructing participants to produce the color (goal condition) or by briefly presenting the color word (prime condition). In both conditions, experienced agency was higher in matching vs. mismatching trials. Furthermore, increased electroencephalography (EEG)-based connectivity strength was observed between parietal and frontal nodes and within the (pre)frontal cortex when color-outcomes matched with goals and participants reported high agency. This pattern of increased connectivity was not identified in trials where outcomes were pre-activated through primes. These results suggest that different connections are involved in the experience and in the loss of agency, as well as in inferences of agency resulting from different types of pre-activation. Moreover, the findings provide novel support for the involvement of a fronto-parietal network in agency inferences.

Keywords: sense of agency, inferences, phase synchronization, EEG, connectivity, goal-directed processes, outcome priming

INTRODUCTION

Humans generally feel in control of their actions and the events that follow from them. This sense of agency plays a key role in self-awareness as well as social interaction (Haggard and Tsakiris, 2009; Ruys and Aarts, 2012). Although experiences of self-agency arise naturally in most individuals, abnormalities in agency processing, such as feeling in control over externally generated outcomes, or, oppositely, experiencing a loss of control over outcomes that one did produce, have been observed in a variety of psychiatric and neurological disorders (Blakemore et al., 2002). Examining the neural substrates underlying self-agency in the healthy brain thus is an important step to comprehend the origin of disturbed agency experiences, and eventually uncover possible ways to alleviate them.

The experience of agency has primarily been studied from the perspective of comparator models that are part of the motor control system (Frith et al., 2000). These models often rely on paradigms in which visual, tactile, or auditory feedback of the participants' action is manipulated (e.g., Sperduti et al., 2011; David, 2012). According to the comparator model, the execution of an action is accompanied by the prediction of sensory action-outcomes based on internal copies of movement-predicting signals (i.e., efference copies) generated by the motor system. Because internal motor predictions are generally fast and reliable, sensory outcomes are readily perceived as self-produced when these predictions correspond with the actual outcome (Frith et al., 2000). This motor prediction process of agency has been found to be associated with brain activity in various areas, including the superior temporal gyrus, the inferior parietal lobe, as well as motor regions such as the pre-supplementary motor area and the cerebellum (for an overview, see Sperduti et al., 2011).

According to the comparator model, experiences of agency are less likely to occur when the motor system cannot produce an efference copy (i.e., when acts are not self-generated) or when these signals are weak or noisy, such as when there is no clear causal relationship between an action and an effect. However, recent research has demonstrated that people can feel in control over externally generated events (Wegner et al., 2004) and in the absence of high action-effect contingency (Moore et al., 2009; Van der Weiden et al., 2011). These findings strongly suggest that agency experiences can also emerge via a different route. This alternative route, specified by the inference model, involves cognitive inferences of the correspondence between action outcomes and prior activation of information about the outcome (Wegner, 2002). Despite the role of these inference processes in the emergence of agency (Moore et al., 2009; Sato, 2009; see also Synofzik et al., 2008, 2013), their neural basis has hitherto received relatively little empirical attention. Another issue that remains unclear from prior work is how brain regions associated with agency interact and exert influence over each other. The present study builds on recent advancement in the quantification of neural communication to examine the interactions between cortical regions during inferences of agency.

AGENCY INFERENCES

The inference model proposes that upon observing an event, people determine whether or not it has resulted from their actions by comparing the outcome with prior activated information or thoughts about action-effects. If there is a match, they ascribe the action-outcome to themselves, whereas, in case of a mismatch, the effect is ascribed to an external cause. Although this account involves a predictive element regarding action-outcomes similar to the comparator model, the prior expectations specified in this model only minimally depend on motor signals. Instead, these expectations pertain to cognitive priors such as intentions and beliefs (Synofzik et al., 2013). Moreover, even though predictive elements are involved in inference processes, the critical information is provided by the action outcome (Synofzik et al., 2013).

It is important to note that inferences of agency are normally thought to result from intentions. That is, if an intention to produce a certain outcome matches the actual sensory consequences following one's action, people tend to experience causal responsibility for these consequences, whereas if the intention mismatches with the observed outcome, a reduced sense of agency is experienced (Wegner, 2002). Intriguingly, however, recent research suggests that prior knowledge regarding action outcomes does not necessarily need to be explicitly activated for agency inferences to occur, but can also consist of outcome primes as a source of agency (Aarts et al., 2005; Linser and Goschke, 2007; Jones et al., 2008; Belayachi and van der Linden, 2010; Dannenberg et al., 2012; Ruys and Aarts, 2012). This evidence possibly accounts for the emergence of experienced agency in everyday situations where people do not produce action-outcomes themselves or lack awareness of the actual causes of their behavior.

Although goals and primes give rise to similar inferences of agency, there is some preliminary evidence to suggest that the two sources produce qualitatively different effects (Van der Weiden et al., 2013). Specifically, pursuing a goal instigates a control process that causes people to focus on the specific outcome one wants to reach and, at the same time, to inhibit all other possible outcomes (Fishbach and Ferguson, 2007; Förster et al., 2007; Aarts, 2012). Consequently, inference processes based on goals are very specific and reliable in the detection of deviations from intended outcomes. These goal-directed control processes are less likely to occur in case of outcome priming, because outcome priming is assumed to merely enhance the accessibility of the outcome representations and other information associated with it (Van der Weiden et al., 2013). This implies that agency inferences based on priming are less sensitive to deviations and hence have a noisier processing mechanism than goal-directed processes (Van der Weiden et al., 2013). Based on these qualitative differences between inferences resulting from goals and primes, we not only examined the neural communication between cortical regions underlying goal-based inferences but, for exploratory purposes, also investigated these neural processes during prime-based inferences.

NEURAL COMMUNICATION AND AGENCY INFERENCES

Cognitive functioning, including inferences of agency, is dependent on the integration of information within and between functionally specialized brain sites (Varela et al., 2001; Stam and van Straaten, 2012a). There is increasing agreement that this integration, or more precisely, the communication between neurons, arises from synchronization of neural activity (Salinas and Sejnowski, 2001; Varela et al., 2001; Buzsáki and Draguhn, 2004; Fries, 2005; Schnitzler and Gross, 2005; Sauseng and Klimesch, 2008). Specifically, neurons' responsiveness has the property to oscillate, referring to fluctuations in excitability of their membrane potential (Buzsáki and Draguhn, 2004). These fluctuations create time windows in which a neuron is most responsive to signals by other neurons (Buzsáki and Draguhn, 2004). Hence, for two neurons to successfully exchange information, their excitability period needs to be aligned, which happens whenever they oscillate in phase (Buzsáki and Draguhn, 2004; Fries, 2005). In contrast, when phase synchronization between the oscillations of two neurons is absent, their communication is inhibited (Fries, 2005). Accordingly, the neural networks underlying agency processing can be studied by examining the synchronization of neural activity, and thus the exchange of information between local and distant groups of neurons (Varela et al., 2001).

Two recent studies using functional magnetic resonance imaging (fMRI) have provided some insights into the neural networks underlying agency processing. In one study, participants were asked to indicate perceived control over actions based on congruent or incongruent movement feedback (David et al., 2007). Increased connectivity was observed between the pre-motor cortex, cerebellum, and posterior parietal cortex (PPC) when movements were correctly identified as externally generated, and between the insula and somatosensory cortex when movements were correctly classified as self-generated (David et al., 2007; David, 2012). In another study, leading and lagging networks were identified during experiences of loss of control in response to incongruent visual feedback (Nahab et al., 2011). The leading network consisted, among others, of the inferior parietal lobe and the insula and was shown to send information to a lagging network consisting of several areas in the posterior parietal and prefrontal lobe. The authors interpreted the leading network as being involved in the comparison of motor predictions with actual effects, whereas the lagging network (in particular the prefrontal lobe) was thought to be responsible for the translation of the outcome of this comparison into higher order processing of agency, such as the conscious awareness of this experience.

Although the aforementioned connectivity studies provide a first glimpse into neural networks underlying experiences of agency and to the direction of information flow between them, they deal with agency processes informed by motor predictive signals, and not by cognitive inferences processes *per se*. A recent fMRI study addressed this notion by examining the neural substrates of goal-based agency inferences (Renes et al., 2013). During the ascription of outcomes to oneself, activation was observed in the inferior parietal lobe, the superior frontal cortex and the medial prefrontal cortex, implying that the lagging network identified by Nahab et al. (2011) might indeed be involved in the previously mentioned higher order agency processing.

THE PRESENT STUDY

In the present study we further examine and extend these findings by analyzing the pattern of information flow during inferences of agency using measures of (directed) phase synchronization. By doing so, we not only build on recent calls for a shift from localization to network perspectives on agency processing (David, 2012), but also expand prior work on the connectivity underlying the sense of agency by employing a more direct measure of neural communication.

To explore the cortical interactions underlying inferences of agency we used an action-outcome task in which participants perform an action (pressing a key) that is followed by a sensory effect (the color word red or blue presented on the computer screen) that either matches or mismatches with pre-activated knowledge of this outcome. After observing the outcome, self-agency over producing the outcome is reported. Importantly, participants learn that the outcome they observe is not always caused by their actions but can be determined by the computer as well. As a consequence, sensorimotor predictive processes are unreliable in this task, allowing us to pinpoint agency experiences that are informed by inferences. Furthermore, pre-activation of knowledge about outcomes in manipulated by explicitly instructed goals to produce the outcome or by briefly presented primes of the outcome, thus allowing us to study goal-based and prime-based agency inferences.

To examine the neural communication of agency inferences we used the electroencephalogram (EEG), which has a temporal resolution that is sufficient to non-invasively examine phase synchronization (Sauseng and Klimesch, 2008; Stam and van Straaten, 2012a). Based on prior work we are particularly interested in coupling strength between parietal and frontal regions and the direction of information flow between them.

METHODS

PARTICIPANTS

Thirty right-handed participants ($M_{age} = 21.03$, $SD_{age} = 3.20$; 22 females) who indicated no current neurological condition, mental illness or use of psychiatric medication took part in the experiment. Participants were asked to refrain from the consumption of caffeine 3 hours prior to the experiment. All participants received course credit or a monetary reward in exchange for their participation. The study received approval from our internal faculty board (Social and Behavioral Sciences) at Utrecht University. Furthermore, written informed consent of each participant was obtained.

AGENCY INFERENCE TASK

The agency inference task was adapted from Renes and Aarts (in preparation). Similar to playing a slot machine, this task required participants to stop a sequence of rapidly presented information to produce a particular outcome (i.e., the color word red or blue) on the computer screen. Specifically, participants pressed a key in response to a cue while viewing alternating letter strings. Upon pressing this key, the stream of letter strings stopped and the color word "red" or "blue" was presented. This outcome could either match or mismatch with prior knowledge regarding the action-effect (i.e., goals or outcome primes; see below). In addition, participants learned that the computer could have caused the presented outcome as well. In other words, the cause of the observed effect was ambiguous (Aarts et al., 2005; Sato, 2009). After viewing the sensory effect following their key press, participants reported experienced agency over causing the perceived effect.

Each trial consisted of five different phases: an exposure phase, a filler interval, an action phase, an outcome phase and a rating phase (see **Figure 1**). The last four phases were identical for all trials. During the filler interval, participants attended to rapidly alternating letter strings. This interval served as a delay between exposure to pre-activated information and the action that was also present in previous work on agency inferences (e.g., Van der Weiden et al., 2013). In the action phase, participants responded to a circle (the letter "o" presented in Arial 24 pt. at an approximate visual angle of 2.10°) that appeared above or below the letter

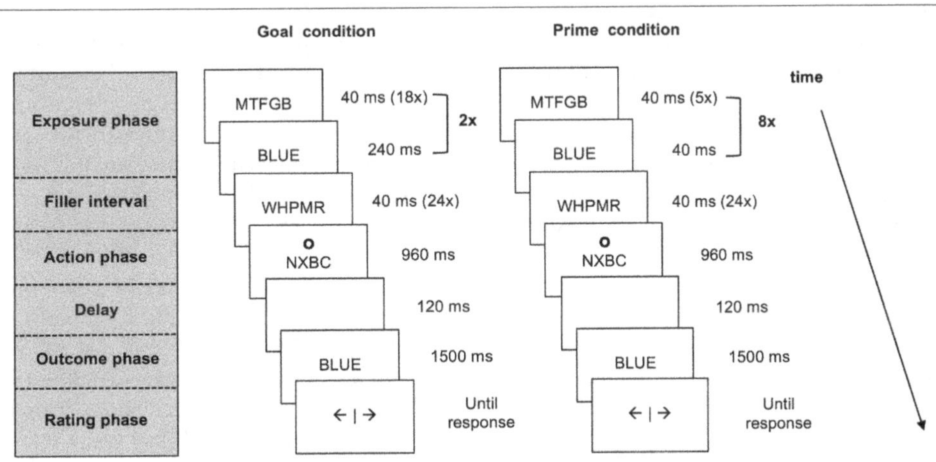

FIGURE 1 | Schematic presentation of a match trial in the agency inference task for the goal condition and the prime condition. Both goal and prime trials start with the pre-activation of a color word that is presented within a stream of letter strings. In the goal trials participants are instructed to produce this outcome. In the prime trials participants are merely exposed to the prime words. After a short interval participants press a key in response to an action cue appearing above or below the letter strings. Upon this key press the stream of information stops and a color word matching or mismatching the pre-activated word is presented. Participants are asked to report experienced self-agency over this outcome.

strings, by pressing the corresponding upper or lower key on a response box with their right index finger. This action cue was included to ensure that participants paid attention to the outcome prime or goal presented amidst of the letter strings. The interval in which a response could be given lasted 800 ms. If participants pressed the key within this interval, the strings continued to alternate until the end of a 960 ms lasting interval, whereas if they pressed too late, an error message occurred and the trial was processed as missing.

Following the action phase, the color word "red" or "blue" (counterbalanced between trials) was shown for 1500 ms, after a short delay of 120 ms. To ensure that participants would maintain looking at the letter strings, participants were told that pressing the key during the presentation of a string containing the letter R (e.g., MWRT) would cause the word "red" to appear, whereas a key press during the presentation of a string containing the letter "B" (e.g., BTSZW) was followed by the word "blue." In reality, the computer determined the presentation of color words.

After each trial, experienced agency was assessed during a rating phase by asking participants to what extent they felt their key press caused the presented color word to occur. They could respond by moving a square on a 9-point analog scale ranging from the Dutch word "*niet*" (in this context roughly corresponding to: "Not at all" to "*wel*" ("Very much"). The square had to be moved at least one position to the left or the right of the scale, starting in the center (i.e., answer "5"). This caused the data to consist of split responses (i.e., data ranging from 1 to 4 and 6 to 9). In order to form a continuous scale ranging from 1 to 8, the agency ratings were recoded (i.e., 9 = 8, 8 = 7, 7 = 6, and 6 = 5).

Pre-activated knowledge about outcomes

As mentioned earlier, the exposure phase was not identical for all trials. Specifically, in this phase knowledge regarding the outcome was activated by either goals or by primes.

In goal trials, participants were exposed to a series of letter strings followed by a color word that was clearly presented on the screen for 240 ms. This sequence was repeated twice (see **Figure 1**), using the same color word. Participants were instructed to form the goal to produce the color word that appeared within the series of letter strings.

In outcome prime trials, participants viewed five random letter strings followed by a briefly presented color word (40 ms). This sequence of events was repeated eight times, resulting in a total of eight identical primes during a 1920 ms period (see **Figure 1**). Importantly, participants were not instructed to formulate a goal in the prime trials.

Note that, in contrast to prior studies (Van der Weiden et al., 2013), the duration and moment of the exposure phase was identical for both types of pre-activated outcome information. Accordingly, differences between prime and goal based inferences could be examined in a more controlled manner.

The goal trials and outcome prime trials were presented in two separated blocks which each consisted of 64 randomly presented trials. All participants started with the prime condition to prevent transference of instructions from the goal condition to the prime condition (i.e., to prevent participants from using the primed information to form a goal). In half of the trials, pre-activated color words corresponded with the actual outcome, whereas in the other half of the trials they did not correspond with this outcome. Participants practiced for both blocks before the onset of the experiment (eight trials per practice block). After completing these practice trials participants completed the outcome-priming block, followed by a practice block for the goal condition (four trials) and the actual goal block. In between the two blocks participants were allowed to have a break. In addition, participants paused for 30 s after completing the first half (i.e., 32 trials) of each block.

EEG RECORDING AND PRE-PROCESSING

EEG was recorded at a sampling rate of 2048 Hz during the entire agency inference task from 32 electrodes positioned according to the international 10/20 system using the BioSemi Active Two EEG system (BioSemi). The Electro-oculogram (EOG) was measured from electrodes placed on the suborbit and supraorbit of the right eye and on the outer canthi of both eyes. Raw EEG data was band pass filtered offline (0.5–50 Hz) with a roll-off of 48 dB/oct and a 50 Hz Notch filter. Time series were re-referenced against an average reference. In order to correct for eye movements, Gratton and Cole's method (Gratton et al., 1983) was used. A semi-automated artifact correction tool (Brain Vision Analyzer software package; Version 2.0), allowing a maximum difference of 50 μV/ms, was employed to detect further artifacts. The corrected data was chunked down to 128 trial-specific segments that started at the onset of the outcome presentation and ended after 1000 ms. This time window corresponds to the interval of interest used in prior work on the neural basis of agency inferences (Renes et al., 2013).

FUNCTIONAL CONNECTIVITY

EEG was employed to assess both bidirectional and directional neural communication during agency inferences; quantified by the phase lag index (PLI; Stam et al., 2007) and directed phase lag index (dPLI; Stam and van Straaten, 2012b) respectively.

Phase lag index

The PLI identifies statistical interdependency of two time series based on the level of asymmetry of the distribution of their phase differences (for mathematical details see Stam et al., 2007). Since the PLI only reflects correlations between signals of which the phase difference deviates from zero, it is less affected by common source problems and amplitude changes than other connectivity measures (however, see Muthukumaraswamy and Singh, 2011). The PLI ranges from 0 to 1, with a score of zero indicating no coupling or coupling that might result from common source problems, and a score of 1 indicating perfect coupling.

BRAINWAVE software (version 9.75) was used to compute the instantaneous phase (using a Hilbert transformation) and PLI between all pairs of electrodes for each trial in the broadband (2–50 Hz), delta band (2–4 Hz), theta band (4–8 Hz), alpha band (8–12 Hz), beta band (13–30 Hz), and gamma band (30–40 Hz). By doing so, trial specific 32 × 32 connectivity matrices were created. Given that the present study aims to examine functional connectivity associated with agency experiences emerging from inferences, rather than connectivity as a function of task conditions, we decided to examine the low vs. high agency contrast within each task condition (i.e., as a function of matching and type of pre-activation). In line with prior research (Renes et al., 2013), the aforementioned 32 × 32 trial matrices were sorted into two groups based on agency ratings (Low agency: rating ≤ 4, High agency: rating ≥ 5). The frequency distributions of agency ratings for matching and pre-activation cells are presented in Supplementary Figure S1. To allow for group comparison, average matrices were created for each possible combination of type of pre-activation, matching and level of agency. This resulted in eight average 3D group matrices comprising PLI values for all possible pairs of electrodes per participant.

Nonparametric permutation tests adapted from Boersma et al. (2013) were used to test for differences in PLI for all possible electrode pairs between low agency and high agency for match and mismatching conditions (i.e., low agency vs. high agency for goals matching the outcome, low agency vs. high agency for goals mismatching the outcome, low agency vs. high agency for primes matching the outcome and low agency vs. high agency for primes mismatching the outcome). These tests involved a resampling method with replacement, which was used to generate ten thousand random pairs of groups from the two originally specified observations (i.e., low and high agency), across participants[1]. By comparing the mean PLI values for all electrode pairs between these random groups, a distribution of differences for all pairwise connections was created. The position of the original difference value in this distribution was used to determine p-values for each contrast. Significant differences (alpha = 0.05) were visualized using a modified version of the topoplot function in the EEGlab toolbox (Delorme and Makeig, 2004). Specifically, networks were plotted in which each node is represented by an EEG electrode and the links between the nodes correspond to a significant difference in connectivity between low and high agency.

Directed phase lag index

dPLIs were calculated to examine the direction of information flow of pairwise connections. Similar to the PLI the dPLI is a measure of the asymmetry of the distribution of phase differences of two signals (Stam and van Straaten, 2012b). However, dPLI also assesses the direction of the asymmetry (i.e., the probability that the phase of the signal measured at electrode X is smaller than the phase of the signal measured at electrode Y), whereas PLI merely determines the presence of absolute asymmetry. The direction of the asymmetry allows one to infer whether a signal recorded from a node is phase leading (i.e., sending information) or phase lagging (i.e., receiving information) compared to the signal recorded from all the other nodes (Stam and van Straaten, 2012b). Specifically, time series measured from a node with a dPLI score larger than 0.5 are thought to be leading in phase, whereas a dPLI score smaller than 0.5 indicates the opposite pattern (Stam and van Straaten, 2012b). In the present study a modified version of the BRAINWAVE software (version 9.70) was used to assess directional connectivity between pairs of nodes.

For each trial, dPLI matrices for all electrode pairs and average group matrices corresponding to each possible combination of matching, type of pre-activation and agency were constructed. These average matrices were used to obtain dPLI values for all participants for each connection that significantly differed in PLI between groups. Exploratory one-sample t-tests were used to examine whether dPLI values of the connections significantly differed from 0.5. Corrections for multiple comparisons were made by means of Benjamini and Hochberg's (1995) false discovery rate procedure. These analyses were performed using SPSS (version 20).

RESULTS

BEHAVIORAL DATA

Agency ratings

One hundred and eleven trials (2.89% of the total amount) were excluded from the analyses due to the absence of a key press within the interval of the action phase. Mean agency ratings were calculated for matches and mismatches in the goal trials and in the prime trials. Visual inspection of the data as well as normality tests indicated non-normality of the data. However, considering the robustness of ANOVA for these departures from normality, we refrained from the use of non-parametric alternatives. The mean ratings were submitted to a 2 (type of pre-activation: goal vs. prime) × 2 (matching: mismatch vs. match) repeated measures ANOVA. This analysis yielded a main effect of matching, $F_{(1, 29)} = 13.06$, $p = 0.001$, $\eta^2_p = 0.31$, indicating higher agency experiences when pre-activated outcome information was consistent as opposed to inconsistent with the actual outcome. Moreover, an interaction between type of pre-activation and matching was observed, $F_{(1, 29)} = 5.39$, $p = 0.03$, $\eta^2_p = 0.16$. The main effect for type of pre-activation was not significant, $F_{(1, 29)} = 1.25$, $p = 0.27$, $\eta^2_p = 0.04$.

To gain further insight into the interaction, simple main effects using Bonferroni correction (corrected alpha = 0.0125) were calculated. These analyses yielded higher agency ratings for matching vs. mismatching in both the goal, $F_{(1, 29)} = 11.36$, $p = 0.002$, $\eta^2_p = 0.28$, and outcome priming condition $F_{(1, 29)} = 10.74$, $p = 0.003$, $\eta^2_p = 0.27$. A marginally significant simple main effect of type of pre-activation was observed within match trials, $F_{(1, 29)} = 6.66$, $p = 0.02$, $\eta^2_p = 0.19$, but not in mismatch trials, $F_{(1, 29)} = 2.22$, $p = 0.15$, $\eta^2_p = 0.07$. The means of the cells are depicted in **Figure 2**.

Key-press reaction times

To check whether participants responded differently to the action cue by pressing the key as a function of the type of trial, mean reaction times were submitted to a 2 (type of pre-activation: goal vs. prime) × 2 (matching: mismatch vs. match) repeated measures ANOVA. This analysis yielded a non-significant main effect of type of pre-activation, $F_{(1, 29)} = 2.68$, $p = 0.11$, $\eta^2_p = 0.09$, indicating no difference in reaction time between goal trials ($M = 436.25$, $SE = 11.85$) and prime trials ($M = 449.28$, $SE =$

[1]The authors are aware that the within-subject nature of the data violates the exchangeability assumption of the permutation tests and thus increases the likelihood of false positives. However, given that the design of the study leads to varying numbers of trials in the low and high agency condition (precluding within-subject permutation), as well as our aspiration to visualize networks, this analytical procedure was deemed most appropriate. Nevertheless, caution is advised when interpreting the results.

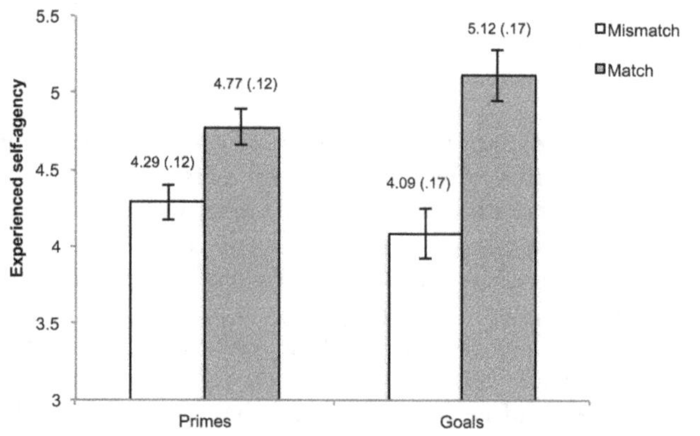

FIGURE 2 | Reported experience of agency as a function of type of pre-activation and matching. The numbers above the bars represent the mean and standard error (also reflected by the error bars) of the corresponding condition.

9.75). In addition, no difference in reaction time was observed between match ($M = 445.43$, $SE = 9.77$) and mismatch trials ($M = 440.10$, $SE = 10.69$), as evidenced by a non-significant main effect of matching, $F_{(1, 29)} = 2.38$, $p = 0.13$, $\eta_p^2 = 0.08$. Finally, the interaction effect between type of pre-activation and matching was not significant, $F_{(1, 29)} = 0.05$, $p = 0.83$, $\eta_p^2 = 0.002$.

Agency rating times

The time participants took to report experienced agency was also assessed by submitting mean rating times (in milliseconds) to a 2 (type of pre-activation: goal vs. primes) × 2 (matching: mismatch vs. match) repeated measures ANOVA. Although the data was non-normally distributed, we refrained from using non-parametric alternatives for previously mentioned reasons. Participants reported experienced agency faster in goal trials ($M = 1470.69$, $SE = 129.57$) than in prime trials ($M = 1669.35$, $SE = 131.58$), $F_{(1, 29)} = 6.51$, $p = 0.02$, $\eta_p^2 = 0.18$. The differences in reaction time between mismatch trials ($M = 1554.70$, $SE = 122.13$) and match trials ($M = 1585.33$, $SE = 130.79$), $F_{(1, 29)} = 0.49$, $p = 0.49$, $\eta_p^2 = 0.02$, as well as the interaction effect between type of pre-activation and matching, $F_{(1, 29)} = 1.95$, $p = 0.17$, $\eta_p^2 = 0.06$, were non-significant.

In short, the behavioral data shows two notable findings. First, participants report higher agency experiences when the observed effect matches vs. mismatches with pre-activated outcome information. This effect tends to be more pronounced in case of goal-based agency inferences than in case of prime-based agency inferences. Moreover, participants provided faster ratings concerning their feeling of agency in goal trials as opposed to prime trials.

EEG DATA

Data exclusion

Visual data inspection led to the detection of noisy data on one or more channels for five participants. These participants were excluded from further EEG analyses to retain the option of analyzing all 32 × 32 channel pairs. In addition, four participants had no trials left in one or more cells that were created by splitting the data in low and high agency ratings; these participants were also excluded. Hence, the total sample for EEG analysis consisted of 21 participants ($M_{age} = 21.43$, $SD_{age} = 3.37$; 17 females). In addition, 1.67% of the trials were excluded based on semi-automated visual artifact rejection. Finally, trials that were characterized as missing in the agency inference task (i.e., trials in which the key was not pressed within the action interval) were omitted from analyses (2.75%)[2].

Connectivity

Figure 3 provides an overview of connectivity for the contrast between low and high agency as a function of matching and type of pre-activation. Re-running the permutation analyses can result in marginal variation in the null distribution of mean differences. As a result, inclusion of connections with PLI differences near the significance threshold (alpha = 0.05; two-tailed) is subject to similar variation. Dashed lines ($0.02 \leq p \leq 0.03$) are used to discriminate these connections from those that are more robust over different runs (i.e., solid lines; $p < 0.02$).

Goal trials. The behavioral data suggests that people experience more self-agency when a goal matches the observed outcome vs. when it does not. In other words, matches are more likely to be associated with high agency, whereas mismatches are associated with low agency[3]. When examining connectivity associated with high agency (vs. low agency) experiences in trials in which goals match with the outcome (**Figure 3**), increased connectivity is observed between parietal and frontal regions as well as within the frontal cortices in the broadband. With regard to specific frequency bands, high agency experiences during match trials seem particularly governed by increased connectivity in the beta band.

Different connections emerge during low-agency experiences in trials in which goals mismatch with the outcome. Specifically, in the broadband frequency increased connectivity for low agency experiences (compared to high agency experiences) is observed within and between parietal and frontal areas. In addition, this increased connectivity can particularly be observed in alpha and gamma bands.

Prime trials. During experiences of high agency (vs. low agency) in trials in which primes match with the observed effect, increased connectivity can be observed between parietal and frontal regions

[2]Although the analyses of behavioral data and EEG data differ (in the sense that different contrasts are assessed), we checked whether the reported findings for behavioral data change when excluding the artifact trials and participants that are excluded from the EEG analysis. The repeated measures ANOVA yielded a main effect of matching, $F_{(1, 20)} = 8.36$, $p = 0.009$, $\eta_p^2 = 0.29$, showing that matching outcomes corresponded with higher agency experiences than mismatching outcomes. The main effect of type of pre-activation, $F_{(1, 20)} = 0.02$, $p = 0.89$, $\eta_p^2 = 0.001$ and the interaction between type of pre-activation and matching, $F_{(1, 20)} = 1.27$, $p = 0.27$, $\eta_p^2 = 0.06$ were not significant.

[3]Note that the behavioral data indicates that participants sometimes report low agency in a match trial and high agency in a mismatch trial. These experiences, and corresponding connectivity, are not likely to reflect agency processes emerging from prime-based or goal-based inferences—and are thus not explicitly discussed in the result section.

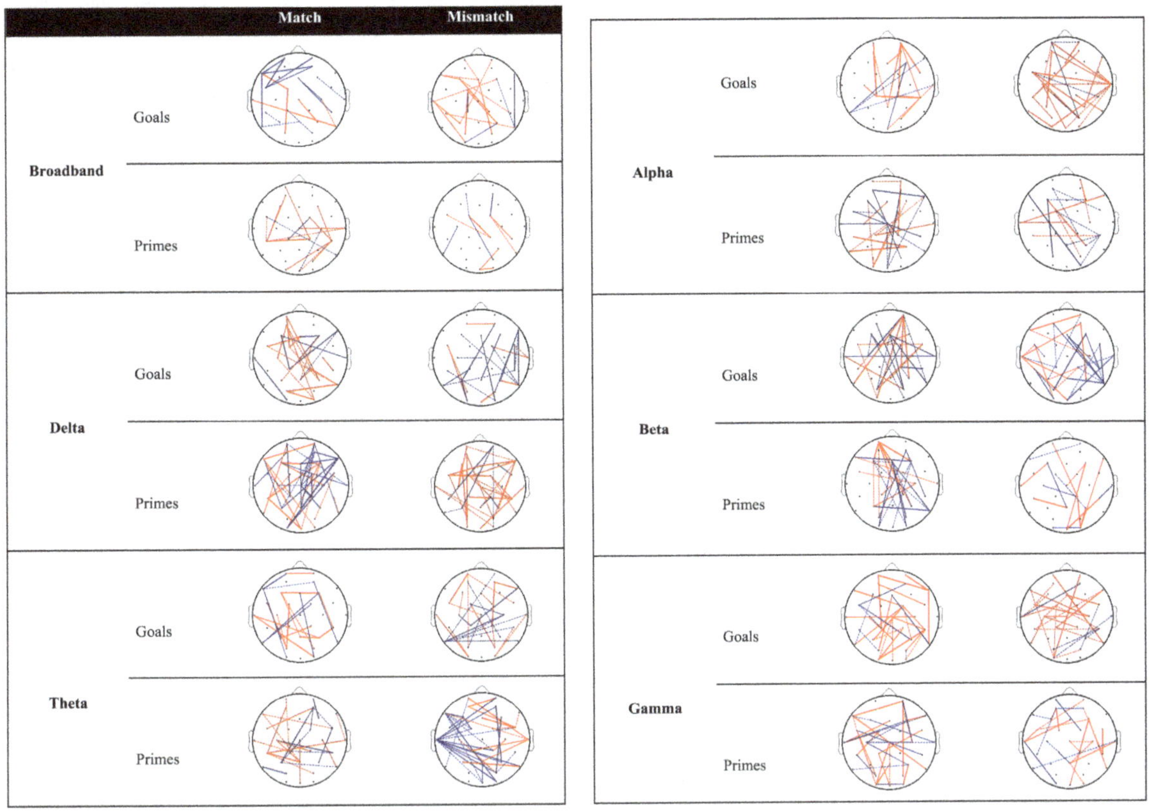

FIGURE 3 | Significant differences in PLI between low and high agency as a function of matching and type of pre-activation across frequency bands. Red lines indicate that PLI low agency > PLI high agency, whereas blue lines represents the opposite pattern. Dashed lines represent PLI differences near the significance threshold ($0.02 \leq p \leq 0.03$) whereas solid lines represent connections that are more robust across re-runs of the permutation analysis ($p < 0.02$).

in the broadband. Increased fronto-parietal connectivity is also present to a larger extent in the delta, theta, alpha, and beta band.

Reports of low agency (as opposed to high agency) during primed mismatch trials are associated with enhanced coupling between parietal and frontal areas. With regard to specific frequency bands, increased connectivity between parietal, and frontal regions during experiences of low agency (vs. high agency) is especially apparent in the delta band.

Direction of information flow

The connectivity pattern that was observed in the broadband during high agency experiences in trials in which goals matched action-effects, is in line with previous findings on the neural basis of agency (e.g., Nahab et al., 2011). To explore whether the information flow between the identified nodes is also consistent with prior work (i.e., directed from parietal to frontal lobes), directed phase lag indices were calculated for all conditions in this frequency range (see **Table 1** for mean PLI values). As can be seen in **Table 2**, the signal measured from the left parietal electrode is leading in phase compared to the signal at the left frontal electrode in trials in which goals match the outcome, suggesting that there is a trend of anteriorly directed information flow in these trials. In the other conditions no clear direction of information flow could be observed. It should be noted that the reported effects are not corrected for multiple comparisons. After implementing this correction, none of the dPLI values were different from 0.5 at the conventional significance level of $p < 0.05$.

DISCUSSION

Building on recent interest in neural networks underlying agency processing (David, 2012), the present study examined cortical information flow during inferences of agency. Whereas some insights into the networks underlying agency processing have been provided by previous studies employing fMRI (David et al., 2007; Nahab et al., 2011), here we offered a first attempt to investigate this connectivity by tapping into the mechanism that is proposed to underlie neural communication (i.e., phase synchronization).

The role of inference processes in self-agency experiences is supported by the current behavioral data. In line with the inference model (Wegner, 2002) and previous work (Wegner and Wheatley, 1999; Aarts et al., 2005; Van der Weiden et al., 2011, 2013), participants reported higher agency experiences when pre-activated knowledge was congruent vs. incongruent with actual outcomes. Importantly, these results cannot be easily accounted for by the comparator account, as predictive motor processes were unreliable (or even absent) due to the experimental set-up. Specifically, there was no causal relation between the key press of

Table 1 | Mean PLI during high (HA) and low experiences of agency (LA) in trials in which (A) goals matched the outcomes, (B) goals mismatched the outcomes, (C) primes matched the outcomes, and (D) primes mismatched the outcomes in broadband frequency.

Connection	PLI (LA)		PLI (HA)	
	M	*SD*	*M*	*SD*
(A)				
PO3_FC1	0.18	0.04	0.15	0.03
FC1_F7	0.16	0.04	0.14	0.03
P7_F7	0.12	0.03	0.15	0.03
F7_AF4	0.11	0.04	0.14	0.04
FC5_FP1	0.12	0.03	0.14	0.03
FC5_FP2	0.11	0.03	0.14	0.03
FC5_AF4	0.11	0.04	0.14	0.03
F7_FP1	0.11	0.03	0.14	0.04
CP6_Fz	0.12	0.03	0.15	0.02
(B)				
PO4_Fz	0.16	0.04	0.13	0.03
PO3_FC1	0.15	0.04	0.12	0.04
P4_FC1	0.16	0.03	0.13	0.04
CP2_F3	0.16	0.03	0.13	0.04
F3_F7	0.15	0.04	0.12	0.04
P8_F8	0.13	0.03	0.16	0.05
CP1_FC1	0.16	0.03	0.18	0.03
(C)				
PO4_CP6	0.16	0.03	0.13	0.03
CP6_FC2	0.17	0.04	0.14	0.03
CP6_F4	0.16	0.05	0.13	0.03
CP2_FP1	0.14	0.04	0.11	0.03
CP2_CP5	0.16	0.03	0.14	0.02
CP5_F3	0.15	0.03	0.13	0.04
CP5_AF3	0.15	0.04	0.12	0.03
CP1_FC2	0.14	0.02	0.16	0.03
(D)				
CP2_FC1	0.16	0.03	0.14	0.03
CP6_FC2	0.16	0.04	0.13	0.03
PO4_FC1	0.13	0.03	0.16	0.04
FC2_AF4	0.13	0.03	0.15	0.04

*Only connections between parietal and frontal electrodes (based on positions in the international 10/20 system) with robust significant PLI group differences are shown (i.e., solid lines in **Figure 3**).*

Table 2 | Results of one-sample *t*-tests for dPLI values during high (HA) and low experiences of agency (LA) in trials in which (A) goals matched the outcomes, (B) goals mismatched the outcomes, (C) primes matched the outcomes, and (D) primes mismatched the outcomes in broadband frequency.

Connection	*t*	*p*	Direction effect
(A)			
LA_PO3_FC1	−0.21	0.83	–
LA_FC1_F7	−0.65	0.53	–
HA_P7_F7	2.46	0.02	↑
HA_F7_AF4	2.11	0.05	↑
HA_FC5_FP1	3.28	0.004	↑
HA_FC5_FP2	3.23	0.004	↑
HA_FC5_AF4	1.40	0.18	–
HA_F7_FP1	2.74	0.01	↑
HA_CP6_Fz	−1.09	0.29	–
(B)			
LA_PO4_Fz	−0.04	0.97	–
LA_PO3_FC1	−0.59	0.56	–
LA_P4_FC1	0.30	0.77	–
LA_CP2_F3	−0.13	0.90	–
LA_F3_F7	−0.81	0.43	–
HA_P8_F8	1.73	0.099	↑
HA_CP1_FC1	0.37	0.72	–
(C)			
LA_PO4_CP6	−0.53	0.60	–
LA_CP6_FC2	−2.89	0.009	↓
LA_CP6_F4	−2.25	0.04	↓
LA_CP2_FP1	−1.91	0.07	↓
LA_CP2_CP5	2.02	0.06	↑
LA_CP5_F3	−0.89	0.38	–
LA_CP5_AF3	0.15	0.88	–
HA_CP1_FC2	0.62	0.54	–
(D)			
LA_CP2_FC1	−0.35	0.73	–
LA_CP6_FC2	−1.40	0.18	–
HA_PO4_FC1	0.09	0.93	–
HA_FC2_AF4	−1.16	0.26	–

*Only connections between parietal and frontal electrodes (based on positions in the international 10/20 system) with robust significant PLI group differences are shown (i.e., solid lines in **Figure 3**). The arrows represent the direction of the information flow between the two nodes (i.e., electrodes) specified in the contrast. Upward arrows indicate that the first node is sending information to the second node, whereas downward arrows indicate that the first node is receiving information of the second node. Arrows are presented for p-values < 0.10.*

participants and the presentation of the outcome, which restricts the motor system in its prediction of sensory action consequences (Sato, 2009). Accordingly, the reported experiences of agency are likely to be informed by cognitive inferences formed upon the occurrence of the outcome.

The results of the EEG data provide insight into neural connectivity underlying agency inferences during matches and mismatches. Increased coupling between parietal and frontal cortices, as well as within frontal areas, was identified in the broadband during high agency experiences in trials in which outcomes matched prior goals. These regions have been associated with agency processing in general (David et al., 2008; Sperduti et al., 2011) and agency inferences in particular (Renes et al., 2013). The PPC has been implicated in the detection of congruence between motor predictions and sensory action consequences, and has mainly been activated during mismatches (David, 2010). Nevertheless, Renes et al. (2013) have also identified activity in this region during matches, suggesting that it might be involved in more general comparative processes between outcome expectations and action-effects. Activity in prefrontal areas has been linked to a conscious monitoring function (i.e., the conscious experience of having caused an outcome or not; David, 2010). Although the observed fronto-parietal connectivity concurs with this prior research, it is important to note that observed connectivity during agency inferences was not restricted to these areas, as can be seen in **Figure 3**.

Connectivity between parietal and frontal areas in the broadband was also observed during low agency experiences in trials in which goals mismatched with the outcome. Notably, however, the coupling within frontal areas that was observed during high agency in match trials was not detected during low agency experiences in mismatch trials. A possible explanation for this finding is that this frontal network is especially involved in the ascription of outcomes to oneself as opposed to external sources. Some indirect support for this idea comes from research on self-referential processing showing increased activity of the medial prefrontal cortex when participants judged personality traits as self-descriptive vs. not self-relevant (Moran et al., 2006; Rameson et al., 2010). This fits with our observation that the frontal network was not involved in case of mismatching outcomes that were not ascribed to oneself (i.e., that were deemed to be non-relevant).

Beyond the mere presence of increased coupling, a trend of directionality pointing toward information flow from parietal to frontal cortices was observed in the broadband during high agency experiences following from outcomes matching goals. This finding is in line with results by Nahab et al. (2011) who speculated that the PPC serves as a low-level congruence detection network that transmits mismatch information to prefrontal cortices in order to give rise to higher order agency processing (i.e., a conscious experience of agency). Although this observation is exciting, it is important to note that the observed directionality in the current study was relatively weak (in terms of statistical significance) and absent in trials in which goals mismatched the actual outcome. That is, whereas increasing coupling between parietal and frontal regions was observed during low agency experiences in these trials, parietal nodes were not leading in phase compared to frontal nodes. Therefore, interpretations with regard to direction of information flow should be made with caution. More generally, it is important to note that there is no unique relationship between the time series recorded by EEG and their underlying source, allowing only crude interpretations concerning underlying brain regions. Importantly, however, the main interest of the present study was to elucidate connectivity between frontal and more posterior parts of the brain, rather than to relate specific brain areas to agency inferences.

In addition to neural communication between cortical regions in the broadband frequency, interactions in specific frequency bands were assessed. Intriguingly, fronto-parietal connections were present across frequency bands, while none of the bands seemed particularly involved in agency inferences as a whole. These observations might be attributable to the complex nature of agency processing, in the sense that it encompasses functions that have been related to specific bands, such as keeping outcome representations active in working memory (associated with theta band oscillations; Klimesch et al., 2005) and, in the case of goal-based inferences, the prioritizing of top-down influence (i.e., goals) over novel events (associated with beta band oscillations; Engel and Fries, 2010). Accordingly, the observed connectivity in the variety of bands might be a reflection of the different dimensions of the integration process involved in agency inferences (Varela et al., 2001).

Recent findings suggest that agency experiences can result from goal-based inferences as well as from primed-based inferences (Van der Weiden et al., 2013). Based on these findings, we examined the neural communication involved in both type of agency inferences. When comparing connectivity patterns between goals and primes in the broadband, frontal connections were observed during high agency experiences in trials in which goals matched the outcome that were absent in trials in which primes matched the outcome. Similarly, more fronto-parietal coupling was observed in goal trials than in prime trials during low agency experiences in mismatch trials. This general decrease in connectivity associated with primes (vs. goals) might be explained by differences in the process underlying the two types of pre-activation (Van der Weiden et al., 2013). In contrast to goals, mere priming of outcome information is not assumed to install an attentional control process that maintains the specific outcome active in mind, while inhibiting other irrelevant (but associated) items at hand. Therefore, the activation of the outcome representation by priming (compared to goals) might be more transient and less stable. The behavioral data provides evidence for this notion. First, the difference in agency experiences resulting from matches and mismatches tends to be more predominantly expressed in goal trials than in prime trials. In addition, participants were significantly faster to report experienced self-agency in the former (vs. the latter) trials. These findings are in line with the notion that agency inferences occurring via priming processes are less stable and noisier than goal-based inferences, which may account for the reduced connectivity associated with the former processes.

This line of reasoning might shed light onto the recent observation that patients suffering from schizophrenia show specific disturbances in prime-based inferences processes whereas their goal-based inferences seem intact (Renes et al., 2013). Schizophrenia has been related to reduced structural connectivity between various brain regions, including reduced integrity of white matter tracts connecting parietal and frontal nodes (Ellison-Wright and Bullmore, 2009; Voineskos et al., 2010; Whitford et al., 2011). Given that anatomical connections restrict the functional networks that can be formed (Fries, 2005), agency inferences that rest on fronto-parietal functional connectivity are likely to be disturbed as well. The present study suggests that functional connectivity related to prime-based inferences is weaker compared to goal-based inferences. When taking into account that only the prime-driven processes are disturbed in schizophrenia patients, it can be speculated that the relatively strong functional connectivity pattern underlying inferences based on goals, might allow schizophrenic patients to experience agency despite decreased anatomical fronto-parietal connectivity. In contrast, inferences based on primes are already associated with weaker functional connectivity and accordingly might not be able to overcome these structural abnormalities. However, the notion that primed-based agency inferences are reduced in schizophrenic patients as a result of the quality of fronto-parietal anatomical connectivity awaits further testing.

There are several methodological limitations that warrant consideration when interpreting the present results. By examining connectivity on the scalp we cannot exclude the possibility that observed differences between conditions have been affected by spontaneous and systematic changes of distant sources. That is, due to the discontinuity PLI, noise induced by these sources can shift phase leads to phase lags, which in turn might give rise to spurious differences or, oppositely, mask real differences in connectivity (Vinck et al., 2011). Future studies incorporating source-localization procedures might provide additional insight into the influence of distant sources. Another factor that might affect PLI measurements is the number of trials used to estimate this index. When this number is small, as in the current study, PLI values tend to be overestimated, especially in case of small PLI values (Vinck et al., 2011). Note, however, that this overestimation of PLI would be expected in both low and high agency conditions. As such, the connectivity difference of interest is relatively unaffected by this issue. A final confounding factor in the present study is the multiple comparisons problem. Statistical analysis of EEG data inherently copes with testing of condition effects at a large number of pairs, across multiple frequency bands. Although there are methods to correct for multiple testing, these methods are either overly conservative when a large number of tests is conducted, or focused on networks rather than individual connections. Given the exploratory aim of the present research, an uncorrected comprehensive overview of connectivity is provided. Accordingly, observed connectivity has to be interpreted with some caution.

CONCLUSION

To conclude, we have demonstrated the potential of recent methodological advances in the quantification of brain dynamics to elucidate the neural basis underlying inferences of agency. In particular, we were able to extend prior research that has mainly focused on localized activation and provide preliminary support for the existence of fronto-parietal interactions involved in sending information from parietal to frontal areas to arrive at the conscious experience of agency. By doing so, we hope that the present results will encourage future research to move beyond mere snapshots of the brain and to further explore the neural networks underlying agentive self-awareness.

AUTHOR NOTE

The work in this paper was supported by a VICI-grant 453-10-003 from the Dutch Organization for Scientific Research.

REFERENCES

Aarts, H. (2012). "Goals, motivated social cognition and behavior," in *SAGE Handbook of Social Cognition,* eds S. Fiske and C. N. Macrae (London: Sage), 75–95. doi: 10.4135/9781446247631.n5

Aarts, H., Custers, R., and Wegner, D. M. (2005). On the inference of personal authorship: enhancing experienced agency by priming effect information. *Conscious. Cogn.* 14, 439–458. doi: 10.1016/j.concog.2004.11.001

Belayachi, S., and van der Linden, M. (2010). Feeling of doing in obsessive–compulsive checking. *Conscious. Cogn.* 19, 534–546. doi: 10.1016/j.concog.2010.02.001

Benjamini, Y., and Hochberg, Y. (1995). Controlling the false discovery rate: a practical and powerful approach to multiple testing. *J. R. Stat. Soc. Series B Stat. Methodol.* 57, 289–300.

Blakemore, S. J., Wolpert, D. M., and Frith, C. D. (2002). Abnormalities in the awareness of action. *Trends. Cogn. Sci.* 6, 237–242. doi: 10.1016/S1364-6613(02)01907-1

Boersma, M., Kemner, C., de Reus, M. A., Collin, G., Snijders, T. M., Hofman, D., et al. (2013). Disrupted functional brain networks in autistic toddlers. *Brain Connectivity* 3, 41–49. doi: 10.1089/brain.2012.0127

Buzsáki, G., and Draguhn, A. (2004). Neuronal oscillations in cortical networks. *Science* 304, 1926–1929. doi: 10.1126/science.1099745

Dannenberg, L., Förster, J., and Jostmann, N. B. (2012). "If only...": when counterfactual thoughts can reduce illusions of personal authorship. *Conscious. Cogn.* 21, 456–463. doi: 10.1016/j.concog.2011.11.008

David, N. (2010). "Functional anatomy of the sense of agency: past evidence and future directions," in *Neuropsychology of the Sense of Agency: From Consciousness to Action,* ed M. Balconi (New York, NY: Springer), 69–80.

David, N. (2012). New frontiers in the neuroscience of the sense of agency. *Front. Hum. Neurosci.* 6, 1–5. doi: 10.3389/fnhum.2012.00161

David, N., Cohen, M. X., Newen, A., Bewernick, B. H., Shah, N. J., Fink, G. R., et al. (2007). The extrastriate cortex distinguishes between the consequences of one's own and others' behavior. *Neuroimage* 36, 1004–1014. doi: 10.1016/j.neuroimage.2007.03.030

David, N., Newen, A., and Vogeley, K. (2008). The "sense of agency" and its underlying cognitive and neural mechanisms. *Conscious. Cogn.* 17, 523–534. doi: 10.1016/j.concog.2008.03.004

Delorme, A., and Makeig, S. (2004). EEGLAB: an open source toolbox for analysis of single-trial EEG dynamics. *J. Neurosci. Methods* 134, 9–21. doi: 10.1016/j.jneumeth.2003.10.009

Ellison-Wright, I., and Bullmore, E. (2009). Meta-analysis of diffusion tensor imaging studies in schizophrenia. *Schizophr. Res.* 108, 3–10. doi: 10.1016/j.schres.2008.11.021

Engel, A. K., and Fries, P. (2010). Beta-band oscillations—signalling the status quo?. *Curr. Opin. Neurobiol.* 20, 156–165. doi: 10.1016/j.conb.2010.02.015

Fishbach, A., and Ferguson, M. J. (2007). "The goal construct in social psychology," in *Social Psychology: Handbook of Basic Principles,* eds A. W. Kruglanski and E. T. Higgins (New York, NY: Guilford Press), 490–515.

Förster, J. A., Liberman, N., and Friedman, R. (2007). Seven principles of goal activation: a systematic approach to distinguishing goal priming from priming of non-goal constructs. *Pers. Soc. Psychol. Rev.* 11, 211–233. doi: 10.1177/1088868307303029

Fries, P. (2005). A mechanism for cognitive dynamics: neuronal communication through neuronal coherence. *Trends. Cogn. Sci.* 9, 474–480. doi: 10.1016/j.tics.2005.08.011

Frith, C. D., Blakemore, S. J., and Wolpert, D. M. (2000). Explaining the symptoms of schizophrenia: abnormalities in the awareness of action. *Brain. Res. Rev.* 31, 357–363. doi: 10.1016/S0165-0173(99)00052-1

Gratton, G., Coles, M. G., and Donchin, E. (1983). A new method for off-line removal of ocular artifact. *Electroencephalogr. Clin. Neurophysiol.* 55, 468–484. doi: 10.1016/0013-4694(83)90135-9

Haggard, P., and Tsakiris, M. (2009). The experience of agency feelings, judgments, and responsibility. *Curr. Dir. Psychol. Sci.* 18, 242–246. doi: 10.1111/j.1467-8721.2009.01644.x

Jones, S. R., de-Wit, L., Fernyhough, C., and Meins, E. (2008). A new spin on the wheel of fortune: priming of action-authorship judgements and relation to psychosis-like experiences. *Conscious. Cogn.* 17, 576–586. doi: 10.1016/j.concog.2007.08.008

Klimesch, W., Schack, B., and Sauseng, P. (2005). The functional significance of theta and upper alpha oscillations. *Exp. Psychol.* 52, 99–108. doi: 10.1027/1618-3169.52.2.99

Linser, K., and Goschke, T. (2007). Unconscious modulation of the conscious experience of voluntary control. *Cognition* 104, 459–475. doi: 10.1016/j.cognition.2006.07.009

Moore, J. W., Lagnado, D., Deal, D. C., and Haggard, P. (2009). Feelings of control: contingency determines experience of action. *Cognition* 110, 279–283. doi: 10.1016/j.cognition.2008.11.006

Moran, J. M., Macrae, C. N., Heatherton, T. F., Wyland, C. L., and Kelley, W. M. (2006). Neuroanatomical evidence for distinct cognitive and affective components of self. *J. Cogn. Neurosci.* 18, 1586–1594. doi: 10.1162/jocn.2006.18.9.1586

Muthukumaraswamy, S. D., and Singh, K. D. (2011). A cautionary note on the interpretation of phase-locking estimates with concurrent changes in power. *Clin Neurophysiol.* 122, 2324–2325. doi: 10.1016/j.clinph.2011.04.003

Nahab, F. B., Kundu, P., Gallea, C., Kakareka, J., Pursley, R., Pohida, T., et al. (2011). The neural processes underlying self-agency. *Cereb. Cortex* 21, 48–55. doi: 10.1093/cercor/bhq059

Rameson, L. T., Satpute, A. B., and Lieberman, M. D. (2010). The neural correlates of implicit and explicit self-relevant processing. *Neuroimage* 50, 701–708. doi: 10.1016/j.neuroimage.2009.12.098

Renes, R. A., Vermeulen, L., Kahn, R. S., Aarts, H., and van Haren, N. E. (2013). Abnormalities in the establishment of feeling of self-agency in schizophrenia. *Schizophr. Res.* 143, 50–54. doi: 10.1016/j.schres.2012.10.024

Ruys, K. I., and Aarts, H. (2012). I didn't mean to hurt you! Unconscious origins of experienced self-agency over others' emotions. *Emotion* 12, 132–141. doi: 10.1037/a0023161

Salinas, E., and Sejnowski, T. J. (2001). Correlated neuronal activity and the flow of neural information. *Nat. Rev. Neurosci.* 2, 539–550. doi: 10.1038/35086012

Sato, A. (2009). Both motor prediction and conceptual congruency between preview and action-effect contribute to explicit judgment of agency. *Cognition* 110, 74–83. doi: 10.1016/j.cognition.2008.10.011

Sauseng, P., and Klimesch, W. (2008). What does phase information of oscillatory brain activity tell us about cognitive processes? *Neurosci. Biobehav. Rev.* 32, 1001–1013. doi: 10.1016/j.neubiorev.2008.03.014

Schnitzler, A., and Gross, J. (2005). Normal and pathological oscillatory communication in the brain. *Nat. Rev. Neurosci.* 6, 285–296. doi: 10.1038/nrn1650

Sperduti, M., Delaveau, P., Fossati, P., and Nadel, J. (2011). Different brain structures related to self-and external-agency attribution: a brief review and meta-analysis. *Brain Struct. Funct.* 216, 151–157. doi: 10.1007/s00429-010-0298-1

Stam, C. J., Nolte, G., and Daffertshofer, A. (2007). Phase lag index: assessment of functional connectivity from multi channel EEG and MEG with diminished bias from common sources. *Hum. Brain. Mapp.* 28, 1178–1193. doi: 10.1002/hbm.20346

Stam, C. J., and van Straaten, E. C. W. (2012a). The organization of physiological brain networks. *Clin. Neurophysiol.* 123, 1067–1087. doi: 10.1016/j.clinph.2012.01.011

Stam, C. J., and van Straaten, E. C. W. (2012b). Go with the flow: use of a directed phase lag index (dPLI) to characterize patterns of phase relations in a large-scale model of brain dynamics. *Neuroimage* 62, 1415–1428. doi: 10.1016/j.neuroimage.2012.05.050

Synofzik, M., Vosgerau, G., and Newen, A. (2008). Beyond the comparator model: a multifactorial two-step account of agency. *Conscious. Cogn.* 17, 219–239. doi: 10.1016/j.concog.2007.03.010

Synofzik, M., Vosgerau, G., and Voss, M. (2013). The experience of agency: an interplay between prediction and postdiction. *Front. Psychol.* 4:127. doi: 10.3389/fpsyg.2013.00127

Van der Weiden, A., Aarts, H., and Ruys, K. I. (2011). Prime and probability: causal knowledge affects inferential and predictive effects on self-agency experiences. *Conscious. Cogn.* 20, 1865–1871. doi: 10.1016/j.concog.2011.09.007

Van der Weiden, A., Ruys, K. I., and Aarts, H. (2013). A matter of matching: how goals and primes affect self-agency experiences. *J. Exp. Psychol. Gen.* 142, 954–966. doi: 10.1037/a0030079

Varela, F., Lachaux, J. P., Rodriguez, E., and Martinerie, J. (2001). The brain-web: phase synchronization and large-scale integration. *Nat. Rev. Neurosci.* 2, 229–239. doi: 10.1038/35067550

Vinck, M., Oostenveld, R., van Wingerden, M., Battaglia, F., and Pennartz, C. (2011). An improved index of phase-synchronization for electrophysiological data in the presence of volume-conduction, noise and sample-size bias. *Neuroimage* 55, 1548–1565. doi: 10.1016/j.neuroimage.2011.01.055

Voineskos, A. N., Lobaugh, N. J., Bouix, S., Rajji, T. K., Miranda, D., Kennedy, J. L., et al. (2010). Diffusion tensor tractography findings in schizophrenia across the adult lifespan. *Brain* 133, 1494–1504. doi: 10.1093/brain/awq040

Wegner, D. M. (2002). *The Illusion of Conscious Will.* Cambridge, MA: MIT Press.

Wegner, D. M., Sparrow, B., and Winerman, L. (2004). Vicarious agency: experiencing control over the movements of others. *J. Pers. Soc. Psychol.* 86, 838–848. doi: 10.1037/0022-3514.86.6.838

Wegner, D. M., and Wheatley, T. (1999). Apparent mental causation: sources of the experience of will. *Am. Psychol.* 54, 480–492. doi: 10.1037/0003-066X.54.7.480

Whitford, T. J., Kubicki, M., and Shenton, M. E. (2011). Diffusion tensor imaging, structural connectivity, and schizophrenia. *Schizophr. Res. Treatment.* 2011:709523. doi: 10.1155/2011/709523

10

Freedom, choice and the sense of agency

Zeynep Barlas and Sukhvinder S. Obhi*

Centre for Cognitive Neuroscience and Department of Psychology, Wilfrid Laurier University, Waterloo, ON, Canada

***Correspondence:**
Sukhvinder S. Obhi, Department of Psychology, Wilfrid Laurier University, Science Building, 75 University Avenue West, Waterloo, ON N2L 3C5, Canada
e-mail: sobhi@wlu.ca

The sense of agency is an intriguing aspect of human consciousness and is commonly defined as the sense that one is the author of their own actions and their consequences. In the current study, we varied the number of action alternatives (one, three, seven) that participants could select from and determined the effects on intentional binding which is believed to index the low-level sense of agency. Participants made self-paced button presses while viewing a conventional Libet clock and reported the perceived onset time of either the button presses or consequent auditory tones. We found that the binding effect was strongest when participants had the maximum number of alternatives, intermediate when they had medium level of action choice and lowest when they had no choice. We interpret our results in relation to the potential link between agency and the freedom to choose one's actions.

Keywords: freedom, action awareness, sense of agency, action choice, intentional binding, authorship

INTRODUCTION

The sense of agency is one of the most pervasive aspects of human consciousness and is commonly defined as the sense that one is author of their own actions and sensory consequences (Haggard and Tsakiris, 2009). Although a full understanding of how we experience the sense of agency remains elusive, research conducted in the last decade has been fruitful in providing the basis for greater insight into agentic experience and the processes that might produce it. At the conceptual level, two competing views emphasizing predictive and retroactive processes, respectively, are slowly being reconciled into a unified framework within which to the study the sense of agency (see Moore and Obhi, 2012). Despite this progress, numerous questions about the neurocognitive architecture underlying agency and the type and variety of factors that affect agency, remain.

It has previously been suggested that the subjective experience of agency occurs at both first order (pre-reflective) and higher order (reflective) levels of processing (Bayne and Pacherie, 2007; Gallagher, 2007, 2010; Synofzik et al., 2008a,b; Obhi and Hall, 2011a,b). The distinction between different forms of agentic experience leads to the question of whether the sense of agency originates at the lower level of sensorimotor operations or at a higher level involving interpretive mechanisms. In this respect, two major accounts have been proposed to explain the origins of the sense of agency. The *predictive* account underlines the role of intrinsic and sensorimotor cues, whereas the inferential account posits the contribution of extrinsic cues and high level inferences (Wegner and Wheatley, 1999; Frith et al., 2000; Blakemore et al., 2002; Wegner, 2002, 2003; Frith, 2005; Sato and Yasuda, 2005; Gallagher, 2007).

Many experiments investigating the neurocognitive basis of agentic experience have used explicit judgments as dependent measures of the sense of agency. Such explicit measures most commonly require participants to state how much control they felt over action outcomes (e.g., Sato and Yasuda, 2005; Balslev et al., 2007; Linser and Goschke, 2007; Metcalfe and Greene, 2007; Ebert and Wegner, 2010; Wenke et al., 2010) or the actions themselves (e.g., Wegner et al., 2004; Sebanz and Lackner, 2007). In some cases participants are asked to make direct judgments about the cause or source of an effect in contexts where source ambiguity is present (i.e., confederate, computer, or participant themselves could have caused the effect; e.g., Wegner and Wheatley, 1999; Aarts et al., 2005, 2009; Dijksterhuis et al., 2008; Spengler et al., 2009; Obhi and Hall, 2011a,b).

However, applying only such explicit measures is highly prone to contamination by issues such as social desirability, impression management and the limits of introspection on the part of participants (Metcalfe and Greene, 2007; Schüür and Haggard, 2011; Obhi, 2012). Alternatively, other experiments have employed "intentional binding" as a potentially implicit measure of the sense of agency. The intentional binding effect refers to the temporal attraction between the perceived times of actions and effects observed in voluntary actions (e.g., Haggard et al., 2002; Haggard and Clark, 2003; Haggard et al., 2009; Moore et al., 2009; Strother and Obhi, 2009; Strother et al., 2010). Since it was first introduced, intentional binding has sparked great interest, due to its purported link relationship to the sense of agency (see Moore and Haggard, 2010; Moore and Obhi, 2012). Although the quest to fully unveil this relationship requires extensive investigation, the progress made by the recent research has been promising (for a recent review of intentional binding research, Moore and Obhi, 2012).

To move closer to understanding the potential relationship between binding and the sense of agency, one approach is to investigate factors that could feasibly be related to agency and assess whether they affect intentional binding. If such factors do indeed affect binding, it would lend support to the notion that binding and agency are indeed linked in some, albeit complex, way.

Agency and freedom are often considered to be tightly intertwined. That is, agency is thought to be strongest in an "environment of opportunities" (Pettit, 2001). Indeed, if a person cannot freely choose a course of action, the very notion that they are an autonomous agent is undermined. Given this, it might be expected that agency and freedom are related such that increasing levels of freedom to choose a course of action correspond to increasing levels of agency. In their study, for example, Wenke et al. (2010) assessed the feeling of control over action outcomes when the proportion of cued and free trials (25% vs. 75%) and the compatibility between two different subliminal action primes and responses were manipulated. In the cued trials participants were required to perform the cued action where in the free trials they could freely choose one of two actions. The results showed that participants' feeling of control was greater when the primes were compatible with the action responses, suggesting the effect of facilitating the action selection processes. Of more interest, the control ratings were higher when the proportion of free trials was high (75/25 ratio). This study suggests an intriguing link between one's freedom to choose an action and their feeling of control over the consequences of their action.

By extension and reducing the general idea of a link between freedom and agency to a testable laboratory task, intentional binding might also be expected to vary with differences in the degree of freedom. Again, agency and freedom are often talked about together and the feeling of freedom has been linked to choice (e.g., Markus and Schwartz, 2010). In this light it is interesting to note that most previous intentional binding experiments have required participants to make a pre-specified action which is followed by a sensory event such as an auditory tone. In such cases, the participant is free to select *when* to make an action, but is not free to select *which* action to make. By simply changing the number of action alternatives that are available to participants, it is possible to parametrically manipulate the "environment of opportunities" (i.e., choice) and thus ascertain the effect that the number of choice alternatives has on intentional binding. The fundamental question is, do more action alternatives produce greater levels of intentional binding than a more constrained choice set, where the agent is less involved in selecting which action to make?

To this end, in the present study we examined how agency as purportedly indexed by intentional binding, is affected when the number of action alternatives is manipulated. To our knowledge, this is the first study that addresses the potential relationship between freedom of action choice and the sense of agency. Accordingly, in the present study participants were requested to make a key press on a seven-button response pad while watching a conventional Libet clock on the screen. They reported their perceived times of key press or the auditory tone that was produced by their key press. In the no choice condition, they were told to press only one specific button on the response pad. In the medium-choice condition, they were free to choose among three buttons and in the high-choice condition they were allowed to press any of the seven buttons. For reports of the timing of actions and effects, we employed a similar paradigm to that of Libet et al. (1983) (see also Haggard et al., 2002; Obhi et al., 2007, 2009).

METHOD

PARTICIPANTS

Twenty-four right handed participants (18 women; age range = 17–22) took part in the study. All participants had normal or corrected-to-normal vision and received partial course credits for their participation. The study was approved by the Research Ethics Board of Wilfrid Laurier University and all participants gave written informed consent prior to beginning the study. One participant's data was not included in the analyses due to not following the experimental instructions.

APPARATUS AND PROCEDURE

The experiment was programmed in Superlab 4.5 (Cedrus Corporation, USA) and ran on a Dell personal computer (3.07 GHz). The stimuli were presented on a 20 inch monitor (1600 × 1200). Participants sat approximately 60 cm away from the computer monitor and the responses were recorded on a laptop by the experimenter. The experiment consisted of baseline and operant conditions in which the number of keys to press (high: 7, medium: 3, no choice: 1) and the critical event (key press, tone) that participants judged the timing were manipulated. Similar to Haggard et al. (2002) study, the baseline condition consisted of single events with either the key presses or the auditory tones. The key press single event condition included seven (high level of choice condition), three (medium level of choice condition) and one (no choice condition) key press choices. In the no choice condition, participants could only press the blue button centrally placed on the response pad. In the medium level of choice condition, they were told to choose one of the three buttons on the right side of the response pad. In the high level of choice condition, participants were free to choose any of the seven buttons on the response pad. When the critical event was the auditory tone, participants did not make any key press but only reported the time when they heard the tone. In the operant conditions, participants' key press was followed by a 1000 Hz tone (duration: 100 ms, bit rate: 160 Kbps) presented after a delay of 200 ms and they were asked to report the time of either their key press or the tone. The condition (2: baseline, operant) together with the level of action choices (3: High, Medium, No choice) and the critical event (2: Key press, Tone) in total were tested in ten separate blocks with 30 trials each (see **Table 1** for a list of different block types). The order of the blocks was randomized across participants. At the beginning of each block, participants were informed which key or keys they were allowed to press and which of the two events' timing (key press or the tone) they were going to report. Participants completed six practice trials prior to the beginning of each block. Sixty practice trials in total thus were excluded from the data analysis.

Each trial began with a warning signal noting that a new trial will begin, which remained on the screen for 1 s. The fixation cross was then presented for 500 ms and followed by the display of the Libet clock (1.8 cm in diameter) with a minute hand pointing to one of 12 positions marked at 5-minute intervals. Participants were told to report their judgments between 0 (12 O'clock position) and 59, including the intermediate values. The minute hand remained stationary at the center of the screen for 500 ms and

Table 1 | Mean judgment errors in each condition.

Level of Choice	Individual Event	Mean Judgment Error	SD
No Choice	Key press alone	−35.96	67.85
	Key* tone	−12.68	81.19
	Key tone*	−106.12	135.21
Medium	Key press alone	−19.24	83.33
	Key* tone	−13.21	63.10
	Key tone*	−141.55	114.60
High	Key press alone	−58.19	62.18
	Key* tone	−11.34	83.65
	Key tone*	−137.73	143.22
	Tone alone	−117.44	97.56

For each event and each condition, perceived times were subtracted from the actual time of the corresponding events.

**Indicates which event was reported in terms of its timing in the operant condition.*

then started rotating clockwise at a 2.5 s period. In the baseline—where the single event was the key press only—and in the operant conditions, participants were told to make the key press at their own pace using their right index finger after the clock started rotating. They were instructed not to give stereotyped responses in the high and medium level of choice conditions and not to press the key at predetermined minute hand positions. In the baseline tone-only condition, participants did not make any key press but reported the onset of the tone occurred at a random time (jittered between 200 and 2000 ms) after the clock hand rotation started. The clock continued rotating for about 2000 ms after the participants reported the timing of the critical event. The perceptual times were verbally reported as minute hand positions and recorded by the experimenter on a laptop. At the end of the experiment, participants were debriefed and thanked for their participation in the study (see **Figure 1** for a sample trial procedure).

RESULTS

The experiment comprised a 2 (Condition: Baseline, Operant) × 3 (Level of choice: High, Medium, No choice) × 2 (Critical Event: Action, Tone) repeated measures design. After converting the clock hand judgments to time values in milliseconds, we calculated the judgment errors for each condition as the difference between perceived and actual times of events (**Table 1**). Trials with key press response time shorter than or equal to 500 ms and with judgment errors three standard deviations away from participant's average judgment error were excluded from the analysis. In addition, trials in which participants made a key press other than the permitted ones were removed from the data. The exclusion criteria resulted in the removal of 3.06% of all trials (range: 1–11%).

We then obtained the perceptual shifts in terms of the difference between judgment errors between operant and the corresponding single event baseline conditions for both key press and tone judgments. For example, the perceptual shift for the high level action choice condition was calculated as the difference between the judgment errors in the operant-high-level condition from the baseline-high-level condition. Similarly, the perceptual shifts for the tone judgments were calculated as the difference between the judgment errors in each choice level-tone judgment condition and baseline-tone only condition. The positive shifts in the key press judgments and the negative shifts in the tone judgments relative to the corresponding baseline conditions demonstrate the temporal attraction, i.e., the intentional binding effect, between actions and effects (**Figure 2**).

We ran a 3 (Level of choice: High, Medium, No choice) × 2 (Critical event: Key press, Tone) repeated measures ANOVA to examine the effect of having different number of action choices on the perceptual shifts. The analysis revealed a significant main effect of key press choice ($F(2,44) = 3.359$, $p < .05$) and a significant main effect of critical event ($F(1,22) = 5.148$, $p < .05$). The interaction between these factors was also significant ($F(2,44) = 3.389$, $p < .05$). We predicted that binding would be least for the no choice condition, strongest for the high level of choice condition and intermediate for the medium level condition. We thus conducted one-tailed Paired Samples t tests to examine the 2-way interaction in more detail.

The t tests performed on the perceived times of actions revealed that when participants had high number of choices among which keys they could press, their perceptual shift in key press judgments from baseline condition was moved significantly further toward the tone compared to when they had medium level of choices ($t(22) = 2.287$, $p < .05$) and to when they had no choice ($t(22) = 1.792$, $p < .05$). The difference between medium level of choice condition and no choice condition was not significant ($p > .05$).

With respect to the tone judgments, the perceptual shifts moved toward the perceived action onsets for both medium and high levels of choices. The size of the shift was greater for the medium level than the high level and it was in the opposite direction for the no choice condition. We found a significant difference in the perceptual shifts between high level of choice and no choice conditions ($t(22) = -2.186$, $p < .05$) and also between medium level of choice and no choice conditions ($t(22) = -2.260$, $p < .05$). The difference in the perceptual shifts between high and medium level of choices was not significant ($p > .05$).

We sought further the effect of choice levels on the mean overall binding by calculating the absolute value of subtraction of the mean key press shift in each condition from the tone shift (Wenke et al., 2009). We conducted a 3 (Level of choice: High, Medium, No choice) repeated measures ANOVA and found a significant main effect of action choice level on overall binding ($F(2,44) = 3.389$, $p < .05$). As expected, we found that overall binding was strongest in the high level of action choice condition, intermediate for the medium level of choice condition and lowest for the no choice condition (**Figure 3**). We ran one-tailed t tests to examine the differences across the three choice levels. The results showed that overall binding in the high level of choice condition was significantly greater compared to no choice ($t(22) = 1.998$, $p < .05$) condition. However, the difference between high level of choice and medium level of choice condition as well as the difference between medium level of choice and no choice conditions were not significant ($p > .05$).

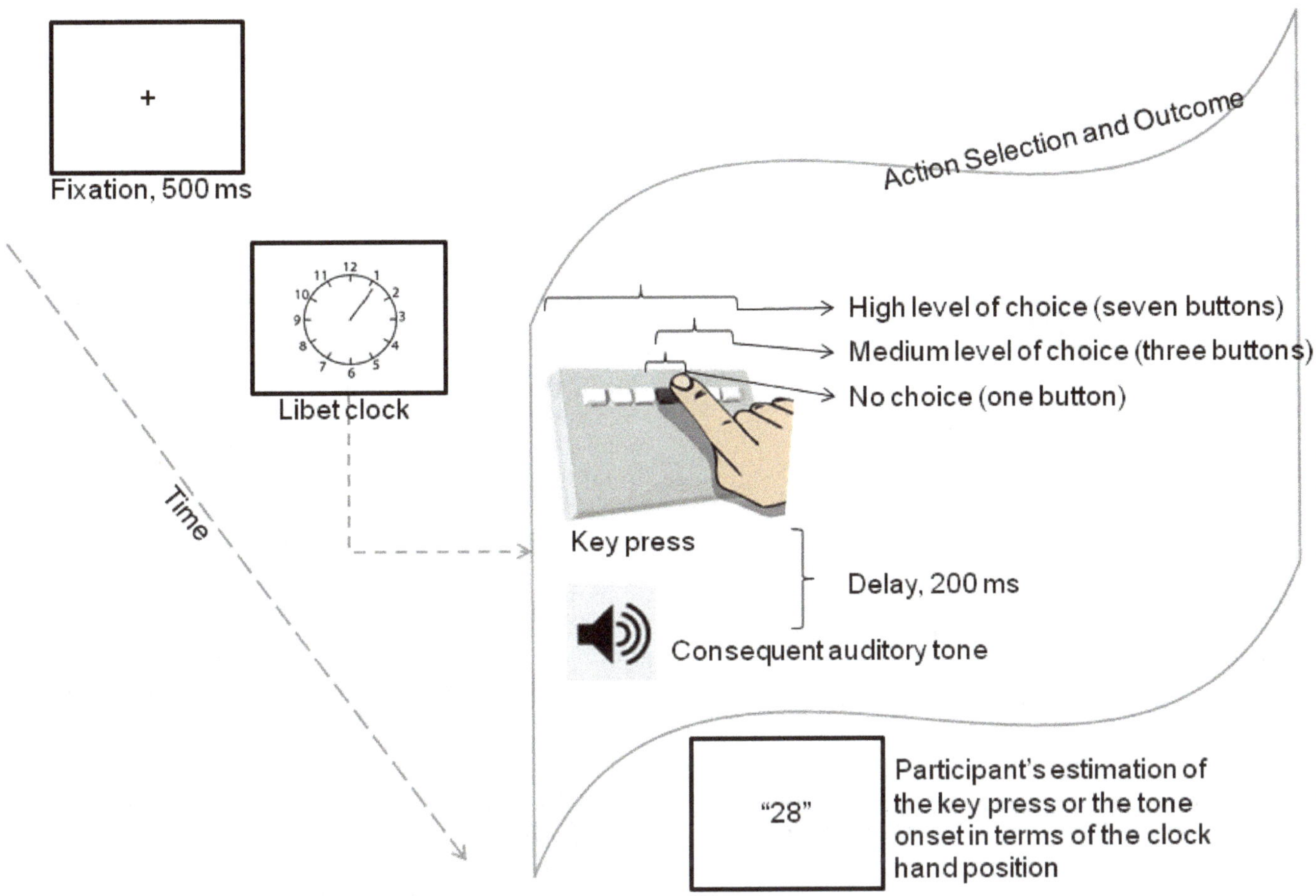

FIGURE 1 | Trial procedure in the operant condition. Each trial began with a fixation cross displayed for 500 ms, participants then made a key press at their own pace after the clock started rotating. They were told to press a specific button in the no-choice condition or select one of three (medium level of choice) or seven (high level of choice) buttons on the response pad. The key press was followed by the auditory tone after a delay of 200 ms. In the baseline condition, participants either made a key press without hearing the tone and judged the timing of their key press, or heard the tone which occurred alone and judged the timing of the tone.

DISCUSSION

Previous research focusing on different forms of the sense of agency has examined the contribution of various factors including predictive and retrospective processes (see Moore and Obhi, 2012, for a full review of these studies). Action selection is a crucial aspect of the agentic experience and has been shown to enhance the explicit feeling of control when facilitated by the subliminal priming of action alternatives (Wenke et al., 2010). The goal of the present study was to examine how intentional binding would be influenced by different levels of action choice. This is an important question given popular notions about how freedom and agency are intertwined (e.g., Pettit, 2001).

We measured the perceived times of individual key press and tone events separately in both baseline and operant conditions which allowed us to compare the size of the perceptual shift between each level of action choice. First, we found that perceived times of key presses for all levels of choices were shifted forward in time. In the medium level and high level conditions, the direction of the perceived time of the tones was shifted toward the key press whereas, somewhat surprisingly, this was not the case for the no-choice condition. Importantly though, as **Figure 2** shows, the overall shift for each individual event (i.e., key press and tone) were in the right direction and demonstrate the intentional binding effect. Of more interest, we found that the degree of overall binding was greatest when participants had the highest level of action alternatives to choose from. In the medium choice condition, binding was not significantly different from the no choice condition, but both these conditions displayed less binding than the high choice condition. Moreover, the magnitude of the binding in three conditions displayed a parametric trend increasing from none to three and seven alternatives (**Figure 3**). Thus, our results provide support for the notion that a high degree of choice is associated with greater action-effect binding than lower degrees of choice. These results serve to connect the sense of agency to free-choice and are also consistent with the common societal notion that the exercise of personal choice, freedom and agency are intimately intertwined (Hirschmann, 2003; Krause, 2012).

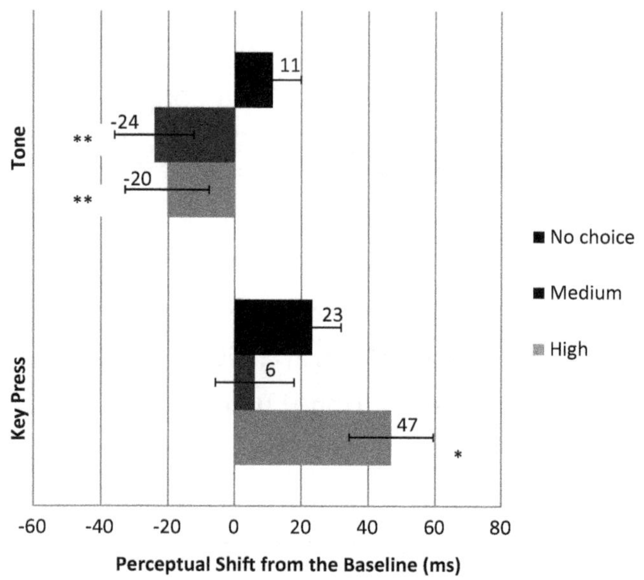

FIGURE 2 | Mean perceptual shift (difference between the judgment errors in the operant and baseline conditions) for key press (lower) and tone (upper) judgments. Error bars represent SEM (*indicates that the perceptual shift for key presses in the high level of choice condition was significantly greater than the medium level of choice and no choice conditions, $p < .05$. The difference between medium level of choice and no choice conditions was not significant, $p > .05$. **Indicates that the perceptual shift for the tone judgments in the high level of choice and the medium level of conditions were significantly greater than no choice condition, $p < .05$. The difference between high and medium levels of choice was not significant, $p > .05$).

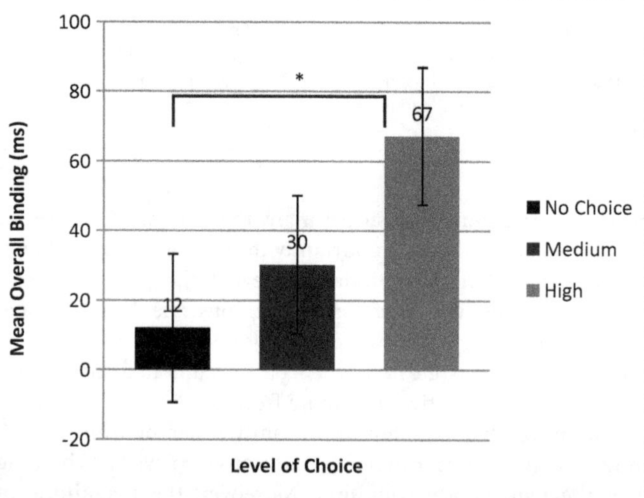

FIGURE 3 | Mean overall binding as a function of action choice. Error bars represent SEM (*indicates that binding is significantly greater in the high level of choice condition than in the no choice condition, $p < .05$).

What could be driving our observed effects of choice on intentional binding and by extension, the sense of agency? Given that all possible actions in the set of alternatives produced the same auditory event, our method could be construed as a true test of action selection on the sense of agency. That is, there is no obvious reason why an individual participant may have chosen one action over another, given that the outcome, or reward value of each possible action was fixed. Several explanations are possible.

First, the results we report here are consistent with the finding that intentional binding is stronger when participants specify both the "what" and the "when" component of a pending action, compared to when they specify just one of these dimensions (i.e., "when" or "what"—Brass and Haggard, 2008; Wenke et al., 2009). Participants in the present study were always responsible for specifying the "when" component, but had varying levels of choice about "what" action to make. Specifically, participants were constrained to just one possible action (no choice condition), three possible actions (medium choice condition) or seven possible actions (high choice condition). Thus, in the no choice condition, the action is completely specified externally by the experimenter whereas in both the medium and high choice conditions, the participant must internally specify which action they will ultimately select. By some accounts, the no choice condition can be thought of as more externally triggered than the medium and high choice conditions (see Obhi and Haggard, 2004; Schüür and Haggard, 2011; Obhi, 2012; Schüür and Haggard, 2012). Correspondingly, it has been shown that activation in areas associated with voluntary preparation to act, such as the supplementary motor area (SMA) is greater for actions that are more internally specified than externally specified (Jahanshahi et al., 1995). Thus one broad explanation for our findings is that more internal, endogenous processing prior to action production is linked to higher levels of agency experience, which manifests as greater intentional binding.

Another interesting framework within which to consider our results is based on the affordance competition hypothesis that models behavior as resulting from competition between different representations of potential actions (Cisek, 2007). In this model, action representations are thought of as distributed neural populations that are activated via selective attentional mechanisms (Tipper et al., 1992). By such a view, the action that is finally selected and executed is chosen based on a dynamic reciprocal process operating largely within fronto-parietal circuits which involves mutual inhibition between potential action representations and is subject to biasing by excitatory inputs, some of which arise from cognitive decision making processes (see Cisek, 2007, for a detailed discussion).

Within this framework, we suggest that high, medium and no choice conditions differ in the degree of this dynamic activation and inhibition process that is ultimately responsible for action selection. Specifically, the no-choice condition may not involve the same degree of this dynamic inhibitory and excitatory activity as the high choice condition. We suggest that this difference might result in stronger activation of the representation of the action selected among many, such as in the high choice condition of the present experiment.

This is akin to more endogenous processing being linked to greater agency, as suggested above, with the endogenous activity being specifically the dynamic interplay between excitatory and inhibitory processes during action selection. This explanation also predicts greater binding for the medium choice condition compared to the no choice condition as reported in our study, although the difference was not significant. From the present study, it appears that when seven alternative actions are available, this is sufficient to change the subjective experience of actions compared to when there is no alternative. However three alternatives demonstrate no difference from seven or no alternatives. Clearly, more work is required to determine if this suggestion is tenable, but at the very least, our data do indicate that high choice affects binding in a way that no choice does not.

One might argue that the cognitive load varied across three levels of action choices in our study, which could have contaminated our results. However, as previous studies discussed this concern in detail, (e.g., Haggard et al., 2002) the errors in time judgments in the operant condition are subtracted from their corresponding baseline conditions (e.g., high level of choice action judgment errors in the baseline condition are subtracted from high level of choice action judgment errors in the operant condition) to calculate the perceptual shifts for each event and condition. Since the potential effect of either cognitive or attentional requirements varying across different levels of choice should be present in both baseline and operant conditions, this effect would diminish as a result of the subtraction we used to obtain the perceptual shifts. We thus feel confident in ruling out the effect of differential cognitive load across conditions.

Having demonstrated that a high degree of choice is linked to increased binding, it is important to consider that there are limitations to the present study. For example, we did not assess the explicit sense of agency in this study and so cannot speak to how the number of action choice alternatives might affect the explicit feeling of agency. In addition, we did not manipulate the outcome of the different action alternatives. This is an obvious extension of the current work and would allow for determining the influence of reward on intentional binding and the sense of agency.

Despite these limitations, showing that intentional binding is influenced by the degree of action choice is an important finding and we believe the current study provides a new set of questions relating to how choice affects the sense of agency, which could apply to many domains that extend beyond a fundamental consideration of how the sense of agency arises.

Finally, the current results, along with other recent results from our and other labs, bolster the notion that intentional binding is linked, in some complex way to agentic experience. Specifically, we have previously shown that priming low power reduces binding and activating memories of depression reduces binding, whereas others have shown that less versus more control of an aircraft, when control is shared with an automatic pilot, reduces binding (Berberian et al., 2012; Obhi et al., 2012a,b). Given that these scenarios are all accompanied by real changes in the degree of control that an individual either perceives themselves as having, or actually has, the idea that binding and agency are linked is strengthened. The key is for future work to understand *why and precisely how* the sense of agency and binding are affected by these kinds of manipulations. For now though, the current results reinforce the suggestion that increased personal choice increases agency which could form the foundation for a sense of freedom.

REFERENCES

Aarts, H., Custers, R., and Marien, H. (2009). Priming and authorship ascription: when nonconscious goals turn into conscious experiences of self-agency. *J. Pers. Soc. Psychol.* 96, 967–979. doi: 10.1037/a0015000

Aarts, H., Custers, R., and Wegner, D. M. (2005). On the inference of personal authorship: enhancing experienced agency by priming effect information. *Conscious. Cogn.* 14, 439–458. doi: 10.1016/j.concog. 2004.11.001

Balslev, D., Cole, J., and Miall, R. C. (2007). Proprioception contributes to the sense of agency during visual observation of hand movements: evidence from temporal judgments of action. J. Cogn. Neurosci. 19, 1535–1541. doi: 10.1162/jocn.2007. 19.9.1535

Bayne, T., and Pacherie, E. (2007). Narrators and comparators: the architecture of agentive self-awareness. *Synthese* 159, 475–491. doi: 10. 1007/s11229-007-9239-9

Berberian, B., Sarrazin, J.-C., Le Blaye, P., and Haggard, P. (2012). Automation technology and sense of control: a window on human agency. PLoS One 7:e34075. doi: 10. 1371/journal.pone.0034075

Blakemore, S. J., Wolpert, D. M., and Frith, C. D. (2002). Abnormalities in the awareness of action. Trends Cogn. Sci. 6, 237–242. doi: 10. 1016/S1364-6613(02)01907-1

Brass, M., and Haggard, P. (2008). The what, when, whether of intentional action. Neuroscientist 14, 319–325. doi: 10.1177/1073858408317417

Cisek, P. (2007). Cortical mechanisms of action selection: the affordance competition hypothesis. Philos. Trans. R. Soc. Lond. B Biol. Sci. 362, 1585–1599. doi: 10.1098/rstb.2007. 2054

Dijksterhuis, A., Preston, J., Wegner, D. M., and Aarts, H. (2008). Effects of subliminal priming of self and god on self-attribution of authorship for events. J. Exp. Soc. Psychol. 44, 2–9. doi: 10.1016/j.jesp.2007.01. 003

Ebert, J. P., and Wegner, D. M. (2010). Time warp: authorship shapes the perceived timing of actions and events. *Conscious. Cogn.* 19, 481–489. doi: 10.1016/j.concog.2009.10.002

Frith, C. (2005). The self in action: lessons from delusions of control. *Conscious. Cogn.* 14, 752–770. doi: 10.1016/j.concog.2005.04.002

Frith, C. D., Blakemore, S. J., and Wol-pert, D. M. (2000). Abnormalities in the awareness and control of action. Philos. Trans. R. Soc. Lond. B Biol. Sci. 355, 1771–1788. doi: 10. 1098/rstb.2000.0734

Gallagher, S. (2007). The natural philosophy of agency. Philos. Compass 2, 347–357. doi: 10.1111/j. 1747-9991.2007.00067.x

Gallagher, S. (2010). Multiple aspects in the sense of agency. New Ideas Psychol. 30, 15–31.

Haggard, P., and Clark, S. (2003). Intentional action: conscious experience and neural prediction. *Conscious. Cogn.* 12, 695–707. doi: 10. 1016/s1053-8100(03)00052-7

Haggard, P., Clark, S., and Kalogeras, J. (2002). Voluntary action and conscious awareness. Nat. Neurosci. 5, 382–385. doi: 10.1038/nn827

Haggard, P., Poonian, S., and Walsh, E. (2009). Representing the consequences of intentionally inhibited actions. Brain Res. 1286, 106–113. doi: 10.1016/j. brainres. 2009.06.020

Haggard, P., and Tsakiris, M. (2009). The experience of agency: feelings, judgments, and responsibility. Curr. Dir. Psychol. Sci. 18, 242–246. doi: 10.1111/j.1467-8721. 2009.01644.x

Hirschmann, N. J. (2003). *The Subject of Liberty: Toward a Feminist Theory of Freedom.* Princeton, NJ: Princeton University Press.

Jahanshahi, M., Jenkins, H., Brown, R. G., Marsden, C. D., Passingham, R. E., and Brooks, D. J. (1995). Self-initiated versus externally triggered movements: I. An investigation using measurement of regional cerebral blood-flow with pet and movement-related potentials in normal and Parkinsons-disease subjects. Brain 118, 913–933. doi: 10. 1093/brain/118.4.913

Krause, S. R. (2012). Plural freedom. Polit. Gend. 8, 238–245. doi: 10. 1017/s1743923x12000220

Libet, B., Gleason, C. A., Wright, E. W., and Pearl, D. K. (1983). Time of conscious intention to act in relation to onset of cerebral activity (readiness potential): the unconscious initiation of a freely voluntary act. Brain 102, 623–642. doi: 10. 1093/brain/106.3.623

Linser, K., and Goschke, T. (2007). Unconscious modulation of the conscious experience of voluntary control. *Cognition* 104, 459–475. doi: 10.1016/j. cognition.2006.07. 009

Markus, H. R., and Schwartz, B. (2010). Does choice mean freedom and well-being? J. Consum. Res. 37, 344–354. doi: 10.1086/651242

Metcalfe, J., and Greene, M. J. (2007). Metacognition of agency. J. Exp. Psychol. Gen. 136, 184–199. doi: 10. 1037/0096-3445.136.2.184

Moore, J. W., and Haggard, P. (2010). Intentional binding and higher order agency experience. *Conscious. Cogn.* 19, 490–491. doi: 10.1016/j.concog.2009.11.007

Moore, J. W., and Obhi, S. S. (2012). Intentional binding and the sense of agency: a review. *Conscious. Cogn.* 21, 546–561. doi: 10.1016/j.concog. 2011.12.002

Moore, J. W., Wegner, D. M., and Haggard, P. (2009). Modulating the sense of agency with external cues. *Conscious. Cogn.* 18, 1056–1064. doi: 10.1016/j.concog.2009.05.004

Obhi, S. S. (2012). The troublesome distinction between self-generated and externally triggered action: a commentary on Schüür and Haggard. *Conscious. Cogn.* 21, 587–588. doi: 10.1016/j.concog.2011.09. 014

Obhi, S. S., and Haggard, P. (2004). Internally generated and externally triggered actions are physically distinct and independently controlled. Exp. Brain Res. 156, 518–523. doi: 10.1007/s00221-004- 1911-4

Obhi, S. S., and Hall, P. (2011a). Sense of agency and intentional binding in joint action. Exp. Brain Res. 211, 655–662. doi: 10.1007/s00221-011-2675-2

Obhi, S. S., and Hall, P. (2011b). Sense of agency in joint action: influ-ence of human and computer coactors. Exp. Brain Res. 211, 663–670. doi: 10.1007/s00221-011-2662-7

Obhi, S. S., Lyons, J., Welsh, T. N., Glazebrook, C. M., Anson, G., and Elliott, D. (2007). The perceived time of voluntary action for adults with and without down syndrome. *Down Syndr.* Q. 9, 4–9.

Obhi, S. S., Planetta, P. J., and Scantlebury, J. (2009). On the signals underlying conscious awareness of action. *Cognition* 110, 65–73. doi: 10.1016/j.cognition. 2008.10.009

Obhi, S. S., Swiderski, K. M., and Brubacher, S. P. (2012a). Induced power changes the sense of agency. *Conscious. Cogn.* 21, 1547–1550. doi: 10.1016/j.concog.2012.06.008

Obhi, S. S., Swiderski, K., and Farquhar, R. (2012b). Activating memories of depression alters the experience of voluntary action. Exp. Brain Res. doi: 10.1007/s00221012-3372-5. [Epub ahead of print].

Pettit, P. (2001). *A Theory of Freedom: From the Psychology to the Politics of Agency.* New York: Oxford University Press.

Sato, A., and Yasuda, A. (2005). Illusion of self-agency: discrepancy between predicted and actual sensory consequences of actions modulates the sense of self-agency, but not the sense of self-ownership. *Cognition* 94, 241–255. doi: 10. 1016/j.cognition.2004.04.003

Schüür, F., and Haggard, P. (2011). What are self-generated actions? *Conscious. Cogn.* 20, 1697–1704. doi: 10.1016/j.concog.2011.09.006

Schüür, F., and Haggard, P. (2012). On capturing the essence of self-generated action: a reply to Obhi. *Conscious. Cogn.* 21, 1070–1071. doi: 10.1016/j.concog.2012.03.003

Sebanz, N., and Lackner, U. (2007). Who's calling the shots? Intentional content and feelings of control. *Conscious. Cogn.* 16, 859–876. doi: 10.1016/j.concog.2006.08.002

Spengler, S., von Cramon, D. Y., and Brass, M. (2009). Was it me or was it you? How the sense of agency originates from ideomotor learning revealed by fMRI. Neuroimage 46, 290–298. doi: 10.1016/j. neuroimage.2009.01.047

Strother, L., and Obhi, S. S. (2009). The conscious experience of action and intention. Exp. Brain Res. 198, 535–553. doi: 10.1007/s00221-009-1946-7

Strother, L., House, K., and Obhi, S. (2010). Subjective agency and awareness of shared actions. *Conscious. Cogn.* 19, 12–20. doi: 10. 1016/j.concog.2009.12.007

Synofzik, M., Vosgerau, G., and Newen, A. (2008a). Beyond the comparator model: a multifactorial two-step account of agency. *Conscious. Cogn.* 17, 219–239. doi: 10.1016/j.concog. 2007.03.010

Synofzik, M., Vosgerau, G., and Newen, A. (2008b). I move, therefore am: a new theoretical framework to investigate agency and ownership. Conscious. Cogn. 17, 411–424. doi: 10.1016/j.concog.2008.03.008

Tipper, S. P., Lortie, C., and Baylis,
G. C. (1992). Selective reaching: evidence for action-centered attention. J. Exp. Psychol. Hum. Percept. Perform. 18, 891–905. doi: 10. 1037/0096-1523.18.4.891

Wegner, D. M. (2002). The Illusion of Conscious Will. Cambridge, MA: MIT Press.

Wegner, D. M. (2003). The mind's best trick: how we experience conscious will. Trends Cogn. Sci. 7, 65–69. doi: 10.1016/S1364-6613(03)00002-0

Wegner, D. M., and Wheatley, T. (1999). Apparent mental causation: sources of the experience of will. Am. Psychol. 54, 481–492. doi: 10. 1037/0003-066x.54.7.480

Wegner, D. M., Sparrow, B., and Winerman, L. (2004). Vicarious agency: experiencing control over the movements of others. *J. Pers. Soc. Psychol.* 86, 838–848. doi: 10.1037/0022-3514.86.6.838

Wenke, D., Fleming, S., and Haggard, P. (2010). Subliminal priming of actions influences sense of control over effects of action. *Cognition* 115, 26–38. doi: 10.1016/j. cognition.2009.10.016

Wenke, D., Waszak, F., and Haggard, P. (2009). Action selection and action awareness. Psychol. Res. 73, 602–612. doi: 10.1007/s00426-009-0240-4

11

What makes us conscious of our own agency? And why the conscious versus unconscious representation distinction matters

***Glenn Carruthers* ***

ARC Centre of Excellence in Cognition and Its Disorders, Macquarie University, Sydney, NSW, Australia

Correspondence:
Glenn Carruthers, ARC Centre of Excellence in Cognition and Its Disorders, Macquarie University, Level 3 Australian Hearing Hub, 16 University Ave., Sydney, NSW 2109, Australia
e-mail: Glenn.rj.carruthers@gmail.com

Existing accounts of the sense of agency tend to focus on the proximal causal history of the feeling. That is, they explain the sense of agency by describing the cognitive mechanism that causes the sense of agency to be elicited. However, it is possible to elicit an unconscious representation of one's own agency that plays a different role in a cognitive system. I use the "occasionality problem" to suggest that taking this distinction seriously has potential theoretical pay-offs for this reason. We are faced, then, with a need to distinguish instances of the representation of one's own agency in which the subject is aware of their sense of own agency from instances in which they are not. This corresponds to a specific instance of what Dennett calls the "Hard Question": once the representation is elicited, *then what happens?* In other words, how is a representation of one's own agency used in a cognitive system when the subject is aware of it? How is this different from when the representation of own agency remains unconscious? This phrasing suggests a Functionalist answer to the Hard Question. I consider two single function hypotheses. First, perhaps the representation of own agency enters into the mechanisms of attention. This seems unlikely as, in general, attention is insufficient for awareness. Second, perhaps, a subject is aware of their sense of agency when it is available for verbal report. However, this seems inconsistent with evidence of a sense of agency in the great apes. Although these two single function views seem like dead ends, multifunction hypotheses such as the global workspace theory remain live options which we should consider. I close by considering a non-functionalist answer to the Hard Question: perhaps it is not a difference in the use to which the representation is put, but a difference in the nature of the representation itself. When it comes to the sense of agency, the Hard Question remains, but there are alternatives open to us.

Keywords: consciousness, self-consciousness, sense of agency (SoA), hard question, functionalism, vehicle theory

INTRODUCTION

In this paper I argue that we, as a community investigating the sense of agency, are not doing enough to answer what Dennett has called the "Hard Question" of consciousness. Our existing models do a very good job of explaining when a representation of own agency is elicited. I illustrate this with two historically important accounts: the comparator model of Frith et al. and Wegner et al. inference to apparent mental state causation. Following Revonsuo, I consider these to be proximal etiological explanations. Although powerful so far as they go, these accounts, on their own, do not provide us with the explanatory resources to distinguish conscious and unconscious representations of one's own agency. This is not a problem we can ignore. I use the "occasionality problem" to suggest that there are potential theoretical benefits to taking this distinction more seriously as conscious and unconscious representations of own agency play very different roles in cognition. I conclude by considering how we might approach the Hard Question for the sense of agency. I consider two Functionalist approaches (i) that a representation of own agency is conscious if it is taken as the object of attention; and (ii) that a representation of own agency is conscious if it is available for verbal report. Although such approaches offer clear research agendas, both of these specific approaches seem non-starters on empirical grounds. That said multifunction hypotheses such as the global workspace theory remain viable Functionalist positions. Finally I consider a Vehicle theory approach to the Hard Question. Such an approach also offers some clear research questions, but currently no clear answers. As of now, the Hard Question remains under-considered for the sense of agency even though there exist a variety of questions we can ask to make progress on it if we take either a Functionalist or a Vehicle approach. These are questions we would all do well to consider.

STANDARD ACCOUNTS OF THE SENSE OF AGENCY

Standard explanations of the sense of agency are of a particular type. Revonsuo (2006, pp. 20–22) calls this type of explanation "proximal etiological explanation". Such explanations have two defining characteristics. First, they enumerate *causes* of the sense of agency. Second, the explanations are *cognitive* explanations. The specific causes posited are mental representations and computations. To understand these accounts as explanations of the sense of agency then, is to understand them as a description of what aspects of the mind, i.e., mental representations and computations, cause a subject to experience their own agency. The sense of agency itself is taken to be just another representation in this causal chain.

These traits are shared by prominent accounts of the sense of agency. Consider first the comparator model. This model gets its name from the use of three hypothetical comparisons performed by the motor control system. Each of these comparisons performs specific functions for motor control and motor learning (Wolpert and Ghahramani, 2000). One of these comparisons also elicits the sense of agency. This is the comparison that will concern us here (for the full account and its broader applicability see Frith et al., 2000a). On this model it is hypothesized that performing an action requires the formation of a goal state or motor intention (Pacherie, 2008), which represents where the body needs to move to in order to perform the action. From this, the motor control system formulates a motor command, which specifies how to move the body from where it is to where it needs to be in order to attain the goal. Two copies of the motor command are formed; one is sent to the periphery and elicits the requisite contractions of the effector muscles to perform the movement needed to attempt the action. This movement, of course, affects the sensory organs, allowing the motor control system to represent the movement after it occurs. The second copy of the motor command, sometimes called the "efference copy" or "corollary discharge", is used by the motor system to form a prediction of what sensory feedback will be received due to the action. This predicted feedback can be used to represent the action as it occurs (Frith et al., 2000a,b; Blakemore et al., 2002).

Now we get to the sense of agency. It is hypothesized that the collection of representations and computations introduced above cause the sense of agency to be elicited. Specifically when feedback from the senses to the motor control system (actual sensory feedback), matches an internally generated prediction of what this feedback will be (predicted sensory feedback), a sense of agency is elicited (Frith et al., 2000a, p. 1784). These two representations matching in this context means that they represent the same action. The comparator model has been considered a promising explanation of the sense of agency and is able to explain some important discoveries (for recent reviews of what and how see Carruthers, 2012).

Wegner et al. have suggested that the sense of agency is elicited by a rather different kind of computation. On their model, the sense of agency is elicited when one infers that one or other of one's mental states caused the action of one's body (Wegner and Wheatley, 1999, p. 480; Wegner, 2003, p. 67). If correct, we can provide a proximal etiological explanation of the sense of agency by explaining how this inference is made. To make the inference the subject needs to represent their mental states *qua* potential causes of action, represent which body in the world is their own (i.e., a sense of embodiment) and represent the action which is occurring or has occurred. Next they must represent that one or other mental state causes the action of their body. This is the role of the inference to apparent mental state causation. According to Wegner et al. this inference is made when three facts about the relationship between the mental state and action are recognized. First, the mental state must be consistent with the action in that it specifies the action that actually occurs. Second, the mental state must seem to occur at an appropriate time before the action occurs, for example a memory of an action won't be inferred as a cause of that action. Third the thought must appear to be the only possible cause of the action, i.e., if something else, another person or gust of wind, say, could have caused the action then the inference will not be made, or at least not made with a high degree of certainty. Wegner et al. call these the principles of "consistency", "priority" and "exclusivity" respectively (Wegner and Wheatley, 1999, pp. 482–487; Wegner, 2003, p. 67). Like the comparator model, this account has been considered a promising approach to the sense of agency and it can explain some important discoveries (see Wegner, 2002 for reviews; Carruthers, 2010).

Numerous authors have followed the general approach of these classic hypotheses. Recently, several authors have proposed that the sense of agency is elicited by a process that integrates the output of several such computations (Synofzik et al., 2008, 2009; Moore and Fletcher, 2012; Carruthers, in press). This work is characterized by considerable progress in investigations into the computations that elicit the sense of agency. However, there is a limitation to this approach. Knowing how the representation of agency is elicited doesn't distinguish between cases where it is elicited but remains unconscious and cases where it is elicited and the subject is aware of it. Unless we are to view the sense of agency as unique amongst all mental representations in that it can only *ever* be conscious, we must allow for the possibility of a representation of own agency to be elicited and remain unconscious. In the next section I consider the occasionality problem which has been presented as an objection to the comparator model, but which is generalizable to other accounts. I use this as an example to show that taking seriously the distinction between unconscious representations and a conscious sense of agency can have theoretical pay-offs in this area as each of these play different roles in the broader cognitive system. In particular I suggest that if we take this distinction seriously then the occasionality problem doesn't arise.

THE OCCASIONALITY PROBLEM AND UNCONSCIOUS REPRESENTATIONS OF ONE'S OWN AGENCY

It would, I take it, be bizarre if there were no unconscious representations of own agency. But, is there any theoretical benefit for sense of agency research as it it currently done to considering this fact explicitly? In this section I argue that there is. That by considering the different roles conscious and unconscious representations of own agency play, in particular that only the absence conscious representations can be noticed by the subject, we can avoid the "occasionality problem". In the next section I consider some ways in which we might attempt to explain the difference between conscious and unconscious representations of own agency. The occasionality problem, it should be noted, was originally formulated as an objection to the comparator model, but it applies equally to Wegner et al. account described above. To see the problem we first need to take a step back and consider clinical phenomena that the above models need to explain.

One of the central explananda for the accounts introduced above is thought to be delusions of alien control. This delusion, commonly seen as a symptom of schizophrenia, is a patient's belief that not they, but rather some other agent, control the patient's actions. This is expressed in reports such as:

> I felt like an automaton, guided by a female spirit who had entered me during it [an arm movement].
> I thought you [the experimenter] were varying the movements with your thoughts.
> I could feel God guiding me [during an arm movement] (Spence, 2001, p. 165).

There is a growing consensus that explanations focusing on the sense of agency alone cannot explain every feature of this delusion (Synofzik et al., 2008; Carruthers, 2009). In particular, such accounts do not have the resources to explain why patients attribute the action to another specific agent. What such accounts can explain is why patients fail to attribute their actions to themselves. According to the comparator model, in healthy subjects the comparison between actual and predicted sensory feedback causes a sense of agency to be elicited for actions the subject performs. However, it is hypothesized that this computation goes wrong for the patient suffering delusions of alien control. They do not represent a match between predicted and actual sensory feedback when they should and so no sense of agency is elicited. Without this sense, the patient has no experiential basis for a self-attribution of action- they do not feel as though they perform the action- and so actions are not self-attributed. For those interested in the details of why this occurs, there is some experimental evidence that these patients have an underlying deficit in forming or using predicted sensory feedback (Frith and Done, 1989; Blakemore et al., 2000; Carruthers, 2012).

As with the comparator model, Wegner et al. inference to apparent mental state causation is unlikely to explain every feature of this delusion. Like the comparator model it may offer an account of how the sense of agency is lost. According to this view the sense of agency would be lost when one of the principles of priority, exclusivity or consistency is not met. I have argued elsewhere (forthcoming) that on this model it is reasonable to hypothesize that it is the principle of priority which is violated, as there is some evidence that patients suffering from delusions of alien control display abnormalities in the representation of the timing of their actions (Voss et al., 2010).

Now we are in a position to examine the occasionality problem (de Vignemont and Fourneret, 2004; Proust, 2006, p. 89; Synofzik et al., 2008). This problem starts from the observation that those suffering from delusions of alien control only attribute *some* of their actions to other agents. None of the models above appear to have, on their own, the resources to explain this observation. At the core of this objection is an accusation of a false prediction. A model like the comparator model predicts patients lack a sense of agency for their actions because they cannot represent a match at the comparison between actual and predicted sensory feedback. This does not offer us principled grounds for distinguishing those actions that the patient self-attributes and those that they attribute to others. If the comparison fails then the model should predict that patients lack a sense of agency for all of their actions. This is not the case, so the comparator model appears to be incorrect. This problem arises again when we consider Wegner et al. account. Hypothesizing that these patients fail to represent their own agency for their actions because they misrepresent the timing of their actions (thus violating the principle of priority) again fails to explain why only some actions are misattributed. In essence these accounts suggest that such patients always lack a representation of their own agency, but it seems that this lack only matters to the subject some of the time.

de Vignemont and Fourneret, (2004, p. 9) have suggested that the system which elicits the sense of agency, whether it be the comparator model or something else, fails only occasionally and in a context specific way. If it is true that the comparator or inference to apparent mental state causation face intermittent failures, then the occasionality problem disappears. However, the questions of how and why the mechanism occasionally fails have not been answered and nothing about the actions themselves or features such as their personal significance affect whether or not they are self-attributed (Proust, 2006, p. 89). More importantly there is no evidence independent of reports of the delusion that the comparator model or the representation of the timing of actions fails only occasionally for such patients. Until such evidence is forthcoming it is difficult for this solution to shake the appearance of being *ad hoc* and it is worth considering other accounts. More so, as I will suggest below, if we consider the different roles conscious and unconscious representations of own agency play in cognition, which we should do anyway, then there is no need to add additional assumptions of this type.

An argument from the occasionality problem against the hypotheses described, like that sketched above, assumes that the result of the process leading to a representation of own agency is a conscious sense of agency. If we drop this assumption the problem needn't arise. To see why this assumption is being made let us consider the relationship between experiences and delusions. So, what is the evidence that patients suffering delusions of alien control lack a sense of agency? One might be tempted to think that they *say so*. But, this isn't typically the case. Rather a deficit in a conscious sense of agency is inferred from the fact that patients attribute their own actions to another agent. This inference is justified by some standard assumptions in the study of delusions. The state of the art in delusions research is strongly influenced by Maher (1988, 1974) hypothesis that delusions are attempts to explain anomalous experience. Now there may be controversy regarding whether this explanatory attempt involves normal or deficient reasoning (Davies et al., 2002; Gerrans, 2002), but both sides agree that the delusion arises from an attempt to make sense of an anomalous experience. This supposition is not universally accepted, of course (Campbell, 2001; Bayne and Pacherie, 2004), but what matters here is that this assumption is needed if we are to justify inferring that patients lack a sense of agency from their acts of other attribution. We can justify this inference if the lack of a sense of agency is the anomalous experience which the delusion of alien control is an attempt to make sense of. So first, why should the absence of a sense of agency be an anomaly that needs to be explained? Well, it would be, if a conscious sense of agency typically accompanied one's actions. If this is the case, we would expect that its absence would be noticed and felt to be in need of explanation. After all, if one feels one's body move, but one does not seem to be the agent behind the movement, then one would naturally search for a reason that one moved.

We see this assumption that there is a conscious sense of agency accompanying all actions at play in the argument from the occasionality problem. The general failure of a process like the comparator should mean that the sense of agency that is usually present is not. This is an anomaly to be explained by the patient. The patient should show delusions of alien control for all of their actions, but they do not, therefore the comparator model (or which ever process we are considering) is false, quod erat demonstrandum (QED).

To avoid this conclusion, all we need do is drop the assumption that a conscious sense of agency always accompanies our actions. Instead, we need only hypothesize that a representation of own agency which may or may not be conscious accompanies our actions. In other words, the output of processes like the comparator or inference to apparent mental state causation is a representation of the subject's agency which is sometimes conscious and sometimes not. An absence of a sense of agency is thus not always an anomaly which the patient need explain. An absence of representation is not a representation of absence, as the saying goes, and it is particularly not a representation of absence *to the subject.* It is the subject noticing (i.e., representing to themselves) that the sense of agency is absent which is hypothesized to lead to delusions of alien control, not it's mere absence. This noticing of the absence will occur when the sense of agency is expected and so we might say the absence of a sense of agency is only an anomaly when the subject expects to experience it.

A possible objection to this line of response is to assert, based on introspection, that a conscious sense of agency accompanies all of our actions in the normal case. As such, it is always expected and any absence is an anomaly to be explained. However, introspection gives us poor grounds to assume that there is a ubiquitous sense of agency. What would lead one to assume that there is a conscious sense of agency accompanying every action? We can see where this assumption comes from, and how poorly grounded it is, by an analogy with visual consciousness. A favorite example purporting to show that we are not conscious of as much as we think we are comes from Dennett (1991). This example is so easy to replicate that given minimal resources you can do it yourself right now. All you need is a well shuffled deck of playing cards. Stare at a point on a wall in front of you. It is important that you continue to stare at this point throughout the entire demonstration. Without looking randomly select a card and hold it out to one side at arm's length. Gradually move it toward the center of your vision. At what point can you see the color and number on the card? The typical finding is that it is only about 2 or 3°[1] from the point one is looking at that these features become visible (Dennett, 1991, p. 54). The reason for this is to do with the nature of photoreceptors outside of the fovea on the retina and need not concern us here. What I wish to draw attention to, however, is that on first experiencing this demonstration most people seem surprised (Dennett, 1991, p. 68). Pre-theoretically, we expect to be able to discriminate objects easily when they are presented in our peripheral vision. Dennett suggests, and I agree, that this expectation is based on a folk-theoretical belief that vision presents us with a relatively uniformly clear and colored world in which objects are easily distinguished. But, as this simple demonstration shows, as do other more rigorous experiments, e.g., Brooks et al. (1980), this is at best only true of the foveated world, and even then with some exceptions (Caplovitz et al., 2008).[2]

Why do we believe this is true of our peripheral vision? We can speculate on many possible reasons for this. One reason might be that things we use as public representations of what we see, e.g., photographs or videos, are somewhat like this. There may be a misbegotten analogy between visual depictions and visual experience. Another more universal proposal comes from Schwitzgebel (2008: p. 255) as well as Dennett (1991: p. 68) who suggests that objects in our peripheral vision appear distinct and colored because they are when we look at them. Whenever one looks to see what object is in one's periphery one finds it clear, distinct and colored. As such we tend to assume that we always experience those objects as such. This claim provides us with a useful analogy for understanding why accounts like the comparator model and Wegner et al. inference to apparent mental state causation needn't suppose that a conscious sense of agency accompanies every action.

If a model like one of those above is right, then it would be true that our actions are normally accompanied by a representation of our own agency. However, the subject need not be aware of their own agency. The representation could be unconscious but, because the representation is formed with every action, it is there whenever we go "looking" for it, or more generally when it is expected to occur to the subject, i.e., consciously. Just as objects in our periphery always appear clear, distinct and colored when we go looking for them, our representation of agency is always experienced when we go looking for it, thus meeting our expectations. Just as this may lead us to believe that objects in our periphery always appear clear, distinct and colored, this may lead us to believe we always experience a sense of agency accompanying our actions rather than merely representing it.

[1]As a rough guide 1 degree is approximately the angle subtended by a point either side of your thumb nail held at arms length.

[2]Now of course in the normal case our eyes saccade constantly allowing us to build a much more detailed visual representation than is possible from staring at a fixation point making the area of clear vision significantly larger than the 2 to 3° observable in a fixation task. This doesn't affect the central Dennettian claim that periphery is not clear and colored in the way that we would typically assume. Nor do we typically reflect on how much moving our eyes is necessary for seeing the way we do.

Accepting this conclusion then, the comparator model or the inference to apparent mental state causation need not suppose that representing one's own agency is always a conscious sense of agency. Still, one may wonder, how exactly does this affect the occasionality problem? After all, it would still seem to be the case that these models predict that the unconscious representation of agency would be missing for every action performed by the patient suffering delusions of alien control, so should the model still predict that the patient would show the delusion for every action?

The answer to this is no. However, to see why, we need to return to the purported role of consciousness in the formation of delusions such as delusions of alien control. Recall Maher's proposal that delusions are attempts to make sense of anomalous experiences. In the case we are interested in here, the delusion of alien control arises because the patient attempts to make sense of the absence of a sense of agency. They expect a sense of agency, but it is not there when they "look", giving rise to an anomalous experience that must be explained. On this view then, an absent sense of agency is only anomalous when it is expected. A subject would not notice the absence of an unconscious representation. It is only when the representation would otherwise become conscious that its absence would be noticeable. Again the absence of the representation is not the same as the subject representing to themselves that something is absent. The upshot of this is that if we hypothesize that the comparator or inference produces an unconscious representation of agency, which only becomes conscious when it is needed by the subject (say in self-recognition or introspecting to see what experiences one has), we find that the occasionality problem is no problem at all.

It is not so much that the problem is solved as it doesn't arise in the first place, all because conscious and unconscious representations of own agency play different roles in cognition. Only conscious representations can be expected by the subject, and only their absence can be noticed by the subject. The normal case is that actions are not accompanied by a conscious sense of agency (only an unconscious representation) and so a lack of this feeling is typically not an anomaly that the patient suffering delusions of control needs to explain. It is only when they would "look for" (however this analogy is to be cashed out mechanistically—see below) this representation that it is expected and so its absence is an anomaly that needs to be explained.

This consideration of the occasionality problem shows us that there are theoretical benefits to taking seriously the distinction between conscious and unconscious representations of own agency. By doing so and considering the different roles conscious and unconscious representations play in cognition we see that the occasionality problem doesn't arise. As such we don't need to add assumptions to our models, such as assuming that they only fail some of the time, which lack supporting evidence. However, we do have a new set of issues to consider. What then is the analogy of "looking for" the representation of agency that produces the expectation of the sense of agency needed to explain delusions of alien control? This question is no less than what distinguishes an unconscious representation of agency from a conscious sense of agency, and this is what Dennett has called the "Hard Question" of consciousness.

THE HARD QUESTION

The approach to the sense of agency used by traditional accounts such as the comparator model and the inference to mental state causation are only designed to answer one question about the sense of agency: how is a representation of one's own agency elicited? This is a vitally important question in the study of the sense of agency, but to think it is the *only* question is to treat awareness as the end of the line of a computation, the dreaded Cartesian Theatre, and to deny the possibility of an unconscious representation of one's own agency. In addition to this question, we also need to ask of accounts of agency what Dennett calls the "Hard Question" [not to be confused with any purported "Hard Problems" (Chalmers, 2003)[3]]: after the representation of own agency is elicited by one or other of these mechanisms, well, then what happens (Dennett, 1991, p. 255)? What is the difference between a representation of my own agency of which I become aware and one that languishes forever in the apparent irrelevance of unconsciousness?

The analogy employed above of "looking" for the sense of agency suggests one possible answer. Perhaps an unconscious representation of agency becomes a conscious representation when the subject's attention is directed to it? In the following section I consider and discuss this possibility. Having found this wanting, I consider a further possibility, that the answer to the Hard Question is that the representation enters into the mechanisms required for verbal report. I argue that this answer is also unsatisfactory, as it is inconsistent with behavioral evidence of a sense of agency in non-verbal animals. These first two options are Functionalist theories. They propose that consciousness is playing a certain role in cognition. Although these two specific proposals seem to fail on empirical grounds it is important to note that other Functionalist theories, notably those that identify consciousness with multiple functional roles remain open. Finally, I propose a radical alternative suggesting that the answer to the Hard Question is to be found not in the uses to which representations are put within a cognitive system, but in the nature of the representations themselves. Regardless of which of the two research agendas individuals chose to pursue, it is clear that we do not have an answer to the Hard Question for the sense of agency nor do we spend enough time thinking about it.

ATTENTION

One potential answer to the Hard Question is *attention.* Such an answer is suggested by well-known cases of inattentional blindness, where subjects fail to see perfectly obvious stimuli (like a woman in a gorilla suit) simply because their attention is directed elsewhere (Mack and Rock, 1998). More specifically,

[3]The supposed "Hard Problem" of consciousness is the problem of explaining how mental and physical states give rise to conscious experience, given that it seems that no explanation in terms of the structure or function of mental states is sufficient to explain this (Chalmers, 2003). This is a problem closely tied with mysterian and dualistic approaches to consciousness. In contrast the "Hard Question" is a question within the materialist tradition, which works from arguments that a structural or functional explanation of consciousness is possible in principle, and asks what is the difference between a conscious and unconscious mental representation.

let us hypothesize that the difference between an unconscious representation of agency and the conscious sense of agency is that the conscious representation is attended to. If this is true then we would have a clear research agenda: understand how and why a representation of agency is selected or not selected for attention and understand the mechanisms of attention.

Such a view has not been developed in detail for the sense of agency; indeed, I am suggesting here that consideration of the Hard Question with respect to the sense of agency has been neglected almost entirely. Notwithstanding, attention based accounts of consciousness do have some currency in the explanation of perceptual consciousness. Prinz (2000, 2012), for example, advocates such a view. Unfortunately evidence is mounting that attention is not a good answer to the Hard Question, at least not on its own, as attention is not sufficient for consciousness. That is, subjects can attend to things of which they are not conscious. Here I discuss one well-studied example.

Norman et al. (2013) have provided compelling evidence that subjects can visually attend to objects, namely two-dimensional shapes, even when they cannot consciously see those objects. They start from prior observations of the effects of taking two-dimensional shapes as the objects of attention in color discrimination tasks. In these tasks, subjects are asked to indicate with a button press the color of a circle. Before the target colored circle appears a supraliminal spatial cue is presented. In the trials of interest here the, cue appears some distance from where the target circle will ultimately appear. However, it may appear in the same shape as the cue or a different shape. See **Figure 1** for an example layout.

When the target appears in the same object as the cue, response times are facilitated (Egly et al., 1994). Norman et al. take this as characteristic of attention to such shapes.

Norman et al. repeated this experiment, but made the shapes invisible. They presented on a screen an array of Gabor patches whose orientation rapidly alternated between vertical and horizontal. Within the array rectangles were defined by Gabor patches flickering out of phase with the remainder of the array (Norman et al., 2013, p. 838). When the background patches were vertical, those defining the rectangle were horizontal, and vice versa. Observing the array subjects reported seeing flickering Gabor patches, but were unable to see the rectangles. Indeed, subjects were no better than chance when asked to guess whether or not such flickering displays contained rectangles (Norman et al., 2013, p. 840). Despite the invisibility of the shapes there was a facilitation effect in the color discrimination task characteristic of attention being directed at the shapes. That is, subjects were faster at responding to targets which appeared in the same shape as the cue, than for targets which appeared the same distance from the cue but in a different shape (Norman et al., 2013, p. 839).

In this study we see an effect characteristic of attention being directed at an object, despite the object being invisible. This demonstrates that subjects can attend to shapes of which they are not conscious. In general, this also suggests that attention is not sufficient for consciousness. Without a reason to think that the sense of agency will be an exception to this, it seems unlikely that attention will answer the Hard Question for the sense of agency.

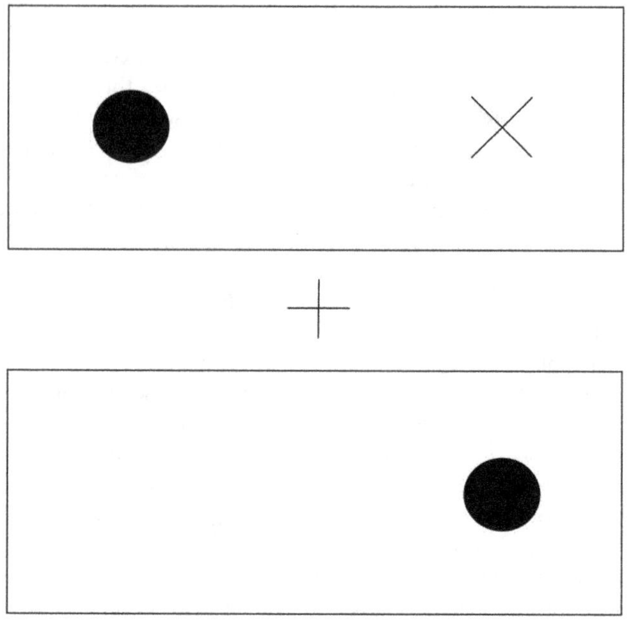

FIGURE 1 | The spatial layout of the stimuli. In the center we see a fixation cross, above and below are two rectangles. A cue appears at the x and disappears, followed by a target at one of the two circles. The subject's task is to indicate the color of the target. Subjects respond faster to cues appearing within the same shape as the cue, even though they are as far from the cue as the target in the other shape.

REPORTABILITY

Often we take it that we can be confident that a subject experiences something if they are able to verbally report it. Although such reports are susceptible to a variety of introspective omissions and commissions (Dennett, 1991, p. 96; Schwitzgebel, 2008), in practise, verbal reports (especially questionnaire responses) are very often treated as the best way to operationalize experience. Indeed the theories of the sense of agency introduced above are built on studies using questionnaires to ask subjects to report their experiences of agency. At the heart of this approach lies an intuition that, however imperfectly, we are able to talk about those things that we experience, but not those things that reside in our unconscious minds. This intuition suggests an approach to the Hard Question: perhaps the difference between conscious and unconscious representations is just that conscious representations are available for report. Although such an approach would be highly controversial (Block, 2007), there is no approach to the Hard Question that is not controversial, and this proposal remains live.

That said, we do have strong reason to doubt that it is reportability that distinguishes conscious and unconscious representations of own agency, as there are many non-verbal animals that display evidence of experiencing a sense of agency. This suggests that being available for verbal report is not necessary for a conscious sense of agency.

Good evidence for this comes from the mirror self-recognition test. This test, first proposed by Gallup (1970), involves marking an animal surreptitiously (usually when anesthetized) with a non-irritating, odorless dye on a part of the animal's body that cannot be seen without a mirror (such as the forehead). An animal is deemed to pass the mirror self recognition test if there is a significant increase in mark directed behavior coincident with the animal observing itself in the mirror (Gallup, 1970, p. 87). Such behavior indicates that the animal has recognized itself in the mirror as it uses the mirror to direct actions towards itself. A sense of agency is needed to pass such tests. To learn to recognize oneself in a mirror one needs to realize that the actions one sees in the mirror are equivalent to the actions one is currently performing (Povinelli, 2001, p. 855). In order to recognize oneself in a mirror, then, one needs to know (amongst many other things) what action one is performing. This is a function of the sense of agency (Povinelli and Cant, 1995). As such, passing the test is good evidence for a sense of agency.

Where this creates a problem for using reportability as an answer to the Hard Question is in the fact that many non-verbal animals pass the mirror self-recognition test. This includes chimpanzees (Gallup, 1970), orang-utans, human raised gorillas (Povinelli and Cant, 1995), bottlenose dolphins (Marten and Psarakos, 1994) and European magpies (Prior et al., 2008). These animals thus show evidence of experiencing a conscious sense of agency. As such, verbal report does not seem necessary for consciousness, and thus investigating how unconscious representations of agency become available for verbal report is a non-starter as a solution to the Hard Question.

The solutions considered so far to the Hard Question are Functionalist theories. They posit that for a representation to be conscious is for it to be used a certain way, say be being attended to or by being made available for report. On such views it is *use* which constitutes consciousness. Whilst the two options considered here do seem like non-starters, there are other Functionalist theories available. Other accounts, such as Dennett (1991) multiple drafts model Dennett (1991) or Baars (1988) global workspace Baars (1988), suggest that consciousness is not a single use within a cognitive system, but rather a conglomeration of many uses and these options remain live. My point here is not to solve the problem of what distinguishes conscious and unconscious representations, but merely to suggest that in sense of agency research this is a problem we should spend more time on. Next, I turn to a theoretical basis for approaching the Hard Question that offers a fundamentally different kind of solution to the options considered so far.

VEHICLE THEORIES

Vehicle theories of consciousness answer the Hard Question in a rather different way. The key issue we are getting at is: what is the difference between an unconscious and a conscious representation of own agency? The proposals considered thus far have followed Dennett in hypothesizing that this difference is a difference between how unconscious and conscious representations are processed (e.g., are they subject to attention or made available for verbal report). In other words the difference is a matter of what is done with the representation. Such approaches are Functionalist theories in that they consider the particular use of a representation within a cognitive system to constitute that representation's being conscious.

Vehicle theories, in contrast, hypothesize that the difference between conscious and unconscious representations is not how they are processed, but in the nature of the representation itself (O'Brien and Opie, 1999, p. 128). The nature of conscious vehicles of representation (also known as representation bearers) is hypothesized to be different to the nature of unconscious representing vehicles. On such views consciousness is a way of representing the world using different kinds of vehicle than those used by unconscious representations. On this kind of view the answer to the Hard Question is not "and then some additional processing occurs" but rather, "and then the vehicle of representation is changed from one form to another".

O'Brien and Opie propose a general answer to this question making use of distinctions in kinds of representing vehicles offered by Dennett (1982). In particular they focus on a distinction between "explicit" representations which are: "physically distinct objects, each possessed of a single semantic value" (O'Brien and Opie, 1999, p. 133) and "potentially explicit" and "tacit"[4] representations which are to be understood in terms of a computational system's *capacity* to make certain information explicit in the above sense. In general, O'Brien and Opie hypothesize that we are conscious of all and only things that are represented in an explicit form. All unconscious representations would then take the form of potentially explicit or tacit representations.

According to this version of a Vehicle Theory, a conscious sense of agency would be an explicit representation of own agency. That is, a discrete vehicle, such as a stable pattern of activity across a layer of neurons (O'Brien and Opie, 1999, p. 138), with that content. An unconscious representation of agency would not be a discrete vehicle, but a disposition in the cognitive system to produce such a representation. To allow for unconscious representations of own agency on such a view, the output of the comparator model or Wegner et al. inference needs to be reconceived. It is not an explicit representation of own agency, but rather a change in the dispositions of a computational system to produce such a representation.

If such an approach is correct then we have a new way to approach the Hard Question for the sense of agency. How is the output of the comparator model, or whichever account we ultimately agree on, made explicit? Why is it the case that it is sometimes not made explicit? Is this a matter of the subject metaphorically "looking for" it, if so, how would that be understood more literally?

The benefit of taking this approach is that it offers a new kind of answer to the Hard Question by offering a new conception of what properties of a computational system distinguish conscious from unconscious representations. With this reconceptualization we can deploy O'Brien and Opie's hypothesis for the sense of

[4]There are differences between "potentially explicit" and "tacit" representations. These differences become important when we consider the kinds of computations being performed within a cognitive system, but won't play a role in this short statement of O'Brien and Opie's hypothesis regarding consciousness (indeed O'Brien and Opie argue that a Vehicle Theory could only be true for connectionist systems and that the "potentially explicit" versus "tacit" distinction does not apply to such systems).

agency and answer the Hard Question in a way that doesn't seem to be falsified like the other answers considered here. In addition, a research agenda is set: why and how is a representation of own agency sometimes made explicit? Of course this question has not yet been answered. Indeed whichever form of the Hard Question we prefer it is clear that we have not yet answered it, although there seem to be two promising avenues to approach it. And so I implore us, as a community to ask of ourselves, now that we have made progress in understanding how a representation of own agency is elicited, *then what happens?*

CONCLUSION

In this paper I have argued that in order to explain the sense of agency we need to move beyond proximal etiological explanations and consider the Hard Question. Although such accounts, including the comparator model and the inference to apparent mental sate causation, are powerful so far as they go, they fail to distinguish between conscious and unconscious representations of own agency. As a consideration of the occasionality problem suggests, not only is this a real distinction, but such representations can play very different roles in cognition. Finally, I have suggested that there are ways we can approach the Hard Question, and although some of the specifics of certain particular approaches might seem like non-starters on empirical grounds it should be clear that there are alternative approaches, both Functionalist and vehicle, available and specific questions to ask. Now what happens?

REFERENCES

Baars, B. J. (1988). *A Cognitive Theory of Consciousness.* Cambridge: Cambridge University Press.

Bayne, T., and Pacherie, E. (2004). Bottom-up or top-down: Campbell's rationalist account of monothematic delusions. *Philos. Psychiatr. Psychol.* 11, 1–11. doi: 10.1353/ppp.2004.0033

Blakemore, S.-J., Smith, J., Steel, R., Johnstone, C. E., and Frith, C. D. (2000). The perception of self-produced sensory stimuli in patients with auditory hallucinations and passivity experiences: evidence for a break-down in self monitoring. *Psychol. Med.* 30, 1131–1139. doi: 10.1017/s0033291799002676

Blakemore, S.-J., Wolpert, D. M., and Frith, C. D. (2002). Abnormalities in the awareness of action. *Trends Cogn. Sci.* 6, 237–242. doi: 10.1016/S1364-6613(02)01907-1

Block, N. (2007). Consciousness, accessibility and the mesh between psychology and neuroscience. *Behav. Brain Sci.* 30, 481–499. doi: 10.1017/s0140525X07002786

Brooks, B., Yates, J. T., and Coleman, R. D. (1980). Perception of images moving at saccadic velocities during saccades and during fixation. *Exp. Brain Res.* 40, 71–78. doi: 10.1007/bf00236664

Campbell, J. (2001). Rationality, meaning and the analysis of delusion. *Philos. Psychiatr. Psychol.* 8, 89–100. doi: 10.1353/ppp.2001.0004

Caplovitz, G. P., Fendrich, R., and Hughes, H. C. (2008). Failures to see: attentive blank stares revealed by change blindness. *Conscious. Cogn.* 17, 877–886. doi: 10.1016/j.concog.2007.08.006

Carruthers, G. (2009). Commentary on Synofzik, Vosgerau and Newen 2008. *Conscious. Cogn.* 18, 515–520. doi: 10.1016/j.concog.2008.05.006

Carruthers, G. (2010). A problem for Wegner and colleagues' model of the sense of agency. *Phenomenology Cogn. Sci.* 9, 341–357. doi: 10.1007/s11097-010-9150-6

Carruthers, G. (2012). The case for the comparator model as an explanation of the sense of agency and its breakdowns. *Conscious. Cogn.* 21, 30–45. doi: 10.1016/j.concog.2010.08.005

Carruthers, G. (in press). Un modello metacognitivo del senso di agentività per le azioni corporee. *Sist. INTELLIGENTI* 26.

Chalmers, D. J. (2003). "Consciousness and its place in nature," in *Blackwell Guide to the Philosophy of Mind*, eds S. Stich and T. Warfield (Malden, MA: Blackwell Publishing), 102–142.

Davies, M., Coltheart, M., Langdon, R., and Breen, N. (2002). Monothematic delusions: towards a two-factor account. *Philos. Psychiatr. Psychol.* 8, 133–158. doi: 10.1353/ppp.2001.0007

de Vignemont, F., and Fourneret, P. (2004). The sense of agency: a philosophical and empirical review of the "Who" system. *Conscious. Cogn.* 13, 1–19. doi: 10.1016/s1053-8100(03)00022-9

Dennett, D. C. (1982). Styles of mental representation. *Proc. Aristotelian Society* 83, 213–226.

Dennett, D. C. (1991). *Consciousness Explained.* New York: Penguin Books.

Egly, R., Driver, J., and Rafal, R. D. (1994). Shifting visual attention between objects and locations: evidence from normal and parietal lesion subjects. *J. Exp. Psychol. Gen.* 123, 161–177. doi: 10.1037/0096-3445.123.2.161

Frith, C. D., Blakemore, S.-J., and Wolpert, D. M. (2000a). Abnormalities in the awareness and control of action. *Philos. Trans. R. Soc. Lond. B Biol. Sci.* 355, 1771–1788. doi: 10.1098/rstb.2000.0734

Frith, C. D., Blakemore, S.-J., and Wolpert, D. M. (2000b). Explaining the symptoms of schizophrenia: abnormalities in the awareness of action. *Brain Res. Brain Res. Rev.* 31, 357–363. doi: 10.1016/s0165-0173(99)00052-1

Frith, C. D., and Done, D. J. (1989). Experiences of alien control in schizophrenia reflect a disorder in the central monitoring of action. *Psychol. Med.* 19, 359–363. doi: 10.1017/s003329170001240x

Gallup, G. G. (1970). Chimpanzees: self recognition. *Science* 167, 86–87. doi: 10.1126/science.167.3914.86

Gerrans, P. (2002). A one-stage explanation of cotard's delusion. *Philos. Psychiatr. Psychol.* 9, 47–53. doi: 10.1353/ppp.2003.0007

Mack, A., and Rock, I. (1998). *Inattentional Blindness.* Cambridge, MA: The MIT Press.

Maher, B. A. (1974). Delusional thinking and perceptual disorder. *J. Individ. Psychol.* 30, 98–113.

Maher, B. A. (1988). "Anomalous experience and delusional thinking: the logic of explanations," in *Delusional Beliefs*, eds T. Oltmanns and B. A. Maher (Chichester: John wiley and Sons), 15–33.

Marten, K., and Psarakos, S. (1994). "Evidence of self-awareness in the bottlenose dolphin (Tursiops truncatus)," in *Self-awareness in Animals and Humans: Developmental Perspectives*, eds S. T. Parker, R. W. Mitchell and M. L. Boccia (New York, NY: Cambridge University Press), 361–379. doi: 10.1017/CBO9780511565526.026

Moore, J. W., and Fletcher, P. C. (2012). Sense of agency in health and disease: a review of cue integration approaches. *Conscious. Cogn.* 21, 59–68. doi: 10.1016/j.concog.2011.08.010

Norman, L. J., Heywood, C. A., and Kentridge, R. W. (2013). Object-Based attention without awareness. *Psychol. Sci.* 24, 836–843. doi: 10.1177/0956797612461449

O'Brien, G., and Opie, J. (1999). A connectionist theory of phenomenal experience. *Behav. Brain Sci.* 22, 127–148; discussion 148–196. doi: 10.1017/s0140525x9900179x

Pacherie, E. (2008). The phenomenology of action: a conceptual framework. *Cognition* 107, 179–217. doi: 10.1016/j.cognition.2007.09.003

Povinelli, D. J. (2001). "The self: elevated in consciousness and extended in time," in *The Development of the Extended Self in Preschool Children: Theory and Research*, eds K. Skene and C. Moore (Mahwah, NJ: Cambridge University Press), 75–95.

Povinelli, D. J., and Cant, J. G. H. (1995). Arboreal clambering and the evolution of self-conception. *Q. Rev. Biol.* 70, 393–421. doi: 10.1086/419170

Prinz, J. (2000). A neurofunctional theory of visual consciousness. *Conscious. Cogn.* 9, 243–259. doi: 10.1006/ccog.2000.0442

Prinz, J. J. (2012). *The Conscious Brain: How Attention Engenders Experience.* New York, NY: Oxford University Press.

Prior, H., Schwarz, A., and Güntürkün, O. (2008). Mirror-induced behavior in the magpie (Pica pica): evidence of self-recognition. *PLoS Biol.* 6:e202. doi: 10.1371/journal.pbio.0060202

Proust, J. (2006). "Agency in Schizophrenia from a control theory viewpoint," in *Disorders of Volition*, eds N. Sebanz and W. Prinz (Cambridge, MA: MIT Press), 87–118.

Revonsuo, A. (2006). *Inner Presence: Consciousness as a Biological Phenomenon.* Cambridge: MIT Massachuusetts.

Schwitzgebel, E. (2008). The unreliability of naive introspection. *Philos. Rev.* 117, 245–273. doi: 10.1215/00318108-2007-037

Spence, S. A. (2001). Alien control: from phenomenology to cognitive neurobiology. *Philos. Psychiatr. Psychol.* 8, 163–172. doi: 10.1353/ppp.2001.0017

Synofzik, M., Vosgerau, G., and Lindner, A. (2009). Me or not me—an optimal integration of agency cues? *Conscious. Cogn.* 18, 1065–1068. doi: 10.1016/j.concog.2009.07.007

Synofzik, M., Vosgerau, G., and Newen, A. (2008). Beyond the comparator model: a multifactorial two-step account of agency. *Conscious. Cogn.* 17, 219–239. doi: 10.1016/j.concog.2007.03.010

Voss, M., Moor, J., Hauser, M., Gallinat, J., Heinz, A., and Haggard, P. (2010). Altered awareness of action in schizophrenia: a specific deficit in predicting action consequences. *Brain* 133, 3104–3112. doi: 10.1093/brain/awQ1252

Wegner, D. M. (2002). *The Illusion of Conscious Will.* Cambridge, MA: MIT Press.

Wegner, D. M. (2003). The mind's best trick: how we experience conscious will. *Trends Cogn. Sci.* 7, 65–69. doi: 10.1016/S1364-6613(03)00002-0

Wegner, D. M., and Wheatley, T. (1999). Apparent mental causation: sources of the experience of will. *Am. Psychol.* 54, 480–492. doi: 10.1037/0003-066x.54.7.480

Wolpert, D., and Ghahramani, Z. (2000). Computational principles of movement neuroscience. *Nat. Neurosci.* 3, 1212–1217. doi: 10.1038/81497

12

Affective coding: the emotional dimension of agency

Antje Gentsch*[1]* and Matthis Synofzik*[2,3]

[1] Research Department of Clinical, Educational and Health Psychology, University College London, London, UK
[2] Department of Neurodegenerative Diseases, Hertie-Institute for Clinical Brain Research, University of Tübingen, Tübingen, Germany
[3] German Research Center for Neurodegenerative Diseases (DZNE), University of Tübingen, Tübingen, Germany

Correspondence:
Antje Gentsch, Research Department of Clinical, Educational and Health Psychology, University College London, Hunter Street 8, London WC1N 1BN, UK
e-mail: a.gentsch@ucl.ac.uk

The sense of agency (SoA) (i.e., the registration that I am the initiator and controller of my actions and relevant events) is associated with several affective dimensions. This makes it surprising that the emotion factor has been largely neglected in the field of agency research. Current empirical investigations of the SoA mainly focus on sensorimotor signals (i.e., efference copy) and cognitive cues (i.e., intentions, beliefs) and on how they are integrated. Here we argue that this picture is not sufficient to explain agency experience, since agency and emotions constantly interact in our daily life by several ways. Reviewing first recent empirical evidence, we show that self-action perception is in fact modulated by the affective valence of outcomes already at the sensorimotor level. We hypothesize that the "affective coding" between agency and action outcomes plays an essential role in agency processing, i.e., the prospective, immediate or retrospective shaping of agency representations by affective components. This affective coding of agency be differentially altered in various neuropsychiatric diseases (e.g., schizophrenia vs. depression), thus helping to explain the dysfunctions and content of agency experiences in these diseases.

Keywords: agency, emotion, prediction, self-awareness, schizophrenia, cue integration, reward

INTRODUCTION

The close relations between emotions and actions are ubiquitous during our active engagement with the world. Emotions are the force initiating and guiding behavior by making people act in certain ways in order to achieve or avoid significant outcomes, and actions in turn change how we are feeling and give rise to particular emotional states. If a person feels in control over her own body or the environment she may experience affective states of pride or guilt, and vice versa, a context of helplessness and depression may alter her predictions and perception of actions and outcomes. It is therefore surprising that the affective dimensions and components of actions have not been taken into the equations of current models of the sense of agency (SoA), i.e., of the registration that I am the initiator of my actions and related events (Gallagher, 2000; Synofzik et al., 2008a,b). The affective dimensions provide the basis for the evaluation of self-controlled actions attributed to one's own agency, leading–for example–to feelings of personal capacity, self-esteem or relevant self-conscious emotions such as guilt, shame, pride, and embarrassment. Moreover, the affective components of our actions (e.g., affective dispositional state of the individual, affective social context, affective value of the action outcome) modulate our inclination to accept our action consequences and outcomes as caused by ourselves or not.

Here our goal is to explore from an affective perspective, what shapes our SoA. Current empirical and theoretical advances in understanding agentive self-awareness from an affective point of view will be discussed in order to stimulate future research and to suggest a necessary extension of current conceptual frameworks of agency to include the affective dimension of action. First, we briefly review recent views suggesting a tight link between emotion, action representation and self-awareness. Second, we provide a review of existing studies explicitly addressing affective influences on the SoA. Third, we discuss different affective determinants and distinguish possible mechanisms underlying the emotion-agency link, introducing the novel concept of "affective coding" of agency which might occur prospectively, immediately or retrospectively (*post-hoc*). The implications of this affective perspective for our understanding of relevant agency disorders will be discussed. We hypothesize that in particular the "affective coding" between agency and action outcomes might play a crucial role in agency processing both in health and disease.

THE ROLE OF EMOTION IN ACTION REPRESENTATION AND SELF-AWARENESS

Recent evidence in cognitive neurosciences suggests that action representation is strongly influenced by emotions and that several brain structures are operating in networks to integrate affectively significant signals with action cognition and relevant behavioral control processes (Pessoa and Adolphs, 2010). The general idea of a direct link between perceptual states and action representation is most familiar from common coding theory in cognitive psychology (Hommel et al., 2001) claiming that actions are represented according to their perceptual consequences. This theoretical approach has been further extended to include affective codes as being part of these action representations and essentially shaping them (Krebs et al., 2010; Eder et al., 2012). It has been shown, for example, that learning of action-effect associations can be modulated by the motivational value of an action during the acquisition phase and the motivational disposition of an individual (Muhle-Karbe and Krebs, 2012). It is worth noting, however, that goal representations associated with motivational states compared to the hedonic experience of the outcome itself might involve dissociable mechanisms and influences on action representations.

Self-awareness in general has frequently been linked to the processing of emotions and bodily states. Affective accounts of selfhood assume that basic pre-reflective forms of self-awareness are grounded in representations of emotions and bodily sensations (Damasio, 1999). This view has recently been formalized within a computational framework of "predictive processing" that links action, sensory perception and interoception (Seth et al., 2011). According to this model of "interoceptive inference", emotion and embodied self-awareness arise from generative models predicting interoceptive signals that result as a consequence of internal autonomic control signals or environmental changes. Agency is considered to be one important predictor of changes in internal bodily states that generate interoceptive signals, for example an increase in heart rate when performing or preparing for a personally challenging action. These prediction signals are thought to give rise to a basic sense of presence and agentive awareness (Seth et al., 2012). That means that, action perception and attribution is thought to be determined not only by exteroceptive and proprioceptive cues but also by their close interplay with interoceptive bodily signals. This multi-cue integration is at the core of an increasingly influential account of agentive self-awareness, the multifactorial weighting account (Synofzik et al., 2008a, 2013; Vosgerau and Synofzik, 2012). Multiple probabilistic cues are thought to be weighted as a function of their predictive accuracy for prospective agency and integrated with action-related signals based on their reliability and salience during action execution and during retrospective processing of the action. Important explanatory gaps still remain, though, with respect to the exact mechanisms of how precisely emotional states may interact with probabilistic and action-related signals to inform feelings and judgments of agency at different levels.

Besides cognitive approaches to self-awareness, a strong motivational and emotional dimension of self-processing has been posited in psychology (Leary, 2007). A number of "self-motives" such as motives for self-enhancement, self-verification, self-expansion, or self-assessment are thought to affect action and cognition, and have been argued to function to protect people's social well-being. These "self-motives" are thought to be strongly linked to different "self-conscious emotions"–including guilt, shame, embarrassment, social anxiety and pride–that emerge from self-representation (Leary, 2007). Experimental studies have shown that although people may prefer objective, accurate information about themselves under certain circumstances, the desire for self-enhancement or verification of pre-existing self-conceptions may override this motive (Sedikides and Strube, 1995). In line with this view, it is well known that our mind has developed ways to maintain the integrity of a positive self-concept even in contexts of failure (Mezulis et al., 2004). Ample evidence indicates the tendency in healthy individuals to make self-serving attributions by relating positive outcomes to the self and negative outcomes to others. This affective shaping of outcome attributions can be altered in different neuropsychiatric diseases; for example, it seems to be lacking in depression (Alloy and Abramson, 1979). These findings can already be taken as first evidence for that fact that the selection of new self-relevant information might follow a differential weighting whereby some cues are weighted more strongly than others (e.g., positive or "self-serving" cues are weighted more strongly than negative or self-detrimental cues) (Synofzik et al., 2009b). Yet this weighting might not always follow the rules of an statistical optimal cue integration, namely the reduction of uncertainty about the self as a cause of sensory input by giving most weight to the objectively most reliable cues, as would be suggested by optimal cue integration accounts (Synofzik et al., 2009b, 2013).

AFFECTIVE INFLUENCES ON THE SENSE OF AGENCY

Based on the above mentioned lines of evidence it is reasonable to generally assume a tight link between emotions and processes underlying agency registration. However, current accounts of the SoA are primarily computational cognitive models, grounded in constructs of motor control theory, without the need for emotional states to be taken into account (Wolpert et al., 1995). Accordingly, the SoA is thought to depend on predictive cues derived from internal forward modeling of upcoming sensory action consequences in the motor system (Frith et al., 2000b). Following first critique of these models as accounts of agency (Synofzik et al., 2008a), a growing body of literature has now started to extend this view by highlighting the importance of a *combination* of *different* cues weighted according to their reliability to signal agency (Moore et al., 2009; Synofzik et al., 2010; Desantis et al., 2012b). Recent models assume a multifactorial weighting process based on some form of Bayesian optimal cue integration (Fletcher and Frith, 2009; Synofzik et al., 2009b; Moore and Fletcher, 2012). However, these models still largely spare out the contribution of emotional and motivational mechanisms, and only recently has empirical work begun to explicitly address the affective influences on specific sensorimotor markers of agency (see also, Synofzik et al., 2013).

Several emerging levels of evidence point toward the importance of emotional influences on both functional and dysfunctional agentive processing. A well-studied phenomenon reflecting the affective influence on agency experience is the "self-serving bias". This refers to the pervasive tendency of healthy individuals to make self-favoring causal attributions when facing significant positive or negative outcomes (Greenberg et al., 1982; Mezulis et al., 2004). Specifically, people tend to attribute causes of positive outcomes more often to internal factors and negative outcomes more often to external factors. This seems to reflect a mechanism for maintaining self-esteem and reducing cognitive dissonance (Harmon-Jones et al., 2009). Clinically depressed patients typically exhibit the inverse pattern of this bias, a "depressive attributional style", reflected in the internalization of responsibility for negative events and externalization of agency for positive events (Alloy and Abramson, 1979).

This evidence for the existence of self-serving attribution biases is based on explicit, retrospective self-report, thus indicating that affective modulation occurs on the level of *judgment* of agency (Synofzik et al., 2008a). These reports are now complemented by recent findings demonstrating that the affective value of action outcomes already influences also the low-level sensorimotor representations of actions and agency in a self-serving way, i.e., the *feeling* of agency (Synofzik et al., 2008a). For example, it was found that participants' perception of pointing actions is biased towards positive and away from negative outcomes (Wilke et al., 2012). Other studies observed reduced temporal binding between actions and consequences signaling monetary loss (Takahata et al., 2012) or eliciting negative emotional vocalizations (Yoshie and Haggard, 2013). These findings suggest the existence of automatic valence specific effects of emotions on implicit low-level measures of the SoA. However, they also have to be interpreted with caution as—in contrast to a long-standing assumption—intentional binding does not necessarily reflect a signature of agency. As we have argued earlier (Synofzik et al., 2009a), the fact that perceived time intervals between movement and effect were decreased by priming also in case of involuntary movements opens up the possibility that the binding between movement and effect might not be specific to agency and intentionality, but can also present—at least in part—a more unspecific effect linked to temporal binding between two external events (in this case between the two congruent sounds, i.e., between prime and effect). Indeed, recent studies suggest that intentional binding is neither linked specifically to motor predictive processes (Desantis et al., 2012a; Hughes et al., 2013) nor to agency (Buehner and Humphreys, 2009; Buehner, 2012; Dogge et al., 2012), but rather to causality in general. However, even if the phenomenon of binding of movements to their effects was not specifically linked to agency, it could still contribute to the experience of agency, for instance, by accentuating subject's perception of the temporal contiguity between movements and their effects (Desantis et al., 2012a).

Notably, any observed emotional modulation of these low-level measures of action perception and SoA could in principle be mediated by predictive influences as well as postdictive reconstruction of the experience (Synofzik et al., 2013). Future studies are needed to clearly modulate only one of these two factors. Alternatively, they could examine valence effects specifically at the early stages of anticipation and outcome processing in order to disentangle predictive and reconstructive components (e.g., by using the high temporal resolution of EEG). Predictive cues are assumed to be weighted according to their reliability to indicate the most likely outcome (Moore et al., 2009; Synofzik et al., 2010). However, cue weighting may further be influenced by activated self-motives in a given social/emotional context. This view is supported by the empirical picture of self-serving biases, which is rather consistent with respect to the tendency to attribute success to the self ("positive bias"), but mixed with respect to the tendency to attribute failure ("negative bias"). It has been argued that this is due to the "negative bias" being moderated by additional self-motives such as self-assessment and self-improvement and the perceived capacity to do so (Duval and Silvia, 2002). Moreover, the weighting of affective predictions and the perception of emotional valence of action outcomes could be affected by the emotional and attentive state of the individual, and may be critically altered in certain psychopathological conditions marked by distorted agency experience, which will be addressed in the following.

EMOTIONS IN AGENCY DISORDERS

Psychopathology research provides abundant evidence for a strong interrelation between emotion and action, suggesting that aberrant sensorimotor awareness could be rooted in deficient emotional processing of action-related signals. In affective disorders, such as mania and depression, action awareness abnormalities are at the core of the phenomenological expression of these disorders. At explicit levels, self-awareness is often dramatically altered towards grandiose delusions and inflated sense of power in periods of mania (Knowles et al., 2011), or towards a depressive realism in depressive episodes (Alloy and Abramson, 1979). Previous studies suggest that already in healthy individuals showing dysphoric compared to non-dysphoric affective states the experience of self-agency and self-serving attributions are reduced (Aarts et al., 2006). Moreover, for depression the possibility has been raised that impaired action monitoring may represent an important depressive endophenotype (Olvet and Hajcak, 2008; Holmes et al., 2010), as reflected for example in impaired post-error behavioral adaptation (Holmes and Pizzagalli, 2008). The role of these monitoring abnormalities for the attenuated self-serving biases in action awareness in these patients, however, remains unclear.

Another indication for emotional influences on agentive awareness comes from neurological patients with anosognosia for hemiplegia (AHP), which can show delusional experience of self-agency despite a complete lack of voluntary movement after brain lesion (Feinberg et al., 2000). These patients may claim that they can move on request or provide excuses (confabulations) for not moving, and some may even believe to have moved ignoring visual, proprioceptive and external cues signaling the absence of an action. Besides models assuming deficits in sensorimotor mechanisms (Heilman et al., 1998; Frith et al., 2000b; Berti et al., 2005), emotion-related explanations have been put forward, stressing the role of motivational factors and emotion regulation mechanisms in generating the unawareness and higher-order confabulations (Vuilleumier, 2004; Turnbull et al., 2005; Fotopoulou, 2010). It has been noted that transient episodes of improved action awareness in these patients are accompanied by an increase in depressive symptoms (Kaplan-Solms and Solms, 2000; Fotopoulou, 2010). AHP patients seem to fail to integrate negative emotions with explicit self-awareness (Fotopoulou et al., 2010). Moreover, recent evidence shows that negative (but not positive) performance feedback can cause improved action awareness in these patients (Besharati et al., submitted). Based on neuroimaging studies reporting damage in anterior parts of the insula (Berti et al., 2005; Karnath et al., 2005), it has been argued that a lack of re-representation of emotional action-related information may lead to the abnormally preserved self-agency experience in these patients (Fotopoulou et al., 2010). It still remains to be explored, however, to which extent this impairment can explain the variations in the clinical presentations of AHP including accompanying confabulations and delusional beliefs around agency and ownership.

Delusions of control in schizophrenia are often seen as the paradigmatic case of a disrupted SoA, and they have typically been explained as motor-cognitive phenomena without relation to emotional and motivational processes (Frith et al., 2000a). However, these frameworks fail to provide an explanation for the often emotionally tuned semantic content and context of delusions in schizophrenia, including delusions of control. Although studies focusing specifically on the thematic content of delusions of influence in schizophrenia patients are still missing, studies analyzing delusions in schizophrenia in general have shown that these refer often not to trivial, non-emotional actions in daily life (e.g., brushing teeth or typing on a computer), but to actions and contexts with high affective and/or moral value, including thematic contents of religion, sex, grandiosity, persecution, and guilt (Frith, 1992; Linskey, 1994; Suhail, 2003). Here the affective and moral valence gains major influence on both the sensorimotor and the cognitive level, such that the action experience and possibly also the action attribution is altered. Many experimentators so far have used mainly simplified non-affective actions (e.g., simple joystick movements (Spence et al., 1997) or simple pointing movements (Synofzik et al., 2010)) to experimentally test and operationalize action monitoring deficits, which they then tried to correlated with the patients' psychopathology of delusions of controls. This testing and operationalization strategy should, of course, not be mistaken as an indicator that the thematic content of the patients' psychopathology *per se* would entail such simple movements.

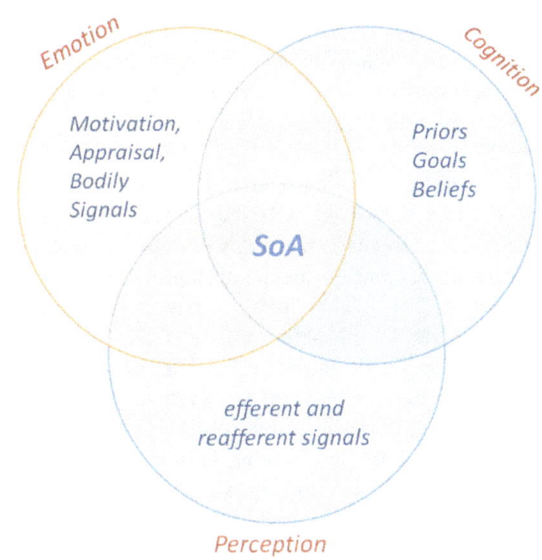

FIGURE 1 | Illustration of the integration of the affective dimension in cognitive-sensorimotor mechanisms underlying agentive awareness. The contribution of emotional cues in synchrony with sensorimotor and cognitive cues in the formation of sense of agency (SoA) is displayed.

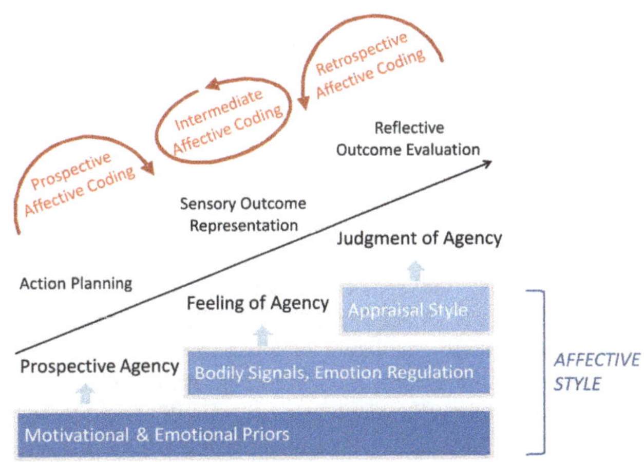

FIGURE 2 | Illustration of the influence of distinct emotional determinants at different stages of agency processing. At the first stage of action planning, priors derived from affective state, affective trait or affective context variables influence prospective representations of agency (prospective affective coding). At the second stage, feelings of agency can be shaped by rapid appraisal of emotionally salient information and emotional bodily responses (intermediated affective coding). Thirdly, positive or negative self-schemas and self-enhancement or self-protection motives may guide *post-hoc* explicit attributions of agency (retrospective affective coding). Finally, individual differences in the degree of emotion regulation during an affective state (affective style) may moderate the interplay between emotion and agency at all three levels of representation.

AFFECTIVE CODING OF AGENCY: HOW AFFECT MAY INFLUENCE THE SENSE OF AGENCY

We suggest "*Affective Coding of Agency*" as an essential extension of current cue integration models of agency. Emotions interact with agency in manifold ways, given the different levels and aspects of emotion representations and the various possible mechanisms mediating the interplay between emotion and action awareness. We hypothesize that both the expected and actual valence of an action outcome act as strong agency cues in synchrony with cognitive and sensorimotor coding of actions (**Figure 1**).

EMOTIONAL DETERMINANTS OF AGENCY

Due to the multifaceted nature of emotions, different components of emotions determine agency processing at different stages. Specifically, emotions can influence agency at the stage of (i) prospective agency; (ii) the immediate feeling of agency; and (iii) the *post-hoc* judgement of agency (**Figure 2**).

1. ***Prospective affective coding***. Emotional and motivational priors of a subject's individual state of an action may strongly shape prospective representations of agency (for example, his depressed vs. euphoric mood or his open-minded vs. buttoned-up attitude; or his positive vs. negative expectation on the affective outcome of an action; or his high vs. low

motivation to perform the upcoming action). Also the affective dimensions of the specific background and context of an action will prospectively shape the agency experience (for example, acting in a friendly vs. hostile environment). This prospective process can be called "prospective affective coding" of agency (**Figure 2**).

2. ***Immediate affective coding***. Fast and automatic emotion processes (LeDoux, 1996) are reflected in immediate emotional bodily responses and early mechanisms of sensory gating based on internal bodily and motivational states (Vuilleumier, 2005; Pourtois et al., 2013). They may construe the immediate pre-reflective feeling of the action (Seth et al., 2011; Synofzik et al., 2013) which is neither fully determined by affective priors nor by the affective *post-hoc* evaluation of the action. Interindividual differences in interoceptive sensitivity may be an important mediator at this level. This immediate shaping of agency by direct affective processes can be called "immediate affective coding" of agency (**Figure 2**).
3. ***Retrospective affective coding***. At the stage of the *post-hoc* evaluation of an action (which might also often occur in rather immediate and automatic manner in everyday life), agency is shaped by the affective appraisal of the actual action outcome (Wilke et al., 2012). Also individual attributional styles as implied by the depressive realism hypothesis (Alloy and Abramson, 1979) and situational self-schema and self-motive activation may influence these *post-hoc* judgments about self-agency (Aarts et al., 2006). This affective *post-hoc* shaping of agency can be called "retrospective affective coding" of agency.

Some affective factors might present general determinants of agency and run across all three different stages of affective agency shaping, modulating all three of them. One of these general determinants might be individual differences in "affective style", that is, the tendency for regulating emotions. Strategies of behavioral re-adjustments, affect suppression or tolerance could also be important general mediators of affective coding of agency. For example, a core feature of depersonalization disorder, self-detachment including a lowered SoA, has been proposed to result from a "shutting down" of emotional responses due increased fronto-insula/limbic inhibitory regulation (Sierra and Berrios, 1998; Phillips et al., 2001).

CONCLUSION

Bringing the affective quality of actions into the empirical picture will provide an important extension to current theoretical accounts of agency experience, and will do justice to the individual differences and pathologies in feelings of self-control. Why do some people have immediate feelings of self-efficacy and others do not when facing the same outcomes? And how deep-rooted are these feelings in embodied social knowledge and actual behavior towards the environment? Self-motives may find their way into an embodied signature by shaping the weight of our predictive codes and the gates through which we perceive the external world. For example, most recent conceptualizations of predictive models hold that the influence of prediction on perception critically depends on the assignment of salience based on dopaminergic neuromodulation of attentional processes (Friston et al., 2012). The degree of self-serving affective biases in agentive awareness may respectively depend on increased attentional resources directed to expected favorable outcomes compared to unfavorable outcomes. For example, one way to regulate emotion or to maximize positivity of the self-concept is through selective withdrawal of attention to unexpected unfavorable outcomes during self-action leading to attenuated outcome salience and reduced belief updating for unfavorable self-generated events. However, the precise nature of salience-weighted perceptual inference in relation to emotions will have to be specified in considerable more detail to understand its contribution to agentive self-awareness. A systematic investigation of discrete aspects of affective processes and emotional regulation strategies could prove a promising avenue in this direction. Importantly, the relation between emotion and agency is bi-directional rather than uni-directional and the concurrent investigation of reciprocal relations between emotion and action awareness at the neural and cognitive level will be the challenge for future investigations.

ACKNOWLEDGMENTS

This work was supported by the "European Platform for Life Sciences, Mind Sciences and Humanities" granted by the Volkswagen Stiftung (to Matthis Synofzik and Antje Gentsch). We acknowledge support by the "Deutsche Forschungsgemeinschaft" (DFG) and the Open Access Publishing Fund of Tuebingen University.

REFERENCES

Aarts, H., Wegner, D. M., and Dijksterhuis, A. (2006). On the feeling of doing: dysphoria and the implicit modulation of authorship ascription. *Behav. Res. Ther.* 44, 1621–1627. doi: 10.1016/j.brat.2005.12.004

Alloy, L. B., and Abramson, L. Y. (1979). Judgment of contingency in depressed and nondepressed students: sadder but wiser? *J. Exp. Psychol. Gen.* 108, 441–485. doi: 10.1037/0096-3445.108.4.441

Berti, A., Bottini, G., Gandola, M., Pia, L., Smania, N., Stracciari, A., et al. (2005). Shared cortical anatomy for motor awareness and motor control. *Science* 309, 488–491. doi: 10.1126/science.1110625

Buehner, M. J. (2012). Understanding the past, predicting the future: causation, not intentional action, is the root of temporal binding. *Psychol. Sci.* 23, 1490–1497. doi: 10.1177/0956797612444612

Buehner, M. J., and Humphreys, G. R. (2009). Causal binding of actions to their effects. *Psychol. Sci.* 20, 1221–1228. doi: 10.1111/j.1467-9280.2009.02435.x

Damasio, A. R. (1999). *The Feeling of What Happens: Body and Emotion in the Making of Consciousness.* San Diego: Harcourt.

Desantis, A., Hughes, G., and Waszak, F. (2012a). Intentional binding is driven by the mere presence of an action and not by motor prediction. *PLoS One* 7:e29557. doi: 10.1371/journal.pone.0029557

Desantis, A., Weiss, C., Schütz-Bosbach, S., and Waszak, F. (2012b). Believing and perceiving: authorship belief modulates sensory attenuation. *PLoS One* 7:e37959. doi: 10.1371/journal.pone.0037959

Dogge, M., Schaap, M., Custers, R., Wegner, D. M., and Aarts, H. (2012). When moving without volition: implied self-causation enhances binding strength between involuntary actions and effects. *Conscious. Cogn.* 21, 501–506. doi: 10.1016/j.concog.2011.10.014

Duval, T. S., and Silvia, P. J. (2002). Self-awareness, probability of improvement and the self-serving bias. *J. Pers. Soc. Psychol.* 82, 49–61. doi: 10.1037/0022-3514.82.1.49

Eder, A. B., Musseler, J., and Hommel, B. (2012). The structure of affective action representations: temporal binding of affective response codes. *Psychol. Res.* 76, 111–118. doi: 10.1007/s00426-011-0327-6

Feinberg, T. E., Roane, D. M., and Ali, J. (2000). Illusory limb movements in anosognosia for hemiplegia. *J. Neurol. Neurosurg. Psychiatry* 68, 511–513. doi: 10.1136/jnnp.68.4.511

Fletcher, P. C., and Frith, C. D. (2009). Perceiving is believing: a Bayesian approach to explaining the positive symptoms of schizophrenia. *Nat. Rev. Neurosci.* 10, 48–58. doi: 10.1038/nrn2536

Fotopoulou, A. (2010). The affective neuropsychology of confabulation and delusion. *Cogn. Neuropsychiatry* 15, 38–63. doi: 10.1080/13546800903250949

Fotopoulou, A., Pernigo, S., Maeda, R., Rudd, A., and Kopelman, M. A. (2010). Implicit awareness in anosognosia for hemiplegia: unconscious interference without conscious re-representation. *Brain* 133(Pt. 12), 3564–3577. doi: 10.1093/brain/awq233

Friston, K. J., Shiner, T., FitzGerald, T., Galea, J. M., Adams, R., Brown, H., et al. (2012). Dopamine, affordance and active inference. *PLoS Comput. Biol.* 8:e1002327. doi: 10.1371/journal.pcbi.1002327

Frith, C. D. (1992). *The Cognitive Neuropsychology of Schizophrenia.* Hillsdale, NJ: Lawrence Erlbaum Associates.

Frith, C. D., Blakemore, S., and Wolpert, D. M. (2000a). Explaining the symptoms of schizophrenia: abnormalities in the awareness of action. *Brain Res. Brain Res. Rev.* 31, 357–363. doi: 10.1016/s0165-0173(99)00052-1

Frith, C. D., Blakemore, S. J., and Wolpert, D. M. (2000b). Abnormalities in the awareness and control of action. *Philos. Trans. R. Soc. Lond. B Biol. Sci.* 355, 1771–1788. doi: 10.1098/rstb.2000.0734

Gallagher, I. I. (2000). Philosophical conceptions of the self: implications for cognitive science. *Trends Cogn. Sci.* 4, 14–21. doi: 10.1016/s1364-6613(99)01417-5

Greenberg, J., Pyszczynski, T. A., and Solomon, S. (1982). The self-serving attributional bias: beyond self presentation. *J. Exp. Soc. Psychol.* 18, 56–67. doi: 10.1016/0022-1031(82)90081-6

Harmon-Jones, E., Amodio, D. M., and Harmon-Jones, C. (2009). "Action-based model of dissonance: a review, integration and expansion of conceptions of cognitive conflict," in *Advances in Experimental Social Psychology* (Vol. 41), ed M. P. Zanna (Burlington: Academic Press), 119–166.

Heilman, K. M., Barrett, A. M., and Adair, J. C. (1998). Possible mechanisms of anosognosia: a defect in self-awareness. *Philos. Trans. R. Soc. Lond. B Biol. Sci.* 353, 1903–1909. doi: 10.1098/rstb.1998.0342

Holmes, A. J., Bogdan, R., and Pizzagalli, D. A. (2010). Serotonin transporter genotype and action monitoring dysfunction: a possible substrate underlying increased vulnerability to depression. *Neuropsychopharmacology* 35, 1186–1197. doi: 10.1038/npp.2009.223

Holmes, A. J., and Pizzagalli, D. A. (2008). Spatiotemporal dynamics of error processing dysfunctions in major depressive disorder. *Arch. Gen. Psychiatry* 65, 179–188. doi: 10.1001/archgenpsychiatry.2007.19

Hommel, B., Musseler, J., Aschersleben, G., and Prinz, W. (2001). The Theory of Event Coding (TEC): a framework for perception and action planning. *Behav. Brain Sci.* 24, 849–878; discussion 878–937. doi: 10.1017/S0140525X01000103

Hughes, G., Desantis, A., and Waszak, F. (2013). Mechanisms of intentional binding and sensory attenuation: the role of temporal prediction, temporal control, identity prediction and motor prediction. *Psychol. Bull.* 139, 133–151. doi: 10.1037/a0028566

Kaplan-Solms, K. L., and Solms, M. (2000). *Clinical Studies in Neuropsychoanalysis: Introduction of a Depth Neuropsychology.* London: Karnac Books.

Karnath, H. O., Baier, B., and Nagele, T. (2005). Awareness of the functioning of one's own limbs mediated by the insular cortex? *J. Neurosci.* 25, 7134–7138. doi: 10.1523/jneurosci.1590-05.2005

Knowles, R., McCarthy-Jones, S., and Rowse, G. (2011). Grandiose delusions: a review and theoretical integration of cognitive and affective perspectives. *Clin. Psychol. Rev.* 31, 684–696. doi: 10.1016/j.cpr.2011.02.009

Krebs, R. M., Boehler, C. N., and Woldorff, M. G. (2010). The influence of reward associations on conflict processing in the stroop task. *Cognition* 117, 341–347. doi: 10.1016/j.cognition.2010.08.018

Leary, M. R. (2007). Motivational and emotional aspects of the self. *Annu. Rev. Psychol.* 58, 317–344. doi: 10.1146/annurev.psych.58.110405.085658

LeDoux, J. E. (1996). *The Emotional Brain.* New York: Simon and Schuster.

Linskey, C. (1994). Theme and content of delusions in asian indian psychotic patients: correlation with diagnosis. *Jefferson J. Psychiatry* 12, 21–28.

Mezulis, A. H., Abramson, L. Y., Hyde, J. S., and Hankin, B. L. (2004). Is there a universal positivity bias in attributions? A meta-analytic review of individual, developmental and cultural differences in the self-serving attributional bias. *Psychol. Bull.* 130, 711–747. doi: 10.1037/0033-2909.130.5.711

Moore, J. W., and Fletcher, P. C. (2012). Sense of agency in health and disease: a review of cue integration approaches. *Conscious. Cogn.* 21, 59–68. doi: 10.1016/j.concog.2011.08.010

Moore, J. W., Wegner, D. M., and Haggard, P. (2009). Modulating the sense of agency with external cues. *Conscious. Cogn.* 18, 1056–1064. doi: 10.1016/j.concog.2009.05.004

Muhle-Karbe, P. S., and Krebs, R. M. (2012). On the influence of reward on action-effect binding. *Front. Psychol.* 3:450. doi: 10.3389/fpsyg.2012.00450

Olvet, D. M., and Hajcak, G. (2008). The error-related negativity (ERN) and psychopathology: toward an endophenotype. *Clin. Psychol. Rev.* 28, 1343–1354. doi: 10.1016/j.cpr.2008.07.003

Pessoa, L., and Adolphs, R. (2010). Emotion processing and the amygdala: from a 'low road' to 'many roads' of evaluating biological significance. *Nat. Rev. Neurosci.* 11, 773–783. doi: 10.1038/nrn2920

Phillips, M. L., Medford, N., Senior, C., Bullmore, E. T., Suckling, J., Brammer, M. J., et al. (2001). Depersonalization disorder: thinking without feeling. *Psychiatry Res.* 108, 145–160. doi: 10.1016/s0925-4927(01)00119-6

Pourtois, G., Schettino, A., and Vuilleumier, P. (2013). Brain mechanisms for emotional influences on perception and attention: what is magic and what is not. *Biol. Psychol.* 92, 492–512. doi: 10.1016/j.biopsycho.2012.02.007

Sedikides, C., and Strube, M. J. (1995). The multiply motivated self. *Pers. Soc. Psychol. Bull.* 21, 1330–1335. doi: 10.1177/01461672952112010

Seth, A. K., Suzuki, K., and Critchley, H. D. (2011). An interoceptive predictive coding model of conscious presence. *Front. Psychol.* 2:395. doi: 10.3389/fpsyg.2011.00395

Seth, A. K., Suzuki, K., and Critchley, H. D. (2012). An interoceptive predictive coding model of conscious presence. *Front. Psychol.* 2:395. doi: 10.3389/fpsyg.2011.00395

Sierra, M., and Berrios, G. E. (1998). Depersonalization: neurobiological perspectives. *Biol. Psychiatry* 44, 898–908. doi: 10.1016/s0006-3223(98)00015-8

Spence, S. A., Brooks, D. J., Hirsch, S. R., Liddle, P. F., Meehan, J., and Grasby, P. M. (1997). A PET study of voluntary movement in schizophrenic patients experiencing passivity phenomena (delusions of alien control). *Brain* 120(Pt. 11), 1997–2011. doi: 10.1093/brain/120.11.1997

Suhail, K. (2003). Phenomenology of delusions in Pakistani patients: effect of gender and social class. *Psychopathology* 36, 195–199. doi: 10.1159/000072789

Synofzik, M., Thier, P., Leube, D. T., Schlotterbeck, P., and Lindner, A. (2010). Misattributions of agency in schizophrenia are based on imprecise predictions about the sensory consequences of one's actions. *Brain* 133(Pt. 1), 262–271. doi: 10.1093/brain/awp291

Synofzik, M., Vosgerau, G., and Lindner, A. (2009a). Me or not me—an optimal integration of agency cues? *Conscious. Cogn.* 18, 1065–1068. doi: 10.1016/j.concog.2009.07.007

Synofzik, M., Vosgerau, G., and Lindner, A. (2009b). Me or not me—an optimal integration of agency cues? *Conscious. Cogn.* 18, 1056–1064. doi: 10.1016/j.concog.2009.07.007

Synofzik, M., Vosgerau, G., and Newen, A. (2008a). Beyond the comparator model: a multifactorial two-step account of agency. *Conscious. Cogn.* 17, 219–239. doi: 10.1016/j.concog.2007.03.010

Synofzik, M., Vosgerau, G., and Newen, A. (2008b). I move, therefore I am: a new theoretical framework to investigate agency and ownership. *Conscious. Cogn.* 17, 411–424. doi: 10.1016/j.concog.2008.03.008

Synofzik, M., Vosgerau, G., and Voss, M. (2013). The experience of agency: an interplay between prediction and postdiction. *Front. Psychol.* 4:127. doi: 10.3389/fpsyg.2013.00127

Takahata, K., Takahashi, H., Maeda, T., Umeda, S., Suhara, T., Mimura, M., et al. (2012). It's not my fault: postdictive modulation of intentional binding by monetary gains and losses. *PLoS One* 7:e53421. doi: 10.1371/journal.pone.0053421

Turnbull, O. H., Evans, C. E., and Owen, V. (2005). Negative emotions and anosognosia. *Cortex* 41, 67–75. doi: 10.1016/s0010-9452(08)70179-5

Vosgerau, G., and Synofzik, M. (2012). Weighting models and weighting factors. *Conscious. Cogn.* 21, 55–58. doi: 10.1016/j.concog.2011.09.016

Vuilleumier, P. (2004). Anosognosia: the neurology of beliefs and uncertainties. *Cortex* 40, 9–17. doi: 10.1016/s0010-9452(08)70918-3

Vuilleumier, P. (2005). How brains beware: neural mechanisms of emotional attention. *Trends Cogn. Sci.* 9, 585–594. doi: 10.1016/j.tics.2005.10.011

Wilke, C., Synofzik, M., and Lindner, A. (2012). The valence of action outcomes modulates the perception of one's actions. *Conscious. Cogn.* 21, 18–29. doi: 10.1016/j.concog.2011.06.004

Wolpert, D. M., Ghahramani, Z., and Jordan, M. I. (1995). An internal model for sensorimotor integration. *Science* 269, 1880–1882. doi: 10.1126/science.7569931

Yoshie, M., and Haggard, P. (2013). Negative emotional outcomes attenuate sense of agency over voluntary actions. *Curr. Biol.* 23, 2028–2032. doi: 10.1016/j.cub.2013.08.034

13

Sense of agency is related to gamma band coupling in an inferior parietal-preSMA circuitry

Anina Ritterband-Rosenbaum[1,2], Jens B. Nielsen[1,2] and Mark S. Christensen[1,2,3]*

[1] Department of Nutrition, Exercise and Sports, University of Copenhagen, Copenhagen, Denmark
[2] Department of Neuroscience and Pharmacology, University of Copenhagen, Copenhagen, Denmark
[3] Cognitive Neuroscience Research Unit, Danish Neuroscience Center, Aarhus University, Aarhus, Denmark

Correspondence:
Mark S. Christensen, Department of Neuroscience and Pharmacology and Department of Nutrition, Exercise and Sports, Copenhagen Neural Control of Movement, Panum Institute, University of Copenhagen, Blegdamsvej 3, Building 33.3, 2200 Copenhagen, Denmark
e-mail: markc@sund.ku.dk

In the present study we tested whether sense of agency (SoA) is reflected by changes in coupling between right medio-frontal/supplementary motor area (SMA) and inferior parietal cortex (IPC). Twelve healthy adult volunteers participated in the study. They performed a variation of a line-drawing task (Nielsen, 1963; Fourneret and Jeannerod, 1998), in which they moved a cursor on a digital tablet with their right hand without seeing the hand. Visual feedback displayed on a computer monitor was either in correspondence with or deviated from the actual movement. This made participants uncertain as to the agent of the movement and they reported SoA in approximately 50% of trials when the movement was computer-generated. We tested whether IPC-preSMA coupling was associated with SoA, using dynamic causal modeling (DCM) for induced responses (Chen et al., 2008; Herz et al., 2012). Nine different DCMs were constructed for the early and late phases of the task, respectively. All models included two regions: a superior medial gyrus (preSMA) region and a right supramarginal gyrus (IPC) region. Bayesian models selection (Stephan et al., 2009) favored a model with input to IPC and modulation of the forward connection to SMA in the late task phase, and a model with input to preSMA and modulation of the backward connection was favored for the early task phase. The analysis shows that IPC source activity in the 50–60 Hz range modulated preSMA source activity in the 40–70 Hz range in the presence of SoA compared with no SoA in the late task phase, but the test of the early task phase did not reveal any differences between presence and absence of SoA. We show that SoA is associated with a directionally specific between frequencies coupling from IPC to preSMA in the higher gamma (ɣ) band in the late task phase. This suggests that SoA is a retrospective perception, which is highly dependent on interpretation of the outcome of the performed action.

Keywords: sense of agency (SoA), supplementary motor area (SMA), right inferior parietal cortex (IPC), dynamic causal model (DCM), γ-activity in SMA-IPC network

INTRODUCTION

When we reach for a cup of coffee we usually feel that we are in control of what we are doing and that we are the agent of the movement. Current research suggests that the sense of agency (SoA) occurs when the sensory consequences (usually in the form of proprioceptive and visual feedback) of the movement correspond to the original intention and plan of the movement, i.e., the comparator model (Gallagher, 2000; Wegner, 2004; Engbert et al., 2008). The comparator model fits within the experimental framework of feedback manipulations, in which (typical) visual feedback is distorted in such a way that there is a mismatch between visual and proprioceptive feedback, and thereby also a mismatch between the intended action outcome and the visual feedback.

The most common way to study the SoA is to expose participants to a situation of ambiguity regarding self-produced movement. This may be done by manipulating the visual feedback that a participant receives regarding performance of a simple hand or arm movement. Nielsen (1963) introduced the first version of this experimental design (known as the Alien Hand paradigm). He was not interested in SoA *per se*, but rather the feeling of volition, which is essential for SoA (Nielsen, 1963). These types of manipulations also allow participants to focus on the judgmental task of determining whether they themselves or an external agent performed the action (Farrer et al., 2003a). Such tasks have led to the notion of a "who"-system (Georgieff and Jeannerod, 1998), which is used in the process of determining "who" is the agent. Several later studies have adapted the paradigm to investigate intentional actions and the neural mechanisms underlying SoA (e.g., Fourneret and Jeannerod, 1998; Farrer and Frith, 2002). However, recent studies suggest that unexpected outcomes of actions are associated with high sense of control if the action leading to the response is compatibly primed (Chambon et al., 2013; Sidarus et al., 2013), suggesting that SoA depends on prospective forms of knowledge relating to action selection processes, and independent of action outcome.

However, the neural circuitry responsible for the experience of agency has not been fully clarified in terms of how brain regions interact and the temporal aspect of activities in specific cortical structures. Several studies have implied that areas in the inferior parietal cortex (IPC) and areas in the supplementary motor area (SMA) are involved in the formation of intentions prior to the movement and evaluation of action outcomes (Sirigu et al., 1999, 2004; Leube et al., 2003; Farrer et al., 2008; Desmurget et al., 2009). Patients with lesions of the posterior parietal cortex (PPC) more often mistake whether they are or an experimenter is responsible for a movement shown on a video screen (Sirigu et al., 1999) and they become aware of their decision with a significant delay compared to healthy participants (Sirigu et al., 2004). Electrical stimulation of the right inferior parietal lobe (IPL) may also make participants falsely believe that they moved or intended to move (Desmurget and Sirigu, 2009), while stimulation of the SMA has been reported to produce an urge to move (Fried et al., 1991). Imaging studies have demonstrated activation in the preSMA and in the right angular gyrus (part of the IPC) when participants experience a discrepancy between intended and observed movements (Farrer and Frith, 2002; Farrer et al., 2008; Yomogida et al., 2010; Nahab et al., 2011; Chambon et al., 2013), which also shows parametric modulations when deviations are increased gradually (Farrer et al., 2003a). Interruption of preSMA by transcranial magnetic stimulation demonstrated disruption of agency (Moore et al., 2010). While these studies provide evidence of the involvement of the respective areas in the generation of the subjective SoA, they reveal nothing about the functional or effective connectivity or the temporal aspect of neural communication in the parietal-SMA network involved in SoA.

In order to elucidate these issues we conducted the present EEG-study of the time course of coupled activity in the right IPC-preSMA network in relation to SoA. The analysis of the study was explorative. However, we hypothesized a modulation of activity between the selected target regions depending on behavior of the participant and the reflective task the participants were exposed to in a modified version of the Alien-Hand Paradigm (Nielsen, 1963). The connectivity between the two regions of interest was disclosed using a dynamic causal model (DCM) (Chen et al., 2008) for induced responses, in which a Bayesian Model Selection (BMS) was used to select the DCM, which explains the activity in right IPC and preSMA and how these are coupled best. The DCM describes how the neural activity, in terms of oscillatory power of one brain region, modulates the activity, again in terms of oscillatory power, of another region. This was investigated in relation to a motor task in which participants were asked to judge whether they themselves were responsible for a cursor movement presented on a computer screen, or whether a computer was responsible. Previous studies have shown that conscious perception of visual input is associated with coupling of neural activity across cortical areas in the γ-band frequency range (Rodriguez et al., 1999; Engel et al., 2001; Palva et al., 2005; Melloni et al., 2007; Siegel et al., 2012). Furthermore, investigations of EEG activity in relation to SoA have focused on modulation of event related potentials (Balconi and Crivelli, 2009; Gentsch et al., 2012), showing increased N1 components for externally-generated visual feedback and increased ERP components around 100 ms for delayed visual feedback respectively. However, to our knowledge no studies have looked at oscillatory coupling in relation to SoA We hypothesized that a network with information flow from preSMA-IPC would be favored in the initial phase of the movement, indicating that formation of intention of the action is formed in frontal regions and fed to parietal regions for later comparison between intended and actual movement outcome. Hence, opposite direction of information flow would be favored in the late phase of the task.

MATERIALS AND METHODS

We included 12 right-handed, healthy adults (10 men/2 women) ranging from 22–32 years (average: 26.4 ± 2.8 years). None of the participants had any history of neurological or psychiatric disorder. Two male participants were excluded from the analysis after initial inspection of the data files revealed that they displayed very odd subjective reports of agency, i.e., reporting YES (or NO) in more than 80% of all trials. Ten participants were therefore included in the analysis. All participants were given written and oral information and all signed a consent form before the start of the experiment. The experiment was carried out according to the Helsinki-declaration and with approval from the local ethics committee of the Capital Region of Copenhagen (protocol number: H-B-2009-17).

EXPERIMENTAL PROCEDURE

The experimental paradigm was adapted from Ritterband-Rosenbaum et al. (2011) and aimed to cause ambiguity as to whether the participant or a computer was responsible for moving a cursor on a computer screen (Ritterband-Rosenbaum et al., 2011). The participants were seated comfortably in a chair with their heads in chin-rests 55 cm away from a computer screen. Vision of participants' own hands was blocked during the entire experiment (see **Figure 1**). Participants were instructed to make a fast (within 1.5 s) straight movement in the sagittal plane away from the center of their body by moving a cursor with a pen on a pen-tablet (Wacom, Intuos 3, Krefeld, Germany). The task was presented in a custom made Matlab (The MathWorks, Natics, MA, USA) program. A cue appeared on the screen indicating when participants were to start the movement. Participants had to move the cursor from the starting position at the bottom of the screen to the target at the top of the screen. When reaching the vertical level of the target, the cursor disappeared and participants had to report as fast as possible (within 1.5 s) whether they felt themselves as the agents of the observed movement. This was done by a key press of either the index finger ("yes, it is me") or middle finger ("no, it is not me") of the left hand. After the key press the participants had 2 s to place the pen to be ready for next trial. Each trial lasted 7 s. All participants performed 2 blocks of 200 trials (25 min) interrupted by a small break of 2–5 min to assure participants were attentive.

Three types of experimental trial types were introduced: Computer manipulated movements, Self-generated movements (trials with no interference of the computer on the observed movement), and Pause trials. The computer manipulated movements consisted of trials where the visual feedback was manipulated 1, 3, 6 (right), −1, −3, and −6 (left) degrees away from target (**Figure 1**), i.e., in parametrical fashion as done previously

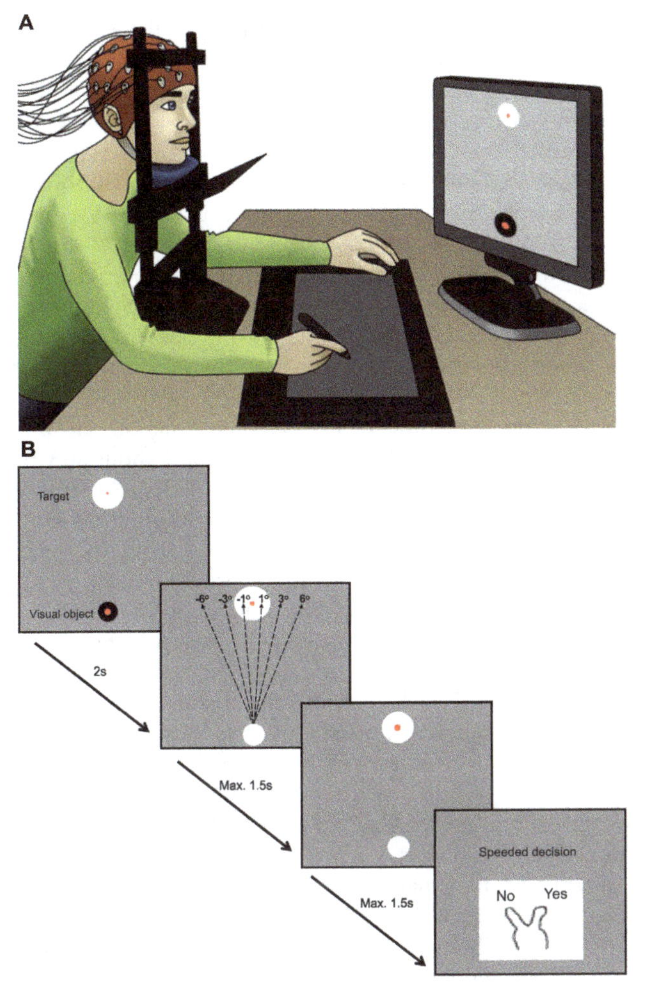

FIGURE 1 | The experimental design. (A) Displays the position of the participants during the experiment. The plate below the chin blocks the view of the hands but participants can follow the consequence of the action on the screen in front of them. **(B)** Illustrates what is occurring on the computer screen. During the experiment the cursor was randomly manipulated from the beginning of the movement by different angles of (−6, −3, −1, 1, 3, 6°). Negative angles refer to manipulation to the left side of the target. Participants had max. 1.5 s to perform the movement, but were instructed to move fast. When reaching the level of the target, the visual object disappeared and participants had to report as fast as possible (within 1.5 s) whether or not they felt they were the agents of the observed movement by a key press of the index or middle finger of the left hand. After key press, participants had 2 s to place the pen on top of the visual object and be ready for the next trial. During the experiment there were no lines visible on the display screen.

in other studies (Fourneret and Jeannerod, 1998; Farrer et al., 2003a,b). The 3/−3° manipulations were presented 80 times, the other angles 40 times. The self-generated movements and Pause trials were presented 40 times each. The Pause trials initially displayed the instruction "Pause" on the screen, after which the cursor moved to the target while participants did not move the hand. The trials were presented in a random order, though the order was the same for all participants. The computer-manipulations were induced from the beginning of the movement and continued in a straight line to the predefined position at the same level as the target. The dimensions of the tablet were 310 × 238 mm and the dimensions of the screen were 380 × 303 mm (with a resolution of 1280 × 1024 pixels). Moving 1 cm on the tablet corresponded to 1.2 cm horizontally and 1.3 cm vertically on the screen. The cursor was placed centrally 20% from the bottom of the screen with a diameter of 0.2 cm. To reach the target, which was located centrally 20% from the top of the screen, participants had to move approximately 15 cm on the tablet, which could easily be done without moving the full body.

We aimed to find movement deviation, which corresponded to 50/50% self-reported agency distribution. Pilot experiments indicated that this ratio was obtained at −3/3° deviations; therefore we exposed the participants to a higher number of −3/3° trials, but in the actual series of experiments the angle of deviation at which this ratio was found differed between participants, and as a consequence data from all angle deviations were pooled across all participants. Trials where the time of the answer was longer than the allowed response time (1.5 s) were excluded from the analysis (1.8% of all trials were excluded corresponding to less than 5.3% from 1 of the participants, less than 2.8% from 9 of the participants, and 0% from 2 participants). A total of 2972 trials with a ratio of roughly 50/50 for agency/no agency reporting were used in the EEG analysis (see also section EEG data analysis for further description). For individual participants the ratio varied from 13 to 72% for agency attribution with an average ratio for attributing the movement to one self of 42%.

DATA ACQUISITION

Continuous EEG was recorded from 64 channels (ActiveTwo, BioSemi, Amsterdam, The Netherlands) using acquisition software ActiView (version 6.05). Active electrodes were mounted in a headcap (headcap BioSemi, The Netherlands). Off-set was kept below 25 microV. Recordings were set to AC and 1 Hz high-pass filtering applied. Sampling rate was 2048 Hz. Markers indicating onset of movement, end of movement, and key-press when reporting experience of agency were co-registered with the EEG.

EEG DATA ANALYSIS

All data were analyzed offline using Matlab R2010a (MathWorks, MA, USA), with the toolbox EEGLab v9.0.4.4b (Swartz Center for Computational Neuroscience; http://sccn.ucsd.edu/eeglab/), and the toolbox Statistical Parametric Mapping (SPM8).

Files were imported to EEGlab, resampled to 256 Hz in order to reduce computation time, re-referenced to average reference. Then 1 Hz high-pass and 80 Hz low-pass filters were applied. Independent Component Analysis (ICA) was applied using the runica algorithm. ICA components reflecting eye-blinks and lateral eye-movements were identified by visual inspection and subsequently removed from the data. If noise components that were visible as noise across the whole scalp image were identified, these were also removed from the data. The EEG data without eye movement and common noise artifacts were exported from EEGlab to BDF-format files.

The new BDF files were imported into SPM8. Data were epoched from −500 to +1000 ms with respect to movement onset for each trial. The epochs were sorted into AgencyYES and

AgencyNo trials. All epochs were visually inspected and in trials with spikes or similar artifacts were declared as "BAD" and left out of further analysis. On average 8% of all epochs were excluded.

The epoched data were then taken into an initial source image analysis using empirical Bayes Methods as implemented in SPM8. EEG data were co-registered with a template T1-weighted magnetic resonance image, and a forward model was constructed using a Boundary Element Model. The forward model was inverted using the multiple sparse priors as hyper priors. Data were limited to a time window from 0 ms to +800 ms with respect to movement onset. Furthermore, the data were limited to frequencies between 4 and 80 Hz. Images of the reconstructed sources were separated into an early (0–400 ms) and late (400–800 ms) task phases, and divided into delta (4–7 Hz), alpha (8–14 Hz), beta (15–30 Hz), low γ (31–50 Hz) and high γ (51–80 Hz) frequency ranges, based on textbook frequency separations which are supposed to reflect different functional properties related to alertness, motor control, attention, conscious thoughts, etc., and into AgencyYES and AgencyNO conditions. Studies suggest that conscious perception depends on transient synchronized activity at frequencies around 30–60 Hz; We therefore found it important to look at different frequency bands and to further separate the γ-band into low and high ranges (Rodriguez et al., 1999; Engel et al., 2001; Palva et al., 2005; Melloni et al., 2007). We chose to separate the early and late task phases as we believed that the two time periods are related to different events of the task presented. The early phase governs the movement as such, whereas the late phase represents evaluation of the movement and therefore a different modulatory activity. These images, reconstructed for each participant, were taken into a second level 3-way ANOVA analysis. An *F*-test was made across all conditions, i.e., the mean of all conditions. Results from this source analysis gave rise to an image of areas that were used to guide the subsequent Dynamic Causal Model (DCM) analysis. Furthermore, we performed a test of the main effect of agency on the source analysis images which was also used to guide the DCM analysis and tests of the main effects of time and frequency.

DCM for induced responses (Chen et al., 2008) was used in order to assess within-frequency and between-frequency coupling between medial frontal and right inferior parietal regions. We were particularly interested in the differences in coupling between the AgencyYES and AgencyNO trials. We therefore tested whether or not ascribing the visually perceived action to one-self would be reflected in different coupling patterns in a network of regions involved in this action.

We selected two regions that have been implicated in motor tasks that include judgments of agency. These were a medial frontal region and right IPC. Two loci, which were used as prior for the DCM source reconstruction procedure, were chosen based on the clusters found in the imaging source analyses (**Figure 2**) described above. These were: right fronto-medial region (preSMA, superior medial gyrus, MNI coordinate: 12, 26, 56) based on the source analysis of the mean across all conditions in the above described ANOVA, and right inferior parietal region (supramarginal gyrus, IPC(PGa), MNI coordinate: 60, −50, 18) based on the analysis of the positive main effect of Agency, i.e., Agency YES > Agency NO. These two regions were used in the subsequent DCM analyses. Furthermore, two different sets of models were constructed, one corresponding to the early part of the task (1–400 ms), and one corresponding to the late part of the task (400–800 ms), covering the time when participants evaluate their movement.

Nine different DCM were constructed from the data from the early task phase (1–400 ms time window) and nine DCMs from the late task phase (400–800 ms). All models included the right preSMA (MNI: 12, 36, 56) and right IPC (MNI: 60, −50, 18) regions. Two types of effects were constructed: the AgencyYES and AgencyNO trials, i.e., SoA condition. These effects were allowed to enter either one or both of the regions; the effects could either influence the coupling from the frontal to the parietal region, the coupling from the parietal to the frontal, or both couplings at the same time. In all models information can "flow" between both regions, but it is the information about SoA that influences the models differently. In models 1–3, SoA can influence both connections between the regions; in models 4–6 it is only information flowing from IPC to preSMA that is influenced by SoA, and in models 7–9 it is only information flowing from preSMA to IPC that is influenced by SoA. Models 1, 4, and 7 are similar with respect to where information about SoA should enter the models, in these cases into both IPC and preSMA. Models 2, 5, and 8 are similar in the sense that information enters preSMA, and in Models 3, 6, and 9 information enters IPC. If any of Models 1–3 are favored by a Bayesian Model Selection (BMS) analyses it indicates that SoA is a process that requires that information between IPC and preSMA has to be reiterated between the two regions. If any of Models 4–6 are favored in a BMS it indicates that intentional information about the predicted consequences of the action, formed in preSMA, is modulated by SoA, and if any of Models 7–9 are favored by a BMS it indicates that actual sensory consequences, or deviations between expected and actual consequences, computed in IPC are modulated by SoA. If models 1, 4, or 7 are favored it indicates that SoA is "generated" simultaneously in IPC and preSMA, which would mean that any distinction of whether SoA depends mainly on information about the intention of the movement or depends on the outcome of the comparison between expected and actual feedback remains unresolved.

For this DCM for induced responses we chose a non-linear coupling, i.e., allowing between-frequency coupling in the range between 4–80 Hz, because this allows modeling both within-frequency coupling and between frequency coupling. This choice was made because "Agency" as a phenomenon incorporates aspects of motor control as well as aspects of conscious self-recognition, and these behaviors are not necessarily associated with EEG oscillations at the same frequencies. These combinations gave rise to the nine different DCMs displayed in **Figure 4**, which then was constructed for the two different task phases (early and late).

In order to determine which of the two times nine models explained the data best, we conducted two separate fixed effect BMS analyses, one for the early task phase (1–400 ms) and one for the late task phase (400–800 ms).

The models that explained the data best selected from the two BMS of the early task phase and late task phase respectively were

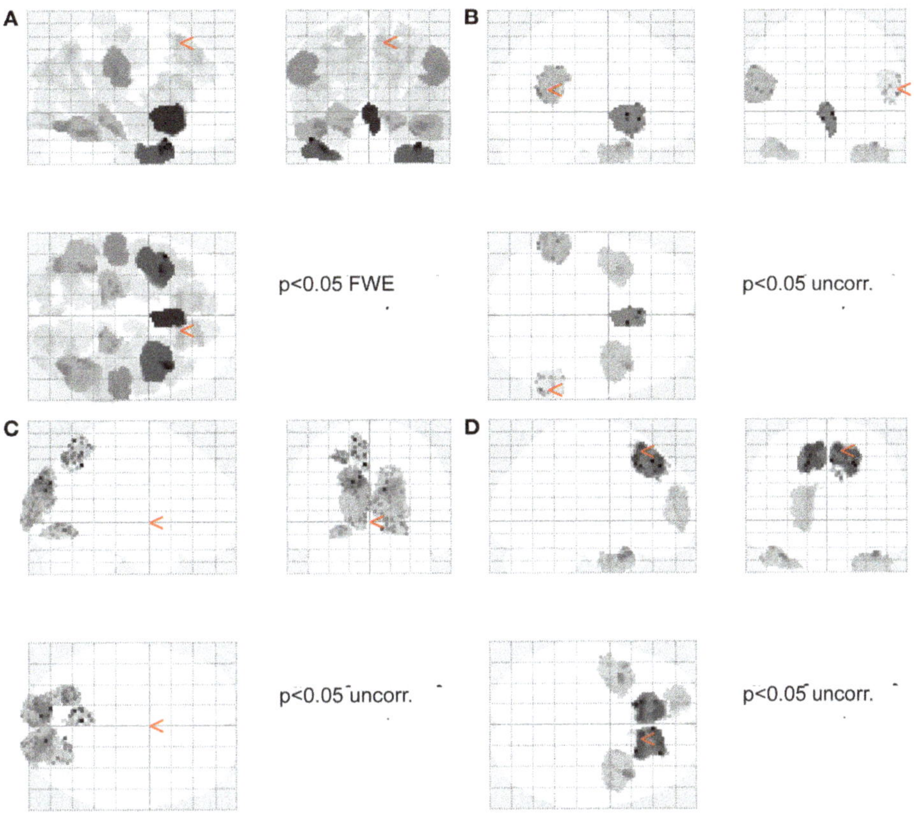

FIGURE 2 | Source localization. (A) Shows the main effect across all conditions ($p < 0.05$ FWE corrected for multiple comparisons). Red arrow points to the location used for the DCM analysis for the preSMA source. **(B)** Shows the main effect of agency ($p < 0.05$ uncorrected threshold). Red arrows point to the location used for the DCM analysis for the IPC source. **(C)** Shows the main effect of time (i.e., early vs. late) ($p < 0.05$ uncorrected threshold) (arrow in MNI 0,0,0). **(D)** Shows the main effect of frequency ($p < 0.05$ uncorrected threshold). Red arrow points to the location used for the DCM analysis for the preSMA source.

used for subsequent comparisons. Here the coupling between the frontal and parietal regions was tested using paired *t*-tests. The *t*-tests compared the frequency-frequency images of the effect of trials on the coupling derived from the respective model.

BEHAVIORAL DATA ANALYSIS

Only data from trials with manipulated angles were used for analysis. Group averages were done after separating data depending on the experience of agency for the different kinematical results. Each trial contains X_{pen}, Y_{pen} coordinates for each individual movement produced by the pen on the tablet, and X_{cursor}, Y_{cursor} coordinates for the trajectory of the cursor on the screen. Each complete set of coordinates was normalized to the size of the pen-tablet and used for further calculations of the kinematic:

(1) Movement time (ms): refers to the time to complete the movement. Movement time is calculated by the start of the movement to the final point on the screen where the visual object reaches the vertical level of the target.
(2) Hit distance (mm): corresponds to the distance between the end position X_{pen} and X_{target} center of the target. Negative and positive values indicate hit distances on the left side and right side of the target, respectively.
(3) Line curvature (mm^{-1}): indicates how curved the actual movement is. It was based on a calculation of the relative distance between the produced movement and the shortest distance to the target. The curvature measure for this purpose is the accumulated local curvature for the entire movement. A lower score represents a more direct movement toward the target. It is calculated by the formula.

$$C = \frac{x'y'' - y'x''}{\left(x'^2 + y'^2\right)^{3/2}}$$

(4) Drift (mm): measures the difference between the movement of the pen on the tablet and the observed cursor movement trajectory on the computer screen. Small values indicate good correspondence between the produced and the observed movement. It was calculated as the Eucledian distance between the X_{pen},Y_{pen} and the X_{object},Y_{object}

$$\text{drift} = \sqrt{(x_{pen} - x_{screen})^2 + (y_{pen} - y_{screen})^2}$$

(5) Answer time (ms): indicates the time from the end of the movement until participants pressed a button to indicate whether they experienced agency or not.

Paired *T*-tests for the behavioral data were used and the alpha level set at 0.05. For non-normally distributed data a Mann-Whitney Rank Sum Test was applied.

RESULTS

BEHAVIORAL FINDINGS

Table 1 reports the kinematics of the performed movement in relation to the subjective experience of agency. The movement time (Mann-Whitney Rank Sum: 49.0, $p = 0.97$), the line curvature (Mann-Whitney Rank Sum: 47.0, $p = 0.583$), the hit distance (Mann-Whitney Rank Sum: 49.0, $p = 0.970$), the drift (Mann-Whitney Rank Sum: 37.0, $p = 0.345$) and the answer time ($t = -0.058$, $p = 0.477$) were all very similar whether the participants experienced agency or not.

Table 1 provides information about group averages of kinematic results separating data into the subjective reporting. Inter-participant variance is given by 1 *SD*.

SOURCE LOCALIZATION

The initial image source localization analysis demonstrated significant sources (*F*-test, across all conditions, voxel threshold $p < 0.05$ Family Wise Error (FWE) corrected for multiple comparisons using Gaussian random field theory, limited to cortical areas associated with gray matter as defined by the SPM anatomy toolbox v1.8) in the right inferior temporal gyrus, right superior parietal lobule (angular gyrus, superior occipital gyrus, middle occipital gyrus, precuneus), left superior parietal lobule (angular gyrus, middle occipital gyrus), bilateral IPC (supramarginal gyrus), right inferior and medial temporal gyrus, left inferior occipital gyrus, bilateral inferior frontal gyrus, left inferior temporal gyrus and temporal pole, bilateral superior medial and superior frontal gyrus (see **Figure 2A**).

Exploratory source localization analyses

The main effect of agency showed significant differences in source strength in bilateral IPC (supramarginal gyrus) albeit at a lenient ($p < 0.05$ uncorrected) threshold (see **Figure 2B**) which was used for the subsequent DCM analysis.

The main effect of task phase (early vs. late) revealed significant albeit at a lenient threshold ($p < 0.05$ uncorrected) source differences in early visual areas and along the dorsal stream (**Figure 2C**).

Table 1 | Kinematic for all deviations divided into the two categories of subjective reporting.

	Yes	No
Movement time (ms)	332 ± 49	327 ± 52
Hit distance (mm)	−24.2 ± 37.4	−25.4 ± 37.2
Line curvature (mm^{-1})	0.033 ± 0.008	0.032 ± 0.007
Drift (mm)	43.8 ± 26.9	51.2 ± 27.5
Answer time (ms)	492 ± 119	489 ± 132

The main effect of frequency revealed significant albeit at a lenient threshold ($p < 0.05$ uncorrected) sources in frontal areas, including the preSMA region, which was used for the subsequent DCM analysis.

Because DCM for EEG incorporates a generative model of the sources that are modeled, these initial source localization analyses are not necessary for the specification of the models. The statistics underlying the sources are not crucial for the specification of the DCM, since the DCM tests specific hypotheses concerning the sources incorporated in the model, and not an unspecific hypothesis concerning any combination of sources in the data. Therefore, these source analyses serve only as guidelines for the loci used in the DCM analyses. As part of the DCM for induced responses, we also employed a step that optimizes source localization. This optimization is based on the initial loci given, but allow for deviations away from the exact loci. The above mentioned source localization analyses of the three main effects serve only as an exploratory test for guidance. We based the IPC and preSMA loci for the DCM on the initial explorative source analyses. However, values based on previous studies would be an alternative, which would serve the same purpose.

DYNAMIC CAUSAL MODEL FIT

The nine models (**Figure 3**), as described in the methods sections, were constructed for all 10 participants and underwent model inversion in SPM8 for the early and late task phase separately. For the early task phase data, all model inversions revealed models that showed time-frequency plots reflecting a simplified version of the actual data (see **Supplementary Figure S1**, which compares data from the two sources with the predictions derived from the models). For the late task phase, model inversions from one participant resulted in nine models without any dynamics, and hence the participant's models were not included in the subsequent BMS for the late phase.

BAYESIAN MODEL SELECTION

The BMS revealed that Model 8 was the winning model for the early task phase, whereas Model 6 was the model that fitted the data best for the late task phase (**Figure 3**). Model 8 for the early task phase is the model in which information about SoA is fed into preSMA, and where SoA modulates the connection from preSMA to IPC. Model 6 for the late task phase is the model in which information about SoA is feed into IPC, and where SoA modulates the connection from IPC to preSMA.

DYNAMIC CAUSAL MODEL OF INDUCED RESPONSES

For the early task phase, where Model 8 was the winning model, the frequency-frequency maps of the couplings from preSMA to IPC revealed no significant ($p > 0.05$ FWE cluster level corrected) (**Figure 4A**) differences between the AgencyYES and AgencyNO conditions.

For the late task phase, where Model 6 was the winning model, the frequency-frequency maps of the couplings from IPC to preSMA revealed significant differences between the AgencyYES and AgencyNO conditions ($p < 0.05$ FWE cluster level corrected). When the power of frequencies in the range from 50–60 Hz in IPC increased, the power in the frequencies 40–70 Hz

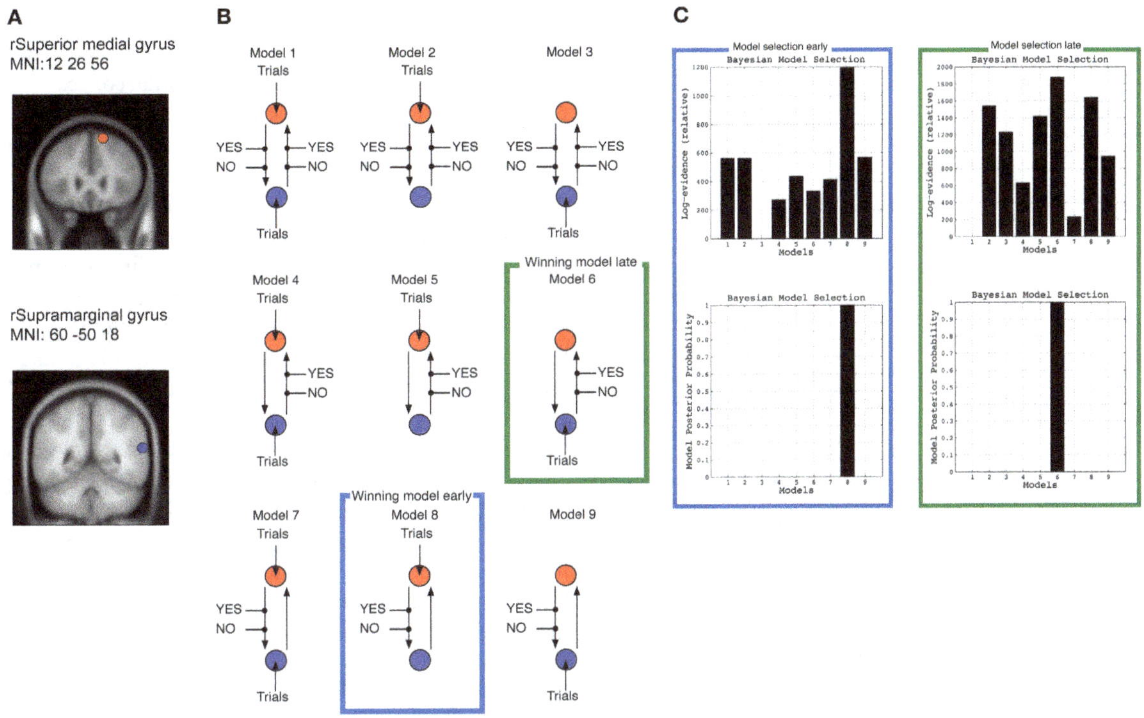

FIGURE 3 | Dynamic causal models. (A) Shows location of the two sources used for the DCM analyses in right medial frontal gyrus ~preSMA and right supramarginal gyrus ~IPC. **(B)** Shows the 9 different DCMs, and **(C)** the results of the Bayesian model selection for the early phase (marked in green square) and late phase (marked in blue square) of the movement (400–800 ms).

increased more in preSMA (**Figure 4B**) for AgencyYES than for AgencyNO.

DISCUSSION

In the present study we have investigated SoA and showed that during a simple goal directed computer cursor movement task, a network consisting of two cortical areas that are believed to be involved in SoA display different coupling patterns depending on the state of the movement. Using DCM and BMS, we have shown that the early and late phases of the task are governed by two different processes as revealed by two different dynamics causal models that explain the data best (Model 8 vs. Model 6). Furthermore, we have shown that only in the late phase of the task, the positive SoA, i.e., "yes I am responsible for the action that I have witnessed on the screen in front of me," is reflected in a change in between-frequency coupling directed from IPC to preSMA in the higher γ frequency range. We interpret these findings in the light of the comparator model in such a way that the preSMA processes the intended outcome of the action, and the IPC is used in sensory integration of the visual and proprioceptive feedback. In the case of correspondence of the comparison between the intended outcome of the action and actual feedback, communication between preSMA and IPC is governed by the increased gamma coupling, which thereby becomes essential in order to form SoA because information about a successful comparison has been achieved. The increase in gamma coupling in the direction from IPC to preSMA may suggests that information about the outcome of the corresponding comparison also is fed back to preSMA in order to update intention formation in preSMA as the specific goal of the action now is accomplished.

LOCALIZATION, TIMING, AND NEURAL ACCOUNTS OF SoA

These two findings suggest on the one hand that information processing in the neural network underlying the early parts of a goal directed movement is a process that preferentially involves information flow from frontal toward parietal areas, as revealed by the results of the Bayesian model selections. Later, the occurrence of SoA seems to require information about the outcome of the action in order to occur as reflected in coupling with an information flow from parietal to frontal areas. This is consistent with the idea that IPC computes the discrepancy between the intended and actual outcome of the movement performed. Theoretical aspects of SoA imply that a central monitoring system is available in order to estimate congruency or incongruency between motor performance and sensory feedback. This comparator model uses predictions of motor output and actual estimated state of movement (Wolpert et al., 1995; David et al., 2008; Synofzik et al., 2008). This discrepancy is reflected in the larger change in coupling from IPC to preSMA in AgencyYES than that in AgencyNO. This is further reflected in the modulation of oscillatory power in preSMA in the 40–70 Hz range by increases in oscillatory power in IPC in the range from 50–60 Hz.

Although the non-specificity of EEG does not permit a precise localization of the signals, we have used approximate source loci

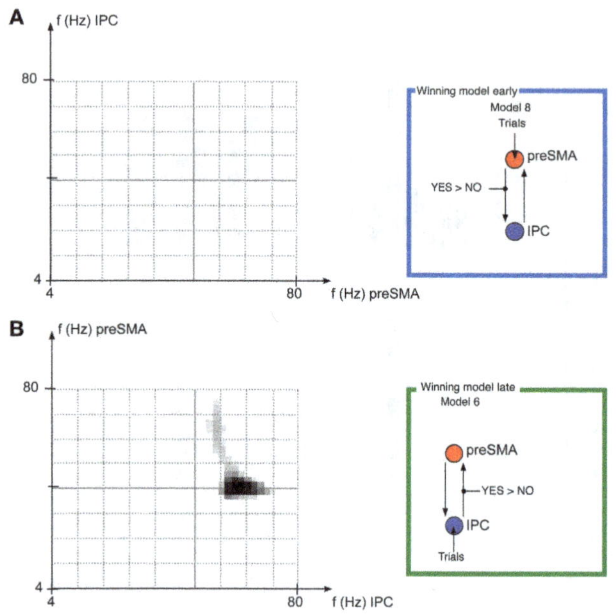

FIGURE 4 | Frequency-Frequency coupling in winning models. Results of the DCM analysis frequency-frequency paired *t*-tests. **(A)** Shows the results of the paired *t*-test of Frequency-pairs for the early task phase, testing whether the coupling from preSMA to IPC is significantly ($p < 0.05$ FWE cluster level, based on $p < 0.05$ uncorrected tests of individual frequency pairs) different for AgencyYES compared with AgencyNO trials. **(B)** Shows the results of the paired *t*-test of Frequency-pairs for the late task phase, testing whether the coupling from IPC to preSMA is significantly ($p < 0.05$ FWE cluster level, based on $p < 0.05$ uncorrected tests of individual frequency pairs) different for AgencyYES compared with AgencyNO trials, which is the case in the 50–60 Hz frequency range for IPC, which then increases the power in the frequencies 40–70 Hz increases in preSMA more for AgencyYES compared with AgencyNO.

for IPC and preSMA, respectively. In general, EEG source localization cannot be used with the same precision as, for instance, fMRI to determine where specific activity is located in the brain. It is therefore also important to stress that the source localizations performed in this study are of exploratory nature, and that the main effect of SoA reflected as a significant, albeit at very lenient threshold, only indicates that IPC may be related directly to SoA. This may also suggest that the approach to look for neural signatures related to SoA is more likely to be found reflected in the network coupling changes rather than in changes in a single brain region. The IPC has been suggested as important for the conscious intention to move (Sirigu et al., 2004; Desmurget and Sirigu, 2009), and lesions including this area induce an inability to recognize visual feedback of one's own movements (Sirigu et al., 1999). This is well in line with the larger coupling that we observed when participants experienced agency. Farrer and Frith (2002), Farrer et al. (2008) suggested that activity in the angular gyrus, which is part of the IPC, is mainly involved in the rejection of agency. In our study this would be the case when participants realized that the computer rather than they themselves was responsible for the movement. This is not in conflict with our findings, since coupling between two areas says little about the overall activity of the involved areas, and vice versa. We cannot decide from our recordings whether the recording over the preSMA reflected activity in the SMA proper, the preSMA, dorsal premotor cortex, or dorsomedial prefrontal cortex. All areas could potentially be involved, but several recent studies have pointed to the preSMA as the most likely area to be involved in generating the experience of agency (Fried et al., 1991; Moore et al., 2010).

We find it likely that the observed coupling reflects the ongoing introspection of the presence or absence of agency imposed by the experimental setup in this study. This finding is supported by the lack of difference in any of the kinematic parameters regardless of whether or not the participants experienced SoA. Since participants did not change their motor output, it is unlikely that they made their decision of SoA during the motor task. They would appear to depend rather on the subsequent perception and integration of neural signals. Participants have also been reported to be unaware of an external perturbation during drawing of a self-produced line (Fourneret and Jeannerod, 1998). In line with this, Synofzik and co-workers argued that the acknowledgment and judgment of SoA is constructed after the motor task has been performed, as it is based on the interpretation of the failure between predicted vs. performed movement (Synofzik et al., 2013).

We are thus aware that we may have revealed an experimental artifact with little relevance to everyday motor control where agency is taken for granted and only noticed by its (rare) absence (Kuhn et al., 2013). However, this does not change the fact that the observation reflects a genuine neural mechanism related to the conscious experience of agency.

FREQUENCY RANGES

Several studies have provided evidence that conscious perception and attention depend on transient synchronized activity in a distributed network at frequencies around 30–60 Hz (Rodriguez et al., 1999; Engel et al., 2001; Palva et al., 2005; Melloni et al., 2007; Siegel et al., 2012).

The increased γ-coupling that we observe seems to be a genuine finding specifically related to participants' perception of agency, because there are no attentional differences associated with the two subjective states imposed by the experimental setup. Furthermore, we base this statement on the fact that there were no behavioral differences with respect to movement time and reaction time in the two different subjective states, which could have indicated different attentional load. One study has revealed that γ-power in cingulate motor areas correlates with performance in a task where participants have to monitor their internal attentional state (Yamagishi and Anderson, 2013). However, this finding was not associated with coupling changes. Neural signatures of attentional mechanisms are indeed also displayed as top down modulation of γ-band coupling (Siegel et al., 2012). However, our findings do differ [from what?] in showing increased γ-coupling in a specific network, with a specific directionality of the coupling. It is not as a top-down controlled mechanism, but rather as a modulation of the bottom-up information giving the flow direction, i.e., from IPC to preSMA, which is in contrast to the more generalized long-distance synchrony observed in the previous studies (Melloni et al., 2007) reflecting a top-down attentional modulation (Siegel et al., 2012). The more generalized long-distance synchrony in the γ-band is probably linked to non-specific conscious awareness or attentional top down mechanisms rather than to processing of specific features of the perceived sensorimotor information. It is likely that conscious detection of other specific sensory features will reveal a specific coupling in different relevant local circuitries similar to what we have seen here.

As seen in **Supplementary Figure S1**, the DCMs models the observed time-frequency content of the two source regions quite well. Importantly it is also evident that the two regions display quite different tempero-frequency dynamics in all participants, suggesting, that coupling is not due to common noise signals in the two regions.

LIMITATIONS TO OUR STUDY

Unfortunately it was not possible to have a single deviation degree that gave rise to a 50/50 distribution of AgencyYES and AgencyNO responses in all participants, and we were therefore forced to collapse all trials across different deviation angles. This will naturally give rise to more small angle (i.e., +/−1°) deviations in the AgencyYES condition and large angle (i.e., +/−6°) deviations in the AgencyNO conditions. However, we do not believe that the difference in coupling between AgencyYES and AgencyNO is a reflection of purely larger visual deviations (+/−1 vs. 6°). As the deviation is initiated shortly after the movement starts, we would also have seen a similar difference in coupling for the early task phase where the visual deviation also is present.

DCM implies causality at the structural level, which means that causality is inferred by how the state equations of the DCM are coupled, and not by temporal precedence of activity in one area and then later in another area. If there is, as we suggest, a different causal relation between the investigated regions in the early and late task phases, it would not have been possible to integrate that into one large DCM covering the full time window of the task. This means that it would not be possible to integrate the dynamics of the whole task into a single model, if one expects that the directional communication changes throughout the task. Therefore, the approach with the split of the data into an early and a late task phase was employed.

CONCLUSION

In conclusion our observations are consistent with the idea that the sense of agency is mainly determined *post-hoc* based on a comparison between the sensory consequences of the movement and the original intention, rather than the ongoing experience during the movement (Kawato and Wolpert, 1998). The sudden absence of agency that we may experience when our interaction with the environment is suddenly altered (defective computer mouse or defective steering in a car) may then be signaled by the absence of high γ coupled activity in IPC and preSMA, when comparison of sensory feedback and motor plan reveals that the desired target was not obtained. This idea requires further testing.

AUTHOR CONTRIBUTIONS

Anina Ritterband-Rosenbaum, Jens B. Nielsen, and Mark S. Christensen designed the experiment and Anina Ritterband-Rosenbaum carried out the data collection. Anina Ritterband-Rosenbaum and Mark S. Christensen analyzed the data, and Anina Ritterband-Rosenbaum, Mark S. Christensen, and Jens B. Nielsen wrote the manuscript.

ACKNOWLEDGMENTS

This study was funded by the Elsass Foundation as a PhD scholarship to Anina Ritterband-Rosenbaum. Mark S. Christensen was funded by the Danish Independent Research Council—Humanities. We thank Morten Lennert Sørensen for making the figure of the experimental design.

SUPPLEMENTARY MATERIAL

Supplementary Figure S1 | Time-frequency plots observed and predicted from DCM. Comparison of time-frequency plots of the observed two source regions (preSMA and IPC) for the **(A)** early and **(B)** late task phases for AgencyYES and AgencyNO trials with the predictions made by the DCMs (model 8 early and model 6 late). Notice for one participant (shaded) no dynamics were predicted by any of the 9 DCMs (here only model 6 is displayed) for the late task phase.

REFERENCES

Balconi, M., and Crivelli, D. (2009). Spatial and temporal cognition for the sense of agency: neuropsychological evidences. *Cogn. Process.* 10(Suppl. 2), S182–S184. doi: 10.1007/s10339-009-0281-z

Chambon, V., Wenke, D., Fleming, S., Prinz, W., and Haggard, P. (2013). An online neural substrate for sense of agency. *Cereb. Cortex* 23, 1031–1037. doi: 10.1093/cercor/bhs059

Chen, C. C., Kiebel, S. J., and Friston, K. J. (2008). Dynamic causal modelling of induced responses. *Neuroimage* 41, 1293–1312. doi: 10.1016/j.neuroimage.2008.03.026

David, N., Newen, A., and Vogeley, K. (2008). The "sense of agency" and its underlying cognitive and neural mechanisms. *Conscious. Cogn.* 17, 523–534. doi: 10.1016/j.concog.2008.03.004

Desmurget, M., Reilly, K. T., Richard, N., Szathmari, A., Mottolese, C., and Sirigu, A. (2009). Movement intention after parietal cortex stimulation in humans. *Science* 324, 811–813. doi: 10.1126/science.1169896

Desmurget, M., and Sirigu, A. (2009). A parietal-premotor network for movement intention and motor awareness. *Trends Cogn. Sci.* 13, 411–419. doi: 10.1016/j.tics.2009.08.001

Engbert, K., Wohlschlager, A., and Haggard, P. (2008). Who is causing what? The sense of agency is relational and efferent-triggered. *Cognition* 107, 693–704. doi: 10.1016/j.cognition.2007.07.021

Engel, A. K., Fries, P., and Singer, W. (2001). Dynamic predictions: oscillations and synchrony in top-down processing. *Nat. Rev. Neurosci.* 2, 704–716. doi: 10.1038/35094565

Farrer, C., Franck, N., Georgieff, N., Frith, C. D., Decety, J., and Jeannerod, M. (2003a). Modulating the experience of agency: a positron emission tomography study. *Neuroimage* 18, 324–333. doi: 10.1016/S1053-8119(02)00041-1

Farrer, C., Franck, N., Paillard, J., and Jeannerod, M. (2003b). The role of proprioception in action recognition. *Conscious. Cogn.* 12, 609–619. doi: 10.1016/S1053-8100(03)00047-3

Farrer, C., Frey, S. H., Van Horn, J. D., Tunik, E., Turk, D., Inati, S., et al. (2008). The angular gyrus computes action awareness representations. *Cereb. Cortex* 18, 254–261. doi: 10.1093/cercor/bhm050

Farrer, C., and Frith, C. D. (2002). Experiencing oneself vs another person as being the cause of an action: the neural correlates of the experience of agency. *Neuroimage* 15, 596–603. doi: 10.1006/nimg.2001.1009

Fourneret, P., and Jeannerod, M. (1998). Limited conscious monitoring of motor performance in normal subjects. *Neuropsychologia* 36, 1133–1140. doi: 10.1016/S0028-3932(98)00006-2

Fried, I., Katz, A., McCarthy, G., Sass, K. J., Williamson, P., Spencer, S. S., et al. (1991). Functional organization of human supplementary motor cortex studied by electrical stimulation. *J. Neurosci.* 11, 3656–3666.

Gallagher, S. (2000). Consciousness in action. *Philos. Psychol.* 13, 127–129.

Gentsch, A., Kathmann, N., and Schutz-Bosbach, S. (2012). Reliability of sensory predictions determines the experience of self-agency. *Behav. Brain Res.* 228, 415–422. doi: 10.1016/j.bbr.2011.12.029

Georgieff, N., and Jeannerod, M. (1998). Beyond consciousness of external reality: a "who" system for consciousness of action and self-consciousness. *Conscious. Cogn.* 7, 465–477. doi: 10.1006/ccog.1998.0367

Herz, D. M., Christensen, M. S., Reck, C., Florin, E., Barbe, M. T., Stahlhut, C., et al. (2012). Task-specific modulation of effective connectivity during two simple unimanual motor tasks: a 122-channel EEG study. *Neuroimage* 59, 3187–3193. doi: 10.1016/j.neuroimage.2011.11.042

Kawato, M., and Wolpert, D. (1998). Internal models for motor control. *Novartis Found. Symp.* 218, 291–304.

Kuhn, S., Brass, M., and Haggard, P. (2013). Feeling in control: neural correlates of experience of agency. *Cortex* 49, 1935–1942. doi: 10.1016/j.cortex.2012.09.002

Leube, D. T., Knoblich, G., Erb, M., and Kircher, T. T. J. (2003). Observing one's hand become anarchic: an fMRI study of action identification. *Conscious. Cogn.* 12, 597–608. doi: 10.1016/S1053-8100(03)00079-5

Melloni, L., Molina, C., Pena, M., Torres, D., Singer, W., and Rodriguez, E. (2007). Synchronization of neural activity across cortical areas correlates with conscious perception. *J. Neurosci.* 27, 2858–2865. doi: 10.1523/JNEUROSCI.4623-06.2007

Moore, J. W., Ruge, D., Wenke, D., Rothwell, J., and Haggard, P. (2010). Disrupting the experience of control in the human brain: pre-supplementary motor area contributes to the sense of agency. *Proc. Biol. Sci.* 277, 2503–2509. doi: 10.1098/rspb.2010.0404

Nahab, F. B., Kundu, P., Gallea, C., Kakareka, J., Pursley, R., Pohida, T., et al. (2011). The neural processes underlying self-agency. *Cerb. Cortex* 21, 48–55. doi: 10.1093/cercor/bhq059

Nielsen, T. I. (1963). Volition - a new experimental approach. *Scand. J. Psychol.* 4, 225–230. doi: 10.1111/j.1467-9450.1963.tb01326.x

Palva, J. M., Palva, S., and Kaila, K. (2005). Phase synchrony among neuronal oscillations in the human cortex. *J. Neurosci.* 25, 3962–3972. doi: 10.1523/JNEUROSCI.4250-04.2005

Ritterband-Rosenbaum, A., Christensen, M. S., Kliim-Due, M., Petersen, L. Z., Rasmussen, B., and Nielsen, J. B. (2011). Altered sense of agency in children with spastic cerebral palsy. *BMC Neurol.* 11:150. doi: 10.1186/1471-2377-11-150

Rodriguez, E., George, N., Lachaux, J. P., Martinerie, J., Renault, B., and Varela, F. J. (1999). Perception's shadow: long-distance synchronization of human brain activity. *Nature* 397, 430–433. doi: 10.1038/17120

Sidarus, N., Chambon, V., and Haggard, P. (2013). Priming of actions increases sense of control over unexpected outcomes. *Conscious. Cogn.* 22, 1403–1411. doi: 10.1016/j.concog.2013.09.008

Siegel, M., Donner, T. H., and Engel, A. K. (2012). Spectral fingerprints of large-scale neuronal interactions. *Nat. Rev. Neurosci.* 13, 121–134. doi: 10.1038/nrn3137

Sirigu, A., Daprati, E., Ciancia, S., Giraux, P., Nighoghossian, N., Posada, A., et al. (2004). Altered awareness of voluntary action after damage to the parietal cortex. *Nat. Neurosci.* 7, 80–84. doi: 10.1038/nn1160

Sirigu, A., Daprati, E., Pradat-Diehl, P., Franck, N., and Jeannerod, M. (1999). Perception of self-generated movement following left parietal lesion. *Brain* 122, 1867–1874. doi: 10.1093/brain/122.10.1867

Stephan, K. E., Penny, W. D., Daunizeau, J., Moran, R. J., and Friston, K. J. (2009). Bayesian model selection for group studies. *Neuroimage* 46, 1004–1017. doi: 10.1016/j.neuroimage.2009.03.025

Synofzik, M., Vosgerau, G., and Newen, A. (2008). Beyond the comparator model: a multifactorial two-step account of agency. *Conscious. Cogn.* 17, 219–239. doi: 10.1016/j.concog.2007.03.010

Synofzik, M., Vosgerau, G., and Voss, M. (2013). The experience of agency: an interplay between prediction and postdiction. *Front. Psychol.* 4:127. doi: 10.3389/fpsyg.2013.00127

Wegner, D. M. (2004). Precis of the illusion of conscious will. *Behav. Brain Sci.* 27, 649–659. doi: 10.1017/S0140525X04000159

Wolpert, D. M., Ghahramani, Z., and Jordan, M. I. (1995). An internal model for sensorimotor integration. *Science* 269, 1880–1882. doi: 10.1126/science.7569931

Yamagishi, N., and Anderson, S. J. (2013). The relationship between self-awareness of attentional status, behavioral performance and oscillatory brain rhythms. *PLoS ONE* 8:e74962. doi: 10.1371/journal.pone.0074962

Yomogida, Y., Sugiura, M., Sassa, Y., Wakusawa, K., Sekiguchi, A., Fukushima, A., et al. (2010). The neural basis of agency: an fMRI study. *Neuroimage* 50, 198–207. doi: 10.1016/j.neuroimage.2009.12.054

The anatomy of choice: active inference and agency

Karl Friston[1]*, Philipp Schwartenbeck[1], Thomas FitzGerald[1], Michael Moutoussis[1], Timothy Behrens[1,2] and Raymond J. Dolan[1]

[1] The Wellcome Trust Centre for Neuroimaging, Institute of Neurology, University College London, London, UK
[2] Centre for Functional MRI of the Brain, The John Radcliffe Hospital, Oxford, UK

Correspondence:
Karl Friston, The Wellcome Trust Centre for Neuroimaging, Institute of Neurology, University College London, 12 Queen Square, WC1N 3BG London, UK
e-mail: k.friston@ucl.ac.uk

This paper considers agency in the setting of embodied or active inference. In brief, we associate a sense of agency with prior beliefs about action and ask what sorts of beliefs underlie optimal behavior. In particular, we consider prior beliefs that action minimizes the Kullback–Leibler (KL) divergence between desired states and attainable states in the future. This allows one to formulate *bounded* rationality as approximate Bayesian inference that optimizes a free energy *bound* on model evidence. We show that constructs like expected utility, exploration bonuses, softmax choice rules and optimism bias emerge as natural consequences of this formulation. Previous accounts of active inference have focused on *predictive coding* and Bayesian filtering schemes for minimizing free energy. Here, we consider *variational Bayes* as an alternative scheme that provides formal constraints on the computational anatomy of inference and action—constraints that are remarkably consistent with neuroanatomy. Furthermore, this scheme contextualizes optimal decision theory and economic (utilitarian) formulations as pure inference problems. For example, expected utility theory emerges as a special case of free energy minimization, where the *sensitivity* or inverse temperature (of softmax functions and quantal response equilibria) has a unique and Bayes-optimal solution—that minimizes free energy. This sensitivity corresponds to the *precision* of beliefs about behavior, such that attainable goals are afforded a higher precision or confidence. In turn, this means that optimal behavior entails a representation of confidence about outcomes that are under an agent's control.

Keywords: active inference, agency, Bayesian, bounded rationality, embodied cognition, free energy, inference, utility theory

INTRODUCTION

This paper addresses the nature of probabilistic beliefs about control that constitute a sense of agency. By separating beliefs about control from action *per se*, one can formulate behavior as a pure inference problem. This allows one to describe goal-directed behavior and decision-making in terms of prior beliefs about how one should behave. It is these beliefs about controlled behavior that we associate with a representation or sense of agency. Here, we take a somewhat formal approach and illustrate the ideas using game theory and Markov decision processes. Our aim is to understand behavior in terms of approximate Bayesian inference and ask whether standard variational schemes can shed light on the functional anatomy of decision-making in the brain.

Our wider aim is to place heuristics in decision theory (in psychology) and expected utility theory (in economics) within the setting of embodied cognition or inference. In brief, we treat the problem of selecting a sequence of behaviors—to optimize some outcome—as a pure inference problem. We assume that policies are selected under the prior belief[1] they minimize the divergence (relative entropy) between a probability distribution over states that can be reached and states agents believe they should occupy—states or goals that agents believe, *a priori*, have high utility. By formulating the problem in this way, three important aspects of optimal decision-making emerge:

- First, because relative entropy can always be decomposed into entropy and expected utility, the ensuing policies maximize expected utility and the entropy over final states. Entropy is a measure of average uncertainty (e.g., the entropy of a coin toss is much greater than the entropy of an unsurprising outcome, like the sun rising tomorrow). This decomposition is closely related to the distinction between extrinsic and intrinsic reward in embodied cognition and artificial intelligence. In this setting, utility or *extrinsic reward* is supplemented with *intrinsic reward* to ensure some efficient information gain, exploratory behavior or control over outcomes. Important examples here include artificial curiosity (Schmidhuber, 1991), empowerment (Klyubin et al., 2005), information to go (Tishby and Polani, 2011) and computational complexity (Ortega and Braun, 2011, 2013). Indeed, the causal generation of entropic forces in nonequilibrium systems has been proposed recently as a general mechanism for adaptive behavior (Wissner-Gross and Freer, 2013). In the present context, an intrinsically rewarding policy maximizes the opportunity to explore (or the entropy of) future states.

[1] In this paper, beliefs about states refer to a probability distribution over states.

- Second, because policies are inferred, they are associated with a confidence or precision that is itself optimized. This furnishes a unique and Bayes-optimal sensitivity or inverse temperature—of the sort associated with softmax choice rules and quantal response equilibria (McKelvey and Palfrey, 1995).
- Third, because policy optimization is absorbed into the more general problem of inferring hidden states of the world, inferences about policies depend upon inferences about hidden states and *vice versa*. This means that beliefs about hidden states depend upon the confidence in policies—leading to an optimism bias (Sharot et al., 2012), in which inferences about ambiguous states are biased toward those that support an optimal policy.

In what follows, we motivate the premises that underlie this formulation and unpack its implications using formal arguments and simulations. The basic idea is that behavior can be cast as inference: in other words, action, and perception are integral parts of the same inferential process and one only makes sense in light of the other. It is fairly straightforward to show that self-organizing systems are necessarily inferential in nature (Friston, 2012). This notion dates back to the writings of Helmholtz and Ashby, who emphasized modeling and inference as necessary attributes of systems—like ourselves—that endure in a changing world (Helmholtz, 1866/1962; Ashby, 1947; Conant and Ashby, 1970). This idea has been formalized recently as minimizing a variational free energy bound on Bayesian model evidence—to provide a seamless link between occupying a limited number of attracting states and Bayesian inference about the causes of sensory input (Dayan et al., 1995; Friston, 2010). In the context of behavior, we suppose that inference underlies a sense of agency.

A corollary of this perspective is that agents must perform some form of active *Bayesian inference*. Bayesian inference can be approximate or exact, where exact inference is rendered tractable by making plausible assumptions about the approximate form of probabilistic representations—representations that are used to predict responses to changes in the sensorium. In general, exact inference is intractable and cannot be realized biophysically. This is because—for non-trivial models—the posterior distributions over unknown quantities do not have an analytic form. This means the challenge is to understand how agents perform approximate Bayesian inference. Conversely, in classical (normative) formulations, it is assumed that agents optimize some expected value or utility function of their states. The question then reduces to how the brain maximizes value (Camerer, 2003; Daw and Doya, 2006; Dayan and Daw, 2008).

Normative approaches assume that *perfectly rational* agents maximize value, without considering the cost of optimization (Von Neumann and Morgenstern, 1944). In contrast, *bounded rational* agents are subject to information processing costs and do not necessarily choose the most valuable option (Simon, 1956). Several attempts to formalize bounded rationality, in probabilistic terms, have focused on the Boltzmann distribution, where optimal behavior corresponds to picking states with a high value or low energy. In this setting, perfect rationality corresponds to choosing states from a low temperature distribution, whose probability mass is concentrated over the state with the highest value (Ortega and Braun, 2011). In particular, quantal response equilibrium (QRE) models of bounded rationality assume that choice probabilities are prescribed by a Boltzmann distribution and that rationality is determined by a *temperature* parameter (McKelvey and Palfrey, 1995; Haile et al., 2008). Boltzmann-like stochastic choice rules have a long history in the psychology and economics literature, particularly in the form of logit choice models (Luce, 1959; Fudenberg and Kreps, 1993). These choice rules are known as *softmax rules* and are used to describe stochastic sampling of actions, especially in the context of the exploration-exploitation dilemma (Sutton and Barto, 1998; Cohen et al., 2007). In this setting, the temperature parameter models the *sensitivity* of stochastic choices to value. This paper suggests that sensitivity can itself be optimized and corresponds to the confidence or precision associated with beliefs about the consequences of choices.

So what does active inference bring to the table? In active inference, there is no value function: free energy is the only quantity that is optimized. This means that bounded rationality must emerge from free energy minimization and the value of a state (or action) is a consequence of behavior, as opposed to its cause. In other words, the consequences of minimizing free energy are that some states are occupied more frequently than others—and these states can be labeled as valuable. We will see later that the frequency with which states are visited depends on prior beliefs—suggesting an intimate relationship between value and prior beliefs. Crucially, in active inference, parameters like sensitivity or inverse temperature must themselves minimize free energy. This means that sensitivity ceases to be a free parameter that is adjusted to describe observed behavior and becomes diagnostic of the underlying (approximate) Bayesian inference (that can be disclosed by observed choices). We will see later that sensitivity corresponds to the *precision* of beliefs about future states and behaves in a way that is remarkably similar to the firing of dopaminergic cells in the brain. Furthermore, QRE, logit choice models and softmax rules can be derived as formal consequences of free energy minimization, using variational Bayes.

Variational Bayes or ensemble learning is a ubiquitous scheme for approximate Bayesian inference (Beal, 2003). Variational Bayes rests on a partition or separation of probabilistic representations (approximate posterior probability distributions) that renders Bayesian inference tractable. A simple example would be estimating the mean and precision (inverse variance) of some data, under the assumption that uncertainty about the mean does not depend upon uncertainty about the variance and *vice versa*. This simple assumption enables a straightforward computation of descriptive statistics that would otherwise be extremely difficult: see (MacKay, 2003, p. 422) for details. In biological terms, a partition into conditionally independent representations is nothing more or less than functional segregation in the brain—in which specialized neuronal systems can be regarded as performing variational Bayesian updates by passing messages to each other. These messages ensure that posterior beliefs about states of (and actions on) the world are internally consistent. We will try to relate variational Bayes to the functional anatomy of inference and action selection in the brain. This provides a functional account of both neuronal representations and functional integration (message passing) among different systems.

Previous accounts of free energy minimization in the brain have focused on continuous time formulations and predictive coding as a neurobiologically plausible variational scheme. In this paper, we take a slightly more abstract approach and consider discrete time representations using variational Bayes. This necessarily implies a loss of biological realism; however, it provides an explicit model of discrete behaviors or choices. In particular, the resulting scheme converges, almost exactly, on the free energy formulation of decision-making under informational costs proposed by (Braun et al., 2011; Ortega and Braun, 2011). These authors accommodate nearly all optimal control, expected utility and evidence accumulation schemes under a single utility-based free energy minimization framework. The free energy minimization considered in this paper can be regarded as a special case of their general formulation, where the utility function is the log-likelihood of outcomes and their causes, under a generative model. This is important, because it connects utility-based schemes to variational Bayes and, more generally, inferential schemes that may underwrite biological self-organization (Ashby, 1947; Friston, 2012).

Although variational Bayes relies upon discrete updates, variational updates still possess a dynamics that can be compared to neuronal responses, particularly dopaminergic responses. In a companion paper (Friston et al., under review), we focus on this, because understanding the computational role of dopamine is important for understanding the psychopathology and pathophysiology of conditions like Parkinson's disease, schizophrenia and autism. In this paper, we focus on the functional anatomy implied by variational message passing in the brain and try to relate this to behavior from a psychological and economic perspective.

This paper comprises six sections: The first introduces active inference and sets up the basic ideas and notation. The second describes a fairly generic model of control or agency, in which purposeful behavior rests on prior beliefs that agents will minimize the (relative) entropy of their final states. We will see that this leads naturally to expected utility theory and exploration bonuses. The third section considers the inversion of this generative model using variational Bayes, with a special focus on mean field assumptions and implicit message passing. The fourth section considers the implications for the functional anatomy of inference and decision-making; namely, reciprocal message passing between systems supporting perceptual inference, action selection and evaluating precision. This section shows how key aspects of classical theory emerge; such as the distinction between perceptual inference about states of the world and action selection, quantal response equilibria, sensitivity and softmax choice rules. The fifth section uses simulations of a particular game (a waiting game with time sensitive contingencies) to illustrate the basic phenomenology of decision-making under active inference. The final section considers the cognitive anatomy of decision-making in terms of temporal discounting and marginal utility.

ACTIVE INFERENCE

In active inference, beliefs about (hidden or fictive) states of the world maximize model evidence or the marginal likelihood of observations. In contrast to classic formulations, active inference makes a distinction between *action* as a physical state of the real world and beliefs about (future) action that we will refer to as *control* states—it is these that constitute a sense of agency. This changes the problem fundamentally from selecting an optimal action (a real variable) to making optimal inferences about control (a random variable). In other words, under the assumption that action is sampled from posterior beliefs about control, we can treat decision-making and action selection as a pure inference problem that necessarily entails optimizing beliefs about behavior and its consequences. This optimization appeals to the principle of free energy minimization.

THE FREE-ENERGY PRINCIPLE AND ACTIVE INFERENCE

The free-energy principle (Friston et al., 2006) tries to explain how agents restrict themselves to a small number of attracting states. This behavior is equivalent to minimizing the Shannon entropy of the distribution over the outcomes they experience. Under ergodic assumptions, this entropy is (almost surely) the long-term time average of self-information or *surprise* (Birkhoff, 1931). Negative surprise $\ln P(\tilde{o}|m)$ is the log likelihood of outcomes $\tilde{o} = (o_0, \ldots, o_t)$, marginalized over their causes—also known as the *Bayesian model evidence* of model m. It is therefore sufficient to minimize surprise—at each point in time—to minimize its time average or Shannon entropy.

However, to evaluate surprise it is necessary to marginalize over the hidden causes of outcomes. This is the difficult problem of exact Bayesian inference. This problem can be finessed by using a proxy for surprise that does not depend on knowing the causes of observations. The proxy is variational free energy that, by construction, is an upper bound on surprise (Feynman, 1972; Hinton and van Camp, 1993). This means that if agents minimize free energy they minimize surprise (approximately). Coincidentally, they maximize model evidence (approximately) and implicitly engage in approximate Bayesian inference (Dayan et al., 1995; Friston, 2010). Put simply, although agents can never know the causes of their observations, the causes can be inferred. Crucially, the free energy that underpins this inference needs a generative model of how observations were caused—a model that can itself be optimized with respect to free energy (cf. Bayesian model selection in statistics).

These arguments suggest that action must minimize variational free energy, because outcomes can only be changed by action. This is *active inference* (Friston et al., 2010), which extends the minimization of free energy implicit in approximate Bayesian inference to include action. This means that behavior minimizes surprise or maximizes model evidence; either exactly—to produce perfectly rational behavior, or approximately—to minimize a variational bound to produce bounded rational behavior. There is a fairly developed literature on variational free energy minimization and active inference; covering things from perceptual categorization of bird songs, through to action observation (Friston, 2010). Most of this work uses generative models based upon differential equations. In this paper, we consider generative models based upon Markovian processes and revisit some of the key results in the context of decision-making and uncertainty.

In what follows, we use the usual conventions of uppercase to denote matrices and lowercase for vectors. In addition, we use bold typeface to indicate true variables in the world and italic typeface for hidden or fictive variables. The sufficient statistics (event probabilities) of categorical distributions over discrete states $\{1, \ldots, J\}$ are denoted by $J \times 1$ vectors $\widehat{s} \in [0, 1]$. The $\sim$ notation denotes collections of variables over time.

Definition

Active inference rests on the tuple $(\Omega, \mathbf{S}, A, P, Q, R, S, U)$:

- A finite set of observations Ω
- A finite set of true states and actions $\mathbf{S} \times A$
- A finite set of fictive or hidden states $S \times U$
- A *generative process* over observations, states and action

$$R(\tilde{o}, \tilde{s}, a) = \Pr(\{o_0, \ldots, o_t\} = \tilde{o}, \{s_0, \ldots, s_t\} = \tilde{s}, A = a)$$

- A *generative model* over observations and hidden states

$$P(\tilde{o}, \tilde{s}, \tilde{u}|m) = \Pr(\{o_0, \ldots, o_t\} = \tilde{o}, \{s_0, \ldots, s_t\} = \tilde{s}, \{u_0, \ldots, u_T\} = \tilde{u})$$

- An *approximate posterior probability* over hidden states with sufficient statistics $\mu \in \mathbf{R}^d$ such that

$$Q(\tilde{s}, \tilde{u}|\mu) = \Pr(\{s_0, \ldots, s_t\} = \tilde{s}, \{u_0, \ldots, u_T\} = \tilde{u}),$$

Remarks

Here, m denotes the form of a generative model or probability distribution entailed by an agent. For clarity, we will omit the conditioning on m unless necessary. In this setup, the *generative process* describes transitions among real states of the world that depend upon action and generate outcomes. The agent is equipped with a *generative model* of this process, where action is replaced by a subset of hidden states called control states U. Although we allow for any action (control) from any state, only a subset may be allowable from any given state. Finally, the sufficient statistics of the approximate posterior encode a probability distribution over hidden states $S \times U$ at times $t \in \{0, \ldots, T\}$. In other words, the sufficient statistics—or parameters of the distribution—represent the probability of hidden states.

As it stands, the above definition does not describe a process. This is because the dependencies among real states and sufficient statistics are not specified. In other words, the agent's generative model of observations $P(\tilde{o}, \tilde{s}, \tilde{u}|m)$ and its approximate posterior distribution over their causes $Q(\tilde{s}, \tilde{u}|\mu)$ does not refer to the process of eliciting outcomes through action $R(\tilde{o}, \tilde{s}, a)$. To couple the agent to its environment, we have to specify how its sufficient statistics depend upon observations and how its action depends upon sufficient statistics. In active inference, the sufficient statistics minimize free energy and the ensuing beliefs about control states prescribe action:

$$\mu_t = \arg\min_{\mu} F(\tilde{o}, \mu)$$
$$\Pr(a_t = u_t) = Q(u_t|\mu_t) \qquad (1)$$

This is usually portrayed in terms of *perception* (inference about hidden states) and *action* (a choice model in which action is a function of inferred states). Usually, sufficient statistics are associated with the internal states of an agent (such as neuronal activity or connection strengths) and action is associated with the state of its effectors. In more general formulations, action would select outcomes with the lowest free energy (Friston et al., 2012a). However, for simplicity, we have assumed that actions are sampled from posterior beliefs about control states—noting that the actions which minimize free energy produce outcomes that are the most likely under posterior beliefs. In short, sufficient statistics and implicit posterior beliefs about the state of the world minimize free energy, while action is selected from posterior beliefs about control states. We will see later that these posterior beliefs depend crucially upon prior beliefs about states that will be occupied in the future.

Figure 1 provides a schematic of the resulting cycle of action and perception, where posterior expectations (sufficient statistics) minimize free energy and prescribe action (left panel). In this setting, free energy is defined in relation to the generative model (right panel). Notice that the generative model does not need to know about action: from its point of view, the world contains (fictive) control states that determine transitions among hidden states generating outcomes. In other words, optimizing posterior beliefs about control states produces action automatically but the agent does not know this—in the sense we are aware of the

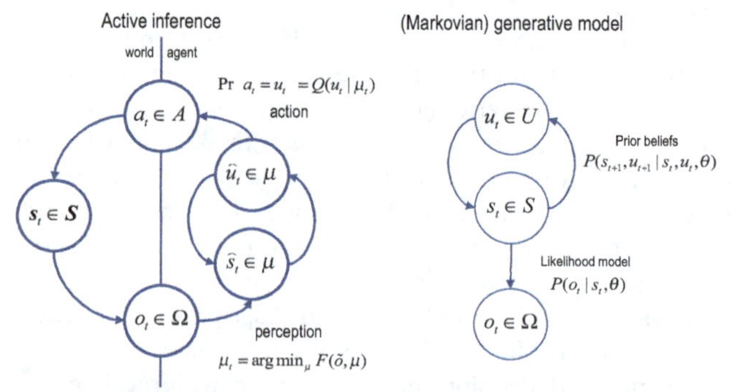

FIGURE 1 | Left panel: this is a schematic of the dependencies among variables underlying active inference. Here, a generative process representing state transitions in the real world generates observations or outcomes that are used to update the internal states of an agent. These internal states encode the sufficient statistics of an approximate posterior distribution over variables defined by a generative model (right panel). Particular sufficient statistics, encoding beliefs about choices or control states are reflexively transcribed into action, which affects real state transitions—thereby closing the action–perception cycle. **Right panel:** notice that the generative model, which defines free energy has a much simpler form. It simply supposes that there are mutually dependent hidden and control states that conspire to produce observations.

sensory consequences of our motor reflexes but not the reflexes *per se*.

One can express free energy in a number of ways:

$$
\begin{aligned}
F(\tilde{o}, \mu) &= E_Q\left[-\ln P(\tilde{o}, \tilde{s}, \tilde{u}|m)\right] - H\left[Q(\tilde{s}, \tilde{u}|\mu)\right] \\
&= D_{KL}\left[Q(\tilde{s}, \tilde{u}|\mu)||P(\tilde{s}, \tilde{u}|\tilde{o})\right] - \ln P(\tilde{o}|m) \\
&= D_{KL}[Q(\tilde{s}, \tilde{u}|\mu)||P(\tilde{s}, \tilde{u}|m)] + E_Q[-\ln P(\tilde{o}|\tilde{s}, \tilde{u})]
\end{aligned} \tag{2}
$$

The first equality expresses free energy as a Gibbs energy (expected under the approximate posterior) minus the entropy of the approximate posterior. This speaks to why it is called a free energy. The second equality shows that free energy is an upper bound on surprise, because the first relative entropy or Kullback–Leibler (KL) divergence term is non-negative by Gibbs inequality (Beal, 2003). This means minimizing free energy corresponds to minimizing the divergence between the approximate and true posterior. This formalizes the notion of unconscious inference in perception (Helmholtz, 1866/1962; Dayan et al., 1995; Dayan and Hinton, 1997) and—under some simplifying assumptions—reduces to predictive coding (Rao and Ballard, 1999). The third equality shows that minimizing free energy is the same as maximizing the expected log likelihood of observations or *accuracy*, while minimizing the divergence between the approximate posterior and prior beliefs about hidden variables. This divergence is known as *model complexity* (Spiegelhalter et al., 2002; Penny et al., 2004), ensuring that inference is both accurate and parsimonious (cf. Occam's razor).

In summary, if agents resist a natural tendency to disorder (occupy a limited number of characteristic states), then they become implicit Bayesian modelers of their environment. This is consistent with the good regulator hypothesis (Conant and Ashby, 1970) and accounts of (unconscious) inference and perception in the brain (Helmholtz, 1866/1962; Gregory, 1968; Dayan et al., 1995). Crucially, this requires agents to entertain beliefs about the control of state transitions producing outcomes. This means we have moved beyond classic formulations—in which deterministic actions are selected—and have to consider posterior beliefs about putative choices. These beliefs determine the states that are eventually sampled. In the next section, we consider the optimization of posterior beliefs; both in terms of their content and the confidence or precision with which they are held.

A GENERATIVE MODEL OF AGENCY

We have seen that a generative model is necessary to furnish a free energy bound on surprise or Bayesian model evidence. This model comprises prior beliefs that determine the states an agent or model will frequent. These beliefs specify the attracting states (goals) that action will seek out. In this section, we consider the form of these beliefs and how they can be understood in terms of expected utility.

THE GENERATIVE MODEL

The Markovian models considered here rest on transitions among hidden states that are coupled to transitions among control states. This is illustrated in terms of a hidden Markov model or finite state (epsilon) machine (Ellison et al., 2011) in the upper panel of **Figure 2**. In the general forms of these models, control states modify the transition probabilities among hidden states, while hidden states modify the transitions among control states (as denoted by the connections with circles). This sort of model allows context-sensitive transitions among states generating outcomes—that themselves can induce changes in the control states providing the context. The lower panels of **Figure 2** illustrate a particular example that we will use later—in which there are two states that control transitions among five hidden states (see figure legend for details).

The generative model used to model these (irreversible Markovian) processes can be expressed in terms of future control states $\tilde{u} = (u_t, \ldots, u_T)$ as follows:

$$
\begin{aligned}
P(\tilde{o}, \tilde{s}, \tilde{u}, \gamma|a,\tilde{}m) &= P(\tilde{o}|\tilde{s})\, P(\tilde{s}, \tilde{u}|\gamma, \tilde{a})\, P(\gamma|m) \\
P(o_0, \ldots, o_t|s_0, \ldots, s_t) &= \prod\nolimits_{i=0}^{t} P(o_i|s_i) \\
P(s_0, \ldots, s_t, \tilde{u}|\gamma, a_0, \ldots, a_{t-1}) &= P(\tilde{u}|s_t)P(s_0|m) \prod\nolimits_{i=1}^{t} \\
&\qquad P(s_i|s_{i-1}, a_{i-1}) \\
\ln P(\tilde{u}|s_t) &= -\gamma \cdot D_{KL}[P(s_T|s_t, \tilde{u})||P(s_T|m)]
\end{aligned} \tag{3}
$$

Remarks

The first equality expresses the model in terms of the likelihood of observations given the hidden and control states (first term) and *empirical* prior beliefs (subsequent terms). Empirical priors are probability distributions over unknown variables that depend on other unknown variables—and are an inherent part of any hierarchical model. The likelihood (second equality) says that observations depend on, and only on, concurrent hidden states. The third equality expresses beliefs about state transitions that embody Markovian dependencies among successive hidden states. For simplicity, we have assumed that the agent knows its past actions by observing them.

The important part of this model lies in the last equality. This describes prior beliefs about control sequences or *policies* that determine which actions are selected. These beliefs take the form of a Boltzmann distribution, where the policy with the largest prior probability minimizes the relative entropy or divergence between the distribution over final states, given the current state and policy, and the marginal distribution over final states. This marginal distribution encodes goals in terms of (desired) states the agent believes it should visit from current state. Crucially, the precision of beliefs about policies is determined by a hidden variable $\gamma \in \mathbb{R}^+$ that has to be inferred. In essence, this model represents past hidden states and future choices, under the belief that control from the current state will minimize the divergence between the distribution over final states and a prior distribution or goal.

PRIOR BELIEFS, ENTROPY AND EXPECTED UTILITY

Basing beliefs about future choices on relative entropy is formally related to optimization schemes based on KL control; particularly risk sensitive control; e.g., (van den Broek et al.,

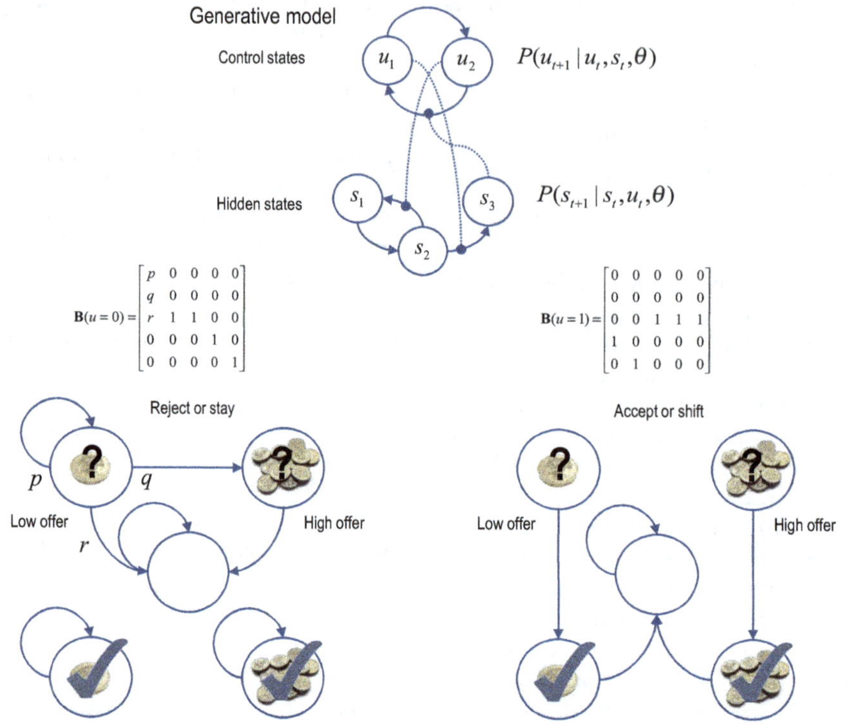

FIGURE 2 | Upper panel: this is an example of a generative model, based on a hierarchical hidden Markov model. The key feature of this model is that there are two sets of states; hidden states and control states. The transitions among one set of states depend upon the state occupied in the other set. **Lower panels**: this provides an example of a particular generative model in which there are two control states; reject (stay) or accept (shift). The control state determines the transitions amongst the hidden states which, in this example, comprise a low offer (first state), a high offer (second state), a no-offer state (third state), and absorbing states that are entered whenever a low (fourth state) or high (fifth state) offer is accepted. The probability of moving from one state to another is one, unless specified by the values of the (control dependent) transition probabilities shown in the middle row. For example, the parameter *r* controls the rate of offer withdrawal (cf. a hazard rate). Note that absorbing states—that re-enter themselves with unit probability—render this Markovian process irreversible. We will use this example in simulations of choice behavior.

2010). This is also a cornerstone of utility-based free energy treatments of bounded rationality (Ortega and Braun, 2011). These schemes consider optimal agents to minimize the KL divergence between controlled and desired outcomes. All we have done here is to equip agents with a sense of agency or prior beliefs that they are KL optimal. These beliefs are then enacted through active inference. The advantage of this is that the precision of beliefs about control can now be optimized—because we have effectively cast the optimal control problem as an inference problem. These arguments may seem a bit abstract but, happily, concrete notions like exploration, exploitation and expected utility emerge as straightforward consequences:

The relative entropy or divergence can be thought of as a prediction error that is nuanced in an important way: it reports the mismatch—not between expected and observed outcomes—but between the final outcomes expected with and without considering the current state: in other words, the difference between what can be attained from the current state and the goals encoded by prior beliefs. Unlike classic reward prediction errors, this probabilistic prediction error is a difference between probability distributions over states. Mathematically, this divergence can be decomposed into two terms that have important implications for behavior. From Equation 3:

$$
\begin{aligned}
\ln P(\tilde{u}|s_t) &= \gamma \cdot \mathbf{Q} \\
\mathbf{Q}(\tilde{u}|s_t) &= -D_{KL}\left[P(s_T|s_t,\tilde{u})||P(s_T|m)\right] \\
&= \sum\nolimits_{s_T} P(s_T|s_t,\tilde{u}) \ln \frac{P(s_T|m)}{P(s_T|s_t,\tilde{u})} \\
&= \underbrace{H\left[P(s_T|s_t,\tilde{u})\right]}_{\text{exploration bonus}} + \sum\nolimits_{s_T} \underbrace{P(s_T|s_t,\tilde{u})\, c(s_T|m)}_{\text{expected utility}} \quad (4)
\end{aligned}
$$

This expresses the log likelihood of a policy as a precision weighted value $Q(\tilde{u}|s_t)$. This *value* is an attribute of policies available from the current state, where the value of a policy is the negative divergence between the states entailed by the policy and goal states. In other words, a valuable policy (or state) minimizes relative entropy. We use $Q(\tilde{u}|s_t)$ to emphasize the analogous role of action value in Q-learning (Watkins and Dayan, 1992). Equation 4 shows that value can be decomposed into terms. The first is the entropy (intrinsic reward) of the distribution over final states, given the current state and policy. The second is the expected *utility* of the final state, where utility (extrinsic reward) or negative cost is the log probability of the final state, under the prior goals $c(s_T|m) = \ln P(s_T|m)$.

These definitions help us connect to classic formulations and highlight an important difference between the value of choices and the utility of states. Utility is a fixed attribute of states that agents are attracted to. In contrast, the value of a policy is context sensitive and depends upon the current state. Because utility is defined in terms of a probability distribution—which sums to one—the utility (log probability) of any state is negative and can be at most zero (i.e., cost is non-negative). This setup highlights the relative nature of utility (Tobler et al., 2005; Jocham et al., 2012), because the value of a policy is determined by the difference among the utilities of outcomes.

EXPLORATION, EXPLOITATION AND NOVELTY

This decomposition of value means that agents (believe they) will maximize the entropy of their final states while maximizing expected utility. The relative contribution of entropy and expected utility depends upon the precision of prior beliefs about the final state or, equivalently, the relative utility of different states. If these beliefs are very precise (informative), they will dominate and the agent will (believe it will) maximize expected utility. Conversely, with imprecise (flat) prior beliefs that all final states are equally valuable, the agent will try to keep its options open and maximize the entropy over those states: in other words, it will explore according to the maximum entropy principle (Jaynes, 1957). This provides a simple account of *exploration-exploitation* that is consistent with expected utility theory. The entropy term implies that (beliefs about) choices are driven not just to maximize expected value but to explore all options in a way that confers an exploratory aspect on behavior. In the absence of (or change in) beliefs about ultimate states, there will be a bias toward visiting all (low cost) states with equal probability. Similarly, the *novelty bonus* (Kakade and Dayan, 2002) of a new state is, in this formulation, conferred by the opportunity to access states that were previously unavailable—thereby increasing the entropy over final states. As indicated in Equation (4), this means that the value of a choice comprises an exploration bonus and an expected utility, where the former depends upon the current state and the latter does not.

In summary, if agents occupy a limited set of attracting states, it follows that their generative models must be equipped with prior beliefs that controlled state transitions will minimize the divergence between a distribution over attainable states and a distribution that specifies states as attractive. These prior beliefs can be expressed in terms of relative entropy that defines the value of policies. This value has exactly the same form as the objective functions in KL control schemes that grandfather conventional utility-based schemes (Kappen et al., 2012; Ortega and Braun, 2011). The value of a policy can be decomposed into its expected utility and an exploration or novelty bonus that corresponds to the entropy over final states. In this setting, notions like value, expected utility and exploration bonus are consequences of the underlying imperative to minimize (relative) entropy, entailed by the priors of an agent's generative model.

The balance between exploration (entropy) and exploitation (expected value) is uniquely determined by the relative utility of future states and not by the temperature parameter—the precision or inverse temperature applies to both exploratory and utilitarian behavior (see Equation 4). In other words, explorative behavior is not just a random version of exploitative behavior but can itself be very precise, with a clearly defined objective (to maximize the entropy of final outcomes). In fact, precision plays a fundamental role in moderating an *optimism bias* when forming beliefs about hidden states of the world (Sharot et al., 2012). To see this clearly, we need to consider the nature of model inversion.

VARIATIONAL BAYESIAN INVERSION

This section illustrates active inference using variational Bayesian inversion of the generative model above. To simplify notation, we will represent allowable policies with $\pi \in \{1, \ldots, K\}$, were each policy prescribes a sequence of control states $(\tilde{u}|\pi) = (u_t, \ldots, u_T|\pi)$. The model considered in the remainder of this paper is parameterized as follows:

$$\begin{aligned} P\left(o_t = i|s_t = j, \mathbf{A}\right) &= \mathbf{A}_{ij} \\ P\left(s_{t+1} = i|s_t = j, \pi, \mathbf{B}\right) &= \mathbf{B}(u_t|\pi)_{ij} \\ \ln P\left(\pi = i|s_t = j, \gamma, \mathbf{Q}\right) &= \mathbf{Q}_{ij} \cdot \gamma - \ln Z_\pi \\ P\left(s_T = i|\mathbf{c}\right) &= \mathbf{c}_i \\ P\left(s_0 = i|\mathbf{d}\right) &= \mathbf{d}_i \\ P\left(\gamma|m\right) &= \Gamma(\alpha, \beta) \end{aligned} \tag{5}$$

$$\begin{aligned} P\left(s_T = i|s_t = j, \pi, \mathbf{c}\right) &= \mathbf{T}(\pi)_{ij} \\ \mathbf{T}(\pi) &= \mathbf{B}(u_t|\pi)\mathbf{B}(u_{t+1}|\pi)\ldots\mathbf{B}(u_T|\pi) \\ \mathbf{Q}_{ij} &= \ln \mathbf{c}^T \cdot \mathbf{T}(\pi = i)_j - \ln \mathbf{T}(\pi = i)_j^T \cdot \mathbf{T}(\pi = i)_j \end{aligned}$$

$$\sum_i \mathbf{A}_{ij} = 1, \sum_i \mathbf{B}(u_t)_{ij} = 1, \sum_i \mathbf{c}_i = 1, \sum_i \mathbf{d}_i = 1$$

Categorical distributions over observations, given the hidden states, are parameterized by the matrix A that maps, probabilistically, from hidden states to outcomes. Similarly, the transition matrices $B(u_t)$ encode transition probabilities from one state to the next, under the current control state of a policy. The vectors $\mathbf{c}$ and $\mathbf{d}$ encode the prior distribution over the last and first states, respectively. The former parameters specify the priors on control, where utility is $c(s_T|m) = \ln P(s_T|m) = \ln \mathbf{c}$. The prior over precision has a gamma distribution with shape and rate parameters (in this paper) $\alpha = 8$ and $\beta = 1$.

The $K \times J$ matrix Q contains the values of allowable policies from current states, where the normalization constant Z_π ensures that the probabilities over policies sum to one. Finally, the matrices $T(\pi)$ encode the probability of transition from the current state to a final state, under a particular policy. This is the composition of transition matrices from the present time until the end of the game. Transition probabilities to the final state determine the entropy and expected utility that comprise value (last equality). Here, $T(\pi = i)_j$ is a column vector of probabilities over final states, under the i-th policy and j-th current state.

APPROXIMATE BAYESIAN INFERENCE

Having specified the exact form of the generative model, we now need to find the sufficient statistics of the approximate posterior density that minimizes free energy. This is equivalent to approximate Bayesian inference about hidden variables $\psi = (\tilde{s}, \tilde{u}, \gamma)$. Variational Bayes now provides a generic and relatively simple scheme for approximate Bayesian inference that finesses the combinatoric and analytic intractability of exact inference (Beal, 2003; Fox and Roberts, 2012).

The efficiency of variational Bayes rests on replacing posterior dependencies among hidden variables with dependencies among the sufficient statistics of marginal probabilities over subsets. This allows one to factorize the (approximate) posterior distribution into marginal distributions, which greatly reduces the size of the state space that has to be represented. This is because one does not have to represent the joint distribution over different subsets. To illustrate this, consider a distribution over all combinations of J hidden states and K control states at every point in time: $Q(\tilde{s}, \tilde{u})$. The underlying state space $S_1 \times U_1 \times \ldots \times S_T \times U_T$ would require an untenable number $(J \times K)^T$ of sufficient statistics or probabilities—the example below would require $(5 \times 2)^{16}$ sufficient statistics, which is more than the number of synapses in the brain.

However, if we exploit the Markovian dependencies among successive states, we can use a *mean field assumption* to reduce the number of sufficient statistics dramatically. The particular mean field assumption we will use is (see also **Figure 3**):

$$
\begin{aligned}
Q(\tilde{s}, \tilde{u}, \gamma|\mu) &= Q(s_0|\hat{s}_0)\ldots Q(s_t|\hat{s}_t)Q(\tilde{u}|\hat{\pi})Q(\gamma|\hat{\beta}) \\
Q(s_t = j|\hat{s}_t) &= \hat{s}_{tj}: \sum_j \hat{s}_{tj} = 1 \\
Q(\tilde{u} = k|\hat{\pi}) &= \hat{\pi}_k: \sum_k \hat{\pi}_k = 1 \\
Q(\gamma|\hat{\beta}) &= \Gamma(\alpha, \hat{\beta})
\end{aligned} \tag{6}
$$

Here, we have assumed a factorization over (past) hidden states, (future) control states and precision. Furthermore, we have factorized successive states over time, which means we only have to represent the current state explicitly. These particular mean field assumptions are not approximations, because the true generative process is Markovian. Conversely, the factorization with respect to precision is an approximation, because the true posterior will show (mild) conditional dependencies between precision and hidden states.

The marginal over control states has not been factorized because the final outcome depends, in general, on the particular history of choices. In other words, generally speaking, any outcome depends upon the sequence of choices in the past. However, there are potentially a vast number of control sequences or policies that could require an enormous number of sufficient statistics. This problem can be finessed by only considering allowable or *a priori* plausible policies. In the example below, there is no point in accepting an offer more than once. Therefore, we

$$P(\tilde{o}, \tilde{s}, \tilde{u}, \gamma | \tilde{a}, m) = P(\tilde{o}|\tilde{s})P(\tilde{s}, \tilde{u}|\gamma, \tilde{a})P(\gamma|m)$$

$$P(\tilde{o}|\tilde{s}) = \prod_{i=0}^{t} P(o_i|s_i)$$
$$P(o_t = i|s_t = j, \mathbf{A}) = \mathbf{A}_{ij}$$
Likelihood

$$P(\tilde{s}, \tilde{u}|\gamma, \tilde{a}) = P(\tilde{u}|s_t)\prod_{i=0}^{t-1} P(s_{i+1}|s_i, a_i)$$
$$P(s_{t+1} = i|s_t = j, \tilde{u}, \mathbf{B}) = \mathbf{B}(u_t|\tilde{u})_{ij}$$
Empirical priors – hidden states

$$\ln P(\tilde{u}|s_t) = -\gamma \cdot D_{KL}[P(s_T|s_t, \tilde{u}) \,||\, P(s_T|m)]$$
$$\ln P(\tilde{u} = i|s_t = j, \gamma, \mathbf{Q}) = \mathbf{Q}_{ij} \cdot \gamma - \ln Z_\pi$$
$$P(s_T = i|s_t = j, \tilde{u}, \mathbf{c}) = \mathbf{T}(\tilde{u})_{ij}$$
Empirical priors – control states

$$P(s_T = i|\mathbf{c}) = \mathbf{c}_i$$
$$P(s_0 = i|\mathbf{d}) = \mathbf{d}_i$$
$$P(\gamma|m) = \Gamma(\alpha, \beta)$$
Full priors

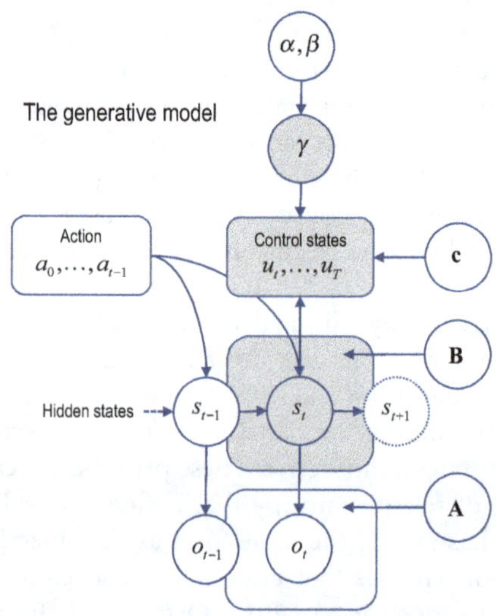

FIGURE 3 | This figure illustrates the temporal dependencies among hidden states and control states in the generative model considered in this paper. This Bayesian graph illustrates the dependencies among successive hidden states and how they depend upon action in the past and control states in the future. Note that future control states depend upon the current state because it depends upon the relative entropy or divergence between distributions over the final state that are, and are not, conditioned on the current state. The resulting choices depend upon the precision of beliefs about control states, which, in turn depend upon the parameters of the model. Observed outcomes depend on, and only on, the hidden states at any given time.

only need to consider policies in which an offer is accepted once during the game. There is nothing lawful about this restriction; however, it is particularly appropriate for irreversible Markovian processes that have absorbing states (that render further action pointless). These processes are ubiquitous in game theory where, having made a choice, there is no going back. This allows one to reduce the number of sufficient statistics for policies from K^T to $(K-1) \times T$ by only allowing policies in which a choice $u_\tau > 1$ is made at $t = \tau$ and $u_t = 1$ otherwise.

The details of the mean field assumption above are not terribly important. The main point here is that the formalism of variational Bayes allows one to specify constraints on the form of the approximate posterior that makes prior assumptions or beliefs about allowable choices explicit. For example, in (Friston et al., 2012a) we used a mean field assumption where every choice could be made at every time point. Equation (6) assumes the approximate marginal over precision is, like its conjugate prior, a gamma distribution; where the shape parameter is the same as the prior $\alpha = 8$ and the rate parameter is optimized. This rate parameter corresponds to temperature in classic formulations. Crucially, it is no longer a free parameter but a sufficient statistic of the unknown precision of beliefs about policies.

VARIATIONAL UPDATES

Variational Bayes optimizes the sufficient statistics $\mu \in \mathbb{R}^+$ with a series of variational updates. It is straightforward to show (Beal, 2003) that the marginal distributions $Q(\psi_i|\mu_i)$ that minimize free energy can be expressed in terms of the *variational energies* $V(\psi_i)$ of each subset:

$$\begin{aligned} \ln Q(\psi_i|\mu_i) &= V(\psi_i) + \ln Z_i \Rightarrow \frac{\partial F(\tilde{o}, \mu)}{\partial \mu_i} = 0 \\ V(\psi_i) &= E_{Q(\psi_{\backslash i})}[\ln P(\tilde{o}, \psi|m)] \\ \psi &= \left(s_0, \ldots, s_t, \tilde{u}, \gamma\right) \\ \mu &= \left(\widehat{s}_0, \ldots, \widehat{s}_t, \widehat{\pi}, \widehat{\beta}\right) \end{aligned} \tag{7}$$

The variational energies are just the (negative) Gibbs energies in Equation (2), expected under the Markov blanket $Q(\psi_{\backslash i})$ of each subset. Loosely speaking, the Markov blanket contains all subsets, apart from the subset in question. The important thing about this result is that it expresses the optimal sufficient statistics of one subset in terms of the others. This allows one to iteratively re-evaluate each subset, given the others, until convergence. This is, in essence, variational Bayes. Given the generative model in Equation (5) and the mean field assumption in Equation (6), Equation (7) furnishes the following remarkably simple updates (starting from prior beliefs):

$$\begin{aligned} \widehat{s}_t &= \sigma\left(\ln A^T \cdot \widehat{o}_t + \ln B(a_{t-1}) \cdot \widehat{s}_{t-1} + \widehat{\gamma} \cdot Q^T \cdot \widehat{\pi}\right) \\ \widehat{\pi} &= \sigma\left(\widehat{\gamma} \cdot Q \cdot \widehat{s}_t\right) \\ \widehat{\beta} &= \beta - \widehat{\pi}^T \cdot Q \cdot \widehat{s}_t \\ \widehat{\gamma} &= \frac{\alpha}{\widehat{\beta}} \\ \sigma(V) &= \frac{\exp(V)}{\sum_{i,j} \exp(V_{ij})} \end{aligned} \tag{8}$$

These expressions follow in a straightforward way from the variational energies in Equation (7): see the **Appendix** and (Beal, 2003) for details. These updates assume the parameters of the model are known. If they are not, then it is relatively straightforward to extend the variational Bayesian scheme above to include variational updates for *learning* unknown parameters, as described in Chapter 3 of (Beal, 2003). The only special consideration is the use of conjugate (Dirichlet) priors over the parameters.

In summary, variational Bayes involves iterating updates to find the sufficient statistics that minimize free energy and, implicitly, provide Bayesian estimates of the hidden variables. This means the sufficient statistics change over two timescales—a fast timescale that updates posterior beliefs given the current observations—and a slow timescale that updates posterior beliefs as new observations become available and action is taken. We have previously speculated (Friston et al., 2012a) that this separation of temporal dynamics may be related to nested electrophysiological oscillations, such as phase coupling between gamma and theta oscillations in prefrontal–hippocampal interactions (Canolty et al., 2006). This speaks to biological implementations of variational Bayes, which we now consider in terms of neuronal and cognitive processing.

THE FUNCTIONAL ANATOMY OF DECISION-MAKING

The variational scheme above has a computational form that resembles many aspects of neuronal processing in the brain. If we assume that neuronal activity encodes sufficient statistics, then the variational update scheme could provide a metaphor for *functional segregation*—the segregation of representations corresponding to the mean field assumption, and *functional integration*—the recursive (reciprocal) exchange of sufficient statistics during approximate Bayesian inference. In terms of the updates themselves, the expectations of hidden states and policies are softmax functions of mixtures of the other expectations. This is remarkable because these updates are derived from basic variational principles and yet they have exactly the form of neural networks that use integrate and fire neurons—and are not dissimilar to real neurons with sigmoid activation functions. Furthermore, the softmax functions are of linear mixtures of sufficient statistics (neuronal activity) with one key exception; namely, the modulation by precision when updating beliefs about the current state of the world and selecting the next action. It is tempting to equate this modulation with the neuromodulation by ascending neurotransmitter systems such as dopamine that send projections to (prefrontal) systems involved in working memory (Goldman-Rakic, 1997; Moran et al., 2011) and striatal systems involved in action selection (O'Doherty et al., 2004; Surmeier et al., 2009). We now consider each of the variational updates from a cognitive and neuroanatomical perspective (see **Figure 4** for a summary):

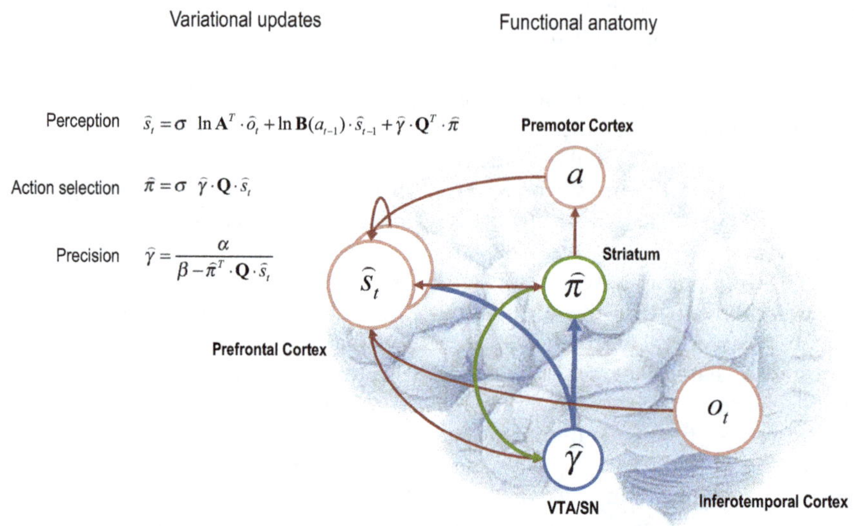

FIGURE 4 | This figure illustrates the cognitive and functional anatomy implied by the variational scheme—or more precisely, the mean field assumption implicit in variational updates. Here, we have associated the variational updates of expected states with perception, of future control states (policies) within action selection and, finally, expected precision with evaluation. The forms of these updates suggest the sufficient statistics from each subset are passed among each other until convergence to an internally consistent (Bayes optimal) solution. In terms of neuronal implementation, this might be likened to the exchange of neuronal signals via extrinsic connections among functionally specialized brain systems. In this (purely iconic) schematic, we have associated perception (inference about the current state of the world) with the prefrontal cortex, while assigning action selection to the basal ganglia. Crucially, precision has been associated with dopaminergic projections from the ventral tegmental area and substantia nigra that, necessarily, project to both cortical (perceptual) and subcortical (action selection) systems. See main text for a full description of the equations.

PERCEPTION

The first variational step updates beliefs about the current state of the world using observed outcomes and representations of the preceding state. This confers a temporal contiguity on inference, where empirical prior beliefs about the current state conspire with sensory evidence to produce posterior beliefs. However, there is a third term that corresponds to expected value of each state, averaged over policies. This term can be thought of as an optimism bias in the sense that, when precision is high, perception is biased toward the state that has the greatest potential to realize the agent's goal. We can now see why precision moderates this bias, much like dopamine (Sharot et al., 2012). **Figure 4** ascribes these updates to the frontal cortex—under the assumption that neuronal populations here encode working memory for the current state of the world (Goldman-Rakic et al., 1992). The functional anatomy in **Figure 4** should not be taken too seriously—it is just used to illustrate the segregation and reciprocal message passing that follows from the computational logic of variational Bayes.

ACTION SELECTION

The second variational update is a softmax function of the expected value of competing choices under the current state. **Figure 4** places this update in the striatum, where the expected value of a policy requires posterior beliefs about the current state from prefrontal cortex and expected precision from the ventral tegmental area. Crucially, this is exactly the softmax choice rule that predominates in QRE theory and other normative models (Haile et al., 2008). Again, it is remarkable that this rule follows directly from basic variational principles. However, utilitarian formulations overlook the symmetry between the expected value over states—that provides the value of a choice, and the expected value over choices—that provides the value of a state. In other words, there are two expected values, one for action $Q \cdot \hat{s}$ and one for perception $Q^T \cdot \hat{\pi}$. Furthermore, the expected value over choices *and* states $\hat{\pi}^T \cdot Q \cdot \hat{s}_t$ specifies the optimal precision or inverse temperature, which is overlooked in classic treatments. Neurobiologically, the softmax policy updates would correspond to a winner-take-all or biased competition among competing choices or policies, where competition is modulated by precision. This is the second key role of precision; namely, to modulate the selection of competing representations of future action: cf. (Cisek, 2007; Frank et al., 2007; Jocham et al., 2012).

EVALUATING PRECISION

The final variational step estimates the precision of prior beliefs about policies, using posterior expectations about hidden states and choices. We have associated expected precision with dopaminergic projections from the ventral tegmental area (and substantia nigra), which must be in receipt of messages from the prefrontal cortex and striatum. One of the key insights, afforded by the variational scheme, is that precision has to be optimized. So what would happen if (estimated) precision was too high or too low? If precision was zero, then perception would be unbiased and represent a veridical representation of worldly states. However, there would be a failure of action selection in the sense that the value of all choices would be the same. One might plausibly associate this with the pathophysiology of Parkinson's disease—that involves a loss of dopaminergic cells and a poverty of action selection. Conversely, if precision was too high, precise choices are made but there would be a predisposition to false perceptual inference—through the augmentation of optimism bias. This might be a metaphor for the positive symptoms of schizophrenia, putatively associated with hyper-dopaminergic states (Fletcher and Frith, 2009). In short, there is an optimal precision for any context and the expected precision has to be evaluated carefully on the basis of current beliefs about the state of the world.

Inspection of the update for expected precision shows that it is an increasing asymptotic function of value, expected under current beliefs about states and choices (see **Figure 5**). This means that the optimal precision depends upon the attainability of goals: if a goal cannot be obtained from the current state, then precision will be small—reflecting a reduced confidence in predictions about behavior. Conversely, if there is a clear and precise path from the current state to a goal, then precision will be high. This means that precision reports the attainability of goals in terms of value. Mathematically, value can never be greater than zero (because the KL divergence is always non-negative). This means that precision increases to its upper bound of α, when value increases to zero (see **Figure 5**). In short, precision reports the expected value over states and policies and plays a dual role in biasing perceptual inference and action selection: on the one hand, it biases perceptual inference toward prior beliefs about future (choice dependent) outcomes. On the other hand, it encodes the confidence that a goal can be attained and increases the precision of action selection.

In summary, this section has considered the implications of variational Bayes for cognitive architectures and functional anatomy. The mean field assumption, enforced by the combinatorics and intractability of exact Bayesian inference, implies a segregation of inference into separable cognitive processes and their neuronal substrates (functional segregation). The particular mean field assumption used here implies distinct perceptual, choice and evaluation processes that can be associated with distributed cortical and subcortical systems in the brain. Crucially, every system (encoding the sufficient statistics of a marginal distribution) must receive signals from every system to which it sends signals. We will now look more closely at this reciprocal message passing.

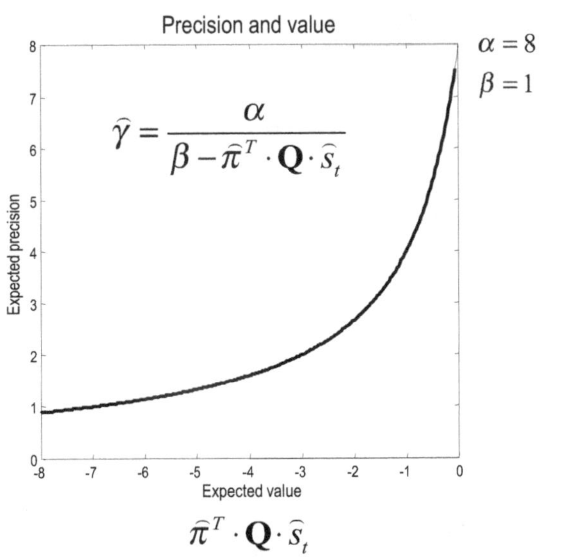

FIGURE 5 | The strictly increasing, monotonic relationship between expected precision and expected value. Note that value never exceeds zero. This is because a Kullback–Leibler divergence can never be less than zero; by Gibbs inequality.

DECISION-MAKING UNDER UNCERTAINTY

This section looks at simulated decision-making using the scheme above. The focus here will be on the circular dependencies between representations of hidden states and precision. This circular causality is one of the most important features of the variational scheme and means that one can consider not just the computational role of precision but also how it is controlled by the representations (posterior expectations) it optimizes.

Figure 2 (lower panels) provides an example of a simple "limited offer" game in which the agent has to choose between a low offer—that might be withdrawn at any time—and a high offer—that may replace the low offer with some fixed probability. The problem the agent has to solve is how long to wait. If it waits too long the low offer may be withdrawn and it will end up with nothing. Conversely, if it chooses too soon, it may miss the opportunity to accept a high offer. The probabilistic contingencies are shown in **Figure 2** in terms of control dependent transition probabilities $B(u_t)$, where there are two control states (reject or accept) and five hidden states (low offer, high offer, no offer, accepted low offer, and accepted high offer). We can specify prior goals over the final states with a softmax function of utilities. Unless otherwise stated we will use:

$$P(s_T|\theta) = \mathbf{c} = \sigma\left([1, 1, 1, 2, 4]^T\right) \tag{9}$$

This means the agent believes it will accept the high offer $\exp(4 - 2) = 7.39$ times more than the low offer, which, in turn is $\exp(2 - 1) = 2.718$ times more likely than having accepted neither. To make things more interesting, we increased the probability of offer withdrawal with time such that the hazard rate: $r = 1 - (1 - \frac{1}{16})^t$. This also illustrates time-dependent transition probabilities that the variational scheme can handle with ease. Finally, the probability that a low offer changes into a high offer (provided it is not withdrawn) was fixed so that the probability of receiving a high offer over $T = 16$ trials was a half. This means the hazard rate in **Figure 2** becomes $q = (1 - r) \cdot (1 - (1 - \frac{1}{2})^{1/T})$. For simplicity, we assumed the sensory mapping was the identity matrix such that $A = I$.

Figure 6, shows the results of a single game after iterating the variational updates of the previous section. In this example, the low offer was replaced with a high offer on the eleventh trial, which the agent accepted. It accepts because this is most probable choice—in the face of a high offer—under its prior beliefs that it is most likely to have accepted the higher offer at the end of the game. The expected probabilities of staying (rejecting) or shifting (accepting) are shown in the upper right panel (in green and blue, respectively), as a function of time for each trial (dotted lines) and the final beliefs (full lines). The interesting thing here is that prior to the high offer, the agent believes that it will accept the low offer three or four trials in the future. Furthermore, the propensity to accept (in the future) increases as time goes on (see dotted lines). This means that it waits, patiently, because it thinks it is more likely to accept an offer in the future than to accept the current offer.

The expected precision of these posterior beliefs is shown in the lower left panel and declines gently until the high offer is made. At this point the expected precision increases markedly, and then remains constant until the end of the game (at its maximum value of eight). This reflects the fact that the final outcome is assured with a high degree of confidence, once the high offer has been made and subsequently accepted. These precisions are the expected precisions after convergence of the variational iterations. The equivalent dynamics in the lower right panel show the expected precision over all updates in terms of simulated dopamine responses. These responses are a least squares deconvolution of the variational updates using an exponentially decaying kernel with a time constant of eight iterations. In other words, convolving the simulated dopamine responses with an exponential decay function would reproduce the Bayes optimal updates. This (de)convolution accounts for the postsynaptic effects of dopamine that, we imagine, decay exponentially after its release. The resulting updates are quite revealing and show phasic responses to the arrival of new sensory information that converge to tonic values, which minimize free energy.

This pattern of precision encoding can be compared with another realization, in which the low offer was withdrawn after the fourth trial: **Figure 7** shows the results of this simulation, where the expected control states and precision are exactly the same as in the previous simulation, until the offer is withdrawn. At this point, the agent moves to the no-offer state and remains there until the end of the game. Notice that there is still an increasing propensity to accept, even though the agent knows that accepting is futile. This is because all allowable policies entail a choice but with no preference for when that choice is made. This is because neither the entropy nor the expected utility of the final state is affected by subsequent choices. In this instance, precision falls at the point the offer is withdrawn and remains low until the last trial. Interestingly, at the point the offer is withdrawn, there is a profound suppression of simulated dopamine firing, followed by phasic bursts on subsequent cues that gently increase with the increasing probability of choosing—despite the fact that nothing can be changed. This illustrates the interdependency of expectations about precision and hidden states of the world—which change after the offer has been withdrawn. Many readers will have noticed a similarity between the dynamics of precision and the firing of dopaminergic cells in reinforcement learning paradigms, which we discuss further in (Friston et al., under review).

For people familiar with previous discussions of dopamine in the context of active inference, the correspondence between precision and dopaminergic neurotransmission will come as no

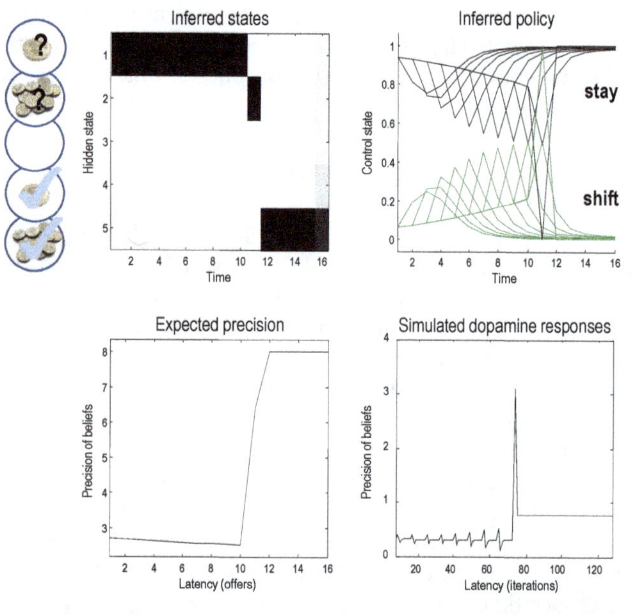

FIGURE 6 | This figure shows the results of a simulation of 16 trials, where a low offer was replaced by high offer on the 11th trial, which was accepted on the subsequent trial. The **upper left** panel shows the expected states as a function of trials or time, where the states are defined in **Figure 2**. The **upper right** panel shows the corresponding expectations about control in the future, where the dotted lines are expectations during earlier trials and the full lines correspond to expectations during the final trial. Blue corresponds to reject (stay) and green to accept (shift). The lower panels show the time-dependent changes in expected precision, after convergence on each trial (**lower left**) and deconvolved updates after each iteration of the variational updates (**lower right**).

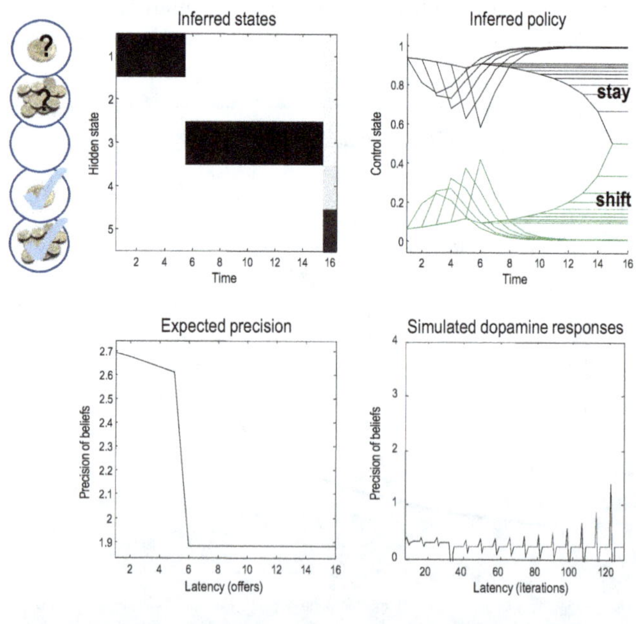

FIGURE 7 | This figure uses the same format as the previous figure; however, here, the low offer was withdrawn on the fifth trial, leading to a decrease in expected precision. Note the difference (divergence) between the expected states on the 15th (penultimate) and 16 (final) trial. It is this large divergence (or more exactly the divergence between distributions over the final state) that leads to a small value and associated precision.

surprise—exactly the same conclusions have been reached when examining predictive coding schemes (Friston et al., 2012b) and hierarchical inference using volatility models (Mathys et al., 2011). "In brief, the emergent role of dopamine is to report the precision or salience of perceptual cues that portend a predictable sequence of sensorimotor events. In this sense, it mediates the affordance of cues that elicit motor behavior (Cisek, 2007); in much the same way that attention mediates the salience of cues in the perceptual domain." (Friston et al., 2012b, p. 2).

TEMPORAL DISCOUNTING AND MARGINAL UTILITY

This section considers the relative contribution of entropy (exploration) and expected utility to choice behavior and how these contribution change with context and time. Generally, when relative utilities are large, they will dominate value (overshadowing entropy) and behavior will conform to expected utility theory. **Figure 8** shows this numerically in terms of the probability of accepting over successive trials with, and without, the entropy term. Here, we precluded withdrawal of the low offer (and its acceptance) and increased the utility of the low offer from zero to eight. Inspection of the upper panels shows that the choice probabilities are essentially the same—with a tendency to wait until the last trial until the low offer becomes more attractive than the high offer (at a utility of four). However, there are subtle differences that are revealed in the lower panels.

These panels show the equivalent results but now in terms of the probability distribution over the latency or number of trials until an offer is accepted. This is simply the cumulative probability of waiting until a particular latency, times the probability of accepting at the latency in question. Here, one sees a slight increase in the latency when value includes the entropy term. This reflects the fact that accepting an offer precludes other outcomes and therefore reduces the entropy of the distribution over final states. Intuitively, there is value in keeping ones options open: cf. a novelty bonus (Krebs et al., 2009).

Figure 9 shows the underlying changes in entropy and expectations as a function of trial number (with a low offer utility of two). The upper left panel shows the probability of staying or accepting and the associated uncertainty or entropy of beliefs about the policy. One can see that this uncertainty increases as the propensity to accept increases. When the agent has in mind a 50–50 probability of accepting, the entropy peaks, shortly before the last offer. The entropy (red) and expected utility (blue) underlying these choices are shown in the right panel and demonstrate—in this example—a complementary dependency on time. As time progresses, the expected utility first falls and then increases, while the entropy does the converse. This suggests that

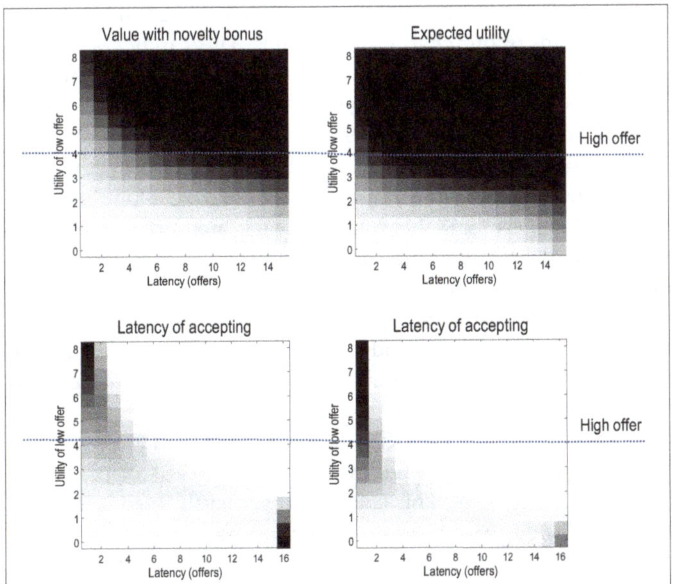

FIGURE 8 | The upper panels show the probability of accepting with (left) and without (right) the entropy or novelty part of value, where the low offer remained available and action was precluded. These probabilities are shown as a function of trial number and the relative utility of the low offer (white corresponds to high probabilities). The lower panels show the same results but in terms of the probability distribution over the latency or time to choice. Note that including the entropy in value slightly delays the time to choice—to ensure a greater latitude of options. This is particularly noticeable in the ambiguous situation when the low offer has the same utility as the high offer (of four).

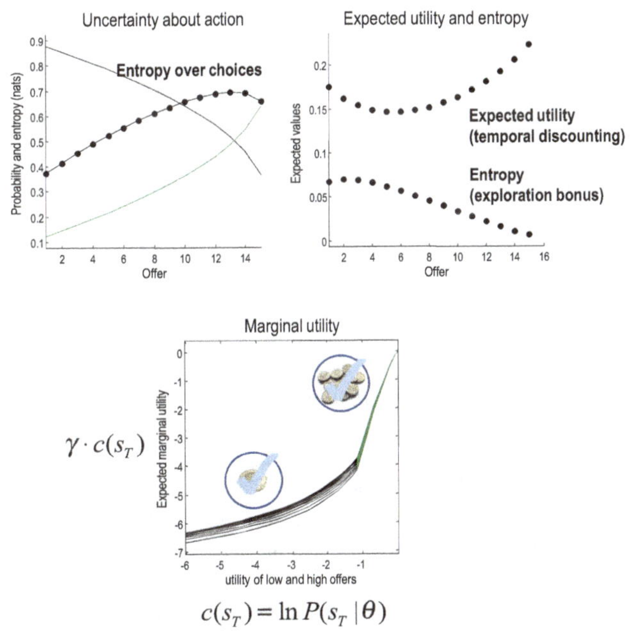

FIGURE 9 | Upper left panel: the probability of accepting an offer as a function of time or trials. Note that the probability of accepting (green) increases over time to approach and surpass the probability of rejection. This produces an increase in the uncertainty about action—shown in red. **Upper right panel**: these are the expected utility and entropy components of expected value as a function of trial number. The key result here is the time-dependent change in expected utility, which corresponds to temporal discounting of the expected utility: i.e., the expected utility of the final state is greater when there are fewer intervening trials. **Lower panel**: the marginal utility of the high offer (green) and low offer (blue) as a function of the relative utility of the high offer. Marginal utility is defined here as expected utility times expected precision. The multiple curves correspond to the marginal utilities as a function of trial number (and do not differ greatly because expected precision changes more slowly over time—for a given utility—than it changes over utility—for a given time).

the agent believes it is more likely to secure an offer later in the game, because it now knows the offer has not been withdrawn; in other words, the possibility of an early withdrawal cannot be discounted at the beginning of the game.

This dynamic speaks directly to temporal discounting in intertemporal choice: consider the expected utility on the eighth trial. This is the utility of a final outcome eight trials in the future. Notice that this is substantially less than the expected utility of the final outcome two trials in the future. In other words, the expected utility of the outcome decreases, the further it recedes into the future. This is the essence of temporal discounting, which—in this example—can be explained simply by prior beliefs that the offer will be withdrawn before the final outcome is reached. This withdrawal probability is known as a *hazard function*, whose rate changes with time in our example (the parameter r in **Figure 2**).

TEMPORAL DISCOUNTING

Temporal discounting is an emergent property of Bayes optimal inference about choice behavior that depends upon the generative model and, implicitly, prior beliefs about time sensitive contingencies—or at least it can be formulated as such (Sozou, 1998). The form of temporal discounting depends upon the generative model and can be quite complicated. This is because the discounting of expected utility depends upon inference about the current state, future choices and precision—all of which change with time in an interdependent fashion. Having said this (economic) hyperbolic discounting can be derived under a simple generative model of losing a reward, given exponential priors on the hazard rate (Sozou, 1998). Although hyperbolic (or exponential) discounting may be sufficient for descriptive purposes, simply optimizing a temporal discounting parameter (Daw and Touretzky, 2002), in light of observed behavior, cannot disambiguate among the prior beliefs an agent may entertain. To understand the nature of temporal discounting, one has to understand the generative model upon which that discounting is based—and use observed choice behaviors to select among competing models or hypotheses.

MARGINAL UTILITY AND PRECISION

We have been careful to distinguish between utility $\ln P(s_T|\theta) = c(s_T)$—an attribute of the final state and value $Q(\tilde{u}|s_t)$—an attribute of choices available from the current state. This means that the value of the current state depends upon how easy it is to access the final state. Furthermore, the ensuing choice depends upon precision, suggesting that the effect of value on choice can be expressed in terms of an effective utility $\gamma \cdot c(s_T)$ that we will call *marginal utility* (for consistency with economic theory). Assuming the entropy term in Equation (4) small enough to be ignored, it is easy to see that expected marginal utility directly informs choices:

$$\ln P(\tilde{u}|s_t) = \sum_{s_T} \underbrace{P(s_T|s_t, \tilde{u})(\gamma \cdot c(s_T))}_{\text{expected marginal utility}} \quad (10)$$

Generally, as the utility of a particular final state increases, precision increases more slowly—because the implicit distribution over final states is less likely to be realized. Intuitively, the marginal utility depends on the confidence that a goal can be reached. This leads to a convex relationship between marginal utility and utility: cf. the law of diminishing marginal utility (Kauder, 1953). The lower panel of **Figure 9** illustrates this relationship. Here, we increased the relative utility of the high offer from two to eight and evaluated the marginal utility of accepting the low and high offers (by precluding offer withdrawal and action). The result is a characteristic convex relationship, in which marginal utility decreases more slowly with the utility of the high offer—reaching its maximum at zero. Conversely, the marginal utility of the low offer decreases more slowly as the utility of the low offer falls. In the current setup, this asymmetry results from the nature of utility and its dependency upon precision. However, there may be interesting connections here with Prospect Theory (Kahneman and Tversky, 1979) that appeal to a reference point for utility—defined here in terms of equiprobable outcomes.

In summary, many classic phenomena in utilitarian and economic theory resurface here as natural consequences of Bayes optimal (active) inference under a relatively simple generative model. This is potentially important, because choice behavior can, in principle, be used to adjudicate among alternative models used by subjects.

CONCLUSION

This paper has considered agency from a rather elementary and formal perspective; namely, that a sense of agency rests upon prior beliefs about how one will behave. Irrespective of how these beliefs are described, they must—in some sense—entail the belief that our behavior will converge on outcomes that define who we are—in terms of our characteristic states. This can be formalized in terms of prior beliefs that controlled state transitions minimize a relative entropy or KL divergence—endowing behavior with a purpose that can be characterized by the states we believe should be occupied. The ensuing scheme appears to have construct validity in relation to normative accounts in psychology and economics. Furthermore, the computational anatomy afforded by variational Bayes fits comfortably with neuronal message passing in the brain.

In reinforcement learning, there is an important distinction between model-free and model-based systems (Daw et al., 2005). In contrast, active inference is quintessentially model-based—so does this preclude model-free schemes? Active inference accommodates the distinction between model-free and model-based by placing model-free schemes at the lower levels of hierarchical generative models. This enables higher levels to contextualize lower level (reflexive or habitual) inference and consequent action selection. We have not addressed this issue in this paper; largely because our focus has been on inference about hidden states, while learning corresponds to optimizing the parameters of the generative model—such as the probability transition matrices that encode environmental contingencies and which hidden states can and cannot be controlled.

The arguments in this paper are based upon—and lead to—a number of points, which we now briefly rehearse:

- Optimal behavior can be cast as a pure inference problem, in which valuable outcomes are defined in terms of prior beliefs about future states. However, exact Bayesian inference (perfect rationality) cannot be realized physically, which means that optimal behavior rests on approximate Bayesian inference (bounded rationality).

- Variational free energy provides a bound on Bayesian model evidence (marginal likelihood) that is optimized by bounded rational behavior. This requires (approximate Bayesian) inference on both hidden states of the world and (future) control states. This mandates beliefs about action (control) that are distinct from action *per se*—beliefs that entail a precision.
- These beliefs can be cast in terms of minimizing the relative entropy or divergence between prior goals—over final states—and conditional distributions, given the current state of the world and future choices.
- Value can be equated with negative divergence and comprises entropy (exploration or novelty bonus) and expected utility (utilitarian) terms that account for exploratory and exploitative behavior respectively.
- Beliefs about the state of the world depend upon expected value over choices, while beliefs about choices depend upon expected value over states. Beliefs about precision depend upon expected value under both states and choices.
- Precision has to be optimized to balance prior beliefs about choices and sensory evidence for hidden states. In other words, precision has to nuance an inherent optimism bias when inferring the current state of the world.
- Variational Bayes provides a formal account of how posterior expectations about hidden states of the world, control states and precision depend upon each other; and may provide a metaphor for message passing in the brain.
- Variational Bayes induces distinct probabilistic representations (functional segregation) of hidden states, control states and precision—and highlights the role of reciprocal message passing. This may be particularly important for expected precision that is required for optimal inference about hidden states (perception) and control states (action selection).

One might ask why these conclusions do not follow from normative accounts of optimal behavior. One reason is that normative accounts do not distinguish between action and beliefs about action (control). These beliefs entail both content (expectations) and uncertainty (precision). This means that both expectations about behavior and the precision of these beliefs have to be optimized. It is the optimization of precision that provides a complete account of bounded rationality (approximate Bayesian inference) and a putative account of the control of dopaminergic firing; cf. (Gurney et al., 2001).

This account considers dopamine to report the precision of divergence or prediction errors (in their nuanced or non-classical sense) and partly resolves the dialectic between dopamine as reporting reward prediction errors (Schultz et al., 1997) and the predictability of rewards (Fiorillo et al., 2003; Redgrave and Gurney, 2006; Schultz et al., 2008). The notion that dopamine encodes precision is now receiving support from several lines of evidence; from purely theoretical treatments of hierarchical Bayesian inference (Mathys et al., 2011), from theoretical neurobiology (Frank et al., 2007; Fletcher and Frith, 2009; Friston et al., 2012b; Pellicano and Burr, 2012) and from empirical studies (Fiorillo et al., 2008; Coull et al., 2011; Galea et al., 2012; Zokaei et al., 2012). Having said this, a proper validation of active inference will require careful model comparison using empirical choice behaviors and a detailed mapping between putative model variables and their neuronal correlates.

Indeed, the aim of this work was to provide a comprehensive but formal model of choice behavior that contextualizes decisions in the more general setting of embodied or active inference about states of the world; e.g., (Pezzulo and Castelfranchi, 2009). In this setting, the ability to compare different formulations of approximate Bayesian inference (in terms of different mean field approximations and prior beliefs) becomes crucial—because different formulations correspond to different hypotheses about how subjects optimize their behavior. We hope to use Bayesian model selection to characterize individual subjects, in terms of their prior beliefs using generative models of the sort introduced in this paper. This may be useful in the study of intersubject variability or indeed differences between normal subjects and those with psychiatric syndromes or addictive behaviors. The advantage of having a variational scheme with dynamics (that can be applied to these models) is that, in principle, one can localize the neuronal correlates of implicit Bayesian updates with neuroimaging. More generally, the theoretical approach adopted in this paper highlights the necessarily intimate relationship between inferring states of the world and optimal behavior (Toussaint and Storkey, 2006; Gläscher et al., 2010), the confidence or precision of that inference (De Martino et al., 2012), and the functional plurality of dopaminergic neuromodulation (Schultz, 2007).

In terms of leveraging active inference to further understand the neurobiology of decision-making, there are several predictions that could be explored—using either choice behavior or functional neuroimaging. One key prediction is that choices will systematically maximize the entropy over outcomes that have the same (relative) utility. In principle, it should be possible to design behavioral experiments that manipulate entropy and expected utility in an orthogonal fashion, to establish whether entropy represents an intrinsic drive. Furthermore, transcribing this sort of paradigm to fMRI should establish the validity of the putative functional segregation implied by the variational message passing scheme considered above. Indeed, we have used the game described in this paper as the basis of an fMRI experiment—and will be reporting the results in the near future. The neurobiological plausibility of variational message passing remains something of an open question. However, there is one comforting point of convergence between variational Bayes and more neurobiologically plausible predictive coding schemes (Bastos et al., 2012): this is the fact that the solution for both is exactly the same. In other words, it may be possible to formulate variational Bayes using neuronal dynamics that implement a gradient descent on variational free energy. Interestingly, this is precisely the (Variational Laplace) scheme used routinely in data analysis (Friston et al., 2007).

ACKNOWLEDGEMENTS

The Wellcome Trust funded this work. Michael Moutoussis is also supported by the NIHR Biomedical Research Centre.

REFERENCES

Ashby, W. R. (1947). Principles of the self-organizing dynamic system. *J. Gen. Psychol.* 37, 125–128. doi: 10.1080/00221309.1947.9918144

Bastos, A. M., Usrey, W. M., Adams, R. A., Mangun, G. R., Fries, P., and Friston, K. J. (2012). Canonical microcircuits for predictive coding. *Neuron* 76, 695–711. doi: 10.1016/j.neuron.2012.10.038

Beal, M. J. (2003). *Variational Algorithms for Approximate Bayesian Inference.* Ph.D. thesis, University College London.

Birkhoff, G. D. (1931). Proof of the ergodic theorem. *Proc. Natl. Acad. Sci. U.S.A.* 17, 656–660. doi: 10.1073/pnas.17.12.656

Braun, D. A., Ortega, P. A., Theodorou, E., and Schaal, S. (2011). "Path integral control and bounded rationality," in *IEEE Symposium on Adaptive Dynamic Programming and Reinforcement Learning (ADPRL)* (Paris: IEEE), 202–209

Camerer, C. F. (2003). Behavioural studies of strategic thinking in games. *Trends Cogn. Sci.* 7, 225–231. doi: 10.1016/ S1364-6613(03)00094-9

Canolty, R. T., Edwards, E., Dalal, S. S., Soltani, M., Nagarajan, S. S., Kirsch, H. E., et al. (2006). High gamma power is phase-locked to theta oscillations in human neocortex. *Science* 313, 1626–1628. doi: 10.1126/science.1128115

Cisek, P. (2007). Cortical mechanisms of action selection: the affordance competition hypothesis. *Philos. Trans. R. Soc. Lond. B Biol. Sci.* 362, 1585–1599. doi: 10.1098/rstb.2007.2054

Cohen, J. D., McClure, S. M., and Yu, A. J. (2007). Should I stay or should I go. How the human brain manages the trade-off between exploitation and exploration. *Philos. Trans R. Soc. Lond. B Biol. Sci.* 362, 933–942. doi: 10.1098/rstb.2007.2098

Conant, R. C., and Ashby, R. W. (1970). Every good regulator of a system must be a model of that system. *Int. J. Systems. Sci.* 1, 89–97. doi: 10.1080/00207727008920220

Coull, J. T., Cheng, R. K., and Meck, W. (2011). Neuroanatomical and neurochemical substrates of timing. *Neuropsychopharmacology* 36, 3–25. doi: 10.1038/npp.2010.113

Daw, N. D., and Doya, K. (2006). The computational neurobiology of learning and reward. *Curr. Opin. Neurobiol.* 16, 199–204. doi: 10.1016/j.conb.2006.03.006

Daw, N. D., Niv, Y., and Dayan, P. (2005). Uncertainty-based competition between prefrontal and dorsolateral striatal systems for behavioral control. *Nat. Neurosci.* 8, 1704–1711. doi: 10.1038/nn1560

Daw, N. D., and Touretzky, D. S. (2002). Long-term reward prediction in TD models of the dopamine system. *Neural Comput.* 14, 2567–2583. doi: 10.1162/08997660 2760407973

Dayan, P., and Daw, N. D. (2008). Decision theory, reinforcement learning, and the brain. *Cogn. Affect. Behav. Neurosci.* 8, 429–453. doi: 10.3758/CABN.8.4.429

Dayan, P., and Hinton, G. E. (1997). Using expectation maximization for reinforcement learning. *Neural Comput.* 9, 271–278. doi: 10.1162/neco.1997.9.2.271

Dayan, P., Hinton, G. E., and Neal, R. (1995). The helmholtz machine. *Neural Comput.* 7, 889–904. doi: 10.1162/neco.1995.7.5.889

De Martino, B., Fleming, S. M., Garrett, N., and Dolan, R. J. (2012). Confidence in value-based choice. *Nat. Neurosci.* 16, 105–110. doi: 10.1038/nn.3279

Ellison, C. J., Mahoney, J. R., James, G., and Crutchfield, J. P. (2011). Information symmetries in irreversible processes. *Chaos* 21, 037107. doi: 10.1063/1.3637490

Feynman, R. P. (1972). *Statistical Mechanics.* Reading, MA: Benjamin. Fiorillo, C. D., Newsome, W. T., and Schultz, W. (2008). The temporal precision of reward prediction in dopamine neurons. *Nat. Neurosci.* 11, 966–973. doi: 10.1038/ nn.2159

Fiorillo, C. D., Tobler, P. N., and Schultz, W. (2003). Discrete coding of reward probability and uncertainty by dopamine neurons. *Science* 299, 1898–1902. doi: 10.1126/science.1077349

Fletcher, P. C., and Frith, C. D. (2009). Perceiving is believing: a Bayesian approach to explaining the positive symptoms of schizophrenia. *Nat. Rev. Neurosci.* 10, 48–58. doi: 10.1038/nrn2536

Fox, C., and Roberts, S. (2012). A tutorial on variational Bayes. *Artif. Intell. Rev.* 38, 85–95. doi: 10.1007/s10462-011-9236-8

Frank, M. J., Scheres, A., and Sherman, J. (2007). Understanding decision-making deficits in neurological conditions: insights from models of natural action selection. *Philos. Trans. R. Soc. Lond. B Biol. Sci.* 362, 1641–1654. doi: 10.1098/rstb.2007.2058

Friston, K. (2010). The free-energy principle: a unified brain theory. *Nat. Rev. Neurosci.* 11, 127–138. doi: 10.1038/nrn2787

Friston, K. (2012). A free energy principle for biological systems. *Entropy* 14, 2100–2121. doi: 10.3390/e14112100

Friston, K., Kilner, J., and Harrison, L. (2006). A free energy principle for the brain. *J. Physiol. Paris.* 100, 70–87. doi: 10.1016/j.jphysparis.2006.10.001

Friston, K., Mattout, J., Trujillo-Barreto, N., Ashburner, J., and Penny, W. (2007). Variational free energy and the Laplace approximation. *Neuroimage* 34, 220–234. doi: 10.1016/j.neuroimage.2006.08.035

Friston, K. J., Daunizeau, J., Kilner, J., and Kiebel, S. J. (2010). Action and behavior: a free-energy formulation. *Biol. Cybern.* 102, 227–260. doi: 10.1007/s00422-010-0364-z

Friston, K., Samothrakis, S., and Montague, R. (2012a). Active inference and agency: optimal control without cost functions. *Biol. Cybern.* 106, 523–541. doi: 10.1007/s00422-012-0512-8

Friston, K. J., Fitzgerald, T., Galea, J. M., Adams, R., Brown, H., Dolan, R. J., et al. (2012b). Dopamine, affordance and active inference. *PLoS Comput. Biol.* 8:e1002327. doi: 10.1371/journal.pcbi.1002327

Fudenberg, D., and Kreps, D. (1993). Learning mixed equilibria. *Game. Econ. Behav.* 5, 320–367. doi: 10.1006/game.1993.1021

Galea, J. M., Bestmann, S., Beigi, M., Jahanshahi, M., and Rothwell, J. C. (2012). Action reprogramming in Parkinson's disease: response to prediction error is modulated by levels of dopamine. *J. Neurosci.* 32, 542–550. doi: 10.1523/JNEUROSCI.3621-11.2012 Gläscher, J., Daw, N., Dayan, P., and O'Doherty, J. P. (2010). States versus rewards: dissociable neural prediction error signals underlying model-based and model-free reinforcement learning. *Neuron* 66, 585–595. doi: 10.1016/j.neuron.2010.04.016

Goldman-Rakic, P.S. (1997). The cortical dopamine system: role in memory and cognition. *Adv. Pharmacol.* 42, 707–711. doi: 10.1016/S1054-3589(08)60846-7

Goldman-Rakic, P. S., Lidow, M. S., Smiley, J. F., and Williams, M. S. (1992). The anatomy of dopamine in monkey and human prefrontal cortex. *J. Neural Transm. Suppl.* 36, 163–177.

Gregory, R. L. (1968). Perceptual illusions and brain models. *Proc. R. Soc. Lond. B Biol. Sci.* 171, 179–196. doi: 10.1098/rspb.1968.0071

Gurney, K., Prescott, T. J., and Redgrave, P. (2001). A computational model of action selection in the basal ganglia. I. A new functional anatomy. *Biol. Cybern.* 84, 401–410. doi: 10.1007/PL00007984

Haile, P. A., Hortaçsu, A., and Kosenok, G. (2008). On the empirical content of quantal response equilibrium. *Am. Econ. Rev.* 98, 180–200. doi: 10.1257/aer.98.1.180

Helmholtz, H. (1866/1962). "Concerning the perceptions in general," in *Treatise on Physiological Optics, 3rd Edn.* Vol. 3. Transl. J. Southall (New York, NY: Dover).

Hinton, G. E., and van Camp, D. (1993). "Keeping neural networks simple by minimizing the description length of weights," in *Proceedings of COLT-93*, 5–13. doi: 10.1145/168304.168306

Jaynes, E. T. (1957). Information theory and statistical mechanics. *Phys. Rev. Ser. II* 106, 620–630. doi: 10.1103/PhysRev.106.620

Jocham, G., Hunt, L. T., Near, J., and Behrens, T. E. (2012). A mechanism for value-guided choice based on the excitation-inhibition balance in prefrontal cortex. *Nat. Neurosci.* 15, 960–961. doi: 10.1038/ nn.3140

Kahneman, D., and Tversky, A. (1979). Prospect theory: an analysis of decision under risk. *Econometrica* 47, 263–291. doi: 10.2307/1914185

Kakade, S., and Dayan, P. (2002). Dopamine: generalization and bonuses. *Neural Netw.* 15, 549–559. doi: 10.1016/S0893-6080(02)00048-5

Kappen, H. J., Gomez, Y., and Opper, M. (2012). Optimal control as a graphical model inference problem. *Mach. Learn.* 87, 159–182. doi: 10.1007/s10994-012-5278-7

Kauder, E. (1953). Genesis of the marginal utility theory: from aristotle to the end of the eighteenth century. *Econ. J.* 63, 638–650. doi: 10.2307/2226451

Klyubin, A. S., Polani, D., and Nehaniv, C. L. (2005). "Empowerment: a universal agent-centric measure of control," in *The 2005 IEEE Congress on Evolutionary Computation.* Vol. 1, 128–135.

Krebs, R. M., Schott, B. H., Schütze, H., and Düzel, E. (2009). The novelty exploration bonus and its attentional modulation. *Neuropsychologia* 47, 2272–2281. doi: 10.1016/ j.neuropsychologia.2009.01.015

Luce, R. D. (1959). *Individual Choice Behavior.* Oxford, UK: Wiley.

MacKay, D. J. (2003). *Information Theory, Inference and Learning Algorithms.* Cambridge, UK: Cambridge University Press.

Mathys, C., Daunizeau, J., Friston, K. J., and Stephan, K. E. (2011). A Bayesian foundation for individual learning under uncertainty. *Front. Hum. Neurosci.* 5:39. doi: 10.3389/fnhum.2011.00039

McKelvey, R., and Palfrey, T. (1995). Quantal response equilibria for normal form games. *Game. Econ. Behav.* 10, 6–38. doi: 10.1006/game.1995.1023

Moran, R. J., Symmonds, M., Stephan, K. E., Friston, K. J., and Dolan, R. J. (2011). An *in vivo* assay of synaptic function mediating human cognition. *Curr. Biol.* 21, 1320–1325. doi: 10.1016/j.cub.2011.06.053

O'Doherty, J., Dayan, P., Schultz, J., Deichmann, R., Friston, K., and Dolan, R. J. (2004). Dissociable roles of ventral and dorsal striatum in instrumental conditioning. *Science* 304,452–454.

Ortega, P. A., and Braun, D. A. (2011).
Information, utility and bounded rationality. *Lect. Notes Artif. Int.* 6830, 269–274. doi: 10.1007/978-3-642-22887-2_28

Ortega, P. A., and Braun, D. A. (2013). Thermodynamics as a theory of decision-making with informationprocessing costs. *Proc. R. Soc. A* 469, 2153. doi: 10.1098/rspa. 2012.0683

Pellicano, E., and Burr, D. (2012). When the world becomes 'too real': a Bayesian explanation of autistic perception. *Trends Cogn. Sci.* 16, 504–510. doi: 10.1016/j.tics.2012.08.009

Penny, W. D., Stephan, K. E., Mechelli, A., and Friston, K. J. (2004). Comparing dynamic causal models. *Neuroimage* 22, 1157–1172. doi: 10.1016/j.neuroimage.2004.03.026

Pezzulo, G., and Castelfranchi, C. (2009). Thinking as the control of imagination: a conceptual framework for goal-directed system. *Psychol. Res.* 73, 559–577. doi: 10.1007/s00426-009-0237-z

Rao, R. P., and Ballard, D. H. (1999). Predictive coding in the visual cortex: a functional interpretation of some extra-classical receptive-field effects. *Nat. Neurosci.* 2, 79–87. doi: 10.1038/4580

Redgrave, P., and Gurney, K. (2006). The short-latency dopamine signal: a role in discovering novel actions. *Nat. Rev. Neurosci.* 7, 967–975. doi: 10.1038/nrn2022

Schmidhuber, J. (1991). "Curious model-building control systems," in *Proceedings in IEEE International Joint Conference on Neural Networks,* Vol. 2, (Singapore), 1458–1463.

Schultz, W. (2007). Multiple dopamine functions at different time courses. *Annu. Rev. Neurosci.* 30, 259–288. doi: 10.1146/ annurev.neuro.28.061604.135722

Schultz, W., Dayan, P., and Montague, P. R. (1997). A neural substrate of prediction and reward. *Science* 275, 1593–1599. doi: 10.1126/science.275.5306.1593

Schultz, W., Preuschoff, K., Camerer, C., Hsu, M., Fiorillo, C. D., Tobler, P. N., et al. (2008). Explicit neural signals reflecting reward uncertainty. *Philos. Trans. R. Soc. Lond. B Biol. Sci.* 363, 3801–3811. doi: 10.1098/rstb.2008.0152

Sharot, T., Guitart-Masip, M., Korn, C.
W., Chowdhury, R., and Dolan, R.
J. (2012). How dopamine enhances an optimism bias in humans. *Curr. Biol.* 22, 1477–1481. doi: 10.1016/j.cub.2012.05.053

Simon, H. A. (1956). Rational choice and the structure of the environment. *Psychol. Rev.* 63, 129–138. doi: 10.1037/h0042769

Sozou, P. D. (1998). A Discounting framework for choice with delayed and probabilistic rewards. *Proc. R. Soc. Lond. B* 265, 2015–2020. doi: 10.1098/rspb.1998.0534

Spiegelhalter, D. J., Best, N. G., Carlin, B. P., and van der Linde, A. (2002). Bayesian measures of model complexity and fit. *J. R. Statist. Soc. B* 64, 583–639. doi: 10.1111/14679868.00353

Surmeier, D., Plotkin, J., and Shen, (2009). Dopamine and synaptic plasticity in dorsal striatal circuits controlling action selection. *Curr. Opin. Neurobiol.* 19, 621–628. doi: 10.1016/j.conb.2009.10.003

Sutton, R. S., and Barto, A. G. (1998). *Reinforcement Learning: An Introduction.* Cambridge, MA: MIT Press.

Tishby, N., and Polani, D. (2011). "Information theory of decisions and actions," in *Perception-Action Cycle Springer Series in Cognitive and Neural Systems*, eds Cutsuridis, A. Hussain, and J. G. Taylor (Berlin: Springer), 601–636.

Tobler, P. N., Fiorillo, C. D., and Schultz, W. (2005). Adaptive coding of reward value by dopamine neurons. *Science* 307, 1642–1645. doi: 10.1126/science.1105370

Toussaint, M., and Storkey, A. (2006). "Probabilistic inference for solving discrete and continuous state markov decision processes," in *Proceedingsof the 23rd International Conference on Machine Learning,* 945–952.

van den Broek, J. L., Wiegerinck, W. A., and Kappen, H. J. (2010). Risksensitive path integral control. *UAI* 6, 1-8.

Von Neumann, J., and Morgenstern, O. (1944). *Theory of Games and Economic Behavior.* Princeton, NJ: Princeton University Press.

Watkins, C. J., and Dayan, P. (1992). Qlearning. *Mach. Learn.* 8, 279–292. doi: 10.1007/BF00992698

Wissner-Gross, A. D., and Freer, C. E. (2013). Causal Entropic Forces. *Phys. Rev. Lett.* 110:168702. doi: 10.1103/PhysRevLett.110.168702

Zokaei, N., Gorgoraptis, N., and Husain, M. (2012). Dopamine modulates visual working memory precision. *J. Vis.* 12, 350. doi: 10.1167/12.9.350

APPENDIX

The variational energies associated with each subset of hidden variables are derived by isolating terms in the generative model that depend upon the subset in question and evaluating their expectation, under their Markov blanket:

$$V(s_t) = E_{Q(\psi\backslash s_t)}\left[\ln P(o_t|s_t) + \ln P\left(s_t|\mathbf{d}\right) + \ln P(s_t|s_{t-1}, a_{t-1}) + \ln P(\tilde{u}|s_t, \gamma)\right]$$
$$= \ln \mathbf{A}^T \cdot \hat{o}_t + [t = 0] \cdot \ln \mathbf{d} + [t > 0] \cdot \ln \mathbf{B}(a_{t-1}) \cdot \hat{s}_{t-1} + \hat{\gamma} \cdot \mathbf{Q}^T \cdot \hat{\pi}$$

$$V(\tilde{u}) = E_{Q(\psi\backslash\tilde{u})}\left[\ln P(\tilde{u}|s_t, \gamma)\right]$$
$$= \hat{\gamma} \cdot \mathbf{Q} \cdot \hat{s}_t$$
$$V(\gamma) = E_{Q(\psi\backslash\gamma)}\left[\ln P(\tilde{u}|s_t, \gamma) + \ln P(\gamma|\beta)\right]$$
$$= \gamma \cdot \hat{\pi}^T \cdot \mathbf{Q} \cdot \hat{s}_t + (\alpha - 1)\ln\gamma - \beta\gamma$$
$$= \ln Q(\gamma) = (\alpha - 1)\ln(\gamma) - \hat{\beta}\gamma - \ln Z_\gamma$$

The Iverson brackets $[t = 0]$ return a value of one when the expression is true and zero otherwise.

15

Individual differences in attributional style but not in interoceptive sensitivity, predict subjective estimates of action intention

Tegan Penton[1,2] *, Guillaume L. Thierry[2] and Nick J. Davis[3]

[1] Department of Psychology, Goldsmiths, University of London, London, UK
[2] School of Psychology, Bangor University, Bangor, UK
[3] Department of Psychology, Swansea University, Swansea, UK

Correspondence:
Tegan Penton, Department of Psychology, Goldsmiths, University of London, New Cross, London, SE14 6NW, UK
e-mail: t.penton@gold.ac.uk

The debate on the existence of free will is on-going. Seminal findings by Libet et al. (1983) demonstrate that subjective awareness of a voluntary urge to act (the W-judgment) occurs before action execution. Libet's paradigm requires participants to perform voluntary actions while watching a clock hand rotate. On response trials, participants make a retrospective judgment related to awareness of their urge to act. This research investigates the relationship between individual differences in performance on the Libet task and self-awareness. We examined the relationship between W-judgment, attributional style (AS; a measure of perceived control) and interoceptive sensitivity (IS; awareness of stimuli originating from one's body; e.g., heartbeats). Thirty participants completed the AS questionnaire (ASQ), a heartbeat estimation task (IS), and the Libet paradigm. The ASQ score significantly predicted performance on the Libet task, while IS did not – more negative ASQ scores indicated larger latency between W-judgment and action execution. A significant correlation was also observed between ASQ score and IS. This is the first research to report a relationship between W-judgment and AS and should inform the future use of electroencephalography (EEG) to investigate the relationship between AS, W-judgment and RP onset. Our findings raise questions surrounding the importance of one's perceived control in determining the point of conscious intention to act. Furthermore, we demonstrate possible negative implications associated with a longer period between conscious awareness and action execution.

Keywords: W-judgment, libet, interoception, locus of control, agency

INTRODUCTION

The concept of free will has long been a controversial topic in both philosophical and scientific domains (Sinnott-Armstrong and Nadel, 2011). Here free will, or volitional action, is defined as conscious awareness of the intention to act. The traditional concept of free will (control of one's actions) has been challenged by the research of Libet et al. (1983); whose results show onset of neural activity associated with an action before an individual becomes aware of their intention to act. In their seminal experiment, Libet et al. (1983) used EEG to record the readiness potentials (RP) of six participants while they completed a computer task. During the task, participants were asked to watch a clock hand rotate around a clock and to press a button only if they felt the urge to act (to emphasize voluntary action). If a response was made during a given trial, the participant was asked to indicate the position of the clock hand when they first became aware of the urge to move (known as the W-judgment). The RP (or Bereitschaftspotential) is characterized by a slow negative shift in potential related to the motor and pre-motor area (Luder Deecke and Kornhuber, 1969) and is often seen before voluntary movements (for example, Waszak et al., 2005; for alternative explanations see Schurger et al., 2012). Libet et al. (1983) showed that, on average, an RP was seen 550 ms before action initiation while W-judgments were seen 206 ms before action initiation (−206 ms). Therefore, Libet et al. (1983) suggested that action intention is not entirely "free" and that conscious awareness may occur as more of a justification of a predetermined action.

Libet (1999) later argued that these findings do not necessarily negate the concept of volition, rather the phenomenon may exist in the period between awareness of the urge to act and action execution. Specifically, Libet (1999) suggested that 200 ms latency between awareness and action execution could allow for conscious inhibition of that action if required. This latency is known as the "veto" period and is used to provide a more observable notion of volition (Haggard and Libet, 2001; Mele, 2008). While the Libet paradigm has been subject to criticism (see Haggard et al., 2002), research accounting for issues related to task constraints (Matsuhashi and Hallett, 2008; RP's 1.42 s prior to action onset) and subjective report (Fried et al., 2011; activity seen 700 ms prior to action onset in single-cell recordings) still replicate the basic findings of Libet's work. However, the precise timing of associated neural activation is disputed (for more replications see, Lau et al., 2004; Soon et al., 2008).

In spite of the wealth of research into the Libet paradigm, the influence of individual differences in response patterns on the

Libet task is relatively unknown. Libet et al. (1983) did take individual differences in response patterns into account (by creating a discrepancy score between a participants average W-judgment and the average time of perceived external touch, determined by another task) in the hope of providing a more reliable estimate of awareness of intention to act, but did not consider other inter-individual differences (e.g., personality). Haggard and Eimer (1999) also addressed variance in W-judgments by investigating variance within a participant's W-judgments and the covariance of associated brain activity (namely, the RP and lateralised RP; a potential calculated by investigating the relative shift in activity between the contralateral and ipsilateral hemisphere to the hand performing the action). They suggest that LRP onset covaries with time of W-judgments in that early W-judgments correlate with early LRP onset and late W-judgments correlate with late LRP onset. In this way, it is clear that research into volition is aware of potential individual differences in the W-judgment. The current research aims to investigate the relationship between aspects of self-awareness (IS, one's awareness of one's internal stimuli), perceived control (AS; the style one uses to explain life events) and one's awareness of one's intention to act. To our knowledge this is the first research investigating personality and perceptual correlates of W-judgments on the Libet task.

Attributional style (AS) refers to the style an individual uses to explain previous positive and negative life events. Peterson et al. (1982) developed the AS Questionnaire (ASQ) to measure perceived control across several modalities. In order to enable a more holistic understanding of an individual's perception of control to be established, the ASQ attempts to define the style that individuals adopt to explain life events across three areas; (1) Internality (whether the individual feels the cause of the event is due to themselves or an external factor), (2) Stability (whether the individual feels this cause is stable over time), and (3) Globality (whether the individual feels the cause will be present across multiple life domains). Those who view the cause of positive life events as internal, stable and global, and the cause of negative life events as external, transient, and specific are said to have a positive or optimistic AS; while those who view the cause of positive life events as external, transient, and specific, and the cause of negative life events as internal, stable and global are thought to have a negative or pessimistic AS. Many benefits of having an optimistic AS have been reported in the literature, such as higher levels of well-being in comparison to those with a negative AS (see Forgeard and Seligman, 2012 for a review). Research into negative AS is more extensive (Seligman et al., 1999; Seligman, 2002) with many reporting a relationship between depression (e.g., Peterson et al., 1982; Stange et al., 2013) and anxiety (e.g., Luten et al., 1997; Mark and Smith, 2012) and negative AS scores. Furthermore research has also shown negative feelings and emotions to correlate with other measures. For example, Critchley et al. (2004) show a positive relationship between "negative emotional experience" and IS.

Interoception refers to one's awareness of one's internal stimuli (e.g., an individual's ability to estimate their own heartbeats over a given time period, Craig, 2002). The somatic-marker hypothesis proposed by Damasio et al. (1996) suggests that emotional and physiological changes elicited by exposure to certain situations or stimuli are bound together. Therefore, when encountering a new stimulus that elicits the same physical arousal/emotion, the individual will evaluate the potential reward or punishment based on prior experience. Werner et al. (2013) supports this theory by showing that increased interoceptive awareness relates to increased processing of somatic markers during a decision making task. Craig (2004) suggests this integration of interoceptive and emotion information occurs within a neural network converging in the insular cortex. Furthermore, he later suggests that integration of this information occurs at each moment in time to create a global, time-locked, sense of self-awareness (Craig, 2010). Relating this to the current research, work by Berlucchi and Aglioti (2010) demonstrate that similar cortical regions, primarily the Insula, are associated with both interoception and agency (a sense of control over one's actions). In this context, one may expect a relationship between performances on the Libet task, AS and IS in the current study.

There is evidence to suggest that perceived control and belief in free will are related, with Baumeister and Brewer (2012) demonstrating a positive correlation between internal Locus of Control (attribution of the cause of life events to the self; LOC; Rotter, 1966) and belief in free will. Furthermore, Stroessner and Green (1990) demonstrate a positive correlation between beliefs in determinism and external LOC (attribution of the cause of life events to external factors). Supporting this, Paulhus and Carey (2011) demonstrate a positive correlation between belief in free will and AS (one's style of explaining life events; a measure of perceived control). As well as this, Orellana-Damacela et al. (2000) suggest that, when more self-aware, one is more likely to consult one's own standards and beliefs during decision-making. It is proposed that this act can be beneficial or detrimental to the individual in question based on their ability to meet their own expectations. This suggests that individual differences in levels of self-awareness can have varying effects on cognition based on top-down factors such as perceived control and decision making. However, little is known about the relationship between one's conscious awareness of intention to act and one's perceived control over life events. Rigoni et al. (2011) attempt to address this issue by investigating the neural correlates associated with manipulating belief in free will. Participants who read a passage of text negating the concept of free will showed decreased RP amplitude, but not W-judgment latency, during the Libet task in comparison to those who read a neutral passage of text. Rigoni et al.'s (2011) work demonstrates the relationship between neural activity associated with action execution and higher level beliefs while demonstrating the malleability of both. However, it is still unclear to what extent pre-existing perceptions of control and awareness of conscious intention to act are related. Therefore, the current research aims to investigate how individual differences in perceived control and self-awareness correlate with one another and with awareness of intention to act.

MATERIALS AND METHODS

ETHICAL APPROVAL

Prior to data collection, ethical approval was granted by Bangor University's Ethics Board. All participants were recruited via the universities recruitment site and were offered printer credits or course credits as compensation for taking part. Written consent was obtained from all participants before beginning the experiment.

TRIALS AND PROCEDURE

A repeated measures design was used to allow for correlational data analysis and to reduce inter-subject variance. Analysis consisted of a multiple regression to assess whether AS and IS predicted performance on the Libet task. A separate correlation was run using Interoceptive sensitivity scores and AS scores. All tasks (clock, questionnaire, and heart-rate) were counterbalanced across participants.

Clock task

The stimuli used were similar to that of Libet et al. (1983), consisting of a black clock hand rotating around a clock-like object on a white background (stimuli remained on screen during inter-trial intervals). The clock hand disappeared during the judgment part of the task (see Procedure). During each trial the clock hand rotated around the clock 3 times (2 s per rotation, 6 s in total). The hand completed three full rotations for every trial (including response trials) to prevent the stop position of the hand from influencing the W-judgment. Participants were instructed to allow one full rotation of the clock hand around the clock and to click the mouse at any point during the final two rotations if they felt the urge to do so. On response trials, following three rotations of the clock hand, the clock hand disappeared and a question mark appeared in the middle of the screen. The participant was instructed to use the mouse to make a retrospective judgment of when they first became aware of the urge to act. "Using the mouse, please mark the point on the clock that the clock hand was at when you first became aware of the urge to act." The next trial began once a mouse click was detected. Trials where no response occurred were excluded from the final analysis. There were 60 trials during the task but, due to the voluntary nature, there was variation in the number of trials included for each individual.

Interoceptive sensitivity task

Participants' heart beat estimates were recorded as well as actual heart beats using an electrocardiogram (electrodes were attached to both wrists and one ankle of the participant). The task consisted of six blocks of varying length (35 s, 45 s, 100 s, repeated) in a randomized order across participants to allow for reliable and varied estimates between participants. Intervals between blocks also varied in length (75 s, 65 s, 55 s and immediate start) – these were also randomized across participants. Participants were instructed to count their heart beats to the best of their ability without taking their pulse. Participants were instructed to close their eyes throughout the experiment and to count their heartbeats to the best of their ability without taking their pulse. Upon hearing a single tone, they were to start counting, upon hearing two short tones; they were required to verbally report the number of heartbeats they had counted.

ASQ

Participants were required to answer the 12 items on the ASQ. Each item consisted of a scenario (for example, "You meet a friend who acts hostilely toward you") followed by four questions (one qualitative – "Write down one major cause for this event") – the questions were the same for all items. The participant was required to give an example of one major cause for the scenario and to rate this cause across three, 7-point, likert scales to assess internality ("Is this cause due to something about you or to something about other people or circumstances?"), stability ("In the future, will this cause again be present?") and globality, respectively ("Is the cause unique to this situation or does it also influence other areas of your life?").

DATA ANALYSIS

Clock task

Only data from response trials was included in the analysis. If number of response trials were more than 2 SD away from the mean, that participant's data was excluded from analysis. The angle of the clock-hand on the clock when the participant made a button press was recorded as well as the angle the mouse was at during the judgment phase of the task. Both angles were converted into time by dividing the angle score by π. To obtain the difference scores, the time of action was taken from the W-judgment time to produce a negative number. Therefore, the closer the difference score was to 0, the smaller the distance between action execution and W-judgment.

Interoceptive sensitivity task

The following formula was used to calculate an average accuracy score (scores were summed for all six trials prior to entry into the formula):

$$\sum 1 - \left[\frac{|\text{Recorded Heartbeats} - \text{Counted Heartbeats}|}{\text{Recorded Heartbeats}}\right]$$

This was then multiplied by 100 to give a percentage accuracy score. Participants who provided more accurate estimates had a higher accuracy score thought to be indicative of better interoceptive sensitivity (Schandry, 1981).

ASQ

It is worth noting that the questionnaire's subscale reliability is low (internality, $r = 0.54$; stability, $r = 0.65$, globality; $r = 0.59$; Peterson et al., 1982), however, when compounding the scales together, the reliability is vastly improved (positive AS, $r = 0.75$, negative AS, $r = 0.72$). As we were concerned with a holistic representation of perceived control, we analyzed response on the questionnaire by taking an average across all the scales for positive and negative questions, respectively. To obtain an overall AS score for each participant, scores from all three subscales for each of the six questions with a positive valence were summed and divided by 18, the same was done for the six questions with a negative valence. The negative composite score was then taken from the positive composite score to obtain an overall composite score of attributional style. Higher scores were indicative of a more positive AS (more likely to attribute positive events to internal, stable, global attributes, and negative events to external, transient, specific attributes).

RESULTS

Three participants were removed due to incomplete data on the heartbeat task (electrode recordings were too noisy) and two participants were removed due to outlier data (one for only completing six trials on the Libet task, and 1 because of an average W-judgment further than 2 SD from the group mean). Due to the voluntary nature of the Libet task, the number of trials completed varied between participants (responses $M = 45.84$, SD $= 12.91$). Data for 25 participants (13 female, Mean age = 23.6, range = 20–39) was included in the analysis. Descriptive statistics from the Libet task represent the latency between W-judgment and action execution in milliseconds (this is a negative number as awareness occurred before action onset in all participants), while percentage scores were used for data from the heartbeat task and composite scores were used to represent performance on the attributional style questionnaire (see **Table 1**).

PREDICTION OF MEAN W-JUDGMENT FROM AS AND IS SCORES

A multiple regression was conducted to establish the relationship between performance on the Libet task, heartbeat accuracy and AS scores. The "Mean W-judgment" variable was used as the outcome variable with the "Attributional Style" and "Heartbeat Accuracy" variables acting as predictors. Predictor variables were entered using the forced entry method due to the exploratory nature of the research. Diagnostic tests did not reveal any violations of the test statistics. Multi-collinearity between predictor variables was not observed during diagnostic tests in the multiple regression ($VIF = 1.22$, $Tolerance = 0.82$) and normality was assumed. The regression model was found to be significant ($R^2 = 0.32$, $F(2,22) = 5.08$, $p = 0.015$) suggesting that the two predictor variables ("Heartbeat Accuracy" and "Attributional Style") explained 31.6% of the variance (see **Table 2**). ASQ score was a significant predictor of mean W-judgment but heartbeat accuracy score was not (see **Figure 1**).

RELATIONSHIP BETWEEN AS AND IS

A separate correlation was run to investigate the relationship between "Attributional Style" and "Heartbeat Accuracy". A medium negative correlation was observed at a 2-tailed significance level, $r(23) = -0.43$, $p = 0.034$ (see **Figure 2**).

DISCUSSION

The results indicate that, while performance on the ASQ can predict performance on the Libet task (consistent with our predictions), IS was not a significant predictor of Libet performance, contrary to our predictions. Specifically, more negative AS scores correlate with more negative W-judgments (further away from action onset). A significant relationship was also observed between AS score and IS.

Table 1 | Descriptive statistics for W-judgment, AS score and heartbeat accuracy.

	W-judgment (ms)	ASQ (7-point Likert)	Heartbeat accuracy (%)
Mean (SD)	−253ms (198 ms)	0.29 (1.06)	65.93 (15.84)
Min/Max	−640/−30	−2.28/1.78	36.41/96.96

Values in parentheses indicate standard deviation.

Table 2 | The unstandardised (u) and standardized (s) beta coefficients as predictors of W-judgment.

Variables	B (u)	β (s)	*p*
ASQ (SE)	0.115 (0.036)	0.617	0.004
Heartbeat accuracy (SE)	0.002 (0.002)	0.198	0.321

Values in parentheses represent the standard error. $R^2 = 0.32$ *(*$p = 0.015$*).*

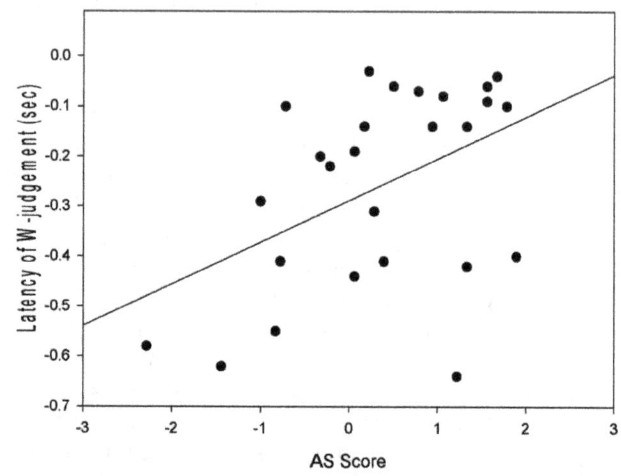

FIGURE 1 | Prediction of Mean W-judgment scores from attributional style scores (AS Score), with linear regression ($R^2 = 0.32$, $p = 0.015$).

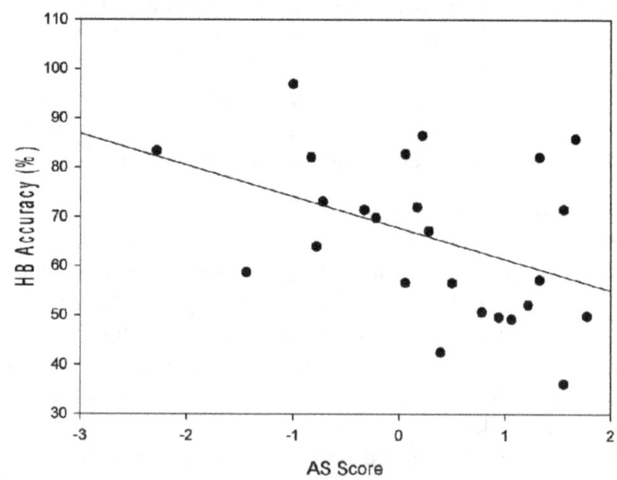

FIGURE 2 | The relationship between AS Score and heartbeat accuracy score (%; HB Accuracy), $r = -0.43$, $p = 0.034$.

Firstly, it is important to note that this research serves as a replication of Libet et al. (1983) original findings in that the mean W-judgment across the entire sample ($M = -253$ ms) was similar to that of Libet's sample ($M = -206$ ms). This is also consistent with other replications of the Libet experiment for example, Lau et al. (2004) reported a $M = -228$ ms while investigating fMRI correlates of voluntary action and Rigoni et al. (2011) also approximately replicate Libet's findings while demonstrating that reducing belief in free will correlates with significant reduction in early RP amplitude, but not with a change in W-judgment (Reduced belief group $M = -242$, Control group $M = -223$). As our data is consistent with the literature, it is possible that individual differences in AS may have had undetected effects on previous findings in the same way as the current research. The large variance of W-judgment values in the literature may be indicative of these individual differences (i.e., Libet et al., 1983). Furthermore, given the direction of the previous literature (for example, Libet et al., 1983; Matsuhashi and Hallett, 2008), it is safe to presume that an overall average W-judgment of −253 ms will follow onset of the RP by several hundred milliseconds.

More negative mean scores are indicative of a larger discrepancy between W-judgment and action execution. This would suggest that those with a more negative AS may be aware of the intention to act sooner than those with a positive AS. It may also be that W-judgment accuracy is affected by these top-down personality factors. This suggests that, even if criticisms surrounding the paradigm were addressed; such as those related to reliance on recall of the urge to act, (for example, Dennett and Kinsbourne, 1992), personality variants may still affect awareness of the urge to act.

This research raises questions surrounding belief in free will – i.e., that a larger veto period may relate to a pessimistic AS. It may be that individuals with a more negative AS may perceive themselves as having less control (and, therefore, less free will) due to a disassociation between action awareness and action execution. Marcel (2003) argues that ownership of action can be separated into ownership of action execution and ownership of action intention. Therefore, a temporal dissociation between the two may reduce the ownership one feels over action execution. In turn, this may lead to a perceived lack of control as intention in the individual's schema is not bound to execution.

It is possible that those with a more pessimistic AS may be more uncertain in the choices they make, as is consistent with research into pessimistic AS (e.g., Bunce and Peterson, 1997; Boudreaux and Ozer, 2013), while those with a more positive AS are more likely to claim ownership over the action resulting in a smaller latency between W-judgment and action onset. Therefore, the pattern in the W-judgments may simply reflect level of self-doubt and uncertainty in those with a negative AS. This theory is consistent with research into negative AS and self-doubt (Heppner et al., 1985; Bunce and Peterson, 1997).

It is most likely that the relationship observed between AS and W-judgment is heavily influenced by aspects of internality (i.e., "is the cause of a life event due to the individual or to an external factor?"). This was not assessed specifically because of the desire to investigate the relationship between a more holistic representation of perceived control and awareness of intention to act. Furthermore, the poor subscale reliability of the ASQ meant that this relationship was not explored in an additional analysis. However, future research should also employ the LOC questionnaire to assess whether individuals with larger latency between W-judgment and action execution have a more external LOC independent of valence. Furthermore, research should investigate whether those with a positive AS will experience greater ownership over their actions than those with a negative AS. To our knowledge, this research is the first to consider the possible negative implications of having a longer "veto" period. Traditional literature into volition implicates the veto period in conscious control of action (Libet, 1999; Mele, 2008), however, until now, no research has investigated individual differences in the veto period. If the above theory is true, it may be that a larger veto period (indicative of greater control over one's actions) correlates with reduced levels of perceived control.

The regression analysis demonstrated that IS did not predict awareness of conscious intention to act. However, the results indicate a medium, negative correlation between IS and AS suggesting that the more negative (or pessimistic) an individual's AS, the better they are at estimating their own heartbeats. Both AS and IS have been shown to correlate with anxiety (Domschke et al., 2010; Mark and Smith, 2012). Therefore, the effect here may relate to a hyper-awareness seen in those with anxiety disorders. It is also possible that, due to the correlation with depressive symptoms (Seligman, 2002), those with a negative AS have a tendency to self-evaluate and, therefore, are more self-aware. It is important to note that researches into the correlates of IS are inconsistent, so more work is still needed in the area (see der Does et al., 2000).

Future research should focus on furthering understanding of individual differences in performance on the Libet task (and other tasks related to awareness of conscious intention to act), and what these differences relate to. More specifically, a causal relationship between AS and W-judgment should be investigated by attempting to manipulate AS (for example, see Anderson, 1983) score and, in turn, modulate performance on the Libet task. This could establish whether perceived control over positive and negative life events may have a causal impact on awareness of conscious intention to act. Manipulating AS score could also be used to investigate a causal relationship between AS and IS. Further investigation is required to uncover latent variables which may modulate the relationships in question. These findings would be strengthened by using EEG to investigate potential neural correlates, specifically the LRP.

Implications of this research are potentially wide ranging; specifically this research informs literature relating to agency, action ownership and AS. Additionally, this research takes a step toward understanding individual differences in awareness of intention to act. More generally, this research suggests that perceived control and volition are related.

In conclusion, it is clear that a relationship exists between performance on the Libet task and performance on the ASQ. It is possible therefore, that some of the variance in the Libet task results from individual differences in top-down traits such as personality variants. The current research highlights potential confounds in the W-judgment related to fluctuations in AS. Furthermore, this research demonstrates that, those with a more negative AS may have a larger latency between W-judgment and action onset. It is proposed that this relationship may result from a discrepancy between conscious awareness of the intention to move, and the consequence of this (action onset) suggesting, for the first time, potential negative implications of a longer veto period.

ACKNOWLEDGMENT

We would like to thank Dr. Julie Davies for her contribution to the statistics used.

REFERENCES

Anderson, C. A. (1983). Motivational and performance deficits in interpersonal settings: the effect of attributional style. *J. Pers. Soc. Psychol.* 45, 1136–1147. doi: 10.1037/0022-3514.45.5.1136

Baumeister, R. F., and Brewer, L. E. (2012). Believing versus disbelieving in free will: correlates and consequences. *Soc. Personal. Psychol. Compass* 6, 736–745. doi: 10.1111/j.1751-9004.2012.00458.x

Berlucchi, G., and Aglioti, S. M. (2010). The body in the brain. *Exp. Brain Res.* 200, 25–35. doi: 10.1007/s00221-009-1970-7

Boudreaux, M. J., and Ozer, D. J. (2013). Goal conflict, goal striving, and psychological well-being. *Motiv. Emot.* 37, 433–443. doi: 10.1007/s11031-012-9333-2

Bunce, S. C., and Peterson, C. (1997). Gender differences in personality correlates of explanatory style. *Pers. Individ. Dif.* 23, 639–646. doi: 10.1016/S0191-8869(97)00072-X

Craig, A. D. (2002). How do You Feel? Interoception: the sense of the physiological condition of the body. *Nat. Rev. Neurosci.* 3, 655–666. doi: 10.1038/nrn894

Craig, A. D. (2004). Human feelings: why are some more aware than others? T*rends Cogn. Sci.* 8, 239–241. doi: 10.1016/j.tics.2004.04.004

Craig, A. D. (2010). The sentient self. *Brain Struct. Funct.* 214, 563–577. doi: 10.1007/s00429-010-0248-y

Critchley, H. D., Wiens, S., Rotshtein, P., Öhman, A., and Dolan, R. J. (2004). Neural systems supporting interoceptive awareness. *Nat. Neurosci.* 7, 189–195. doi: 10.1038/nn1176

Damasio, A. R., Everitt, B. J., and Bishop, D. (1996). The somatic marker hypothesis and the possible functions of the prefrontal cortex [and discussion]. *Philos. Trans. R. Soc. Lond. B Biol. Sci.* 351, 1413–1420. doi: 10.1098/rstb.1996.0125

Dennett, D., and Kinsbourne, M. (1992). Time and the observer: the where and when of consciousness in the brain. *Behav. Brain Res.* 15, 210–274. doi: 10.1017/S0140525X00068229

der Does, V., Willem, A. J., Antony, M. M., Ehlers, A., and Barsky, A. J. (2000). Heartbeat perception in panic disorder: a reanalysis. *Behav. Res. Ther.* 38, 47–62. doi: 10.1007/s00221-004-2183-8

Domschke, K., Stevens, S., Pfleiderer, B., and Gerlach, A. L. (2010). Interoceptive sensitivity in anxiety and anxiety disorders: an overview and integration of neurobiological findings. *Clin. Psychol. Rev.* 30, 1–11. doi: 10.1016/j.cpr.2009.08.008

Fried, I., Mukamel, R., and Kreiman, G. (2011). Internally generated preactivation of single neurons in human medial frontal cortex predicts volition. *Neuron* 69, 548–562. doi: 10.1016/j.neuron.2010.11.045

Forgeard, M. J. C., and Seligman, M. E. P. (2012). Seeing the glass half full: a review of the causes and consequences of optimism. *Prat. Psychol.* 18, 107–120. doi: 10.1016/j.prps.2012.02.002

Haggard, P., Clark, S., and Kalogeras, J. (2002). Voluntary action and conscious awareness. *Nat. Neurosci.* 5, 382–385. doi: 10.1038/nn827

Haggard, P., and Eimer, M. (1999). On the relation between brain potentials and the awareness of voluntary movements. *Exp. Brain Res.* 126, 128–133. doi: 10.1007/s002210050722

Haggard, P., and Libet, B. (2001). Conscious intention and brain activity. *J. Conscious. Stud.* 8, 47–64.

Heppner, P. P., Baumgardner, A., and Jackson, J. (1985). Problem-solving self-appraisal, depression, and attributional style: are they related? *Cogn. Ther. Res.* 9, 105–113. doi: 10.1007/BF01178754

Lau, H. C., Rogers, R. D., Haggard, P., and Passingham, R. E. (2004). Attention to intention. *Science* 303, 1208–1210. doi: 10.1126/science.1090973

Libet, B. (1999). Do we have free will? *J. Conscious. Stud.* 6, 47–57.

Libet, B., Gleason, C. A., Wright, E. W., and Pearl, D. K. (1983). Time of conscious intention to act in relation to onset of cerebral activity (readiness-potential) the unconscious initiation of a freely voluntary act. *Brain* 106, 623–642. doi: 10.1093/brain/106.3.623

Luder Deecke, P. S., and Kornhuber, H. H. (1969). Distribution of readiness potential, pre-motion positivity, and motor potential of the human cerebral cortex preceding voluntary finger movements. *Exp. Brain Res.* 7, 158–168. doi: 10.1007/BF00235441

Luten, A. G., Ralph, J. A., and Mineka, S. (1997). Pessimistic attributional style: is it specific to depression versus anxiety versus negative affect? *Behav. Res. Ther.* 35, 703–719. doi: 10.1016/S0005-7967(97)00027-2

Marcel, A. (2003). "The sense of agency: awareness and ownership of action," in *Agency and Self-Awareness*, eds J. Roessler and N. Eilan (Oxford: Clarendon Press), 48–93.

Mark, G., and Smith, A. P. (2012). Effects of occupational stress, job characteristics, coping, andattributional style on the mental health and job satisfaction of university employees. *Anxiety Stress Coping* 25, 63–78. doi: 10.1080/10615806.2010.548088

Matsuhashi, M., and Hallett, M. (2008). The timing of conscious intention to move. *Eur. J. Neurosci.* 28, 2344–2351. doi: 10.1111/j.1460-9568.2008.06525.x

Mele, A. R. (2008). "Psychology and free will: a commentary," in *Are We Free?* eds J. Baer, J. C. Kaufman, and R. F. Baumeister (New York: Oxford University Press), 325–346.

Orellana-Damacela, L. E., Tindale, R. S., and Suárez-Balcázar, Y. (2000). Decisional and behavioral procrastination: how they relate to self-discrepancies. *J. Soc. Behav. Pers.*15, 225–238.

Paulhus, D. L., and Carey, J. M. (2011). The FAD-Plus: measuring lay beliefs regarding free will related constructs. *J. Pers. Assess.* 93, 96–104. doi: 10.1080/00223891.2010.528483

Peterson, C., Semmel, A., Von Baeyer, C., Abramson, L. Y., Metalsky, G. I., and Selgiman, M. E. P. (1982). The attributional style questionnaire. *Cognit. Ther. Res.* 6, 287–300. doi: 10.1007/BF01173577

Rigoni, D., Kühn, S., Sartori, G., and Brass, M. (2011). Inducing disbelief in free will alters brain correlates of preconscious motor preparation: the brain ninds whether we believe in free will or not. *Psychol. Sci.* 22, 613–618.

Rotter, J. B. (1966). Generalized expectancies of internal versus external control of reinforcements. *Psychol. Monogr.* 80, 1–28. doi: 10.1037/h0092976

Schandry, R. (1981). Heart eat perception and emotional experience. *Psychophysiology* 18, 483–488. doi: 10.1111/j.1469-8986.1981.tb02486.x

Schurger, A., Sitt, J. D., and Dehaene, S. (2012). An accumulator model for spontaneous neural activity prior to self-initiated movement. *Proc. Natl. Acad. Sci. U.S.A.* 109, E2904–E2913. doi: 10.1073/pnas.1210467109

Seligman, M. E. P. (2002). "Positive psychology, positive prevention, and positive therapy," in *Handbook of Positive Psychology*, eds E. R. Snyder and S. J. Lopez (New York: Oxford University Press), 1–9.

Seligman, M. E. P., Schulman, P., DeRubeis, R. J., and Hollon, S. D. (1999). The prevention of depression and anxiety. *Prev. Treat.* 2:8a.

Sinnott-Armstrong, W., and Nadel, L. (2011). "Introduction," in *Conscious Will and Responsibility*, eds W. Sinnott-Armstrong and L. Nadel (New York: Oxford University Press), 11–16.

Soon, C. S., Brass, M., Heinze, H. J., and Haynes, J. D. (2008). Unconscious determinants of free decisions in the human brain. *Nat. Neurosci.* 11, 543–545. doi: 10.1038/nn.2112

Stange, J. P., Sylvia, L. G., da Silva Magalhaes, P. V., Miklowitz, D. J., Otto, M. W., Frank, E., et al. (2013). Extreme attributions predict the course of bipolar depression: results from the STEP-BD randomised controlled trial of psychosocial treatment. *J. Clin. Psychiatry* 74, 249–255. doi: 10.4088/JCP.12m08019

Stroessner, S. J., and Green, C. W. (1990). Effects of belief in free will or determinism on attitudes toward punishment and locus of control. *J. Soc. Psychol.* 130, 789–799. doi: 10.1080/00224545.1990.9924631

Waszak, F., Wascher, E., Keller, P., Koch, I., Aschersleben, G., Rosenbaum, D. A., et al. (2005). Intention-based and stimulus-based mechanisms in action selection. *Exp. Brain Res.* 162, 346–356. doi: 10.1007/s00221-004-2183-8

Werner, N. S., Schweitzer, N., Meindl, T., Duschek, S., Kambeitz, J., and Schandry, R. (2013). Interoceptive awareness moderates neural activity during decision-making. *Biol. Psychol.* 94, 498–506. doi: 10.1016/j.biopsycho.2013.09.002

16

The experience of agency in human-computer interactions

Hannah Limerick[1], David Coyle[1]* and James W. Moore[2,3]

[1]
[2] Department of Computer Science, Bristol Interaction and Graphics, University of Bristol, Bristol, UK
[3] Department of Psychology, Goldsmiths, University of London, London, UK
School of Experimental Psychology, University of Bristol, Bristol, UK

***Correspondence:**
David Coyle, Department of Computer Science, Bristol Interaction and Graphics, University of Bristol, Merchant Ventures Building, Woodland Row, Bristol, BS8 1UB, UK
e-mail: david.coyle@bristol.ac.uk

The sense of agency is the experience of controlling both one's body and the external environment. Although the sense of agency has been studied extensively, there is a paucity of studies in applied "real-life" situations. One applied domain that seems highly relevant is human-computer-interaction (HCI), as an increasing number of our everyday agentive interactions involve technology. Indeed, HCI has long recognized the feeling of control as a key factor in how people experience interactions with technology. The aim of this review is to summarize and examine the possible links between sense of agency and understanding control in HCI. We explore the overlap between HCI and sense of agency for computer input modalities and system feedback, computer assistance, and joint actions between humans and computers. An overarching consideration is how agency research can inform HCI and vice versa. Finally, we discuss the potential ethical implications of personal responsibility in an ever-increasing society of technology users and intelligent machine interfaces.

Keywords: sense of agency, human computer interaction, control, technology, computer assistance, joint action

INTRODUCTION

The sense of agency is the experience of controlling both one's body and the external environment. This experience has received a considerable amount of attention in the field of cognitive neuroscience, due in part to the recognition that a disordered sense of agency is central to illnesses such as schizophrenia (Frith, 1992). The sense of agency is also an important part of human consciousness more generally, forming a fundamental aspect of self-awareness (Gallagher, 2002). In this review, we will primarily focus on the sense of agency for control over the external environment. This is because it is most pertinent to the human-computer-interaction (HCI) issues we consider.

The sense of agency is a vital consideration for assessing how people experience interactions with technology, a core focus for research in the field of HCI. The seventh of Shneiderman's Rules of Interface Design states that designers should strive to create computer interfaces that *"support an internal locus of control"* (Shneiderman and Plaisant, 2004). This is based on the observation that users *"strongly desire the sense that they are in charge of the system and that the system responds to their actions"*. What makes our understanding of agency in HCI especially pertinent is the fact that an increasing number of our everyday agentive interactions involve technology. During interactions with technology, the simple process of producing an action to cause an intended outcome is endowed with a whole host of possible variables that can alter the agentive experience dramatically. Thus both cognitive neuroscience and HCI seek to understand how humans experience agency and control over action execution. The aim of this review is to examine the links between sense of agency in cognitive neuroscience and HCI and highlight some possible new research directions.

We pose that an interdisciplinary combination of HCI research and cognitive neuroscience to investigate the sense of agency can provide a rich and promising new research area that has the potential to inform both fields in novel ways. Research into the sense of agency stands to benefit from the new interaction techniques rapidly being developed in the field of HCI such as gestural input, physiological or intelligent interfaces and assistance methods. Thus enabling novel ways of producing actions to be incorporated into such research. Moreover, testing agency in more "real-world" settings can lead to new insights regarding the nature and parameters of agentive experiences in everyday interactions. Equally, HCI research can take advantage of the relative maturity of neurocognitive research and the reliable metrics for the experience of volitional control that have been developed. An incorporation of such metrics will encourage the HCI researcher to consider the sense of agency as a quantifiable experience in future research. Furthermore, understanding the neurocognitive processes and mechanisms that support this experience provides an important evidence base and guide for interface design. The first section of this paper briefly considers the theoretical and methodological background of research on the sense of agency. We then discuss the potential implications and areas of overlap of these theories and methods for three specific areas of HCI research: (1) input modalities and system feedback;

(2) computer assistance; and (3) collaboration and attribution of agency.

THEORETICAL AND METHODOLOGICAL BACKGROUND INTO THE SENSE OF AGENCY

As stated above, the sense of agency is the experience of controlling both one's body and the external environment. On this definition, control is central to the experience of being an agent. In the psychological literature a number of studies have investigated the relationship between control and agency. For example, it has been shown that sense of agency is altered by a manipulation of the statistical relationship between actions and effects (Moore et al., 2009) and by a manipulation of the perception of control over action (Desantis et al., 2011). More recent work by Kumar and Srinivasan (2014) has also looked at how sense of agency is influenced by control specified at different hierarchical levels. This work shows, in part, that when higher-level control is exercised (i.e., goal-level control) lower level control processes (i.e., perceptuo-motor control) have no influence on sense of agency. This relationship between control and sense of agency is highly relevant in the context of HCI, given the fact that different HCI applications involve different kinds of control manipulations.

A phenomenological distinction has been made between the "Feeling of Agency" and the "Judgement of Agency" (Synofzik et al., 2008). The feeling of agency refers to the implicit, pre-reflective, low-level feeling of being the agent of an action. The judgement of agency describes the explicit judgement and attribution of agency to oneself or another on a conceptual level. Traditionally there are two theoretical views regarding the neurocognitive processes underlying the sense of agency. Some have suggested that the sense of agency arises principally from internal processes serving motor control (Blakemore et al., 2002; Haggard, 2005). On the other hand, external situational cues have been emphasized (Wegner, 2002, 2003). However, it is now becoming increasingly recognized that this is a false dichotomy and that various cues contribute to the sense of agency (Wegner and Sparrow, 2004; Wegner et al., 2004; Moore et al., 2009; Moore and Fletcher, 2012; Kranick and Hallett, 2013). These cues include internal sensorimotor signals and external situational information (Moore and Fletcher, 2012). Moreover, it has been suggested that the influence of these cues depends on their reliability (Moore and Fletcher, 2012), implying some form of optimal cue integration. According to the cue integration concept, multiple agency cues are weighted by their relative reliability and then optimally integrated to reduce the variability of the estimated origins of an action.

Researchers have developed numerous ways of measuring the components of the sense of agency experimentally. The explicit judgement of agency is typically measured by verbal report by asking participants to rate their feeling of agency during a task or simply state whether they were the agent or not. Measures have also been developed to probe implicit aspects of sense of agency. These include sensory attenuation paradigms (e.g., Blakemore et al., 1998) and intentional binding (e.g., Haggard et al., 2002). In this review we focus primarily on intentional binding. In this paradigm participants report the perceived time of voluntary action initiation and the consequent effects using the so-called Libet clock. Haggard et al. (2002) found that when participants caused an action, their perceived time of initiation and the perceived time of the outcome where brought closer together, i.e., the perceived interval between voluntary actions and outcomes was shorter than the actual interval (**Figure 1**). In the case of involuntary actions the perceived interval was found to be longer than the actual interval. This phenomenon is known as "intentional binding", and is seen as an implicit metric for the sense agency.

Intentional binding is a widely used implicit measure of the sense agency and the effect has been replicated widely and in a number of settings (e.g., see Wohlschläger et al., 2003; Engbert and Wohlschläger, 2007; Moore et al., 2009; Aarts and van den Bos, 2011). More recently, alternative intentional binding measures have been developed, such as the direct interval estimation procedure where the participant is required to estimate the interval between actions and outcomes (e.g., see Moore et al., 2009; Humphreys and Buehner, 2009; Coyle et al., 2012). As stated above, intentional binding is the predominant measure considered in this review. The main reason for this is that while it seems particularly well suited to the nature of agent interaction during many interactions with technology, it has not yet been widely applied in the HCI domain. One key advantage of intentional binding in the context of HCI is that it is typically measured at sub-second sensorimotor timescales, which are common in HCI. An additional benefit of intentional binding in the context of HCI is that it offers a measure of the *degree* of sense of agency the individual experiences, rather than being a binary "me" vs. "not me" measure. However, it is important to note that intentional binding may not be best suited for assessing sense of agency for all types of tasks within HCI, such as those agentive interactions operating at much longer timescales (although see Faro et al., 2013, for review of literature suggesting that binding may operate at longer timescales).

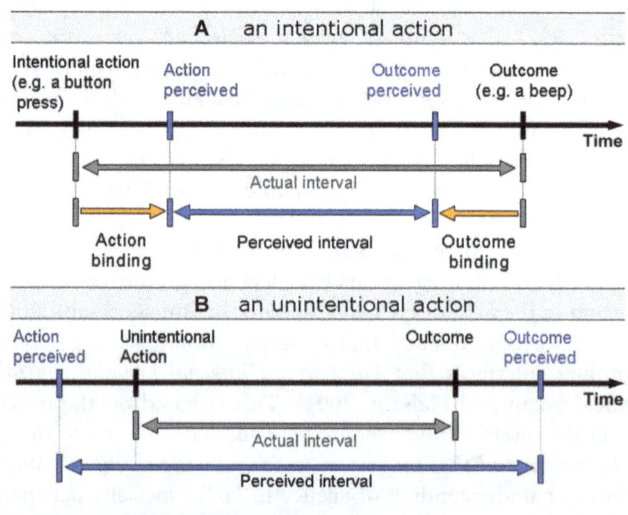

FIGURE 1 | Intentional Binding. (A) During voluntary action, the perceived time of action and outcome are shifted toward one another, resulting in a shorter perceived interval between action and outcome. **(B)** During involuntary actions, the perceived time interval between action and outcome is longer than the actual delay.

INPUT MODALITIES AND SYSTEM FEEDBACK

The first point of contact between the sense of agency and HCI we wish to consider is the importance of input modalities. Input modalities are the sensors or devices by which the computer receives input from the human, e.g., a keyboard or mouse. The input modality is central to the process of producing actions in order to bring about the user's desired state changes in the computer and thus also central to the sense of agency over the action. HCI research is interested in how to optimally turn psychological states (such as intentions) into state changes within the computer. The user's intentions and the system's state differ considerably in form and content and one of the challenges of HCI is to bridge this gap. This separation is known as the Gulf of Execution (Norman, 1986). The input modality of the system is central to bridging the Gulf of Execution. Norman (1986) states:

> *"Execution of an action means to do something, whether it is just to say something or perform a complex motor sequence. Just what physical actions are required is determined by the choice of input devices on the system, and this can make a major difference in the usability of the system. Because some physical actions are more difficult than others, the choice of input devices can affect the selection of actions which in turn affects how well the system matches with intentions".*

More recently a similar message has been emphasized by Williamson et al. (2009) who state:

> *"A computer interface facilitates control. It provides a set of mechanisms by which a human can drive the belief of a system about a user's intentions towards a desired state over a period of time. Control requires both display to the user and input from the user; computers feedback state to a user, who modifies his or her actions to bring about the required change of state".*

In recent years HCI researchers have developed a wide range of new interaction techniques and devices such as speech and gestural control. These are rapidly becoming common place, with everyday devices having the option of being controlled by such interaction including, smart phones (Apple's Siri), televisions (Samsung's Smart TV), computers (Leap Motion) and games consoles (Microsoft Kinect). Each new method of controlling technology presents new challenges to HCI researchers. New input modalities offer different ways of "bridging the Gulf of Execution" including distinct action initiation requirements, feedback mechanisms, and device capabilities (**Figure 2**). This has the potential to dramatically reshape the experience of control and agency. In this section we consider some of the ways in which agency research can help to inform such issues. From a cognitive neuroscience perspective different modes of action execution pose interesting questions. Experimental investigations into the sense of agency have typically involved participants controlling their environment via conventional input devices such as a keyboard or mouse. Altering the sensorimotor requirements for action execution presents an opportunity to further investigate the sense of agency during distinctly new sensorimotor requirements.

INPUT MODALITIES

To begin addressing the impact of input modalities on the sense of agency, Coyle et al. (2012) conducted an experiment employing intentional binding as an implicit measure of users' sense of agency for two distinctive input techniques. In one condition participants pressed a button on a keyboard to cause an outcome (a beep). In the second condition participants wore a skin-based input device and tapped their arm to cause a beep (**Figure 3**). Results show that intentional binding was significantly greater for skin-based input than the keyboard input, thus indicating a stronger sense of agency with skin-based input. From an input design perspective this is interesting as it indicates that skin-based input is experienced as significantly more responsive than button-based input. More broadly, Coyle et al. provided evidence that different interaction techniques can provide different experiences of agency to those offered by traditional mouse or keyboard interactions. It also demonstrated the potential of intentional binding to quantify this difference. In future this method can be used to assess and quantify the differences for a larger range of interaction techniques, including changes more subtle than those assessed here. We could for example assess the difference in the experience of agency during interactions with a touch screen via a stylus vs. direct finger interaction, or differences in interactions that incorporate techniques such as haptic, embodied or physiological input. We can also compare the different interaction experiences for a specific input technique when other conditions of the interactions change, e.g., when conditions such as system feedback, reliability or latency are varied. Greater consideration is given to these possibilities below.

The finding that skin-based input results in greater intentional binding also raises interesting questions regarding the underlying cognitive processes for the sense of agency. One possible explanation for the higher sense of implicit agency measured in the skin-based input is that, with a self directed, skin-based action, there is a higher degree of congruence between the internally predicted sensory output of the action and the actual sensory output of the action. Intentional binding may be strengthened when the individual is more sensorially aware of their action. Another possible explanation in line with the cue integration theory for agency is that for the skin-input conditions, participants receive additional sensory agency cues from the passive limb, which is acting as the input modality. This may serve to increase sense of agency. A final possible explanation is linked to the finding that actions aimed at the self are associated with increased activity within the motor system (Master and Tremblay, 2010). Given that the sense of agency is closely tied to sensorimotor processes, increased activity within this system might increase the sense of agency. These are all possibilities that we are currently exploring. Whatever the explanation, this study shows how the new modes of interaction being developed in HCI can open up new avenues of enquiry for the neurocognitive understanding of the sense of agency.

RELIABILITY

Coyle et al. (2012) represents an early application of intentional binding to explicitly address an HCI research question. But there are many more specific input design questions and trade offs that

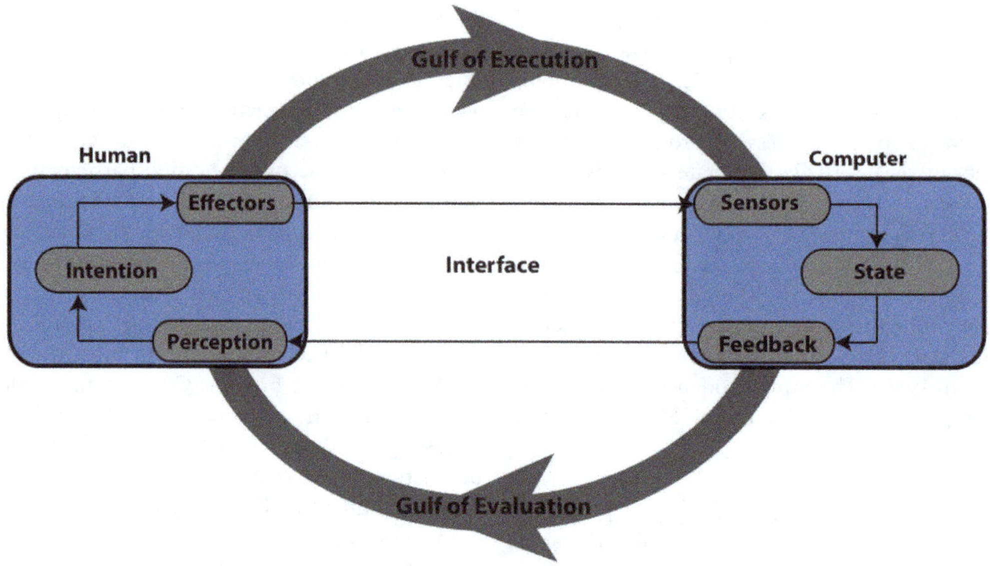

FIGURE 2 | A closed loop input system, based on Norman (1986) and Williamson et al. (2009).

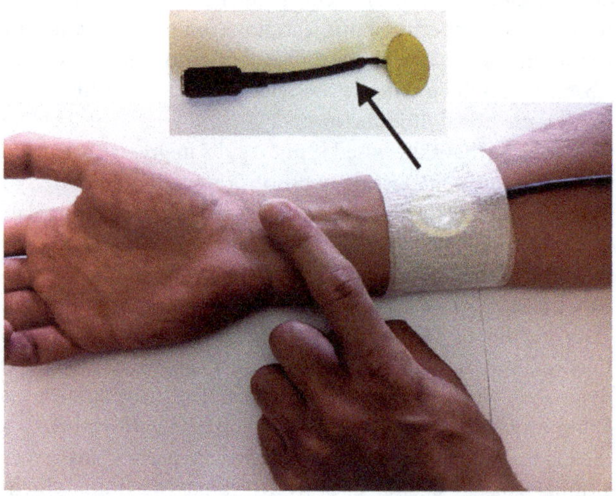

FIGURE 3 | In Coyle et al. (2012) a piezo-electric contact microphone was placed on the user's arm and connected to a computer. Vibrations on the user's arm were monitored to detect when the user tapped on their arm.

can be informed by their approach. System reliability is one such issue.

Many input techniques suffer from varying degrees of reliability, due to the fact that the interaction requires the computer's sensors to recognize and then classify the intention of the user, which is not always clear-cut and often noisy. Consider for example a speech interface and the various possible accents the user may have. A speech system designed to accommodate many different accents is likely to result in more incorrect classifications of peoples' utterances. Speech systems could be made more reliable through initial training periods or by allowing the system more time to classify utterances. But this reduces the responsiveness of the speech input system. In a similar vein a gesture recognition system like the Microsoft Kinect is required to recognize a wide range of mid-air gestures. Even for simple gestures there are variations in the way different people will execute the gesture. A system that allows leeway for variations in action execution will be more flexible, but again may result in more misclassifications of peoples' actions. Designers of such systems are therefore required to make trade-offs between constraints such as accuracy and flexibility, both of which affect system reliability.

Reliability is analogous to the predictability of an action and has been found in neurocognitive research to affect sense of agency. Empirical evidence suggests that participants experience a lower sense of agency for unexpected outcomes of their actions (Sato and Yasuda, 2005). Moore and Haggard (2008) investigated inference and prediction for conditions where there was either a high or low probability of an outcome. The results indicated that in both probability conditions, participants exhibited binding for situations where the action was followed by the outcome. For high probability conditions, participants also exhibited intentional binding for trials where the action was not followed by an outcome, suggesting that a strong prediction was sufficient to generate the binding effect. With regard to input modalities and reliability, these results suggest that the more reliable an input method is, both in terms of matching the intended outcome and in predictability, the greater the sense of agency experienced by the user. In future similar approaches may provide HCI researchers with a concrete means of investigating how reliable a system needs to be before people begin to experience significant reductions in their sense of agency. Evidence from such studies will help designers to make more informed decisions regarding the reliability trade-offs in new input systems.

SYSTEM FEEDBACK

In addition to the input modality, control over a computer system requires feedback to inform the user of the system's current state, the actions required to bring about changes in the system's state in line with their intentions and the success of those actions. The user can then use this feedback to modify their consequent actions to bring about the next desired outcome. In HCI, the mode of feedback and the information the interface provides regarding the system's state is again an important consideration. Parallel to the Gulf of Execution, Norman describes the Gulf of Evaluation (Norman, 1988), which refers to the mismatch between the system's feedback regarding it's actual state and how this state is perceived by the user in terms of their expectations and intentions (see **Figure 2**). The Gulf of Evaluation will differ depending on the particular interface, context, requirements and user expectations. For example, a mobile phone interface and an automatic flight deck will have distinctly different Gulfs of Evaluation and therefore require different forms of feedback to be presented to the user.

Typically, when interacting with technology users make an action and then receive sensory feedback about their action. Consistency between predicted sensory feedback and actual sensory feedback during action execution has been the focus of several studies in cognitive neuroscience. Interestingly, empirical evidence indicates that the sense of agency is malleable and feedback can be distorted to lead participants to misattribute their own actions as being caused by another agent or visa versa. In cases where the outcome of an action is incongruent with participants' predicted sensory outcome, agency can be misattributed to an external source (Sato and Yasuda, 2005). Conversely Sato and Yasuda (2005) also induced a false sense of agency for an externally generated action that matched participants' predictions. Farrer et al. (2008) found that deviations in the visual feedback of a moving curser associated with joystick movement beyond 50° led participants to explicitly attribute their movements to another agent irrespective of their implicit sensorimotor movements. System feedback presented to the user may also be in the form of contextual information. Such feedback might have a profound effect on the user's experience of agency. For example, Desantis et al. (2011) demonstrated that prior causal beliefs about the agent of an action led participants to experience less implicit sense of agency for self-generated actions that they believed to be caused by another agent.

In order to achieve optimal control over an interface it will be beneficial to the interface designer to understand how sensory feedback of the interface modulates the sense of agency in various contexts. Evidence regarding the degree to which sensory feedback should match the user's predicted feedback is valuable for developing effective input modalities. This is especially so, considering the evidence that mismatches between predicted outcome and actual outcome can actually lead to misattributed sense of agency.

LATENCY

Another factor to note when considering input modalities and the sense of agency is the latency imposed between the action and it's consequent outcome. Latency is commonly presented as an issue in HCI due to technological constraints within the system. This can interfere with perceptual constraints such as attention span or memory load. Therefore another key question in HCI research is how best to overcome latency in a way that suits the user's perceptual capacities. An example would be the Roto and Oulasvirta (2005) early work on web browsing on a mobile phone. They identified several temporal constraints, including the speed of the network connection, the phone's processing abilities, and the user's visual attention span. They found that a user's attention typically shifts away from a screen after 4–8 s. At the time of their research, mobile web browsing suffered from page download times being over 5 s. Roto and Oulasvirta suggested that a solution to this is multimodal feedback, with tactile feedback (vibration) helping to reduce the need for visual attention beyond which is natural.

In a similar vein to the web-browsing example, neurocognitive experimental techniques have the potential to validate design decisions regarding latencies in a range of contexts. Empirical evidence indicates that the intentional binding phenomenon breaks down beyond 650 ms for a simple button-pressing task (Haggard et al., 2002). However, there is also evidence for intentional binding still being intact at 2250 ms for a conflict resolution task (Berberian et al., 2012). In order to optimally overcome the effect that latency has on control, an understanding of how the sense of agency behaves and is modulated over time-scales is important. In many cases decisions on latency will also involve trade-offs regarding system feedback and system reliability. For example, an input classification system can be made more reliable by allowing it more time to make an accurate classification of peoples' actions, but this will increase the latency of the system.

BRAIN MACHINE INTERFACES

We conclude this section on input modalities and system feedback by considering one final input technique that has relevance for all of the issues we have discussed above. Brain Machine Interfaces (BMI) use different aspects of the brain's cortical activity such as P300 (Farwell and Donchin, 1988) or slow cortical potentials (Hinterberger et al., 2004) to control objects such as prosthetic arms (Velliste et al., 2008), external devices (Wolpaw and McFarland, 2004) and computer cursers (Kennedy et al., 2000). BMI suffers from variable reliability largely due to the fact that it is EEG based and therefore the bandwidths involved are slow, noisy and suffers variable delays between action and outcome (Williamson et al., 2009). The field of HCI is currently attempting to improve control in BMI to make it more effective in therapeutic contexts. One aspect of this is faster command execution (Minnery and Fine, 2009). Neurocognitive research into the sense of agency may offer insights into ways to modify agency under such latencies. Metrics used to measure the sense of agency can also provide guidance regarding optimum time delays a system can take to respond to an action, beyond which agency starts to break down. BMI has broad feedback channels with the possibility of providing the user with rich sensory feedback (Williamson et al., 2009) and thus these feedback channels could be exploited to provide sensory cues or external contextual cues which increase the experience of agency despite the latencies involved.

COMPUTER ASSISTANCE

Computer systems that assist us in completing tasks are increasingly common and are likely to become ever more commonplace given the increasing capabilities of technology and with the development of a broader range of intelligent machine interfaces. The degree to which computers assist us can vary from "high-assistance", such as fully automatic flight decks, to "low assistance", such as the smoothing or snap to point techniques that are used to make pointing with a mouse on a desktop computer more accurate. The manner in which the computer "assistant" is presented can also vary considerably and be made more or less explicit to the human user. Terveen (1995) identified two broad forms of computer assistance. The first is human emulation, where a computer assistant is endowed with human like abilities and an anthropomorphic representation, which is designed to ultimately mirror human-human interaction. We consider this form of assistance in Section Collaboration and Attribution of Agency below. In the present section we consider Terveen's second category of computer-assisted action. Here the computer assistance is not presented in an anthropomorphic form and the assistance is not always made explicit to the user. The aim of such systems is generally to combine both the human and computer's unique abilities to more effectively achieve a particular goal.

Intelligent interfaces and computer-assisted actions are interesting for many reasons, not least because of the varying degrees of control given to the user and the potential to introduce a grey area between voluntary and involuntary action. HCI research is interested in the many interactions now occurring in this grey area. For example, what happens to a person's sense of agency when they voluntarily initiate an action, but a computer then steps in to complete the action? This agentive ambiguity in interactions with intelligent technologies also presents interesting challenges for research into the sense of agency.

TASK AUTOMATION

Many tasks are now automated by computers and machines, requiring the user to simply monitor the activity and intervene when required. Some automated tasks are already common in everyday life, e.g., aircraft control and factory automation. Other examples, which once seemed like science fiction, are now commonplace in research settings and close to becoming an everyday occurrence, including self-driving cars and robotic surgery. In developing such systems designers need to think carefully about the optimal balance between computer assistance and human sense of agency. This is particularly important in safety critical systems and in semi-automated systems where a human supervising the task is held responsible for task failures.

Berberian et al. (2012) investigated the participants' sense of agency when performing the complex task of flying a plane using a flight simulator under different levels of automation. The task required the participant to observe a flight plan and after a random time interval, a conflict occurred due to the presence of another plane. The participant was required to decide an appropriate command and implement it using a button-based interface. The action was followed by visual and auditory feedback informing the user whether they were successful in their conflict resolution. Participants were asked to estimate the time interval between the keypress and the auditory feedback. There were varying levels of automation of the task, from the user having complete control (no automation) to the computer executing the entire task with the participant simply observing (full automation). Berberian et al. found that with increasing levels of automation the participant's estimate of action-outcome time interval duration increased—indicating that more assistance leads to less implicit sense of agency during the task. The authors concluded that the intentional binding measure of agency is a promising metric for HCI research and can assist in the optimal development of such operator control interfaces.

COMPUTER ASSISTED MOVEMENTS

A vast majority of our interactions with computers require us to make motor actions. Therefore interface designers have focused efforts into optimally developing interfaces to compliment the dynamics of human motor actions. Coyle et al. (2012) investigated how the sense of agency is effected when a computer assists user's mouse movements. Participants undertook a task in which they were required to point and click on an onscreen target using a standard mouse. During the experiment the computer gave participants different levels of targeting assistance in achieving this task. Once the participant clicked the target, an auditory tone occurred after a random interval. Implicit sense of agency was measured during this task by incorporating an interval estimation based intentional binding measure between clicking the target and hearing the tone. The results indicated that, although participants were aware of the varying assistance levels, at mild level of computer assistance they still experienced intentional binding, suggesting an implicit level of agency occurring for the action. The intentional binding measure for two further assistance levels (medium and high assistance) indicated a significant loss of agency. This suggests that, when interacting with a computer via assisted mouse movements, there is a point up to which users can be assisted and still feel a sense of agency, however beyond this point the experience of agency breaks down, even in situations where the computer correctly executes the human's intentions.

Similarly, Kumar and Srinivasan (2013) ran an experiment in which participants were asked to click targets on a screen, using a joystick and trigger button. They manipulated the level of control provided to the user at the sensorimotor level–and measured the impact control has over implicit (intentional binding) and explicit (verbal report) sense of agency. The level of control provided to the joystick movements was varied from low, medium and full control. Once the trigger button was pressed (action), a blue circle would appear on the screen (outcome) and participants were asked to estimate the action-outcome interval. Participants also verbally reported their sense of authorship for the action. For tasks where the participants were unsuccessful in hitting the target and thus not achieving high-level goal, the results are consistent with that of Coyle et al. (2012) and Berberian et al. (2012) where intentional binding decreases as a function of automaticity provided during the task. However, when the goal was achieved, intentional binding did not show the same pattern.

The investigations above highlight that the sense of agency may be a graded experience in situations where the line between voluntary and assisted action is gradually blurred. We suggest that metrics for the sense of agency applied in the development of assisted control tasks would allow the interface designer to address the point where the experience of agency becomes disrupted. With regard to the cognitive basis for the sense of agency, the finding that there is a graded loss of sense of agency with increasing assistance is potentially consistent with our current understanding of sensorimotor prediction. For example, increasing assistance may result in internal sensorimotor predictive models becoming less accurate at predicting the next sensory state; this could therefore give rise to reduced congruence between the predicted sensory state and that actual sensory state. Therefore resulting in a reduced sense of agency for the action, of course, this requires further investigation.

COLLABORATION AND ATTRIBUTION OF AGENCY

Finally we turn to more explicit forms of computer assistance and the subject of human emulation. Here a computer agent is endowed with human like abilities and often an anthropomorphic representation that is designed to ultimately mirror human-human interaction (Terveen, 1995). We explore the relevance of the perceptual representation of a computer agent and the impact this has on the sense of agency when collaborating with computer agents as co-actors to achieve a shared goal. We also consider the process of attributing agency to a computer agent and how research into the sense of agency may help inform these areas within HCI and joint action.

The question of collaboration and attributed agency is also particularly relevant to the branch of HCI that focuses on humans' interaction with robots—Human Robot Interaction (HRI). Robotics has made significant advances and is progressing to integrate robot entities into people's everyday lives (Murphy et al., 2010). Effective and optimal implementation of human-robot collaboration techniques rely on HCI research to provide an understanding of the cognitive mechanisms involved in representing, understanding and communicating shared intentions between a human and a computer. HRI is faced with the same challenges in reciprocally representing and communicating human intentions and the system state of the robot. We believe the sense of agency and how we attribute it is an important cognitive consideration for HRI research when assessing how humans relate to robot co-actors.

The sense of agency is also an important consideration for the design of embodied virtual agents. Embodied agents are virtual humans that can engage with people in a human like manner and aim to both understand and generate speech, gestures and facial expressions (Cassell, 2000). Cassell states: "*they are a type of software agent insofar as they exist to do the bidding of their human users, or to represent their human users in a computational environment*". Such agents have been investigated in application areas including education (Cassell, 2004; Ogan et al., 2012), healthcare (Bickmore and Gruber, 2010) and entertainment (Lim and Reeves, 2010).

The relevance of this section extends to cognitive science research. A burgeoning area of research on sense of agency investigates it in social settings (Sebanz et al., 2006; Sebanz, 2007; Pacherie, 2013). One key area of interest is how social context modifies the individual's sense of agency. A number of important consequences of social context have been identified (Pacherie, 2013). One of these is a quantitative effect: social context can alter the strength of sense of agency. For example, in a sensorimotor learning study by van der Wel et al. (2012), they found little difference in sense of agency between participants acting along and with another at the beginning of the task. However as participants became more acquainted with the task significant differences emerged, with the joint action setting associated with a weaker sense of agency.

The majority of this work has so far focused on joint action between human agents. However, joint action between human and *computer* agents is now an important consideration both for agency and HCI research. In the following section we explore this issue in more detail.

COMPUTERS VS. HUMAN CO-ACTORS

One significant consideration is how our sense of agency for actions differ when collaborating with computer vs. human partners. A study by Obhi and Hall (2011) addressed this idea by measuring intentional binding in a joint action task with both a computer partner and a human partner. The findings suggest that humans implicitly consider human-human joint actions very differently to human-computer joint actions. The task involved a participant acting with either a hidden human or computer partner making silent key-presses from behind a screen to cause a tone. Explicit information regarding who was actually responsible for the tone was given. Intentional binding measures were recorded for the action-outcome interval along with the subject's explicit beliefs about who caused the tone. The results showed that the intentional binding was present when paired with another human, regardless of whether they explicitly knew they were the agent or not. This suggests an implicit sense of agency for their co-actor's actions and thus indicating a "we-agency" for the action. For trials with the computer, no intentional binding occurred, even for trials where participants explicitly knew that they were the agent. These findings are compelling because they suggest that implicit agency for self-generated actions are overridden or inhibited when the participant is aware that a computer is the co-actor. The authors speculate that the breakdown in implicit agency here suggests that participants subconsciously develop a belief that when paired with a computer they have no control over the task. Furthermore, they suggest that the criteria for forming "we-agency" are based on comprehending other's intentions in a similar way to one's own, which may be more difficult with computers.

A similar investigation by Wohlschläger et al. (2003) found analogous effects. They measured the perceived onset time of self, other-human and machine generated actions. The results indicated that the participants had a delayed awareness of action for the self and other-human conditions. However, participants had an anticipatory awareness of actions in the machine conditions. In a second experiment Wohlschläger et al. (2003) controlled for the fact that during the machine-action condition there was a lack of visual information corresponding to the hand movement seen in the self and other-human conditions. Therefore, the study was repeated using a rubber hand for the machine-action trials. This change to the procedure reduced the anticipatory effect seen in the first experiment but did not induce the delayed awareness of action seen for the self and other-human actions. These findings indicate that intentions are attributed to others but not to machines. Interestingly, Wohlschläger et al. suggest that, in the machine action condition, modifying the sensory feedback in the form of a rubber hand *"may have activated to some extent a system for understanding biological actions"*.

The investigations above suggest that participants implicitly consider non-biological actions as distinct to self and other actions. This poses potential challenges in the development of such agents in order to facilitate optimal collaboration with humans. One such way to alter this may be the perceptual representation of the computer agent. Metrics used to measure the sense of agency, such as intentional binding offer opportunities to further test perceptual aspects of computer agents and their affect on the sense of agency during collaboration.

EMBODIED AGENTS

The perceptual representation of computer co-actors is a crucial consideration in HCI research. Within HCI there are two theoretical positions regarding this, the first holds that the "humanness" of the agent is key and that we feel fundamentally less connected to computer agents compared to other humans and avatars (Sheehan, 1991). The intentional binding studies outlined above (Wohlschläger et al., 2003; Obhi and Hall, 2011) feed into this human centric idea because they indicate that the emergence of "we-agency" is tightly linked to the nature of the "other" in joint action tasks. In addition, fMRI studies indicate that the brain regions activated during a collaborative task are more significantly activated by human partners compared to computer partners (Rilling et al., 2004). A contrasting perspective posits that humans automatically treat computers as social actors (Reeves and Nass, 1996); this is known as the Media Equation. This idea is based on the observation that humans orient socially to computers in the same manner as with other humans due to the fact that humans are "*very liberal in assigning humanity to an artificial stimulus as long as they have at least minimal human features and if they follow a social rule governing human-to-human interaction*" (Lee and Nass, 2003). The Media Equation goes further and suggests that designers of computer agents should focus on developing the cues that elicit the desired perceptions and responses from humans. There is empirical evidence to support this view. For example, the emotion conveyed in a computer agent's tone of voice (happy or sad) affected the user's perceived emotion of the content being conveyed (Nass et al., 2001).

These perspectives differ in the extent of the affect a biological resemblance of the computer agent has on our ability to attribute agency to the other. Typically these investigations explicitly assess attribution of agency through *post hoc* questionnaires (e.g., Nowak and Biocca, 2003). However, we have seen that explicit and implicit experiences of agency differ when co-acting with a computer partner (Obhi and Hall, 2011). Therefore, using implicit metrics such as intentional binding and sensory attenuation have the potential to yield important insights in this area of HCI research. Experimentally, computational techniques such as virtual reality offer promising new avenues to investigate the sense of agency in joint action by modifying and controlling the perceptual and motor requirements of tasks.

DISCUSSION AND CONCLUSION

This review has highlighted a new area of application for agency research-HCI. We have focused this review on a selection of opportunities to investigate the sense of agency in HCI settings; however this is certainly not intended to be an exhaustive list. Interaction techniques are evolving at a rapid rate. Once the validity and benefits of neurocognitive experimental techniques and implicit metrics such as intentional binding are established in HCI settings, they have the potential to inform the design of a wide range of new technologies. They will also provide valuable insights into how people experience interactions with technology and allow designers to more effectively tailor interaction experiences.

HCI is concerned with developing new or improving existing interfaces that sit between humans and computers. Thus this paper proposes that when developing novel interfaces or improving existing interfaces the user's experience of agency is an important consideration. Whilst explicit measures, such as verbal report are currently utilized in HCI to assess agency, implicit measures are far less utilized. The relatively small number of prior studies that crossover between HCI and sense of agency research have been reviewed here. Of the studies reviewed, intentional binding has been the primary measure for implicit sense of agency. Intentional binding has been well replicated for tasks that require actions and outcomes on a sensorimotor (e.g., sub-second) timescale. Therefore, it is an ideal measure for assessing sense of agency in the many HCI tasks that involve agentive interactions at this timescale. However, we recognize that there are tasks in HCI that necessarily play out over longer timescales and for these tasks intentional binding may be less useful. Consider for example a computer game or robotic surgery in which individual actions combine to achieve a longer-term goal. Both the immediate experience of agency in individual actions and the user's control over the longer-term goal will have an effect on the user experience. Further investigation will determine whether alternative measures, both implicit and explicit, may be better suited to HCI research on these kinds of scenarios.

We have also discussed both implicit and explicit computer assistance and the impact this has on a user's sense of agency. For implicit assistance, research on agency can help to determine the extent to which users can be assisted whist still maintaining their experience of agency. For explicit assistance, the questions raised are different and surround the notion of how a system presents assistance to the user and how the user will attribute agency to an explicit computer co-actor. Sense of agency during joint-action is a current avenue of research, of which HCI techniques could provide assistance. Techniques such as virtual reality offer promising new avenues to investigate the sense of agency in joint action by modifying and controlling the perceptual and motor requirements of tasks. Within the context of virtual environments the notion of the virtual self is another interesting area for sense of agency research. It is commonplace for individuals to take actions and influence a virtual environment, by proxy, through a virtual representation of their self.

Ultimately we believe that HCI researchers can benefit from an increased understanding of underlying mechanisms involved in HCI tasks. Understanding these mechanisms will provide an additional evidence base for the design of interaction systems and this, in turn, may improve the efficiency of the design process and maximize the effectiveness of the end product. This understanding may prove particularly important for the growing body of HCI research focused on developing technology for groups whose sense of agency may differ from that of the normal population. This includes systems designed to support people with psychotic difficulties (Bickmore and Gruber, 2010; Gleeson et al., 2014) and Parkinson's disease (Bächlin et al., 2010; Espay et al., 2010; Mazilu et al., 2014). We also think that HCI can benefit from new neurocognitive interventions that are being developed. For example, there is a burgeoning interest in cognitive enhancement through physiological interventions (such as non-invasive brain stimulation and psychopharmacology). This opens up new avenues for the HCI community, for example, by offering ways to artificially modify and improve user experience.

Finally, there is another dimension to investigating the sense of agency and HCI and that is one of personal responsibility in an ever-increasing society of technology users and intelligent machine interfaces. Situations where the distinction between computer and human controlled actions are blurred during computer assistance or joint action raise important legal and social questions for the sense of agency and responsibility. This is particularly so in safety critical scenarios. Consider for example self-driving cars, which automate the process of driving. One challenge in HCI is to develop optimal ways in which the interface can be presented to keep the distal feeling of control intact, but enable people to leave the proximal sensorimotor control to the machine. However a balance must also be struck such that the human "driver" retains a sufficient sense of responsibility to ensure the safe operation of the car. Understanding how the sense of agency is modified over time, when interacting with a semi-automated system, will also be important and may help to guide the recommended time spent using such interfaces. Within the HCI literature there are numerous examples of the consequences of poor interface design in safety critical situations, perhaps the most infamous of which was recorded in the partial nuclear meltdown at Three Mile Island. In this case conflicting information from a control panel, which operators had come to trust and rely on, contributed to initial operator inaction and delayed the response to the escalating crisis (Norman, 1988, pp. 43–44). Whilst the consequences will rarely be of such significance, the potential reduction in human responsibility as a consequence of increased interaction with intelligent interfaces is an important subject for further investigation. Research on HCI and agency will play a key role in shaping and informing decisions made in this area. The initial work of Berberian et al. (2012) showing operators' diminished sense of agency in highly automated flight control scenarios offers a sense of the risk inherent in such situations.

REFERENCES

Aarts, H., and van den Bos, K. (2011). On the foundations of beliefs in free will intentional binding and unconscious priming in self-agency. *Psychol. Sci.* 22, 532–537. doi: 10.1177/0956797611399294

Bächlin, M., Plotnik, M., Roggen, D., Maidan, I., Hausdorff, J. M., Giladi, N., et al. (2010). Wearable assistant for Parkinson's disease patients with the freezing of gait symptom. *IEEE Trans. Inf. Technol. Biomed.* 14, 436–446. doi: 10.1109/TITB.2009.2036165

Berberian, B., Sarrazin, J. C., Le Blaye, P., and Haggard, P. (2012). Automation technology and sense of control: a window on human agency. *PLoS One* 7:e34075. doi: 10.1371/journal.pone.0034075

Bickmore, T., and Gruber, A. (2010). Relational agents in clinical psychiatry. *Harv. Rev. Psychiatry* 18, 119–130. doi: 10.3109/10673221003707538

Blakemore, S., Wolpert, D., and Frith, C. (1998). Central cancellation of self-produced tickle sensation. *Nat. Neurosci.* 1, 635–640. doi: 10.1038/2870

Blakemore, S., Wolpert, D., and Frith, C. (2002). Abnormalities in the awareness of action. *Trends Cogn. Sci.* 6, 237–242. doi: 10.1016/S1364-6613(02)01907-1

Cassell, J. (Ed.) (2000). *Embodied Conversational Agents.* Boston: MIT Press.

Cassell, J. (2004). Towards a model of technology and literacy development: story listening systems. *J. Appl. Dev. Psychol.* 25, 75–105. doi: 10.1016/j.appdev.2003.11.003

Coyle, D., Moore, J., Kristensson, P. O., Blackwell, A. F., and Fletcher, P. C. (2012). "I did that! Measuring users' experience of agency in their own actions," in *CHI, ACM Conference on Human Factors in Computing Systems* (Austin, Texas, USA), 2025–2034.

Desantis, A., Roussel, C., and Waszak, F. (2011). On the influence of causal beliefs on the feeling of agency. *Conscious. Cogn.* 20, 1211–1220. doi: 10.1016/j.concog.2011.02.012

Engbert, K., and Wohlschläger, A. (2007). Intentions and expectations in temporal binding. *Conscious. Cogn.* 16, 255–264. doi: 10.1016/j.concog.2006.09.010

Espay, A. J., Baram, Y., Dwivedi, A. K., Shukla, R., Gartner, M., Gaines, L., et al. (2010). At-home training with closed-loop augmented-reality cueing device for improving gait in patients with Parkinson disease. *J. Rehabil. Res. Dev.* 47, 573–582. doi: 10.1682/jrrd.2009.10.0165

Faro, D., McGill, A. L., and Hastie, R. (2013). The inflence of perceived causation on judgments of time: an integrative review and implications for decision-making. *Front. Psychol.* 4:217. doi: 10.3389/fpsyg.2013.00217

Farrer, C., Bouchereau, M., Jeannerod, M., and Franck, N. (2008). Effect of distorted visual feedback on the sense of agency. *Behav. Neurol.* 19, 53–57. doi: 10.1155/2008/425267

Farwell, L. A., and Donchin, E. (1988). Talking off the top of your head: toward a mental prosthesis utilizing event-related brain potentials. *Electroencephalogr. Clin. Neurophysiol.* 70, 510–523. doi: 10.1016/0013-4694(88)90149-6

Frith, C. (1992). *The Cognitive Neuropsychology of Schizophrenia.* Hove: Lawrence Erlbaum Associates.

Gallagher, S. (2002). Experimenting with introspection. *Trends Cogn. Sci.* 6, 374–375. doi: 10.1016/s1364-6613(02)01979-4

Gleeson, J. F., Lederman, R., Wadley, G., Bendall, S., McGorry, P. D., and Alvarez-Jimenez, M. (2014). Safety and privacy outcomes from a moderated online social therapy for young people with first-episode psychosis. *Psychiatr. Serv.* 65, 546–550. doi: 10.1176/appi.ps.201300078

Haggard, P. (2005). Conscious intention and motor cognition. *Trends Cogn. Sci.* 9, 290–295. doi: 10.1016/j.tics.2005.04.012

Haggard, P., Clark, S., and Kalogeras, J. (2002). Voluntary action and conscious awareness. *Nat. Neurosci.* 5, 382–385. doi: 10.1038/nn827

Hinterberger, T., Schmidt, S., Neumann, N., Mellinger, J., Blankertz, B., and Curio, G. (2004). Brain-computer communication and slow cortical potentials. *IEEE Trans. Biomed. Eng.* 51, 1011–1018. doi: 10.1109/tbme.2004.827067

Humphreys, G. R., and Buehner, M. J. (2009). Magnitude estimation reveals temporal binding at super-second intervals. *J. Exp. Psychol. Hum. Percept. Perform.* 35, 1542–1549. doi: 10.1037/a0014492

Kennedy, P. R., Bakay, R. A., Moore, M. M., Adams, K., and Goldwaithe, J. (2000). Direct control of a computer from the human central nervous system. *IEEE Trans. Rehabil. Eng.* 8, 198–202. doi: 10.1109/86.847815

Kranick, S. M., and Hallett, M. (2013). Neurology of volition. *Exp. Brain Res.* 229, 313–327. doi: 10.1007/s00221-013-3399-2

Kumar, D., and Srinivasan, N. (2013). "Hierarchical control and sense of agency: differential effects of control on implicit and explicit measures of agency," in *Proceedings of 35th Annual Meeting of the Cognitive Science Society.* Berlin, Germany.

Kumar, D., and Srinivasan, N. (2014). Naturalizing sense of agency with a hierarchical event-control approach. *PLoS One* 9:e92431. doi: 10.1371/journal.pone.0092431

Lee, K. M., and Nass, C. (2003). "Designing social presence of social actors in human computer interaction," in *Proceedings of the SIGCHI Conference on Human Factors in Computing Systems* (Fort Lauderdale, Florida: ACM), 289–296. doi: 10.1145/642611.642662

Lim, S., and Reeves, B. (2010). Computer agents versus avatars: responses to interactive game characters controlled by a computer or other player. *Int. J. Hum. Comput. Stud.* 68, 57–68. doi: 10.1016/j.ijhcs.2009.09.008

Master, S., and Tremblay, F. (2010). Selective increase in motor excitability with intraactive (self) verses interactive touch. *Neuroreport* 21, 206–209. doi: 10.1097/WNR.0b013e328335b530

Mazilu, S., Blanke, U., Hardegger, M., Troster, G., Gazit, E., and Hausdorff, J. M. (2014). "GaitAssist: a daily-life support and training system for Parkinson's disease patients with freezing of gait," in *Proceedings of the 32nd Annual ACM Conference on Human Factors in Computing Systems* (Toronto, Canada: ACM), 2531–2540.

Minnery, B., and Fine, M. (2009). Neuroscience and the future of human-computer interaction. *Interactions* 16, 70–75. doi: 10.1145/1487632.1487649

Moore, J., and Fletcher, P. (2012). Sense of agency in health and disease: a review of cue integration approaches. *Conscious. Cogn.* 21, 59–68. doi: 10.1016/j.concog.2011.08.010

Moore, J., and Haggard, P. (2008). Awareness of action: inference and prediction. *Conscious. Cogn.* 17, 136–144. doi: 10.1016/j.concog.2006.12.004

Moore, J. W., Wegner, D. M., and Haggard, P. (2009). Modulating the sense of agency with external cues. *Conscious. Cogn.* 18, 1056–1064. doi: 10.1016/j.concog.2009.05.004

Murphy, R. R., Nomura, T., Billard, A., and Burke, J. L. (2010). Human-robot interaction. *IEEE Rob. Autom. Mag.* 17, 85–89. doi: 10.1109/MRA.2010.936953

Nass, C., Foehr, U., Brave, S., and Somoza, M. (2001). "The effects of emotion of voice in synthesized and recorded speech," in *Proceedings of the AAAI Symposium Emotional and Intelligent II: The Tangled Knot of Social Cognition.* North Falmouth, MA.

Norman, D. A. (1986). "Cognitive engineering," in *User Centred System Design*, eds D. A. Norman and S. W. Draper (Hillsdale, NJ: Lawrence Erlbaum Associates), 31–61.

Norman, D. (1988). *The Design of Everyday Things.* New York: Basic Books.

Nowak, K. L., and Biocca, F. (2003). The effect of the agency and anthropomorphism on users' sense of telepresence, copresence and social presence in virtual environments. *Presence Teleoperators Virtual Environ.* 12, 481–494. doi: 10.1162/105474603322761289

Obhi, S. S., and Hall, P. (2011). Sense of agency in joint action: influence of human and computer co-actors. *Exp. Brain Res.* 211, 663–670. doi: 10.1007/s00221-011-2662-7

Ogan, A., Finkelstein, S., Mayfield, E., D'Adamo, C., Matsuda, N., and Cassell, J. (2012). "Oh dear stacy!: social interaction, elaboration and learning with teachable agents," in *Proceedings of the SIGCHI Conference on Human Factors in Computing Systems* (Austin, Texas: ACM), 39–48. doi: 10.1145/2207676.2207684

Pacherie, E. (2013). How does it feel to act together? *Phenomenol. Cogn. Sci.* 13, 25–46. doi: 10.1007/s11097-013-9329-8

Reeves, B., and Nass, C. (1996). *The Media Equation: How People Treat Computers, Television and New Media Like Real People and Places.* New York: Cambridge University Press.

Rilling, J. K., Sanfey, A. G., Aronson, J. A., Nystrom, L. E., and Cohen, J. D. (2004). The neural correlates of theory of mind within interpersonal interactions. *Neuroimage* 22, 1694–1703. doi: 10.1016/j.neuroimage.2004.04.015

Roto, V., and Oulasvirta, A. (2005). "Need for non-visual feedback with long response times in mobile HCI," in *Special Interest Tracks and Posters of The 14th International Conference on World Wide Web* (Chiba, Japan: ACM), 775–781. doi: 10.1145/1062745.1062747

Sato, A., and Yasuda, A. (2005). Illusion of sense of self-agency: discrepancy between the predicted and actual sensory consequences of actions modulates the sense of self-agency, but not the sense of self-ownership. *Cognition* 94, 241–255. doi: 10.1016/j.cognition.2004.04.003

Sebanz, N. (2007). The emergence of the self: sensing agency through joint action. *J. Conscious. Stud.* 14, 234–251.

Sebanz, N., Beckering, H., and Knoblich, G. (2006). Joint action: bodies and minds moving together. *Trends Cogn. Sci.* 10, 70–76. doi: 10.1016/j.tics.2005.12.009

Sheehan, J. (1991). "Introduction: humans and animals," in *The Boundaries of Humanity: Humans, Animals, Machines*, eds J. Sheehan and M. Sosna (Oxford, England: University of California Press), 27–35.

Shneiderman, B., and Plaisant, C. (2004). *Designing the User Interface: Strategies for Effective Human-Computer Interaction.* 4th Edn. Reading, MA: Pearson Addison-Wesley.

Synofzik, M., Vosgerau, G., and Newen, A. (2008). Beyond the comparator model: a multifactorial two-step account of agency. *Conscious. Cogn.* 17, 219–239. doi: 10.1016/j.concog.2007.03.010

Terveen, L. G. (1995). Overview of human-computer collaboration. *Knowl. Based Syst.* 8, 67–81. doi: 10.1016/0950-7051(95)98369-h

van der Wel, R. P., Sebanz, N., and Knoblich, G. (2012). The sense of agency during skill learning in individuals and dyads. *Conscious. Cogn.* 21, 1267–1279. doi: 10.1016/j.concog.2012.04.001

Velliste, M., Perel, S., Spalding, M. C., Whitford, A. S., and Schwartz, A. B. (2008). Cortical control of a prosthetic arm for self-feeding. *Nature* 453, 1098–1101. doi: 10.1038/nature06996

Wegner, D. (2002). *The Illusion Of Conscious Will.* Cambridge: MIT Press.

Wegner, D. (2003). The mind's best trick: how we experience conscious will. *Trends Cogn. Sci.* 7, 65–69. doi: 10.1016/s1364-6613(03)00002-0

Wegner, D. M., and Sparrow, B. (2004). "Authorship processing," in *The Cognitive Neurosciences III*, ed M. Gazzaniga (Cambridge, MA: MIT Press), 1201–1209

Wegner, D., Sparrow, B., and Winerman, L. (2004). Vicarious agency: experiencing control over the movements of others. *J. Pers. Soc. Psychol.* 86, 838–848. doi: 10.1037/0022-3514.86.6.838

Williamson, J., Murray-Smith, R., Blankertz, B., Krauledat, M., and Muller, K. R. (2009). Designing for uncertain, asymmetric control: interaction design for brain-computer interfaces. *Int. J. Hum. Comput. Stud.* 67, 827–841. doi: 10.1016/j.ijhcs.2009.05.009

Wohlschläger, A., Haggard, P., Gesierich, B., and Prinz, W. (2003). The perceived onset of time of self and other generated actions. *Psychol. Sci.* 14, 586–591. doi: 10.1046/j.0956-7976.2003.psci_1469.x

Wolpaw, J. R., and McFarland, D. J. (2004). Control of a two- dimensional movement signal by a noninvasive brain-computer interface in humans. *Proc. Natl. Acad. Sci. U S A* 101, 17849–17854. doi: 10.1073/pnas.0403504101

17

Agency over a phantom limb and electromyographic activity on the stump depend on visuomotor synchrony

Shu Imaizumi[1,2], Tomohisa Asai[3], Noriaki Kanayama[4], Mitsuru Kawamura[5] and Shinichi Koyama[1,5,6]*

[1] Graduate School of Engineering, Chiba University, Chiba, Japan
[2] Japan Society for the Promotion of Science, Tokyo, Japan
[3] NTT Communication Science Laboratories, NTT Corporation, Kanagawa, Japan
[4] Institute of Biomedical and Health Sciences, Hiroshima University, Hiroshima, Japan
[5] School of Medicine, Showa University, Tokyo, Japan
[6] Division of Systems and Engineering Management, Nanyang Technological University, Singapore

***Correspondence:**
Shinichi Koyama, Graduate School of Engineering, Chiba University, 1-33 Yayoicho, Inage, Chiba 263-8522, Japan
e-mail: skoyama@faculty.chiba-u.jp

Most patients, post-amputation, report the experience of a phantom limb. Some even sense voluntary movements when viewing a mirror image of the intact limb superimposed onto the phantom limb. While delayed visual feedback of an action is known to reduce a sense of agency, the effect of delayed visual feedback on phantom motor sensation (i.e., sense of controlling a phantom limb) has not been examined. Using a video-projection system, we examined the effect of delayed visual feedback on phantom motor sensation in an upper-limb amputee (male; left upper-limb amputation). He was instructed to view mirrored video images of his intact hand clasping and unclasping during a phantom limb movement. He then rated the intensity of the phantom motor sensation. Three types of hand movement images were presented as follows: synchronous, asynchronous with a 250-ms delay, and asynchronous with a 500-ms delay. Results showed that phantom motor sensation decreased when the image was delayed by 250 and 500 ms. However, when we instructed the patient to adjust the phase of phantom limb movement to that of the image with a 500-ms delay, phantom motor sensation increased. There was also a positive correlation between intensity of phantom motor sensation and electromyographic (EMG) activity on deltoids at the patient's stump. These results suggest that phantom motor sensation and EMG activity on the stump depend on visuomotor synchrony and top-down effects.

Keywords: phantom limb, motor sensation, sense of agency, delayed visual feedback, mirror therapy

INTRODUCTION

We may often feel that an action triggers a change in the external environment. Such feelings are referred to as a "sense of agency" (Gallagher, 2000; David et al., 2008; Moore and Obhi, 2012). Although recent studies have described many aspects to a sense of agency (e.g., Synofzik et al., 2008), the key concept is a sense of controlling one's own actions and, therefore, the external proxy or tool (Haggard and Chambon, 2012). A sense of agency emerges not only through voluntarily generating an action but also by having temporal contiguity between the action and outcome (Blakemore et al., 1999; Bays et al., 2005). The internal forward model in the central motor system has been adopted to help explain the origin of this sense of agency based on sensorimotor processes (Wolpert et al., 1995; Wolpert, 1997; Frith et al., 2000). This model is based on efference copy, which is generated as a copy of the motor commands from a self-produced action (von Holst and Mittelstaedt, 1950) and predicted sensory consequences of motor commands before actual afferent feedback. These consequences are matched against actual feedback. If this prediction does not match the feedback, the perceived sense of agency will decrease. For instance, previous studies suggest that delayed visual feedback when voluntarily handling tools decreases a sense of agency (Franck et al., 2001; Asai and Tanno, 2007).

Although there are several studies assessing a sense of agency manifesting with *intact* limbs, few studies have approached how a sense of agency emerges with *affected* limbs (i.e., phantom limbs). After the amputation of a limb, up to 98% of patients report phantom limb awareness (Ramachandran and Hirstein, 1998). Furthermore, 50–80% of amputees feel pain at the phantom limb site (Kooijman et al., 2000). It has been suggested that neural plasticity plays a key role in the emergence of phantom limb sensations (Flor et al., 2006, 2013). Some patients report that they can voluntarily move the phantom limb. Voluntary movements of a phantom limb have been described as imaginary movements (Ersland et al., 1996; MacIver et al., 2008). Recently, Raffin et al. (2012a) demonstrated that amputees are capable of performing motor execution and motor imagery with their phantom limbs. Furthermore, they suggest that distinct cortical networks contribute to voluntary phantom motor execution (Raffin et al., 2012b). However, it is still unclear how an individual produces voluntary movement in a phantom limb.

Voluntary movement of a phantom limb could be interpreted based on a sense of agency. Ramachandran and Rogers-Ramachandran (1996) developed a technique for providing visual feedback of a moving, intact limb corresponding to the phantom limb while using a mirror placed upright on a table and vertical to an amputee's chest (mirror therapy). The amputee moves his/her intact limb and looks at the mirrored image of the intact limb superimposed on the phantom limb. Subsequently, the amputee can experience control of the phantom limb. Blakemore et al. (2002) suggested that mirrored visual feedback matches sensory feedback predicted by the forward model. Coincidently, this is an efference copy of motor commands generating change in the predicted position of the phantom limb corresponding to mirrored visual feedback.

Mirror therapy was originally developed to relieve phantom limb pain (Ramachandran and Rogers-Ramachandran, 1996; Chan et al., 2007). During therapy, amputees view their unaffected limb in a mirror so that the mirrored image superimposes on their contralateral affected limb behind the mirror. Amputees are encouraged to synchronize their phantom limb with visual feedback from the mirror. Visual feedback of a mirrored-intact limb provides predicted sensory feedback corresponding to motor commands; consequently, this coherent sensorimotor integration might alleviate phantom limb pain (Harris, 1999; McCabe et al., 2005; Ramachandran and Altschuler, 2009). Because a sense of agency plays an important role in the formation of a coherent body image based on visuo-proprioceptive interaction (Tsakiris et al., 2006), it is assumed that a sense of agency is an important factor for determining the effects of mirror therapy and an individual's ability to move a phantom limb. However, few studies have directly examined the relationship between sense of agency and phantom limb movements.

A previous study suggested that phantom limb pain was attenuated when amputees perceived sense of agency toward a moving hand-image superimposed on a phantom limb in an immersive virtual environment (Cole et al., 2009). Conversely, phantom limb pain did not decrease when amputees did not perceive a sense of agency. While Cole et al. (2009) suggest that a sense of agency is linked to alleviating phantom limb pain, the authors used semi-structured interviews to assess (rather than quantify) a sense of agency. Moreover, the authors had no means to modulate an induced sense of agency. To manipulate and investigate a sense of agency, previous studies adopted systematically delayed visual feedback of an action from an intact limb (Franck et al., 2001; Asai and Tanno, 2007). For instance, participants were asked to judge whether they felt they had produced the action outcome. The proportion of "yes" responses was an index of a sense of agency. The authors then quantitatively showed that longer visual feedback delays decreased the sense of agency. Other studies have measured a sense of agency by asking participants to rate, on a numerical scale, to what extent the participant felt that he/she was the one who caused the action outcome (e.g., Sato and Yasuda, 2005).

The present case study examined how temporal congruence between phantom limb movement and visual feedback modulates a sense of controlling a phantom limb (i.e., a sense of agency over a phantom limb). We refer to this sensation as "phantom motor sensation" in order for the amputee to quantify sensory information more easily. Our first hypothesis was that the delayed visual feedback on phantom movement decreases or even extinguishes phantom motor sensation. We also examined how phantom motor sensations could be modulated by spontaneous effort to adjust phantom limb movement to delayed visual feedback. Previous studies suggested that a sense of effort could facilitate a sense of agency among individuals with intact limbs (Demanet et al., 2013; Damen et al., 2014). When an individual's action can be seen as his/her own action, he/she can misattribute the viewed action, which can affect actual movement (Nielsen, 1963; Fourneret and Jeannerod, 1998). Thus, our second hypothesis was that a reduction in the subjective intensity of phantom motor sensation by delayed visual feedback would be less when an amputee receives an instruction to adjust the phantom limb movement phase to that of the delayed feedback. Finally, our third hypothesis was that phantom motor sensations positively correlate with electromyographic (EMG) activity on stump muscles. Previous studies found that stump muscles are activated during phantom motor execution, and waveforms show consistent phases with that of phantom limb movement (Reilly et al., 2006; Gagné et al., 2009; Kawashima and Mita, 2009; Raffin et al., 2012a; Kawashima et al., 2013). Furthermore, muscles are inactive during motor imagery (Raffin et al., 2012a). A recent study also suggested that subjective movability of a phantom limb is positively correlated with EMG activity in stump muscles (Kawashima et al., 2013).

To test our hypotheses, we investigated an upper-limb amputee who obtained visual feedback from filmed images of intact limb movements. This is a technique used in previous studies (Giraux and Sirigu, 2003; Mercier and Sirigu, 2009) that has been validated as an alternative to traditional mirror therapy. This technique allowed the manipulation of the presentation onset of visual feedback in milliseconds, as well as present delayed visual feedback of an action to the participant. To test the first and second hypotheses, subjective intensities of phantom motor sensation from the amputee were compared across conditions varying in visual feedback delay and the amputee's mental set. Then, to test the third hypothesis, we analyzed the correlation between the intensities of phantom motor sensation and EMG activity on stump muscles. Finally, we confirmed that EMG responses from a group of control participants' deltoids were not evoked by motor imagery (Gandevia et al., 1997; Hashimoto and Rothwell, 1999; Raffin et al., 2012a) with visual feedback.

MATERIALS AND METHODS

CASE HISTORY

The patient was a 67-year-old right-handed male. He was recruited from the outpatient clinic of Showa University Hospital. His left arm was amputated 5 cm below the shoulder due to a car accident 39 years prior. He had been using a prosthesis for esthetic purposes. For 31 years after the accident, he had phantom limb pain with numbness and perceived his hand with a clenching spasm as frequently as 10 times a month. The pain lasted for a few hours on average and was very strong; once this pain arose, he was unable to work. Seven years before, he started mirror therapy for approximately 10 min per day, which relieved his pain. More recently, he experienced mild phantom limb pain about once a month, but pain was relieved by mirror therapy. After recovery from the phantom limb pain, he still had phantom limb experiences. Work with the patient for the current study was undertaken while he was not experiencing phantom limb pain. He had corrected-to-normal eyesight and no history of neurological or psychiatric illness except for the limb amputation and phantom limb sensations.

CONTROL PARTICIPANTS

Six healthy male volunteers (age 22.33 ± 0.82 years) participated in the same EMG recording scenario as the patient. Five were self-declared right-handed, and one was left-handed. All had normal or corrected-to-normal eyesight and no history of neurological or psychiatric illness. Since it has been established that delayed visual feedback decreases a perceived sense of agency over intact limbs (e.g., Asai and Tanno, 2007), these volunteers participated only in the EMG recording portion of the experiment.

ETHICS STATEMENT

The ethics committee of the School of Medicine, Showa University, approved this study, which was conducted according to principles outlined by the Declaration of Helsinki. The patient and controls received an explanation of the research protocol and gave written informed consent.

EXPERIMENTAL SETUP

This is shown in **Figures 1A,B**. A participant sat at a table and put his right elbow on the table. The dorsum of the right hand was recorded by a color video camera (STC-TC33USB-AS, Sensor Technologies America, Inc.) at 60 frames per second, from approximately 45 cm directly above the hand. The tabletop was covered with a black cloth so that the camera captured the hand isolated against a black background. To prevent the camera from capturing fluorescent light flickers in the room, LED lighting (Z-6600, Yamada Shomei Lighting, Ltd.) illuminated the space near the right hand to be captured.

We developed an image-processing program to generate video images with or without systematic delay (0, 250, or 500 ms) using Hot Soup Processor version 3.32 (Onion Software). These images were horizontally flipped so that the image of the right hand appeared to look like the left hand. The filmed images were processed, and then simultaneously displayed on a 23-inch LED monitor (i2353Ph, AOC) with a resolution of 1920 × 1080 pixels and a refresh rate of 60 Hz. The monitor was placed on a table in front of the participant with an 8 cm gap from the table surface. A personal computer (CF-SX1, Panasonic Corporation) controlled image recording with the camera, image processing, and stimulus presentation on the monitor. The hand images were presented at an almost identical size on the monitor. In the experiment with the control group, participants put their intact left hand into this gap. Participants sat with their head approximately 35 cm from the monitor. To obstruct the direct view of the right hand, each participant's right hand was placed behind a black standing screen aligned with the mid-sagittal plane on the table.

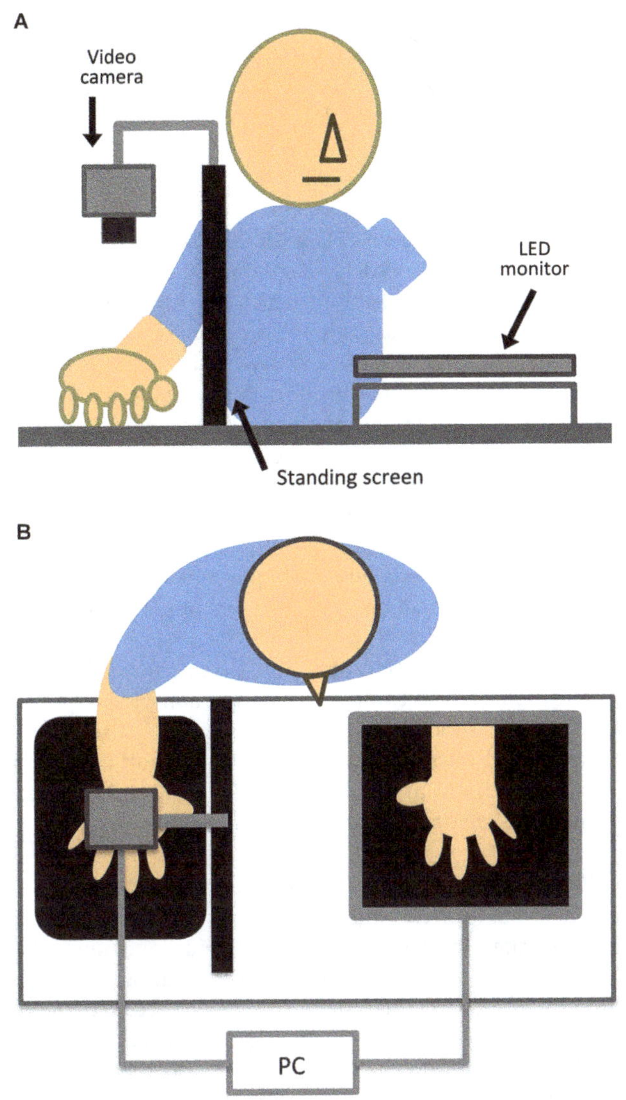

FIGURE 1 | Experimental setup depicted in (A) elevated and (B) horizontal views. Participants sat at the table and placed their right hand on the tabletop. Control participants placed their left hand in the gap between the LED monitor and table. A steel framework fixed the video camera and black standing screen. LED lighting lit the space near the right hand.

PROCEDURE

We conducted tasks in which participants repetitively clasped and unclasped their right hand for 10 s set to a metronome (120 beats per minute). At the same time, the patient intended to move his phantom limb at the same rate as the right hand. Control participants were to *imagine* the movement of their left hand in the same manner. The experimenter told the participants to start and stop the task. The reason for using the clasp/unclasping task was that the patient was familiar with this task for his mirror therapy.

The study consisted of five experimental and two control conditions. The patient performed a single trial in each experimental and control condition, whereas controls only performed a single trial in each experimental condition. To minimize patient fatigue, a single trial in each condition was carried out. We followed a previous study that adopted single trials to examine the effect of mirrored visual feedback on phantom limb sensations (Hunter et al., 2003).

During the experimental conditions, participants viewed three types of video images of the participant's own hand movement: 0 ms (synchronous), 250-ms delayed, and 500-ms delayed images. In the 250-ms and 500-ms delayed conditions, the patient viewed the image with a mental set in which he adjusted the phase of the phantom limb clasping and unclasping to that of the delayed image (adjusted action) and viewed the image without this mental set (unadjusted action). For example, in the 500-ms delay condition with adjusted action, the patient clasped and unclasped alternately the left phantom and right intact limbs. During unadjusted action, the patient also clasped and unclasped the left phantom and right intact limbs at the same rate as the right hand movement. On the other hand, controls adopted a mental set in which they adjusted the phase of motor imagery of the left arm clasping and unclasping to that of the delayed image during adjusted action.

During the control conditions, the patient performed the same clasp/unclasping task in two ways. One was a non-video condition in which a blank monitor with a black screen was presented. The other was a real mirror condition, similar to traditional mirror therapy, in which a transportable mirror (25 × 40 cm) was placed in the patient's sagittal plane against the standing screen.

SUBJECTIVE RATINGS OF PHANTOM MOTOR SENSATION

The patient subjectively rated phantom motor sensations after each trial. After the patient stopped clasping and unclasping, the intensity of felt motor sensation in the phantom limb using magnitude estimation was rated. The patient received the following instructions: "How strongly did you feel like controlling your phantom limb during the task?" Prior to these trials, the patient experienced phantom motor sensation in the synchronous condition without a delay. Next, the patient performed a trial in one of the experimental and control conditions, and then rated the intensity of the phantom motor sensation in the condition relative to the synchronous condition, which was supposed to have a rating of 10. To rate the subjective intensity of phantom motor sensation, the patient was allowed to use arbitrary scores above 0. Higher scores indicated stronger intensity of phantom motor sensation, and 0 indicated no sensation at all.

ELECTROMYOGRAPHIC RECORDING

To examine the relationship between phantom motor sensation and actual muscle activity, we recorded muscle activity in the left anterior and posterior deltoid of both the patient and control group during the trials. Because the patient had a limb amputation below the left shoulder, and showed obvious movement of the deltoid during motor execution of the phantom limb during mirror therapy, we chose the deltoid for EMG recordings.

To compare the EMG waveform of the left deltoid with the phase of alternation in the right hand clasping and unclasping, we also recorded EMG of the right flexor digitorum superficialis (FDS) and extensor digitorum communis (EDC) in both the patient and control group after completion of all trials. During this recording, participants kept clasping and unclasping their right hand for 10 s along with the metronome but without a video image.

EMG signals were captured with disposable Ag/AgCl surface electrodes (P-150, Nihon Koden Corporation) placed in a bipolar configuration. EMG data were recorded using a data acquisition system (MP150, BIOPAC Systems Inc.) and an electromyogram amplifier (EMG2, BIOPAC Systems Inc.). EMG signals were recorded at a frequency of 1000 Hz and band pass filtered between 20 and 400 Hz.

DATA ANALYSIS

Subjective ratings regarding the intensity of phantom motor sensation and EMG recordings for single trials in each experimental and control conditions were obtained from the patient. The patient's ratings were reported descriptively and compared across conditions without statistics. To corroborate ratings varying across conditions by consistent EMG variations, we used a Pearson's product-moment correlation coefficient to determine the relationship between the ratings of phantom motor sensation and EMG indices from the patient's stump muscles, using maximum peak amplitude (MAX) and root mean square amplitude (RMS) during each trial. Finally, we confirmed that EMG activity from control participants' deltoids was not observed across the experimental conditions by visual inspection.

RESULTS

SUBJECTIVE RATINGS OF PHANTOM MOTOR SENSATION

Figure 2 presents the patient's results from single trials in the experimental and control conditions. In the 250-ms and 500-ms delayed conditions, sensations decreased to 2.50 and 3.25, respectively, relative to the standard in the synchronous condition (10.00). The patient reported an odd feeling regarding the delayed appearance of the hand images during debriefing. However, when

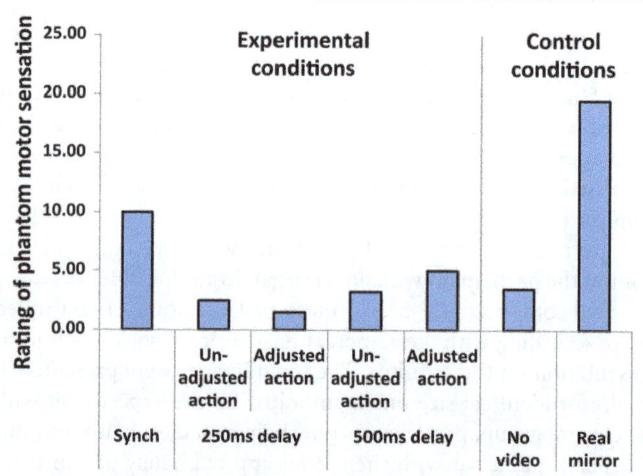

FIGURE 2 | The patient's subjective ratings of intensity in phantom motor sensation as a function of condition.

the patient performed action in which he adjusted the phantom movement to visual feedback with a 500-ms delay, the rating increased to 5.00. This effect due to the adjusted action was not observed in the 250-ms delayed condition (the rating slightly decreased to 1.50). When the patient performed the task while viewing his hand in the real mirror, the rating increased to 19.50. The patient was comfortable during the real-mirror condition and reported vivid phantom motor sensation during debriefing. In the non-video condition in which the monitor presented only a black screen, the rating was 3.50.

ELECTROMYOGRAPHIC RECORDING

The EMG recorded on the patient's left anterior and posterior deltoid showed greater activity during each condition than at rest. **Figure 3A** shows a waveform of EMG activity in the left deltoid and right FDS and EDC in the patient and one control participant. Overall, EMG at the patient's left deltoid showed sinusoidal waveforms corresponding to phase alternation of clasping and unclasping. Thus, we attributed this muscle activity to phantom motor sensations.

Figures 3B,C present the patient's EMG activity results from single trials in both experimental and control conditions. EMG activity was greater when subjective sensation ratings were higher: there was high correspondence between phantom motor sensation and EMG activity. We also analyzed the relationships between subjective ratings of phantom motor sensation and the MAX and RMS of EMG during each trial. We found significant and strong positive correlations between subjective ratings and MAX at the anterior deltoid (Pearson's coefficient $r = 0.90$, $p < 0.01$), MAX at the posterior deltoid ($r = 0.97$, $p < 0.01$), RMS at the anterior deltoid ($r = 0.92$, $p < 0.01$), and RMS at the posterior deltoid ($r = 0.87$, $p < 0.01$).

In the control group, no EMG activity was observed at both the anterior and posterior left deltoid during all conditions (**Figure 3A**). For further demonstration of a lack of EMG activity among control participants, we conducted two additional tasks. First, we removed the monitor and then asked control participants to repetitively clasp and unclasp their left hand with the left elbow placed on the table during EMG recording at the left deltoid. No EMG activity was observed at the left deltoid. Second, we recorded EMG activity at the left FDS and EDC while performing the same task in the same experimental conditions. Again, no EMG activity was observed in the FDS and EDC. These results confirmed that EMG activity was uniquely evoked in the patient's left deltoid and was related to phantom limb sensations.

DISCUSSION

Using a video-projection system, the present case study investigated the effect of visual feedback on perceived phantom motor sensation (i.e., a sense of controlling a phantom limb). Our results suggest three findings. First, delayed visual feedback reduced phantom motor sensation in our patient. The patient perceived decreased phantom motor sensation when visual feedback was delayed by 250 and 500 ms. These results are consistent with previous findings suggesting that delayed sensory feedback of an action decreases a sense of agency (Franck et al., 2001; Sato and Yasuda, 2005; Asai and Tanno, 2007). Since temporal contiguity between an action and sensory feedback predicted by the internal forward model is necessary for generating a sense of agency (Wolpert et al., 1995; Wolpert, 1997; Frith et al., 2000), action through a phantom limb should also predict sensory feedback if temporally matched. Several previous studies investigated the relationship between visual feedback of an action and phantom motor sensation. For instance, Kawashima et al. (2013) reported that amputees perceived stronger phantom motor sensation with mirrored visual feedback than without such feedback. However, to our knowledge, no study has examined the relationship between the temporal properties of visual feedback for phantom limb movement and phantom motor sensation. For the first time, we show that phantom motor sensation requires temporal contiguity between the motor intention and visual feedback.

Second, we found that even if delayed visual feedback reduced phantom motor sensation, the patient's spontaneous effort to adjust the phase of phantom movement to that of delayed feedback (adjusted action) helped restore phantom motor sensations. This result was consistent with previous findings suggesting that a sense of effort enhances a sense of agency among healthy individuals (Demanet et al., 2013; Damen et al., 2014). However, the restoration was observed only during a 500-ms delay. We assumed that difficulty in spontaneously adjusting phantom limb movement to delayed visual feedback would affect phantom motor sensation. That is, for the hand image paired with a 500-ms delay, the actual hand appeared to be alternately clasping and unclasping at a tempo of 120 beats per minute. However, the 250-ms delayed image presented a lag with an alternation of clasping and unclasping with two hands. In this sense, a larger delay seems advantageous for generating a sense of agency. However, more delayed visual feedback tends to increase the discrepancy between the action and sensory feedback, subsequently inducing a decreased sense of agency (Sato and Yasuda, 2005; Asai and Tanno, 2007). Thus, our results may reflect the influence of top-down processing (Synofzik et al., 2008) in which the patient intended to judge the 500-ms delayed image as self-produced movement. A recent study also reported that delayed visual feedback decreased manual task performance (Fujisaki, 2012). Performance sharply decreased with increasing delay up until 490 ms and decreased more gradually as the delay increased up to 2120 ms. In a sense, this previous finding is consistent with ours in that the adjusted action to a delayed hand image can only be influential during a certain time window (500 ms); however, there are apparent differences in the time window and phantom/intact limbs used in Fujisaki (2012) and the present study. Our results suggest that the patient's mental set toward mirrored visual feedback might help elicit phantom motor sensation, which is necessary for therapeutic benefits (e.g., alleviate phantom limb pain) during both mirror (Ramachandran and Rogers-Ramachandran, 1996) and video-projection system therapy (Giraux and Sirigu, 2003; Mercier and Sirigu, 2009), as well as virtual reality (Murray et al., 2007; Cole et al., 2009).

Finally, we observed that EMG activity in the patient's stump muscles correlated with the phase of phantom limb clasp/unclasping movements, consistent with previous findings

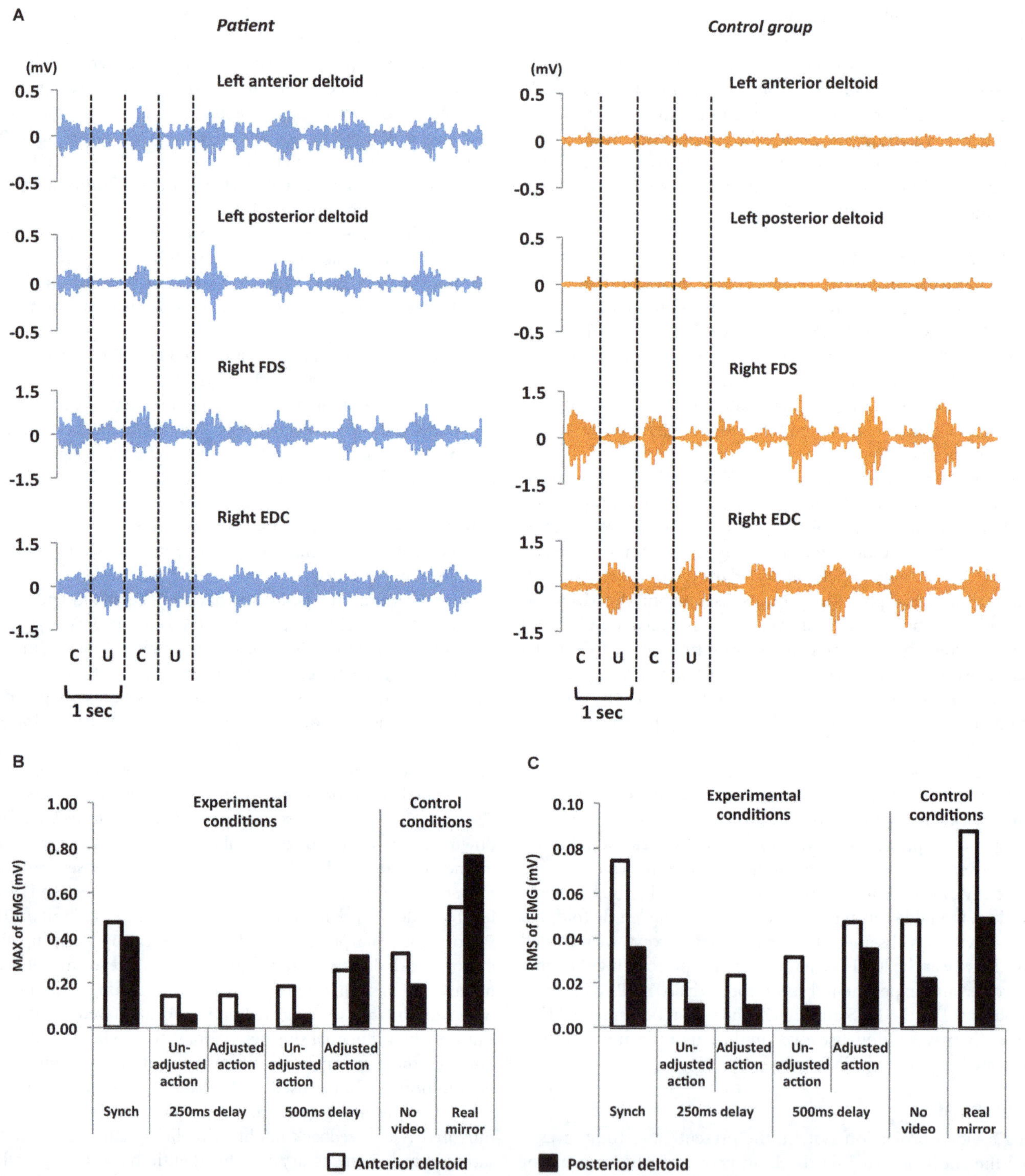

FIGURE 3 | (A) EMG activity in the left anterior and posterior deltoids, and right FDS and EDC in the patient (left column) and one control participant (right column). EMG waveforms of the left deltoid were obtained when participants performed the task with synchronous visual feedback. The sinusoidal EMG waveforms correspond to phase clasping (C) and unclasping (U). **(B)** MAX of EMG activity recorded at the patient's anterior and posterior deltoid as a function of condition. **(C)** RMS of EMG activity recorded at the patient's anterior and posterior deltoid as a function of condition. The ratings significantly and positively correlated with each MAX and RMS at both the anterior and posterior deltoid ($r \geq 0.87$, $p < 0.01$).

that upper-limb stump EMGs correlate with the phantom limb movement phase (Kawashima and Mita, 2009; Raffin et al., 2012a; Kawashima et al., 2013). More importantly, our results showed that EMGs were highly correlated with modulations in both phantom motor sensation through visual feedback and the intention to adjust phantom movement to delayed visual feedback. A recent study also reported that ease of phantom limb motor execution is positively correlated with EMG activity in a forearm stump when compared with and without mirror visual feedback (Kawashima et al., 2013). Furthermore, we confirmed that this modulated EMG activity in the deltoid was not observed among healthy controls. Consistent with previous findings (Gagné et al., 2009), these results suggest that phantom motor sensation is involved in certain motor commands targeted at stump muscles originally not targeted prior to amputation. These motor commands are capable of not only decreasing when perceived phantom motor sensation attenuates, but also increasing when the individual intends to facilitate phantom limb movement.

Our study has three limitations of note. First, in our single-case study, one patient performed one trial in each condition. Consequently, while a significant correlation between subjective ratings of phantom motor sensation and EMG activity on the stump was demonstrated, we were unable to determine statistically significant differences among conditions. Therefore, further research with a larger sample size is necessary to examine the reliability of our results. Second, because the patient was not experiencing phantom limb pain at the time of the study, we could not investigate the therapeutic effect of the video-monitor technique. Further investigations should be conducted to identify how phantom motor sensations remedy phantom limb pain, comparing the efficacy of a video-projection system and mirror therapy. Since mirror therapy requires a sensorimotor coherence (Ramachandran and Altschuler, 2009), phantom motor sensation in terms of producing a sense of agency should be important in the treatment of phantom limb pain. Finally, we did not examine whether a sense of body-ownership toward the hand images could have emerged in the patient. This was because we measured only phantom motor sensation as one of the components related to a sense of agency. Given that coherent body-ownership is based on a sense of agency (Tsakiris et al., 2006), future studies should investigate the relationship between phantom motor sensations and a sense of ownership toward an external alternative to a phantom limb. Additional studies should also examine how a sense of agency and body-ownership contribute to mirror therapy effects.

Given that the strongest sensations were observed for the real mirror condition, the video-projection system cannot easily replace traditional mirror therapy. For instance, our system could not precisely reproduce the appearance of an object (e.g., spatial resolution and three-dimensional effects). Since it has been suggested that susceptibility to visual feedback might relate to the effectiveness of virtual visual feedback for therapeutic use (Mercier and Sirigu, 2009), video-projection visual feedback must be able to reproduce more vivid and exact feedback. However, the video-projection system, which can manipulate the timing of visual feedback unlike a real mirror, might be beneficial for not only the investigation of relationships between a phantom limb and a sense of agency but also for the development of new therapeutic approaches that use top-down processing, such as a sense of effort (Demanet et al., 2013; Damen et al., 2014) and contextual prediction (Blakemore et al., 1998). Moreover, this system, which can present pre-recorded visual feedback of an action, might be beneficial for bilateral amputees and patients with bilateral motor impairment.

In conclusion, the present single-case study suggests that a sense of agency over a phantom limb and EMG activity on stump muscles depends on visuomotor synchrony and a mental set for adjusting phantom limb movement to delayed visual feedback. This indicates that a sense of controlling an external proxy (e.g., hand images) can be generated even though the agent does not have an effector (e.g., intact limb). Several findings regarding a sense of agency can be applied to investigate mechanisms related to a phantom limb, providing therapeutic applications based on future studies.

ACKNOWLEDGMENTS

We would like to thank all the participants for their cooperation, Yoshihiro Shimomura for his technical help during EMG recording, and two anonymous reviewers for their helpful comments. This work was supported by Grant-in-Aids for Young Scientists (B) and Scientific Research (B) to Shinichi Koyama (21730586, 23330218 respectively), a Grant-in-Aid for Scientific Research (C) to Mitsuru Kawamura (23591283), a Grant-in-Aid for JSPS Fellows to Shu Imaizumi (13J00943) from the Japan Society for the Promotion of Science, and Grant-in-Aids for Scientific Research on Innovative Areas "Face Perception and Recognition" and "the Science of Mental Time" to Mitsuru Kawamura (23119720, 25119006 respectively) from the Ministry of Education, Culture, Sports, Science, and Technology, Japan. This work was also supported in part by the Showa University Medical Foundation and the Research Funding for Longevity Sciences (25-13) from the National Centre for Geriatrics and Gerontology, Japan.

REFERENCES

Asai, T., and Tanno, Y. (2007). The relationship between the sense of self-agency and schizotypal personality traits. *J. Mot. Behav.* 39, 162–168. doi: 10.3200/jmbr.39.3.162-168

Bays, P. M., Wolpert, D. M., and Flanagan, J. R. (2005). Perception of the consequences of self-action is temporally tuned and event driven. *Curr. Biol.* 15, 1125–1128. doi: 10.1016/j.cub.2005.05.023

Blakemore, S. J., Frith, C. D., and Wolpert, D. M. (1999). Spatio-temporal prediction modulates the perception of self-produced stimuli. *J. Cogn. Neurosci.* 11, 551–559. doi: 10.1162/089892999563607

Blakemore, S. J., Goodbody, S. J., and Wolpert, D. M. (1998). Predicting the consequences of our own actions: the role of sensorimotor context estimation. *J. Neurosci.* 18, 7511–7518.

Blakemore, S. J., Wolpert, D. M., and Frith, C. D. (2002). Abnormalities in the awareness of action. *Trends Cogn. Sci.* 6, 237–242. doi: 10.1016/s1364-6613(02)01907-1

Chan, B. L., Witt, R., Charrow, A. P., Magee, A., Howard, R., Pasquina, P. F., et al. (2007). Mirror therapy for phantom limb pain. *N. Engl. J. Med.* 357, 2206–2207. doi: 10.1056/NEJMc071927

Cole, J., Crowle, S., Austwick, G., and Slater, D. H. (2009). Exploratory findings with virtual reality for phantom limb pain: from stump motion to agency and analgesia. *Disabil. Rehabil.* 31, 846–854. doi: 10.1080/09638280802355197

Damen, T. G. E., Dijksterhuis, A., and van Baaren, R. B. (2014). On the other hand: nondominant hand use increases sense of agency. *Soc. Psychol. Personal. Sci.* 5, 680–683. doi: 10.1177/1948550614527626

David, N., Newen, A., and Vogeley, K. (2008). The "sense of agency" and its underlying cognitive and neural mechanisms. *Conscious. Cogn.* 17, 523–534. doi: 10.1016/j.concog.2008.03.004

Demanet, J., Muhle-Karbe, P. S., Lynn, M. T., Blotenberg, I., and Brass, M. (2013). Power to the will: how exerting physical effort boosts the sense of agency. *Cognition* 129, 574–578. doi: 10.1016/j.cognition.2013.08.020

Ersland, L., Rosen, G., Lundervold, A., Smievoll, A. I., Tillung, T., Sundberg, H., et al. (1996). Phantom limb imaginary fingertapping causes primary motor cortex activation: an fMRI study. *Neuroreport* 8, 207–210. doi: 10.1097/00001756-199612200-00042

Flor, H., Diers, M., and Andoh, J. (2013). The neural basis of phantom limb pain. *Trends Cogn. Sci.* 17, 307–308. doi: 10.1016/j.tics.2013.04.007

Flor, H., Nikolajsen, L., and Jensen, T. S. (2006). Phantom limb pain: a case of maladaptive CNS plasticity? *Nat. Rev. Neurosci.* 7, 873–881. doi: 10.1038/nrn1991

Fourneret, P., and Jeannerod, M. (1998). Limited conscious monitoring of motor performance in normal subjects. *Neuropsychologia* 36, 1133–1140. doi: 10.1016/s0028-3932(98)00006-2

Franck, N., Farrer, C., Georgieff, N., Marie-Cardine, M., Dalery, J., d'Amato, T., et al. (2001). Defective recognition of one's own actions in patients with schizophrenia. *Am. J. Psychiatry* 158, 454–459. doi: 10.1176/appi.ajp.158.3.454

Frith, C. D., Blakemore, S. J., and Wolpert, D. M. (2000). Abnormalities in the awareness and control of action. *Philos. Trans. R. Soc. Lond. B Biol. Sci.* 355, 1771–1788. doi: 10.1098/rstb.2000.0734

Fujisaki, W. (2012). Effects of delayed visual feedback on grooved pegboard test performance. *Front. Psychol.* 3:61. doi: 10.3389/fpsyg.2012.00061

Gagné, M., Reilly, K. T., Hetu, S., and Mercier, C. (2009). Motor control over the phantom limb in above-elbow amputees and its relationship with phantom limb pain. *Neuroscience* 162, 78–86. doi: 10.1016/j.neuroscience.2009.04.061

Gallagher, S. (2000). Philosophical conceptions of the self: implications for cognitive science. *Trends Cogn. Sci.* 4, 14–21. doi: 10.1016/s1364-6613(99)01417-5

Gandevia, S. C., Wilson, L. R., Inglis, J. T., and Burke, D. (1997). Mental rehearsal of motor tasks recruits alpha-motoneurones but fails to recruit human fusimotor neurones selectively. *J. Physiol.* 505, 259–266. doi: 10.1111/j.1469-7793.1997.259bc.x

Giraux, P., and Sirigu, A. (2003). Illusory movements of the paralyzed limb restore motor cortex activity. *Neuroimage* 20, S107–S111. doi: 10.1016/j.neuroimage.2003.09.024

Haggard, P., and Chambon, V. (2012). Sense of agency. *Curr. Biol.* 22, R390–R392. doi: 10.1016/j.cub.2012.02.040

Harris, A. J. (1999). Cortical origin of pathological pain. *Lancet* 354, 1464–1466. doi: 10.1016/s0140-6736(99)05003-5

Hashimoto, R., and Rothwell, J. C. (1999). Dynamic changes in corticospinal excitability during motor imagery. *Exp. Brain Res.* 125, 75–81. doi: 10.1007/s002210050660

Hunter, J. P., Katz, J., and Davis, K. D. (2003). The effect of tactile and visual sensory inputs on phantom limb awareness. *Brain* 126, 579–589. doi: 10.1093/brain/awg054

Kawashima, N., and Mita, T. (2009). Metal bar prevents phantom limb motion: case study of an amputation patient who showed a profound change in the awareness of his phantom limb. *Neurocase* 15, 478–484. doi: 10.1080/13554790902950442

Kawashima, N., Mita, T., and Yoshikawa, M. (2013). Inter-individual difference in the effect of mirror reflection-induced visual feedback on phantom limb awareness in forearm amputees. *PLoS One* 8:e69324. doi: 10.1371/journal.pone.0069324

Kooijman, C. M., Dijkstra, P. U., Geertzen, J. H., Elzinga, A., and van der Schans, C. P. (2000). Phantom pain and phantom sensations in upper limb amputees: an epidemiological study. *Pain* 87, 33–41. doi: 10.1016/s0304-3959(00)00264-5

MacIver, K., Lloyd, D. M., Kelly, S., Roberts, N., and Nurmikko, T. (2008). Phantom limb pain, cortical reorganization and the therapeutic effect of mental imagery. *Brain* 131, 2181–2191. doi: 10.1093/brain/awn124

McCabe, C. S., Haigh, R. C., Halligan, P. W., and Blake, D. R. (2005). Simulating sensory-motor incongruence in healthy volunteers: implications for a cortical model of pain. *Rheumatology (Oxford)* 44, 509–516. doi: 10.1093/rheumatology/keh529

Mercier, C., and Sirigu, A. (2009). Training with virtual visual feedback to alleviate phantom limb pain. *Neurorehabil. Neural Repair* 23, 587–594. doi: 10.1177/1545968308328717

Moore, J. W., and Obhi, S. S. (2012). Intentional binding and the sense of agency: a review. *Conscious. Cogn.* 21, 546–561. doi: 10.1016/j.concog.2011.12.002

Murray, C. D., Pettifer, S., Howard, T., Patchick, E. L., Caillette, F., Kulkarni, J., et al. (2007). The treatment of phantom limb pain using immersive virtual reality: three case studies. *Disabil. Rehabil.* 29, 1465–1469. doi: 10.1080/09638280601107385

Nielsen, T. I. (1963). Volition: a new experimental approach. *Scand. J. Psychol.* 4, 225–230. doi: 10.1111/j.1467-9450.1963.tb01326.x

Raffin, E., Giraux, P., and Reilly, K. T. (2012a). The moving phantom: motor execution or motor imagery? *Cortex* 48, 746–757. doi: 10.1016/j.cortex.2011.02.003

Raffin, E., Mattout, J., Reilly, K. T., and Giraux, P. (2012b). Disentangling motor execution from motor imagery with the phantom limb. *Brain* 135, 582–595. doi: 10.1093/brain/awr337

Ramachandran, V. S., and Altschuler, E. L. (2009). The use of visual feedback, in particular mirror visual feedback, in restoring brain function. *Brain* 132, 1693–1710. doi: 10.1093/brain/awp135

Ramachandran, V. S., and Hirstein, W. (1998). The perception of phantom limbs. The D. O. Hebb lecture. *Brain* 121, 1603–1630. doi: 10.1093/brain/121.9.1603

Ramachandran, V. S., and Rogers-Ramachandran, D. (1996). Synaesthesia in phantom limbs induced with mirrors. *Proc. Biol. Sci.* 263, 377–386. doi: 10.1098/rspb.1996.0058

Reilly, K. T., Mercier, C., Schieber, M. H., and Sirigu, A. (2006). Persistent hand motor commands in the amputees' brain. *Brain* 129, 2211–2223. doi: 10.1093/brain/awl154

Sato, A., and Yasuda, A. (2005). Illusion of sense of self-agency: discrepancy between the predicted and actual sensory consequences of actions modulates the sense of self-agency, but not the sense of self-ownership. *Cognition* 94, 241–255. doi: 10.1016/j.cognition.2004.04.003

Synofzik, M., Vosgerau, G., and Newen, A. (2008). Beyond the comparator model: a multifactorial two-step account of agency. *Conscious. Cogn.* 17, 219–239. doi: 10.1016/j.concog.2007.03.010

Tsakiris, M., Prabhu, G., and Haggard, P. (2006). Having a body versus moving your body: how agency structures body-ownership. *Conscious. Cogn.* 15, 423–432. doi: 10.1016/j.concog.2005.09.004

von Holst, E., and Mittelstaedt, H. (1950). Das reafferenzprinzip. *Naturwissenschaften* 37, 464–476. doi: 10.1007/bf00622503

Wolpert, D. M. (1997). Computational approaches to motor control. *Trends Cogn. Sci.* 1, 209–216. doi: 10.1016/S1364-6613(97)01070-X

Wolpert, D. M., Ghahramani, Z., and Jordan, M. I. (1995). An internal model for sensorimotor integration. *Science* 269, 1880–1882. doi: 10.1126/science.7569931

18

Loss of agency in apraxia

***Mariella Pazzaglia*[1,2]* *and Giulia Galli*[2]**

[1] *Department of Psychology, University of Rome 'La Sapienza', Rome, Italy*
[2] *IRCCS Fondazione Santa Lucia, Rome, Italy*

Correspondence:
Mariella Pazzaglia, Department of Psychology, University of Rome 'La Sapienza', Via dei Marsi 78, 00185 Rome, Italy
e-mail: mariella.pazzaglia@uniroma1.it

The feeling of acting voluntarily is a fundamental component of human behavior and social life and is usually accompanied by a sense of agency. However, this ability can be impaired in a number of diseases and disorders. An important example is apraxia, a disturbance traditionally defined as a disorder of voluntary skillful movements that often results from frontal-parietal brain damage. The first part of this article focuses on direct evidence of some core symptoms of apraxia, emphasizing those with connections to agency and free will. The loss of agency in apraxia is reflected in the monitoring of internally driven action, in the perception of specifically self-intended movements and in the neural intention to act. The second part presents an outline of the evidences supporting the functional and anatomical link between apraxia and agency. The available structural and functional results converge to reveal that the frontal–parietal network contributes to the sense of agency and its impairment in disorders such as apraxia. The current knowledge on the generation of motor intentions and action monitoring could potentially be applied to develop therapeutic strategies for the clinical rehabilitation of voluntary action.

Keywords: agency, apraxia, fMRI, rehabilitation, action

EVIDENCE FOR THE LOSS OF SENSE OF AGENCY IN APRAXIA

The sense of agency implies the subjective experience of elaboration, monitoring, and control of external events through one's own motor actions, as well as the neural intention to act. Using cognitive neuroscience techniques, researchers have attempted to elucidate this interesting phenomenon (Farrer et al., 2003b; David et al., 2007; Spengler et al., 2009; Tsakiris et al., 2010; Salomon et al., 2013; Weiss et al., 2014) distinguishing, at the conceptual level, between two important aspects of agency: a retrospective component (the outcome of action—objective) and prospective signal (from the self-perception of generated actions to the intention to move—subjective) (Moore and Obhi, 2012; Chambon et al., 2013). Agency research has attracted investigators and theorists, although the mechanism appears very natural, critical voices have questioned the validity of studying agency via conventional scientific paradigms (David, 2012). An alternate approach is to investigate how brain damage may alter the awareness of being causally involved in an action (de Jong, 2011).

A prime neurological example is apraxia, a disturbance characterized by a marked impairment in performing volitional movements (de Jong, 2011; Dovern et al., 2011; Wolpe et al., 2014). In essence, apraxia encompasses a broad spectrum of higher-order *purposeful* movement disorders (Leiguarda and Marsden, 2000) that affect both sides of the body, even though neurological damage is more frequently associated with unilateral left frontal and parietal lesions (Haaland et al., 2000; Leiguarda and Marsden, 2000; Hermsdörfer et al., 2003). The traditional definition includes deficits in performing, imitating, and recognizing skilled actions known as meaningless or meaningful gestures (Rothi and Heilman, 1984; Pazzaglia et al., 2008a,b). The pathological condition is identified on the basis of an inability to execute both transitive (using an object) and intransitive (without an object) gestures with different body effectors (mouth, hand, or foot) (Leiguarda and Marsden, 2000). This failure to move intentionally cannot be explained by primary motor or sensory impairments, or by deficits in memory or comprehension (De Renzi and Lucchelli, 1988).

Apraxia has been, and is still, subject to intense debate about its deficits to sensorimotor function and higher-level cognitive processes (Goldenberg, 2013). In this perspective article, we will discuss just one of the possible pathological perspectives of the apraxic disturbance: whether the emerging concept of "agency" is consistent with the presentation of neurological symptoms due to apraxia. Distinct from other clinical disturbances such as anosognosia for hemiplegia—where the symptom of disownership (Karnath and Baier, 2010) with consequent disorders of motor awareness of the paralyzed parts have been interpreted in relation to agency (Pia et al., 2013)—the framework we offer here specifically involves a more global and genuine action volitional disorder that typically affects the two sides of the body. Until recently, a limited number of experimental studies have identified the essential aspects of agency that can be objectively quantified in apraxia by the following three lines of evidence: (i) a genuine incapacity with respect to the voluntary control of one's action bound closer to its outcome; (ii) a disordered subjective experience of actions both performed and not; and (iii) altered predictive signals generated during motor planning.

The first evidence is related to the fundamental importance of performing an intentional action with an outcome and, secondly, to the subjective sense of control in the selection of actions. Consider, for example, the active action of taking a cigarette from a pack, opening a book of matches, and then lighting and drawing on the cigarette. A variety of movements may be similarly effective when it comes to performing the given aim of smoking. However, if an apraxic patient attempts to smoke, he typically exhibits poor control over actions, and has difficulty in movement selection, which is compatible with slow, incorrect, and ineffective motor acts ("put a match to the mouth in an attempt to smoke", Pick, 1905). Given that the patient showed intact knowledge of functional uses of objects and a disturbance of the mental control of deliberate motor actions, Pick interpreted this disorder as a sign of apraxia. The patient generally recognizes that the action performed does not unfold as expected, and reports his disappointment. Phenomenologically, we can distinguish at least two aspects interpretable in relation to the sense of agency. The first aspect is a disorder of volitional movement where non volitional movement is spared. In the first description of apraxia, Jackson (1866) observed the core pathology as a motor purposeful deficit [*"the patient seems to have lost much of his power to do anything intentionally, even with those muscles that are not paralyzed"]*. The second aspect, related to the first, is the incapacity to select the correct action leads to a weak power over the outcome itself. Apraxic patients not only have problems with purposeful object manipulation in everyday activities, but also in selecting actions (Rumiati et al., 2001), demonstrating impairments not related to mere movement execution (Hermsdörfer, 2014), nor to a loss of functional semantic knowledge or resource limitation (Rumiati, 2014). In motor act selection, patients with apraxia lose much of their power to perform intentional actions, are more prone to errors and have typically prolonged response times compared to neurological controls without apraxia (Goldenberg and Hagmann, 1998; Goldenberg et al., 2004; Hermsdörfer et al., 2006; Rumiati, 2014). The fragility of the deliberate control of their own actions may substantially depend on the interference caused by the competition between varieties of degraded movements (Sirigu et al., 2004; Pazzaglia et al., 2008b; Botvinick et al., 2009; Buxbaum and Kalenine, 2010; Jax and Buxbaum, 2010; Nelissen et al., 2010). Thus, weakened movement representation impedes correct and fast action selection processing by reducing freedom and power in selecting between possible movement options, thereby contributing to a reduced fluency (Haggard and Chambon, 2012, for a review) and sense of agency over one's own action effects (Wenke et al., 2010). Consistent with a deficit that implies a failure to select or retrieve stored internal representations, apraxia should affect the subjective perception of generated actions.

Another evidence is the disorder of self-generated action essential to establishing a sense of agency. A seminal paper showed experimentally that a sample of patients who had developed apraxic symptoms exhibited deficits in judging whether they did or did not cause a specific movement of their own body (Sirigu et al., 1999). With a more traditional experimental paradigm such as the explicit attribution in agency task, the patients were asked to execute simple and complex hand–finger movements with their unseen, gloved hand, and to observe in real time hand movements relayed on a video display. The display showed either the patient's own hand or that of a model who performed the same movements. The apraxic patients were selectively impaired in deciding whether the hand moving on the screen was their own or belonged to someone else and become aware of their decision with a significant delay compared to healthy participants (Sirigu et al., 2004).

Different authors questioned the validity of these explicit judgments when studying agency, suggesting a more reliable, implicit quantitative measure for the awareness of action based on an intriguing relationship between voluntary action and subjective time (Haggard et al., 2002). This so-called "intentional binding" measure has been studied in patients with corticobasal degeneration, some with clinical apraxia (Wolpe et al., 2014). Participants were asked to report either when they pressed a button or when they heard a tone. In the case of apraxic patients the intentional binding is associated with a subjective contraction of time between an action and its effect. This change in judgment is proportional to disease severity of apraxia but not to other motor features or cognitive impairments and occurs for the reduced sense of ownership of the action (Wolpe et al., 2014). Increased binding of action in patients is therefore more likely to reflect a deficit in control of actions by the anticipation of their effects. This possibility is explored by closer examination of action prediction in patients with apraxia.

The third evidence are disordered predictive signals, which are critical to the sense of agency (Blakemore et al., 2001). According to the "comparator" model, one makes a choice on the basis of a match between the predicted and actual sensory effect of one's action (Chambon et al., 2013). It is possible that in previous studies, patients failed to compare between an internal model and the expected and actual sensory consequence of the action (Sirigu et al., 2004). Indeed, patients with apraxia are unable to mentally simulate movements of their own hands, (Sirigu et al., 1995) and in monitoring the early phases of movement planning (Sirigu et al., 2004), thus suggesting an impairment in anticipating the sensory consequences of manual movements. The readiness potential (RP), a marker of motor preparation that increases just before an observed movement (Kilner et al., 2003), was explored using electroencephalography in an elegant study on apraxic patients (Sirigu et al., 2004; Fontana et al., 2012). Apraxic patients passively viewed a series of short video clips showing a predictable hand moving on the basis of changes of colored objects. The results revealed a clear association between deficits typically present in patients with apraxia and the alteration to monitor the early planning phases of self-generated actions. Specifically, instead of showing the marker of motor preparation to self-generated movement observation-related events that was exhibited in control participants, no such RP was observed in patients with apraxia. Research has revealed that RP results from forward model predictions of the motor system precisely automatically preceding the movement's onset (Kilner et al., 2003). Within this context, the lack of RP exhibited by patients indicates that the inability to predict the consequences of one's own motor actions lead to inadequate online updating during actions (Pazzaglia, 2013a,b). The online information about movement is a prerequisite for the capacity to feel that one's own body generates the event and has control over it and the discrepancy between the predicted and actual sensory feedback is directly associated to a distorted phenomenology in the experience of agency.

Separately, the results from these studies reaffirm the objective difficulty in voluntary control of action and thereby its consequences by predictive mechanisms, and the ever-expanding apraxia picture on perturbation of agentive awareness. Despite few direct studies on agency, the disorder of the processes promoting agency that may co-occur in apraxia could fully explain the higher-order computations (e.g., related to intention to act and to the experience of controlling one's own actions, and, through them, events in the outside world) that likely interact with low-level motor mechanisms (e.g., the automatic selection of action primitives on which conscious experience corresponding to efficiency of action selection is based). This hypothetical processing, necessary to account the different form of apraxia observed, may be predicted on the basis of an internal model (see **Figure 1**) that attributes, evaluates, controls, or predicts the consequences of one's own actions, and compares these predictions to actual outcomes.

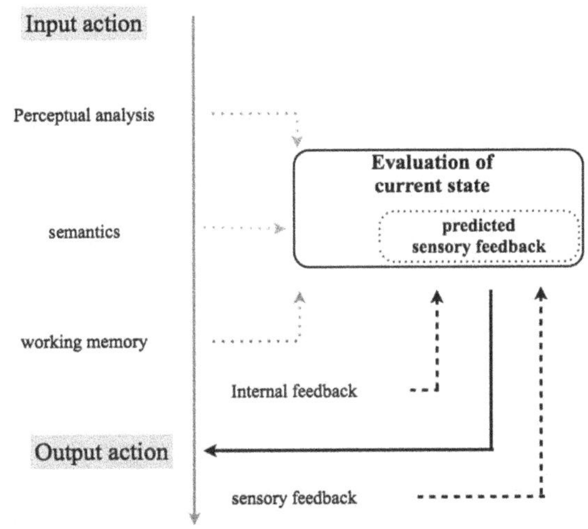

FIGURE 1 | Hypothetical model for performing and recognizing self-produced movements. The model has been adapted from Rothi and Heilman (1997) within the internal model adapted from Sirigu et al. (2003). Failures in performing or in recognizing gestures may occur because of damage at any stage in the directional flow of action between perceiving (input) and performing (output) an action. Successful completion of any gesture-related task (e.g., execution, imitation or recognition of either correctly or incorrectly, transitive (using objects) or intransitive (without objects) meaningful conventional limb gestures, etc.) requires access to an internal model. A prominent theory in motor control proposes the use of internal models with capacity to control or predict the consequences of one's own actions, and comparing these predictions to actual outcomes (Wolpert et al., 1995) adapted from Sirigu et al. (2003) to the putative level of dysfunction in apraxia. An efference copy of the motor command is used by forward models to predict the sensory feedback. The discrepancy between the predicted and actual sensory feedback is directly associated to a distorted phenomenology in the experience of agency. Hhypothetical models for performing and recognizing self-produced movements highlight the role of an internal model that attributes, evaluates, controls, or predicts the consequences of one's own actions, and compares these predictions to actual outcomes.

DOES AGENCY PLAY A CRUCIAL CAUSATIVE ROLE IN THE LEFT FRONTAL–PARIETAL NETWORK?

By examining both fMRI data on voluntary actions that are usually accompanied by an experience of agency and data on the anatomical localization of altered awareness and the control of volitional action in apraxia, it is possible to begin uncovering the neural substrates related to the sense of agency. FMRI allows the detection of brain activity changes that are *correlated* with motor intentions and subsequent action monitoring. It does not, however, clarify whether such activations play a *causal role.* In contrast, lesion-mapping analysis can highlight brain areas or circuits actively involved in the process of deriving actions from the original intention and plan of the movement. Several fMRI studies have suggested that the sense of agency, including action monitoring (Matsuzawa et al., 2005; Schnell et al., 2007; Farrer et al., 2008; Kontaris et al., 2009; Tsakiris et al., 2010; Chambon et al., 2013; Koban et al., 2013), prediction (Leube et al., 2003b; Ramnani and Miall, 2004; Spengler et al., 2009; Yomogida et al., 2010; Nahab et al., 2011), self-other coding (Blakemore et al., 1998; Leube et al., 2003a; Balslev et al., 2006; David et al., 2006, 2007; Ogawa and Inui, 2007; Fukushima et al., 2013; Lee and Reeve, 2013), and intentional binding (Kühn et al., 2013; Moore et al., 2013) involve the exchange of signals across a frontal–parietal network that voxel-based lesion symptom mapping (VLSM) analysis demonstrated is typically affected in apraxia (Pazzaglia et al., 2008a,b; Dovern et al., 2011). In particular, the posterior parietal cortex (PPC; Fink et al., 1999; Chaminade and Decety, 2002; Farrer and Frith, 2002; Farrer et al., 2003b, 2008; Chaminade et al., 2005) and the angular gyrus (AG) monitor signals related to action selection in the dorsolateral prefrontal cortex and the ventral premotor cortex (vPM) to prospectively signal subjective experience control over a coming action (Grossman et al., 2000; Leube et al., 2003a; Pelphrey et al., 2004; Ramnani and Miall, 2004; Saxe et al., 2004).

Healthy subjects report a decreased sense of agency when their intentions do not match the outcomes of their actions. In this case, activity in the temporo-parietal junction (TPJ) and AG regions increased as a function of the degree of retrospective action-intention mismatch (Farrer et al., 2008; Spengler et al., 2009), and might represent a self-indicator of volition prior to movement itself (Chambon et al., 2013). Therefore, direct electrical stimulation applied to the parietal cortex (AG and supramarginal gyrus, SMG) in patients undergoing awake surgery for tumor removal elicits the subjective experience of an "intention to move" the contralesional hand, arm, or foot (Desmurget et al., 2009).

Direct evidence of the anatomical and functional association on three different levels (the choice of action where ambiguity is present; self-perception/intentional binding; and the intention to act) has been obtained in patients with apraxia. Neurological investigations into the intention to move in apraxic participants have shown that the AG, in the inferior parietal lobule of the parietal cortex, may be essential for anticipating the multisensory consequences of predicted movements (Sirigu et al., 2004;

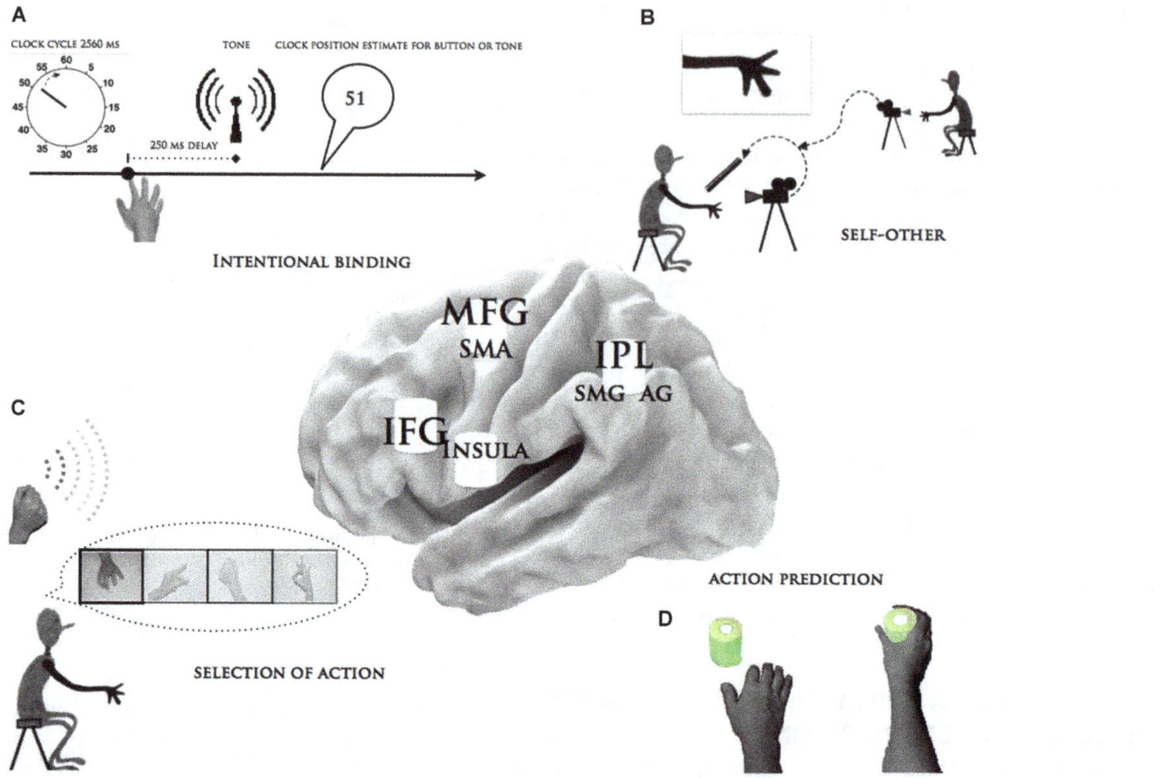

FIGURE 2 | Summary of the functional and anatomical link between the essential aspects of agency and apraxia. This figure describes some of the objective measures of agency obtained in patients with apraxia: **(A)** The *"intentional binding"* paradigm, in particular the chronometric approach for volition. **(B)** The *"self vs. other"* paradigm, specifically the differentiation of self-generated movements from experimenter-generated actions. **(C)** The *"selection of action paradigm"*, particularly the feeling of less power over efficacy of one's own action. **(D)** The *"neural intention to act"* in which EEG signals were recorded while the subjects passively watched a series of short videos showing the voluntary actions of an actor's hand. The central brain illustration depicts the critical brain areas for apraxia, which are alluded to in these paradigms. MFG = middle frontal gyrus, SMA = supplementary motor area, IFG = inferior frontal gyrus, insula, IPL = inferior parietal lobe, SMG = supra marginal gyrus, AG = angular gyrus.

Fontana et al., 2012). Similarly, both frontal and parietal structures may differentially code for self-generated actions as well as for action selection (Sirigu et al., 1999; Pazzaglia et al., 2008b). Patients with apraxia, who systematically identified the hand of a model that performed their same movement as their own, demonstrated mainly fronto-parietal lesions (Sirigu et al., 1999). A clear association was identified between the impairment in selection of four versions of actions to the gesture-sound with lesions mainly involving the inferior parietal region, SMG, and AG, but also extending as far as the frontal lobe (Pazzaglia et al., 2008b). Yet, impairments in correct selection of three versions of the same visual gesture presented within the same trial were related to the gray matter volume of the left anterior inferior parietal cortex extending into the posterior superior temporal gyrus (Nelissen et al., 2010).

Another circuit, anchored in the frontal lobe involving the supplementary motor area (SMA) and its most anterior portion, the pre-SMA (Farrer and Frith, 2002; Farrer et al., 2003a,b; Haggard and Clark, 2003; Haggard and Whitford, 2004; Cunnington et al., 2006; Lau et al., 2006), together with the dorsolateral prefrontal cortex (Fink et al., 1999; Slachevsky et al., 2001; Schnell et al., 2007; Synofzik et al., 2008), has been proposed to play a role in intentional binding and the judgment of agency, as has the insula (Karnath and Baier, 2010). Only recent behavioral, structural, and functional results converge to reveal the frontal network for altered awareness and the control of voluntary actions in patients with apraxia (Wolpe et al., 2014). Structural neuroimaging of voxel-based morphometry and diffusion tensor imaging showed that the volitional signals that drive internally generated actions in an intentional binding task were modulated by gray and white matter degeneration in the medial frontal-prefrontal network, with its hub in the pre-SMA (Wolpe et al., 2014). In apraxic patients, the dorsal premotor cortex may be essential for intentionally retrieving motor knowledge (Dovern et al., 2011). Although a substantial proportion of right-hemisphere damaged patients also showed apraxia (Donkervoort et al., 2000), involvement of the right hemisphere lesions to the sense of agency is currently lacking. Thus, two regions in the left hemisphere process different information (**Figure 2**), while the parietal lobe's principal functions might be to self-monitor motor intentions, the frontal lobe might be directly involved in forming, monitoring, and control intentions. Nonetheless, other cortical areas, such as the insula (Pazzaglia et al., 2008a,b), have been implicated in selecting different actions, so that the agentic experience in apraxia is likely to be sustained by a distributed left brain network rather than by a single brain center. For a schematic representation of the functional and anatomical link between the essential aspects of agency and apraxia see **Figure 2**.

AUTOMATIC RETRIEVAL STRATEGIES IN THERAPY FOR APRAXIA REHABILITATION

The loss of a sense of control over one's own movements plays, in apraxic patients, an important role in many purposeful actions that are an inherent part of daily life. It affects the self-care routines (Foundas et al., 1995; Hanna-Pladdy et al., 2003; Walker et al., 2004; Smania et al., 2006) with respect to, for example, personal hygiene (Goldenberg and Hagmann, 1998), preparing food (van Heugten et al., 2006), eating (Foundas et al., 1995), and dressing (Walker et al., 2004). Occasionally, the inability to predict the consequences of one's own motor acts can have devastating effects that jeopardize the autonomy and safety of the individual (Giovannetti et al., 2002; Hanna-Pladdy et al., 2003; Bettcher et al., 2011). A person with apraxia might be able to safely eat candy, but when attempting to smoke, risks getting burnt on the palm of the hand, cheeks, or elsewhere. From an adaptive point of view, intentional selection about incorrect actions could be deeply pervasive in a patient's life, and sometimes dangerous for their own safety (Hanna-Pladdy et al., 2003).

It is clear that progress in understanding action awareness and control represents a significant opportunity to strengthen the automatic rather than intentional retrieval strategies in the treatment of apraxic patients. After a stroke, patients with apraxia must increase the capacity to automatically retrieve learned motor knowledge by restoring the congruency between sensory-motor and intention systems. The prospective sense of agency might only develop once the brain has automatically re-learned. Matching or mismatching between visual but also multimodal signals and motor output re-stabilizes the relation between actions and outcomes. Automatically re-learning the appropriate responses to familiar action situations using closely associated perceptual-motor codes permits patients with apraxia to improve their selection of action (Smania et al., 2006), and thus function independently, but also, more importantly, can block the generation of unsafe motor patterns (Hanna-Pladdy et al., 2003).

CONCLUDING REMARKS

Taken together, the studies discussed in our perspective article seem to reveal a picture of apraxia that, although probably still incomplete, demonstrates how altered mechanisms that underlie awareness and control can be detrimental to agency. As such, these studies disclose more about agency itself. The prospective framework we offer here for apraxia renew the interpretation of the puzzling aspect generally viewed as apraxia, and encourage the advancement of novel and effective treatments to cure the disorder. Moreover, for agency, we provided support for the existence of a left parietal–frontal network underlying agentive self-awareness that continues to be a valuable way for gathering conclusive evidence on the role of agency in motor control and cognition as a natural part of human life, and thus provide ecologically valid data. Future studies focusing specifically on the thematic content of the sense of agency (e.g., related to the control of one's own action or to intention to act to social and cultural conditions in which the idea of responsibility is central for our own actions) may help to understand the wide and complex range of human actions in both normal and pathological conditions.

FUNDING INFORMATION

This work was supported by the University of Rome "Sapienza" and the Italian Ministry of Health [grant RC13.G] by IRCCS Fondazione Santa Lucia.

REFERENCES

Balslev, D., Nielsen, F. Å., Lund, T. E., Law, I., and Paulson, O. B. (2006). Similar brain networks for detecting visuo-motor and visuo-proprioceptive synchrony. *Neuroimage* 31, 308–312. doi: 10.1016/j.neuroimage.2005.11.037

Bettcher, B. M., Giovannetti, T., Libon, D. J., Eppig, J., Wambach, D., and Klobusicky, E. (2011). Improving everyday error detection, one picture at a time: a performance-based study of everyday task training. *Neuropsychology* 25, 771–783. doi: 10.1037/a0024107

Blakemore, S. J., Frith, C. D., and Wolpert, D. M. (2001). The cerebellum is involved in predicting the sensory consequences of action. *Neuroreport* 12, 1879–1884. doi: 10.1097/00001756-200107030-00023

Blakemore, S. J., Wolpert, D. M., and Frith, C. D. (1998). Central cancellation of self-produced tickle sensation. *Nat. Neurosci.* 1, 635–640. doi: 10.1038/2870

Botvinick, M. M., Buxbaum, L. J., Bylsma, L. M., and Jax, S. A. (2009). Toward an integrated account of object and action selection: a computational analysis and empirical findings from reaching-to-grasp and tool-use. *Neuropsychologia* 47, 671–683. doi: 10.1016/j.neuropsychologia.2008.11.024

Buxbaum, L. J., and Kalenine, S. (2010). Action knowledge, visuomotor activation and embodiment in the two action systems. *Ann. N Y Acad. Sci.* 1191, 201–218. doi: 10.1111/j.1749-6632.2010.05447.x

Chambon, V., Wenke, D., Fleming, S. M., Prinz, W., and Haggard, P. (2013). An online neural substrate for sense of agency. *Cereb. Cortex* 23, 1031–1037. doi: 10.1093/cercor/bhs059

Chaminade, T., and Decety, J. (2002). Leader or follower? Involvement of the inferior parietal lobule in agency. *Neuroreport* 13, 1975–1978. doi: 10.1097/00001756-200210280-00029

Chaminade, T., Meltzoff, A. N., and Decety, J. (2005). An fMRI study of imitation: action representation and body schema. *Neuropsychologia* 43, 115–127. doi: 10.1016/j.neuropsychologia.2004.04.026

Cunnington, R., Windischberger, C., Robinson, S., and Moser, E. (2006). The selection of intended actions and the observation of others' actions: a time-resolved fMRI study. *Neuroimage* 29, 1294–1302. doi: 10.1016/j.neuroimage.2005.09.028

David, N. (2012). New frontiers in the neuroscience of the sense of agency. *Front. Hum. Neurosci.* 6:161. doi: 10.3389/fnhum.2012.00161

David, N., Bewernick, B. H., Cohen, M. X., Newen, A., Lux, S., Fink, G. R., et al. (2006). Neural representations of self versus other: visual-spatial perspective taking and agency in a virtual ball-tossing game. *J. Cogn. Neurosci.* 18, 898–910. doi: 10.1162/jocn.2006.18.6.898

David, N., Cohen, M. X., Newen, A., Bewernick, B. H., Shah, N. J., Fink, G. R., et al. (2007). The extrastriate cortex distinguishes between the consequences of one's own and others' behavior. *Neuroimage* 36, 1004–1014. doi: 10.1016/j.neuroimage.2007.03.030

de Jong, B. M. (2011). Neurology of widely embedded free will. *Cortex* 47, 1160–1165. doi: 10.1016/j.cortex.2011.06.011

De Renzi, E., and Lucchelli, F. (1988). Ideational apraxia. *Brain* 111(Pt. 5), 1173–1185. doi: 10.1093/brain/111.5.1173

Desmurget, M., Reilly, K. T., Richard, N., Szathmari, A., Mottolese, C., and Sirigu, A. (2009). Movement intention after parietal cortex stimulation in humans. *Science* 324, 811–813. doi: 10.1126/science.1169896

Donkervoort, M., Dekker, J., van den Ende, E., Stehmann-Saris, J. C., and Deelman, B. G. (2000). Prevalence of apraxia among patients with a first left hemisphere stroke in rehabilitation centres and nursing homes. *Clin. Rehabil.* 14, 130–136. doi: 10.1191/026921500668935800

Dovern, A., Fink, G. R., Saliger, J., Karbe, H., Koch, I., and Weiss, P. H. (2011). Apraxia impairs intentional retrieval of incidentally acquired motor knowledge. *J. Neurosci.* 31, 8102–8108. doi: 10.1523/JNEUROSCI.6585-10.2011

Farrer, C., Franck, N., Georgieff, N., Frith, C. D., Decety, J., and Jeannerod, A. (2003a). Modulating the experience of agency: a positron emission tomography study. *Neuroimage* 18, 324–333. doi: 10.1016/s1053-8119(02)00041-1

Farrer, C., Franck, N., Paillard, J., and Jeannerod, M. (2003b). The role of proprioception in action recognition. *Conscious. Cogn.* 12, 609–619. doi: 10.1016/s1053-8100(03)00047-3

Farrer, C., Frey, S. H., Van Horn, J. D., Tunik, E., Turk, D., Inati, S., et al. (2008). The angular gyrus computes action awareness representations. *Cereb. Cortex* 18, 254–261. doi: 10.1093/cercor/bhm050

Farrer, C., and Frith, C. D. (2002). Experiencing oneself vs. another person as being the cause of an action: the neural correlates of the experience of agency. *Neuroimage* 15, 596–603. doi: 10.1006/nimg.2001.1009

Fink, G. R., Marshall, J. C., Halligan, P. W., Frith, C. D., Driver, J., Frackowiak, R. S. J., et al. (1999). The neural consequences of conflict between intention and the senses. *Brain* 122, 497–512. doi: 10.1093/brain/122.3.497

Fontana, A. P., Kilner, J. M., Rodrigues, E. C., Joffily, M., Nighoghossian, N., Vargas, C. D., et al. (2012). Role of the parietal cortex in predicting incoming actions. *Neuroimage* 59, 556–564. doi: 10.1016/j.neuroimage.2011.07.046

Foundas, A. L., Macauley, B. L., Raymer, A. M., Maher, L. M., Heilman, K. M., and Gonzalez Rothi, L. J. (1995). Ecological implications of limb apraxia: evidence from mealtime behavior. *J. Int. Neuropsychol. Soc.* 1, 62–66. doi: 10.1017/s1355617700000114

Fukushima, H., Goto, Y., Maeda, T., Kato, M., and Umeda, S. (2013). Neural substrates for judgment of self-agency in ambiguous situations. *PLoS One* 8:e72267. doi: 10.1371/journal.pone.0072267

Giovannetti, T., Libon, D. J., Buxbaum, L. J., and Schwartz, M. F. (2002). Naturalistic action impairments in dementia. *Neuropsychologia* 40, 1220–1232. doi: 10.1016/s0028-3932(01)00229-9

Goldenberg, G. (2013). *Apraxia: The Cognitive Side of Motor Control.* Oxford, New York: Oxford University Press.

Goldenberg, G., and Hagmann, S. (1998). Tool use and mechanical problem solving in apraxia. *Neuropsychologia* 36, 581–589. doi: 10.1016/s0028-3932(97)00165-6

Goldenberg, G., Hentze, S., and Hermsdörfer, J. (2004). The effect of tactile feedback on pantomime of tool use in apraxia. *Neurology* 63, 1863–1867. doi: 10.1212/01.wnl.0000144283.38174.07

Grossman, E., Donnelly, M., Price, R., Pickens, D., Morgan, V., Neighbor, G., et al. (2000). Brain areas involved in perception of biological motion. *J. Cogn. Neurosci.* 12, 711–720. doi: 10.1162/089892900562417

Haaland, K. Y., Harrington, D. L., and Knight, R. T. (2000). Neural representations of skilled movement. *Brain* 123(Pt. 11), 2306–2313. doi: 10.1093/brain/123.11.2306

Haggard, P., and Chambon, V. (2012). Sense of agency. *Curr. Biol.* 22, R390–R392. doi: 10.1016/j.cub.2012.02.040

Haggard, P., and Clark, S. (2003). Intentional action: conscious experience and neural prediction. *Conscious. Cogn.* 12, 695–707. doi: 10.1016/s1053-8100(03)00052-7

Haggard, P., Clark, S., and Kalogeras, J. (2002). Voluntary action and conscious awareness. *Nat. Neurosci.* 5, 382–385. doi: 10.1038/nn827

Haggard, P., and Whitford, B. (2004). Supplementary motor area provides an efferent signal for sensory suppression. *Brain Res. Cogn. Brain Res.* 19, 52–58. doi: 10.1016/j.cogbrainres.2003.10.018

Hanna-Pladdy, B., Heilman, K. M., and Foundas, A. L. (2003). Ecological implications of ideomotor apraxia: evidence from physical activities of daily living. *Neurology* 60, 487–490. doi: 10.1212/wnl.60.3.487

Hermsdörfer, J. (2014). Role of manipulation knowledge in routine tool use. *Cortex* 57, 292–293; discussion 306–308. doi: 10.1016/j.cortex.2014.02.016

Hermsdörfer, J., Blankenfeld, H., and Goldenberg, G. (2003). The dependence of ipsilesional aiming deficits on task demands, lesioned hemisphere and apraxia. *Neuropsychologia* 41, 1628–1643. doi: 10.1016/s0028-3932(03)00097-6

Hermsdörfer, J., Hentze, S., and Goldenberg, G. (2006). Spatial and kinematic features of apraxic movement depend on the mode of execution. *Neuropsychologia* 44, 1642–1652. doi: 10.1016/j.neuropsychologia.2006.03.023

Jackson, H. (1866). Notes on the physiology and pathology of language. *Brain* 38, 48–58.

Jax, S. A., and Buxbaum, L. J. (2010). Response interference between functional and structural actions linked to the same familiar object. *Cognition* 115, 350–355. doi: 10.1016/j.cognition.2010.01.004

Karnath, H. O., and Baier, B. (2010). Right insula for our sense of limb ownership and self-awareness of actions. *Brain Struct. Funct.* 214, 411–417. doi: 10.1007/s00429-010-0250-4

Kilner, J. M., Paulignan, Y., and Blakemore, S. J. (2003). An interference effect of observed biological movement on action. *Curr. Biol.* 13, 522–525. doi: 10.1016/s0960-9822(03)00165-9

Koban, L., Corradi-Dell'Acqua, C., and Vuilleumier, P. (2013). Integration of error agency and representation of others' pain in the anterior insula. *J. Cogn. Neurosci.* 25, 258–272. doi: 10.1162/jocn_a_00324

Kontaris, I., Wiggett, A. J., and Downing, P. E. (2009). Dissociation of extrastriate body and biological-motion selective areas by manipulation of visual-motor congruency. *Neuropsychologia* 47, 3118–3124. doi: 10.1016/j.neuropsychologia.2009.07.012

Kühn, S., Brass, M., and Haggard, P. (2013). Feeling in control: neural correlates of experience of agency. *Cortex* 49, 1935–1942. doi: 10.1016/j.cortex.2012.09.002

Lau, H. C., Rogers, R. D., and Passingham, R. E. (2006). On measuring the perceived onsets of spontaneous actions. *J. Neurosci.* 26, 7265–7271. doi: 10.1523/jneurosci.1138-06.2006

Lee, W., and Reeve, J. (2013). Self-determined, but not non-self-determined, motivation predicts activations in the anterior insular cortex: an fMRI study of personal agency. *Soc. Cogn. Affect. Neurosci.* 8, 538–545. doi: 10.1093/scan/nss029

Leiguarda, R. C., and Marsden, C. D. (2000). Limb apraxias: higher-order disorders of sensorimotor integration. *Brain* 123(Pt. 5), 860–879. doi: 10.1093/brain/123.5.860

Leube, D. T., Knoblich, G., Erb, M., Grodd, W., Bartels, M., and Kircher, T. T. (2003a). The neural correlates of perceiving one's own movements. *Neuroimage* 20, 2084–2090. doi: 10.1016/j.neuroimage.2003.07.033

Leube, D. T., Knoblich, G., Erb, M., and Kircher, T. T. J. (2003b). Observing one's hand become anarchic: an fMRI study of action identification. *Conscious. Cogn.* 12, 597–608. doi: 10.1016/s1053-8100(03)00079-5

Matsuzawa, M., Matsuo, K., Sugio, T., Kato, C., and Nakai, T. (2005). Temporal relationship between action and visual outcome modulates brain activation: an fMRI study. *Magn. Reson. Med. Sci.* 4, 115–121. doi: 10.2463/mrms.4.115

Moore, J. W., and Obhi, S. S. (2012). Intentional binding and the sense of agency: a review. *Conscious. Cogn.* 21, 546–561. doi: 10.1016/j.concog.2011.12.002

Moore, J. W., Teufel, C., Subramaniam, N., Davis, G., and Fletcher, P. C. (2013). Attribution of intentional causation influences the perception of observed movements: behavioral evidence and neural correlates. *Front. Psychol.* 4:23. doi: 10.3389/fpsyg.2013.00023

Nahab, F. B., Kundu, P., Gallea, C., Kakareka, J., Pursley, R., Pohida, T., et al. (2011). The neural processes underlying self-agency. *Cereb. Cortex* 21, 48–55. doi: 10.1093/cercor/bhq059

Nelissen, N., Pazzaglia, M., Vandenbulcke, M., Sunaert, S., Fannes, K., Dupont, P., et al. (2010). Gesture discrimination in primary progressive aphasia: the intersection between gesture and language processing pathways. *J. Neurosci.* 30, 6334–6341. doi: 10.1523/JNEUROSCI.0321-10.2010

Ogawa, K., and Inui, T. (2007). Lateralization of the posterior parietal cortex for internal monitoring of self- versus externally generated movements. *J. Cogn. Neurosci.* 19, 1827–1835. doi: 10.1162/jocn.2007.19.11.1827

Pazzaglia, M. (2013a). Does what you hear predict what you will do and say? *Behav. Brain Sci.* 36, 370–371. doi: 10.1017/s0140525x12002804

Pazzaglia, M. (2013b). Impact commentaries. Action discrimination: impact of apraxia. *J. Neurol. Neurosurg. Psychiatry* 84, 477–478. doi: 10.1136/jnnp-2012-304817

Pazzaglia, M., Pizzamiglio, L., Pes, E., and Aglioti, S. M. (2008a). The sound of actions in apraxia. *Curr. Biol.* 18, 1766–1772. doi: 10.1016/j.cub.2008.09.061

Pazzaglia, M., Smania, N., Corato, E., and Aglioti, S. M. (2008b). Neural underpinnings of gesture discrimination in patients with limb apraxia. *J. Neurosci.* 28, 3030–3041. doi: 10.1523/JNEUROSCI.5748-07.2008

Pelphrey, K. A., Morris, J. P., and McCarthy, G. (2004). Grasping the intentions of others: the perceived intentionality of an action influences activity in the superior temporal sulcus during social perception. *J. Cogn. Neurosci.* 16, 1706–1716. doi: 10.1162/0898929042947900

Pia, L., Garbarini, F., Fossataro, C., Fornia, L., and Berti, A. (2013). Pain and body awareness: evidence from brain-damaged patients with delusional body ownership. *Front. Hum. Neurosci.* 7:298. doi: 10.3389/fnhum.2013.00298

Pick, A. (1905). *Studienüber Motorische Apraxie und ihre Nahe Stehende Erscheinungen.* Leipzig: Deuticke.

Ramnani, N., and Miall, R. C. (2004). A system in the human brain for predicting the actions of others. *Nat. Neurosci.* 7, 85–90. doi: 10.1038/nn1168

Rothi, L. J., and Heilman, K. M. (1984). Acquisition and retention of gestures by apraxic patients. *Brain Cogn.* 3, 426–437. doi: 10.1016/0278-2626(84)90032-0

Rothi, L. J., and Heilman, K. M. (1997). *Apraxia, the Neuropsychology of Action.* Hove, UK: Psychology Press.

Rumiati, R. I. (2014). One or two things I know about apraxia. *Cortex* 57, 279–280; discussion 306–308. doi: 10.1016/j.cortex.2014.03.004

Rumiati, R. I., Zanini, S., Vorano, L., and Shallice, T. (2001). A form of ideational apraxia as a delective deficit of contention scheduling. *Cogn. Neuropsychol.* 18, 617–642. doi: 10.1080/02643290126375

Salomon, R., Lim, M., Kannape, O., Llobera, J., and Blanke, O. (2013). "Self pop-out": agency enhances self-recognition in visual search. *Exp. Brain Res.* 228, 173–181. doi: 10.1007/s00221-013-3549-6

Saxe, R., Xiao, D. K., Kovacs, G., Perrett, D. I., and Kanwisher, N. (2004). A region of right posterior superior temporal sulcus responds to observed intentional actions. *Neuropsychologia* 42, 1435–1446. doi: 10.1016/j.neuropsychologia.2004.04.015

Schnell, K., Heekeren, K., Schnitker, R., Daumann, J., Weber, J., Hesselmann, V., et al. (2007). An fMRI approach to particularize the frontoparietal network for visuomotor action monitoring: detection of incongruence between test subjects' actions and resulting perceptions. *Neuroimage* 34, 332–341. doi: 10.1016/j.neuroimage.2006.08.027

Sirigu, A., Cohen, L., Duhamel, J. R., Pillon, B., Dubois, B., and Agid, Y. (1995). A selective impairment of hand posture for object utilization in apraxia. *Cortex* 31, 41–55. doi: 10.1016/s0010-9452(13)80104-9

Sirigu, A., Daprati, E., Buxbaum, L. J., Giraux, P., and Pradat-Diehl, P. (2003). "How the human brain represents manual gestures: effect of brain damage," in *Taking Action: Cognitive Neuroscience Perspectives on Intentional Acts*, ed S. H. Johnson-Frey (Cambridge, MA: MIT Press), 167–183.

Sirigu, A., Daprati, E., Ciancia, S., Giraux, P., Nighoghossian, N., Posada, A., et al. (2004). Altered awareness of voluntary action after damage to the parietal cortex. *Nat. Neurosci.* 7, 80–84. doi: 10.1038/nn1160

Sirigu, A., Daprati, E., Pradat-Diehl, P., Franck, N., and Jeannerod, M. (1999). Perception of self-generated movement following left parietal lesion. *Brain* 122, 1867–1874. doi: 10.1093/brain/122.10.1867

Slachevsky, A., Pillon, B., Fourneret, P., Pradat-Diehl, P., Jeannerod, M., and Dubois, B. (2001). Preserved adjustment but impaired awareness in a sensory-motor conflict following prefrontal lesions. *J. Cogn. Neurosci.* 13, 332–340. doi: 10.1162/08989290151137386

Smania, N., Aglioti, S. M., Girardi, F., Tinazzi, M., Fiaschi, A., Cosentino, A., et al. (2006). Rehabilitation of limb apraxia improves daily life activities in patients with stroke. *Neurology* 67, 2050–2052. doi: 10.1212/01.wnl.0000247279.63483.1f

Spengler, S., von Cramon, D. Y., and Brass, M. (2009). Was it me or was it you? How the sense of agency originates from ideomotor learning revealed by fMRI. *Neuroimage* 46, 290–298. doi: 10.1016/j.neuroimage.2009.01.047

Synofzik, M., Vosgerau, G., and Newen, A. (2008). Beyond the comparator model: a multifactorial two-step account of agency. *Conscious. Cogn.* 17, 219–239. doi: 10.1016/j.concog.2007.03.010

Tsakiris, M., Longo, M. R., and Haggard, P. (2010). Having a body versus moving your body: neural signatures of agency and body-ownership. *Neuropsychologia* 48, 2740–2749. doi: 10.1016/j.neuropsychologia.2010.05.021

van Heugten, C., Visser-Meily, A., Post, M., and Lindeman, E. (2006). Care for carers of stroke patients: evidence-based clinical practice guidelines. *J. Rehabil. Med.* 38, 153–158. doi: 10.1080/16501970500441898

Walker, C. M., Sunderland, A., Sharma, J., and Walker, M. F. (2004). The impact of cognitive impairment on upper body dressing difficulties after stroke: a video analysis of patterns of recovery. *J. Neurol. Neurosurg. Psychiatry* 75, 43–48.

Weiss, C., Tsakiris, M., Haggard, P., and Schutz-Bosbach, S. (2014). Agency in the sensorimotor system and its relation to explicit action awareness. *Neuropsychologia* 52, 82–92. doi: 10.1016/j.neuropsychologia.2013.09.034

Wenke, D., Fleming, S. M., and Haggard, P. (2010). Subliminal priming of actions influences sense of control over effects of action. *Cognition* 115, 26–38. doi: 10.1016/j.cognition.2009.10.016

Wolpe, N., Moore, J. W., Rae, C. L., Rittman, T., Altena, E., Haggard, P., et al. (2014). The medial frontal-prefrontal network for altered awareness and control of action in corticobasal syndrome. *Brain* 137, 208–220. doi: 10.1093/brain/awt302

Wolpert, D. M., Ghahramani, Z., and Jordan, M. I. (1995). An internal model for sensorimotor integration. *Science* 269, 1880–1882. doi: 10.1126/science.7569931

Yomogida, Y., Sugiura, M., Sassa, Y., Wakusawa, K., Sekiguchi, A., Fukushima, A., et al. (2010). The neural basis of agency: an fMRI study. *Neuroimage* 50, 198–207. doi: 10.1016/j.neuroimage.2009.12.054

19

Tickle me, I think I might be dreaming! Sensory attenuation, self-other distinction and predictive processing in lucid dreams

Jennifer M. Windt[1]*, Dominic L. Harkness[2] and Bigna Lenggenhager[3,4]

[1] *Theoretical Philosophy Group, Department of Philosophy, Johannes Gutenberg-University of Mainz, Mainz, Germany*
[2] *Institute of Cognitive Science, University Osnabrück, Osnabrück, Germany*
[3] *Department of Neurology, University Hospital Zurich, Zurich, Switzerland*
[4] *Institute of Physiology and Zurich Center for Integrative Human Physiology (ZIHP), University of Zurich, Zurich, Switzerland*

***Correspondence:**
Jennifer M. Windt,
Philosophisches Seminar,
Johannes Gutenberg-Universität,
D-55099 Mainz, Germany
e-mail: windt@uni-mainz.de

The contrast between self- and other-produced tickles, as a special case of sensory attenuation for self-produced actions, has long been a target of empirical research. While in standard wake states it is nearly impossible to tickle oneself, there are interesting exceptions. Notably, participants awakened from REM (rapid eye movement-) sleep dreams are able to tickle themselves. So far, however, the question of whether it is possible to tickle oneself and be tickled by another *in* the dream state has not been investigated empirically or addressed from a theoretical perspective. Here, we report the results of an explorative web-based study in which participants were asked to rate their sensations during self-tickling and being tickled during wakefulness, imagination, and lucid dreaming. Our results, though highly preliminary, indicate that in the special case of lucid control dreams, the difference between self-tickling and being tickled by another is obliterated, with both self- and other produced tickles receiving similar ratings as self-tickling during wakefulness. This leads us to the speculative conclusion that in lucid control dreams, sensory attenuation for self-produced tickles spreads to those produced by non-self dream characters. These preliminary results provide the backdrop for a more general theoretical and metatheoretical discussion of tickling in lucid dreams in a predictive processing framework. We argue that the primary value of our study lies not so much in our results, which are subject to important limitations, but rather in the fact that they enable a new theoretical perspective on the relationship between sensory attenuation, the self-other distinction and agency, as well as suggest new questions for future research. In particular, the example of tickling during lucid dreaming raises the question of whether sensory attenuation and the self-other distinction can be simulated largely independently of external sensory input.

Keywords: agency, self-other distinction, dreaming, lucidity, tickling, self-tickling, sensory attenuation, predictive processing

> "*. . . from the fact that a child can hardly tickle itself, or in a much less degree than when tickled by another person, it seems the precise point to be touched must not be known. . .*"
>
> (Darwin, 1859)

INTRODUCTION

Why is it almost impossible to tickle oneself, and so easy to be tickled by others? And what can tickling tell us about the sense of agency, ownership and the self-other distinction? At least since Darwin, it has been thought that the inability to self-tickle—especially to the point of inducing laughter—is linked to the unpredictability and uncontrollability of other- as opposed to self-tickling. The advent of tickling machines enabled researchers to identify and isolate the relevant factors in an experimentally controlled manner. In a seminal study, Weiskrantz et al. (1971) devised an apparatus that could be used for active (motor command plus proprioceptive feedback) or passive (proprioceptive feedback *without* motor commands) self-tickling as well for being tickled by another person. They found that active self-tickling was least effective, with passive self-tickling being intermediate between active self-tickling and being tickled by another. This result, which has been confirmed in a number of follow-up studies (e.g., Blakemore et al., 2000b), suggests that sensory feed-forward information, but also proprioceptive feedback from the tickling hand are crucial for sensory attenuation during self-tickling and for the self-other distinction. The general idea is that sensory attenuation, in which the sensory consequences of self-generated actions are dampened, underlies the ability to distinguish between self and others (Blakemore et al., 2000a; Frith et al., 2000). Because the sensory consequences of self-produced tickling match our predictions and thus are unsurprising, they also *feel* less ticklish than the more unexpected tickles produced by others. Indeed, on this view, the felt ticklishness of other-produced tickles alerts us to the fact that we have been tickled by another, and not by ourselves.

TICKLING IN A PREDICTIVE PROCESSING FRAMEWORK

The theoretical framework proposed by predictive processing accounts now offers a new perspective on Darwin's claim that sensory attenuation during self-tickling depends on the predictability of the stimulus. According to this framework (e.g., Clark, 2013b; Hohwy, 2013), the brain is essentially involved in hypothesis testing and prediction error minimization, with prediction errors resulting from a mismatch between predicted and actual sensory input. While prediction error minimization has been suggested to operate on many different levels of the cortical hierarchy and to underlie a wide range of cognitive processes, including perception, beliefs, learning and attention to illusions, hallucinations and delusions (Mumford, 1992; Hohwy, 2010), there are principally two different ways in which it can be achieved. First, incoming sensory inputs can be used to optimize internal predictions (or generative models) about the brain's next possible states, as in perception. Second, action, or active inference, ensues when the organism changes its sensory inputs in order to better match its predictions (Friston et al., 2011). What the brain abhors, on this account, is surprise: the amount of surprise, or more technically free energy (Friston and Kiebel, 2009), signals that the internal predictions were insufficiently accurate or outright false. Less surprise, on this view, indicates a better fit of the internal models.

This view offers a new way of making sense of sensory attenuation during self-tickling. On the classical model, a copy (the so-called efference copy) of motor commands is used to compare the predicted and actual sensory consequences of self-generated movement; when the discrepancy is minimal, sensory attenuation occurs (Blakemore et al., 1998a,b, 2003; Frith et al., 2000). By contrast, predictive processing accounts do away with the need for an efference copy, suggesting that in ambiguous situations, the attribution of agency can be resolved by attending away from the consequences of self-generated movements. On this view, "sensory attenuation is a necessary consequence of reducing the precision of sensory evidence during movement to allow the expression of proprioceptive predictions that incite movement" (Brown et al., 2013, p. 413). Attenuation, in other words, is the phenomenal mark of self- as opposed to other-generated action.

A recent study (van Doorn et al., 2014) contrasted these two accounts by investigating self-tickling and being tickled by another person in a highly surprising context—namely an experimentally induced self-other confusion involving the illusion of having swapped bodies with someone else (cf. Petkova and Ehrsson, 2008) and of experiencing another person's hand as one's own (cf. rubber hand illusion; Botvinick and Cohen, 1998). The background idea was that this would be a way of testing whether confrontation with a highly non-standard, surprising situation might undermine the precision with which the exact pattern of proprioceptive and tactile feedback during self-tickling could be predicted—thus enabling it to feel more like being tickled by someone else. Whereas this would fit the classical efference copy model, van Doorn and colleagues' findings suggest that this is not the case: "even as participants shift their first-person perspective to someone else's, or experience having a baseball bat as a hand, or an invisible hand, there is no change in the characteristic pattern of feeling less tickle sensation when producing the touch themselves, and more tickle sensation when the touch is produced by someone else" (van Doorn et al., 2014, p. 8). The authors conclude that because sensory attenuation during self-tickling remains robust even in these highly surprising conditions, active inference, rather than context, is crucial for sensory attenuation, thus favoring predictive processing over the classical efference copy model.

THE PHENOMENAL-FUNCTIONAL CHARACTERISTICS OF DREAMING

In the following, we argue that dreams are a unique contrast condition for investigating the relationship between agency and the self-other distinction not just in specific experimental setups in waking participants, but across the sleep-wake cycle. In particular, the example of dreaming can extend existing work on sensory attenuation and the self-other distinction within the framework of predictive processing.

First, while paradigms investigating full-body illusions such as the body-swap illusion aim to disturb the mechanisms underlying the self-other distinction in healthy, waking subjects, dreaming involves a more profound and naturally occurring breakdown of the distinction between self and non-self, or between internally and externally generated sensory information. In the dream state, what is in fact an internally generated world-model—the dream world—is not experienced as self-generated, but simply as real (Metzinger, 2003; Revonsuo, 2006), typically including the experience of interacting with mind-independent characters and objects. Dreams are, in other words, *immersive spatiotemporal hallucinations* (Windt, 2010, 2015): they involve the robust sense of presence in a world that is experienced as real; yet, at the same time, this experienced world is only weakly constrained by sensory inputs from the sleeping subject's actual environment and is largely the product of internal signal generation, and hence hallucinatory. Because of this profound confusion of internally and externally produced stimuli, dreaming has even been suggested to be a model of delusional and hallucinatory wake states, such as those arising in schizophrenia (see Hobson, 1999; Gottesmann, 2006; see Windt and Noreika, 2011, for critical discussion).

Second and relatedly, social imagery is abundant in dreams, with non-self (usually human) dream characters being described in over 95% of adults' dream reports and the average dream involving 2–4 non-self dream characters (Kahn et al., 2000; see Nielsen and Lara-Carrasco, 2007, for details and further references). These are typically experienced as being highly realistic and clearly distinct from the self. Social interactions are actually even more frequent in dream reports than in randomly timed waking reports (McNamara et al., 2005) and are often experienced as emotionally engaging (Kahn et al., 2002). In particular, non-self dream characters are often experienced as having a mind of their own, with dream reports frequently describing cases in which the dreamer engages in theory-of-mind attributions by ascribing emotions, beliefs and desires to other dream characters (McNamara et al., 2007). This suggests that dreaming involves not only a breakdown of the distinction between internally and externally generated sensory information, but also specific disturbances in self-other distinctions.

Third, while both dreaming and wakefulness are characterized, on the phenomenological level of description, by the experience of interacting with a world, the transition from wakefulness to dreaming is accompanied by important functional changes. During the dream state, conscious experience is comparatively shielded from and only weakly constrained by external stimuli. While external stimuli are occasionally incorporated in dreams, the pattern of incorporation is often indirect, resembling sensory illusions rather than veridical perception (as in a dream of hearing a siren that is triggered by the sound of one's alarm clock; cf. Nielsen et al., 1995; see Windt, 2015, for theoretical discussion). Moreover, REM-sleep paralysis, or the near-complete absence of muscle tone during REM sleep, prevents the outward enactment of internally experienced movements (for a discussion of important exceptions involving dream-enactment behavior, see Schenck, 2005; Nielsen et al., 2009; Leclair-Visonneau et al., 2010). This unique phenomenal-functional configuration, as will become clear below, is particularly interesting from a predictive processing perspective.

PREDICTIVE PROCESSES IN DREAMS

Recent attempts to accommodate REM-sleep dreaming in a predictive processing framework suggest that alterations in the monitoring and generation of sensory predictions might be crucial to dreaming. As noted above, these accounts owe some of their attraction to the ambitious claim that not just veridical perception, but also imagination, hallucinations and nocturnal dreams are the outcome of a process of hypothesis testing and prediction error minimization. In this framework, dreaming, due to the comparative attenuation of external stimulus processing, has been described as a state in which hypothesis testing and prediction error minimization can be rehearsed and optimized (Clark, 2013a,b; Hohwy, 2013; cf. Hobson and Friston, 2012, 2014).

For the same reason, however, dreaming also presents a challenge for predictive processing accounts. Recall that the key claim of these accounts is that internal predictions are tested against incoming sensory stimuli, resulting either in the optimization of the internal, generative models themselves (as in perception) or in changing the incoming stimuli to better fit the internal models (as in active inference). In dreams, however, both types of processes are disturbed: because dreams unfold largely independently of sensory input and motor output, the crucial ingredient for either model optimization or active inference is lacking. Yet, because dreaming nonetheless involves the vivid phenomenology of perceiving and interacting with a mind-independent world rather than with one of our own making, both processes must be simulated, as it were, largely offline. Indeed, it has been suggested that dream bizarreness might result from the fact that dreams are largely unconstrained by external stimuli and hence by prediction errors, leading to the loss of representational accuracy, for instance of visual dream imagery (cf. Fletcher and Frith, 2009; Hobson and Friston, 2012). This does not explain, however, why large portions of dream experience are not bizarre, but are experienced as highly realistic (including, as noted above, non-self dream characters). This in itself is a remarkable computational achievement, suggesting that in the special case of dreaming, the processes of prediction error minimization and hypothesis testing are simulated largely internally, but nonetheless in a fairly realistic manner. Dreams thus offer a unique opportunity for investigating the interplay between hypothesis testing and prediction error minimization on the one hand and the sensory stimuli they are tested against, in standard wake states, on the other hand, suggesting that this relationship changes dramatically over the sleep-wake cycle.

SELF TICKLING IN DREAMS?

In sum, the presented literature suggests that a transient breakdown in the ability to discriminate, on the level of phenomenal experience, between self- and other-generated actions, mediated by disturbances in the sense of agency and the precision of sensory predictions, might be crucial to the unique phenomenology of dreaming. Here, we suggest that questions about the process of hypothesis testing and prediction error minimization in dreams can be sharpened by focusing on the special question of why, in dreams, self-produced actions are experienced as if they were caused by others. Again, sensory attenuation for self-tickling as opposed to being tickled by another is a promising example. In particular, schizophrenics, unlike healthy participants, are able to tickle themselves (Blakemore et al., 2000a,b), presumably due to a disturbance in self-other distinctions. Similarly, Blagrove et al. (2006) found that participants awakened from REM sleep dreams are able to tickle themselves, which they explained by saying that "a deficit in self-monitoring and a confusion between self- and external-stimulation accompany REM dream formation" (Blagrove et al., 2006, p. 291).

The logical next question to ask, we suggest, is whether it is possible to tickle oneself in dreams. Here, it is important to note that the evidence presented by Blagrove and colleagues is indirect at best, as the effect was only observed after awakening and not during the dream state itself. Moreover, participants were only asked about the presence or absence of dream recall, but the content of their dreams was not analyzed. This points to an important methodological limitation, namely the practical impossibility of obtaining systematic ticklishness ratings for self- as compared to other-administered tickles during dreams. Lucid dreams, however, are an important exception, as they involve not only insight into the fact that one is now dreaming, but often also the ability to control the dream narrative, including the actions of non-self dream characters (LaBerge, 1985, 1990; Voss et al., 2013). Lucid insight into the fact that one is dreaming often coexists alongside vivid visual and motor hallucinations and social imagery, sometimes even leading lucid dreamers to think they are sharing their dream with another (Levitan, 1994). This is important, because it suggests that the disturbances in self-other distinctions that characterize nonlucid dreams largely remain intact in lucid dreams.

Our study aimed to exploit this fact by asking participants to contrast self- and other-administered tickles in three conditions: wakefulness, imagination, and lucid dreaming. Based on theoretical considerations on lucid dreams, but also on findings on self-tickling in healthy participants, schizophrenics, and following REM-sleep dreams, we predicted that while our participants would rate other-administered tickles as more ticklish than self-administered ones in wakefulness (*prediction 1*), this difference would be diminished in dreams (*prediction 2*). We also expected that in dreams, self-tickling would feel more like being tickled by another than like self-tickling in wakefulness (*prediction 3*). By contrast, we expected the distinction between self- and other-administered tickles to be preserved for imagined tickles (*prediction 4*), though we expected that both would be rated as less ticklish than their actual (and dreamed) counterparts (*prediction 5*).

AN EXPLORATIVE STUDY OF SELF-TICKLING IN LUCID DREAMS

This explorative online study aimed to rate how ticklish it feels to tickle oneself as compared to being tickled by someone else in three different conditions: actual self-tickling vs. actually being tickled during wakefulness; imagined self-tickling vs. imagining being tickled; and self-tickling vs. being tickled by another in a lucid dream.

PARTICIPANTS

Participants were recruited via a German Internet platform for lucid dreamers (www.klartraum.de). Sixty-one persons participated in the first part of the study (questionnaire on actual and imagined tickling in wakefulness), but only 9 participated in the second part (tickling in lucid dreams). From our data we cannot judge whether this high drop-out rate was due to the difficulty of the task or the time-consuming nature of the study as whole. We did, however, ask participants to fill out the lucid dreaming questionnaire even if they did not manage to tickle themselves in their dream. Out of the 9 dream responses, 7 (4 female, average age 20.7) were able to complete the task and were thus included in the analysis.

PROCEDURE

The experiment was entirely web-based. Written instructions were given to the participants before they started the experiment. Participants were instructed to complete the experiment in two sessions. Actual tickling and imagined tickling were performed in a first session during the daytime, followed by dream tickling in a second session during a lucid dream. In all conditions, participants were asked to use (or imagine using, respectively) a feather, brush or a similar tool to first tickle their own foot, then to ask (or imagine asking) someone else to tickle their foot. Immediately after each task (respectively after waking up from a lucid dream), they completed an online questionnaire, adapted from the study conducted by Blagrove et al. (2006), in which they were asked to rate how "intense," "ticklish," "pleasant," and "irritating" the stimulation felt on a discrete scale from 0 (not at all) to 10 (extremely). For the dream condition, they were additionally asked to give a free dream report (see supplementary material). In order to minimize the risk of forgetting, we emphasized the importance of filling in the questionnaire and reporting their dream immediately after awakening.

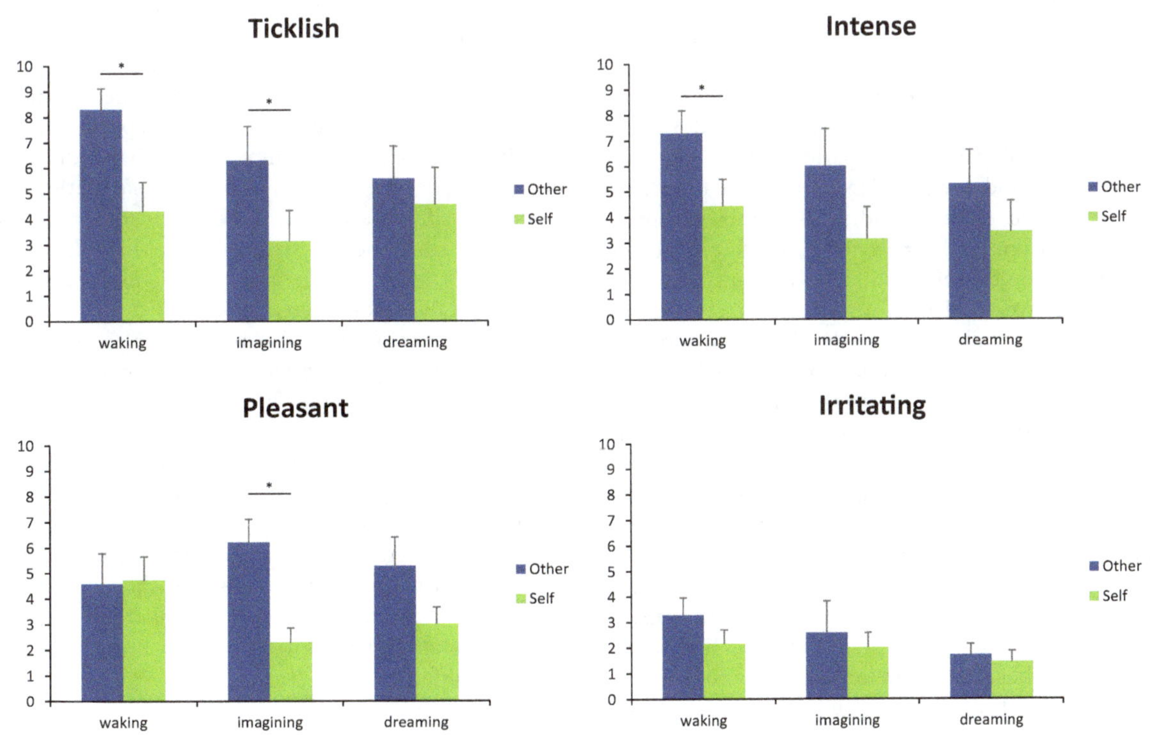

FIGURE 1 | Mean and standard error of the participants' ratings for each of the four scales in the three different conditions (waking, imagining, dreaming). *Indicates $p < 0.05$ according to an uncorrected, non-parametric comparison between ratings for self-tickling and ratings for being tickled by another person.

Table 1 | Results of the Wilcoxon comparisons.

Scale	State	Mean other	Mean self	Z-score	*p*-value
Intense	Waking	7.3	4.4	2.06	0.04
	Imagining	6.0	3.1	1.90	0.06
	Dreaming	5.3	3.4	1.46	0.14
Ticklish	Waking	8.3	4.3	2.02	0.04
	Imagining	6.3	3.2	2.00	0.046
	Dreaming	5.6	4.6	1.29	0.20
Pleasant	Waking	4.6	4.7	0.41	0.68
	Imagine	6.2	2.3	2.20	0.03
	Dreaming	5.3	3.0	1.60	0.11
Irritating	Waking	3.3	2.1	1.84	0.07
	Imagining	2.6	2.0	0.45	0.66
	Dreaming	1.7	1.4	1.41	0.16

Red color = significant value ($p < 0.05$).

RESULTS

The results are depicted in **Figure 1**, which shows mean and standard errors for each of the four scales in the three different conditions (waking, imagining, dreaming). Uncorrected wilcoxon tests (see **Table 1**) were done for each scale in each of the conditions in order to test whether there was a difference between self-tickling and being tickled by another person.

Confirming previous findings (e.g., Weiskrantz et al., 1971) and in line with *prediction 1*, participants' ratings of the ticklishness of other-administered tickles were higher than for self-tickling when the task was performed during wakefulness. A similar pattern was found for imagined self- and other-administered tickling, though both had a lesser absolute intensity than actual tickling (thus confirming *predictions 4* and *5*). This makes us confident that participants performed the test correctly and that the method was sufficient to replicate the results found by a number of existing studies. By contrast, during lucid dreams, and in line with *prediction 2*, we found no significant difference between self- and other-administered tickling. Interestingly, however, ticklish sensations in dreams still felt less ticklish than actually being tickled by another person during wakefulness and were comparable to waking self-tickling (Wilcoxon test, $Z = 0.82$, $p = 0.41$)—thus contradicting *prediction 3*. This effect was specific to ticklishness ratings, and dream tickles were rated as similarly intense, irritating and pleasant as imagined and/or actual tickles. Our highly preliminary conclusion is that both being tickled and tickling oneself, at least in a lucid dream, feel much like tickling oneself in wakefulness, but weaker than being tickled by another. This, in turn, suggests that in the special case of lucid control dreams, sensory attenuation characterizes not just self-administered tickles, but also those experienced as being administered by another. This stands in interesting contrast to the findings that schizophrenic participants rate self-tickling as being as intense as being tickled by another, and that the same is true for participants who have awakened from (presumably nonlucid) REM-sleep dreams.

LIMITATIONS

Clearly, this study is subject to important limitations and the results should be taken with caution. Yet, we think that considering these in detail is interesting in itself, because it helps illustrate what we take to be the larger theoretical implications of this study. Though this may sound somewhat paradoxical, we think that the value of our study lies, in part, in the insights that can be derived from a careful consideration of what it did *not* show, and why. Indeed, this is also why we take the main value of this study to be of a theoretical rather than of an empirical nature. In particular, a discussion of these limitations also suggests a number of specific challenges and questions for future research.

PRACTICAL AND METHODOLOGICAL LIMITATIONS

To begin with, there are a number of practical and methodological limitations. Due to the demanding nature of the task, only a very small number of participants succeeded in completing the tickle-test in a lucid dream. Because this was an online study, we could not control whether the task was indeed carried out according to our instructions (though reports no. 4 and 5 suggest that this was the case), which sleep stage the lucid dreams occurred in, or how soon after awakening participants actually reported their dreams. This situation could be improved by conducting a laboratory study, insisting on signal verified lucid dreams and obtaining polysomnographic measurements to determine the sleep stages in which the dreams occurred (cf. LaBerge et al., 1981).

Furthermore, unlike the studies of self-tickling in waking participants, we were not able to use a tickling machine and thus to standardize the procedure. Rather, as shown by the dream reports, our participants dreamt up different tickling devices, such as wooden spoons, pens, or branches (cf. reports no. 1, 4, 6) and were also occasionally tickled elsewhere than on the foot (cf. reports no. 5, 8). A number of dream reports describe difficulties with dream-character compliance, such that dream characters refused to carry out the tickling task or poked rather than tickled the dream self (cf. report no. 1). Some dream reports are also too short to be sure whether dreamers were really lucid (cf. reports no. 3, 7, 8), and even when lucid, participants occasionally forgot to carry out the task (cf. report no. 9).

Expectation may have also biased our results. For instance, Guiguère and LaBerge (1995) found that pinching in a lucid dream was not really painful, possibly due to expectation and motivation bias; moreover, at least one dream report (cf. report no. 2) suggests that the dreamer was theorizing about the outcome and implications of the experiment even during the lucid dream. Yet, the fact that ticklish-ratings for lucid dreams did not simply mirror ratings for actual and imagined tickling and specifically that the characteristic gap between self- and other administered tickles was preserved during imagined, but obliterated during dreamed task performance suggests that our study nonetheless tapped into a genuine difference.

THEORETICAL LIMITATIONS

A further limitation that is not specific to our study but characterizes lucid dream research in general is that the generalizability of results from lucid to nonlucid dreams is unclear. Indeed, it is possible that *prediction 3*, which was contradicted by our study, accurately characterizes nonlucid dreams. Because the phenomenal property of agency and the resulting ability to control both one's own and others' actions differ strongly between lucid and nonlucid dreams (Metzinger, 2003; Windt and Metzinger, 2007; Voss et al., 2013), and because of the suggested link between agency and sensory attenuation, it could well be that in nonlucid dreams, there would be no sensory attenuation for self-tickling.

A first step toward answering this question might be to compare ticklish sensations after waking up from lucid as compared to non-lucid dreams. If the attenuation of ticklish sensations in lucid dreams is indeed related to the increased sense of agency that characterizes lucid dream control, then one might expect both self- and other-administered tickles to be attenuated even after awakening from a lucid dream. Alternatively, the pattern observed in dreams might also be reversed, and participants awakened from a lucid dream might show the same ticklish ratings as participants awakened from nonlucid REM-sleep dreams, namely an increased ability to tickle themselves. It could also be the case, however, that after awakening from a lucid dream, ticklish ratings are the same as in standard wakefulness, but different from the pattern observed following nonlucid REM-sleep dreams. Indeed, lucid dreams are often described as involving a shift toward wake-like cognitive activity and agentive control and might even be regarded as subjective states in a much stronger sense than nonlucid dreams (Metzinger, 2003; Windt and Metzinger, 2007). It has also been suggested that lucidity occurs during a hybrid state between nonlucid REM-sleep dreams and wakefulness (Voss et al., 2009). Whatever the outcome, contrasting ticklishness ratings after awakening from lucid and nonlucid dreams might tell us something about the relationship between lucid insight, agency and sensory attenuation, as well as about the generalizability of our results from lucid to nonlucid dreams.

DISCUSSION

Given the limitations discussed above, the results of our study are highly preliminary. Yet, we think they give rise to a number of interesting, albeit speculative, considerations, as well as to some new hypotheses and perspectives for future research. In order to describe these in a maximally clear manner, we will assume, *purely for the sake of argument*, that our results had been substantiated by further studies. Skeptical readers are invited to regard the following as a theory-based thought experiment loosely inspired by some preliminary empirical observations.

DOES SENSORY ATTENUATION REALLY UNDERLIE THE SELF-OTHER DISTINCTION IN DREAMS?

Even if they are taken at face value, it is important to note that the interpretation of our results is hampered by an underlying theoretical ambiguity. Spelling this out in some detail is instructive, because it helps illustrate a more general difficulty in comparing dreams and wakefulness. This is especially important given our claim that the example of lucid dreaming extends research on sensory attenuation in wakefulness. So far we have assumed that the weak ticklishness ratings found in our study are indeed an example of sensory attenuation specific to self-generated actions. However, because dream actions unfold largely independently both of the actual execution of dream movements (with the exception of dream-enactment) and of appropriate proprioceptive feedback, it is not clear that it makes sense to say that in dreams, the consequences of self-produced actions are attenuated in the first place. Moreover, while dreams typically involve the experience of phenomenal selfhood, or of being or having a self, bodily experiences are characteristically underrepresented in dreams, and body and body-part representations can also differ from the waking body (cf. report no. 4, which describes that the dreamer's toe looked like a banana, as well as difficulty controlling leg movements; for details and further references, see Windt, 2010, 2015). Consequently, it is possible that the attenuation of ticklish sensations observed in our study is an artifact of the more general phenomenal-functional characteristics of bodily experience in the dream state. On this view, sensory attenuation would only be present for the sensory consequences of actual movements and would not be applicable to the case of dreamed actions unfolding independently of their outward counterparts.

We do not, however, think that this alternative explanation, in itself, offers an entirely satisfying account of our findings. To begin with, studies of lucid dreaming suggest that dream movements continue to be associated with muscle twitches in the respective limbs (LaBerge et al., 1981; Fenwick et al., 1984) as well as with activation of the sensorimotor cortex (Erlacher and Schredl, 2008; Dresler et al., 2011). Moreover, while touch, thermal and pain sensations are only rarely described in dream reports (Hobson, 1988), both lucid and nonlucid dreams do at least occasionally include vivid tactile or even pain sensations (e.g., Voss et al., 2011). This was also the case in at least some of the dreams reported by our participants, who described either varying degrees of ticklishness or other sensations such as pain (cf. reports no. 1, 4, 5, 6). Also, a questionnaire-based study similar to our own found that dream caressing was rated as having equal intensity as actual (but not as imagined) caressing (Giguère and LaBerge, 1995). It at least seems possible, then, that our results can be compared to sensory attenuation of the type that is otherwise specific to the sensory consequences of self-generated actions in wakefulness.

A recent review of the factors underlying sensory attenuation further supports the claim that sensory attenuation is not wholly determined by motor predictions. As Hughes et al. (2013) suggest, the ability to predict or even control the timing of sensory events may also modulate sensory attenuation. As most existing studies have not controlled for these factors, it is unclear, according to the authors, that sensory attenuation, for instance during self-tickling, is driven by motor rather than temporal predictions or temporal control. They also tentatively suggest that temporal predictions may play a role in explaining schizophrenics' hallucinations and delusions of control. This leads us to speculate that a similar factor might be driving our results in lucid dreams.

A first conclusion, then, would be that lucid control dreams are the special case in which sensory attenuation spreads to actions initiated by "others," at least in the sense in which non-self dream characters are experienced as distinct from the self, thus dampening other-generated tickles to a level comparable to self-generated ones. It is noteworthy that in dreams, this is not, however, associated with a complete obliteration of the experienced self-other distinction. By contrast, in wakefulness, *illusory* feelings of agency, or the experience of being able to control another's actions (e.g., *vicarious agency* Wegner et al., 2004) typically also result in an illusory feeling of ownership for these actions and in disturbed self-other distinctions (Tsakiris et al., 2006). For fully lucid dreams, the situation seems to be different: even though in such dreams, dreamers *know* that they are dreaming and are aware that non-self dream characters (including their actions) are ultimately creatures of their own making, they still continue to experience these as clearly distinct from themselves (see also our dream reports). Contrary to what one might expect based on studies of vicarious agency and full-body illusions in wakefulness, in dreams, controlling a body does not, it would seem, induce one to experience this body as one's own.

A fascinating question that we at present have no answer for is how to explain this difference. In order to be able even to gesture toward an explanation, one would have to know whether agency and/or sensory attenuation for dream tickles is prior to self-other distinction of the type involved, for instance, in experiencing another dream character as distinct from oneself (i.e., the dream self), whether the opposite is true, or whether these processes are independent. Whereas in wakefulness, ownership seems, at least occasionally, to follow on the heels of agency (such as in motor versions of the rubber-hand illusion; see Tsakiris et al., 2006), it is also possible that the purely phenomenological distinction between dream self and non-self dream characters taps into more basic and robust processes.

SENSORY ATTENUATION AND SELF-OTHER DISTINCTIONS IN DREAMS FROM A PREDICTIVE PROCESSING PERSPECTIVE

The problem of how to describe the relationship between sensory attenuation and self-other distinctions in dreams can be nicely sharpened by describing it from the perspective of predictive processing. Recall that predictive processing accounts suggest that in dreaming as in waking, we only have access to our generative models, but are never in direct perceptual contact with the world. Hence, the direct comparison between these states within a predictive processing framework seems permissible—with the exception, noted above, that in dreams, the predictions are not kept in check by the outer world, thus being able to "roam free." Conscious experience in dreams, then, may be seen as isolating our prior convictions from the ability to test them against incoming sensory input. On this view, dreaming is even more strongly constrained by our prior convictions about the world because we lack the means to check and adjust them to sensory input during perception and active inference.

Moreover, recent attempts to account for self-consciousness in a predictive processing framework highlight the probabilistic nature of self-representation, including the representation of one's physical body (Limanowski and Blankenburg, 2013; Apps and Tsakiris, 2014). What is experienced as the self is, on this view, highly plastic and constrained not only by low-level influences, such as multisensory stimuli and even interoceptive cues (on the latter, see Seth et al., 2012; Aspell et al., 2013; van Elk et al., 2014), but also by high-level processes such as long-term beliefs. In particular, as Apps and Tsakiris (2014, p. 92) put it, "the free-energy account argues that information prior to an event will nuance predictions about the likely sensory input, and when sensory input is received, the prior information biases the probabilistic inferences that are made causes of an event." Self-other distinctions in dreams, on this view, reflect sensory predictions operating under non-standard conditions of highly unstable and mostly internally generated sensory information and driven to a considerable extent by long-standing and shorter-term contextual beliefs.

What, then, are the priors driving the experience of self-tickling and being tickled by another in dreams? One of these, it would seem, is the conviction that we cannot fully control, or at least not directly and via acts of will, any bodily agent other than ourselves. Indeed, given that participants were asked to control the actions of dream characters they were already experiencing as distinct from the self, this might explain why the task investigated in our study was so difficult to complete in a lucid dream—and perhaps even the low response rate and the varying success of our participants. Perhaps, the type of control exerted over non-self dream characters in lucid dreams is sufficient to induce sensory attenuation for ticklish sensations, but not to obliterate the experience that other dream characters are distinct from oneself—and perhaps, the very nature of the task prevented our participants from developing this stronger form of control in the first place. This is also borne out by the fact that lucid dream control is often incomplete or has unintended results (Stumbrys et al., 2012). Yet, another interpretation is also possible. In particular, a strong conviction driving these effects in lucid dreams might be that to the extent that one is able to control an agent, this agent cannot be fully distinct from oneself. This would plausibly lead the sensory results of movements generated by these agents—such as tickling—to be experienced similarly to instances of tickling oneself. As Apps and Tsakiris (2014) note, the mere expectation or predictability of a self-stimulus might be sufficient to lead to sensory attenuation. As being tickled by another in a lucid control dream is predictable, this might account for the spread of sensory attenuation to tickles generated by non-self dream characters. This also fits in well with the finding that authorship beliefs about the causes of sensory changes in the environment may be one of the factors underlying sensory attenuation (Desantis et al., 2012).

But yet another and perhaps even more basic prior is needed to explain why the self-other distinction is not obliterated completely in lucid control dreams. This is that at any given moment, there should not only be a self, but also no more than a single self. Indeed, dreams exacerbate the computational problem of determining which one among a number of different body models is the unit of identification (Metzinger, 2013) and hence experienced as the self. Recall that dreams are not only rich with social imagery, but also that input from the physical body, typically a primary source of information for self-representation (Apps and Tsakiris, 2014), is only intermittently available. Yet, it is telling that even in lucid control dreams, where multiple (visual) body models are simultaneously active and under one's own control, only one of these is typically experienced as being the self, whereas the others are experienced as distinct from the self. This fits in well with the finding that in wakefulness, instances of bi-location and of identification with more than one body-model at the same time are rare and typically unstable (as in heautoscopy; see Blanke and Mohr, 2005; see also Furlanetto et al., 2013). Research is only beginning to investigate the feeling of *dis*owning one's own body in full-body illusions, and again, there is some indication that the experience of owning a different body comes at the price of disowning one's own (Guterstam and Ehrsson, 2012). Taken together with our evidence from lucid control dreams, this suggests that at its most basic, the self-other distinction is driven neither by agency nor by multisensory integration, but by the assumption that there is always exactly one unit of identification, the self. Dreams thus might be a good research model for investigating the simplest form of phenomenal selfhood (cf. Windt, 2010, 2015; Metzinger, 2013) as well as the most basic forms of modeling and understanding others (for a discussion of the applicability of predictive processing to social cognition, see Limanowski and Blankenburg, 2013).

In addition, note that in lucid dreams, there is also an interplay of long-standing and probably largely unconscious expectations of the type described above, and short-term, unconscious and conscious expectations about the specific situation encountered in the dream (for the effect of unconscious priming on sensory attenuation, see Gentsch and Schütz-Bosbach, 2011). Lucid dream control is a learnable skill (Stumbrys et al., 2012), and the complexity of the tickling task investigated in our study leads us to expect that our participants were likely experienced lucid dreamers, equipped with specific expectations about lucid dreams in general and non-self dream characters in particular. Indeed, as suggested by report no. 2, at least one participant was considering the theoretical implications of the dream experiment even while dreaming. At the very least, our participants, to the extent that they were indeed lucid, knew that they were dreaming and that they were controlling non-self dream characters that were not in fact real. They also may have had specific background beliefs about the autonomy of other dream characters, their own ability to control them, etc. Hence, it is quite possible that these lucid-dream-specific convictions colored our results as well. Indeed, dream report no. 4 describes that when the dreamer was unexpectedly tickled by another dream character, this felt more ticklish than willing the non-self dream character to perform the tickle-test. Expectations may have also been driving the dreamer's discovery, in the same dream report, that, following an initially weak tickling sensation, he or she had a Band-Aid on the foot—almost as if the process of dream imagery production were automatically explaining away the unexpected weakness of the sensation. Seen from a predictive processing perspective, it thus seems possible that the role of expectation in lucid dreams was not so much, as indicated above, a limitation as a factor contributing to sensory attenuation for self- and other-administered tickles.

While it seems difficult or even near-impossible, for practical reasons, to tease these different factors apart in future studies of lucid dreaming, the way forward, we suggest, might be to create an experimental setup that could be performed with waking participants, but that would nonetheless mimic the situation involved in lucid control dreams as closely as possible. We suggest that this might be a fruitful way of evaluating the different explanations briefly sketched above and thus of extending existing research on sensory attenuation during self-tickling.

THE WAY FORWARD? TOWARD A NEW EXPERIMENTAL PARADIGM

The question, then, is whether a similar effect, involving sensory attenuation for other-administered tickling, whilst leaving the phenomenological distinction between self and non-self intact, might exist in standard wake states as well. To begin with, note that in a sense, our explorative study can be regarded as the mirror image of the study conducted by van Doorn et al. (2014). While they asked whether swapping bodies with another enables one to tickle oneself, our study investigated not only whether one can tickle oneself in a dream, but also, at least implicitly, whether one can tickle oneself by controlling, indirectly and via thought, the movements of a non-self dream character. The waking analog to this situation in lucid dreams would be to create a virtual reality (VR) setup in which participants can be tickled by avatars that are under their voluntary control for an extended period of time, but without simultaneously identifying with them or experiencing ownership for their bodies and bodily actions.

How might this be done? Standard VR setups and full-body and body-part illusions rely heavily on multisensory and sensorimotor coherence (for a review, see Bohil et al., 2011). Here, e.g., synchronous visuotactile stimulation leads participants to experience a virtual body (Lenggenhager et al., 2007) or body part (Botvinick and Cohen, 1998) as their own. The same is true for setups in which participants control an avatar by making real-body movements (Slater et al., 2010). In order to mimic the situation in lucid dreams, a first step would be to dissociate bodily imagery from real-body movement. Indeed, several studies have used brain-computer interfaces to enable participants to control avatars or robots via bodily imagery (i.e., merely imagined movement; cf. Pfurtscheller et al., 2006; Friedman et al., 2007a,b), thus approximating the type of thought control involved in lucid dreams. Here, the general finding, once more in keeping with newer accounts of self-other distinctions in a predictive processing framework (cf. Apps and Tsakiris, 2014), is that even these more abstract, imagistic forms of control lead participants to identify with the avatar. In order to mimic lucid control dreams, then, something more would be needed. In particular, VR would have to create a situation in which participants, perhaps thanks to sensorimotor coherence and bodily agency, first identified with one avatar, and then were given the ability to additionally control, perhaps via bodily imagery within the dream, the movements of another, such that the non-self avatar were now acting toward the self, e.g., by tickling its foot. We would now, as in a lucid dream, have two different avatars, driven by different kinds of control (e.g., bodily imagery vs. real-body movement and sensorimotor contingency), only one of which would be the target of ownership and identification. One could then investigate in more detail and in a more carefully controlled manner whether this would result, as in our study, in sensory attenuation for being tickled by the non-self avatar—and one could thereby make progress on isolating and experimentally manipulating the relevant factors underlying agency, ownership and the self-other distinction, as well as participants' prior expectations, both conscious and unconscious. A careful prediction would be that once participants had been induced to identify with one avatar, the unit of identification should remain stable even as they gain the ability to control another, which would continue to be experienced as distinct from the self. In particular, they should not, we submit, simultaneously identify with more than one avatar at the same time.

Even beyond the delicate matter of self-tickling, this type of experiment might have profound theoretical implications. In particular, it might help sharpen, both conceptually and experimentally, the distinction between different types of agency, ranging from agency for bodily movement under conditions of appropriate sensorimotor coherence, to bodily imagery in the absence of real-body enactment and sensorimotor coherence, to, perhaps, more abstract and conceptual forms of control, such as simply willing the avatar to tickle one's foot. It might also shed light on the degree of precision of temporal and motor predictions required for bringing about sensory attenuation for the actions of a non-self character (e.g., in a dream or an avatar in a virtual environment) that is under participants' indirect control (for an excellent review of factors underlying sensory attenuation, see Hughes et al., 2013). And finally, it might help identify (and tamper with) general, longer-term as well as context-specific, shorter-term expectations about the ability to control others in natural and virtual environments. At the same time, this type of experimental setup, though inspired by our findings in lucid dreams, might circumvent some of the methodological difficulties encountered by our study.

SENSORY ATTENUATION REVERSED: TOWARD A NEW THEORETICAL PERSPECTIVE

More generally, if our results are taken at face value, they suggest a new perspective on the investigation of sensory attenuation. Much existing research has tried to create conditions in which the attenuation of self-generated actions is obliterated, raising them to the level of other-generated actions and events. We submit that this research strategy could be complemented by attempts to isolate the conditions under which other-generated actions are dampened to the level of self-generated ones—but apparently without thereby being experienced as one's own.

Studies investigating agency and self-other distinction during joint action (cf. Sebanz et al., 2006) indicate that sensory attenuation is indeed modulated by social interactions. Weiss et al. (2011) presented the first-ever evidence that sensory attenuation is not exclusively determined intra-individually, but also modulated by social interactions. Intriguingly, they found that sounds generated in an interactive context in which another person was acting on the participant's request were significantly attenuated, suggesting that "the other person may become an integral part of one's own internal sensorimotor loop that then specifies the relation between one's own transmitting action, the other's responsive action and sensory consequence" (Weiss et al., 2011, p. e22723). They also found that attenuation was strongest for self-produced sounds generated, interestingly, on request of another, possibly "due to a kind of contrastive enhancement of self-agency in the interactive action context" (Weiss et al., 2011, p. e22723). Yet, this is not to say that the difference between self- and other-generated actions is wholly obliterated in social interaction. Recently, it has been suggested that even in joint actions, such as in ensemble music performance, sensory attenuation helps distinguish one's own contributions to a shared goal from that of others (Loehr, 2013).

One way of explaining the results of our explorative study, consequently, might be to say that lucid dream control over the actions of non-self dream characters leads to sensory attenuation for other-administered tickles because this involves an incomplete simulation of joint action, where the non-self character is incompletely distinguished from the self. If this is correct, an intriguing possibility is that one way of investigating sensory attenuation during joint action may be to investigate cases in which no social interaction is actually taking place, but where social interactions are either simulated internally, as in lucid dreams, or technologically, as in the hypothetical VR experiment sketched above.

CONCLUSIONS

To conclude, can you tickle yourself in a dream? At least for the special case of lucid control dreams, the answer seems to be no. And neither, apparently, can anyone else. Given the limitations of our explorative study, this result might be somewhat too weak to constitute a genuine test of whether one is now dreaming or awake, and thus to provide a palpable alternative to the better-known pinching test. Even though the tickle-test will likely not convince the determined skeptic, we still think, however, that the main value of this result is to suggest a new theoretical perspective on the problem of sensory attenuation for self- and other-generated actions, as well as new questions for future research. In investigating the factors contributing to sensory attenuation, future studies might focus not just on self-generated actions and events, but might also investigate the conditions under which sensory attenuation spreads to the sensory consequences of actions generated by others than the self. It might also focus on cases of simulated as opposed to actual social interaction and investigate in more detail how sensory attenuation and self-other distinctions change when they are simulated largely offline, as in dreams.

Finally, note that this also leads to an interesting metatheoretical observation. This is that aside from their specific results, lucid dream studies, even of the wholly exploratory nature presented here, may be theoretically valuable even when, as in our case, they are too speculative to warrant any strong conclusions in their own right. In particular, one reason for being interested in lucid dreams, if we are correct, is that the theoretical discussion of lucid dreaming is a kind of playground for dreaming up new and theoretically interesting experimental setups and suggesting new perspectives for future research, for instance on virtual reality, full-body illusions, sensory attenuation and the self-other distinction. If this is all we have achieved with this paper, we think it will have been well worth its while.

ACKNOWLEDGMENTS

We would like to thank Daniel Erlacher for his help recruiting participants and for allowing us to run the study on klartraum.de, as well as all those who participated in our study. Bigna Lenggenhager was founded the Swiss National Science Foundation.

REFERENCES

Apps, M. A. J., and Tsakiris, M. (2014). The free-energy self: a predictive coding account of self-recognition. *Neurosci. Biobehav. Rev.* 41, 85–97. doi: 10.1016/j.neubiorev.2013.01.029

Aspell, J. E., Heydrich, L., Marillier, G., Lavanchy, T., Herbelin, B., and Blanke, O. (2013). Turning body and self inside out: visualized heartbeats alter bodily self-consciousness and tactile perception. *Psychol. Sci.* 24, 2445–2456. doi: 10.1177/0956797613498395

Blagrove, M., Blakemore, S.-J., and Thayer, B. R. J. (2006). The ability to self-tickle following Rapid Eye Movement sleep dreaming. *Conscious. Cogn.* 15, 285–294. doi: 10.1016/j.concog.2005.06.007

Blakemore, S. J., Goodbody, S. J., and Wolpert, D. M. (1998a). Predicting the consequences of our own actions: the role of sensorimotor context estimation. *J. Neurosci.* 18, 7511–7518.

Blakemore, S.-J., Oakley, D. A., and Frith, C. D. (2003). Delusions of alien control in the normal brain. *Neuropsychologia* 41, 1058–1067. doi: 10.1016/S0028-3932(02)00313-5

Blakemore, S. J., Smith, J., Steel, R., Johnstone, C. E., and Frith, C. D. (2000a). The perception of self-produced sensory stimuli in patients with auditory hallucinations and passivity experiences: evidence for a breakdown in self-monitoring. *Psychol. Med.* 30, 1131–1139. doi: 10.1017/S0033291799002676

Blakemore, S. J., Wolpert, D., and Frith, C. (2000b). Why can't you tickle yourself? *Neuroreport* 11, R11–R16. doi: 10.1097/00001756-200008030-00002

Blakemore, S. J., Wolpert, D. M., and Frith, C. D. (1998b). Central cancellation of self-produced tickle sensation. *Nat. Neurosci.* 1, 635–640. doi: 10.1038/2870

Blanke, O., and Mohr, C. (2005). Out-of-body experience, heautoscopy, and autoscopic hallucination of neurological origin: implications for neurocognitive mechanisms of corporeal awareness and self-consciousness. *Brain Res. Rev.* 50, 184–199. doi: 10.1016/j.brainresrev.2005.05.008

Bohil, C. J., Alicea, B., and Biocca, F. A. (2011). Virtual reality in neuroscience research and therapy. *Nat. Rev. Neurosci.* 12, 752–762. doi: 10.1038/nrn3122

Botvinick, M., and Cohen, J. (1998). Rubber hands "feel" touch that eyes see. *Nature* 391, 756. doi: 10.1038/35784

Brown, H., Adams, R. A., Parees, I., Edwards, M., and Friston, K. (2013). Active inference, sensory attenuation and illusions. *Cogn. Process.* 14, 411–427. doi: 10.1007/s10339-013-0571-3

Clark, A. (2013a). Dreaming the whole cat: generative models, predictive processing, and the enactivist conception of perceptual experience. *Mind* 121, 753–771. doi: 10.1093/mind/fzs106

Clark, A. (2013b). Whatever next? Predictive brains, situated agents, and the future of cognitive science. *Behav. Brain Sci.* 36, 181–204. doi: 10.1017/S0140525X12000477

Darwin, C. (1859). *The Origin of Species.* Hertfordshire: Wordsworth Editions Ltd.

Desantis, A., Weiss, C., Schütz-Bosbach, S., and Waszak, F. (2012). Believing and perceiving: authorship belief modulates sensory attenuation. *PLoS ONE* 7:e37959. doi: 10.1371/journal.pone.0037959

Dresler, M., Koch, S. P., Wehrle, R., Spoormaker, V. I., Holsboer, F., Steiger, A., et al. (2011). Dreamed movement elicits activation in the sensorimotor cortex. *Curr. Biol.* 21, 1833–1837. doi: 10.1016/j.cub.2011.09.029

Erlacher, D., and Schredl, M. (2008). Do REM (lucid) dreamed and executed actions share the same neural substrate? *Int. J. Dream Res.* 1, 7–14. doi: 10.1016/j.cub.2011.09.029

Fenwick, P., Schatzmann, M., Worsley, A., Adams, J., Stone, S., and Backer, A. (1984). Lucid dreaming: correspondence between dreamed and actual events in one subject during REM sleep. *Biol. Psychol.* 18, 243–252. doi: 10.1016/0301-0511(84)90056-5

Fletcher, P. C., and Frith, C. D. (2009). Perceiving is believing: a Bayesian approach to explaining the positive symptoms of schizophrenia. *Nat. Rev. Neurosci.* 10, 48–58. doi: 10.1038/nrn2536

Friedman, D., Leeb, R., Dikovsky, L., Reiner, M., Pfurtscheller, G., and Slater, M. (2007a). "Controlling a virtual body by thought in a highly-immersive virtual environment—a case study in using a brain-computer interface in a virtualreality cave-like system," in *GRAPP 2007, Proceedings of the Second International Conference on Computer Graphics Theory and Applications*, eds J. Braz, P.-P. Vázquez and J. M. Pereira (Barcelona: INSTICC-Institute for Systems and Technologies of Information, Control and Communication), 83–90.

Friedman, D., Leeb, R., Guger, C., Steed, A., Pfurtscheller, G., and Slater, M. (2007b). Navigating virtual reality by thought: what is it like? *Presence Teleoper. Virtual Environ.* 16, 100–110. doi: 10.1162/pres.16.1.100

Friston, K., and Kiebel, S. (2009). Predictive coding under the free-energy principle. *Philos. Trans. R. Soc. Lond. B Biol. Sci.* 364, 1211–1221. doi: 10.1098/rstb.2008.0300

Friston, K., Mattout, J., and Kilner, J. (2011). Action understanding and active inference. *Biol. Cybern.* 104, 137–160. doi: 10.1007/s00422-011-0424-z

Frith, C. D., Blakemore, S. J., and Wolpert, D. M. (2000). Abnormalities in the awareness and control of action. *Philos. Trans. R. Soc. Lond. B Biol. Sci.* 355, 1771–1788. doi: 10.1098/rstb.2000.0734

Furlanetto, T., Bertone, C., and Becchio, C. (2013). The bilocated mind: new perspectives on self-localization and self-identification. *Front. Hum. Neurosci.* 7:71. doi: 10.3389/fnhum.2013.00071

Gentsch, A., and Schütz-Bosbach, S. (2011). I did it: unconscious expectation of sensory consequences modulates the experience of self-agency and its functional signature. *J. Cogn. Neurosci.* 23, 3817–3828. doi: 10.1162/jocn_a_00012

Giguère, B., and LaBerge, S. (1995). To touch a dream: an experiment in touch, pain, and pleasure. *Nightlight* 7, 1–6, 11.

Gottesmann, C. (2006). The dreaming sleep stage: a new neurobiological model of schizophrenia? *Neuroscience* 140, 1105–1115. doi: 10.1016/j.neuroscience.2006.02.082

Guterstam, A., and Ehrsson, H. H. (2012). Disowning one's seen real body during an out-of-body illusion. *Conscious. Cogn.* 21, 1037–1042. doi: 10.1016/j.concog.2012.01.018

Hobson, J. A. (1988). *The Dreaming Brain.* New York, NY: Basic Books.

Hobson, J. A. (1999). *Dreaming as Delirium. How the Brain Goes Out of Its Mind.* Cambridge, MA: MIT Press.

Hobson, J. A., and Friston, K. J. (2012). Waking and dreaming consciousness: neurobiological and functional considerations. *Prog. Neurobiol.* 98, 82–98. doi: 10.1016/j.pneurobio.2012.05.003

Hobson, J. A., and Friston, K. J. (2014). Consciousness, dreams, and inference the cartesian theatre revisited. *J. Conscious. Stud.* 21, 6–32.

Hohwy, J. (2010). "The hypothesis testing brain: some philosophical applications" in *Presented at the Proceedings of the 9th Conference of the Australasian Society for Cognitive Science* (Macquarie Centre for Cognitive Science), 135–144.

Hohwy, J. (2013). *The Predictive Mind.* Oxford: Oxford University Press.

Hughes, G., Desantis, A., and Waszak, F. (2013). Mechanisms of intentional binding and sensory attenuation: the role of temporal prediction, temporal control, identity prediction, and motor prediction. *Psychol. Bull.* 139, 133–151. doi: 10.1037/a0028566

Kahn, D., Pace-Schott, E. F., and Hobson, J. A. (2002). Emotion and cognition: feeling and character identification in dreaming. *Conscious. Cogn.* 11, 34–50. doi: 10.1006/ccog.2001.0537

Kahn, D., Stickgold, R., Pace-Schott, E. F., and Hobson, J. A. (2000). Dreaming and waking consciousness: a character recognition study. *J. Sleep Res.* 9, 317–325. doi: 10.1046/j.1365-2869.2000.00213.x

LaBerge, S. (1985). *Lucid Dreaming.* New York, NY: Ballantine Books.

LaBerge, S. (1990). "Lucid dreaming: psychophysiological studies of consciousness during REM sleep," in *Sleep and Cognition*, eds R. Bootzin, J. Kihlstrom, and D. Schacter (Washington, DC: American Psychological Association), 109–126.

LaBerge, S., Nagel, L. E., Dement, W. C., and Zarcone, V. P. (1981). Lucid dreaming verified by volitional communication during REM sleep. *Percept. Mot. Skills* 52, 727–732. doi: 10.2466/pms.1981.52.3.727

Leclair-Visonneau, L., Oudiette, D., Gaymard, B., Leu-Semenescu, S., and Arnulf, I. (2010). Do the eyes scan dream images during rapid eye movement sleep? Evidence from the rapid eye movement sleep behaviour disorder model. *Brain* 133, 1737–1746. doi: 10.1093/brain/awq110

Lenggenhager, B., Tadi, T., Metzinger, T., and Blanke, O. (2007). Video ergo sum: manipulating bodily self-consciousness. *Science* 317, 1096–1099. doi: 10.1126/science.1143439

Levitan, L. (1994). A fool's guide to lucid dreaming. *Nightlight* 6.

Limanowski, J., and Blankenburg, F. (2013). Minimal self-models and the free energy principle. *Front. Hum. Neurosci.* 7:547. doi: 10.3389/fnhum.2013.00547

Loehr, J. D. (2013). Sensory attenuation for jointly produced action effects. *Front. Psychol.* 4:172. doi: 10.3389/fpsyg.2013.00172

McNamara, P., McLaren, D., Kowalczyk, S., and Pace-Schott, E. F. (2007). "'Theory of Mind' in REM and NREM dreams," in *The New Science of Dreaming*, eds D. Barrett and P. McNamara (Westport: Praeger Perspectives), 201–220.

McNamara, P., McLaren, D., Smith, D., Brown, A., and Stickgold, R. (2005). A "Jekyll and Hyde" within: aggressive versus friendly interactions in

REM and non-REM dreams. *Psychol. Sci.* 16, 130–136. doi: 10.1111/j.0956-7976.2005.00793.x

Metzinger, T. (2003). *Being No One*. Cambridge; London: MIT Press.

Metzinger, T. (2013). Why are dreams interesting for philosophers? The example of minimal phenomenal selfhood, plus an agenda for future research. *Front. Psychol.* 4:746. doi: 10.3389/fpsyg.2013.00746

Mumford, D. (1992). On the computational architecture of the neocortex. II. The role of cortico-cortical loops. *Biol. Cybern.* 66, 241–251. doi: 10.1007/BF00198477

Nielsen, T. A., and Lara-Carrasco, J. (2007). "Nightmares, dreaming, and emotion regulation: a review," in *The New Science of Dreaming*, eds D. Barrett and P. McNamara (Westport, CT: Praeger Perspectives), 253–284.

Nielsen, T. A., Ouellet, L., and Zadra, A. L. (1995). Pressure stimulation during REM sleep alters dream limb activity and body bizarreness. *Sleep Res.* 24, 134.

Nielsen, T. A., Svob, C., and Kuiken, D. (2009). Dream-enacting behaviors in a normal population. *Sleep* 32, 1629–1636.

Petkova, V. I., and Ehrsson, H. H. (2008). If I were you: perceptual illusion of body swapping. *PLoS ONE* 3:e3832. doi: 10.1371/journal.pone.0003832

Pfurtscheller, G., Leeb, R., Keinrath, C., Friedman, D., Neuper, C., Guger, C., et al. (2006). Walking from thought. *Brain Res.* 1071, 145–152. doi: 10.1016/j.brainres.2005.11.083

Revonsuo, A. (2006). *Inner Presence*. Cambridge; London: MIT Press.

Schenck, C. (2005). *Paradox Lost*. Minneapolis, MN: Extreme Nights, LLC.

Sebanz, N., Bekkering, H., and Knoblich, G. (2006). Joint action: bodies and minds moving together. *Trends Cogn. Sci.* 10, 70–76. doi: 10.1016/j.tics.2005.12.009

Seth, A. K., Suzuki, K., and Critchley, H. D. (2012). An interoceptive predictive coding model of conscious presence. *Front. Psychol.* 2:395. doi: 10.3389/fpsyg.2011.00395

Slater, M., Spanlang, B., Sanchez-Vives, M. V., and Blanke, O. (2010). First person experience of body transfer in virtual reality. *PLoS ONE* 5:e10564. doi: 10.1371/journal.pone.0010564

Stumbrys, T., Erlacher, D., Schadlich, M., and Schredl, M. (2012). Induction of lucid dreams: a systematic review of evidence. *Conscious. Cogn.* 21, 1456–1475. doi: 10.1016/j.concog.2012.07.003

Tsakiris, M., Prabhu, G., and Haggard, P. (2006). Having a body versus moving your body: how agency structures body-ownership. *Conscious. Cogn.* 15, 423–432. doi: 10.1016/j.concog.2005.09.004

van Doorn, G., Hohwy, J., and Symmons, M. (2014). Can you tickle yourself if you swap bodies with someone else? *Conscious. Cogn.* 23, 1–11. doi: 10.1016/j.concog.2013.10.009

van Elk, M., Lenggenhager, B., Heydrich, L., and Blanke, O. (2014). Suppression of the auditory N1-component for heartbeat-related sounds reflects interoceptive predictive coding. *Biol. Psychol.* 99, 172–182. doi: 10.1016/j.biopsycho.2014.03.004

Voss, U., Holzmann, R., Tuin, I., and Hobson, J. A. (2009). Lucid dreaming: a state of consciousness with features of both waking and non-lucid dreaming. *Sleep* 32, 1191–1200.

Voss, U., Schermelleh-Engel, K., Windt, J. M., Frenzel, C., and Hobson, J. A. (2013). Measuring consciousness in dreams: the lucidity and consciousness in dreams scale. *Conscious. Cogn.* 22, 8–21. doi: 10.1016/j.concog.2012.11.001

Voss, U., Tuin, I., Schermelleh-Engel, K., and Hobson, A. (2011). Waking and dreaming: related but structurally independent. Dream reports of congenitally paraplegic and deaf-mute persons. *Conscious. Cogn.* 20, 673–687. doi: 10.1016/j.concog.2010.10.020

Wegner, D. M, Sparrow, B., and Winerman, L. (2004). Vicarious agency: experiencing control over the movements of others. *J. Pers. Soc. Psychol.* 86, 838–848. doi: 10.1037/0022-3514.86.6.838

Weiskrantz, L., Elliott, J., and Darlington, C. (1971). Preliminary observations on tickling oneself. *Nature* 230, 598–599. doi: 10.1038/230598a0

Weiss, C., Herwig, A., and Schütz-Bosbach, S. (2011). The self in social interactions: sensory attenuation of auditory action effects is stronger in interactions with others. *PLoS ONE* 6:e22723. doi: 10.1371/journal.pone.0022723

Windt, J. M. (2010). The immersive spatiotemporal hallucination model of dreaming. *Phenom. Cogn. Sci.* 9, 295–316. doi: 10.1007/s11097-010-9163-1

Windt, J. M. (2015). *Dreaming. A Conceptual Framework for Philosophy of Mind and Empirical Research*. Cambridge; London: MIT Press. (forthcoming).

Windt, J. M., and Metzinger, T. (2007). "The philosophy of dreaming and self-consciousness: what happens to the experiential subject during the dream state?" in *The New Science of Dreaming. Vol. 3: Cultural and Theoretical Perspectives*, eds D. Barrett and P. McNamara (Westport; London: Praeger Perspectives), 193–248.

Windt, J. M., and Noreika, V. (2011). How to integrate dreaming into a general theory of consciousness—a critical review of existing positions and suggestions for future research. *Conscious. Cogn.* 20, 1091–1107. doi: 10.1016/j.concog.2010.09.010

20

10 Hz rTMS over right parietal cortex alters sense of agency during self-controlled movements

***Anina Ritterband-Rosenbaum*[1,2*†], *Anke N. Karabanov*[2,3†], *Mark S. Christensen*[1,2,4] and *Jens Bo Nielsen*[1,2]**

[1] *Department of Nutrition, Exercise and Sports, Panum Institite, University of Copenhagen, Copenhagen, Denmark*
[2] *Department of Neuroscience and Pharmacology, Panum Institite, University of Copenhagen, Copenhagen, Denmark*
[3] *Danish Research Center for Magnetic Resonance, Copenhagen University Hospital Hvidovre, Hvidovre, Denmark*
[4] *Danish Neuroscience Center, Cognitive Neuroscience Research Unit, Aarhus University, Aarhus, Denmark*

Correspondence:
Anina Ritterband-Rosenbaum, Department of Neuroscience and Pharmacology, Panum Institute 33.3, University of Copenhagen, Blegdamsvej 3, 2200 Copenhagen, Denmark
e-mail: aninari@sund.ku.dk

† These authors have contributed equally to this work.

A large body of fMRI and lesion-literature has provided evidence that the Inferior Parietal Cortex (IPC) is important for sensorimotor integration and sense of agency (SoA). We used repetitive transcranial magnetic stimulation (rTMS) to explore the role of the IPC during a validated SoA detection task. 12 healthy, right-handed adults were included. The effects of rTMS on subjects' SoA during self-controlled movements were explored. The experiment consisted of 1/3 self-controlled movements and $^2/_3$ computer manipulated movements that introduced uncertainty as to whether the subjects were agents of an observed movement. Subjects completed three sessions, in which subjects received online rTMS over the right IPC (active condition), over the vertex (CZ) (sham condition) or no TMS but a sound-matched control. We found that rTMS over right IPC significantly altered SoA of the non-perturbed movements. Following IPC stimulation subjects were more likely to experience self-controlled movements as being externally perturbed compared to the control site ($P = 0.002$) and the stimulation-free control ($P = 0.042$). The data support the importance of IPC activation during sensorimotor comparison in order to correctly determine the agent of movements.

Keywords: sense of agency (SoA), self-controlled movement, repetitive TMS, inferior parietal cortex (IPC), sensorimotor comparison

INTRODUCTION

Distinguishing one's own actions from actions of others is a key component of social interaction and usually happens effortlessly even in the most complex situations like playing a fourhanded piano piece. The ability to correctly identify self-produced movement is called sense of agency (SoA) and is based on integration of sensory (most often visual and proprioception) and motor information (Gallagher, 2000). An altered sense of agency can occur both in mental illness and following brain injury and can severely impact the ability to control movements and alter self-consciousness (Farrer and Frith, 2002; Ritterband-Rosenbaum et al., 2011).

Neuropsychological evidence and brain imaging data associate the sense of agency with areas in the Inferior Parietal Cortex (IPC) which are generally important for a multitude of complex sensory and motor tasks (e.g., visuo-motor integration, visual attention, spatial representations, reaching and grasping movements, action observation) (Andersen et al., 1987; Culham and Kanwisher, 2001; Culham and Valyear, 2006; Iacoboni, 2006; Rushworth and Taylor, 2006). Neuropsychological data from lesion studies often associate damage in IPC to distortions in self-awareness such as hemi-spatial neglect (unawareness of the visual field and body side contralateral to the lesion) (Mort et al., 2003), asomatognosia (loss of ownership over a limb) (Baier and Karnath, 2008) or alien-limb syndrome (distorted sense of agency over own movements) (Franck et al., 2001; Fourneret et al., 2002). In experimental settings, neurological patients (all with lesions involving the left parietal lobe) also show changes in awareness of voluntary action (Sirigu et al., 2004). However, since brain damage may be functionally more extensive than what can be determined by imaging techniques and usually involve adaptations to compensate for lost functions, it is hard to make spatially precise inferences about the role of the individual cortical areas in agency attribution in the healthy brain from such studies.

Several brain-imaging studies have studied the role of the IPC during agency attribution in healthy individuals (Farrer and Frith, 2002; Farrer et al., 2008; Nahab et al., 2011). Since spontaneous misattributions of agency are rare in healthy participants all these studies use external perturbations of the feedback either temporally or spatially to challenge the agency attribution. These studies consistently show that activation of the IPC and the adjacent areas increase with a subjective loss of agency. In a recent EEG study (Ritterband-Rosenbaum et al. submitted and planned to appear in this issue) we were able to identify an IPC-pre supplementary motor area (preSMA) network, which showed coupled activity when subjects experienced agency over their movements. Results from the study suggest that the IPC supplies the preSMA with information about a mismatch of sensorimotor and visual information after the movement has been performed.

TMS allows that conclusions regarding the causal relationship between a brain region and behavior may be made by producing a transient and localized disruption in normal brain activity (Pascual-Leone et al., 2000). Some previous TMS studies have investigated the role of the IPC and the adjacent parietal areas in temporal and spatial aspects of agency attribution (MacDonald and Paus, 2003; Preston and Newport, 2008). MacDonald and colleagues investigated the temporal assessment of self-controlled movements and showed that participants' awareness of movement onset was disrupted after stimulation of the left superior parietal lobule. Preston et al. investigated the outcome assessment of reaching movements and reported a decreased tendency for self-attribution for spatially perturbed and un-perturbed trials after TMS of the right IPC (Preston and Newport, 2008). However, in that study participants were only able to observe the start and end point of the movement with the largest part of the movement trajectory occluded. A noticeable difference between the imaging literature and some of the brain stimulation results is that whereas imaging work consistently reports increased activity of the IPC with increasing levels of external perturbation (e.g., when participants do not experience agency), the TMS work seems to suggest that disrupting this region modulates agency relatively unspecifically whether the observed movement is externally generated (e.g., a manipulated movement) or not (e.g., a self-controlled movement).

The goal of the present study was to further disentangle the role the IPC has in agency perception during different degrees of spatial feedback perturbations. Since we did not perturb the temporal movement feedback we cannot draw conclusions about the role of the IPC in temporal agency perception. We used a validated arm-reaching paradigm (Ritterband-Rosenbaum et al., 2011, 2012). In two thirds of trials different levels of spatial perturbation (10 and 15°) were added to introduce uncertainty as to whether the subjects were the agent of the observed movement or not. Participants performed three different sessions during which online rTMS (rTMS) was given over the right IPC or over the vertex. In the third session a sound-matched, stimulation-free control was applied.

Imaging studies consistently report that activity in the IPC decreases in trials with high-perceived agency, rTMS, on the other hand is assumed to be state-dependent and may influence less active neural populations most strongly (Silvanto and Pascual-Leone, 2008; Silvanto et al., 2008). This is why we hypothesize that the self-controlled movements might be most susceptible to rTMS, since in this condition there is most scope for the IPC firing rate to be increased by stimulation. On a first glance, this seems counterintuitive but the notion of a higher degree of firing rate modulability might offer a neural basis for the state-dependency phenomena. The idea is also consistent with clinical observations reporting that normal brain activity can interfere with the spread of an epileptic discharge (Wilkins et al., 2004).

MATERIALS AND METHODS

POPULATION

Fourteen healthy, naïve, right-handed adults (mean age: 25.6 ± 6.7 years, SD, 5 males) participated in the study. None of the participants had a history of neurological or psychiatric disorders. None of them had metal implants. Handedness was assessed prior to the experiment using the Edinburgh Inventory questionnaire (Oldfield, 1971). All participants in the study had an anatomical MRI scan made within the past 2 years. One participant had to be excluded due to failure to perform the task properly and one withdrew after completing 2 of the 3 sessions because of discomfort with the TMS; therefore, only 12 participants were included in further analysis. Subject selection and all TMS procedures were in accordance with the TMS safety guide lines (Rossi et al., 2009). Written informed consent was obtained for each subject prior to the experiment. The study was conducted according to the Helsinki declaration and was approved by the local ethics committee in Copenhagen, Denmark (protocol number: H-A-2008-029).

GENERAL PROCEDURE

Subjects were seated comfortably in a chair with their head resting in a chin rest 55 cm in front of a computer screen and vision of the arms blocked by a blind (see **Figure 1A**), so they were not able to see the digital tablet placed in front of them. On the screen, participants could see a target in the upper center and a circle in the lower center of the screen. The task was to move the circle toward the target by placing a digital pen on the tablet. As subjects did not see their own movement on the

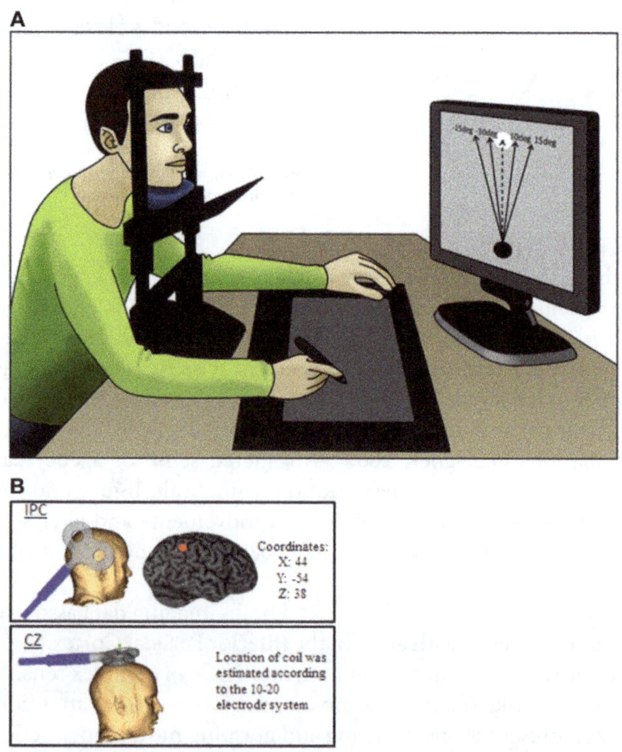

FIGURE 1 | The experimental setup. (A) The subject is not able to see his own arms as vision is blocked. The dotted line is representing the self-controlled movement where subjects have full control of the object and the black lines represent the possible perturbations. During the experiment there were no visible lines or text on the display screen. **(B)** Illustrate coil orientation and placement.

tablet, they received visual feedback about their movement from the trajectory of the circle on the screen. In two-thirds of all trials, the circle was manipulated to deviate by 10, −10, 15, and −15° away from the target regardless of the movement of the subject. The manipulations were intermingled with movements which were completely controlled by the subject (self-controlled movement). After each finished movement subjects were asked to make a quick intuitive decision whether they felt being responsible for the observed movement or if they thought the circle was externally manipulated. This decision was communicated by pressing one of two buttons with the left hand. A total number of 120 trials (80 trials evenly divided between the computer deviations and 40 self-controlled movements) were performed per session.

The paradigm design was presented in a validated custom-made program (using F#) (Ritterband-Rosenbaum et al., 2011). In accordance with the TMS safety guidelines (Rossi et al., 2009) inter-trial intervals of 3 s were added to the original paradigm to ensure sufficient breaks between rTMS trains. The sizes of the screen and tablet were 380 × 303 mm (with a resolution of 1280 × 1024 pix) and 310 × 238 mm, respectively (Tablet: Wacom, Intuos 3, Krefeld, Germany http://www.wacom.com/en/de/). Subjects were instructed to move the circle by straight, fast movements. The size of the circle and the target was 3.8 × 3.6 cm (120 × 116 pix) resulting in an actual movement distance of approximately 15 cm, which could be achieved without moving the head or torso. Three successive sessions (TMS on active site (IPC), TMS on control site (CZ) and noTMS) were conducted with 1 h of break in between. The break was added to avoid any carry-over effect of the TMS stimulation and sessions were randomized. Prior to each session, subjects were given a short introduction to familiarize themselves with the task and the TMS. For the noTMS session we placed the TMS coil in close proximity (approximately 25 cm away from the subjects' right side of the head) to the subject to keep the auditory input constant. This baseline control was chosen to confirm that TMS over CZ did not affect agency experience. Participants in the noTMS condition were aware that no direct stimulation was given; this allowed us to verify that behavior during control stimulation over CZ was not influenced by either diffuse general effects of stimulation (e.g., stimulation sensation, placebo) or by a stimulation specific effect. Since we did not expect any effect of CZ stimulation, differentiation between diffuse and specific effects in this condition was not the focus of the experimental design.

TMS STIMULATION

Neuronavigation (Brainsight, Magstim Ltd) was used for precise positioning of the coil. Magnetic resonance imaging (MRI) data specific to each participant were used to ensure correct placement of the coil. Each individual MRI was normalized onto the Montreal Neurological Institute (MNI) brain template from the Brainsight software. The IPC location was found using the MNI coordinates: 44,-54, 38 (Farrer et al., 2008), whereas the control site was CZ measured by the 10–20 electrode system (Herwig et al., 2003).

Magnetic stimulation was delivered using a custom-made figure of-eight coil (external diameter of coil wing: 115 mm), connected to a MagstimRapid stimulator (Magstim Ltd, Whitland, Dyfed, UK). 1 s trains of 10 Hz TMS were given for each individual trial. This frequency was chosen because it has proven effective in modulating cognitive functions in a wide range of previous studies (Devlin et al., 2003; Leyman et al., 2009; Manenti et al., 2010; Acheson et al., 2011). The stimulation started 500 ms after the pen was placed on the tablet on top of the visual object and participants were instructed and trained to start the movement as soon as the stimulation started. Hence TMS stimulation stopped 1500 ms after the pen was placed on the tablet exceeding average trial time (mean: 643 ± 216 ms). The intensity of the TMS was set to 120% of resting motor threshold of the first dorsal interosseous muscle (FDI) (Rossini et al., 1994). During the experiment the coil was kept in position by a TMS-holder (see **Figure 1B**) and continuously monitored by neuronavigation.

DATA ANALYSIS

All analysis was done off-line after the experiment using Excel, SigmaPlot 12 (Systat Software Inc) and Matlab R2012a (MathWorks, Natics, MA, USA). All X,Y-coordinates from the pen on the tablet and the object on the screen were combined in order to extrapolate data from each completed trial. Agency scores and kinematic data were calculated as follows:

(1) Subjective agency score (%) was calculated from the participants reporting of whether they experienced being responsible for the observed movement trajectory. A higher score corresponds to a higher rate of reporting "No, I was not responsible for the observed movement."
(2) Line curvature (mm^{-1}) referred to how much the movement of the pen on the tablet deviated from the direct straight line from initial object position to the target. The smaller the value the more straight the subjects made the movement. The equation for the values is as follow:

$$c = \frac{x'y'' - y'x''}{\left(x'^2 + y'^2\right)^{3/2}}$$

(3) Hit distance (mm) is the difference between the target and the end position of the pen on the tablet, i.e., the difference between the coordinates of X_{pen} and $X_{center\ of\ target}$. Absolute values were used to evaluate the distance independent of which side of the target was hit.
(4) Movement time (ms) corresponded to the time for moving the visual object to the target.
(5) Answer time (ms) corresponded to the time it took subjects to decide about their agency after the movement was completed.

EXCLUDED DATA

Trials where the answer time was longer than 2 s or where the whole trial time was over 3 s were excluded from further analysis (30 trials). Additionally, trials were excluded if the curvature was more than 2 SD above that of the participant's average curvature within the same manipulation group (56 trials). In total, less than 2% of all trials were excluded.

For the kinematic data we focused the analysis on an area above and below a horizontal level of 20% from the bottom and top of the screen. The included area covered the top of the object to the bottom of the target. The cutoff meant that contaminated data which could derive from picking up the visual object or when hitting the horizontal level of the target would not affect the active cursor movement.

STATISTICS

All data were checked for normality distribution and equal variance using the Shapiro-Wilk test. To test for changes in agency attribution and kinematic measures after TMS stimulation repeated-measures ANOVAS were done. In a first step a repeated measures ANOVA (rmANOVA) with the factors Site (IPS, CZ, and noTMS) and Perturbation (no perturbation, 10 and 15°) was run. In a second step, agency scores were analyzed in separate rmANOVAs for each level of perturbation (self-controlled movement, 10 and 15°). We chose to investigate conditions separately for two reasons: first, the SoA ratings reflect antagonistically on correct agency detection in non-perturbed and perturbed trials (e.g., in unperturbed trials high "self" ratings reflect good performance, in perturbed trials low "self" ratings reflect good performance). Second, the state-dependency of TMS predicts that high activity levels can "protect" from the effects of TMS (Silvanto and Pascual-Leone, 2008). This is why we hypothesized that the self-controlled movements might be most susceptible to rTMS. For those movements where a significant effect of TMS was observed, differences in kinematic parameters (curvature, hit distance, movement time) and answer time depending on TMS *and* agency attribution were explored. Only 8 participants were included in this analysis since the other participants did not have both answer types (yes/no) for some of the conditions. All *Post-hoc* comparisons were done using Holm-Sidak corrected *t*-tests. All Statistical analysis was done in SigmaPlot 12.

RESULTS

In the 3 × 3 rmANOVA including all levels of perturbation only a main effect for perturbation could be detected [$F_{(2)} = 64.95$; $P < 0.001$] neither the main effect for Stimulation Site [$F_{(2)} = 0.289$; $P = 0.75$] or the interaction between stimulation site and deviation reached significance [$F_{(2)} = 0.558$; $P = 0.75$]. When running a separate analysis for each perturbation level, a main effect for TMS [$F_{(2)} = 4.62$; $P = 0.02$] was detected for unperturbed movements (see **Figure 2**). *Post-hoc* testing confirmed higher rates of agency rejection for IPC stimulation compared to CZ stimulation and no TMS ($P = 0.007$ and $P = 0.045$, respectively) and no difference in agency rejection between CZ and no TMS ($P = 0.421$). Only the IPC-CZ comparison remained significant following Holm-Sidak correction for multiple comparisons. For perturbed movements no significant main effects was found ([$F_{(2)} = 0.18$; $P = 0.83$] and [$F_{(2)} = 0.38$; $P = 0.68$] respectively for the 10 and 15° perturbations) (see **Figure 3**).

We did not find any statistical differences between the different TMS sessions for the self-controlled movements when dividing the data according to the subjective reporting for $\text{Curvature}_{\text{Self}}$ [$F_{(2)} = 1.278$; $P > 0.5$], Movement $\text{time}_{\text{Self}}$[$F_{(2)} = 0.712$; $P > 0.5$], Answer $\text{time}_{\text{Self}}$[$F_{(2)} = 1.06$; $P > 0.3$] or Hit $\text{distance}_{\text{Self}}$ ([$F_{(2)} = 0.901$; $P > 0.4$]). However,

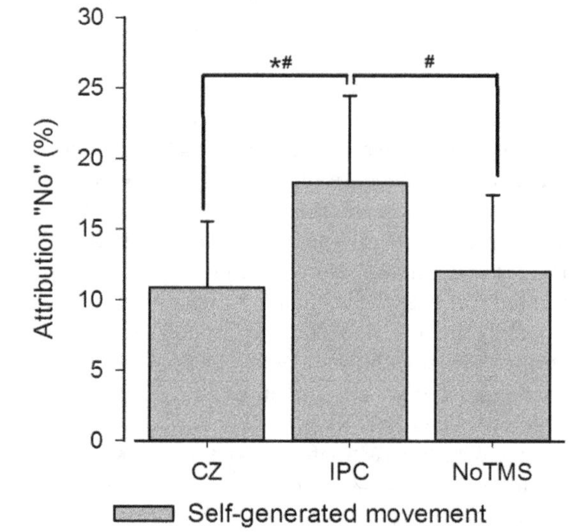

FIGURE 2 | Group averages for SoA for self-controlled movements. The figure displays the group averaged level of agency rejection in percentage for self-controlled movements. The * indicates a significant difference when corrected for Holm-Sidak *post-hoc* test. The # identifies a significant *p*-value prior to the Holm-Sidak correction. Error bars depict inter-subject s.e.m.

for Hit $\text{distance}_{\text{Self}}$ we were able to detect a significant main effect of assessment (yes/no) ([$F_{(1)} = 11.67$; $P = 0.01$]) indicating that the hit distance was smaller when subjects attributed the movement to themselves. None of the other variables (Hit $\text{distance}_{\text{Manipulated}}$, $\text{Curvature}_{\text{Manipulated}}$, Movement $\text{time}_{\text{Manipulated}}$, or Answer $\text{time}_{\text{Manipulated}}$) showed a significant assessment effect.

Table 1 illustrates the averaged kinematics (curvature, hit distance and movement time) and answer time for self-controlled movement in the three individual sessions. The table only contains data from eight subjects, as four subjects did not have both Yes and No assessments. Variation is depicted as 1 inter-subjects SD.

DISCUSSION

When rTMS was applied over the IPC subjects were more likely to reject agency for unperturbed movements than when rTMS was given over a control site. Rejection rate for these movements increased from around 11 to 19% after IPC stimulation, and the same pattern was observed when comparing IPC stimulation with noTMS. The sense of agency for the externally perturbed movements was unaffected by IPC stimulation. The observed effect was only significant when analyzing the perturbed and unperturbed movements separately. We argue that separating movements is appropriate for two reasons: first, the SoA ratings reflect antagonistically on correct agency detection in non-perturbed and perturbed trials and errors in agency detection reflect antagonistically on attribution-errors: in the self-controlled movements participants commit errors of under-attribution whereas in the perturbed movements the participant commits errors of over-attribution. Second, we specifically hypothesized that rTMS influences the self-controlled trials more due to the state-dependency

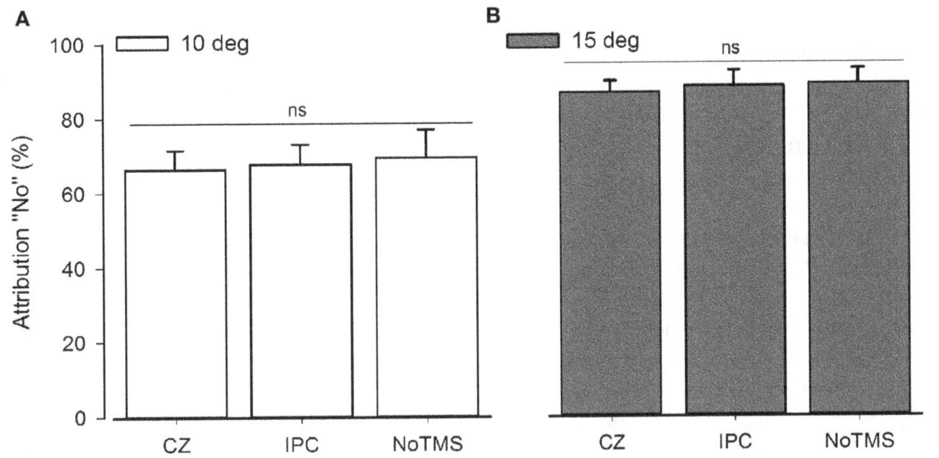

FIGURE 3 | Group average for SoA for computer-manipulated movements. The graphs display the agency rejection for computer-manipulated movements. NS, Non-significant. **(A)** Shows 10° perturbations. **(B)** Shows 15° perturbation. The error bars depict the inter-subject s.e.m.

Table 1 | Kinematic.

Table for kinematic (self–controlled movements)						
	CZ		**No TMS**		**IPC**	
	Yes	**No**	**Yes**	**No**	**Yes**	**No**
Curvature (mm^{-1})	0.046 ± 0.032	0.047 ± 0.032	0.038 ± 0.018	0.046 ± 0.032	0.039 ± 0.025	0.042 ± 0.025
Hit distance (mm)	−2.8 ± 10.6	−8.6 ± 16.7	−4.8 ± 9.3	−8.0 ± 10.6	−5.9 ± 12.0	−11.2 ± 13.6
Movement time (ms)	200.5 ± 65.3	213.0 ± 71.6	200.5 ± 60.3	205.1 ± 59.5	197.3 ± 45.7	206.4 ± 53.5
Answer time (ms)	376.4 ± 105.6	421.9 ± 197	405.5 ± 203.9	529.8 ± 241.9	404.7 ± 203.4	493.8 ± 277.4

of brain stimulation (Silvanto and Pascual-Leone, 2008; Silvanto et al., 2008).

Our data for the non-perturbed movements are in line with results from Preston and Newport (2008) reporting decrease in agency for self-controlled movements after right IPC stimulation. Preston et al. also reported changes in agency perception for computer manipulated movements but it has to be noted that these changes were not significantly greater than the difference induced by TMS over a control site (Preston and Newport, 2008) suggesting that, as in our study, only the effects observed during own movements were truly site specific. In our study, *post-hoc* testing showed that increases in agency rejection were significant between the control site and the IPC and a similar pattern was found when comparing IPC and no TMS (significant when uncorrected). It is worth noting, that the significant difference between the IPC and control site was not driven by a TMS induced change in the control region since no difference could be detected between the control region and the stimulation free condition. Our data indicates that TMS over the IPC does not result in a non-specific tendency to reject agency or misattribute the observed movements across different levels of perturbations. Rather it selectively affects conditions where the feeling of agency is very high.

Comparator Models (CM) (Wolpert et al., 1995; Frith et al., 2000) have often been proposed as the underlying mechanisms of agency attribution, and can help to explain why the shift in agency perception was only observed where the feeling of agency was high (self-controlled movements). According to the CM, every movement outcome is compared to an "internal model" of the movement, which consists of the movement intention and a prediction about the movement outcome. If the error between the internal model and the actual outcome of the movement is low we perceive agency. In the case of the 10 and 15° perturbations the error between the predicted and the actual sensory feedback is high causing participants to reject agency for these movements. Potentially, IPC stimulation is not able to increase the mismatch between the predicted and observed movement for the movement types of 10 and 15° computer manipulations, and hence does not further impact agency judgments. On the other hand, for the self-controlled movements the error signal is usually small and stimulating the right IPC adds significant noise to the comparison, which creates difficulties for the subjects when determining movement agency. This could lead to higher rates of misattribution (increased agency rejection) when compared to baseline. It is probable that very challenging perturbations, with only minimal prediction-outcome errors would show significant agency alterations after interfering with normal activity in right IPC with TMS.

The IPC and the surrounding area has also been implicated in many aspects of visually guided movement control (Rushworth and Taylor, 2006) and stimulation of the posterior parietal cortex can disrupt visually guided reaching movements and the ability to correct for perturbations during reaching movements (Desmurget et al., 1999; Johnson and Haggard, 2005; Chib et al., 2009; Reichenbach et al., 2011). Since neither curvature, hit distance nor movement time were significantly affected by TMS our kinematic data suggest that the change in agency attribution was not merely caused by an altered ability to control movements. We can however not exclude the possibility that TMS had a minor effect on visual movement control that was not picked up by our kinematic analysis.

We cannot determine if subjects' based their agency decision on an online sensorimotor comparison of performance and feedback or on a post-movement evaluation of the movement outcome but the difference in hit distance (end point of the movements) between accepted and rejected agency trials (irrespective of TMS) suggests that post-movement visuo-spatial cues were used by the participants to determine agency. This notion is supported by a recent EEG-study (Ritterband-Rosenbaum et al. submitted and planned to appear in this issue), showing increased parietal-prefrontal directional coupling during the agency judgment phase, after reaching movements had been concluded. These findings and the fact that the parietal lobule has been suggested to act as an interface between retrospective reflections and online sensorimotor comparisons (Jeannerod, 2009), suggests that TMS stimulation covering both, the movement and the decision phase, as applied in this study, likely yields the strongest effect on agency detection since it is able to impact both online sensory-motor comparisons and retrospective reflections.

It is interesting that imaging studies have consistently reported increased activity in the right IPC or more specifically in the right angular gyrus with higher level of feedback perturbations (Farrer and Frith, 2002; Farrer et al., 2008; Nahab et al., 2011) whereas both our study and the work of Preston and Newport (2008) suggest that IPC stimulation is most disruptive during unperturbed movements. This is in line with the state-dependent theory of rTMS effects postulating that brain stimulation effects neural populations more when their baseline activity is low.

Generally, care has to be taken when directly comparing increases in BOLD activity with behavioral performance during TMS. First of all, the exact mechanisms of online rTMS during task performance are not completely understood: the "virtual-lesion" method assumes that trains of rTMS during performance adds external noise to the stimulated area and thereby disrupt any internal processes (Pascual-Leone et al., 2000). This approach has been shown to be state-dependent with effects depending on the underlying behavioral task. Furthermore, concurrent TMS-fMRI experiments have shown that rTMS does not necessarily result in measurable changes in bold activity at the stimulated site and can show task-specific bold-effects in remote, connected brain areas (Sack et al., 2007; Heinen et al., 2011). Our results indicating that the right IPC is most vulnerable to stimulation during the self-controlled movements are in line with the idea of state-dependent brain-stimulation but it is also possible that the observed behavioral effect was caused by effects on larger parts of a fronto-parietal network.

As mentioned earlier, the IPC is part of a larger directionally specific IPC-preSMA network (Ritterband-Rosenbaum et al., submitted and planned to appear in this issue) where SoA is associated with stronger coupling from IPC to preSMA during late task phase. These inter-regional connections indicate that "self" vs. "other" attributions should not be seen purely as increased or decreased activity in single cortical areas. Rather it is the coupled activity in a specific frequency band in the network that is needed to determine sense of agency. Our rTMS-results complement the results of the EEG-study by demonstrating that stimulation of the IPC node of the parietal-premotor network alters the sensorimotor interpretation of self-controlled movements. In this context it is interesting to speculate over the different roles of the preSMA and the IPC in creating a SoA. Moore and co-workers (Moore et al., 2010) showed that disrupting the preSMA reduced the temporal link between action and effect, an implicit measure of SoA. The authors speculate that the preSMA may use motor information to generate predictions over the sensory consequences of actions. The results of the presented study and the associated EEG study are at least consistent with this idea and may suggest that the IPC feeds the sensory feedback needed for comparison to the preSMA.

Taken together, our findings suggest that interference with rTMS alters recognition of self-controlled movements in a simple drawing task. It needs to be further clarified to what extend more complex *natural* movements are being affected by external disturbance in the IPC or in the IPC-SMA network. This could help explain behavior of patients with lesions in the areas around IPC, e.g., angular gyrus, intraparietal sulcus, supramarginal gyrus etc., which also seem important for agency detection.

AUTHOR CONTRIBUTIONS

Anina Ritterband-Rosenbaum, Anke N. Karabanov, Mark S. Christensen, and Jens Bo Nielsen designed the experiment while Anina Ritterband-Rosenbaum and Anke N. Karabanov completed the data collection, analyzed the data and wrote the manuscript. All authors approved the final version of the manuscript.

ACKNOWLEDGMENTS

Anke N. Karabanov was founded by the Swedish Research Council. Anina Ritterband-Rosenbaum was funded by the University of Copenhagen, Denmark and the Helene Elsass Foundation. Mark S. Christensen was funded by the Danish Independent Research Council Humanities.

REFERENCES

Acheson, D. J., Hamidi, M., Binder, J. R., and Postle, B. R. (2011). A common neural substrate for language production and verbal working memory. *J. Cogn. Neurosci.* 23, 1358–1367. doi: 10.1162/jocn.2010.21519

Andersen, R. A., Essick, G. K., and Siegel, R. M. (1987). Neurons of area 7 activated by both visual stimuli and oculomotor behavior. *Exp. Brain Res.* 67, 316–322. doi: 10.1007/BF00248552

Baier, B., and Karnath, H. O. (2008). Tight link between our sense of limb ownership and self-awareness of actions. *Stroke* 39, 486–488. doi: 10.1161/STROKEAHA.107.495606

Chib, V. S., Krutky, M. A., Lynch, K. M., and Mussa-Ivaldi, F. A. (2009). The separate neural control of hand movements and contact forces. *J. Neurosci.* 29, 3939–3947. doi: 10.1523/JNEUROSCI.5856-08.2009

Culham, J. C., and Kanwisher, N. G. (2001). Neuroimaging of cognitive functions in human parietal cortex. *Curr. Opin. Neurobiol.* 11, 157–163. doi: 10.1016/S0959-4388(00)00191-4

Culham, J. C., and Valyear, K. F. (2006). Human parietal cortex in action. *Curr. Opin. Neurobiol.* 16, 205–212. doi: 10.1016/j.conb.2006.03.005

Desmurget, M., Epstein, C. M., Turner, R. S., Prablanc, C., Alexander, G. E., and Grafton, S. T. (1999). Role of the posterior parietal cortex in updating reaching movements to a visual target. *Nat. Neurosci.* 2, 563–567. doi: 10.1038/9219

Devlin, J. T., Matthews, P. M., and Rushworth, M. F. (2003). Semantic processing in the left inferior prefrontal cortex: a combined functional magnetic resonance imaging and transcranial magnetic stimulation study. *J. Cogn. Neurosci.* 15, 71–84. doi: 10.1162/089892903321107837

Farrer, C., Frey, S. H., Van Horn, J. D., Tunik, E., Turk, D., Inati, S., et al. (2008). The angular gyrus computes action awareness representations. *Cereb. Cortex* 18, 254–261. doi: 10.1093/cercor/bhm050

Farrer, C., and Frith, C. D. (2002). Experiencing oneself vs another person as being the cause of an action: the neural correlates of the experience of agency. *Neuroimage* 15, 596–603. doi: 10.1006/nimg.2001.1009

Fourneret, P., Paillard, J., Lamarre, Y., Cole, J., and Jeannerod, M. (2002). Lack of conscious recognition of one's own actions in a haptically deafferented patient. *Neuroreport* 13, 541–547. doi: 10.1097/00001756-200203250-00036

Franck, N., Farrer, C., Georgieff, N., Marie-Cardine, M., Dalery, J., D'Amato, T., et al. (2001). Defective recognition of one's own actions in patients with schizophrenia. *Am. J. Psychiatry* 158, 454–459. doi: 10.1176/appi.ajp.158.3.454

Frith, C. D., Blakemore, S. J., and Wolpert, D. M. (2000). Abnormalities in the awareness and control of action. *Philos. Trans. R. Soc. Lond. B Biol. Sci.* 355, 1771–1788. doi: 10.1098/rstb.2000.0734

Gallagher, S. (2000). Consciousness in action. *Philos. Psychol.* 13, 127–129.

Heinen, K., Ruff, C. C., Bjoertomt, O., Schenkluhn, B., Bestmann, S., Blankenburg, F., et al. (2011). Concurrent TMS-fMRI reveals dynamic interhemispheric influences of the right parietal cortex during exogenously cued visuospatial attention. *Eur. J. Neurosci.* 33, 991–1000. doi: 10.1111/j.1460-9568.2010.07580.x

Herwig, U., Satrapi, P., and Schonfeldt-Lecuona, C. (2003). Using the international 10–20 EEG system for positioning of transcranial magnetic stimulation. *Brain Topogr.* 16, 95–99. doi: 10.1023/B:BRAT.0000006333.93597.9d

Iacoboni, M. (2006). Visuo-motor integration and control in the human posterior parietal cortex: evidence from TMS and fMRI. *Neuropsychologia* 44, 2691–2699. doi: 10.1016/j.neuropsychologia.2006.04.029

Jeannerod, M. (2009). The sense of agency and its disturbances in schizophrenia: a reappraisal. *Exp. Brain Res.* 192, 527–532. doi: 10.1007/s00221-008-1533-3

Johnson, H., and Haggard, P. (2005). Motor awareness without perceptual awareness. *Neuropsychologia* 43, 227–237. doi: 10.1016/j.neuropsychologia.2004.11.009

Leyman, L., De, R. R., Vanderhasselt, M. A., and Baeken, C. (2009). Influence of high-frequency repetitive transcranial magnetic stimulation over the dorsolateral prefrontal cortex on the inhibition of emotional information in healthy volunteers. *Psychol. Med.* 39, 1019–1028. doi: 10.1017/S0033291708004431

MacDonald, P., and Paus, T. (2003). The role of parietal cortex in awareness of self-generated movements: a transcranial magnetic stimulation study. *Cereb. Cortex* 13, 962–967. doi: 10.1093/cercor/13.9.962

Manenti, R., Tettamanti, M., Cotelli, M., Miniussi, C., and Cappa, S. F. (2010). The neural bases of word encoding and retrieval: a fMRI-guided transcranial magnetic stimulation study. *Brain Topogr.* 22, 318–332. doi: 10.1007/s10548-009-0126-1

Moore, J. W., Ruge, D., Wenke, D., Rothwell, J., and Haggard, P. (2010). Disrupting the experience of control in the human brain: pre-supplementary motor area contributes to the sense of agency. *Proc. Biol. Sci.* 277, 2503–2509. doi: 10.1098/rspb.2010.0404

Mort, D. J., Malhotra, P., Mannan, S. K., Rorden, C., Pambakian, A., Kennard, C., et al. (2003). The anatomy of visual neglect. *Brain* 126, 1986–1997. doi: 10.1093/brain/awg200

Nahab, F. B., Kundu, P., Gallea, C., Kakareka, J., Pursley, R., Pohida, T., et al. (2011). The neural processes underlying self-agency. *Cereb. Cortex* 21, 48–55. doi: 10.1093/cercor/bhq059

Oldfield, R. C. (1971). Assessment and analysis of handedness edinburgh inventory. *Neuropsychologia* 9, 97–113. doi: 10.1016/0028-3932(71)90067-4

Pascual-Leone, A., Walsh, V., and Rothwell, J. (2000). Transcranial magnetic stimulation in cognitive neuroscience–virtual lesion, chronometry, and functional connectivity. *Curr. Opin. Neurobiol.* 10, 232–237. doi: 10.1016/S0959-4388(00)00081-7

Preston, C., and Newport, R. (2008). Misattribution of movement agency following right parietal TMS. *Soc. Cogn. Affect. Neurosci.* 3, 26–32. doi: 10.1093/scan/nsm036

Reichenbach, A., Bresciani, J. P., Peer, A., Bulthoff, H. H., and Thielscher, A. (2011). Contributions of the PPC to online control of visually guided reaching movements assessed with fMRI-guided TMS. *Cereb. Cortex* 21, 1602–1612. doi: 10.1093/cercor/bhq225

Ritterband-Rosenbaum, A., Christensen, M. S., Kliim-Due, M., Petersen, L. Z., Rasmussen, B., and Nielsen, J. B. (2011). Altered sense of agency in children with spastic cerebral palsy. *BMC Neurol.* 11:150. doi: 10.1186/1471-2377-11-150

Ritterband-Rosenbaum, A., Christensen, M. S., and Nielsen, J. B. (2012). Twenty weeks of computer-training improves sense of agency in children with spastic cerebral palsy. *Res. Dev. Disabil.* 33, 1227–1234. doi: 10.1016/j.ridd.2012.02.019

Rossi, S., Hallett, M., Rossini, P. M., Pascual-Leone, A., and The Safety of TMS Consensus Group. (2009). Safety, ethical considerations, and application guidelines for the use of transcranial magnetic stimulation in clinical practice and research. *Clin. Neurophysiol.* 120, 2008–2039. doi: 10.1016/j.clinph.2009.08.016

Rossini, P. M., Barker, A. T., Berardelli, A., Caramia, M. D., Caruso, G., Cracco, R. Q., et al. (1994). Non-invasive electrical and magnetic stimulation of the brain, spinal cord and roots: basic principles and procedures for routine clinical application. Report of an IFCN committee. *Electroencephalogr. Clin. Neurophysiol.* 91, 79–92. doi: 10.1016/0013-4694(94)90029-9

Rushworth, M. F., and Taylor, P. C. (2006). TMS in the parietal cortex: updating representations for attention and action. *Neuropsychologia* 44, 2700–2716. doi: 10.1016/j.neuropsychologia.2005.12.007

Sack, A. T., Kohler, A., Bestmann, S., Linden, D. E., Dechent, P., Goebel, R., et al. (2007). Imaging the brain activity changes underlying impaired visuospatial judgments: simultaneous FMRI, TMS, and behavioral studies. *Cereb. Cortex* 17, 2841–2852. doi: 10.1093/cercor/bhm013

Silvanto, J., Muggleton, N., and Walsh, V. (2008). State-dependency in brain stimulation studies of perception and cognition. *Trends Cogn. Sci.* 12, 447–454. doi: 10.1016/j.tics.2008.09.004

Silvanto, J., and Pascual-Leone, A. (2008). State-dependency of transcranial magnetic stimulation. *Brain Topogr.* 21, 1–10. doi: 10.1007/s10548-008-0067-0

Sirigu, A., Daprati, E., Ciancia, S., Giraux, P., Nighoghossian, N., Posada, A., et al. (2004). Altered awareness of voluntary action after damage to the parietal cortex. *Nat. Neurosci.* 7, 80–84. doi: 10.1038/nn1160

Wilkins, A. J., Bonanni, P., Porciatti, V., and Guerrini, R. (2004). Physiology of human photosensitivity. *Epilepsia* 45(Suppl. 1), 7–13. doi: 10.1111/j.0013-9580.2004.451009.x

Wolpert, D. M., Ghahramani, Z., and Jordan, M. I. (1995). An internal model for sensorimotor integration. *Science* 269, 1880–1882. doi: 10.1126/science.7569931

21

Personality and intentional binding: an exploratory study using the narcissistic personality inventory

Ann (Chen) Hascalovitz[1] and Sukhvinder S. Obhi[2]*

[1] Department of Physiology, Development and Neuroscience, Behavioural and Clinical Neuroscience Institute, University of Cambridge, Cambridge, UK
[2] Social Brain, Body and Action Lab, Department of Psychology, Neuroscience and Behaviour, McMaster University, Hamilton, ON, Canada

***Correspondence:**
Sukhvinder S. Obhi, Social Brain, Body and Action Lab, Department of Psychology, Neuroscience and Behaviour, McMaster University, 1280 Main Street West, Hamilton, ON L8S 4L8, Canada
e-mail: obhi@mcmaster.ca

When an individual estimates the temporal interval between a voluntary action and a consequent effect, their estimates are shorter than the real duration. This perceived shortening has been termed "intentional binding", and is often due to a shift in the perception of a voluntary action forward towards the effect and a shift in the perception of the effect back towards the action. Despite much work on binding, there is virtually no consideration of individual/personality differences and how they affect it. Narcissism is a psychological trait associated with an inflated sense of self, and individuals higher in levels of subclinical narcissism tend to see themselves as highly effective agents. Conversely, lower levels of narcissism may be associated with a reduced sense of agency. In this exploratory study, to assess whether individuals with different scores on a narcissism scale are associated with differences in intentional binding, we compared perceived times of actions and effects (tones) between participants with high, middle, and low scores on the narcissistic personality inventory (NPI). We hypothesized that participants with higher scores would show increased binding compared to participants with lower scores. We found that participants in our middle and high groups showed a similar degree of binding, which was significantly greater than the level of binding shown by participants with the lowest scores. To our knowledge, these results are the first to demonstrate that different scores on a personality scale are associated with changes in the phenomenological experience of action, and therefore underscore the importance of considering individual/personality differences in the study of volition. Our results also reinforce the notion that intentional binding is related to agency experience.

Keywords: intentional binding, agency, narcissism, narcissism and agency, narcissism and intentional binding, subjective time, awareness of action

INTRODUCTION

Whereas there is large body of research on the production and control of human action, there is less work devoted to understanding the subjective experience of action (Rosenbaum, 1991; Haggard, 2001; Obhi and Goodale, 2005). The sense of agency refers to the feeling of control over self-produced actions and, as a consequence, the feeling of being a causal agent capable of effecting change in the environment (Gallagher, 2012; Moore and Obhi, 2012). The sense of agency can be either an explicit phenomenologically rich conscious experience of control, or can be relatively phenomenologically "thin", such as when a person "knows" that they acted to cause some effect, but such knowledge does not become the focus of conscious awareness. Understanding the neurocognitive processes that underlie both forms of agency experience has become an important goal for cognitive neuroscience and experimental psychology.

To the extent that actions produce effects in the environment, they can be considered as operant. From over a decade of research, an important finding is that, when such operant actions are made volitionally, the actor perceives the time interval between the action and the consequent effect to be shorter than its true value (Haggard et al., 2002; see Moore and Obhi, 2012 for a review). More specifically, this illusory interval compression usually manifests as a perception that the initiation of action occurs later than it actually did, and a perception that the effect occurred earlier than it actually did, although in certain cases effects have been found on the percept of one component of the action-effect complex and not the other. Interestingly, if the person is *made* to perform the action (and thus produce the effect) involuntarily, either by transcranial magnetic stimulation (TMS) of the motor cortex, or by other mechanical means, the perceived shortening of the action-effect interval does not occur (Tsakiris and Haggard, 2003). The apparent dependence of this temporal illusion on intention seems to support the notion that the illusion may be linked to the sense of agency. The illusion has thus been referred to as "intentional binding". The potential link between intentional binding and the sense of agency is intriguing and has spawned considerable interest from researchers in experimental psychology and cognitive neuroscience, although it is noteworthy that some researchers have exercised caution in interpreting the effect in terms of intentional processes and instead consider it as a special case of more general cause-effect processing (Buehner, 2012).

In this light, and in order to better understand whether intentional binding is linked to agency, it is necessary to investigate the conditions under which intentional binding occurs, with specific regard to the personal and situational factors that modulate the magnitude of the effect. This has often been done using experimental manipulations of action-effect contingency which influence the ability to predict the outcome of actions, and has even extended into questions about the moral status of an outcome, joint actions and the effects of recalling memories of power and depression (Moore et al., 2009; Moretto et al., 2011; Obhi and Sebanz, 2011; Obhi et al., 2012, 2013).

Another approach has been to assess binding in patients who are known to have deficits in the production, control and subjective experience of action. In this regard, patients such as those with schizophrenia, Parkinson's disease and psychogenic conversion disorders have been found to display "abnormal" patterns of binding (Haggard et al., 2003; Kranick et al., 2013). However, despite some limited work in patient populations, to date, there has been no research investigating the effects of variation in specific personality traits on binding. Indeed, more generally, the question of how action is experienced by individuals with different psychological profiles remains largely ignored.

Similar to the patient approach, studying the relationship between personality traits and binding could be useful in shedding light on the purported link between binding and agency. Specifically, individuals who possess traits that are linked to differences in the tendency to act, or to the perception of the self as a powerful entity, might be expected to show differences in binding. In the present study, to further investigate the notion that binding is linked to agency, we contrasted neurologically normal individuals who differ on their scores on the narcissistic personality inventory (NPI), a commonly used index of sub-clinical narcissism in social psychological research. Narcissism is a personality trait that has been linked to an inflated sense of self, a tendency toward high levels of dominance motivation and dominance behavior, and a perception of the self as a powerful agent (Kohut, 1977; Raskin et al., 1991; Morf and Rhodewalt, 2001). Despite this stereotypical view of the powerful and dominant narcissist, it is worth noting that accounts of clinical narcissists often reveal a rather fragile picture in which narcissists are prone to feelings of emptiness, a lack of belonging and fluctuating self-esteem. Indeed, Kohut has argued that behind the grandiosity, lies low self-esteem (Kohut, 1971). Others suggested that narcissists overcome this situation via greater than normal self-enhancement (John and Robins, 1994). In their proposal for an integrated model of narcissism, Dimaggio et al. (2002) observe that narcissists often engage in an ever-escalating process of self-enhancement, which they employ to protect fragile self-esteem. These authors suggest that narcissists do not have the requisite metacognitive skills to understand why they don't fit in, and they tend to deal with such situations which leave them feeling disconnected and separate, by self-administering self-esteem tests, which they tend to pass due to self-enhancement. This process has been associated with threatening swings in self-esteem, which further contribute to the fragility of the narcissistic mindset (Ronningstam, 2011a; for more on manifestation of clinical narcissism see Dimaggio et al., 2006, 2008). However, individuals with sub-clinical levels of narcissism, do appear to maintain a higher level of self-esteem and self-agency and are therefore somewhat more stable than their clinical coutnerparts (Ackerman et al., 2011). Individuals who score higher on subclinical narcissism have been shown to pursue dominance behaviors in order to maintain their grandiose sense of self, and from an evolutionary perspective, to gain better access to resources via increased social status (Baumeister et al., 2000; Kirkpatrick et al., 2002). Indeed, when scores on measures such as the NPI are examined in relation to scores on self-report measures of agency, there is a strong positive correlation between the two (Campbell et al., 2007). This finding, coupled with the purported link between agency and intentional binding, makes it important to characterize the relationship between narcissism and intentional binding.

In the current study, to shed more light on the link between scores on the NPI, intentional binding and agency, we recruited individuals who had previously completed the NPI. We allocated individuals to a high, middle, and low groups based on the range of NPI scores in our sample and ran each participant through an intentional binding experiment. During this intentional binding task, participants were asked to judge the onset time of actions and consequent effects. The task involved making an action (clicking a mouse), experiencing an effect (hearing a tone), and making an action that resulted in a subsequent effect (clicking the mouse to produce the tone), while watching clock hand rotate on a computer screen (Haggard et al., 2002). During the different conditions, participants reported where the clock hand was when they clicked the mouse or heard the tone. By calculating the difference between the perceived time of the action when it did not produce a tone against when it did produce a tone, and the perceived time of the tone when it was preceded by an action against when it was not preceded by an action, we determined the intentional binding effect. Importantly, intentional binding is thought to represent an implicit measure of the sense of agency (see Moore and Obhi, 2012 for a review). Given the purported link between narcissism and agency, we predicted that individuals with higher NPI scores would demonstrate significantly greater levels of intentional binding compared to those with lower NPI scores.

METHODS

PARTICIPANTS

Twenty-seven university students (nine males and 18 females, age 17–20, Mean 18.3, SD 0.73) participated in the study for a course credit or $11 compensation. Each participant was run individually in a single cubicle with the researcher present. The participants had all been previously screened online using the NPI and grouped into the high and low narcissism group prior to the experiment based on the distribution of scores on the NPI taken as part of mass testing. Specifically, participants were allocated to the "high" group if their score on the NPI was over 21 out of a possible 40, and participants were allocated to the "low" group if their NPI score was less than 10. The middle group was created based on the distribution of scores between the high and low groups, and was comprised of individuals who scored between 11–17 on the NPI. This resulted in the inclusion of nine participants in each of the three groups. All participants completed a written consent form at the beginning of the study. It is important to note that being placed into the high group does not correspond to being a pathological "narcissist" and we are not making any claims in this paper about narcissistic personality disorder (NPD). Indeed, the label "high" in this paper simply refers to a relatively high score in the range of scores we obtained in the current sample. Our simple aim in this exploratory study was to assess whether there are measurable differences in intentional binding associated with individuals whose score on the NPI differs.

APPARATUS AND STIMULI

The experiment was programmed using Superlab version 4.5 (Cedrus Corporation, San Pedro, CA, USA) and was run on a Lenovo computer, with stimuli displayed on a 19-inch LCD monitor. A Microsoft serial mouse was used to register the voluntary key press (left click). Auditory tones (100 ms, 1000 Hz, were presented over Dell Desktop speakers situated either side of the computer monitor).

PROCEDURE

Participants completed the experiment one at a time with the experimenter present in a testing cubicle. Participants were instructed to watch a small clock (2.5 cm diameter, marked at 5 min intervals) rotate on the computer screen and, depending on the condition, to report where the clock hand was when they either pressed the key or heard the tone (between 0 and 59, see Haggard et al., 2002; Obhi and Hall, 2011 for a similar approach). There were four different conditions, or blocks, that each subject completed in a pseudo-random order: baseline action, baseline effect, operant action and operant effect (**Figure 1**). Each block had 60 trials and clock hand starting position was pseudo-randomly varied. In the baseline action condition, participants were instructed to click the mouse at a time of their own choosing (and not in response to position of the clock hand). After their key press, the clock hand continued to rotate for a variable amount of time. At the end of the trial, participants were asked to report to the researcher where the clock hand was when they initiated their voluntary action. In the baseline effect condition, participants were asked not to produce a key press, but instead watch the clock and report the clock hand position at the time a randomly occurring tone sounded (tone could occur between 1600 and 3600 ms after the appearance of the clock). In the operant action condition, participants were again instructed to click the mouse at a time of their own choosing after the appearance of the clock. Upon clicking the mouse, a tone sounded and, at the end of the trial, participants were asked to report where the clock hand was when they clicked the mouse, not when they heard the tone. Finally, in the operant effect condition, participants again clicked the mouse at a time of their own choosing, which again produced a tone. On these trials however, participants were asked to report where the clock hand was when they heard the tone, not when they clicked the mouse. At the beginning of each block, participants completed five practice trials to familiarize themselves with the procedure. Practice trials were not included in the analysis.

RESULTS

For each participant, action and tone judgments that deviated more than 2.5 standard deviations from the mean judgment for a particular condition were excluded. This resulted in the removal of less than 1% of trials. Remaining action and tone judgment data were subjected to inferential statistical analysis.

CALCULATING ACTION, TONE AND TOTAL SHIFTS

To determine perceptual shifts, we first calculated judgment errors by quantifying the difference between judgments of actions and tones compared to their veridical onset times, for both baseline and operant conditions. The difference between these judgment errors for baseline and operant conditions was taken as the perceived shift. In addition, the overall "degree of binding" (or "total shift") was determined by calculating the extent to which the perceived times of actions and tones moved towards each other. This was calculated as: (Action shift) + (−1xTone shift) (see **Figure 2**).

NPI SCORE AND AGENCY

The three groups were classified as follows: High NPI score, who had scores greater than 21, Middle NPI scores who had scores between 11–17, and Low NPI scores, who had scores between 3–9. Participant binding data from the three groups were entered into three separate one-way ANOVAs for analysis. There was a main effect of group on Tone shift ($F_{(2,24)} = 3.759$, $p < 0.05$), as well as on Total shift ($F_{(2,24)} = 3.643$, $p < 0.05$). However there was no effect of group on Action shift ($F_{(2,24)} = 0.319$, $p > 0.05$). Follow up independent samples t-tests were run to investigate the difference in the degree of shift between High, Middle and Low groups (mean shift data for actions and effects are presented in **Figure 3**, overall binding data is presented in **Figure 4**).

HIGH VS. LOW NPI SCORES

Follow up independent samples t-tests were run to investigate the difference in the degree of shift between High and Low NPI score participants (mean shift data for actions and effects is presented in **Figure 3**, and overall binding is presented in **Figure 4**). The t-test revealed a significant difference for tone shifts (High: Mean = −130.97, SD = 46.25 < Low: Mean = −65.18, SD = 71.20, $t_{(16)} = 2.325$, $p = 0.034$) and overall binding (High: Mean = 157.40, SD = 51.08 > Low: Mean = 100.20, SD = 45.94, $t_{(16)} = -2.498$, $p = 0.024$), but not for action shifts (High: Mean = 26.36, SD = 26.73 < Low: Mean = 18.62, SD = 13.03, $t_{(15)} = -0.304$, $p = 0.765$).

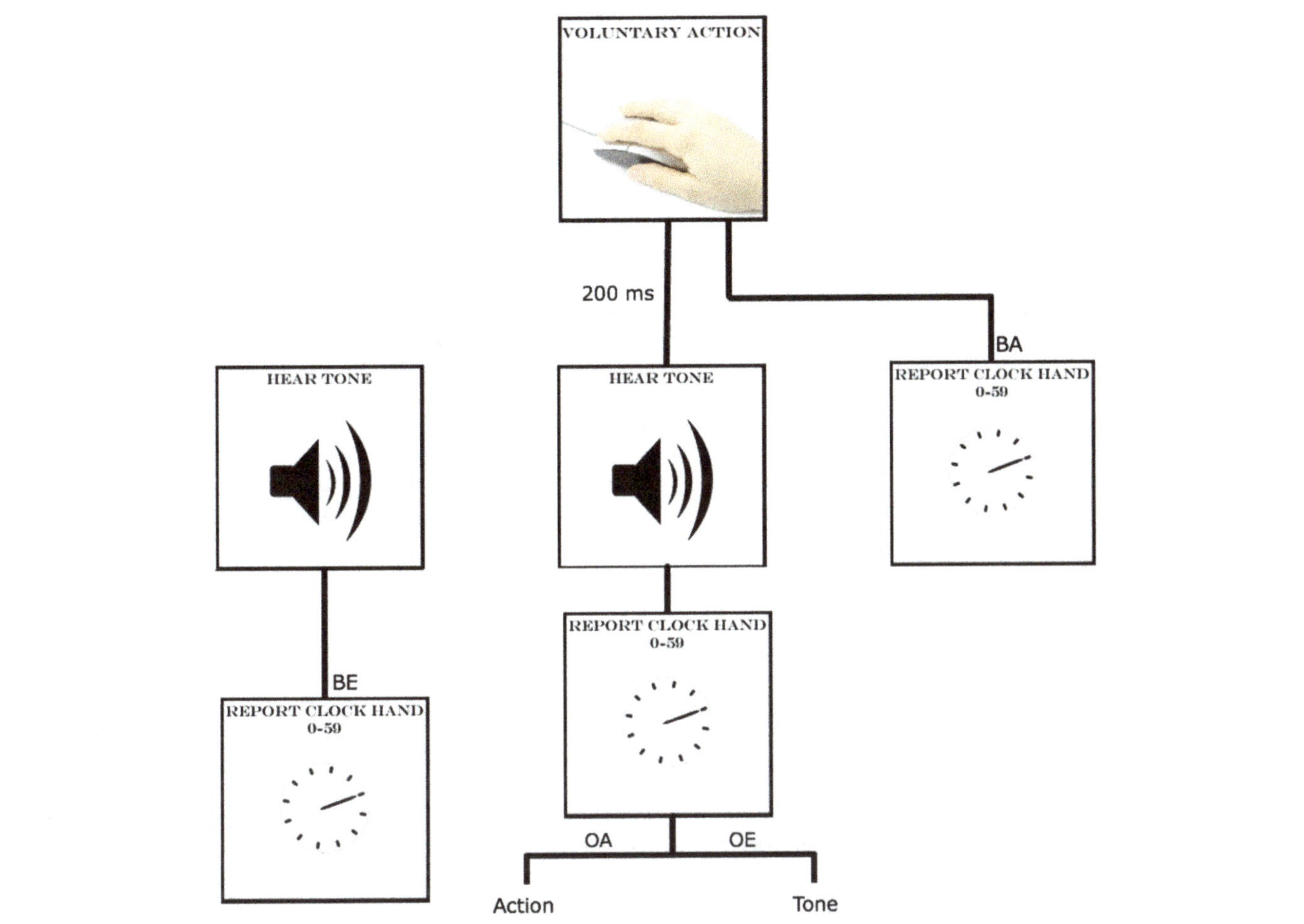

FIGURE 1 | Procedure for the intentional binding experiment, labeled BA, BE, OA and OE for: baseline action, baseline effect, operant action and operant effect conditions.

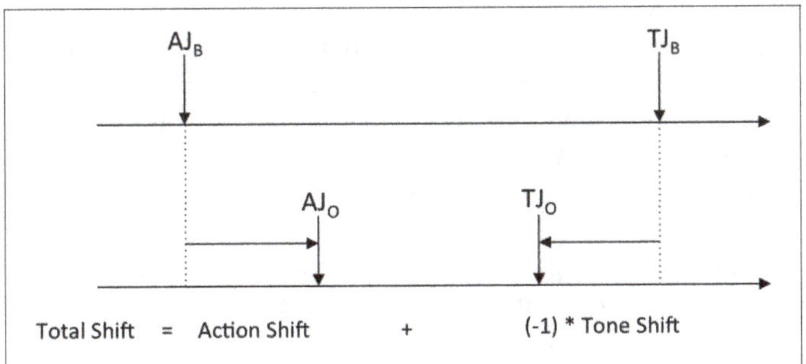

FIGURE 2 | Illustrates how action, tone, and overall degree of binding (i.e., total shift) are calculated. AJ_B: Action judgment in baseline condition, TJ_B: Tone judgment in baseline condition. AJ_O: Action judgment in operant condition, TJ_O: Tone judgment in operant condition.

LOW VS. MIDDLE NPI SCORES

The *t*-tests also revealed a significant difference for tone shifts between Middle and Low groups (Middle: Mean = −131.05, SD = 56.28 < Low: Mean = −65.18, SD = 71.20, $t_{(16)} = 2.177$, $p = 0.045$) (see **Figure 3**), and for overall degree of binding (Middle: Mean = 152.67, SD = 52.45 > Low: Mean = 100.20, SD = 45.94, $t_{(16)} = -2.258$, $p = 0.038$) (see **Figure 4**), but not action shift (Middle: Mean = 21.62, SD = 25.02 > Low: Mean = 18.62, SD = 13.03, $t_{(15)} = -0.304$, $p = 0.765$) (see **Figure 3**).

MIDDLE VS. HIGH NPI SCORES

The High and Middle groups did not significantly differ on the action (Middle: Mean = 21.62, SD = 25.02 < High: Mean = 26.36, SD = 26.73, $t_{(16)} = -0.388$, $p = 0.703$) or effect shifts (Middle: Mean = −131.05, SD = 56.28 < High: Mean = −130.97, SD = 46.25, $t_{(16)} = -0.003$, $p = 0.998$) (see **Figure 3**), nor on overall binding (Middle: Mean = 152.67, SD = 52.45 < High: Mean = 157.40, SD = 51.08, $t_{(16)} = -0.914$, $p = 0.849$) (see **Figure 4**).

DISCUSSION

The current study investigated whether individuals who differ on their score on the NPI also show different patterns of intentional binding when making judgments about the onsets of voluntary actions and their effects. Given that narcissistic traits are associated with increased dominance motivation and behavior,

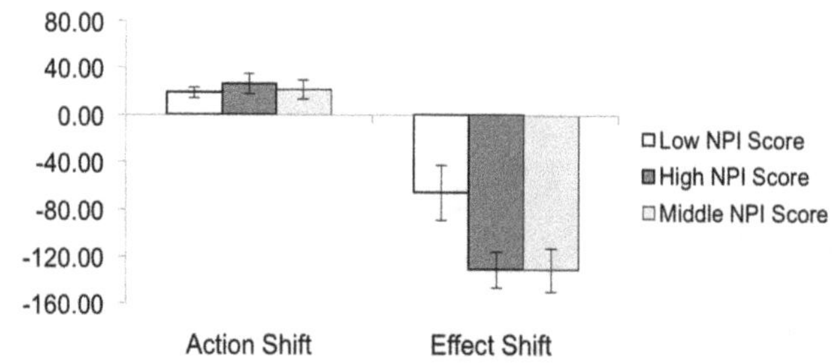

FIGURE 3 | The mean action shift and mean tone shift for the low, middle and high NPI score group. Tone shift was significantly greater in the high and middle groups compared to the low group. Error bars are SEM. See text for statistics.

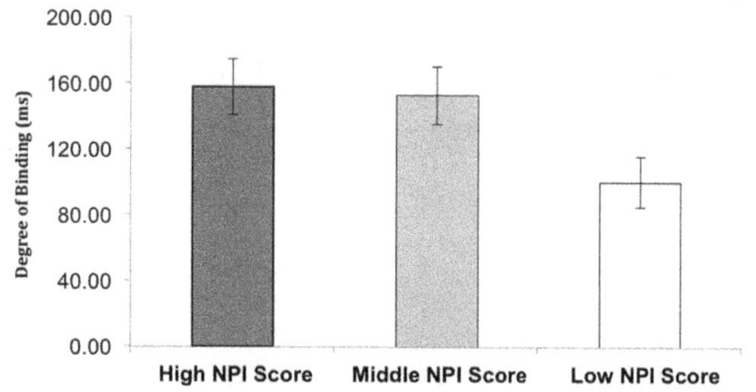

FIGURE 4 | The mean total degree of binding (in ms) for the low, middle, and high NPI score groups; the high and middle group showed significantly more binding than the low group. Error bars are SEM. See text for statistics.

an over-inflated sense of self-importance and a tendency to seek out social power as a means to maintain high social status, we hypothesized that those who scored higher on the NPI would exhibit a correspondingly greater degree of intentional binding.

Our prediction was borne out by the results. Individuals with higher NPI scores did indeed display greater levels of binding than those with low NPI scores, although the effect was entirely driven by shifts in perception of the tone. Interestingly the middle group displayed tone binding that was indistinguishable from the high group. This is most likely due to the fact that none of our participants scored anywhere near the maximum NPI score of 40. Thus, one limitation of the current initial study, is that our groups, although split on the basis of the range of NPI scores we obtained, did not include scores at the upper end of the NPI scale itself. Thus, high and middle levels of narcissism in our sample, perhaps corresponded to a single "moderate" group and may reflect healthy levels of narcissism (Maxwell et al., 2011). Indeed, it could be argued that, in the absence of obtaining scores right at the high end of the NPI scale, we are not dealing with narcissism at all in the current sample. However, we do have different ranges of NPI scores and to avoid mislabeling a moderate NPI score as a moderate level of narcissism, we simply refer to moderate NPI scores instead of middle and high narcissism, for the remainder of the discussion.

Not withstanding the lack of high NPI scores, our results show a clear difference in binding between individuals with moderate NPI scores and low NPI scores. Importantly the low group did contain scores as low as 3, and therefore our results are consistent with reduced agency for individuals at the low end of the NPI scale. Indeed, low scores on the NPI may be comorbid with other psychological characteristics such as low self-esteem, anxiety and/or depression, which have been shown to be related to a reduced sense of agency (Barlow, 1991; Keeton et al., 2008; Obhi et al., 2012, 2013). Despite the lack of very high NPI scores in the current study, overall, our results provide the first evidence that different scores on a personality trait are associated with differences in the degree of binding of effects to voluntary actions, and by extension, pre-reflective agentic experience.

Our results suggest that even moderate scores on the NPI might be linked to a stronger sense of agency and increased intentional binding for voluntary actions and outcomes, compared to lower levels of narcissism. Furthermore, while it is well known that narcissists often over-estimate their intelligence and their academic abilities (Robins and Beer, 2001; Campbell et al., 2002), among other things, it may be that those who score very low on the NPI may correspondingly under-estimate their abilities. Specifically, the decreased level of tone binding they display suggests that they may particularly under-estimate the degree of control they have over the outcomes that their actions produce. Given that low self-esteem has been linked to risk for depression (Orth et al., 2008), and that we recently showed that activating memories of depression reduces intentional binding (Obhi et al., 2013), one plausible explanation for the current pattern of data is indeed that individuals with low NPI scores are less psychologically "healthy" than their moderate scoring counterparts, and one consequence of this is that they have diminished agentic experience. Binding is an intriguing method for examining differences in the experience of voluntary action and further research is required to clarify the precise relationship between narcissism, psychological health and agency. This study represents an initial demonstration that such a relationship may exist, and is therefore worthy of further investigation. More generally, this study underscores that personality differences do impact the experience of voluntary action and thereby open up a new area of inquiry for researchers working on volitional action.

A noteworthy aspect of the current results is that the action-outcome complex that was employed in the experiment was arbitrary (a key press followed by an auditory tone) and did not involve control over other social agents. An obvious and potentially illuminating extension of this work involves comparing binding for arbitrary action outcomes such as lights and tones, with social outcomes such as "winning", "losing" or influencing the actions of another individual (see Obhi et al., 2012 for a similar approach). Indeed, previous authors have commented on the tendency for narcissists to subjugate others in their social environment and "use" them in the service of their own goals (Dimaggio et al., 2002). One prediction is that such manipulations would increase the influence of narcissism on binding.

Future work might consider investigating intentional binding in patients with clinical narcissism. Since NPD has been more recently associated with a deeply held sense of low self-esteem (Ronningstam, 2011b), the intentional binding effect in patients may mimic those who had abnormally low scores on the NPI. Unlike trait anxiety, which is highly correlated to anxiety disorder (Grupe and Nitschke, 2013), narcissism as a personality trait (measured on the NPI) is often not well correlated to the full-blown experience of narcissistic disorder. Thus, non-patients tend to score lower on the NPI than healthy participants, and higher scoring on the NPI by narcissists could simply be a function of response bias (John and Robins, 1994; Pincus and Lukowitsky, 2010). Furthermore, some researchers have suggested that the sense of agency in NPD is more vulnerable and experiences more fluctuations than that in non-narcissists. In view of this it would be beneficial to test clinical narcissists on the intentional binding task and to measure how the degree of binding changes after receiving criticism, or other types of feedback. Changes in binding, as a function of the social circumstance, may explain the variability experienced in self-agency by narcissists, and can further aid to explain why narcissists tend to shift between different periods of high and low functioning (Ronningstam, 2013; Ronningstam and Baskin-Sommers, 2013). Again though, we underline that in the current study we simply measured NPI scores and determined whether different scores were associated with differences in binding. We likely did not have "real" narcissists in our sample and thus our ideas for future work on clinical samples must be treated as speculative.

There has been considerable research interest in intentional binding since it was first reported in 2002 (Haggard et al., 2002; Moore and Obhi, 2012). Out of this research, strong support for the notion that preparatory and predictive, processes play an important role in binding, and particularly tone binding, has emerged. The comparator model is an influential model of motor control that posits interaction between a prediction of the sensory consequences of pending movement and the actual sensory consequences of the movement (Blakemore et al., 1999). This comparator model has been invoked in the study of agency and it has been shown that when accurate prediction is not possible, the sense of agency, and intentional binding is reduced (Haggard and Clark, 2003; Tsakiris and Haggard, 2003). Specifically, an influential model of agency proposes that when the prediction of the sensory consequences of an action and the actual sensory consequences match, agency is experienced, whereas, when they do not match, the action is not attributed to the self (Blakemore et al., 2002).

The supplementary motor area (SMA) is thought to be a key region involved in action preparation and prediction as well as the conscious experience of motor intentions (Fried et al., 1991; Makoshi et al., 2011; Moore and Obhi, 2012). Interestingly, theta burst TMS over the pre-supplementary motor area (pre-SMA) has been shown to reduce tone binding in neurologically normal participants, apparently confirming a key role for the pre-SMA in subjective experience of action effects (Moore et al., 2010). More generally, prediction has been purported as a fundamental brain process that enables successful navigation of the environment, both physical and social (e.g., Bubic et al., 2010). Taken together these studies lend support to the notion that premotor processing is strongly tied the phenomenology of action and effect binding. Thus, it is possible that individuals with low NPI scores experience lower levels of motor preparation or differ in their predictive processing compared to those with moderate NPI scores.

In addition to the possible role of prediction, it has also been shown that the binding of outcomes back toward actions can be the result of inferential processes that take into account the probability of actions producing effects. In this sense, binding is brought about not by prediction, but by a postdictive process (e.g., Wegner, 2002). For example, when additional effects occur that are not linked to actions, effect binding is reduced compared to when these additional non-action related effects do not occur (Moore et al., 2009). The manner in which the pre-SMA might contribute to postdictive processes remains to be elucidated, and given current knowledge of pre-SMA function, a predictive influence on binding may be more likely. Another important finding that fits well with our current results is that when an agent has a strong prior belief that they will cause an outcome, they show stronger effect binding (Desantis et al., 2011). In our experimental context, this result suggests that those with low NPI scores may have a chronically weak belief in themselves as causal agents, whereas those with moderate NPI scores have a stronger chronic belief in themselves as causal agents. As Desantis et al. (2011) suggested this difference in the strength of a priori beliefs could affect the reliability that the brain places on predictions of a forward model. Future work should consider this possibility further.

Future work could also address these possibilities by employing neuroimaging to assess the level of preparatory activity in the SMA (among other areas) in clinical narcissists and by manipulating the ability to predict sensory consequences of actions (by varying the probability of an effect occurring, for example). The suggestion that differences in trait narcissism may be linked with differences in sensorimotor prediction is, to our knowledge, relatively novel, and warrants further investigation.

The initial study we present here suffers from several limitations, some of which have been mentioned above. First, our sample was smaller than ideal and did not contain any individuals who scored above 33/40 on the NPI. This may have reduced differences in between our high and middle group in particular, which might account for the similar levels of binding displayed by these groups. Thus, one important follow-up study will be to recruit individuals whose scores fall along the full range of the NPI scale with at least 12 participants per group, and it must be underlined that this study cannot directly shed light on how clinical narcissists might manifest in intentional binding tasks. Second, we did not assess other psychological characteristics that may be correlated with different levels of narcissism (e.g., self-esteem). Another possibility is that different facets of narcissism are associated with different facets of cognition, including agentic dominance or causal reasoning; involving adaptive and/or maladaptive outcomes (Vonk et al., 2013). Measuring binding in relation to the subscales of the NPI may shed further light on variability in perceptual shifts within the three groups; although it is still unclear how many and to what extent the factors in these subscales exist (Ackerman et al., 2011). We also had a sample that was heavily biased towards females, who may experience narcissism differently, as gender differences have been described in other mental illnesses or trait characteristics (Greaves-Lord et al., 2010; McLean et al., 2011).

In sum, we report seminal results demonstrating a relationship between scores on a personality scale, the NPI and intentional binding. These results show that different scores on the NPI are associated with changes in the subjective experience of sensory effects produced by voluntary actions. Thus, to the extent that binding indexes agency, our results also provide evidence that low-level, pre-reflective agency is lower in individuals who score lower on the NPI compared to their counterparts who have moderate scores on the NPI. In future studies, measuring the degree of intentional binding in clinically diagnosed narcissists could provide insight to their inner most state: are they overly agentic, confident, and self loving; or are they over compensating for feelings of worthlessness, low self-esteem and lack of control (see Bosson et al., 2008)? Indeed, the development of agency measures that circumvent self-presentational biases could eventually be valuable in the diagnosis of personality disorders and may be relevant to new ideas regarding levels of functioning and assessment criteria in the diagnostic and statistical manual of mental disorders (DSM-5; see Skodol, 2012). These are questions that would be hard to address via the use of more traditional explicit measures that are hampered by self-presentation issues. Finally, the present work underscores the importance of assessing individual/personality differences in the performance and experience of volitional action, which allows the field to move beyond reliance on group level data.

ACKNOWLEDGMENTS

This research was supported by funds from a NSERC Discovery grant held by Sukhvinder S. Obhi. The authors thank Jeremy Hogeveen and Zeynep Barlas for assistance with data analysis.

REFERENCES

Ackerman, R. A., Witt, E. A., Donnellan, M. B., Trzesniewski, K. H., Robins, R. W., and Kashy, D. A. (2011). What does the narcissistic personality inventory really measure? *Assessment* 18, 67–87. doi: 10.1177/1073191110382845

Barlow, D. H. (1991). "The nature of anxiety: anxiety, depression and emotional disorders," in *Chronic Anxiety: Generalized Anxiety Disorder and Mixed Anxiety Depression*, eds R. M. Rapee and D. H. Barlow (New York: Guilford Press), 1–28.

Baumeister, R. F., Bushman, B. J., and Campbell, W. K. (2000). Self-esteem, narcissism and aggression: does violence result from low self-esteem or from threatened egotism? *Curr. Dir. Psychol. Sci.* 9, 26–29. doi: 10.1111/1467-8721.00053

Blakemore, S., Frith, C. D., and Wolpert, D. M. (1999). Spatio-temporal prediction modulates the perception of self-produced stimuli. *J. Cogn. Neurosci.* 11, 551–559. doi: 10.1162/089892999563607

Blakemore, S., Wolpert, D. M., and Frith, C. D. (2002). Abnormalities in the awareness of action. *Trends Cogn. Sci.* 6, 237–242. doi: 10.1016/s1364-6613(02)01907-1

Bosson, J. K., Lakey, C. E., Campbell, W. K., Zeigler-Hill, V., Jordan, C. H., and Kernis, M. H. (2008). Untangling the links between narcissism and self-esteem: a theoretical and empirical review. *Soc. Personal. Psychol. Compass.* 2, 1415–1439. doi: 10.1111/j.1751-9004.2008.00089.x

Bubic, A., von Cramon, D. Y., and Schubotz, R. I. (2010). Prediction, cognition and the brain. *Front. Hum. Neurosci.* 4:25. doi: 10.3389/fnhum.2010.00025

Buehner, M. J. (2012). Understanding the past, predicting the future: causation, not intentional action, is the root of temporal binding. *Psychol. Sci.* 23, 1490–1497. doi: 10.1177/0956797612444612

Campbell, W. K., Bosson, J. K., Goheen, T. W., Lakey, C. E., and Kernis, M. H. (2007). Do narcissists dislike themselves "deep down inside?". *Psychol. Sci.* 18, 227–229. doi: 10.1111/j.1467-9280.2007.01880.x

Campbell, W. K., Rudich, E. A., and Sedikides, C. (2002). Narcissism, self-esteem and the positivity of self-views: two portraits of self-love. *Pers. Soc. Psychol. Bull.* 28, 358–368. doi: 10.1177/0146167202286007

Desantis, A., Roussel, C., and Waszak, F. (2011). On the influence of causal beliefs on the feeling of agency. *Conscious. Cogn.* 20, 1211–1220. doi: 10.1016/j.concog.2011.02.012

Dimaggio, G., Fiore, D., Lysaker, P. H., Petrilli, D., Salvatore, G., Semerari, A., et al. (2006). Early narcissistic transference patterns: an exploratory single case study from the perspective of dialogical self theory. *Psychol. Psychother.* 79, 495–516. doi: 10.1348/147608305x63089

Dimaggio, G., Nicolo, G., Fiore, D., Centenero, E., Semerari, A., Carcione, A., et al. (2008). States of minds in narcissistic personality disorder: three psychotherapies analyzed using the grid of problematic states. *Psychother. Res.* 18, 466–480. doi: 10.1080/10503300701881877

Dimaggio, G., Semerari, A., Falcone, M., Nicolò, G., Carcione, A., and Procacci, M. (2002). Metacognition, states of mind, cognitive biases and interpersonal cycles: proposal for an integrated narcissism model. *J. Psychother. Integr.* 12, 421–451. doi: 10.1037//1053-0479.12.4.421

Fried, I., Katz, A., McCarthy, G., Sass, K. J., Williamson, P., Spencer, S. S., et al. (1991). Functional organization of human supplementary motor cortex studied by electrical stimulation. *J. Neurosci.* 11, 3656–3666.

Gallagher, S. (2012). Multiple aspects in the sense of agency. *New Ideas Psychol.* 30, 15–31. doi: 10.1016/j.newideapsych.2010.03.003

Greaves-Lord, K., Tulen, J., Dietrich, A., Sondeijker, F., Van Roon, A., Oldehinkel, A., et al. (2010). Reduced autonomic flexibility as a predictor for future anxiety in girls from the general population: the TRAILS study. *Psychiatry Res.* 179, 187–193. doi: 10.1016/j.psychres.2009.04.014

Grupe, D. W., and Nitschke, J. B. (2013). Uncertainty and anticipation in anxiety: an integrated neurobiological and psychological perspective. *Nat. Rev. Neurosci.* 14, 488–501. doi: 10.1038/nrn3524

Haggard, P. (2001). The psychology of action. *Br. J. Psychol.* 92, 113–128. doi: 10.1348/000712601162121

Haggard, P., and Clark, S. (2003). Intentional action: conscious experience and neural prediction. *Conscious. Cogn.* 12, 695–707. doi: 10.1016/s1053-8100(03)00052-7

Haggard, P., Clark, S., and Kalogeras, J. (2002). Voluntary action and conscious awareness. *Nat. Neurosci.* 5, 382–385. doi: 10.1038/nn827

Haggard, P., Martin, F., Taylor-Clarke, M., Jeannerod, M., and Franck, N. (2003). Awareness of action in schizophrenia. *Neuroreport* 14, 1081–1085. doi: 10.1097/00001756-200305230-00035

John, O. P., and Robins, R. W. (1994). Accuracy and bias in self-perception: individual differences in self-enhancement and the role of narcissism. *J. Pers. Soc. Psychol.* 66, 206–219. doi: 10.1037//0022-3514.66.1.206

Keeton, C. P., Perry-Jenkins, M., and Sayer, A. G. (2008). Sense of control predicts depressive and anxious symptoms across the transition to parenthood. *J. Fam. Psychol.* 22, 212–221. doi: 10.1037/0893-3200.22.2.212

Kirkpatrick, L. A., Waugh, C. E., Valencia, A., and Webster, G. D. (2002). The functional domain specificity of self-esteem and the differential prediction of aggression. *J. Pers. Soc. Psychol.* 82, 756–767. doi: 10.1037//0022-3514.82.5.756

Kohut, H. (1971). *The Analysis of the Self: A Systematic Approach to the Psychoanalytic Treatment of Narcissistic Personality Disorders.* Chicago, IL: University of Chicago Press. Available online at: http://search.proquest.com/docview/622249253?accountid=12347

Kohut, H. (1977). *The Restoration of the Self.* Chicago, IL: University of Chicago Press.

Kranick, S. M., Campen, C. J., Kasner, S. E., Kessler, S. K., Zimmerman, R. A., Lustig, R. A., et al. (2013). Headache as a risk factor for neurovascular events in pediatric brain tumor patients. *Neurology* 80, 1452–1456. doi: 10.1212/wnl.0b013e31828cf81e

Makoshi, Z., Kroliczak, G., and van Donkelaar, P. (2011). Human supplementary motor area contribution to predictive motor planning. *J. Mot. Behav.* 43, 303–309. doi: 10.1080/00222895.2011.584085

Maxwell, K., Donnellan, M. B., Hopwood, C. J., and Ackerman, R. A. (2011). The two faces of narcissus? An empirical comparison of the narcissistic personality inventory and the pathological narcissism inventory. *Pers. Individ. Dif.* 50, 577–582. doi: 10.1016/j.paid.2010.11.031

McLean, C. P., Asnaani, A., Litz, B. T., and Hofmann, S. G. (2011). Gender differences in anxiety disorders: prevalence, course of illness, comorbidity and burden of illness. *J. Psychiatr. Res.* 45, 1027–1035. doi: 10.1016/j.jpsychires.2011.03.006

Moore, J. W., Lagnado, D., Deal, D. C., and Haggard, P. (2009). Feelings of control: contingency determines experience of action. *Cognition* 110, 279–283. doi: 10.1016/j.cognition.2008.11.006

Moore, J. W., and Obhi, S. S. (2012). Intentional binding and the sense of agency: a review. *Conscious. Cogn.* 21, 546–561. doi: 10.1016/j.concog.2011.12.002

Moore, J. W., Ruge, D., Wenke, D., Rothwell, J., and Haggard, P. (2010). Disrupting the experience of control in the human brain: pre-supplementary motor area contributes to the sense of agency. *Proc. Biol. Sci.* 277, 2503–2509. doi: 10.1098/rspb.2010.0404

Moretto, G., Walsh, E., and Haggard, P. (2011). Experience of agency and sense of responsibility. *Conscious. Cogn.* 20, 1847–1854. doi: 10.1016/j.concog.2011.08.014

Morf, C. C., and Rhodewalt, F. (2001). Unraveling the paradoxes of narcissism: a dynamic self-regulatory processing model. *Psychol. Inq.* 12, 177–196. doi: 10.1207/s15327965pli1204_1

Obhi, S. S., and Goodale, M. A. (2005). Bimanual interference in rapid discrete movements is task specific and occurs at multiple levels of processing. *J. Neurophysiol.* 94, 1861–1868. doi: 10.1152/jn.00320.2005

Obhi, S. S., and Hall, P. (2011). Sense of agency and intentional binding in joint action. *Exp. Brain Res.* 211, 655–662. doi: 10.1007/s00221-011-2675-2

Obhi, S. S., and Sebanz, N. (2011). Moving together: toward understanding the mechanisms of joint action. *Exp. Brain Res.* 211, 329–336. doi: 10.1007/s00221-011-2721-0

Obhi, S. S., Swiderski, K. M., and Brubacher, S. P. (2012). Induced power changes the sense of agency. *Conscious. Cogn.* 21, 1547–1550. doi: 10.1016/j.concog.2012.06.008

Obhi, S. S., Swiderski, K. M., and Farquhar, R. (2013). Activating memories of depression alters the experience of voluntary action. *Exp. Brain Res.* 229, 497–506. doi: 10.1007/s00221-012-3372-5

Orth, U., Robins, R. W., and Roberts, B. W. (2008). Low self-esteem prospectively predicts depression in adolescence and young adulthood. *J. Pers. Soc. Psychol.* 95, 695–708. doi: 10.1037/0022-3514.95.3.695

Pincus, A. L., and Lukowitsky, M. R. (2010). Pathological narcissism and narcissistic personality disorder. *Annu. Rev. Clin. Psychol.* 6, 421–446. doi: 10.1146/annurev.clinpsy.121208.131215

Raskin, R., Novacek, J., and Hogan, R. (1991). Narcissistic self-esteem management. *J. Pers. Soc. Psychol.* 60, 911–918. doi: 10.1037/0022-3514.60.6.911

Robins, R. W., and Beer, J. S. (2001). Positive illusions about the self: short-term benefits and long-term costs. *J. Pers. Soc. Psychol.* 80, 340–352. doi: 10.1037/0022-3514.80.2.340

Ronningstam, E. (2011a). Complex case: narcissistic personality disorder. *Personal. Ment. Health* 5, 222–227. doi: 10.1002/pmh.172

Ronningstam, E. (2011b). Narcissistic personality disorder: a clinical perspective. *J. Psychiatr. Pract.* 17, 89–99. doi: 10.1097/01.pra.0000396060.67150.40

Ronningstam, E. (2013). An update on narcissistic personality disorder. *Curr. Opin. Psychiatry* 26, 102–106. doi: 10.1097/YCO.0b013e328359979c

Ronningstam, E., and Baskin-Sommers, A. R. (2013). Fear and decision-making in narcissistic personality disorder-a link between psychoanalysis and neuroscience. *Dialogues Clin. Neurosci.* 15, 191–201.

Rosenbaum, D. (1991). *Human Motor Control.* San Diego, California: Academic Press.

Skodol, A. E. (2012). Personality disorders in DSM-5. *Annu. Rev. Clin. Psychol.* 8, 317–344. doi: 10.1146/annurev-clinpsy-032511-143131

Tsakiris, M., and Haggard, P. (2003). Awareness of somatic events associated with a voluntary action. *Exp. Brain Res.* 149, 439–446. doi: 10.1007/s00221-003-1386-8

Vonk, J., Zeigler-Hill, V., Mayhew, P., and Mercer, S. (2013). Mirror, mirror on the wall, which form of narcissist knows self and others best of all? *Pers. Individ. Dif.* 54, 396–401. doi: 10.1016/j.paid.2012.10.010

Wegner, D. M. (2002). *The Illusion of Conscious Will.* Cambridge, MA: MIT Press. Available online at: http://search.proquest.com/docview/619864394?accountid=12347

22

Noisy visual feedback training impairs detection of self-generated movement error: implications for anosognosia for hemiplegia

Catherine Preston[1,2] * and Roger Newport[1]

[1] *Brain, Body and Self Laboratory, Department of Neuroscience, Karolinska Institutet, Stockholm, Sweden*
[2] *University of Nottingham, Nottingham, UK*

***Correspondence:**
Catherine Preston, Brain, Body and Self Laboratory, Department of Neuroscience, Karolinska Institutet, Retzius Väg, Stockholm 17177, Sweden
e-mail: catherine.preston@ki.se

Anosognosia for hemiplegia (AHP) is characterized as a disorder in which patients are unaware of their contralateral motor deficit. Many current theories for unawareness in AHP are based on comparator model accounts of the normal experience of agency. According to such models, while small mismatches between predicted and actual feedback allow unconscious fine-tuning of normal actions, mismatches that surpass an inherent threshold reach conscious awareness and inform judgments of agency (whether a given movement is produced by the self or another agent). This theory depends on a threshold for consciousness that is greater than the intrinsic noise in the system to reduce the occurrence of incorrect rejections of self-generated movements and maintain a fluid experience of agency. Pathological increases to this threshold could account for reduced motor awareness following brain injury, including AHP. The current experiment tested this hypothesis in healthy controls by exposing them to training in which noise was applied the visual feedback of their normal reaches. Subsequent self/other attribution tasks without noise revealed a decrease in the ability to detect manipulated (other) feedback compared to training without noise. This suggests a slackening of awareness thresholds in the comparator model that may help to explain clinical observations of decreased action awareness following stroke.

Keywords: agency, motor awareness, anosognosia for hemiplegia, comparator model, forward models

INTRODUCTION

Under normal circumstances we have no difficulty in recognizing our own movements and knowing when we have, or have not, performed an action. However, this can be disrupted following brain injury or stroke. One such disorder that has been well described is anosognosia for hemiplegia (AHP) and is characterized as a disorder, normally following right hemisphere stroke, in which the patient is not aware of their contralateral (left) motor deficit (Jenkinson et al., 2011). Such patients claim to be able to perform actions normally despite their obvious paralysis, even to the extent that when asked to execute an action some can claim to be doing so when their limb is motionless (paralyzed) at their side (Ramachandran, 1996).

Most of the current theories explaining AHP focus on forward models originally described to explain motor control. These forward models incorporate comparators, which compare motor commands and intentions with actual and predicted sensory feedback. Normally the errors detected are small and do not reach conscious awareness but allow the motor system to correct and fine-tune our movements (Miall and Wolpert, 1996; Wolpert, 1997). Another role ascribed to the comparators is for the discrimination between *Self* and *Other* generated actions (agency attribution). When the discrepancies detected at the comparators are large they reach conscious awareness and influence the experience of agency (the feeling of causation over an action). There is a general consensus within theories based on the comparator model that in AHP, erroneous feelings of agency over actions that are never executed are based solely on comparisons between intact intentions and motor predictions. Such that these patients retain the ability to form motor intentions and produce an efference copy of the action on which a prediction of the next state of the motor system is formed. However, due to their paralysis AHP patients never actually initiate the action. With normal functioning of the comparators, the lack of movement from the paralyzed limb would highlight large discrepancies with that intended or predicted, thus informing the individual of their paralysis. However, AHP patients do not appear to detect these discrepancies and thus remain unaware of their motor deficit.

Exactly why these large discrepancies do not reach conscious awareness is as yet unclear. Frith et al. (2000) suggested that these discrepancies are ignored, which may in part be due visual neglect that is frequently a co-morbid deficit of AHP. This explanation cannot fully account for this; however, given that double dissociations of neglect and AHP have been identified (Bisiach et al., 1986; Jehkonen et al., 2006). Other explanations for ignoring these discrepancies are not fully described and so difficult to test experimentally. Berti and Pia (2006) suggested that, although the rest of the comparator functions normally, the comparators monitoring sensory feedback are broken. Although this explains why the inability to produce movement is not detected, if the comparators are destroyed it does not adequately account for reinstatement of awareness, which commonly occurs in AHP after a few weeks

(Jenkinson et al., 2011). Recently, a third hypothesis was put forward suggesting that these comparators, rather than being broken, have pathological slackening of awareness thresholds (Preston et al., 2010). As stated above, most discrepancies detected by the comparator model are used for fine-tuning movements and do not reach conscious awareness and as such it is logical to assume that there is a threshold that needs to be reached in order to penetrate consciousness. It is also logical to assume that any threshold should be greater than the inherent noise in the system, a threshold, which is likely to be seriously increased following brain damage. It was thus suggested that in AHP the threshold is pathologically increased to the extent that all movements, and indeed no movement at all, do not reach threshold and so are accepted as successful *Self* produced actions.

Preston et al. (2010) found support for this theory from a single AHP patient, GG. Interestingly it was found that GG, in addition to a lack of awareness for his left sided paralysis, was also unaware of actions produced with his intact (right) arm [an observation that had only previously been reported anecdotally, Ramachandran (1995)]. This allowed experimental investigation of comparator functioning of a moving limb in terms of low-level motor control as well as high-level awareness of action. It was found that, following large spatial perturbations being applied to visual feedback of his right handed reaching movements, GG was able to make crude motor corrections to his reaches in an attempt to compensate for the visual perturbation, whilst remaining unaware of large inaccuracies in his movements, any corrective movements he was making (including large secondary movements), or that any such perturbations were applied. A control sample of hemiplegic neglect patients without AHP did perform worse than young healthy controls, but were able to detect some larger perturbations (unlike GG who never reported being aware). The fact that GG was able to make some corrections to his movements, albeit poorly, implies that the comparators are working to an extent and thus arguing against broken comparators as suggested by Berti and Pia (2006). However, as these motor corrections never reached consciousness, such findings are in line with a slackening of comparator thresholds – something that was observable to an extent in the neglect control group, but was extreme in the AHP patient. However, this was based on observations of a single AHP patient and a small control group so further research is clearly needed.

The aim of the current study was to further test the threshold theory of AHP using neurologically intact controls. If comparator thresholds of motor awareness are governed by inherent noise in the system (i.e., the threshold should be at least as great as the noise) increasing noise to feedback of movements made by healthy controls should serve to increase thresholds and so leading them to accept greater discrepancies between their actual movement and the visual feedback as true representations of their actions.

An important factor found to inform judgments of agency involves conscious motor intention, such that you are more likely to attribute an observed action as self-generated if it accurately attains your intended movement goal (e.g., accurately reaches the target). Systematic visual distortions applied across a series of reaches can induce motor learning such that adjustments are made to the motor commands in order to compensate for the distortions and maintain accuracy of the reach (e.g., Izawa and Shadmehr, 2011). Through such paradigms, dissociations between low-level motor planning and high-level motor awareness have been demonstrated. Gradually increasing systematic distortions to visual feedback of reaches produces gradual changes in reach trajectory without conscious awareness to the extent that when shown veridical feedback of the actual reach participants deny that it is a true representation of their action (Synofzik et al., 2006; Preston and Newport, 2010). Thus visual perturbations applied to feedback of reaches can modulate conscious error detection (agency) through changes to reach trajectory via unconscious (sub threshold) motor correction mechanisms. Distortions applied to the visual feedback of reaches that, rather than being systematic, are randomly selected from a distribution leads to learning the mean of that distribution (Scheidt et al., 2001). Therefore if the mean of the distribution is veridical feedback (no perturbation), there should be no effect on reach accuracy as participants retain highest accuracy for unperturbed reaches. Therefore any changes to observed conscious error detection as a result should not be an indirect effect of reach accuracy, but a direct modulation of conscious awareness thresholds.

Participants received visual feedback of reaching movements using a vBOT robotic manipulandum. All participants took part in a self/other detection task similar to that described in Preston et al. (2010). This was completed after both noise and no-noise training with each participant. It was predicted that the percentage *Self* judgments to visually perturbed trials in the detection task would increase following noise training compared to following no-noise training, without any significant effect on reach accuracy.

MATERIALS AND METHODS

PARTICIPANTS

Twenty-two neurologically healthy participants (seven males) took part in the experiment with a median age of 20 years (range 20–55 years). All were right hand handed and had normal or corrected to normal vision. The experiment was conducted in accordance with the local ethics committee and the declaration of Helsinki.

MATERIALS

Participants' reaches were represented by the movements of a white cursor (20 mm in diameter) that was projected, along with the target location, onto a horizontal semi-transparent screen positioned 450 mm above the reaching limb. Participants viewed the cursor via a horizontal mirror that was positioned equidistant between the limb and projection such that visual feedback of their movements appeared in the same spatial plane as the actual reaching limb (see **Figure 1**). The location of the cursor was calculated on-line using position data recorded by a vBOT 2D robotic manipulandum sampling at 1000 Hz (see Howard et al., 2009 for a comprehensive description of this device).

PROCEDURE

Participants sat looking down into the mirror and held onto the vBOT handle with their right hand. Before the beginning of each trial the vBOT moved the limb to a start location just out of view and directly in front of the body midline then there was a 500 ms delay before the trail commenced. At the beginning of each trial a blue circular target with a diameter of 30 mm appeared for

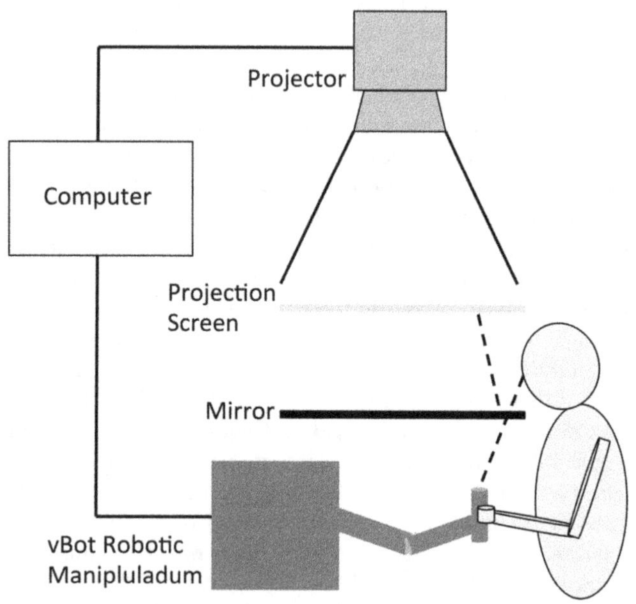

FIGURE 1 | The experimental set-up was similar to that described in Preston et al. (2010). Participants viewed the cursor via a horizontal mirror that was positioned equidistant between the limb and projection screen such that visual feedback of their movements appeared in the same spatial plane as the actual reaching limb.

1000 ms at randomly varying locations on the screen averaging 210 mm forward from the start location and directly inline with the start position. 200 ms following the disappearance of the target a tone sounded to indicate that the participants should begin their reach. The participants then had 1250 ms to complete their reach before the cursor disappeared and the vBOT move the limb back to the start location (see **Figure 2**). Visual feedback of the reaching movements was represented by the movements of the white cursor and was either an exact representation of their actual movement (*Self*) or had an angular perturbation applied (*Other*), for which the angle of the cursor trajectory was rotated relative to the actual reach trajectory by varying degrees. *Other* actions were defined as actions under the control of the computer (i.e., not the same as the movement performed), as opposed to the actions of another human being. This was made clear to, and understood by, all participants prior to the experiment.

The experiment contained two conditions, *Noise* and *No-Noise*, the order of which was counterbalanced between participants. For each condition participants first completed a training block, in which the experimental variable was modulated (and which differed between conditions) followed by a judgment block, which was identical for both conditions. Training blocks consisted of 80 trials in which participants were required to execute reaching movements whilst instructed only to be as accurate as possible to the target. For the *Noise* condition the visual feedback in the training block was equally divided between –2°, –4°, –6°, –8°, –10°, 2°, 4°, 6°, 8°, and 10° perturbations (eight trials per perturbation size, with negative values indicating leftward perturbations. Degrees of perturbation refers to the angle between the start and end point of the cursor trajectory relative to the actual reach trajectory). In the *No-Noise* condition, all reaches were veridical to the actual movements. Judgment blocks consisted of 56 trials equally divided between –12°, –8°, –4°, 0°, 4°, 8°, and 12° perturbations (eight per perturbation size). Following each reach, participants were required to make a forced choice verbal judgment as to whether the visual feedback had been controlled by themselves (*Self*) or by the computer (*Other*). Only trials in which the participant failed to initiate a reach within the time window were rejected (<2% of total trials).

Prior to the experimental conditions, participants took part in three practice blocks in order to familiarized them with the vBOT, the timing of the reaching movements, and what was meant by *Other* visual feedback. The first practice block contained 10 trials of only veridical visual feedback (*Self* trials). For this block participants were informed that all visual feedback was an exact representation of their actual reaches and so were not required to give self/other judgments. The second practice block also consisted of 10 trials but with perturbation sizes of 0°, 10°, –10°, 20° and –20° (two trails per perturbation). Participants were required to make a self/other judgment at the end of each trial as in the judgment blocks. The third practice block consisted of 56 trials and was identical to the judgment block described above. The trial order in all the individual blocks was randomized.

RESULTS

SUBJECTIVE JUDGMENTS

The self/other judgment data were converted into a percentage *Self* score for each perturbation size (collapsed across left/right direction) and entered in a 2 × 4 repeated measures ANOVA with the factors condition (*Noise, No-Noise*) and perturbation (0°, 4°, 8°, 12°).

There was a significant main effect of condition [$F(1,21) = 8.69$, $p = 0.008$] with the *Noise* condition having a higher percentage of *Self* judgments (mean = 68.71%, SD = 14.24%) compared to the *No-Noise* condition (mean = 62.86%, SD = 9.9%; see **Figure 3A**). There was also a main effect of perturbation [$F(3,63) = 145.89$, $p < 0.001$] with 0° having the greatest percentage of *Self* responses (mean = 92.77, SD = 9.81), followed by 4° (mean = 85.88%, SD = 12.86%), 8° (mean = 54.91%, SD = 16.7%) then 12° (mean = 28.49%, SD = 19.71%). There was no significant interaction [$F(3,57) = 1.19$, $p = 0.321$].

REACHING ACCURACY

Mean endpoint and midpoint errors were calculated for reaches in the judgment blocks for both training and no-training conditions. Errors were calculated as the angle in degrees between a straight line from the start point to the target and from the start point to the cursor position at the end or midpoint of the reach for endpoint and midpoint errors, respectively. Because of the inclusion of both left and right sided perturbations, endpoint errors were calculated as absolute values and then entered in separate 2 × 4 repeated measures ANOVAs with the factors condition (*Noise, No-Noise*) and perturbation (0, 4, 8 and 12°).

ENDPOINT ERROR

There was a significant main effect of perturbation [$F(3,63) = 204.8$, $p < 0.001$] with 0° having the smallest errors (mean = 2.56°,

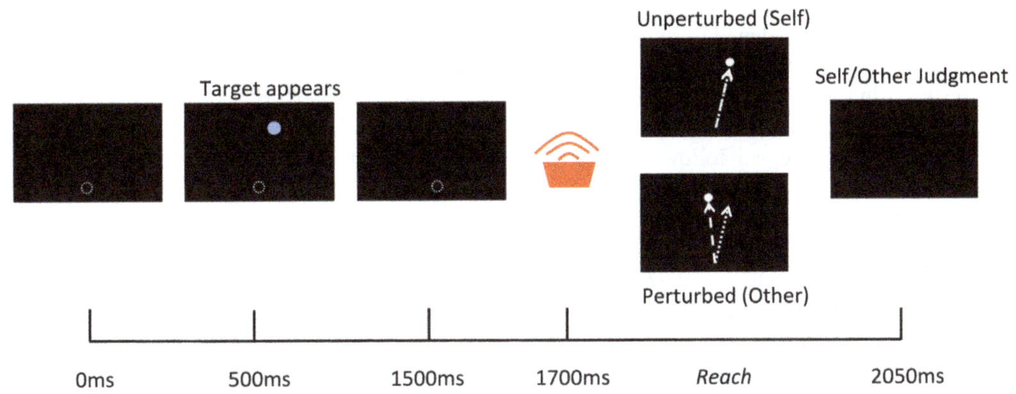

FIGURE 2 | Schematic of a single trial. 500 ms after the vBOT moved the limb to the start location a target appeared for 1000 ms followed by a tone indicating for participants to begin their reach. A white cursor represented the movements of the real limb and was either an exact representation of the actual movement (*Self*) or had a spatial perturbation applied (*Other*). At the end of the reach participants were required to give a verbal forced choice judgment as to whether the observed movement was that of *Self* or *Other*.

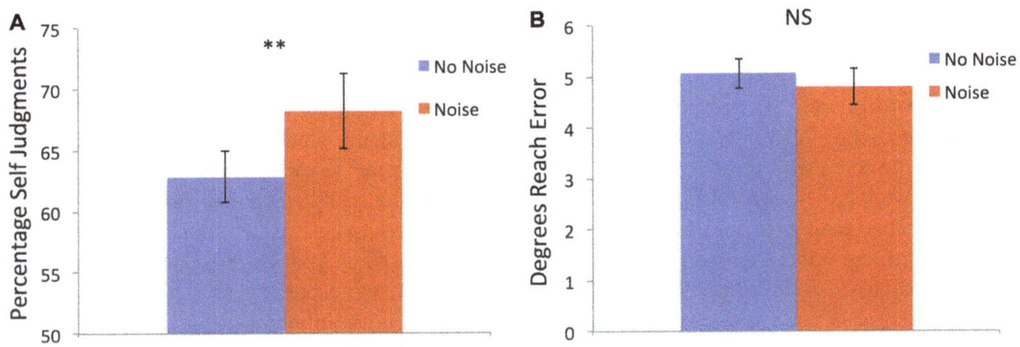

FIGURE 3 | (A) Percentage of *Self* judgments was significantly higher following *Noise* training compared to *No-Noise* training across all perturbation sizes. **(B)** Absolute degrees of end point reach error did not differ between the different training conditions. Error bars show SE and ** denotes significant difference < 0.01.

SD = 1.15°), followed by 4° (mean = 3.31°, SD = 1.13°), 8° (mean = 5.44, SD = 1.73) then 12° (mean = 8.4°, SD = 2.29°). Importantly there was no significant effect of training condition [$F(1,21) = 1.7$, $p = 0.206$; see **Figure 3B**] and there was also no significant interaction [$F(3,57) = 2.03$, $p = 0.121$].

MIDPOINT ERROR

There was a significant main effect of perturbation [$F(3,63) = 334$, $p < 0.001$] with 0° having the smallest errors (mean = 3.93°, SD = 1.48°), followed by 4° (mean = 4.95°, SD = 1.02°), 8° (mean = 7.94°, SD = 0.756°) then 12° (mean = 11.25°, SD = 0.698°). There was no significant effect of training condition [$F(1,21) = 0.037$, $p = 0.849$] and there was no significant interaction [$F(3,57) = 0.665$, $p = 0.577$].

DISCUSSION

The current results demonstrate that following a period of training in which noise was added to visual feedback, participants were less able to perceive perturbations to their movements on a subsequent detection task: that is, a greater number of trials were judged by participants as being controlled by themselves (*Self*) across all perturbations. This suggests that the threshold at which we become consciously aware of discrepancies between our actions and sensory feedback can be increased by introducing noise to the motor system. It has long been suggested that comparator based forward models of motor control have a threshold below which discrepancies detected by the system do not reach consciousness (Frith et al., 2000). Moreover, the fact that we are largely unaware of small corrections to our actions has been consistently demonstrated using different paradigms (e.g., Goodale et al., 1986; Fourneret and Jeannerod, 1998), but this is the first demonstration that the level of unawareness can also be increased at will.

The current data lends support to the threshold theory as an explanation for AHP. Within current explanations of AHP based on forward model comparator systems there is a general agreement that awareness of action in these patients is dictated by motor predictions rather than sensory feedback. Due to limited experimental evidence there is disagreement as to why such large discrepancies caused by hemiplegia go undetected by consciousness awareness. The threshold theory suggests that such unawareness occurs due to a pathological slackening of the normal comparator thresholds. Here, it has been demonstrated in neurologically intact participants, that the threshold at which a visual/motor mismatch reaches conscious awareness can be broadened by experimentally increasing noise of visual feedback. This therefore demonstrates that consciousness thresholds in the motor system can be manipulated and hence it is plausible that this normal adaptability of thresholds can be pathologically increased following extensive brain damage.

In terms of implicated brain regions, AHP does not have a clear-cut pathology. Unawareness for left sided hemiplegia has been associated with larger lesion sizes (Orfei et al., 2007) as well as numerous co-morbid deficits (although none have be found to fully account for AHP symptomology; Jehkonen et al., 2006). Due to these factors it is unsurprising that various brain areas have been identified in AHP pathology, including frontal parietal networks (Pia et al., 2004), premotor areas (Berti et al., 2005) and the insula cortex (Berti et al., 2005; Karnath et al., 2005; Vocat et al., 2010). Although evidence from healthy controls places the comparator in the right parietal lobe (Farrer et al., 2003; Preston and Newport, 2008), all of these brain areas have been independently associated with motor control and/ or action awareness (e.g., Haggard and Magno, 1999; Farrer and Frith, 2002; Farrer et al., 2003). If AHP is caused by a pathological increase in awareness thresholds due to increased inherent noise, this could be a result of damage to multiple sites associated with action planning and execution and not just regions specifically involved with the comparator. Therefore, extensive lesion sites covering various combinations of motor related regions, as are associated with AHP, may feasibly result in a greater increase in noise throughout the entire system, explaining why no single brain area has been uniformly identified in the etiology of AHP.

Importantly there was no effect of the noise training on reach accuracy. Previously it has been suggested that goal attainment and motor intention (accurately reaching the target) are strong predictors for judgments/feelings of agency (Farrer et al., 2008; Preston and Newport, 2010). Indeed post hoc analysis of reach accuracy for perturbed trails judged as *Self* vs. those judged to be *Other*, find the former to be significantly more accurate for both training [$t(21) = 6.19$, $p < 0.001$] and non-training [$t(21) = 6.57$, $p < 0.001$] conditions. However, due to the lack of difference in accuracy between the conditions, the observed increase in *Self* judgments following noise training cannot be explained by participants being more accurate to the target. This suggests that following noise training, participants accepted larger reach errors as accurate representations of their own movements; in other words a general broadening of what is accepted as *Self*.

Other implications of these results include the interpretation of agency and movement recognition experiments. Experimental paradigms that include numerous different perturbation sizes over the same or several consecutive blocks, by their very nature increase noise in the visual feedback and so are likely to result in poorer detection of discrepancies. Similarly, when fewer different discrepancies are used, detection may become more sensitive. For example, Preston and Newport (2008) report fewer than 50% *Self* judgments for perturbations of 4° when only presenting feedback of 0° and 4°. In the current experiment, however, which uses a greater number of perturbation sizes, the mean percentage of *Self* judgments to a 4° perturbation is over 80%, even before noise training. Moreover, these values are also different to those observed by Farrer and colleagues (Farrer et al., 2003, 2008) when using a broad range of perturbations, but with shorter reach distances (resulting in relatively smaller end-point errors). Caution must be applied, therefore, when comparing across different experimental paradigms.

A possible limitation of the current study concerns implementation of motor correction during reaching. Because the cursor was visible throughout the reach, low-level (unconscious) motor correction mechanisms could have been recruited that maintained accuracy to the target despite the visual perturbations – thereby influencing self/other judgments. While mean midpoint errors were larger than endpoint errors, this is to be expected due the curvature observed in normal reaching. It should also be noted that any online corrections that may have occurred were incomplete as both mid and endpoint errors increased with perturbation size. Moreover, any correction that did occur was equivalent for both conditions as accuracy at mid and endpoint were not significantly different between training and no-training conditions. Future studies, however, could further deconstruct the mechanisms of low and high level processes in motor awareness by modulating the visibility of the cursor at the beginning and end of the reach. Another consideration for future studies is to vary the range of noise applied in the training blocks. In the current study a smaller range of noise was applied in the training compared to test blocks. This meant that although the awareness threshold for error detection was expanded it still followed the same pattern as under normal reaching conditions, such that noise inherent in the system (training block) would be smaller than the range of errors that could occur during every day reaching (test block). However, with AHP it is suggested that the thresholds are expanded beyond the inherent noise so that no perturbations are consciously perceived. Future studies could investigate the effect of larger noise ranges in the training blocks relative to test blocks so as to be more comparable to AHP.

A further point of interest for future research is the role of oculomotor strategies. Previous studies have shown that eye movements can effect perception of limb movements (Ariff et al., 2002; Scherberger et al., 2003). However, to date little is known about eye movements during agency attribution tasks or during action (and attempted action) in AHP patients. Monitoring eye movements during tasks such as that described in the current study with both healthy and brain damaged participants may help shed light on the role of eye movements for action awareness and how this might be effected by noise training.

In conclusion, the current study demonstrates that exposing neurologically intact participants to noisy visual feedback can reduce their ability to consciously detect visual discrepancies applied to the feedback of their actions in a subsequent self/other action recognition task. This provides support for the threshold theory of AHP, which suggests that the disorder may be caused by pathological slackening of comparator thresholds within the motor system. These data also have implications concerning experimental models of action awareness given that awareness thresholds can be so easily manipulated by experimental design.

AUTHOR CONTRIBUTIONS

Both authors contributed equally to the design of the experiment and the interpretation of the data. Catherine Preston conducted the data analysis and wrote the initial draft, which was iteratively edited by Roger Newport and Catherine Preston. Both authors approved the final version of the manuscript and are fully accountable for the work.

ACKNOWLEDGMENTS
This research was funded by the ESRC (RES-000-22-3455). The Authors would also like to thank Erica Boylett for data collection.

REFERENCES

Ariff, G., Donchin, O., Nanayakkara, T., and Shadmehr, R. (2002). A real-time state predictor in motor control: study of saccadic eye movements during unseen reaching movements. *J. Neurosci.* 22, 7721–7729.

Berti, A., Bottini, G., Gandola, M., Pia, L., Smania, N., Stracciari, A., et al. (2005). Shared cortical anatomy for motor awareness and motor control. *Science* 309, 488–491. doi: 10.1126/science.1110625

Berti, A., and Pia, L. (2006). Understanding motor awareness through normal and pathological behavior. *Curr. Dir. Psychol. Sci.* 15, 245–250. doi: 10.1111/j.1467-8721.2006.00445.x

Bisiach, E., Vallar, G., Perani, D., Papagno, C., and Berti, A. (1986). Unawareness of disease following lesions of the right hemisphere: anosognosia for hemiplegia and anosognosia for hemianopia. *Neuropsychologia* 24, 471–482. doi: 10.1016/0028-3932(86)90092-8

Farrer, C., Bouchereau, M., Jeanerrod, M., and Franck, N. (2008). Effect of distorted visual feedback on the sense of agency. *Behav. Neurol.* 19, 53–57. doi: 10.1155/2008/425267

Farrer, C., Franck, N., Georgieff, N., Frith, C. D., Decety, J., and Jeannerod, M. (2003). Modulating the experience of agency: a positron emission tomography study. *Neuroimage* 18, 324–333. doi: 10.1016/S1053-8119(02)00041-1

Farrer, C., and Frith, C. D. (2002). Experiencing oneself vs another person as being the cause of an action: the neural correlates of the experience of agency. *Neuroimage* 15, 596–603. doi: 10.1006/nimg.2001.1009

Fourneret, P., and Jeannerod, M. (1998). Limited conscious monitoring of motor performance in normal subjects. *Neuropsychologia* 36, 1133–1140. doi: 10.1016/S0028-3932(98)00006-2

Frith, C. D., Blakemore, S. J., and Wolpert, D. M. (2000). Abnormalities in the awareness and control of action. *Philos. Trans. R. Soc. Lond. B Biol. Sci.* 355, 1771–1788. doi: 10.1098/rstb.2000.0734

Goodale, M. A., Pélisson, D., and Prablanc, C. (1986). Large adjustments in visually guided reaching do not depend on vision of the hand or perception of target displacement. *Nature* 320, 748–750. doi: 10.1038/320748a0

Haggard, P., and Magno, E. (1999). Localising awareness of action with transcranial magnetic stimulation. *Exp. Brain Res.* 127, 102–107. doi: 10.1007/s002210050778

Howard, I. S., Ingram, J. N., and Wolpert, D. M. (2009). A modular planar robotic manipulandum with end-point torque control. *J. Neurosci. Methods* 181, 199–211. doi: 10.1016/j.jneumeth.2009.05.005

Izawa, J., and Shadmehr, R. (2011). Learning from sensory and reward prediction errors during motor adaptation. *PLoS Comput. Biol.* 7:e1002012. doi: 10.1371/journal.pcbi.1002012

Jehkonen, M., Laihosalo, M., and Kettunen, J. E. (2006). Anosognosia after stroke: assessment, occurrence, subtypes and impact on functional outcome reviewed. *Acta Neurol. Scand.* 114, 293–306. doi: 10.1111/j.1600-0404.2006.00723.x

Jenkinson, P. M., Preston, C., and Ellis, S. J. (2011). Unawareness after stroke: a review and practical guide to understanding, assessing, and managing anosognosia for hemiplegia. *J. Clin. Exp. Neuropsychol.* 33, 1079–1093. doi: 10.1080/13803395.2011.596822

Karnath, H. O., Baier, B., and Nägele, T. (2005). Awareness of the functioning of one's own limbs mediated by the insular cortex? *J. Neurosci.* 25, 7134–7138. doi: 10.1523/JNEUROSCI.1590-05.2005

Miall, R. C., and Wolpert, D. M. (1996). Forward models for physiological motor control. *Neural Netw.* 9, 1265–1279. doi: 10.1016/S0893-6080(96)00035-4

Orfei, M. D., Robinson, R. G., Prigatano, G. P., Starkstein, S., Rüsch, N., Bria, P., et al. (2007). Anosognosia for hemiplegia after stroke is a multifaceted phenomenon: a systematic review of the literature. *Brain* 130, 3075–3090. doi: 10.1093/brain/awm106

Pia, L., Neppi-Modona, M., Ricci, R., and Berti, A. (2004). The anatomy of anosognosia for hemiplegia: a meta-analysis. *Cortex* 40, 367–377. doi: 10.1016/S0010-9452(08)70131-X

Preston, C., Jenkinson, P. M., and Newport, R. (2010). Anosognosia for hemiplegia as a global deficit in motor awareness: Evidence from the non-paralysed limb. *Neuropsychologia* 48, 3443–3450. doi: 10.1016/j.neuropsychologia.2010.07.027

Preston, C., and Newport, R. (2008). Misattribution of movement agency following right parietal TMS. *Soc. Cogn. Affect. Neurosci.* 3, 26–32. doi: 10.1093/scan/nsm036

Preston, C., and Newport, R. (2010). Self-denial and the role of intentions in the attribution of agency. *Conscious Cogn.* 19, 986–998. doi: 10.1016/j.concog.2010.04.005

Ramachandran, V. S. (1995). Anosognosia in parietal lobe syndrome. *Conscious Cogn.* 4, 22–51. doi: 10.1006/ccog.1995.1002

Ramachandran, V. S. (1996). The evolutionary biology of self-deception, laughter, dreaming and depression: some clues from anosognosia. *Med. Hypotheses* 47, 347–362. doi: 10.1016/S0306-9877(96)90215-7

Scheidt, R. A., Dingwell, J. B., and Mussa-Ivaldi, F. A. (2001). Learning to move amid uncertainty. *J. Neurophysiol.* 86, 971–985.

Scherberger, H., Goodale, M. A., and Andersen, R. A. (2003). Target selection for reaching and saccades share a similar behavioral reference frame in the macaque. *J. Neurophysiol.* 89, 1456–1466. doi: 10.1152/jn.00883.2002

Synofzik, M., Thier, P., and Lindner, A. (2006). Internalizing agency of self-action: perception of one's own hand movements depends on an adaptable prediction about the sensory action outcome. *J. Neurophysiol.* 96, 1592–1601. doi: 10.1152/jn.00104.2006

Vocat, R., Staub, F., Stroppini, T., and Vuilleumier, P. (2010). Anosognosia for hemiplegia: a clinical–anatomical prospective study. *Brain* 133, 3578–3597. doi: 10.1093/brain/awq297

Wolpert, D. M. (1997). Computational approaches to motor control. *Trends Cogn. Sci.* 1, 209–216. doi: 10.1016/S1364-6613(97)01070-X

23

Beyond the "urge to move": objective measures for the study of agency in the post-Libet era

Noham Wolpe[1,2]* and James B. Rowe[1,2,3]

[1] Department of Clinical Neurosciences, University of Cambridge, Cambridge, UK
[2] Medical Research Council, Cognition and Brain Sciences Unit, Cambridge, UK
[3] Behavioural and Clinical Neuroscience Institute, University of Cambridge, Cambridge, UK

***Correspondence:**
Noham Wolpe, Department of Clinical Neurosciences, University of Cambridge, Herchel Smith Building, Robinson Way, Cambridge CB2 0SZ, UK
e-mail: n.wolpe@gatesscholar.org

The investigation of human volition is a longstanding endeavor from both philosophers and researchers. Yet because of the major challenges associated with capturing voluntary movements in an ecologically relevant state in the research environment, it is only in recent years that human agency has grown as a field of cognitive neuroscience. In particular, the seminal work of Libet et al. (1983) paved the way for a neuroscientific approach to agency. Over the past decade, new objective paradigms have been developed to study agency, drawing upon emerging concepts from cognitive and computational neuroscience. These include the chronometric approach of Libet's study which is embedded in the "intentional binding" paradigm, optimal motor control theory and most recent insights from active inference theory. Here we review these principal methods and their application to the study of agency in health and the insights gained from their application to neurological and psychiatric disorders. We show that the neuropsychological paradigms that are based upon these new approaches have key advantages over traditional experimental designs. We propose that these advantages, coupled with advances in neuroimaging, create a powerful set of tools for understanding human agency and its neurobiological basis.

Keywords: agency, voluntary action, Libet, objective measures, intentional binding, motor control, active inference, neuroimaging

INTRODUCTION

For centuries, the topic of human volition has been the playground and battlefield for philosophers and religious thinkers to debate the existence of "free will", its role in driving human behavior, and its incompatibility with determinism. However, alongside its conceptual importance in the philosophical discourse, impairments in volition have also prompted the scientific investigation of the psychological processes and neurobiology of the sense of agency.

The sense of agency refers to the conscious experience that one has volitional or willed control over one's own actions, and through these actions one can influence the environment. Agency is hence one component of the experience of awareness of actions, which includes, among other qualia, the sense of ownership over one's body parts (Synofzik et al., 2008c). Agency research has attracted investigators and theorists for many years, but it is only in recent decades that human agency has become an active field of neuroscientific research (Haggard, 2008). This is partly due to the major challenges associated with capturing voluntary movements in an ecologically relevant state while in a research environment. Based upon this research, several theories have been developed to explain the origins of the sense of agency.

One prominent theory emphasizes the importance of predictive signals to agency (Blakemore et al., 2002). According to this "comparator" model, the sense of agency arises as a result of a comparison between predictive signals generated during motor planning and the actual sensory effect of one's action. An action is perceived as self-caused in the case where there is a match between the predicted and actual sensory effect. A second account describes the experience of agency as a postdictive or retrospective insertion to consciousness—that is, an "editing" of the conscious experience after the action has already occurred (Wegner and Wheatley, 1999). In this "apparent mental causation" theory, an action is self-attributed when it follows one's intention; has no other plausible causes and is consistent with the perceived outcome. There can be an integration of these predictive and postdictive cues (Synofzik et al., 2013), possibly through an optimal "cue integration" process (Moore and Fletcher, 2012), in which more reliable cues are given a larger weight for determining if an action is one's own. These theories will be discussed in this Review in the context of specific agency measures.

The development of neurobiological theories for the sense of agency is largely the result of a recent boost in agency research. The seminal work of Libet et al. (1983) has substantially contributed to this growth, as it paved the way towards establishing a neuroscientific approach to studying human agency. Libet's study differed from the early investigations of agency that were dominated by the use of *explicit* reports of intentionality and control by participants. For example, such experimental paradigms involve asking subjects to rate how much they felt in control of a certain movement, or whether a sensory stimulus was felt to be the result of their own action (Wegner and Wheatley, 1999; Wegner, 2003). As we discuss below, the application of such tasks is problematic, especially in the clinical population (e.g., Franck et al., 2001). The indirect and quantitative approach of Libet's study has thus inspired the development of novel agency measures.

Over the last decade, new paradigms which draw upon emerging concepts from cognitive and computational neuroscience have been developed to investigate awareness and control of voluntary action without depending on subjective reports. Here we review the principal methods for examining agency with objective measures, including: (1) intentional binding which has its origins in the chronometric approach embedded in Libet's study; (2) motor control theory and the comparator model; and (3) current and potential application of active inference theory.

We start off with Libet's experiment as the key step triggering the development of indirect and quantitative measures for the neuroscience of agency, but also describe its caveats that have highlighted the need for objective measures. We then present the advantages that have made objective measures of agency so effective and review the three principal methods. Lastly, we show that when combined with advances in neuroimaging, these methods provide critical insights into agency in healthy individuals and in patients.

LIBET'S EXPERIMENT AND QUANTITATIVE MEASURES OF AGENCY

The study of Libet et al. (1983) was a landmark in the neuroscience of agency. The novelty of the experiment lies in the successful combination of an ingenious behavioral task with a neuroimaging technique (electroencephalogram) that provides neural markers of critical neurophysiological events in volitional actions. Libet's pioneering experiment epitomizes the *chronometric* approach for agency.

To address the intricate questions surrounding voluntary actions, one can fractionate the process leading up to the execution of a movement. Voluntary action becomes a set of decision processes about, for example, what action to perform, when to perform it, or whether to perform it at all (Brass and Haggard, 2008). Libet's experiment focused on the component of "when" in a voluntary action.

A generalized Libet task involves a self-paced movement, such as a button press, together with the use of a "clock" for estimating either the time of a movement or the time of being aware of the intention to move. In the original paradigm, subjects were asked to flex their right wrist or finger while attending a clock face made up of a revolving dot on a screen. There were three conditions in which subjects reported the clock position in three events: (i) when they felt an "urge to move" (called "W judgement"); (ii) when they moved ("M judgement"); and (iii) when they felt an unexpected skin stimulation ("S judgements"). Using electromyography to measure muscle activity, the judgements were compared against the veridical time of movement initiation. It was found that subjects perceive the time of their intention to move to occur about 200 ms prior to movement. Time of movement was perceived about 85 ms before movement onset, and time of sensory stimulation about 50 ms prior to stimulation.

Electrical brain activity was recorded by electroencephalography (EEG). The main aim was to compare subject judgement errors to the time of the readiness potential, the reliable negative potential measured by EEG before a voluntary movement (Kornhuber and Deecke, 1965). The conscious intention lagged the initiation of the readiness potential by about 300–500 ms. The finding indicates that brain activity in preparation for action starts before people are aware they want to perform an action, and therefore conscious awareness is unable to cause the brain activity for action execution.

Libet's experiment kindled two main lines of research. First, many studies went on to investigate the behavioral and neural mechanisms of agency by examining the underlying mechanisms of the task, taking advantage of the quantitative nature of its measures. Second, because Libet's paradigm measures the perceived times of events surrounding voluntary actions, the paradigm has provided indirect and arguably more objective measures of agency, compared to the self-reports of agency that have been traditionally used. These indirect and quantitative measures have been adopted for the study of patient populations, where reliable self-reports are often difficult to obtain. The emergence of an indirect approach for examining agency in Libet's task was thus an important step towards the development of objective measures for agency.

The first line of research has examined the mechanisms of agency through Libet's task. Although it remains debateable what exactly the W and M judgements reflect (Lau et al., 2006; Banks and Isham, 2009), neuroimaging studies have exploited the continuous and quantitative measures in order to link them with activity of specific brain regions. EEG data showed that the W judgement is more closely related to the lateralized component of the readiness potential, suggesting that it is linked to the time when a motor plan is specified (Haggard and Eimer, 1999). Functional MRI has been used to examine the roles of attention to intention and attention to action in the task (Lau et al., 2004). Relative to attention to the M judgement, attention to the W judgement is associated with increased activity in the pre-supplementary motor area (pre-SMA), dorsolateral prefrontal cortex (PFC) and intra parietal sulcus of the posterior parietal cortex (PPC; Lau et al., 2004). In contrast, the M judgement is associated with activity in the cingulate motor cortex in the mid-posterior aspect of the medial frontal cortex (Lau et al., 2006).

Striking evidence for an association between the W judgment and neural activity comes from Fried et al. (2011), using single cell neuron recording in humans. Neurons in the SMA, pre-SMA and anterior cingulate cortex predicted the time of W judgements. The authors proposed that an integration of these signals leads to conscious awareness of intentionality. Interestingly, an earlier study showed that stimulation of similar areas induces a similar experience of "urge to move" a specific body part (Fried et al., 1991). Taken together, these results reveal some of the complex neural substrate of agency.

The second line of research following up Libet's paradigm has successfully used the task as a quantitative measure to study changes in awareness of action in clinical population (reviewed in Rowe and Wolpe, in press). For example, the sense of agency might be altered in Tourette's syndrome by the repeated occurrence of involuntary movements or vocalizations known as tics, which are not perceived by patients as self-caused (Singer, 2005). This has motivated the investigation of agency in tic disorders and Tourette's syndrome, demonstrating for example that the M judgement is unaffected in Tourette's patients, whereas the W judgement is shifted positively towards the time of the movement. This change in W judgement is proportional to disease severity (Moretto et al., 2011).

The W judgement is also positively shifted towards the time of movement in patients with psychogenic movement disorders (PMD; Edwards et al., 2011). PMD is a constellation of movement disorders that result from a psychological or psychiatric disturbance, in which patients report the experience of motor symptoms without their control, although there is no organic neurological cause (Schrag et al., 2013). PMDs manifest a positive shift in the W judgement compared to controls, and also show a small shift in the M judgement, perceiving the time of movement as later than controls. The shift in W judgement is larger than that in M judgement, such that overall the two judgements do not differ in PMDs. The authors suggested the lack of temporal distinction between intention and action could explain how PMD patients perceive their psychogenic actions as involuntary, although these actions share similar neurophysiological correlates as healthy voluntary movements (Schrag et al., 2013).

Clinical studies suggest that Libet's task can detect and quantify changes in the sense of agency. However, although Libet's main results have been replicated in numerous studies (e.g., Matsuhashi and Hallett, 2008), studies using the paradigm have also raised methodological and interpretative limitations, which should be taken into account (e.g., see review of Roskies, 2010). One major criticism relates to the large individual differences in the use of the "clock" and potential biases in the time estimation procedure (Lau et al., 2006). This drawback hinders the interpretation of results from patient studies such as those presented above, which may simply represent different strategies to the task between patients and controls.

Another criticism surrounds the ambiguity in judging the time of an "urge to move". As described above, the great advantage of Libet's task was its indirect and somewhat more objective nature compared to direct judgements of agency, as it looks at the perceived times of events surrounding a voluntary action. However, particularly the W judgement requires an introspection of a conscious experience. Even if this conscious event of feeling an urge to move is real and discrete, the subjective account inherent in the Libet task retains the drawbacks of a direct approach, underscoring the need for fully objective measures.

In conclusion, Libet's task has been subjected to the scrutiny of a multitude of replication studies and has given important insights by providing quantitative measures related to agency. However, due to its limitations and dependence on subjective experience of agency, there is a need for more objective measures of volitional actions, which we discuss in the next section.

BEYOND THE "URGE TO MOVE": ADVANTAGES OF OBJECTIVE MEASURES OF AGENCY

Emerging concepts from cognitive and computational neuroscience (**Figure 1**) have led to novel experimental paradigms that indirectly map onto awareness and control of action through *objective* measures. Although the sense of agency is by definition a subjective conscious experience, it has been demonstrated that agency arises from the activity and interaction of different sensory and motor brain areas (Fried et al., 1991, 2011; Desmurget et al., 2009). An indirect approach exploits the integration of the sensory and motor systems in the central nervous system, and the effect of this integration in shaping and perceiving behavior (e.g., Hamilton et al., 2004; reviewed in Schütz-Bosbach and Prinz, 2007). Therefore, instead of metacognitive judgements of agency or time of intentions as in Libet's task, these paradigms use low-level perceptual changes that are associated with volitional actions.

There are three principal advantages for such objective measures, particularly in patient populations. First, the implementation of quantitative and *objective* paradigms is not reliant on subjective reports and introspection, which might be biased or confounded. For example, there might be critical differences between the "feeling of agency" and "judgement of agency" (Synofzik et al., 2008b). A feeling of agency is the low-level perceptual experience of whether an action is self-caused, and it is proposed to be dependent on distinct processes in sensorimotor control (see next section). In contrast, judgement of agency is the explicit, high-order interpretation of being the agent of an action. The interpretation is dependent on the feeling of agency and additional signals, such as contextual information (Synofzik et al., 2008b). Moreover, the judgement of agency might indirectly influence the feeling of agency (Synofzik et al., 2013). Therefore, probing explicit agency reports through the judgement of agency might in fact introduce confounding factors, while biasing the measures of interest.

Second, in patient groups, metacognitive insights and self-monitoring can themselves be impaired, as seen in PMDs (de Lange et al., 2007; Pareés et al., 2012) and schizophrenia (Frith and Done, 1989). Such impairments are difficult to measure, but may interfere with direct measures of agency. For example, schizophrenia patients over-attribute sensory events to their own actions (Franck et al., 2001). However, these patients also tend to "jump into conclusions" based on less evidence, and ignore new evidence that supports an alternate inference (e.g., see review by Fletcher and Frith, 2009). The over-attribution of action might thus reflect abnormalities in decision making rather than in agency, and it is not straightforward to separate such metacognitive processes from the processes that are linked to agency.

Third, new objective paradigms can be designed to probe *specific* mechanisms within the volitional operation, in conjunction with the recent mechanistic insights into both normal and

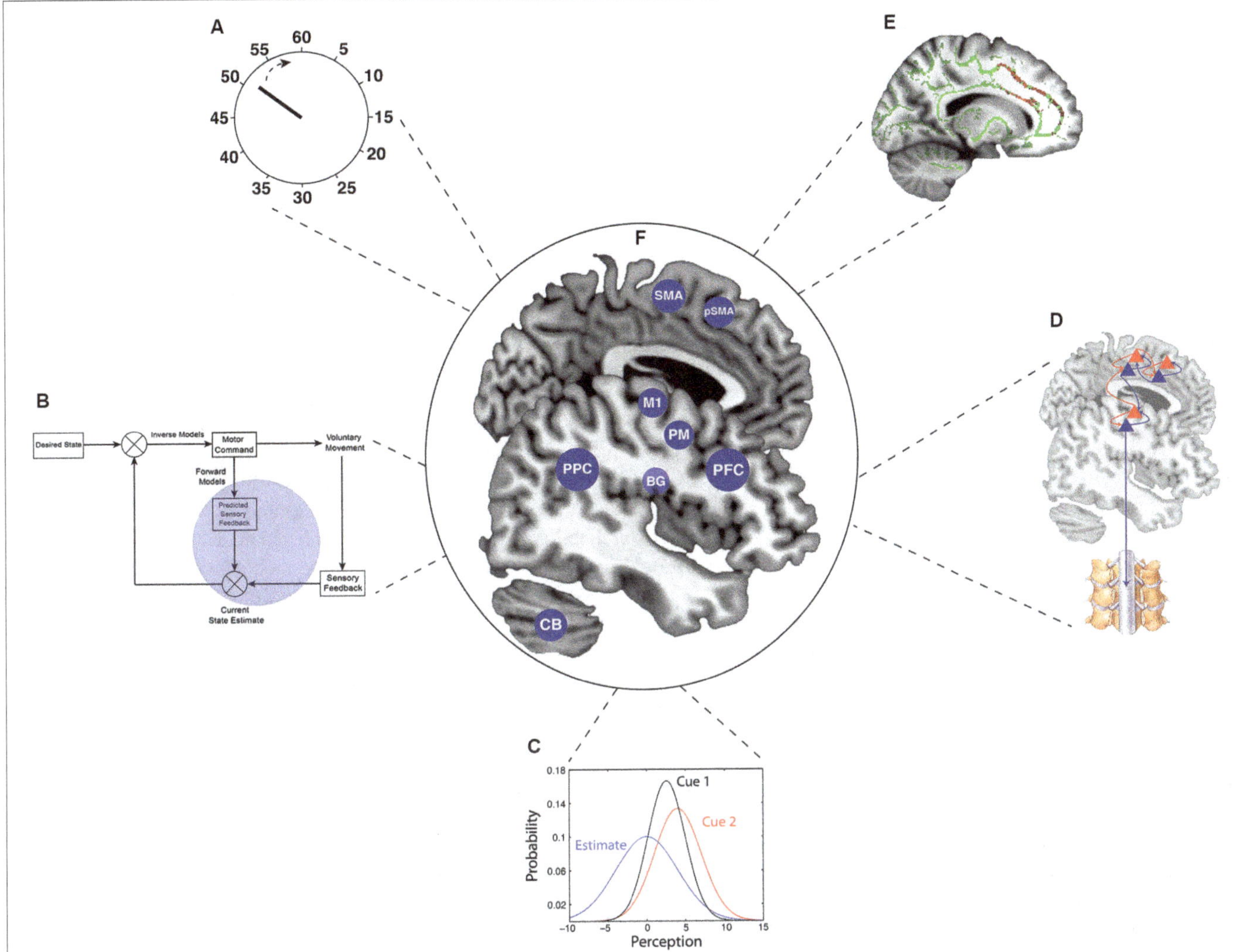

FIGURE 1 | Summary of the key theoretical concepts and neuroanatomy in the study of agency. This review describes some of the key emerging neuroscientific concepts that have facilitated the acquisition of more objective measures in agency research. **(A)** The "clock" represents developments cognitive neuroscience paradigms, particularly the chronometric approach for volition that is embedded in Libet's paradigm and in "*intentional binding*". **(B)** *Comparator model* of agency within *optimal motor control* theory (enlarged in **Figure 2**). **(C)** Precision-dependent cue integration, following optimal Bayesian integration. **(D)** The recently developed theory of *active inference*, implementing Bayesian principles for voluntary action (enlarged in **Figure 3**). **(E)** Combination of structural and functional *neuroimaging* (inset adapted from Wolpe et al., 2014), which when considered together with these behavioral paradigms, provides a powerful tool for linking behavior to its underlying brain mechanisms. **(F)** The central brain illustration depicts the critical brain areas for voluntary action, which are alluded to in this Review. BG = basal ganglia; CB = Cerebellum; M1 = primary motor cortex; PFC = prefrontal cortex; PM = Premotor cortex; PPC = posterior parietal cortex; pSMA = pre-supplementary motor area; SMA = supplementary motor area.

abnormal voluntary control. In patients, this advantage facilitates the achievement of two critical aims: (i) improving the understanding of clinical phenomenology by addressing more specific questions about the nature of disorders of agency and by providing candidate biomarkers for treatments; and (ii) using disorders as a model for testing mechanistic hypotheses regarding the neural substrates of agency. Meeting the latter aim could not only help mapping the functional anatomy for agency, but also test for causality (i.e., whether a brain area is causally involved in agency) and necessity (whether it is required for agency).

Together, these advantages have made objective measures appealing for the neuroscience of agency. We next review the main three advances in cognitive and computational neuroscience that have facilitated this research approach.

INTENTIONAL BINDING: OBJECTIVE CHRONOMETRY IN THE STUDY OF AGENCY

The "intentional binding" paradigm evolved from Libet's task: subjects use a "Libet clock" to report the time of either an action, such as pressing a button, or the time of a sensory event, such as a tone. When the action and the sensory event are coupled together, subjects tend to perceive their action as occurring later in time and the consequent sensory event as occurring earlier in time, relative to when both events occur separately. Importantly, this temporal attraction or the binding of an action and its sensory consequence does not occur for passive or involuntary TMS-induced actions (Haggard et al., 2002; Engbert et al., 2008), and is interestingly related to explicit judgement of control in some cases (Ebert and Wegner, 2010).

Intentional binding can be generalized to actions and sensory consequences of different modalities (Engbert et al., 2008), but most studies use an auditory tone. The principal measures include binding of action (the delay in the perception of action and its attraction towards the time of tone) and binding of tone (the earlier perception of tone and its attraction towards the time of action) (Haggard et al., 2002). One can also examine "composite" binding, in terms of the sum of action binding and tone binding (Moore et al., 2010b; Moore and Obhi, 2012), although there are caveats to this approach (see below).

Intentional binding measures have already proved advantageous in the study of agency (Moore and Obhi, 2012). The paradigm elegantly overcomes some of the innate limitations of Libet's task. As binding is a relative measure, the paradigm successfully addresses many critical confounds of Libet's task, mainly the individual differences in strategy or biases in time estimation procedure. Crucially, it does not require subjects to report conscious reflections, as in an urge to move, making it an objective chronometric measure for the study of agency.

There are, however, unresolved issues and limitations of the paradigm that should also be carefully considered. Temporal binding is not limited to one's own actions, and can also occur when observing the actions of another agent (Wohlschläger et al., 2003) or even when observing a predicted action-effect sequence generated by a machine (Buehner, 2012). These findings suggest that intentional binding might simply reflect the temporal binding resulting from learning the causal relations between actions and their effects, and cast doubts on the specificity of binding to one's own actions and sense of agency. Further, intentional binding is usually observed on a group level, but there is a large single-subject variability, and many individuals do not show the effect (e.g., Wolpe et al., 2013). The source of this high variability remains largely unknown. Lastly, the paradigm can be subjected to a similar criticism as Libet's task with regard to the need for dividing attention between the action and the clock, as well as the tone event in the binding task. These concerns emphasize the importance of examining the underlying mechanisms of binding.

Since it was introduced, the mechanisms of intentional binding have been extensively investigated. The relative contribution of predictive and postdictive or retrospective processes to binding of action has been examined using a modified intentional binding task. Moore and Haggard (2008) included two operant conditions: one in which the action triggered a tone in 50% of the trials; and another in which the action triggered a tone in 75% of the trials. Baseline measures were subtracted from the operant conditions as in the typical binding task. Binding of action was stronger for higher tone probability, but still occurred in trials with lower tone probability when the action was followed by a tone. These results suggest that binding of action results from a combination of predictive and postdictive signals (Moore and Haggard, 2008). Predictive signals for binding of action could come from an "efference copy" of motor commands (see next section). In contrast, the postdictive contribution to binding of action could be mediated through a precision-dependent integration of predictive signals with the time of action itself and its sensory effect (Wolpe et al., 2013).

Interestingly, a similar precision-dependent integration of predictive and postdictive signals has also been suggested to govern the correct attribution of actions (Moore and Fletcher, 2012), both in terms of the "feeling" and "judgement" of agency (Synofzik et al., 2013). The argument is that with optimal cue integration one can make better estimates by combining different sources of information, for example about the most likely time or cause of an action. The relative contribution of each source of information depends on its reliability (i.e., whether it is variable or noisy). As in binding of action (Wolpe et al., 2013), the sense of agency itself can be the outcome of a combination of predictive cues related to motor planning processes and postdictive signals, driven from sensory and high-level contextual agency cues. The cues are integrated as a function of their reliability and availability in each particular situation (Synofzik et al., 2013). The combination of such cues is an intriguing link between the mechanisms of binding of action and the sense of agency.

In contrast to binding of action, binding of tone might be more directly associated with sensorimotor prediction (Waszak et al., 2012; Wolpe et al., 2013). According to this notion, preparatory motor processes normally lead to a pre-activation of the neural representation of the predicted sensory effect of one's action. When the sensory effect occurs, it reaches the perceptual threshold faster due to the increased excitability of the appropriate sensory representation (Waszak et al., 2012), resulting in a shortening of the perceptual latency (Wolpe et al., 2013). The magnitude of this effect can be shaped by high-level beliefs about the cause of the action, which in turn does not influence binding of action (Desantis et al., 2011). These examples for a mechanistic discrepancy between action and tone binding suggest that these measures could be more informative when considered separately, which is illustrated next as we review studies of intentional binding.

Wolpe et al. (2014) have used the intentional binding paradigm in combination with multimodal brain imaging, to study the mechanisms of agency through the disorders of agency associated with the corticobasal syndrome (CBS; Wolpe et al., 2014). CBS is a progressive asymmetric movement disorder often caused by cortical and subcortical degeneration (Gibb et al., 1989). CBS is associated with two disorders of volitional actions: alien limb (the performance of semi-purposeful movements in the absence of "will") and apraxia (in this case the impairment in the performance of complex movements despite the understanding of their goal). We used intentional binding to investigate possible abnormalities in agency in the more severely affected limb.

In CBS patients, tone binding was normal in both hands compared to controls. In contrast, there was a specific increase in binding of action in the more-affected hand. Binding was normal in the less-affected hand, providing a crucial internal control condition that rules out general task deficits. Moreover, the magnitude of action binding correlated with the severity of alien limb and apraxia. The substantial increase in action binding was interpreted through the lens of cue integration theory: a low reliability (or high uncertainty) in the perception of time of action could lead to an over-reliance on the sensory effect for the perception of one's own action. Supporting this interpretation, the precision of time estimates in baseline conditions correlated with action binding, as predicted by the cue integration theory (Wolpe et al., 2013). The authors proposed that the volitional signals that drive internally generated actions (and suppress actions triggered by the environment) were imprecise due to gray and white matter degeneration.

Intentional binding is also abnormal in patients with PMDs (Kranick et al., 2013). In these patients, however, there was no difference in binding of action, but a consistent reduction in the binding of tone. As binding of tone is strongly reliant on intact predictive processes for agency, the results suggest a specific prediction abnormality in PMD which has been confirmed by complementary methods as illustrated in the next sections.

Abnormal binding is found in patients with schizophrenia in proportions to symptoms of delusions (Voss et al., 2010). Almost 80% of schizophrenia patients present with delusions or false beliefs, many of which implicate the sense of agency, such as delusions of control or passivity phenomena (Andreasen and Flaum, 1991). Voss et al. (2010) used the modified binding task from Moore and Haggard (2008) that is described above and quantified the relative contribution of predictive and postdictive signals. The predictive component was calculated by subtracting judgement errors in the "action only" trials (i.e., when actions were not followed by tones) in the 50% tone probability condition, from judgement errors in "action only" trials in the 75% tone probability condition. The retrospective component was calculated by subtracting judgement errors in the "action only" trials in the 50% tone probability condition from judgement errors in the "action and tone" trials (i.e., when actions were followed by tones) in the 50% tone probability condition. Patients showed a substantially diminished predictive contribution, but an increased retrospective contribution for the perception of time of action in binding of action. Interestingly, the reduction in the predictive component was related to severity of positive symptoms. The authors suggested that the abnormally high association between actions and effects in schizophrenia results from an over-reliance on retrospection, due to impaired prediction (Voss et al., 2010).

A recent development has been the characterization of pharmacological contributors to agency. For example, the NMDA antagonist ketamine enhances binding of action (Moore et al., 2011), while dopamine replacement therapy in Parkinson's disease (PD) increases overall intentional binding (Moore et al., 2010b). These results suggest that dopamine (or its interactions with NMDA) can modulate the sense of agency. Further development of this pharmacological perspective is anticipated in the next few years, with major implications for treating disorders of agency.

Despite the potential limitations of the paradigm, intentional binding can objectively quantify essential aspects of agency in health and disease. The task can improve the understanding of agency when considered together with its underlying mechanisms of postdictive and predictive volitional processes, the importance of which is further emphasized in the next section.

OPTIMAL MOTOR CONTROL THEORY AND THE COMPARATOR MODEL OF AGENCY

The indirect investigation of agency and awareness of action has drawn on concepts from optimal motor control theory. The principles underlying this line of research are: (a) awareness of action arises from specific processes in motor control (the "comparator" model); and (b) experimental tools that probe motor control processes are applicable to the awareness of action (Frith et al., 2000; Blakemore et al., 2002). In this section we expand these principles, and illustrate how they have been implemented in clinical populations.

Optimal motor control theory draws on engineering principles and a general hypothesis of internal models (**Figure 2**): to optimize motor control, the central nervous system internally represents the dynamics of one's own body and its interaction with the external world (Wolpert, 1997; Wolpert and Ghahramani, 2000). These models are learned and updated to reliably represent the relationship between motor commands and their sensory effects.

An inverse model generates the appropriate motor command for movement according to a comparison between the current state of the body and the goal. Optimization balances performance accuracy and the motor costs (Todorov and Jordan, 2002; Scott, 2004), while a forward model uses an "efference copy" of the motor command (von Holst, 1954) to predict the sensory effect of an action. The predicted sensory effect is integrated with the actual sensory feedback by precision-dependent Bayesian integration (see **Figure 1C**). The combination of prior knowledge (predictions of the forward model) with sensory evidence (actual sensory feedback) generates a "posterior" distribution for the state estimate (Wolpert et al., 1995), which in turn is used to update the motor command.

Within these processes, the comparator model suggests that the sense of agency arises from the comparison between the predicted and actual sensory feedback (Frith et al., 2000). If the predicted sensory effect matches the actual sensory effect, a sensation is perceived as self-caused. However, when there is a large discrepancy, a sensation is perceived as externally generated, independent of one's own volition. In turn, deficits in any of the processes of the comparator may underlie abnormalities in the awareness and control of action (Frith et al., 2000; Blakemore et al., 2002). The comparator model within optimal motor control theory has thereby provided a useful framework for addressing questions surrounding the mechanisms that underlie agency in health and disease (Rowe and Wolpe, in press).

The comparator model, however, cannot explain some aspects of the experience of agency. For example, not all divergences from the predicted sensory effect reach awareness, and small sensory discrepancies or their ensuing motor adjustments do not necessarily influence the sense of agency (Castiello et al., 1991; Fourneret and Jeannerod, 1998). The model has also been criticized for not encompassing external contextual cues, such

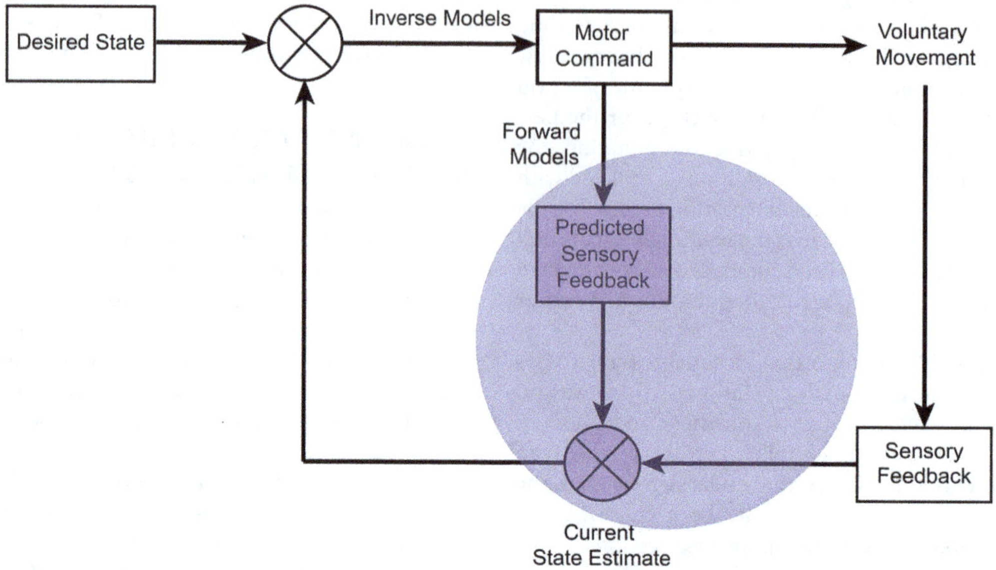

FIGURE 2 | Schematic of the "comparator model" within optimal motor control theory. A prominent theory in motor control proposes the use of internal models, which represent the dynamics of the body in the environment. To generate a voluntary movement, the central nervous system represents a desired state of the body. This is compared with the estimated current state, and is converted to a motor command through inverse models by an optimal feedback controller, so as to minimize both the difference and the motor costs. An efference copy of the motor command is used by forward models to predict the sensory effect. The predicted sensory effect is compared and integrated with the actual sensory feedback from the moving body part to generate an optimal state estimate. According to the comparator model, the sense of agency arises from the comparison between the predicted and actual sensory feedback (opaque blue). When the discrepancy is small, the sensory effect is attributed to one's own volition, but when the discrepancy is large, the sensory effect is interpreted as externally generated.

as the emotional valence of sensory effect or high level beliefs about an action (Synofzik et al., 2008b, 2013). The importance of such postdictive indicators of agency is emphasized in the "apparent mental causation" theory (Wegner and Wheatley, 1999; Wegner, 2003). These cues have been demonstrated to influence not only the explicit judgement of agency (Wegner, 2003), but also the lower experience of feeling of agency as measured by intentional binding (Moore et al., 2009; Desantis et al., 2011).

Nevertheless, there is currently little doubt as for the importance of action planning signals, particularly sensorimotor prediction, and the processing of sensory feedback for the sense of agency. The most recent theories of agency have thus argued for an integration between the sensorimotor signals embedded in the comparator model and the high-level postdictive cues for generating a sense of agency (Moore and Fletcher, 2012; Synofzik et al., 2013).

In what follows, we review the current research looking at the role of the sensorimotor signals rooted in the comparator model for impairments of agency. We first consider studies that have pointed to an abnormal sensorimotor prediction, followed by studies of abnormal processing of sensory feedback and their implications for the sense of agency in patients.

SENSORIMOTOR PREDICTION

Intact sensorimotor prediction is typically linked to the fundamental difference between the perception of self-generated and externally triggered sensory stimuli. For example, the inability to tickle oneself is dependent on accurate spatio-temporal predictions (Blakemore et al., 1999). Such difference between the perception of self- and externally triggered sensations is captured by "sensorimotor attenuation", i.e., the reduction in the perceived intensity of the consequences of one's own actions relative to externally caused sensations (Shergill et al., 2003). The attenuation is temporally centered on the time of the action, and relies on accurate sensorimotor prediction (Bays et al., 2005, 2006).

Two main explanations for attenuation have been put forward. One suggests that it is directly linked to the efference copy that is used by an internal model to generate a predicted sensory intensity. The predicted sensory intensity is in turn removed from the actual sensory feedback for the perception of the consequences of one's action (Bays et al., 2006). A more recent account posits that attenuation results from a predictive activation of the sensory representations of the prospective sensation. This "pre-activation" reduces the sensitivity to the actual sensory stimulus (Roussel et al., 2013). In either case, attenuation has a critical behavioral role, facilitating the distinction between the effects of self-generated actions and external sensory events. Normal sense of agency thus relies on intact prediction and its consequent sensorimotor attenuation, which may in turn provide a measure for the integrity of agency.

A robust method to measure sensorimotor attenuation is a "force matching" task. In the original task of the haptic modality, varying forces were applied to subjects' left index finger by a lever attached to a torque motor. Subjects were asked to reproduce the forces by pressing the lever with their right index finger (Shergill et al., 2003). Typically, the reproduced forces are larger than the forces that are actually applied by the torque motor. The degree of overcompensation has been used as a proxy for sensorimotor attenuation and the integrity of agency.

In PMDs, the extent of overcompensation is reduced compared to controls, such that patients show a more "accurate" perception of the sensory consequences of their actions, similar to external sensory events (Pareés et al., in press). These prediction deficits in PMD may thus lead to the abnormal perception that their movements are involuntary and not self-caused (Schrag et al., 2013), as suggested by the results from Libet's task.

Reduced attenuation is also reported in schizophrenia (Shergill et al., 2005), and has been linked to delusions of agency. This association is further supported by the correlation between visual sensory attenuation and the severity of delusions (Lindner et al., 2005). Thus, increasing impairments in sensorimotor prediction in schizophrenia and the inability to "remove" self-caused sensory information for perception are tightly linked to delusions of influence and abnormalities in agency.

Sensorimotor prediction was elegantly probed by Lindner et al. (e.g., Synofzik et al., 2006), drawing on the methodology of classic motor adaptation paradigm. Subjects performed out-and-back ballistic pointing movements, and receive visual feedback through a mirrored computer screen, while the true position of their hand was not visible. A deviation in the visual feedback was introduced, and subjects learned to correct for this perturbation. Two additional components were added to this conventional motor adaptation task: a perceptual component, wherein subjects indicate the perceived position of their action outcome; and a motor test component, wherein subjects point to a target in the absence of feedback (Synofzik et al., 2006).

Subjects normally learn to correct their movement in the presence of an initial deviation in the visual feedback. Interestingly, after learning to correct for the deviation, subjects perceive their movement as deviant even when no visual feedback is given, and move accordingly when asked to point to a target, suggesting they internally update their predictions. Predictions are thus adaptable, enabling the correct attribution of new sensory outcomes to one's own action (Synofzik et al., 2006). The authors used the task to test awareness of action in patients with cerebellar lesions (Synofzik et al., 2008a) and in schizophrenia (Synofzik et al., 2010).

Cerebellar patients of mixed pathologies showed intact discrimination thresholds for detecting feedback perturbation in the sensory effect of their movement. Patients also adapted their movement similarly to controls when visual feedback was given throughout the movement (Synofzik et al., 2008a). However, when no online feedback was given, the cerebellar group showed reduced perceptual adaptation than controls. Patients also compensated less for the experienced deviation when asked to point to a target. These results suggest that awareness of action in cerebellar patients could remain intact, but might be affected when predictions require adjustments, e.g., when the dynamics with the environment change (Synofzik et al., 2008a).

In contrast, schizophrenia patients demonstrated increased thresholds for detecting feedback perturbation in movements. The magnitude of the increase positively correlated with the severity of delusions of influence (Synofzik et al., 2010). Moreover, schizophrenia increased adaptation to the deviated feedback when it was displayed, but when no feedback was given their updated perception and adjusted movements were similar to controls (Synofzik et al., 2010). The results corroborate force matching and intentional binding data, highlighting an over-reliance on sensory feedback for the perception of actions in schizophrenia.

PROCESSING OF SENSORY FEEDBACK

According to the comparator model, impaired agency could also arise from impairments in sensory processing (see **Figure 2**). Changes in sensory processing in relation to awareness of action has been investigated in the context of kinaesthetic deficits in PD. PD is associated with neuronal dysfunction and loss in the substantia nigra, which can result in muscular rigidity, resting tremor, bradykinesia and slowness in the initiation of voluntary movements (Hughes et al., 1992). PD also affects a wide range of sensory and cognitive functions, including the perception of one's own movement.

Kinaesthesia (the awareness of the position and movement of one's body parts) is impaired by PD. For example, patients require larger passive limb displacements for becoming aware of such displacement (Konczak et al., 2007). By optimal motor control theory, kinaesthesia might rely on efferent signals from sensorimotor prediction, as well as afferent signals from the moving body part, such as proprioceptive and haptic information. The origins of kinaesthetic abnormalities was investigated by Konczak et al. (2012).

An age-related decline in haptic perception was found, with a strong trend towards an increase in detection thresholds, but stable discrimination thresholds. In PD, both detection thresholds and discrimination thresholds were increased (Konczak et al., 2012). The thresholds were similarly increased both when patients actively explored a virtual contour surface and when their hand was passively moved on the surface. As both conditions require intact processing of sensory feedback, this shared deficit is likely to arise mainly from impaired low-level processing of afferent signals. Abnormal afferent signals could thus contribute to abnormal kinaesthesia and awareness of movement and position of one's body limb in PD (Konczak et al., 2012).

To sum up, a growing number of studies employ concepts from optimal motor control theory in the comparator model to investigate agency. In addition to their objective nature, the additional value of these studies lies in their capacity to reveal specific mechanisms that are required for normal sense of agency and its changes in patient populations. We next review an alternative theory to optimal motor control for voluntary action, and its current and potential applications for the study of agency.

ACTIVE INFERENCE: A NEW APPROACH TO THE UNDERSTANDING OF AGENCY

The previous section underscored the importance of sensorimotor prediction for voluntary control and for the sense of agency. It also emphasized the role of prediction deficits in disorders of agency, e.g., in PMDs and in schizophrenia. Prediction in the brain can also be framed in terms of the "free energy" principle, according to which the brain constantly seeks to minimize its "surprise" (Friston, 2010). Surprise in this context amounts to unexpected sensations or "prediction errors", including those that are contingent on one's own action (Friston, 2010). This principle can explain several perceptual phenomena and in recent years has been extended to encompass voluntary actions (Friston, 2011) and disorders of agency (e.g., Edwards et al., 2012) under a unifying "active inference" theory.

In order to explain how prediction errors give rise to voluntary action and agency, it helps to first consider the origins of this theory in predictive coding for perception. Helmholtz proposed that perception is a process of probabilistic inference, whereby the brain infers the sensory causes based on certain sensory effects (von Helmholtz, 1860). Combined with the free energy principle, it has been proposed that perceptual inference relies on hierarchical predictive processing (Friston, 2010; Clark, 2013). Accordingly, higher levels in a cortical hierarchy adjust their predictions so as to "explain away" sensory samples from the lower levels (**Figure 3A**).

Specifically, at each level of the cortical hierarchy there is a set of neurons encoding predictions, and another set encoding prediction errors ("prediction units" and "prediction error units"). Prediction units encode the "belief" at that level, i.e., the probabilistic representation of the causes of sensation, and provide prediction signals through top-down (backward) projections to prediction error units at the level below (Feldman and Friston, 2010; Friston, 2010; Clark, 2013). Prediction error units receive prediction signals from the level above and compare them to the sensory belief at that level. The discrepancy constitutes the prediction error, which is projected forward to the higher cortical level that adjusts its predictions, so as to minimize the prediction

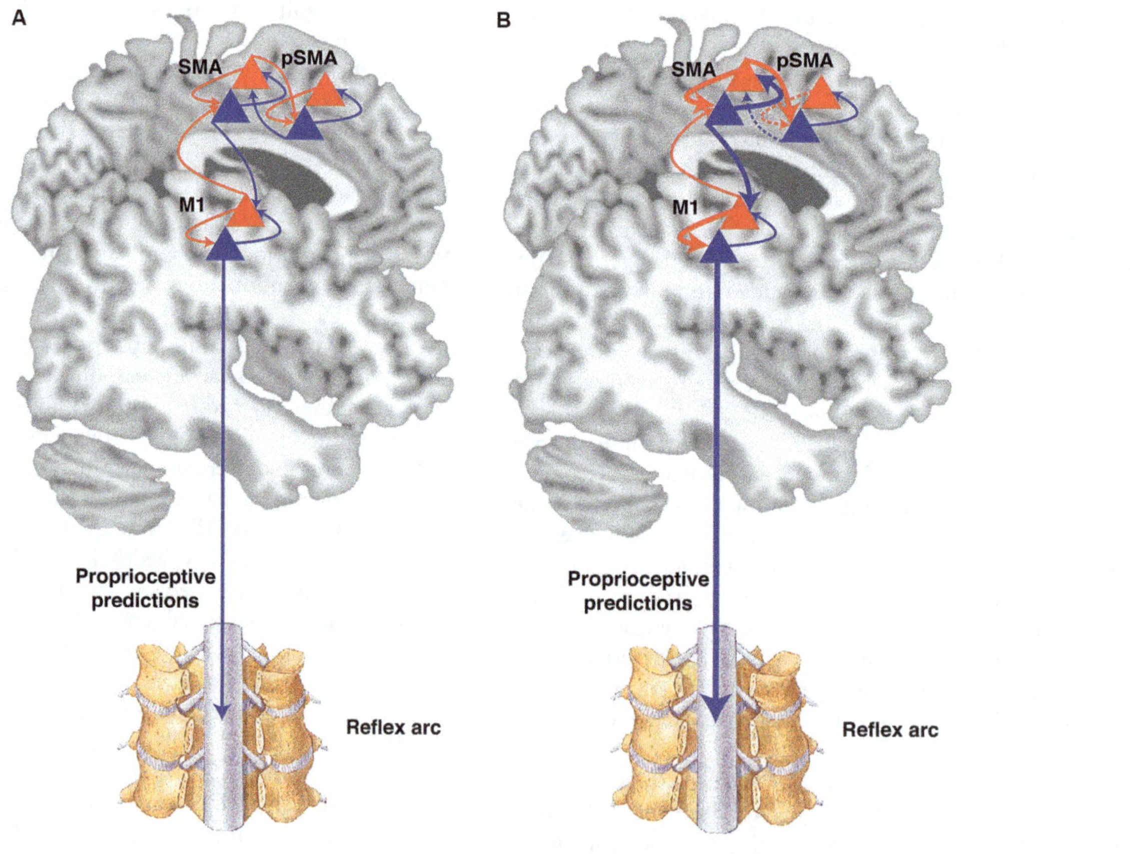

FIGURE 3 | Active inference and the sense of agency. (A) According to the active inference theory, at each level of the cortical hierarchy, there are prediction units (blue triangles) representing the "belief" at each level, which modulate their activity so as to predict the "belief" or inference of the state at the level below. Backward projection (blue arrows), signal the belief to prediction error units (red triangles) at the same level and at the level below. The prediction error units project the error forward (red arrows). This hierarchical network converges on a minimized prediction error. Minimizing prediction errors can be achieved by adjusting the sensory information through movement. High level areas in a motor hierarchy, such as the pre-SMA (pSMA), signal beliefs or goal states as represented by their expected sensations to lower level areas, such as the SMA, which in turn project to the primary motor cortex (M1). Even lower level predictions are sent to the spinal cord, inducing movements through reflex arcs. The sense of agency arises from the consistency between predictions in high level and lower level sensory data, balancing precision across the network. **(B)** In psychogenic movement disorders (PMD) for example, there is a misallocation of attention, and intermediate-level areas gain abnormally high precision (thick arrows) (Edwards et al., 2012). Consequently, prediction errors at that level induce movements through lower levels of the hierarchy, and overwhelm the higher intentional levels that initially did not predict the movement (dashed arrows). This discrepancy makes the network converge on the most likely explanation that a movement was externally caused. The figure is based on Friston et al. (2012).

error it receives (Feldman and Friston, 2010; Friston, 2010; Clark, 2013). The process of minimizing prediction errors by adjusting predictions at each level of the hierarchy allows different levels of representation of the causes of the sensory input—and that is perception.

Hierarchical predictive processing is implicitly Bayesian in that the sensory representation or belief at each hierarchical level is analogous to the Bayesian posterior distribution. It is derived from a precision-dependent combination of both prior beliefs (prediction signals) and likelihood or sensory evidence (prediction error signals) (Friston, 2010). The precision of the prediction error at each level is important for determining the balance between prior beliefs and sensory evidence for perception. The relative precision of prediction errors is suggested to be determined as a function of post-synaptic gain, modulated by neuromodulators, and optimized through attention (Feldman and Friston, 2010).

Predictive coding can be extended to explain voluntary action in the "active inference" theory (Friston et al., 2010). In the sensory system, perception is proposed to result from minimization of prediction errors in different levels of the cortical hierarchy through the adjustment of predictions (or beliefs). In the motor system, minimizing prediction errors is achieved by adjusting the sensory data through movement (**Figure 3A**). Expectations of the sensory consequence thus drive the movement of limbs through classical motor reflex arcs, so as to "fulfil" the prediction signals. In other words, movement is specified in terms of the expected sensation (Friston et al., 2010). This theory for voluntary action has been applied to explain movement disorders and abnormalities in the sense of agency in patients.

PMD has been suggested to result from a misallocation of attention (Edwards et al., 2012) with abnormally high precision of prior beliefs at intermediate levels of the cortical hierarchy (**Figure 3B**). As a result, the abnormally precise intermediate priors are spread down the hierarchy to the spinal cord where they induce abnormal movements through the reflex arcs. In parallel, the abnormally precise prediction errors are propagated forward to higher "intentional" levels in the hierarchy (i.e., levels where activity is more directly related to conscious awareness of action), such as the pre-SMA. As the relative precision of representations at the higher levels is reduced, prediction errors at the intermediate levels overwhelm the high-level intentional priors, and indicate a movement that was not predicted by the higher levels. The discrepancy between high intentional levels that do not predict movements and the abnormally precise intermediate levels leading to movements, causes the abnormal movements to be interpreted as involuntary, without one's sense of agency (Edwards et al., 2012).

In psychosis, abnormal awareness of action has been proposed to result from a perturbed inference as a result of aberrant encoding of precision (Adams et al., 2013). Here, abnormal release of neuromodulators, such as dopamine, together with altered post-synaptic NMDA receptor densities in PFC, lead to reduced precision of high-level prior predictions. These may lead to false perceptual inferences and catatonia. For example, the suppression of high-level predictions result in their inability to induce movements, and consequently in akinesia (Adams et al., 2013). The catatonic state could be rescued by a compensatory increase in the precision of probabilistic representations in intermediate levels. In this case, low-level proprioceptive data does not predominate, allowing top-down prediction from the intermediate levels to induce movements. However, the compensatory increase in intermediate precision now leads to a mismatch between intentional and lower levels of the hierarchy as in PMD, making the patient prone to a misattribution of action and abnormal agency (Adams et al., 2013).

On these active inference accounts, the sense of agency arises from the capacity of higher intentional levels of the cortical hierarchy (e.g., pre-SMA, PFC) to predict sensory data from lower levels (SMA, M1) through movement. Critically, normal agency depends on a balance in the precision of prediction errors within the cortical hierarchy for action, and the ability of this balanced hierarchy to converge on the most likely cause of a sensation. The theory thus offers a different and novel research avenue for the objective investigation of agency, focusing on testing parameters of brain connectivity within hierarchical networks.

A similar approach has been successfully implemented to investigate the sensory system. For example, the hypothesized modulation of the precision of prediction errors by the neuromodulator acetylcholine has been supported in a multimodal study (Moran et al., 2013) incorporating the mismatch negativity paradigm (Näätänen et al., 1978), dynamic causal modeling (Friston et al., 2003; Rowe et al., 2010a) and a pharmacological manipulation. Moreover, it has been shown that individual differences in connectivity in a hierarchical sensory network can not only underlie behavioral changes in a perceptual task, but also relate to delusional ideation of healthy participants (Schmack et al., 2013).

Although the active inference theory has not yet been applied experimentally for the study of agency, this approach can already be implemented in the research lab. Experiments of active inference on agency could include a behavioral task involving a voluntary action, such as a simple action selection task (Rowe et al., 2010b), which triggers activity in the key areas for action (as in **Figure 1F**). One could then use dynamic causal modeling to reveal variability in connectivity measures within hierarchical networks for agency, resulting from either individual differences, pharmacological manipulation or disease state. Moreover, new sensorimotor paradigms that probe different levels of prediction for voluntary action will be able to shed light on their underlying neural mechanisms and on the differential contribution of distinct levels of prediction to the sense of agency.

Active inference provides an appealing attempt to develop mechanistic accounts for the sense of agency, among diverse cognitive and motor phenomena. Importantly, it offers a unified account by integrating psychophysical and clinical observations with structural and functional brain imaging. The advantages of combining neuroimaging with new agency studies are discussed in the final section.

AN APERTURE TO AGENCY: COMBINING OBJECTIVE MEASURES WITH NEUROIMAGING TECHNIQUES TO UNRAVEL THE MECHANISMS OF AGENCY

As highlighted in the previous section, human brain imaging enables one to study the widely distributed networks related to agency. However, early neuroimaging studies of agency focused on contrasting self vs. externally triggered movements and contrasting different levels of perturbations to the sensory feedback. These univariate analyses implicated several areas, including the insular cortex, premotor cortex, cerebellum and the SMA and pre-SMA of the medial frontal cortex (Deiber et al., 1999; Farrer and Frith, 2002; Wiese et al., 2004; Rowe et al., 2010a, 2008; Rowe and Siebner, 2012).

As more advanced neuroimaging techniques have evolved, and in combination with computational modeling methods, neuroimaging studies have begun to point at more specific mechanisms of agency. Multivariate pattern analysis enabled the decoding of intentions from the frontopolar cortex several seconds before they reached awareness (Soon et al., 2008). Other methods include the application of accumulation-to-threshold models for predicting neuronal or BOLD signal in relation to voluntary actions (Zhang et al., 2012). This approach has shown that based on an increase in the firing rate of single neurons in the medial frontal cortex, it is possible to predict the time of awareness of the urge to move in Libet's task (Fried et al., 2011). Such data suggest that the sense of agency emerges when activity of neurons in high-level areas, such as the pre-SMA reaches a certain threshold.

The advances in neuroimaging methods can be combined with lesions or clinical disorders. For example, Wolpe et al. (2014) studied patients with alien limb and apraxia resulting from the neurodegenerative CBS (Wolpe et al., 2014). They combined multimodal brain imaging with two of the three main advances discussed throughout this Review, namely: (i) the quantitative and objective measure of agency of intentional binding and (ii) a mechanistic account of agency that draws on optimal motor control theory. They showed how such a combination leads to a clear and integrated model of agency and its abnormality.

Patients with CBS showed a specific increase in binding of action measure of intentional binding in their more-affected hand, relative to their less-affected hand and to controls. The extent of the increase correlated with severity of alien limb and apraxia, suggesting that abnormally enhanced binding of action reflected the abnormalities in agency in CBS (Wolpe et al., 2014). Structural neuroimaging of voxel-based morphometry and diffusion tensor imaging showed that the gray matter volume in the pre-SMA and the white matter tract integrity of its connections, were associated with the specific behavioral change in action binding. Finally, functional connectivity at rest between the pre-SMA and PFC was increased as a function of enhanced action binding. Drawing upon the contribution of a precision-weighted integration to binding of action (Wolpe et al., 2013), the results suggest that there is reduced precision in the volitional signals that drive movements in CBS patients. The reduced precision was associated with impairments in a medial frontal-prefrontal network for agency and volitional control, with its hub in the pre-SMA (Wolpe et al., 2014).

Intentional binding was also combined with temporary "lesions" in healthy adults by transcranial magnetic stimulation. Stimulation over the pre-SMA, reduced intentional binding of the outcome tone (Moore et al., 2010a). As binding of the outcome tone is mainly driven by a reduction of perceptual latencies through sensorimotor prediction (Waszak et al., 2012; Wolpe et al., 2013), these results further suggest that the pre-SMA contributes to the sense of agency through the processing of specific predictions of the sensory effect.

We propose that the combination of advanced neuroimaging techniques with recent developments in the study of agency, and particularly the objective measures of agency, provide a powerful tool for an integrated study of agency. This approach can be applied to clinical and pharmacological investigations, thereby improving treatments for disorders of agency.

CONCLUSIONS

We have reviewed the development and use of objective measures in the study of agency. We began by showing how Libet's experiment was central to the development of the neuroscience of agency by providing indirect quantitative measures, and by inspiring the development of objective measures. These indirect objective measures are based on the chronometric approach in intentional binding, the comparator model of optimal motor control and the emerging active inference theory. We have discussed the advantages of objective measures especially in combination with advanced structural and functional neuroimaging techniques. We propose that this combination of methods and their application to patient populations will be important in the ongoing endeavor to discover the mechanisms of human agency.

ACKNOWLEDGMENTS

The work was funded by the James S. McDonnell Foundation 21st Century Science Initiative, Scholar Award in Understanding Human Cognition, with additional support from the Wellcome Trust [088324] and the Medical Research Council [MC-A060-5PQ30].

REFERENCES

Adams, R. A., Stephan, K. E., Brown, H. R., Frith, C. D., and Friston, K. J. (2013). The computational anatomy of psychosis. *Front. Psychiatry* 4:47. doi: 10.3389/fpsyt.2013.00047

Andreasen, N. C., and Flaum, M. (1991). Schizophrenia: the characteristic symptoms. *Schizophr. Bull.* 17, 27–49. doi: 10.1093/schbul/17.1.27

Banks, W. P., and Isham, E. A. (2009). We infer rather than perceive the moment we decided to act. *Psychol. Sci.* 20, 17–21. doi: 10.1111/j.1467-9280.2008.02254.x

Bays, P. M., Flanagan, J. R., and Wolpert, D. M. (2006). Attenuation of self-generated tactile sensations is predictive, not postdictive. *PLoS Biol.* 4:e28. doi: 10.1371/journal.pbio.0040028

Bays, P., Wolpert, D., and Flanagan, J. (2005). Perception of the consequences of self-action is temporally tuned and event driven. *Curr. Biol.* 15, 1125–1128. doi: 10.1016/j.cub.2005.05.023

Blakemore, S. J., Frith, C. D., and Wolpert, D. M. (1999). Spatio-temporal prediction modulates the perception of self-produced stimuli. *J. Cogn. Neurosci.* 11, 551–559. doi: 10.1162/089892999563607

Blakemore, S. J., Wolpert, D. M., and Frith, C. D. (2002). Abnormalities in the awareness of action. *Trends Cogn. Sci.* 6, 237–242. doi: 10.1016/S1364-6613(02)01907-1

Brass, M., and Haggard, P. (2008). The what, when, whether model of intentional action. *Neuroscientist* 14, 319–325. doi: 10.1177/1073858408317417

Buehner, M. J. (2012). Understanding the past, predicting the future: causation, not intentional action, is the root of temporal binding. *Psychol. Sci.* 23, 1490–1497. doi: 10.1177/0956797612444612

Castiello, U., Paulignan, Y., and Jeannerod, M. (1991). Temporal dissociation of motor responses and subjective awareness. A study in normal subjects. *Brain* 114, 2639–2655. doi: 10.1093/brain/114.6.2639

Clark, A. (2013). Whatever next? Predictive brains, situated agents and the future of cognitive science. *Behav. Brain Sci.* 36, 181–204. doi: 10.1017/S0140525X12000477

de Lange, F. P., Roelofs, K., and Toni, I. (2007). Increased self-monitoring during imagined movements in conversion paralysis. *Neuropsychologia* 45, 2051–2058. doi: 10.1016/j.neuropsychologia.2007.02.002

Deiber, M. P., Honda, M., Ibañez, V., Sadato, N., and Hallett, M. (1999). Mesial motor areas in self-initiated versus externally triggered movements examined with fMRI: effect of movement type and rate. *J. Neurophysiol.* 81, 3065–3077.

Desantis, A., Roussel, C., and Waszak, F. (2011). On the influence of causal beliefs on the feeling of agency. *Conscious. Cogn.* 20, 1211–1220. doi: 10.1016/j.concog.2011.02.012

Desmurget, M., Reilly, K. T., Richard, N., Szathmari, A., Mottolese, C., and Sirigu, A. (2009). Movement intention after parietal cortex stimulation in humans. *Science* 324, 811–813. doi: 10.1126/science.1169896

Ebert, J. P., and Wegner, D. M. (2010). Time warp: authorship shapes the perceived timing of actions and events. *Conscious. Cogn.* 19, 481–489. doi: 10.1016/j.concog.2009.10.002

Edwards, M. J., Adams, R. A., Brown, H., Pareés, I., and Friston, K. J. (2012). A Bayesian account of "hysteria". *Brain* 135, 3495–3512. doi: 10.1093/brain/aws129

Edwards, M. J., Moretto, G., Schwingenschuh, P., Katschnig, P., Bhatia, K. P., and Haggard, P. (2011). Abnormal sense of intention preceding voluntary movement in patients with psychogenic tremor. *Neuropsychologia* 49, 2791–2793. doi: 10.1016/j.neuropsychologia.2011.05.021

Engbert, K., Wohlschläger, A., and Haggard, P. (2008). Who is causing what? The sense of agency is relational and efferent-triggered. *Cognition* 107, 693–704. doi: 10.1016/j.cognition.2007.07.021

Farrer, C., and Frith, C. (2002). Experiencing oneself vs another person as being the cause of an action: the neural correlates of the experience of agency. *Neuroimage* 15, 596–603. doi: 10.1006/nimg.2001.1009

Feldman, H., and Friston, K. J. (2010). Attention, uncertainty and free-energy. *Front. Hum. Neurosci.* 4:215. doi: 10.3389/fnhum.2010.00215

Fletcher, P. C., and Frith, C. D. (2009). Perceiving is believing: a Bayesian approach to explaining the positive symptoms of schizophrenia. *Nat. Rev. Neurosci.* 10, 48–58. doi: 10.1038/nrn2536

Fourneret, P., and Jeannerod, M. (1998). Limited conscious monitoring of motor performance in normal subjects. *Neuropsychologia* 36, 1133–1140. doi: 10.1016/s0028-3932(98)00006-2

Franck, N., Farrer, C., Georgieff, N., Marie-Cardine, M., Daléry, J., d'Amato, T., et al. (2001). Defective recognition of one's own actions in patients with schizophrenia. *Am. J. Psychiatry* 158, 454–459. doi: 10.1176/appi.ajp.158.3.454

Fried, I., Katz, A., McCarthy, G., Sass, K. J., Williamson, P., Spencer, S. S., et al. (1991). Functional organization of human supplementary motor cortex studied by electrical stimulation. *J. Neurosci.* 11, 3656–3666.

Fried, I., Mukamel, R., and Kreiman, G. (2011). Internally generated preactivation of single neurons in human medial frontal cortex predicts volition. *Neuron* 69, 548–562. doi: 10.1016/j.neuron.2010.11.045

Friston, K. (2010). The free-energy principle: a unified brain theory? *Nat. Rev. Neurosci.* 11, 127–138. doi: 10.1038/nrn2787

Friston, K. (2011). What is optimal about motor control? *Neuron* 72, 488–498. doi: 10.1016/j.neuron.2011.10.018

Friston, K. J., Daunizeau, J., Kilner, J., and Kiebel, S. J. (2010). Action and behavior: a free-energy formulation. *Biol. Cybern.* 102, 227–260. doi: 10.1007/s00422-010-0364-z

Friston, K. J., Harrison, L., and Penny, W. (2003). Dynamic causal modelling. *Neuroimage* 19, 1273–1302. doi: 10.1016/S1053-8119(03)00202-7

Friston, K. J., Shiner, T., FitzGerald, T., Galea, J. M., Adams, R., Brown, H., et al. (2012). Dopamine, affordance and active inference. *PLoS Comput. Biol.* 8:e1002327. doi: 10.1371/journal.pcbi.1002327

Frith, C. D., Blakemore, S. J., and Wolpert, D. M. (2000). Abnormalities in the awareness and control of action. *Philos. Trans. R. Soc. Lond. B Biol. Sci.* 355, 1771–1788. doi: 10.1098/rstb.2000.0734

Frith, C. D., and Done, D. J. (1989). Experiences of alien control in schizophrenia reflect a disorder in the central monitoring of action. *Psychol. Med.* 19, 359–363. doi: 10.1017/s003329170001240x

Gibb, W. R., Luthert, P. J., and Marsden, C. D. (1989). Corticobasal degeneration. *Brain* 112, 1171–1192. doi: 10.1093/brain/112.5.1171

Haggard, P. (2008). Human volition: towards a neuroscience of will. *Nat. Rev. Neurosci.* 9, 934–946. doi: 10.1038/nrn2497

Haggard, P., Clark, S., and Kalogeras, J. (2002). Voluntary action and conscious awareness. *Nat. Neurosci.* 5, 382–385. doi: 10.1038/nn827

Haggard, P., and Eimer, M. (1999). On the relation between brain potentials and the awareness of voluntary movements. *Exp. Brain Res.* 126, 128–133. doi: 10.1007/s002210050722

Hamilton, A., Wolpert, D., and Frith, U. (2004). Your own action influences how you perceive another person's action. *Curr. Biol.* 14, 493–498. doi: 10.1016/j.cub.2004.03.007

Hughes, A. J., Daniel, S. E., Kilford, L., and Lees, A. J. (1992). Accuracy of clinical diagnosis of idiopathic Parkinson's disease: a clinico-pathological study of 100 cases. *J. Neurol. Neurosurg. Psychiatry* 55, 181–184. doi: 10.1136/jnnp.55.3.181

Konczak, J., Krawczewski, K., Tuite, P., and Maschke, M. (2007). The perception of passive motion in Parkinson's disease. *J. Neurol.* 254, 655–663. doi: 10.1007/s00415-006-0426-2

Konczak, J., Sciutti, A., Avanzino, L., Squeri, V., Gori, M., Masia, L., et al. (2012). Parkinson's disease accelerates age-related decline in haptic perception by altering somatosensory integration. *Brain* 135, 3371–3379. doi: 10.1093/brain/aws265

Kornhuber, H. H., and Deecke, L. (1965). Changes in the brain potential in voluntary movements and passive movements in man: readiness potential and reafferent potentials. *Pflugers Arch. Gesamte Physiol. Menschen Tiere* 284, 1–17.

Kranick, S. M., Moore, J. W., Yusuf, N., Martinez, V. T., Lafaver, K., Edwards, M. J., et al. (2013). Action-effect binding is decreased in motor conversion disorder: implications for sense of agency. *Mov. Disord.* 28, 1110–1116. doi: 10.1002/mds.25408

Lau, H. C., Rogers, R. D., and Passingham, R. E. (2006). On measuring the perceived onsets of spontaneous actions. *J. Neurosci.* 26, 7265–7271. doi: 10.1523/jneurosci.1138-06.2006

Lau, H. C., Rogers, R. D., Haggard, P., and Passingham, R. E. (2004). Attention to intention. *Science* 303, 1208–1210. doi: 10.1126/science.1090973

Libet, B., Gleason, C. A., Wright, E. W., and Pearl, D. K. (1983). Time of conscious intention to act in relation to onset of cerebral activity (readiness-potential). The unconscious initiation of a freely voluntary act. *Brain* 106, 623–642. doi: 10.1093/brain/106.3.623

Lindner, A., Thier, P., Kircher, T. T. J., Haarmeier, T., and Leube, D. T. (2005). Disorders of agency in schizophrenia correlate with an inability to compensate for the sensory consequences of actions. *Curr. Biol.* 15, 1119–1124. doi: 10.1016/j.cub.2005.05.049

Matsuhashi, M., and Hallett, M. (2008). The timing of the conscious intention to move. *Eur. J. Neurosci.* 28, 2344–2351. doi: 10.1111/j.1460-9568.2008.06525.x

Moore, J. W., and Fletcher, P. C. (2012). Sense of agency in health and disease: a review of cue integration approaches. *Conscious. Cogn.* 21, 59–68. doi: 10.1016/j.concog.2011.08.010

Moore, J., and Haggard, P. (2008). Awareness of action: inference and prediction. *Conscious. Cogn.* 17, 136–144. doi: 10.1016/j.concog.2006.12.004

Moore, J. W., and Obhi, S. S. (2012). Intentional binding and the sense of agency: a review. *Conscious. Cogn.* 21, 546–561. doi: 10.1016/j.concog.2011.12.002

Moore, J. W., Ruge, D., Wenke, D., Rothwell, J., and Haggard, P. (2010a). Disrupting the experience of control in the human brain: pre-supplementary motor area contributes to the sense of agency. *Proc. Biol. Sci.* 277, 2503–2509. doi: 10.1098/rspb.2010.0404

Moore, J. W., Schneider, S. A., Schwingenschuh, P., Moretto, G., Bhatia, K. P., and Haggard, P. (2010b). Dopaminergic medication boosts action–effect binding in Parkinson's disease. *Neuropsychologia* 48, 1125–1132. doi: 10.1016/j.neuropsychologia.2009.12.014

Moore, J. W., Turner, D. C., Corlett, P. R., Arana, F. S., Morgan, H. L., Absalom, A. R., et al. (2011). Ketamine administration in healthy volunteers reproduces aberrant agency experiences associated with schizophrenia. *Cogn. Neuropsychiatry* 16, 364–381. doi: 10.1080/13546805.2010.546074

Moore, J. W., Wegner, D. M., and Haggard, P. (2009). Modulating the sense of agency with external cues. *Conscious. Cogn.* 18, 1056–1064. doi: 10.1016/j.concog.2009.05.004

Moran, R. J., Campo, P., Symmonds, M., Stephan, K. E., Dolan, R. J., and Friston, K. J. (2013). Free energy, precision and learning: the role of cholinergic neuromodulation. *J. Neurosci.* 33, 8227–8236. doi: 10.1523/JNEUROSCI.4255-12.2013

Moretto, G., Schwingenschuh, P., Katschnig, P., Bhatia, K. P., and Haggard, P. (2011). Delayed experience of volition in Gilles de la Tourette syndrome. *J. Neurol. Neurosurg. Psychiatry* 82, 1324–1327. doi: 10.1136/jnnp.2010.221143

Näätänen, R., Gaillard, A. W. K., and Mäntysalo, S. (1978). Early selective-attention effect on evoked potential reinterpreted. *Acta Psychol. (Amst)* 42, 313–329. doi: 10.1016/0001-6918(78)90006-9

Pareés, I., Brown, H., Nuriki, A., Adams, R. A., Davare, M., Bhatia, K. P., et al. (in press). "It's not me": loss of sensory attenuation in patients with functional (psychogenic) neurological symptoms.

Pareés, I., Saifee, T. A., Kassavetis, P., Kojovic, M., Rubio-Agusti, I., Rothwell, J. C., et al. (2012). Believing is perceiving: mismatch between self-report and actigraphy in psychogenic tremor. *Brain* 135, 117–123. doi: 10.1093/brain/awr292

Roskies, A. L. (2010). How does neuroscience affect our conception of volition? *Annu. Rev. Neurosci.* 33, 109–130. doi: 10.1146/annurev-neuro-060909-153151

Roussel, C., Hughes, G., and Waszak, F. (2013). A preactivation account of sensory attenuation. *Neuropsychologia* 51, 922–929. doi: 10.1016/j.neuropsychologia.2013.02.005

Rowe, J. B., and Siebner, H. R. (2012). The motor system and its disorders. *Neuroimage* 61, 464–477. doi: 10.1016/j.neuroimage.2011.12.042

Rowe, J. B., and Wolpe, N. (in press). "Disorders of volition from neurological disease: altered awareness of action in neurological disorders," in *The Sense of Agency*, eds B. Eitam and P. Haggard (Oxford: Oxford University Press).

Rowe, J. B., Hughes, L. E., Barker, R. A., and Owen, A. M. (2010a). Dynamic causal modelling of effective connectivity from fMRI: are results reproducible and sensitive to Parkinson's disease and its treatment? *Neuroimage* 52, 1015–1026. doi: 10.1016/j.neuroimage.2009.12.080

Rowe, J. B., Hughes, L., and Nimmo-Smith, I. (2010b). Action selection: a race model for selected and non-selected actions distinguishes the contribution of premotor and prefrontal areas. *Neuroimage* 51, 888–896. doi: 10.1016/j.neuroimage.2010.02.045

Rowe, J., Hughes, L., Eckstein, D., and Owen, A. M. (2008). Rule-selection and action-selection have a shared neuroanatomical basis in the human prefrontal and parietal cortex. *Cereb. Cortex* 18, 2275–2285. doi: 10.1093/cercor/bhm249

Schmack, K., Gòmez-Carrillo de Castro, A., Rothkirch, M., Sekutowicz, M., Rössler, H., Haynes, J.-D., et al. (2013). Delusions and the role of beliefs in perceptual inference. *J. Neurosci.* 33, 13701–13712. doi: 10.1523/JNEUROSCI.1778-13.2013

Schrag, A. E., Mehta, A. R., Bhatia, K. P., Brown, R. J., Frackowiak, R. S. J., Trimble, M. R., et al. (2013). The functional neuroimaging correlates of psychogenic versus organic dystonia. *Brain* 136, 770–781. doi: 10.1093/brain/awt008

Schütz-Bosbach, S., and Prinz, W. (2007). Perceptual resonance: action-induced modulation of perception. *Trends Cogn. Sci.* 11, 349–355. doi: 10.1016/j.tics.2007.06.005

Scott, S. H. (2004). Optimal feedback control and the neural basis of volitional motor control. *Nat. Rev. Neurosci.* 5, 532–546. doi: 10.1038/nrn1427

Shergill, S. S., Bays, P. M., Frith, C. D., and Wolpert, D. M. (2003). Two eyes for an eye: the neuroscience of force escalation. *Science* 301:187. doi: 10.1126/science.1085327

Shergill, S. S., Samson, G., Bays, P. M., Frith, C. D., and Wolpert, D. M. (2005). Evidence for sensory prediction deficits in schizophrenia. *Am. J. Psychiatry* 162, 2384–2386. doi: 10.1176/appi.ajp.162.12.2384

Singer, H. S. (2005). Tourette's syndrome: from behaviour to biology. *Lancet Neurol.* 4, 149–159. doi: 10.1016/s1474-4422(05)70018-1

Soon, C. S., Brass, M., Heinze, H.-J., and Haynes, J.-D. (2008). Unconscious determinants of free decisions in the human brain. *Nat. Neurosci.* 11, 543–545. doi: 10.1038/nn.2112

Synofzik, M., Lindner, A., and Thier, P. (2008a). The cerebellum updates predictions about the visual consequences of one's behavior. *Curr. Biol.* 18, 814–818. doi: 10.1016/j.cub.2008.04.071

Synofzik, M., Thier, P., and Lindner, A. (2006). Internalizing agency of self-action: perception of one's own hand movements depends on an adaptable prediction about the sensory action outcome. *J. Neurophysiol.* 96, 1592–1601. doi: 10.1152/jn.00104.2006

Synofzik, M., Thier, P., Leube, D. T., Schlotterbeck, P., and Lindner, A. (2010). Misattributions of agency in schizophrenia are based on imprecise predictions about the sensory consequences of one's actions. *Brain* 133, 262–271. doi: 10.1093/brain/awp291

Synofzik, M., Vosgerau, G., and Newen, A. (2008b). Beyond the comparator model: a multifactorial two-step account of agency. *Conscious. Cogn.* 17, 219–239. doi: 10.1016/j.concog.2007.03.010

Synofzik, M., Vosgerau, G., and Newen, A. (2008c). I move, therefore I am: a new theoretical framework to investigate agency and ownership. *Conscious. Cogn.* 17, 411–424. doi: 10.1016/j.concog.2008.03.008

Synofzik, M., Vosgerau, G., and Voss, M. (2013). The experience of agency: an interplay between prediction and postdiction. *Front. Psychol.* 4:127. doi: 10.3389/fpsyg.2013.00127

Todorov, E., and Jordan, M. I. (2002). Optimal feedback control as a theory of motor coordination. *Nat. Neurosci.* 5, 1226–1235. doi: 10.1038/nn963

von Helmholtz, H. (1860). *Treatise on Physiological Optics* (Vol. 3), ed J. P. C. Southall (New York, NY: Dover; published in English in1962).

von Holst, E. (1954). Relations between the central nervous system and the peripheral organs. *Br. J. Anim. Behav.* 2, 89–94. doi: 10.1016/s0950-5601(54)80044-x

Voss, M., Moore, J., Hauser, M., Gallinat, J., Heinz, A., and Haggard, P. (2010). Altered awareness of action in schizophrenia: a specific deficit in predicting action consequences. *Brain* 133, 3104–3112. doi: 10.1093/brain/awq152

Waszak, F., Cardoso-Leite, P., and Hughes, G. (2012). Action effect anticipation: neurophysiological basis and functional consequences. *Neurosci. Biobehav. Rev.* 36, 943–959. doi: 10.1016/j.neubiorev.2011.11.004

Wegner, D. (2003). The mind's best trick: how we experience conscious will. *Trends Cogn. Sci.* 7, 65–69. doi: 10.1016/S1364-6613(03)00002-0

Wegner, D. M., and Wheatley, T. (1999). Apparent mental causation. Sources of the experience of will. *Am. Psychol.* 54, 480–492. doi: 10.1037/0003-066x.54.7.480

Wiese, H., Stude, P., Nebel, K., de Greiff, A., Forsting, M., Diener, H. C., et al. (2004). Movement preparation in self-initiated versus externally triggered movements: an event-related fMRI-study. *Neurosci. Lett.* 371, 220–225. doi: 10.1016/j.neulet.2004.08.078

Wohlschläger, A., Haggard, P., Gesierich, B., and Prinz, W. (2003). The perceived onset time of self- and other-generated actions. *Psychol. Sci.* 14, 586–591. doi: 10.1046/j.0956-7976.2003.psci_1469.x

Wolpe, N., Haggard, P., Siebner, H. R., and Rowe, J. B. (2013). Cue integration and the perception of action in intentional binding. *Exp. Brain Res.* 229, 467–474. doi: 10.1007/s00221-013-3419-2

Wolpe, N., Moore, J. W., Rae, C. L., Rittman, T., Altena, E., Haggard, P., et al. (2014). The medial frontal-prefrontal network for altered awareness and control of action in corticobasal syndrome. *Brain* 137, 208–220. doi: 10.1093/brain/awt302

Wolpert, D. M. (1997). Computational approaches to motor control. *Trends Cogn. Sci.* 1, 209–216. doi: 10.1016/S1364-6613(97)01070-X

Wolpert, D. M., and Ghahramani, Z. (2000). Computational principles of movement neuroscience. *Nat. Neurosci.* 3, 1212–1217. doi: 10.1038/81497

Wolpert, D. M., Ghahramani, Z., and Jordan, M. I. (1995). An internal model for sensorimotor integration. *Science* 269, 1880–1882. doi: 10.1126/science.7569931

Zhang, J., Hughes, L. E., and Rowe, J. B. (2012). Selection and inhibition mechanisms for human voluntary action decisions. *Neuroimage* 63, 392–402. doi: 10.1016/j.neuroimage.2012.06.058

Permissions

All chapters in this book were first published by Frontiers; hereby published with permission under the Creative Commons Attribution License or equivalent. Every chapter published in this book has been scrutinized by our experts. Their significance has been extensively debated. The topics covered herein carry significant findings which will fuel the growth of the discipline. They may even be implemented as practical applications or may be referred to as a beginning point for another development.

The contributors of this book come from diverse backgrounds, making this book a truly international effort. This book will bring forth new frontiers with its revolutionizing research information and detailed analysis of the nascent developments around the world.

We would like to thank all the contributing authors for lending their expertise to make the book truly unique. They have played a crucial role in the development of this book. Without their invaluable contributions this book wouldn't have been possible. They have made vital efforts to compile up to date information on the varied aspects of this subject to make this book a valuable addition to the collection of many professionals and students.

This book was conceptualized with the vision of imparting up-to-date information and advanced data in this field. To ensure the same, a matchless editorial board was set up. Every individual on the board went through rigorous rounds of assessment to prove their worth. After which they invested a large part of their time researching and compiling the most relevant data for our readers.

The editorial board has been involved in producing this book since its inception. They have spent rigorous hours researching and exploring the diverse topics which have resulted in the successful publishing of this book. They have passed on their knowledge of decades through this book. To expedite this challenging task, the publisher supported the team at every step. A small team of assistant editors was also appointed to further simplify the editing procedure and attain best results for the readers.

Apart from the editorial board, the designing team has also invested a significant amount of their time in understanding the subject and creating the most relevant covers. They scrutinized every image to scout for the most suitable representation of the subject and create an appropriate cover for the book.

The publishing team has been an ardent support to the editorial, designing and production team. Their endless efforts to recruit the best for this project, has resulted in the accomplishment of this book. They are a veteran in the field of academics and their pool of knowledge is as vast as their experience in printing. Their expertise and guidance has proved useful at every step. Their uncompromising quality standards have made this book an exceptional effort. Their encouragement from time to time has been an inspiration for everyone.

The publisher and the editorial board hope that this book will prove to be a valuable piece of knowledge for researchers, students, practitioners and scholars across the globe.

List of Contributors

Valérian Chambon
Laboratoire de Neurosciences Cognitives, INSERM U960, Paris, France
Institut Jean Nicod, Ecole Normale Supérieure-EHESS, CNRS UMR-8129, Paris, France
Institute of Cognitive Neuroscience, University College London, London, UK

Nura Sidarus and Patrick Haggard
Institute of Cognitive Neuroscience, University College London, London, UK

Lauren Swiney
School of Anthropology, Institute of Cognitive and Evolutionary Anthropology, University of Oxford, Oxford, UK

Paulo Sousa
Department of History and Anthropology, Institute of Cognition and Culture, Queen's University Belfast, Belfast, UK

Annachiara Cavazzana
Department of General Psychology, University of Padua, Padova, Italy

Chiara Begliomini and Patrizia S. Bisiacchi
Department of General Psychology, University of Padua, Padova, Italy
Center for Cognitive Neuroscience, University of Padua, Padova, Italy

Han-Gue Jo and Stefan Schmidt
Department of Psychosomatic Medicine, University Medical Center Freiburg, Freiburg, Germany
Institute for Transcultural Health Studies, European University Viadrina, Frankfurt (Oder), Germany

Marc Wittmann
Institute for Frontier Areas of Psychology and Mental Health, Freiburg, Germany

Thilo Hinterberger
Department of Psychosomatic Medicine, Research Section of Applied Consciousness Sciences, University Medical Center Regensburg, Regensburg, Germany

Roland Pfister
Department of Psychology III, Julius Maximilians University of Würzburg, Würzburg, Germany

Sukhvinder S. Obhi
Department of Psychology, Wilfrid Laurier University, Waterloo, ON, Canada
Centre for Cognitive Neuroscience and Department of Psychology, Wilfrid Laurier University, Waterloo, ON, Canada
Social Brain, Body and Action Lab, Department of Psychology, Neuroscience and Behaviour, McMaster University, Hamilton, ON, Canada

Martina Rieger
Institute for Psychology, UMIT, University for Health Sciences, Medical Informatics and Technology, Hall in Tirol, Austria
Department of Psychology, Max-Planck-Institute for Human Cognitive and Brain Sciences, Leipzig, Germany

Dorit Wenke
Department of Psychology, Max-Planck-Institute for Human Cognitive and Brain Sciences, Leipzig, Germany
Department of Psychology, Humboldt University at Berlin, Berlin, Germany

Takahiro Kawabe
NTT Communication Science Laboratories, Atsugi, Japan

Karl J. Friston
Wellcome Trust Centre for Neuroimaging, University College London, London, UK

Nelson J. Trujillo-Barreto
Brain Dynamics Department, Cuban Neuroscience Centre, Havana, Cuba

Wael El-Deredy
School of Psychological Sciences, University of Manchester, Manchester, UK

Anna Stenzel and Roman Liepelt
Institute for Psychology, University of Muenster, Muenster, Germany

Thomas Dolk
Department of Psychology, Max-Planck-Institute for Human Cognitive and Brain Sciences, Leipzig, Germany
Research Group: Heterogeneity and Inclusion, Faculty of Human Science, University of Potsdam, Potsdam, Germany

Lorenza S. Colzato, Roberta Sellaro and Bernhard Hommel
Institute for Psychological Research and Leiden Institute for Brain and Cognition, Leiden University, Leiden, Netherlands

Myrthel Dogge
Department of Psychiatry, University Medical Center Utrecht, Utrecht, Netherlands

Dennis Hofman, Maria Boersma, H. Chris Dijkerman and Henk Aarts
Department of Psychology, Utrecht University, Utrecht, Netherlands

Zeynep Barlas
Centre for Cognitive Neuroscience and Department of Psychology, Wilfrid Laurier University, Waterloo, ON, Canada

Glenn Carruthers
ARC Centre of Excellence in Cognition and Its Disorders, Macquarie University, Sydney, NSW, Australia

Antje Gentsch
Research Department of Clinical, Educational and Health Psychology, University College London, London, UK

Matthis Synofzik
Department of Neurodegenerative Diseases, Hertie-Institute for Clinical Brain Research, University of Tübingen, Tübingen, Germany
German Research Center for Neurodegenerative Diseases (DZNE), University of Tübingen, Tübingen, Germany

Jens B. Nielsen
Department of Nutrition, Exercise and Sports, University of Copenhagen, Copenhagen, Denmark
Department of Neuroscience and Pharmacology, University of Copenhagen, Copenhagen, Denmark

Mark S. Christensen
Department of Nutrition, Exercise and Sports, University of Copenhagen, Copenhagen, Denmark
Department of Neuroscience and Pharmacology, University of Copenhagen, Copenhagen, Denmark
Cognitive Neuroscience Research Unit, Danish Neuroscience Center, Aarhus University, Aarhus, Denmark
Department of Nutrition, Exercise and Sports, Panum Institute, University of Copenhagen, Copenhagen, Denmark
Department of Neuroscience and Pharmacology, Panum Institute, University of Copenhagen, Copenhagen, Denmark

Karl Friston, Philipp Schwartenbeck, Thomas FitzGerald, Michael Moutoussis and Raymond J. Dolan
The Wellcome Trust Centre for Neuroimaging, Institute of Neurology, University College London, London, UK

Timothy Behrens
The Wellcome Trust Centre for Neuroimaging, Institute of Neurology, University College London, London, UK
Centre for Functional MRI of the Brain, The John Radcliffe Hospital, Oxford, UK

Tegan Penton
Department of Psychology, Goldsmiths, University of London, London, UK
School of Psychology, Bangor University, Bangor, UK

Guillaume L. Thierry
School of Psychology, Bangor University, Bangor, UK

Nick J. Davis
Department of Psychology, Swansea University, Swansea, UK

Hannah Limerick and David Coyle
Department of Computer Science, Bristol Interaction and Graphics, University of Bristol, Bristol, UK

James W. Moore
Department of Psychology, Goldsmiths, University of London, London, UK
School of Experimental Psychology, University of Bristol, Bristol, UK

Shu Imaizumi
Graduate School of Engineering, Chiba University, Chiba, Japan
Japan Society for the Promotion of Science, Tokyo, Japan

Tomohisa Asai
NTT Communication Science Laboratories, NTT Corporation, Kanagawa, Japan

Noriaki Kanayama
Institute of Biomedical and Health Sciences, Hiroshima University, Hiroshima, Japan

Mitsuru Kawamura
School of Medicine, Showa University, Tokyo, Japan

Shinichi Koyama
Graduate School of Engineering, Chiba University, Chiba, Japan
School of Medicine, Showa University, Tokyo, Japan
Division of Systems and Engineering Management, Nanyang Technological University, Singapore

Mariella Pazzaglia
Department of Psychology, University of Rome 'La Sapienza', Rome, Italy
IRCCS Fondazione Santa Lucia, Rome, Italy

Giulia Galli
IRCCS Fondazione Santa Lucia, Rome, Italy

Jennifer M. Windt
Theoretical Philosophy Group, Department of Philosophy, Johannes Gutenberg-University of Mainz, Mainz, Germany

Dominic L. Harkness
Institute of Cognitive Science, University Osnabrück, Osnabrück, Germany

Bigna Lenggenhager
Department of Neurology, University Hospital Zurich, Zurich, Switzerland
Institute of Physiology and Zurich Center for Integrative Human Physiology (ZIHP), University of Zurich, Zurich, Switzerland

Anina Ritterband-Rosenbaum and Jens Bo Nielsen
Department of Nutrition, Exercise and Sports, Panum Institute, University of Copenhagen, Copenhagen, Denmark
Department of Neuroscience and Pharmacology, Panum Institute, University of Copenhagen, Copenhagen, Denmark

Anke N. Karabanov
Department of Neuroscience and Pharmacology, Panum Institute, University of Copenhagen, Copenhagen, Denmark
Danish Research Center for Magnetic Resonance, Copenhagen University Hospital Hvidovre, Hvidovre, Denmark

Mark S. Christensen
Department of Nutrition, Exercise and Sports, Panum Institute, University of Copenhagen, Copenhagen, Denmark
Department of Neuroscience and Pharmacology, Panum Institute, University of Copenhagen, Copenhagen, Denmark
Danish Neuroscience Center, Cognitive Neuroscience Research Unit, Aarhus University, Aarhus, Denmark

Ann (Chen) Hascalovitz
Department of Physiology, Development and Neuroscience, Behavioural and Clinical Neuroscience Institute, University of Cambridge, Cambridge, UK

Sukhvinder S. Obhi
Social Brain, Body and Action Lab, Department of Psychology, Neuroscience and Behaviour, McMaster University, Hamilton, ON, Canada

Catherine Preston
Brain, Body and Self Laboratory, Department of Neuroscience, Karolinska Institutet, Stockholm, Sweden
University of Nottingham, Nottingham, UK

Roger Newport
Brain, Body and Self Laboratory, Department of Neuroscience, Karolinska Institutet, Stockholm, Sweden

Noham Wolpe
Department of Clinical Neurosciences, University of Cambridge, Cambridge, UK
Medical Research Council, Cognition and Brain Sciences Unit, Cambridge, UK

James B. Rowe
Department of Clinical Neurosciences, University of Cambridge, Cambridge, UK
Medical Research Council, Cognition and Brain Sciences Unit, Cambridge, UK
Behavioural and Clinical Neuroscience Institute, University of Cambridge, Cambridge, UK

Index

R

S

T

V

W

www.ingramcontent.com/pod-product-compliance
Lightning Source LLC
LaVergne TN
LVHW082216200926
848484LV00008B/2263